And There We Were
The Baker's Son and Sawyer's Daughter

By

Robert L. Lent

Text and Photographs © 2021 Robert L. Lent
All rights reserved.

Cover Art © 2021 Joey Freund

Library of Congress Control Number: 2021902085

Published: February 2021
Dog Soldier Press, PO Box 1782,
Ranchos de Taos, NM 87557
dogsoldierpress.com

Graphic Design: book interior and cover
Ananda M. Sundari, Alchemy Arts
AlchemyArtsllc.com

Printing: Ingram Sparks
Print ISBN: 978-1-7362743-8-5
ePub ISBN: 978-1-7362743-7-8

*This book is dedicated to
Tobin Lent and Taran Lent,
our two 'noble' sons.*

ACKNOWLEDGMENTS

I wish to thank John Pruit with Dog Soldier Press for his invaluable efforts in taking my efforts from a manuscript to a published book. John's efforts with regard to editing and expediting were much appreciated.

I would also like to acknowledge Ananda Sundari at Alchemy Arts for the book layout and formatting, the creative dust cover design, and her collaborative efforts with the printer, Ingram Sparks. Ananda made the book be all that it could be.

TABLE OF CONTENTS

Chapter 1	A Formulation of Dreams	1
Chapter 2	Big Summit Prairie	5
Chapter 3	The Sawyer and His Family	13
Chapter 4	An End to Migratory Work	21
Chapter 5	Prineville, Oregon	25
Chapter 6	Bob Lent and Shirley Hill in The 1950s	29
Chapter 7	Beauty and Beautiful	49
Chapter 8	Prineville, Oregon in The 1950s	55
Chapter 9	Courtship and Marriage	67
Chapter 10	Family and a Career, The Denver Years	79
Chapter 11	Oklahoma City	89
Chapter 12	Welcome to the United Kingdom, A London Landing	95
Chapter 13	"England, My Beloved England"	147
Chapter 14	Memorable People Encountered in The United Kingdom	149
Chapter 15	A Few of Our Favorite Places in The United Kingdom	209
	Cliveden	209
	Compleat Angler, Marlow, Buckinghamshire	222
	Windsor Great Park, Berkshire	227
	Frogmore House Gardens and Mausoleum	234
	The Ritz Hotel London, Claridge's, and Harrods	237
	The Thames	244
	The Tower of London	271
	The English Public Houses	276
	Ascot and Windsor Villages	289

Chapter 16	Memorable Excursions in The United Kingdom, Ireland, and Continental Europe		315
	Valentine's Day on the Venice Simplon Orient-Express		317
	A Weekend in Venice, Italy		320
	The Tall Ship Races		322
	The British Open, July 1996		325
	Travels to Ireland		329
	Rugby, Football (Soccer), Horse Races, and Outdoor Opera		339
	Horse Races (Other than Ascot)		342
	Glyndebourne Festival Opera		344
	AWBS Trips to Europe		345
	The Paul Smith Wedding		350
	Pheasant Hunts		352
	Across the Sea to Norway		356
	Through the Channel Tunnel to Brussels and Paris		360
	A Trip to The United States		363
	Through Sherwood Forest to Nottingham		365
	Out to Sea, A Visit to the Gryphon FPSO		367
	Supper With the King and Queen at Hatfield House		370
	Thrice to Copenhagen, Denmark		372
Chapter 17	Leaving the United Kingdom		377
Chapter 18	The Search for a Home, Meeting Our Business Partners, and the Move to China		387
Chapter 19	The People of China		383
Chapter 20	Memorable Observations of Animals, Crops, Transport, and Roadside Activities		425
	Pigs		426
	Geese		427

	Cows and Cattle	428
	Chickens	430
	Horses and Donkeys	431
	Fish	434
	Ducks	436
	Sheep	436
	Crops and Transport	437
Chapter 21	Our Stay in China. Events Not to be Forgotten	441
	Black Tie Dinner and Dance on the Great Wall of China	441
	River Li and Guilin	444
	Turnandot	449
	Tobin and Ha Lent's Wedding in Hanoi	451
	Honored in the Great Hall of The People	458
Chapter 22	Other Memorable Chinese Experiences	471
	Longqing Gorge	471
	Fragrant Hills	475
	Ming Tombs, Summer Palace, Temple of Heaven, Drum and Bell Towers, and The Forbidden City (Imperial Palace)	478
	July 4th Celebration, Dinner at The United States Ambassador's Home, New Year Celebration at the Australian Embassy, St. Patrick's Day Ball, and New York Philharmonic Performance in The Great Hall of The People	479
	Casablanca Theme Night and a Performance by Rondo' Veneziano	482
Chapter 23	Leaving China	485
Chapter 24	Becoming Texans	491
Chapter 25	Bohai Bay. Bob's Give-Back to China and to Kerr-McGee	493

Chapter 26	A New Assignment, A New World of Adventure	499
	Rio de Janeiro, Brazil	499
	Paris, France	504
Chapter 27	Retirement. Travels and Adventures in the First Year	507
	New England and the Maritime Provinces of Canada	508
	Niagara Falls (Canada/New York), Buffalo, and Ithaca, New York	512
	West Coast Trip, San Jose, California to Vancouver Island, Canada and Back	515
	Northern Nevada and Montana Fishing Trips	545
	Kansas City and Branson, Missouri (September 20-27, 2004)	554
	San Antonio on the Occasion of Shirley's 60th Birthday (October 8-11, 2004)	572
Chapter 28	An Unexpected Journey, A Trip to France, and Riverboat Float Through the Wine Region of Burgundy (July 30 - August 11, 2008)	581
Chapter 29	Fifteen Years of Retirement and The End of the Story	607
List of Photographs		609

Chapter 1

A Formation of Dreams

*W*hen you are 16 going on 17, the world outside your hometown can be viewed as very interesting, if not downright exciting. Reading about foreign places, governments, and people fueled my imagination and imparted in my psyche a desire to travel and sample all that was 'out there'. I had been introduced to the magic of the written word by my grandmother, May Lent, who always took the time to read to me and my two younger brothers. I was hooked on books early and I have been an avid reader ever since the day I entered grade school. Reading opened tantalizing doors which provided glimpses of a wondrous world that existed outside the series of small towns where I was born and where I attended grammar and high schools.

Small town number one was Canby, Oregon where my father John built a home following his marriage to my mother Mabel. My parents lived in Canby, but I was born in Oregon City, Oregon, home of the closest hospital and located near the Falls on the historic Willamette River. Father was a baker and when I was age 3 he decided he would rather own a bakery than just work in one so we moved 15 miles to Molalla. We lived in an apartment located above the bakery. What chance did I ever have of being a thin child? I would wake up in the morning walk downstairs with sleep in my eyes and see trays of hot rolls, Danish pastries, and my all-time favorite, maple bars. Dad was a hard worker and at six foot two inches he was a rather tall man. But he was thin and no matter what he ate he stayed thin. When I joined him in the morning, we usually had a glass of cream (in those days the cream was on top of the milk in the gallon jugs delivered to the bakery) and a maple bar. Bobby was a chubby boy.

We remained in Molalla until the middle of my fifth year in elementary school. During this fifth grade year, 1952-53, Dad moved us three times and on January 1, 1953 we moved into our new home in Prineville, Oregon. The move my parents had made from Canby to Molalla was an easy one, both physically and emotionally. But the move to Prineville in the more distant Central Oregon took mother away from her parents and her seven brothers and sisters.

The moves were also a bit traumatic for me. By the fifth grade I was already a tall boy and I was large, not necessarily fat but certainly approaching "fat". I do not know what it is, but when a big kid shows up at a new school the resident 'big kid' has to fight him to see if the pecking order is correct, or if there needs to be an adjustment. I enrolled in two new schools during my fifth-grade year and on the first day of attendance at each I was involved in a fight. I remember fighting Lyle and Billy, the two resident big men and bullies at their respective schools. It turns out I had latent athletic ability, and I acquitted myself quite well, although neither of the big boys would say more than, "You did alright" or "I think I taught you a few moves". To tell you the truth I thought I beat the crap out of them. My peers had seen enough: I never had to fight after day one.

After the first day there were often fights, but never between the reigning big boy, me, and another new big boy. That is not to say that sometimes a pack of kids would not surround a big boy and taunt him. On one occasion, at Crooked River Elementary School in Prineville, an incident like this did occur. The encircled big boy flicked a right fist into the face of one of the miscreants and bloodied his nose. When one of the other kids in the circle said, "Hey, You can't do that." the big guy reached out and bloodied his nose. End of game.

I had long ago learned my lesson, and I was not a part of

that fiasco. Some people wonder why big kids tend to be pacifists. What have we got to gain? If we beat up on a small kid, we get scorned for beating him up; if we perform poorly, we are disdained for losing to the wee one. When a fight involves a person of equal size, we are talking about serious injuries no matter who wins. To paraphrase an old axiom, "The bigger they are the harder they hit." Long live pacifism. I am with Albert Einstein.

After dad sold his bakery in Molalla, he bought another one in Prineville. One might ask, "Why would a man make a move like that?" The move had nothing to do with baking or economics. The fact is Dad was an avid fisherman. Maybe avid is an understatement. His one overriding passion in life was fishing, especially trout fishing. He had developed this passion as a youth when he found he could escape the throes and angst that came from his being the son of an alcoholic father by walking along a river with a fly rod in hand. His life was wonderful when he was fishing and that is probably what fueled his love of the sport. His identity as a person and self-worth came from his growing status as a *great* fisherman. He had found an avocation in which he excelled. As a young married man and as a father, he wanted to move to a community where he could fish quality streams and lakes. He not only wanted to fish these streams, he wanted to fish at least one of them every day. Prineville, in Central Oregon, was the perfect place.

By the middle of my junior year at Crook County High School (Prineville) it was apparent to me that there was a world beyond Central Oregon and I really had a yearning to get a taste of what it might be like traveling in Mexico or in Canada. I often drove my best friend Jerry Riley to a viewpoint atop a basaltic rim overlooking the city, and there, with either a cigarette or beer (we were too young to legally possess either), we would kick back and talk of making a trip to Mexico. What fun it was to talk about routes, where we might stay, girls we would surely meet, and most of all, how we would avoid the Mexican banditos. We would plan a trip for spring break, and when spring break had come and gone, we would drive back up on the mesa and talk about a journey in the summer, vowing that this time we would really do it. Of course, we never did. I think those early, and failed, attempts at international travel made the experiences I had later much sweeter, for they fulfilled a dream I never really expected to see come true. I have, with my very precious wife, gone places and done things that surprised both of us.

I could say the journey, and narrative I am about to undertake, began up on that rim rock with its wonderful vista of Prineville, but the story actually began a number of years before. In the early summer of 1955, my Grandpa Lent (then a reformed alcoholic) and I became fishing buddies. We would fish in many places, but fishing with grandfather Fred placed an emphasis on accessibility. With Grandpa the rugged terrain and roaring rock bottomed streams were to be avoided, no matter how many fish might be present. I mention this because my father had told Grandpa there was a fish pond high up in the Ochoco Mountains near Big Summit Prairie where fish could be taken in both a pond and in a nearby creek. And we could drive right up to the fishing areas.

Chapter 2

BIG SUMMIT PRAIRIE

*A*s one heads east of Prineville and into the Ochoco Mountains, it is not long before the change in elevation brings a transition from sage and juniper to the wonderful grass carpeted forests of ochre-barked and majestically tall Ponderosa pines. Even today I marvel at how unique these forests are. It is like someone planted pine seedlings in a grassy meadow and then allowed the trees to grow over fifteen stories high. In contrast to the massive forests of Douglas fir growing along the west slopes of the volcano dotted Cascade Range, the Ponderosa forests are relatively barren of undergrowth. Consequently, it is always refreshing to travel along any mountain road, paved or not, and to be able to view the wide expanse of forest. I know if I had been a deer I would have wanted to be a Central Oregon mule tail as I could have run forever and could have had grass and clean water without end. Such is how I viewed these forests in the 1950's and how I still view them.

As Grandpa's 1945 Ford gained elevation we came to a junction where Highway 20 East makes an uphill departure from the Ochoco Creek valley. The valley is not wide, maybe only a quarter to half a mile from hillside to hillside, and the grass lands and meadows that flank the creek exist only because of the water has been diverted from the creek into the fields. The pine forests flanking the creek meadows are not as large, and the grass not as green, as they are once the elevation increases. We turned off Highway 20 and followed the creek up to a fork in the road where we took the road sign-posted *Summit Prairie*. By now the road was a narrow two lanes and the pavement had given way to gravel. We progressed up the narrowing valley and along the increasingly winding road. The trees became much taller and the creek much reduced in size. The mountains closed in on us and then came countless switch backs as we gained elevation. When you are fourteen these turns and slow speeds make for an endless trip, but in reality, we probably only climbed 3000 feet in elevation over a five-mile stretch.

And then there it was, stretching out before us like a massive ocean carved out of forest - Big Summit Prairie. As Grandpa and I rounded a curve that gave us our first glimpse of the prairie I wondered how the forest could so quickly be replaced by such a wide expanse of grasslands. We could see a number of creeks fanning out before us like a horsetail with all the small tributaries funneling to a single outlet located far to the southeastern edge of the prairie. But most of all, we saw no one. There were seemingly no cows, no horses, and no people. How very strange. I think sometimes the magnitude of a vista masks reality and the imagination paints a tainted picture. There were a few fences that partitioned parts of the grassy plain and there were cattle, but mostly the animals were hidden up in the woodlands that feathered into the grasslands.

Big Summit Prairie covers more than 40 square miles with high alpine meadows. In the spring these meadows explode in an eruption of colors when the wildflowers (Indian Paint Brush, Lupines, etc.) burst into bloom. Although it is difficult to come up with an accurate estimate of the total number of small creeks that drain the prairie there are at least 13 which all drain southeast into the Crooked River. From Summit Prairie, the Crooked River gradually makes a turn to the west and then it makes a more abrupt turn to the north as it works its way through Crook County to the City of Prineville. Downstream from Prineville the Crooked River once again heads west, flowing through irrigated meadows and farms. After slowly moving past the cliffs forming Smith Rocks National Monument the river enters a narrow basalt-bounded canyon. Within this deep canyon the Crooked River loses its identity when it merges with the Deschutes River and its even more impressive canyon.

Some of the creeks in Summit Prairie have sign-posted names. Howard Creek, Dudley Creek, and Johnson Creek are but three of these. The creek by the old abandoned sawmill has no name that I know of, although it appears to be a tributary of Johnson Creek.

As we descended to the level of the prairie, we came upon the sawmill pond. With the boards and timbers bleached by the sun, the mill itself was only a gray skeleton of what it had been. The iron carriages, saws, and anything else of value had been stripped away years ago. The skid deck was still intact and there were certainly enough surviving wooden platforms from which one could drop a line into the deep green waters. The pond had to be deep since it once held the massive Ponderosa pine logs that were dumped off logging trucks. The logs floated in the pond until they were poled to the skid ramp and brought up and into the mill for processing.

I remembered looking around and wondering how long it had been since the mill had cut its last log. Nearby, there were a few abandoned shacks that did not seem to be too badly damaged. I was also surprised to see a considerable number of large trees standing in the immediate vicinity of the old mill. There were stumps of harvested giants, but the panoramic view was mostly "forest" with its ever-present grassy undergrowth. I guess where there is an open forest, trees can be selectively harvested and the resulting impact is not like in the western Oregon logging areas where clear cut (if it grows, it goes) was, and is, an operative practice. Still, I could not help but wonder why one would leave tall standing pines so close and accessible to the mill.

Standing there with Grandpa I did not reflect too long on the shacks, the mill, or the people who might have lived and worked in the area. I hustled over to the creek that meandered down a meadow and then along the southwestern edge of the abandoned sawmill. I peeked at the slow-moving stream with grass lined and grasshopper infested banks. There was a very strong scent of wild mint. Yes, there would be fish here.

And There We Were

Grandpa and I assembled our fly rods and walked over to one of the wooden platforms. Fishing lines were baited with giant salmon eggs, our bait of choice, and the hooks lowered into one area after another. I do not remember catching any fish, or even having a hook-up, in that pond. We caught several small trout out of the creek, but I am quite sure we did not even get a strike in the pond. Still, Grandpa and I, and later myself and my school buddies, made numerous journeys to fish this mill pond. I think we returned because the scenery was so beautiful and because of the incredible solitude. Only the wind blowing through the tops of the pines disturbed the quiet. Even the sound of the moving water in the creek was undetectable, like it did not wish to disturb Mother Nature's chapel.

One might inquire as to how an abandoned mill pond fits into this tale of travels. The answer is that if I marvel at what a boy from Prineville did and saw during his working career, I am humbled by the adventures of a little curly haired blond girl who once lived in that sawmill camp. A girl who lived in a one room cabin with no running water and no electricity; who loved the forest and the outdoors; and who had the freedom to walk anywhere and was able to play and be alone beneath the tall whispering pines. Her sanctuary was only violated when the mill whistle blew and the mill operations commenced.

My future wife, and life-long companion, was that little girl. Our paths, although not coeval, crossed for the first time in that remote little sawmill camp. Shirley Hill, the curly haired and freckled face country lass grew up to be a beautiful (I can be biased if you will allow me) and regal lady whose charm captivated royalty, premiers, and street vendors with equal aplomb. But I get ahead of the story.

Shirley Hill lived in the sawmill camp because her father, Virgil "Son" Hill, was the mill sawyer. Son and Marie, Shirley's mother, lived in a one room cabin no more than a quarter of a mile from the mill. In 1949 the population at the camp was approximately 30. Most of these were single men, many of whom lived in a crude dormitory. The four, going on five, year old blonde was in her element. She could walk and play in an outdoors many have never seen and will probably never see. The sweet smell of pine and the wildflowers, and the freedom to find solitude were indelibly etched into the young girl's being. The carefree nature of her youthful existence must also have been responsible, at least in part, for the embedding in her personality a longing for adventure where dreams and imaginations were never ending. When one comes from such simple origins, it is no wonder that the world seems so amazing, and each new experience pales in comparison to the next. If you believe life is a series of great adventures, then even the simplest of worldly activities elicit excitement and are to be pursued to their fullest. Such was the building of a personality typified by effervescence, a sense of inquiry, and imagination. Humor and wit completed the package but those were traits probably developed in later years.

Their stay in Summit Prairie was only one stop in the migrant career of the Hill family.

And There We Were

FIGURE 1. AERIAL VIEW OF BIG SUMMIT PRAIRIE
OCHOCO MOUNTAINS, CENTRAL OREGON

FIGURE 2. PONDEROSA PINE FOREST WITH
GRASS AND WILD FLOWER UNDERGROWTH

Big Summit Prairie

Figure 3. The aged one room cabin near the Big Summit Prairie Sawmill

Figure 4. Shirley Hill (age 4) when the Hill family lived at the sawmill camp

And There We Were

Chapter 3

THE SAWYER AND HIS FAMILY

Shirley's mother, Marie Taylor, met Virgil "Son" Hill when he was 19 and she was a 15-year-old sophomore in high school. During the summer of her sophomore year the Taylor family was living near a mill along Bridge Creek, Central Oregon. Marie Taylor was a high school student in Prineville and her father, Clifford, was a pond worker at the Bridge Creek Mill. One evening around dusk Marie went down to the stream to get a bucket of water so she could wash her hair. She looked downstream and could not believe her eyes. There were two handsome young men sitting along the stream bank watching the sun set. One of these was Son Hill and the other was his brother-in-law, Roy Flanary. Roy, saw the attractive young girl and ran over to help her with the water. She told Roy where she was staying and that is all that Son Hill needed to know. He dropped by the next evening to say "Hello" and the sparks flew.

Once, in an attempt to embarrass Marie, I suggested that the two boys she met along Bridge Creek must have been stunned by her beauty. Her giggling response was, "Not really, it was just that girls were scarce around those parts." Still Son and Marie quickly found themselves in love. Marie returned to Prineville when school started, and in her own words, "Son was a very handsome man and I loved his personality. The road between Mitchell (Bridge Creek) and Prineville was hot."

Son Hill had left home when he was fourteen. Both his

mother and his father had remarried, and the burden of this young boy was too much for either family. Times were tough and Son's father, Port Hill, did not want to do anything that would jeopardize his second marriage. That is not to say that Port did not love his son. He did. And Son Hill worshiped his father.

Out on his own at such a young age Son Hill picked up bad habits. Drinking and gambling were two of these. It was these sins that alienated Son to Marie's parents. The age difference (he was 19 and she 15) was a concern but they were more concerned that Marie was getting involved with a young man who would ultimately cause her considerable unhappiness. For all they knew he was also a womanizer. Their advice was to stay away from him until she was a bit older. Marie had loved school but when she fell in love with Son she found herself hating it. Marie decided one way to get her parents to accept Son was to become pregnant, and that she did. Bye, Bye high school.

Shirley's brother, Larry was born in 1943 and Shirley arrived in October of 1944. When Shirley was 3 months old Marie moved to Point Richmond outside of San Francisco so she could be with Son who at the time had been drafted into the navy. In mid 1945, with the war winding down, Son was discharged from the Navy and the family moved back to Prineville where Son and Port began a series of sawmill ventures that took the Hill clan to a number of localities. The only constant theme during the next 8 years was that after every failed business venture or completed job assignment the Son Hill family returned to the Melrose area of Prineville, home of Marie's mother and father, Clifford and Jennie Taylor.

For the most part, Son's saw-milling moves were related to Port Hill's decisions. When Grandpa Hill said he was moving, to another sawmill camp or to another town, it was given Shirley and her parents were moving too. It was family, and family worked and lived together. This dedication to family came out of the dust bowl days and the trying times that "Okies" like Virgil and Port Hill endured. They came from Oklahoma to Oregon in search of a better life. I once, with a bit of trepidation, asked if they had come in trucks like those portrayed in the caravans depicted in John Steinbeck's *Grapes of Wrath*. The proud answer was, "Pretty much that way." They brought their dreams and they lived as honest, hardworking, and God-fearing citizens in a country where an Oklahoman heritage was not something the locals looked up to. An Okie and those who lived in "Okieville" were second class citizens: this was really odd, for in Prineville and in Central Oregon in the 1940s and 1950s the gap between second class and upper class must have been mighty thin. Still the sentiment was there and my Shirley, by heritage, if not by geography, was an Okie.

In late 1945 Son and Port jointly leased a sawmill in Sweet Home, Oregon. This Willamette Valley venture did not work out (they were under-capitalized) and in the end Son and Marie lost everything. Of those times Marie says, "We all lost our shirts but we sure did have a lot of fun!" They lost more than there shirts! They lost their small home in Prineville and even their car. It was back to the Prineville refuge. Clifford and Jennie Taylor came to Sweet Home and drove the family back "home". This time home meant living with Marie's parents. The failed 1945-46 Sweet Home venture would be repeated a number of times over the coming years, so it was good that the Hills had the wherewithal to pick themselves up off the turf and keep coming back. Son and Port Hill were knowledgeable and valued sawmill workers, and it was only a short time before they were back earning a salary at a Prineville mill.

After a year of steady employment in Prineville (enough so that Son and Marie had once again moved into their own home) Port Hill had his eye on a milling operation near Mountain Creek, located in the mountains above Mitchell, Oregon. The money looked good and Port wanted his family together. He had his way. The Port Hills, the Son Hills, and the Roy Flanary family which included Son's sister, Mildred, moved to Mountain Creek. At the end of the next year, 1946-47, with steady incomes by all, the Hill entourage was ready for its next adventure. The wand of wanderlust touched Port, and the clan was once again on the move.

This time the new venture was a leased sawmill near Izee, Oregon, another one of those seemingly endless small towns in

And There We Were

the back reaches of Central Oregon. Port and Son seemed to be on their way to financial success. Marie and Son had a new purpose built home with separate areas for bedroom, kitchen, and bathing. They even had a porch looking out over a small stream. Marie loved the wide-open spaces and her new home. Ray and Lois Ball, Son's other sister, had joined the group and Ray became part of the Hill work force. But all was lost when, in 1948, the mill burned to the ground. Once again it was time to start over. For Son and Marie, it was back to the Melrose area and the family safety net, the Clifford Taylors.

After a bit of work in Prineville Son Hill took on work in John Day, Oregon where the house they lived in had a piano. When this work played out, the family moved for a short stay in nearby Prairie city. It was now early in the year 1949. In the rare instance when Son opted to move without his father it was "for the money". One of these "for the money" moves was to Big Summit Prairie.

In early spring of 1949 Son Hill accepted the job to be the sawyer at the mill along "No Name" creek in Big Summit Prairie. The owner of the mill had sought out Son as he needed a good man and a sawyer. Son Hill had never been a sawyer but he knew enough about milling that the job was a challenge he could accept. The mill had been operating for years, although milling only occurred from early spring until late fall. Each year the mill was shut down for the winter. The snowfall in the Ochoco Mountains resulted in mandatory closures by the National Forest Service who had jurisdiction over the timber being harvested.

The Hill family's home was a one room cabin located near the Big Summit Prairie sawmill. There was no running water, electricity, or indoor plumbing. The cabin was approximately 20 feet long and 12 feet wide. The walls were built with rough-hewn pine logs whose ends were milled and notched to provide a solid fit where the walls came together. The log walls were caulked and/or filled in with smaller limbs or willow branches. A front door and a window greeted those approaching the front of the cabin. A rear door opened into a small covered area used for storage of dry goods and firewood. An additional window provided an outward view from the end of the cabin. The outhouse was accessed out the front door and then via a short path around the side of the house towards the area with the densest vegetation.

What the cabin may have lacked in appearance and in amenities it made up for in location. Ponderosa Pines and smaller Douglas fir or White fir trees enclosed the cabin on all four sides, but not so densely as to occlude views of the nearby meadows where there were a multitude of colored flowers, birch trees, and willows. Where people had not walked or parked a car, the grass grew up to one's knees. Shirley Hill could walk out of her front door and immediately be in a scenic wonderland. The air was fresh with a strong scent of freshly cut pine and wild mint. As long as she stayed away from the mill and the trucks moving in and out of that area she could pretty much go where she pleased, and this she did. There were deer in the meadows but there were no bears or other predators to fear. The noise coming from the sawmill operations had driven all of the nasty animals to higher ground.

The typical day in the sawmill camp and at the Hill cabin began with a wake up around 5:00 am. A fire was built and then biscuits were prepared for the morning meal. If the family had been to Prineville over the weekend (a journey of 50 miles), there would be eggs and maybe bacon for breakfast. All other times it was biscuits and gravy. Son would walk back to the cabin for lunch which almost invariably was cornbread and beans. The evening meal, served after the mill shut down at 5:30 was once again cornbread and beans with occasional servings coming from canned vegetables and canned fruit. Meat, since the cabin lacked any refrigeration, was notably lacking. Venison was available at their doorstep, but when Marie was asked if Son had ever poached any of the "camp" deer she replied with a slight smile, "Not here."

During the day Marie mostly cooked and cleaned the cabin and washed clothes. She was a fanatic about cleanliness and even the outhouse received a daily scrubbing with brush and bleach. The plank floors were bleached white and they smelled clean. In the evening Son came home for dinner, the dishes were done, and the kids were put into a circular galvanized tub. This tub was used by both the children and by Son who stepped in after the kids had been bathed. Shirley remembered she got the first bath and the cleanest water. After all of the bathing, it was time for bed. There was no television and no lights. When it was dark all were in bed. If you think that this early to bed promoted a certain amount of "frisky business" you would be wrong. During the week both Marie and Son were too tired to think about such foolishness. Of course, the weekend was another matter.

With Marie busy cooking and cleaning the cabin the children were free to wander. Even though there were several other cabins for married couples, there were no other children. Shirley remembered playing in the meadows, picking flowers, and taking walks along the slow-moving creek. She felt free and unconfined. Later, when we had moved to Ascot, England, Shirley would go for long walks in the Windsor Great Park, and she would often return remarking how much these walks reminded her of the walks she took in the meadows and forests of the Ochoco Mountains.

Brother Larry, age 6, was into boy activities and one of his favorite pursuits involved the capture of chipmunks. With only the patience a young boy could muster, he would find a hole into which a chipmunk had darted and then he would lie on his stomach with his hands around the hole. After what must have been an incredible amount of time, a chipmunk would eventually stick its head out and Larry would grab it. Son had built a wire pen where Larry could put his captured "pets". Mostly he would grab the younger and less wary chipmunks and these never bit. However, one day he grabbed a mad mother and she chomped down on his index finger and would not let go. For animal lovers, it should be noted that all the chipmunks were returned to their wild habitat after three or four weeks.

Trips to town, Prineville, were big events. It was a chance to see family, to get provisions, and for Son, a chance to go drinking and gambling with his male friends and relatives. There was no drinking in camp, but come time for a weekend spent in town it was "Katy, bar the door". Momma Taylor had been right about two things, the gambling and the drinking.

One weekend when the family was in town Shirley learned a new ice cream parlor, Dairy Queen, had opened and that this establishment served ice cream "with a curl on top". She said they just had to go so she could see this "curl". The only curls Shirley knew were those she had in her hair. Marie and Son loved to see Shirley in ringlets so her hair was periodically curled. Shirley was proud of her curls. To mollify Shirley, Marie loaded the kids into grandma's car and off they went to Dairy Queen. What an imagination and what a disappointment it was for the little blonde. The "curl on top" it was not at all like what she thought it would be. There were no ringlets. The ice cream was more than good enough.

Although Marie was happy working hard taking care of the children, cooking, and cleaning the Big Summit Prairie cabin, Shirley remembers she thought it must be awfully hard to work like this week in and week out. The work her mother did just did not seem to be a lot of fun, and she always seemed to be so tired. Such was born the seed that grew and the philosophy of fun and play that Shirley carried with her through elementary and high school. She would eventually find her role model in her Aunt Mildred who knew how to dress and how to play. But that comes later.

In the fall of 1949 Marie took the children to Prineville where she enrolled Larry in the first grade. A place to live was found in a home in the Melrose area near Grandma and Grandpa Taylor's home. Son continued to work in the mountains until the snow closed the mill in late October. The family never went back to Summit Prairie. With Larry and, the next year Shirley, in elementary school it was mandatory work be found in small towns or cities with schools.

And There We Were

Chapter 4

An End to Migratory Work

*L*arry Hill finished the first year of school in Prineville, and the following year, 1950, Shirley entered the first grade. Son was employed at a local sawmill as was Port Hill, but after another year of "steady" work Port decided the extended Hill family should move to Prairie City, Oregon. The surprising part of this move was the business endeavor Port chose to pursue. He would own and operate a restaurant in Prairie City. It seems that the many milling failures had led him to believe he could make a better living operating a restaurant. Son Hill, wanting to be near his father, opted to lease a service station. So early in 1951 Son moved his family from Prineville, and from Clifford and Jennie Taylor, to Prairie City. Now all the Port Hill clan were together. Son and his two sisters, Lois and Mildred, along with the second family of Port and Irene Hill were all in one village. Lois and Mildred worked in the restaurant alongside Port and Irene. Marie added bookkeeper to her role as mother and homemaker. Son worked long hours attending the service station.

After about a year it became apparent to Port Hill that the restaurant business was not all it was cracked up to be and the work was certainly not as much fun nor as challenging as the work found in the milling industry. After all was said and done, the Hills were sawmill guys. It was now time for the Hills to move to Pendleton, Oregon where Port had once again leased a sawmill. Shirley, in 1953, thus began her third year of elementary school in Pendleton. Of Port's first family, only Mildred was missing.

Port was once again under-capitalized and the Pendleton milling operation failed after only a few months of operation. It was time for Son Hill to take his family back to Prineville and the ever-used safety net offered by Clifford and Jennie.

This last move to Prineville, in 1953, marked the end of Son Hill's migratory work habits. He would no longer follow the *wandering star* and Port Hill. Marie was persuasive in her argument that it was time to settle down. Son hired on at the Pine Products sawmill in Prineville and he remained there until his tragic illness in 1978. His next 25 years of employment were with this one company. Wanderlust had been expelled from his system.

With a steady job in hand the Son Hill family moved into a new home in what the locals call "Okieville". The home on Locust Street in the western part of Prineville had running water and electricity but no indoor plumbing. But with Marie, ever the fastidious one, the outdoor facilities always smelled of bleach and were memorable for their cleanliness. Shirley could describe the toiletry in extreme detail even after 65 years.

With the family now firmly ensconced in Prineville one might wonder how all of the travels and business ventures Son Hill undertook played out at the Taylor residence. Clifford and Jennie had always been concerned about the wayward ways of Son Hill, and his constant departures chasing after Port Hill and his family had to have been a bit irritating. Whenever there was a setback, it was always to the Taylor home that the Son Hill family retreated. One would think Marie and Son would have wanted something more stable in their lives, and that they would have wanted to remain around the Taylors rather than chase after the Hills. But the truth of the matter is Son Hill loved his father and the Hill entourage was one that was fun to be around. Clifford and Jennie were stable but they were not "fun" and so, no matter what the outcome, Marie was willing to pack up and take the children wherever Son wished to go. I think it is true in most families that all are loved but few are really fun to be around. Those that are fun to be around are the ones with whom most time is spent. Clifford and Jennie were stable and loved, but when it came time for adventure they chose to remain rooted in their comfortable and spacious Melrose home. At a whim, Son and Marie packed up and hit the road. But until the day she passed, Shirley would tell you that the grandparent she loved the most was Jennie Taylor. Port Hill comes in a close second, but no one matched Jennie for number one.

I too had a preference for time spent with grandmothers. I loved both of mine, but May Lent is the finest woman I have ever been around. And I do not diminish at all the feelings and respect I have for both my own mother and for the mother of my children. Blanche Hepler, my maternal grandmother, was loved by all of us, but she was just not fun to be around. When, as a youngster we traveled from Molalla to Canby, we would always make our first stop to see Grandma Hepler, but the moment I walked in the door I could hardly wait to get leave to walk across town and spend time with Grandma Lent and my cousins, the Macks. There was always something going on when you were around Grandma Lent. She would read to us, take us down to the creek to catch frogs and crawdads, or pack us a lunch so we could go into the forest to build a fort or an Indian village. There were a hundred things to do and Grandma Lent encouraged us to do them all.

I believe Son and Marie found fun and excitement being around the Port Hill family and that is why they packed up and left at a moment's notice. It is interesting to note that when Son and Marie finally settled down in Prineville, Oregon it was the Clifford and Jennie Taylor home where the family gathered for the holidays and special occasions. Even though the Port Hills lived near Son and Marie in Okieville (i.e., on Locust Street) there were few occasions when the families got together. Part of this was because Port Hill and his second wife, Ivene, had four children of their own who were now of an age where most of Port and Ivene's time was focused on them. Eventually Port Hill packed up his second family and moved to Arizona, where he once again went back into the restaurant business. That

And There We Were

left only Son as the lone remaining sawmiller in the Hill family.

In midyear 1953 Shirley Hill enrolled in the third grade at Ochoco Elementary School, Prineville, Oregon. The "Okie girl" was about to get her first taste of discrimination.

Chapter 5

PRINEVILLE, OREGON

Prineville, located in Central Oregon, is approximately 30 miles from the geographic center of the Oregon. It is the county seat for Crook County, named after the U.S. Army Indian fighter, Major-General George Crook. The county was established in 1882 and covers approximately 3,000 square miles.

Until late in the 1860's, few white men had traveled through this part of the Indian Territory. Barney Prine, the town's namesake, built a cabin near the confluence of the Crooked River and Ochoco Creek, and by 1871 this cabin had grown into a store and saloon. Having such amenities to serve a now rapidly expanding populace of settlers also demanded a United States post office, and one was established in the same year, 1871.

Prineville is located in a verdant valley surrounded by mesas and tablelands. When one travels east after crossing the Cascade Range and its many snow-covered volcanic peaks, the rapid change from forest to sagebrush and juniper is striking. The Cascades provide a high barrier to the flow of moist air, and little moisture makes it into the skies over the high and dry lands of Central Oregon. Rainfall is minimal, somewhere around 15 inches per year in the non-mountainous regions.

The initial view of Prineville is breathtaking. The striking contrast between the dry semi-desert juniper-dominated wastelands and the green valley of the Crooked River and Ochoco Creek, when viewed from a car, occurs in an instant.

And There We Were

The panorama unfolds as soon as one begins a descent through the basaltic tablelands. Where a few moments ago there were only dry lands, there is suddenly an oasis of grass, trees, and streams.

The 1890 population in Crook County was a little over 3,200, but in the census taken that year Indians were not counted. The population in the County is now approximately 23,000 and Indians are counted. However, they are hard to find. More than 95 percent of the population is Caucasian (7% of whom are Hispanic) and most of these can trace ancestry back to Europe.

Two other points worthy of note involve the construction of a railroad spur and a county courthouse in 1910. The courthouse is remarkable because the three-story building is built out of massive blocks carved from basalt. I was proud of this building when I was growing up in Prineville and I am proud of it today. Of course, being a geologist, I think most rock is special. Even a casual traveler cannot but be impressed by the structure.

The City of Prineville Railway provided a market outlet for the City's commercial products, mostly lumber and timber. Without this rail spur connecting to the Union Pacific and Great Northern line 20 miles to the west, it is likely Prineville would have become a minor player in the growth and development of Central Oregon.

Prineville, Oregon

Figure 5. Prineville, Oregon as seen from View Point, circa 1950

Figure 6. Crook County Courthouse, Prineville, Oregon

And There We Were

Chapter 6

BOB LENT AND SHIRLEY HILL IN THE 1950S

John and Mabel Lent moved to Prineville in January of 1953, the same year Son Hill settled his family for the last time in the city of Shirley Hill's birth. Dad Lent was a baker who came to Central Oregon for one reason only. And we know what that was. There was no place better to fish than in Central Oregon, and my father's wish to fish every day was one he fulfilled until he was 80.

The five of us (I had two brothers) moved into a two-bedroom house in one of the better neighborhoods, "The Ochoco Heights". When I think back on this move - three boys into a two bedroom house - it baffles me that mom and dad thought it would work. But it did work, sometimes with bunks and single beds and sometimes with one of us sleeping out in the garage.

Prineville in the early 50's was a bustling little town whose citizens gained employment from numerous sawmills. Back then there were at least seven mills that cut logs into lumber. Four of them were major mills employing hundreds of people. There were "teepee" burners scattered throughout the town where sawdust and end pieces moved steadily up from the mill floors and into fires that rarely died. The smell of pine sawdust and smoke were pleasing especially in the summer when the scent from nearby alfalfa hay fields was added to the mixture. The sounds of the saws, the whistles for shift changes, and the movement of trains echoed throughout the city. Prineville, small by most standards, was vibrant.

Dad sold the bakery sometime around 1955. He said it was too much work for him and mother, but I really think the demands were cutting into the time he had to fish. He had come to Central Oregon to fish the many wonderful streams, lakes, and creeks. He wanted a job that would allow him to fish every day. He found that job in a laundry. He could go to work at 2:00 in the morning and have the laundry washed for the co-workers who would come in at 8:00. By 10:00 a.m. dad was done with most of his work. He might have to come back and work a few hours in the late evening, but he had the day free to fish. And fish he did. No one was as proficient as he was. It was his life's passion, and he could catch fish if you threw rocks in the stream... which I did on occasion just to see if he could. He could and did. I never had the nerve to tell Dad I had done such a dastardly deed. Imagine, going around the bend in the river, tossing big rocks in a riffle, and then waiting for your dad to come wading downstream to fish it. He caught fish like they had been lined up and starving for days on end.

I do not know how my mother put up with dad spending all of his time either at work or on a stream, but she did. She would not clean the fish. I think that after some 5 or 6 thousand cleanings she finally said enough is enough. So the Lent boys cleaned the fish or dad gave them to friends and acquaintances. God help you if you told John Lent you would like a few trout. In more than one instance people had to tell Dad that they really had had enough fish for the time being.

Both of my parents worked and there were many times that we did not see either of them until late at night. Dad was most likely fishing or down at the laundry and mom usually worked the late shift at a local drugstore. Her normal time for arrival at home was around 9:30 p.m. My brothers and I loved our parents, but they worked hard, and in my father's case, worked and played hard.

You might wonder when dad slept. Sleep was usually had in front of the television. He had to have strong neck muscles since his head was always bobbing up and down as he drifted into and out of sleep. Heaven help you if you suggested he might get more rest if he just went into the bedroom. A nap or a needed sleep was something he did not want no matter how tired he was. He would pick huckleberries and sell them, gather pinecones to sell to the forest service, or work on his massive and productive garden. Sometimes he would paint other's houses, even though the paint was chipping off our own. But for sleep, just forget it.

Most of my early memories of Prineville and Crook County relate to the many, many fishing and hunting trips I took with my father. I was always game to go and, being the oldest son, I found that I had preference over my brothers. All of us could go but I was the one who had the passion and was willing to be awakened before dawn.

An early arrival at a stream or pond was imperative. To this day I wonder if it really mattered. I can still feel the cold that cut into my fingers like stinging nettles. There were innumerable weekends when we would load into dad's pickup and drive up along the banks of the Crooked River. One April morning, on the opening day of fishing season, we found ourselves walking along slippery rocks during a snowstorm. That it was biting cold and that the fish were themselves hunkered down in a non-eating mode mattered not a whit to dad. We fished.

I also found I could get on my bike and ride to nearby streams. What a great feeling this was. McKay Creek was only four or five miles north of Prineville and the creek was full of small to medium sized trout. But it was the trip there that was fun. I had the freedom to go by myself. And I was an egg fisherman. We had such disdain for anyone who would use a worm. How weird is that?

I was expected to work even when I was in grade school. Dad always found a way for me to help a bread distributor deliver bread, acquire a paper route, clean the dry-cleaning room at the laundry, or assist in delivering of the laundry. To this day I am not quite sure why he was so darned persistent in getting me work. I did not have to give the money to him, and I did not need it for myself. It was only when I got into high school that it became important for me to have money. I then needed it for a car, girls, and clothes. But dad must have had a master plan for me, and he always made sure that I was "employed".

On the laundry route I was the runner. I would take the clean linen, towels, diapers, shirts, or whatever into business establishments or into homes. The people would give me the money owed the laundry and I would hustle back out to the laundry truck. The only place dad would not let me make a delivery was the local brothel, "Jane's Place". I did not know it was a brothel at the time but when it was raided and closed down, I read about this house of ill repute in the local newspaper. Dad seemed to take longer than usual when he made the deliveries to the "house", and I often wondered what was taking him so long. But he did not take *that* long. I believe he just wanted to chat up the naughty ladies. Dad had a gift of gab and that gift was with him to the end.

As I grew older, I worked in the hay fields tossing bales of hay onto trucks and then offloading these same bales in open field haystacks. During the summer of 1957, between my freshman and sophomore years of high school, the hay crew I was working with hauled and stacked alfalfa, rye, and grass bales in the high meadow country along the upper reaches of the Crooked River. Each bale weighed between 60 and 120 pounds, the light ones coming from the dusty and dry rye fields and the heavy ones from alfalfa meadows. We slept in the hay fields and ate in nearby ranch kitchens. We, there were 10 of us, put up an average of 100 tons of hay per day that summer and we were each paid $1 per hour. A 10-hour work day netted me $7 since $3 was deducted for the three meals we ate.

The time spent in the high country was hard work, but it was fun and proved to be very interesting. I became knowledgeable about my fellow man and I smoked my first cigarette. Looking back on it, a first cigarette is not something to be proud of, but at the time I thought it was quite venturesome. I had not yet kissed a girl, felt a breast, or even had a beer so a first cigarette was a pretty big deal. I had nothing else to compare it to. My first smoke came one evening when all of us were lying on the grassy meadow following our late evening meal. One of the older boys offered me an unfiltered Lucky Strike. I took it like I was a professional smoker, struck a match, and then took my first big drag. I remember my lungs hurt and I coughed violently. I wonder if everyone reacts as I did to their first cigarette. If so, it probably is a defining moment, and we ought then to realize this activity is not really all that good for our body. Who needs science and statistics? The body is telling us "Houston, we have a problem".

As for lessons related to people, I learned during the summer in the high country that if you were big and strong enough, most people would not pick a fight with you, especially at the Saturday night dances held in the nearby town of Paulina. This was really just an affirmation of what I learned in the 5th grade, but I had no idea that it applied to young adults. I thought we all grew up and probably just left that kind of behavior behind us. Nearly all of the tough ranchers, cowboys, and lumber men used the dances as an excuse to drink copious quantities of beer and spirits. Holding a beautiful gal, and there were few of those, by their narrow waist was only secondary. By the shank of the evening, when bravado was at its fuzzy peak, it was time to find out who was the meanest and the toughest. As a 15-year-old I could not really understand this desire to abuse yourself or others. I picked up quickly on the "big and strong enough" ticket out of a fight. I made sure I ate a lot. I was now about 6' 3" tall and weighed approximately 220 pounds. That size and my rapidly developing muscle mass got me passes when it came to fights. There are times when being big is a bonus. Of course I was young, too, but I never ever thought being aged 15 would excuse me from fisticuffs. It might have but the thought never then crossed my mind. Obviously it does now, but not then.

In 1958 during the summer following my sophomore year dad found me a job in a local meat market. I was only a cleanup boy, but I thought this was the best job ever. I could stay at home and I made $1.25 an hour. I had to clean the saws, the meat grinders, and the rotisserie. I also waited on the public as this retail market sold only unpackaged meat. I did not know it at the time, but this job was, indeed, the best thing that could have happened to me. I applied myself, and by the time I went to college I had become a journeyman meat cutter, capable of earning enough money to fund my entire college education.

What my father did was instill in me a work ethic that has served me well in life. I regret I spent so much of my time in high school working at the meat market, but it did prove to be fun. I just wish I could have had more of the free time my fellow students had. I worked weekends and then after school (or after football/basketball practice) until we closed at 9:00 p.m. My dates, when I had them, came after I left the meat market, went home to bathe, and then dressed. When you start a date at 10:00 p.m. in a small town your options for entertainment are somewhat limited. Sometimes it was just lying on a blanket near an irrigation canal looking up at the stars listening to music. As to basketball games on weekends, I can remember working all day and then traveling to a nearby town to play a game. After spending 8 hours on my feet at the meat market my legs were throbbing during our half time rest period and the coach's exhortations went unheeded.

My love of athletics, as did my increasing interest in books, developed during grade school. By the time I reached the 7th and 8th grade, my friends, peers, and teachers called me Robert which I always thought was kind of scholarly. And I did very well in my studies. Mind you that I did not have a great environment at home in which to study. With the three of us boys banging around and Dad with the television blaring there really was no place to lay open a book. Yet grades had come easy.

When I began to excel in football and basketball my grades suffered. In 1959 I had my first girlfriend, the job in the meat market, and was otherwise totally consumed with athletics. Dad mentioned that I had become a somewhat marginal fishing companion what with my desire to leave the stream or lake early so I could get back home to see my sweetheart. With all that was going on in my life I went from getting mostly A's to mostly B's and C's. My friends dropped the more scholarly "Robert" for "Bob". Actually, I think my athletic teammates called me "animal" but that has little relevance in this tale.

Bob Lent and Shirley Hill in the 1950s

I do not wish to dwell on my athletic achievements, and they were certainly modest compared to the achievements of the two sons Shirley and I had, but I can tell you now that during the first three years of my high school athletic career, I lived for football and basketball. If my father found his self-worth through fishing, I found mine being an athlete. I could not spend enough time in the gym shooting hoops. During my lunch breaks and after school, before I went to the meat market, I would shoot ball after ball. Sometimes I would shoot 100 left-handed hook shots and then 100 right-handed hooks shots. I loved athletics.

When I started varsity football and basketball games as a sophomore I thought I had died and gone to heaven. One of the great memories in my life remains a road trip we took to The Dalles, Oregon, after learning I would be in the starting lineup for the varsity basketball game we were playing that night. I remember the songs on the radio, the conversations with my teammates, and each play that occurred that evening. I think I scored 12 points which did not make me the star, but I was plenty happy. I never once closed my eyes on the way home even though we did not get back into Prineville until after midnight.

Before leaving the topic of high school athletics, I have to bring up an event that changed my entire life. Going into my senior year, 1959-60, I had every expectation that I would attain special honors for my play in football and/or basketball. I had been contacted by university coaches and I knew that I would probably have the opportunity to play college football, maybe even college basketball. I was a senior leader on a team that was expected to be very good. We had beaten the 5th ranked team in Oregon in our last football game the preceding year and all our key players were returning.

But something cruel happened to me and my dreams. The week before the first football game of my senior season I was running laps around the track during practice when I was suddenly gripped by a very sharp pain in my chest. I bent over and found it difficult to walk back to the locker room. When I was taken to the doctor's office a number of tests were run, including an EKG, and it was determined I had pericarditis, which is an inflammation of the sack surrounding the heart. The doctors were worried I might have a heart attack if I continued to participate in athletics. I have never known such despair. I had lived for athletics, and it was all over. I was facing my mortality, an awful situation when you are only 17. I remember crying in the doctor's office and my father wanting me to take it like a man. There was no way I could be consoled. I had never loved anything as much as I did competitive athletics.

The doctors had me lose 35 pounds and confined me to bed for several weeks. Team representatives came up to the house to see me before they made their road trip to Coos Bay where they were to play one of the powerhouse teams in Oregon, Marshfield High School. Grandma Lent was by my side. She was always there for me.

I had to do a lot of serious thinking as to what my life was going to be. I decided first of all that I could once again be a great student. I would study hard, even if it meant having to go to the library every night where it would be quiet. I broke up with my girlfriend. I did not think anyone would want to be with a person who was already an "invalid", aged 17. I liked being thin but I missed being a participant in athletics. I eventually went on several visits to big time football schools and most of them said that if I wanted to play major college football, I would have to go to a junior college program where I could prove myself. I decided that my athletic career was over.

When I graduated from Crook County High School in 1960, I set off for the University of Oregon. I intended to be a good student and I would work my way through school being a meat cutter. My years in Prineville, 1953-1960, had been good to me. But I left for University with a hollow spot in my heart for now I had to find a new passion in life. Athletics were a thing of the past.

The sad thing is that we now know more about pericarditis than we did when I was diagnosed with the disease. Football All Americans Louie and Dewie Selmon both had it during their careers at the University of Oklahoma, and they only missed a few weeks of action. I am not a Doctor of Medicine, but I think the most common cause of pericarditis is a virus, and that virus can be treated. I have always wondered what my life would have been like had I been able to continue on with an athletic career. It more than likely would never have matched the life I have had. But one can wonder.

If the time from 1953-1960 was an eventful one for me, it was even more so for my some-day-wife-to-be. During the same year that the John Lent family moved to Prineville (1953) Son and Marie moved into their home on Locust Street in "Okieville". As mentioned previously their two-bedroom home was modest and lacked indoor plumbing. In later years, following my marriage to Shirley, she took me back to her old home. It was always my understanding that she had lived near Okieville. After that first visit, I remember looking at her and remarking, "Shirley, you did not live in Okieville, you were Okieville." I can tell you that I meant no disrespect for Shirley, her parents, or those that lived in her neighborhood. The Okieville residents were people of strong character, and it is also the neighborhood that turned out one of the most special individuals who ever came out of Prineville.

In 1953 the Son Hill family lived in Okieville. The Port Hills were nearby and Grandpa and Grandma Taylor still lived in the Melrose area approximately 4 miles away. All of the family members were now fairly close together. There were aunts, uncles, cousins, and other families nearby all with an Oklahoma heritage. By this time, it was fairly easy to get a job in Prineville if you were from Oklahoma. One of the richest men in town and certainly one of the major mill operators was John Hudspeth. John was a fellow Oklahoman who had made it big. Unlike what happened to Son and Port Hill, John Hudspeth's mill never burned and he was always adequately capitalized. His one standing order was that if a man needed a job and he was from Oklahoma every effort should be made to help get him get one. That all of these Oklahoma workers settled into Okieville was no surprise. They had a common heritage and in many cases were related to a number of others living in this close-knit community. That these workers may have taken jobs from other locals was not lost on the locals, one of the reasons so much scorn was heaped on the Okies.

And There We Were

When Shirley transferred into Ochoco Elementary School during third grade she could not understand why people were so prejudiced against those who lived in Okieville. It bothered her that there were taunts and that she was referred to as "gypsy girl". She had her ears pierced and she wore earrings, but then so did all of her aunts and nieces. She was taunted for the way she dressed and for the ringlets she wore. But it was the disparaging remarks made of her parents, grandparents, aunts, and uncles that really surprised and hurt her. The finest people she had ever known lived around her and it was difficult to understand why her fellow students could have such a callous disregard for her family and the others who lived in her neighborhood.

But for all of the taunting, school was a magnificent experience for the little Okie girl. School was a place where there was elegance. The girls wore dresses and had their hair done up in braids or in ponytails, sometimes even with ribbons. Ringlets might not have been the in or appropriate hair style, but most of the young girls, or more appropriately their mothers, still found a way to have a flair in the way their hair was done. After living in sawmill camps the variations in style were exciting. Shirley made many friends: not all of her classmates were bent on alienating or ridiculing the curly-haired little blonde. Some children are just plain mean and in the third grade these taunting children tend to have a disproportionate influence on what other children think of others.

The most memorable part of Shirley's first year at Ochoco Elementary was the "Maypole Dance". This remained one of Shirley's fondest memories of her early school years. She never forgot the elegance and exquisite beauty of that dance, and the colorful weaving of ribbons. The beauty of the dance captured her and never let go. She found many of the other school activities to be equally fun, especially when she compared these events to those that occupied her time when she lived in the small cabins and isolated communities that came with sawmilling.

School was easy and Shirley made straight A's. This ease with studies continued throughout her elementary and secondary education. When she graduated from high school she was a member of the honor society and was in the top 10 of her class.

During the 1950's life was tough for the family and Son Hill, Shirley's dad, never took a vacation. He chose to work rather than take time off since the pay was double time when one exercised that option. When a trip was made, the family would load up the car and head for Grandma Woods (Port Hill's first wife and Son Hill's mother) in Crescent City, California. No more than three days were allocated for the trip down to California and back. Sandwiches were prepared and put in a hamper for in-car eating. The eight-hour journey was a one stop trip with the one stop required for gasoline or for an absolutely necessary (screaming and crying required) stop at a rest facility. If one was not about to pee his or her pants it was not necessary to pull over. And if gasoline could not be purchased a stop would not even be considered.

In 1956 the family made a big decision and opted to move into a new neighborhood and into a three-bedroom home. Still modest, the home had indoor plumbing and it was closer to the junior high school where Shirley would be going to school. Money was now very tight. Son Hill made good money at the mill but he had not yet cured his drinking and gambling habits. There was precious little money left for the necessities of life let alone for frivolous expenditures. Many of Shirley's clothes were made by her mother. In fact, it was not until she was in her sophomore year of high school that Shirley purchased a store-bought dress. This dress, an orange chiffon formal, remains in Shirley's personal closet in our home to this day. During grade school most of Shirley's dresses were made from flower sacks which had beautiful flower patterns on them. She was teased, but the dresses were well made by her mother and Shirley found them to be wonderful.

The Hill refrigerator usually contained a half gallon of milk and both Shirley and her brother, Larry, could have one glass a day with dinner. There were no snacks. Meals were strictly meat and potatoes. And the meat was primarily venison that was taken during the fall hunting season. Hunting in the Hill family was now very serious business. Once, and this skips ahead a bit, Shirley had a boyfriend over to her house. He said he was hungry and wondered if there might be something in the refrigerator that he could eat. Shirley saw two slices of bologna and she made him a sandwich out of one of them. She was worried since she knew that these two slices were needed for Son Hill's lunch the next day. When the young man asked for a second sandwich, Shirley was mortified. She made it knowing full well that there would be a serious admonition from her mother. And that is what she got. Her mother could not believe Shirley would give away her father's lunchmeat. The truth of the matter is the young man who asked for the sandwich did not ever, in his wildest dreams, think he was creating a crisis in the Hill family. Both his father and Son worked in the same sawmill and they both made about the same amount of money. The only thing is that the young boy's dad did not drink or gamble and there was never a shortage of good things to eat and to snack on in his home.

In the 7th grade Shirley found that she had special talents with respect to dancing, swimming, and tumbling. She tried out for the 7th grade cheerleading team and was met with the same hostile prejudice she had endured at Ochoco Elementary School. One girl said that if an Okie makes the team she was not going to be a member of it. Well, Shirley made the team; and the girl ate her words and became a member of the team too.

In the 8th grade Shirley found that she loved to dance. There was always music in her home and she would grab her brother and mimic what she saw on *American Bandstand.* She became an excellent dancer, talented beyond her years. In 1958, the summer before she enrolled in high school, Shirley went to many summer dances and had her first serious boyfriend. The young lad was an exceptional athlete two years her senior and he loved to dance as much as she did. Since this boy ran in an older group Shirley became an accepted member of the high school clique even before she entered school.

In the fall of 1958 Shirley, then a freshman, tried out for and made Rally squad at Crook County High School, the only underclass girl to do so. She had by this time blossomed into a beautiful young lady. She was not only pleasing to look at but a person who could and would laugh at the drop of a hat. She had an infectious enthusiasm and a wonderful love of life. One could but like her. She was fun to be around. She had charm and vivacity.

I met Shirley in 1958. She was the girlfriend of my best friend, Jerry Riley, the aforementioned first love of Shirley's life. I enjoyed being in Shirley's presence and we found that it was easy for each of us to make the other laugh. I had my own girlfriend so there was no romantic inclination on either part. The only thing I tucked back in my mind was the fact that Shirley was the most beautiful, charming, and talented girl I had ever known. I felt she was so far above my head that it was not even remotely possible we would ever be romantically linked.

But we did have one date (1959) during my senior year and her sophomore year in high school. It was the Christmas formal and this is the dance for which the first store bought orange chiffon dress was purchased. Shirley had had a falling out with her boyfriend, and me with my girlfriend, so Shirley asked if I would escort her to the formal. Despite the fact that I was not an accomplished dance partner, I was not about to say "no". We went and I had but two dances with her. She filled out her dance card and danced with everyone. I had the first and last dance. In between she spun to the rock music and glided to the soft sound of the "Platters". She had won many dance contests, so it was not surprising that she wanted to dance with everyone but me. I did not feel disappointed although I very much enjoyed holding her when I got the chance.

After the dance we went up on the View Point, the table rock overlooking Prineville, and there we talked about our mutual love interests. I never kissed her, and we never had another date in high school. I was sure that was how things should be. She would be a good friend forever, but we would never be lovers.

During the formative years in middle school and undergraduate high school, Shirley became acutely aware of how a young lady could dress and wear makeup. Her role model was her Aunt Mildred who loved to dance and to wear nice clothing. The dresses and shoes Aunt Mil wore were unlike anything found in the Hill household. And Mildred would spend hours filing her nails and painting them bright red. Shirley decided someday she, too, would have fancy nails and paint them red. Mildred was also a bit of a rogue in that she worked to earn her own money, and this brought to her a degree of independence. She was very outspoken and opinionated. Shirley loved that spunk.

Mildred also liked to stay up late, and she was inclined to go out dancing until the wee hours of the morning. The contrast between Mildred and Shirley's hard-working mother, Marie, was simply startling to Shirley. Her mother's life seemed to be so monotonous and it was dominated with cleaning, cooking, and washing. There just did not seem to be very much fun in Marie's life. Shirley was appreciative of the life her mother provided for the family, but she felt there had to be more to life than cleaning and cooking.

Aunt Mildred was living proof life could be fun and full of elegance. To Shirley it seemed the only time Marie came alive was during some of the late evening chats Marie and Mildred had. Shirley loved those chats because, one she was allowed to stay up late, and two, she saw a spark in her mother's eyes that was rarely there.

As for Shirley, it was rare that she did not dig into her meager wardrobe to put on and model the best of what she had during those late-night chats. Shirley wanted Aunt Mildred to know that she was not the only one who had elegance in her life. So, with Mildred's influence, the natural beauty Shirley possessed became enhanced with a very sophisticated degree of femininity. This combination of beauty and femininity made Shirley Hill, at age 15, an absolute knockout. Once again, I may be prejudiced but I would dare say that most who knew my dear wife would not argue the point.

With Shirley's growing status as a student body leader, athlete, yell leader, and scholar she was invited by her friends into many of the better homes in the Prineville area. This exposure to the life styles of others was a real eye opener to her. One of her friends on the Rally Squad came from a wealthy family, and Shirley could not believe the things she saw when she visited this friend's home. There might be a half gallon of ice cream in the refrigerator or even a gallon or two of milk. There were hand lotion and perfumes in the guest bathrooms.

One evening Son and Marie informed Shirley that they were going to go to a dance and then out to a local cafe. Shirley was so excited she stayed up until 2:00 a.m. just so she could ask all of the questions she had about what a cafe was like. "Did they really serve you?" "What did you order?" Shirley remembers her mother saying she had ordered chicken fried steak. As unbelievable as it seems, this trip to the cafe took place when Shirley was in high school.

Shirley's first dinner in a restaurant came when her rich friend's mother took the two of them to Portland and they ate in a restaurant at the Imperial Hotel. Shirley had an elegant meal and when she was told she could have dessert she ordered "Cherry pie ala mode with ice cream". When it came time to pay the bill, her friend's mother pulled a $100 bill from her purse. Right then and there Shirley decided that someday she would always have a hundred-dollar bill in her purse. And this she did.

When Shirley graduated, she was voted by her classmates to be Most Popular, Most Athletic, Best Personality, and Most Likely to Succeed. The school decided she should not be acknowledged in all categories, so they let her choose the one she wanted most. She chose Most Athletic and the school allocated the other "Mosts" to the classmates who were runners-up in the voting. The fact that Shirley chose Most Athletic over the other choices does make one wonder where priorities are when you are so young.

By the time she had graduated from high school, Shirley had been Rally Queen, President of PEP Club, President of the Honor Society, President of Girls Club, Miss Year Book, Captain of the Tumbling Team, and active in number of other student political and social organizations.

Her father and mother never watched Shirley cheerlead. It was a frivolous activity. Son and Marie both loved Shirley but they could not relate to what she had accomplished. A girl's place was in the home with her mother and eventually, with her husband. Virgil went to a Father and Daughter Tea with her, Marie spoke at Girls League, and both parents once chaperoned a dance. That was the limit of their involvement in Shirley's high school activities.

Son Hill was concerned the family might not be able to afford the outfits needed for Rally Squad, but the team members selected skirts and sweaters that could either be made or purchased cheaply. Still, it broke Shirley's heart when, on one occasion, her dad drove her to the High School and said he felt her extracurricular activity was a waste of time. It hurt her because she knew how much he loved her; he just did not have any idea of the wonderful things she had in her school life, and no realization of how very happy she was. Son Hill was a good man, but life had been tough on him and frivolity was not something he could condone.

I graduated from high school and went to the University of Oregon in 1960. Shirley graduated from Crook County High in 1962 and she enrolled at Oregon State University. Shirley loved her first term at university. She made the honor roll, was nominated for sweetheart of Sigma Chi Fraternity, and had aspirations to become a college cheerleader. All of this came tumbling down for Shirley Hill when her father gambled, and lost, a significant amount of the funds set aside for the education of Shirley and her brother Larry. After the Fall Quarter of her freshman year, Shirley was told there was no money left for her and the family would not be able to afford to send her back to school. The hurt Shirley felt at this time was comparable to that I had experienced when I learned I would no longer be able to participate in athletics. The sad thing is that Shirley accepted the decision and dropped out of college.

Shirley had always been made to feel life was difficult and that she should be grateful for what she had. It was a given that if she asked for something then something else had to be taken away from the family or from a family member. You did not make waves in the Hill household. Life was difficult and everyone knew that to be the case. The money that was left had to go for brother Larry's college education. What was unsaid, but also a given, was the prevailing belief in the family that Shirley should not be so inconsiderate of the family as to expect the family to spend money on her education when it was needed for Larry's education. Any argument to the contrary, had it been raised, would have been met with, "You are just going to get married anyway so why should we waste money sending you to college."

Shirley, of course, did get married and she did make an incredible wife. She also turned out to be an outstanding parent. Shirley agreed she had a wonderful life, but she still often contemplated what might have been if only ..

It is too bad that there was not someone there to help Shirley with the ins and outs of financial aid available at Oregon State University. With her grades, her charm, and her infectious personality, I am sure she could have acquired the scholarships necessary for her to continue her education. But Shirley just bit her lip and decided college was not going to be a part of her life. She enrolled in Lawton Dental School in Los Angeles where she graduated as a Dental Assistant.

When I think back on what Shirley had to give up at a time when she seemed to be on the brink of such a wonderful college experience, I cannot help but think of all the minority parents who sacrifice everything so their children can have a better life. One reads these stories all the time. I think it requires a special type of parent, one who understands and is willing to make untold sacrifices so the next generation has a better life than the previous one. Education is more than sending one off to become a professional. Some people understand this and some do not. An educated person has doors that open in many areas and it is really an obligation of every parent to give their child a key to an unknown door behind which, perhaps, may be unknown opportunity.

If you could know Son (now deceased) and Marie you would not find them to be selfish people. They are as loving and caring as anyone you could meet. They just had a difference in opinion as to what was important in life. A college education for a daughter, no matter how talented she might be, just did not make any sense to them. Son Hill eventually gave up drinking and gambling, and Marie went to work, first in a box factory and then as a secretary. After these two events took place the family finally began to live like all those other families who made a decent wage.

My father John Lent suffered from having an alcoholic father and he recovered from that horrible episode in his life. Shirley's dad drank and gambled and this inflicted unnecessary pain on the family. Marie was the glue that held things together until Son came to his senses. In the end Marie had the man she loved, and the comfortable lifestyle she was entitled to have. To this day I think Son Hill was one of the most decent and fun gentlemen I have ever been around. You could see why he was such a beloved man. Marie today is a beautiful and elegant lady, almost a mirror image of her daughter.

Bob Lent and Shirley Hill went separate ways after our graduations from Crook County High School. We lived in a small town and our parents remained in Prineville even after we left to pursue our life ambitions. We never really lost touch with each other but our chats, if any, were few and far between. Obviously, something happened to bring us together but that remains for another chapter in this tale of adventure and travels.

Bob Lent and Shirley Hill in the 1950s

FIGURE 7. YELL QUEEN SHIRLEY HILL AT CROOK COUNTY HIGH SCHOOL IN PRINEVILLE, OREGON

FIGURE 8. BOB LENT CROOK COUNTY HIGH SCHOOL BASKETBALL PHOTO

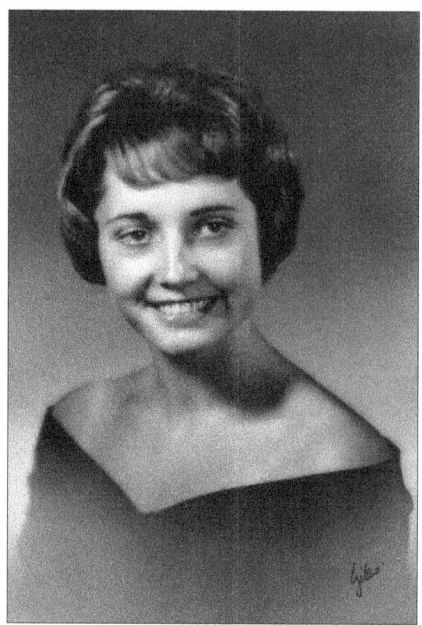

Figure 9. Shirley Hill high school graduation photo, Class of 1962

Figure 10. Bob Lent high school graduation photo, Class of 1960

Chapter 7

BEAUTY AND BEAUTIFUL

*I*n previous paragraphs references have been made as to Shirley Hill being a beautiful, even gorgeous, young lady. Perhaps that allusion needs a bit of elucidation. After we review those attributes that made Shirley, at least to me, a beautiful woman, the reader is likely to agree with the comment, "she probably was a looker". That there are also many other "beautiful women" who are not even cute may cause the reader to pause and scratch his or her head. And then again maybe this last seemingly paradoxical statement will not bother you at all. Perhaps you learned a lesson long ago that took me years to learn. But first, let me explain the attraction of "my" beauty.

If you go back and look at the early photographs of Shirley Hill, you can see that she is attractive. She has a heart shaped face, a well-proportioned nose, high cheek bones, beautiful hazel eyes, perfect teeth, blonde hair, soft lips, and a peaches and cream complexion. Her body was well proportioned, but she was not necessarily *endowed*. She had a very sweet and pleasing voice. You might see many similar attributes in any number of other young women in Shirley's High School Year Book. Some of the girls appear to be cute, some beautiful, and some gorgeous. Which brings us to what does it mean to be irresistibly beautiful? It is my opinion that the connotation of *beautiful* includes the whole package relating to an individual.

Shirley Hill in high school blossomed into a beautiful young woman. Yes, she was stunningly attractive, and you could not help but look at her and be drawn to that beauty. But what of the other *gorgeous* young girls who somehow could not be labeled with the moniker, *stunningly attractive*? The answer is it takes personality to project true beauty. Shirley had and retained a certain charm and poise that came from a self confidence that rests deep in the soul; a foundation from within that gives rise to poise. Poise when matched with beauty, wit, and seemingly endless energy and exuberance, becomes intoxicatingly attractive. Vivacity is an aphrodisiac, both to boys and men.

Even as a young lady Shirley could captivate with her smile and her charm. What a marvelous trait it is to have the ability to engage those in one's presence and to be with one whom conversation comes easily. Shirley grabbed your attention with her abundance of exuberance and energy. When she laughed she had you heart and soul. Most of Shirley's laughter was directed at her shortcomings or her misadventures, but she could laugh with you, at you, and for you. What can possibly be more charming?

In high school she made you feel like you were a very special person and no matter what was said, you were the one who was humorous. What a gift! I think that is why we were such good friends at such an early age. I liked the generally accepted perception that I was "funny", and when I was with Shirley she made me feel I was such a funny guy. We were many years into our marriage before I realized that I was not as funny as I thought I was. Shirley laughed at what I said and my feeling of being "funny" came simply because she made me feel that way. But Shirley made everyone laugh, and as previously stated, she laughed hardest when she laughed at herself.

Shirley was a warm, sensual female. She loved to touch people. She would hold your arm or tastefully lay a hand on you when she was up close and personal. And you did not necessarily have to be her close friend for her to show this subtle almost flirtatious affection. Some attractive women are seemingly aloof, and part of their extraordinary physical beauty is diluted by seemingly absence of warmth and charm. They are almost like dolls: no personality and no emotion.

Beautiful is also about taking care of your body and your apparel. Clothing is important but by itself is not a single determining factor. I think it is more about knowing how you look and also about caring how you look. Shirley had very few store-bought clothes when she was in high school, but she came to class wearing clean, well pressed, and perfectly coordinating clothing. She cared about how she looked. She wore a very subtle lip stick, and this made her lips look soft and inviting. Her teeth, a gift from above, were perfectly formed, but she took this gift and made sure, through personal hygiene that they were always bright white. No one, but no one, brushed their teeth as religiously as Shirley.

So beautiful, as it relates to my Shirley covers a lot of territory. She turned heads everywhere we lived and traveled. When she walked into a room or passed through a gathering of people she became a polarizing attraction. She was approached by innumerable strangers who complemented her on her hair, her complexion, her clothing, her smile, her voice... you name it. And what is more surprising, once someone had been in contact with Shirley, they rarely forgot her. People that saw her on television, whether in China or in Houston, or who met her at a business establishment would come up to her and begin talking as if they had known her for many years. Many times Shirley would come back from a shopping excursion only to tell me some very nice lady had approached her and had begun an engaging conversation, and Shirley did not have a clue who the person was. In the end it often turned out to be a sales clerk, someone who had seen her at a business or social function, or a friend of a friend. Shirley learned to talk around this lack of connection, and it made both her and her "friend" quite comfortable. Shirley exuded a profound beauty of heart. She was a very good person.

Shirley's mother and father rarely, if ever, told her she was beautiful. I asked Marie once if it was true that she never mentioned to Shirley that she was beautiful. Her answer was, "We did not want her to be vain, so we stayed away from such references." Marie once mentioned to me that she thought Shirley, at age 23, had become a classical beauty. It was only in the last few years that I heard Marie (then aged 92) mention to Shirley that she was beautiful.

Now please allow me to address something else that is even more amazing; at least it is to me. I began courting Shirley when I was aged 25 and she aged 22. She remarked at the time that I was the first person who had ever told her she was beautiful. She had been in several serious relationships. I found it very hard to believe that not one of her lovers had mentioned on numerous occasions how beautiful she was. The more I think about this, I think it comes from the fact that when you are with someone who is an absolute knockout you do not mention it to them because you do not want to come across as someone who is overtly solicitous. I wonder how many other women who are achingly beautiful go deep into their lives before they hear such sweet words. It came naturally for me to look at Shirley and to blurt out that she just looked stunning. And more often than not she was just that.

I must address another part of *beautiful* that comes to mind. Any number of young ladies and mature women can say, "It is nice to be a beauty, but beauty is God given and it does not describe me. Shirley is one of the lucky ones." But I have something to say to you. I believe that a very high percentage of the female population can be beautiful.

When Shirley and I lived in Denver, Colorado I would ride the bus to and from work. There was a lady who rode this same bus with me, and I found myself always looking at her. It was almost embarrassing: I usually sat 10 or 15 rows behind her, and I could not take my eyes off of her. She took exceptional care of herself. Her clothes were perfectly tailored, and they were always neatly pressed. She wore make-up, not so ostentatiously as to be garish, just enough to highlight certain aspects of her face, to bring out the best of what she had. Her weight was perfect for her build: her body was not particularly provocative. What caught my attention was that this lady, and she was not even particularly cute, was incredibly "attractive". She had an engaging smile, a warm personality, and she absolutely exuded a modest sensuality. Those around her were engaged and they were caught up in her exuberance and her wonderful personality.

This was the first time that I had come across a person that broadened my definition of *beautiful*. I think in my mind's eye I realized then that there are many women who could have this type of beauty, a beauty that is just as attractive to a male as is the classical beauty. I pass this along since I do not want my Shirley, who is a classical beauty, to take the brunt of those who say, "Yes, all of these things that happened to her in her lifetime came about simply because she was a beauty." To those who may think that way I take you back to the lady on the bus. I never learned her name, but I shall never, ever, forget her. John Keats had it right when he wrote, "*Beauty is in the eye of the beholder.*" Beautiful women are pleasing to the eye, the ear, and the mind. Shirley was a beauty. But more than that she was incredibly beautiful.

And There We Were

Chapter 8

PRINEVILLE, OREGON IN THE 1950S

Somehow a descriptive narrative of the city of Prineville does not capture what is special about this small community. It is one thing to describe the setting and to give the factual data on such a community. But what made, or even today makes, this town special is not unlike what makes every "special" town the way it is.

To get a feeling for what it was like growing up in Prineville during the 1950's one needs to understand why those who lived in this Central Oregon community had what might be viewed by outsiders as an "arrogance of pride". I cannot speak for everyone, but after the John Lent family arrived in Prineville in 1953 I quickly came to believe there was not a better place to live on the entire planet. Why?

Civic pride is something a community has or it does not have. If the citizens feel strongly about their community, they make sure it represents them. You can drive down the western coast of, say, Washington State. You pass through one community and see nothing but trash and buildings in disrepair. The feeling that comes forth is that this community is the home of a "I don't give a damn" attitude. Yet only 15 or 20 miles down the road you come across another village, town, or city where civic pride is everywhere. Flowered pots hang from posts along the street, the houses are all painted, and the citizens walk a little straighter and with a little more purpose. Each town is underpinned with the same financial base, a sawdust economy. Such variation in communities has always puzzled me. I once wondered why those of us living in Prineville were so damned arrogant. In retrospect, there were a number of reasons and I think they were all valid. No one thing was really all that special but when all were put into the mix, Prineville came out "special".

In the 1950's the economic base for the community was strong. The city owned its own railway, so sawmills flourished. The old growth Ponderosa forests were nearby and the harvest from the national forests was sufficient to keep the mills running day and night. The other industries, farming and ranching were also prospering. Many of the prosperous businesses in town were run by strong personalities. John Hudspeth, playing off success with his mill, Hudspeth Pine, became one of the largest private landowners in Oregon. If you wanted a job you had one. Prineville dwarfed the other nearby communities of Madras, Redmond, and even the more populated Bend. For the most part the milling plants in the city were union free and proud of it. The local economy was basically spared from debilitating strikes. In an earlier chapter I had said the city was vibrant. It was, to be sure. Prineville was the economic powerhouse in Central Oregon.

The city government benefited from an expansive tax base and from the profits of the City of Prineville Railway which moved timber, farm, and ranch products to market. For a small community, the town was indeed well off. You could see prosperity in the way people walked and the way they talked. Even displaced Oklahomans walked around with money in their pockets. Few individuals were wealthy, but many were comfortable with their finances.

As for the City of Prineville Railway, no other community in Oregon owned its own railway. How about those apples?

Economic prosperity may have left the populace with a bounce in their steps, but it was the success of the high school football teams in the 1950s that made individuals walk around with their chests stuck out so far they were in danger

Prineville, Oregon in the 1950s

of toppling over. In 1952 Crook County High School (Prineville) won its first ever state football championship when it won the Class 2-A title beating St. Helens 25-12. Banquets were held and the head football coach at Oregon State led the community in honoring and praising the champions. The team defended its state title again in 1953 and at the banquet following the season, the University of Oregon football coach was the keynote speaker. When one went into the barbershop all the talk consisted of commentary on the team, the players, and the coaches. Everyone loved to recall their version of the game. Yeah, we are from Prineville, home of the state champs. It is that way when you live in a small community. The town shuts down for key games and the citizens, most of them anyway, live for Friday nights. Success continued in 1954 when the team went deep into the playoffs, but did not win the state title. After three years, it was known that Prineville was special. It was the home of championship football teams. It takes a while for this aura to pass even when the teams are no longer "championship" caliber. After the mid 50's it would be 30 years before Crook County won another state football championship.

Crook County was also known to be a weathervane for presidential hopefuls. In the 1950s there were only a handful of counties throughout the United States where the incoming elected president had always carried the county. The community took this to mean that Crook County was the pulse of the national heartbeat. I remember in high school listening to one of my classmates (she went on to become a medical doctor) tell me she had just heard a speech by a man who would be the next president of the United States. She had gone to a political rally in nearby Powell Butte where Senator John F. Kennedy had delivered a speech to 20,000 plus Central Oregonians attending the annual Lord's Acre Sale. The Sale is held each year and the local church sells items that come from what its parishioners have raised on one acre of their land during the year. The funds from the Lord's Acre Sale are used to pay church expenses throughout the year. When Senator Kennedy won the presidency, he carried Crook County. Crook County was special, and Senator Kennedy knew it.

And There We Were

People in Prineville loved their lifestyle. They could boat, fish, hunt, and do just about anything they wished in the great outdoors. On the opening day of deer hunting season, the town was host to 20-25,000 hunters who traveled through the city on their way to the nearby Ochoco Mountains and the open range lands beyond. The community geared up for visitors by supplying them with free coffee, doughnuts, and pancakes. Of course, the community benefited from the frenzied way these nimrods purchased groceries, gasoline, ammunition, and apparel. But it was not lost on the citizenry of Prineville that the hunters were coming from many parts of western Oregon to hunt in the Prineville area. We lived here and did not have to make such long trips. Here is where you wanted to live.

The outdoors is not just about the mountains, rivers, and lakes. In Central Oregon it is also about the skies. When you look up into the skies over Central Oregon, you see the brightness of stars so clearly it actually stuns you. The Milky Way is an entity, and the constellations are more than names. You can actually see them. Watching the sky was so popular that the local paper, The Central Oregonian, carried a column by a local science teacher, Miss Fay Van Schoiack, informing readers of what was on display during a given week. There was hardly a student in Crook County who, beyond the seventh grade, could not go out at night and identify at least a dozen constellations.

Prineville, Oregon was also host to one of Oregon's premier rodeos. In the 1950s the rodeo, The Crooked River Roundup, was indeed a big event. The parades were long and full of interesting individuals and vehicles, and there were any number of marching bands. Indians from the nearby Warm Springs Reservations were annual participants in the parade and in the rodeo. They often put their teepees up in a field adjacent to the rodeo arena. In later years the Indians stopped coming (the wave of social indignation for exploitation of the Indian that swept the nation also hit Central Oregon). In the 1950s we loved having the Indians, and there was great pride in our Crooked River Roundup. We felt there was none better in Oregon, although that was not necessarily a true assessment.

Prineville, Oregon in the 1950s

Still, we felt the way we did, and we were proud of it.

I will leave the why Prineville is the best recitation with this last bit of information. The geology of Central Oregon is such that there are many quality agate beds under both private and public lands. Each year there was a gathering in Prineville of rockhounds who came from all around the country to trade, sell, and dig agates. Next to the rodeo and hunting seasons this gathering of agate hunters brought the largest annual influx of tourists into the city.

Shirley and I grew up in Prineville and we could not help but be impacted by the civic pride that prevailed at the time. I personally think this civic pride has greatly diminished over the years. The town has seen its traditional financial base eroded. Most sawmills have closed down and the City of Prineville Railway is now a liability rather than an asset. A local man, Les Schwab, stepped up and built a significant tire industry which for many years had its national headquarters in Prineville. Without the efforts of Les Schwab I fear the city would be a shell of its former self.

Television did not come to Prineville until 1955 and the John Lent family did not get a TV set until 1957. When we did get our television set, it was not turned off for the next 40 years. Or at least so it seemed.

News of the outside world came to us through the radio, the local and state newspapers, and finally television. The Lent family bought a television set when a relay station, on the summit of Grizzly Mountain, allowed signals to be re-transmitted into our community.

My earliest recollection of world events came during a 1950 broadcast of my favorite children's radio show, *The Squirrel Cage*. I remember running home from school - we lived in Molalla at the time - to turn on the radio. One day, instead of *The Squirrel Cage* there was news of American troops and ships moving into Korea. I do not know why but the thought of submarines heading into war terrified me. I remember watching my father listen to the news and the very serious face he had. I knew that wherever this Korea was, it was not good for us.

And There We Were

Once the Korea War began there were a number of comic books that came out showing the Chinese hoards charging the GIs. The Americans fired their guns at the quilt- uniformed Chinese until GI's guns melted down. The images were of battles fought in frozen and snow-covered terrain. I did not like the radio news, and the comic books did not make the situation seem any better. How could those Chinese make such suicidal charges? What is wrong with those people?

The atomic bomb had been known to us and as the cold war heated up, we were aware of the destruction caused by such thermo-nuclear devices. When the United States dropped the hydrogen bomb on the Island of Eniwetok in 1952 and I saw the results on Movie Tone News at the local theater, I was terrified. It did not help matters when we were asked to conduct drills in school where we crouched beneath our school desks and covered ourselves with a white sheet. I always wondered how a white sheet was going to help me if an atomic or hydrogen bomb exploded. When the Russians exploded their version of the hydrogen bomb in 1953, I began to wonder if it was even safe to live in Prineville.

That thought stayed with me until the day the Soviet Union dissolved and the Cold War became a thing of the past. One day, at a time of unusually bad rhetoric between the Soviet Premier and our President, I remember thinking, "This could be it!" And then I looked west over the Cascade Range and saw this huge mushroom looking cloud. My heart raced like it never had before. "Is it possible war has come and the Soviets have bombed Portland?" Such was my thinking. The fluffy mushroom was only an unusual storm cloud. But the fear of what could have been absolutely terrified me.

When King George VI died in 1952 and his daughter Elizabeth became Queen of England there were clips of the ceremony at the local theater. The new queen appeared to be very young. The election of Dwight D. Eisenhower in the same year was exciting and he carried Crook County. The local newspapers said that if Ike was elected there was a good chance that we would get a much-needed dam built on the Crooked River upstream from Prineville.

Prineville, Oregon in the 1950s

Father took my brother and I to see the movie, *Quo Vadis*, and I made a big scene when we returned home, crying about the lions eating the Christians. My mother admonished father for taking his kids to see such a spectacle. How things come full circle. In the 1970s I took my boys to see the movie *Jaws*. When we got home our youngest son, Taran, ran into the house and burst out crying, "Mama, the shark ate the little boy." And I got the same admonishment that my father received some 20 years earlier. Of course, father also took us to see *The African Queen* and that was very good, but I did not like it when Humphrey Bogart got all of those leeches on him.

It is funny what you remember about different years. For me 1953 was wonderful in that the New York Yankees won another World Series (their 6th in a row), and Edmund Hillary and his guide, Tenzing Norgay, became the first men to climb Mount Everest in Nepal. Fighting stopped in Korea and that was a big relief, but it did not impact me like the news in 1950 when the fighting had begun. Maybe it is the uncertainty about what the future portends that makes the beginning of a war so gripping and terrifying. When it looks like the war is coming to an end it is joyous and not nearly so traumatic. Joseph Stalin died and Nikita Khrushchev became the leader of the Soviet Union, but neither one really mattered to me. They were both bad guys and I figured one could drop a bomb on us just as easily as the other.

The year 1954 pretty much went by me and I cannot remember world events being such a big deal. We still did not have TV and the movies were not exceptional, although Prineville had three theaters at the time: two were indoors and one was a drive-in. Whenever the movie changed my brothers and I would talk father into going. It was always that way. Boy did we see some bad ones. Sometimes we would lie to father about how good the movie was just so he would take us. On several occasions we ended up walking out. Thinking back on this I think walking out was the 1950's equivalent of changing channels on the television set.

Some people will say that 1955 is famous for the year that McDonald's (in California) opened its doors for the first time.

I, however, will remember it as the year I had musical awakenings. We had dances in the 8th grade and there were a number of great songs that played on the local radio station, KRCO. Who can ever forget the following: *Rock Around the Clock* (Bill Haley and the Comets), *The Yellow Rose of Texas* (Mitch Miller), *Love is a Many Splendid Thing* (The Four Aces), *Autumn Leaves* (Roger Williams), and *Sixteen Tons* (Tennessee Ernie Ford). Wow! Now that was great music! And I did not even know how to dance to it although I did hug a girl or two and did the "two step". That year a very special movie came to the local theater. I could not believe how excited I felt when I walked out of the Pine Theater after watching, *20,000 Leagues Under the Sea*. And I did not even know what a league was. I remember blurting out *20,000 Leagues Under the Sea* when a sweet young junior high school interviewer asked me to name my all-time favorite movie.

Who can forget 1956? This was the year that the youngsters in Prineville learned of the guitar playing idol, Elvis Presley. We had read about him in the newspaper, heard his songs on the radio (*Heartbreak Hotel, I Want You, I Need You, I Love You, Don't Be Cruel, Hound Dog,* and *Love Me Tender*), and saw his first movie. The Pine Theater was packed and when the first scene with Elvis Presley came up on the screen (he was behind a mule, maybe it was a horse, in the background, plowing a field) in *Love Me Tender*, the whole place erupted as young girls began screaming and yelling. I could not believe it. I still can't. Two great movies won Academy Awards that year (*Around the World in Eighty Days* and *Giant*). *Love Me Tender* was not a contender. The year 1956 also saw Egypt try to take control of the Suez Canal, and that precipitated a battle for the Sinai Peninsula, one that seemed to be a lopsided victory for the Israeli forces. We saw it on the news, but Egypt and Israel sure seemed a long way away and it was hard to figure out what the relevance was to us.

Mom and Dad bought our first television set in 1957 and our whole lifestyle changed. We watched the news on television. When the Russians launched Sputnik, we all rushed out to see if we could see it in the skies. I think we did but that memory may be a little jaundiced. I remember that it scared me that the Russians controlled the skies and that they seemed to be ahead of us in technical prowess. With the advent of television in our local community we began to become more aware of domestic and international news. There was something going on in China with Mao Zedong but it was difficult to sort out. His new program, *Let a Thousand Flowers Bloom*, sounded good but it still seemed like he was a dictator. I do not think Mao ever intended there to really be a *hundred schools of thought*. China seemed to be mystical and far away. I could not help but think that it was still the same country that had, in Korea, sacrificed so many of its people simply because they had so many of them and because they could.

When President Eisenhower sent troops to Little Rock, Arkansas to implement court-ordered segregation it was hard to see the relevance to our way of life. There was not a colored family living in Prineville or in Crook County, and I had never met one. I read about and cheered colored athletes and I loved the music they made, but I really could not empathize with what was happening in the South.

The popular music in 1957, 1958, and 1959 now had a much greater impact on my life, and on my one-day-to-be bride. The music popular in those years was the music we heard when we danced, petted, and dragged main. To this day I can visualize places I was when the following music was played: 1957 – *Too Much* (Elvis Presley), *Young Love* (Tab Hunter), *Party Doll* (Buddy Knox), *Love Letters in the Sand* (Pat Boone), *Teddy Bear* (Elvis Presley), and *Tammy* (Debbie Reynolds); 1958 – *At the Hop* (Danny and the Juniors), *Don't I Beg of You* (Elvis Presley), *Twilight Time* (The Platters), *All I Have to Do is Dream* (Everly Brothers), and *Volare* (Domenico Modugno); 1959 - *Smoke Gets in Your Eyes* (The Platters), *Stagger Lee* (Lloyd Price), *Come Softly to Me* (The Fleetwoods), and *Venus* (Frankie Avalon). I think each generation has a special attachment to music that was popular during the impressionable years of maturation. The music listed was like magic during our high school years. I hope that each class, each generation has equally moving music that they think back on.

And There We Were

Music notwithstanding, I think the launch of the United States Explorer I in 1958 was exciting and also necessary. We needed that: I thought, "Maybe we are not out of the space race yet." When television became an important part of our lives, we found we did not go to as many movies. The local drive-in theater, The Patio, was good for going out on a date. It was so fun to hold your gal and watch the movie. We still went to the downtown theater, there was only one now, and when *The Bridge on the River Kwai* played the theater was packed. But we did not, and probably could not, get father to go to many movies. He had television and he would not miss *Gunsmoke, Wagon Train, Have Gun Will Travel, The Rifleman, Maverick,* or *Tales of Wells Fargo* for anything. I think dad watched re-runs of these programs until the day he died. So now we went to the movies to be with our friends and with our dates. But I was also working at a local meat market, so I missed many of the good movies. Not many started after 10:00 pm and that was about the time I was showered, dressed, and had my girlfriend in my 1958 Chevy.

The year 1959 was disappointing to me. The music was good, but this was the year I found out that competitive athletics was not going to be a part of my ongoing life. Alaska and Hawaii were added as the 49th and 50th states that year. Somehow that bothered me. How can a country be scattered all around the globe? It just seems that if we are going to be a United States, we ought to be contiguous. It was not until many years later that I came to accept the fact it was right and proper for Alaska and Hawaii to be a part of our United States. Change is never easy, and it is harder for some than it is for others. Fidel Castro took over Cuba at about the same time the United States was adding two more states. I do not remember being too upset about Mr. Castro's revolution, but his ascendancy to power certainly was one of defining moments for life in the western hemisphere. Someday we will normalize relations with Cuba. Even with the evil Fidel Castro dead and gone we still hold a grudge. When the United States gets mad at a country or a dictator, we stay mad a long time.

Life in Central Oregon in the 1950s was pretty good. Shirley and I lived in a great community that had great civic pride. Our families, humble as they were, gave us both good homes and we were loved by our parents. Shirley and I were aware of what was happening in the rest of the world but neither of us would ever have thought that we would someday be on the world stage, or that we would cherish our memories of the time we spent living and working in England and in China. We would eventually get to know the peoples and members of the governments of both countries, and that seemed like a remote possibility as the year 1959 wound down.

We had heard about the revolutionary, Mao Zedong, in China who was kicking Chiang Kaishek all the way to Formosa. We knew a revolution was sweeping China and there were many people who were starving, especially young children. Many youngsters in Prineville, as well as the rest of the nation, heard the admonition that we had better eat up and not waste our food. We should remember, the starving children in China. But for most of us China meant Chinese food at one of two or three local eateries. I think there are very few towns in the western United States that do not have a Chinese restaurant. To most of us growing up in the 1950s China was a big black hole.

We knew little of England, only that it was the ancestral home to many of our ancestors. In 1776, when King George III was around, we rebelled and became a country. That there was another King George (VI) who had died in 1952 and who had been replaced by a young queen (Elizabeth II) was of passing interest. We were aware of the great sacrifices that had been made by the British citizenry during World War II, and the of role that Americans had played when they first went to Great Britain and from there onto the beaches and battlefields of Europe. England, in its own way, was also a black hole, for it was about the past and not the future. Little did we know that the island country would become a very, very significant part of Bob and Shirley's future.

As 1959 wound down I made an application to attend the University of Oregon. Once more I would try my hand at becoming a scholar. In the spring of 1960 Bob graduated from

And There We Were

Crook County High School and Shirley was looking forward to another two exciting years in high school.

Chapter 9

COURTSHIP AND MARRIAGE

W hen I enrolled at the University of Oregon, I had no idea I would be spending the next nine years at this institution of higher learning. I came to campus with great expectations and none of them were reality checked. My father mandated I get a college education so that I would have a chance to get ahead. Dad had graduated from high school and that was quite an accomplishment in his family. Mother dropped out after her freshman year in high school so neither parent had been to university. They both knew their boys must go to college. And we did. All three of us graduated from the University of Oregon. The problem with me is I graduated (B.A. Geology in 1964), graduated (B.S. Mathematics in 1967), and graduated (Ph.D. Geology in 1969).

Looking back, it is somewhat interesting that I spent nine years in college studying geology, then 34 years working in the oil and gas business as a geologist, and I got into the field of geology for an almost absurd reason. During registration for the fall term of my freshman year (1960), we were required to sign in with an academic advisor. The lines for advisors at McArthur Court were very long except for one. I walked over to the short line and found the table to be manned by a professor of geology. I signed up to have this gentleman as my freshman advisor. Since he was my advisor, I thought it would be a good idea if I took his course. The professor was James Stovall, probably the most interesting professor I had during my matriculation at the University of Oregon. He had me hooked on geology. I got straight A's in his class. More than that, I got the highest grade in his class – all three terms. I must also clarify that I was not a straight A student. I got good grades, but I had to work very hard to get what I got.

Grades were good my freshman year and then I ran into a juggernaut in the form of a failed relationship with a long-time girlfriend. I lost my way. I changed majors from geology to pre-medicine and then found that I really did not have the heart to be a doctor. I think the stretch from meat cutter to a doctor is a bit much. When I went home to work in the meat market during the summer after my sophomore year, I found myself standing at the meat counter, honing my knife on a steel and relating to a customer my plans to go on to medical school. I think that dual image brought a new meaning to "the doctor is in."

When I returned to college for my junior year, I switched my major back to geology. Grades were still hard to come by. I think once you lose focus it is hard to come back to being a good student. It takes a bit of character rebuilding to get back the needed discipline. I always admired those students who were so damned smart they breezed through their classes with straight A's. It must be great to be that smart. You can go out drinking beer and chasing women, all the time knowing you can ace any class you take. I was not so gifted.

I did find that whenever I took a mathematics class, I usually got an A or a B. Mathematics came easy and I enjoyed the classes. Each academic quarter I would sign up for a mathematics class or two as electives. I had pretty much worked my way through most of the applied mathematics courses, but I had not had any that took me into the theoretical domain.

In 1964 I graduated from the University of Oregon with a B.A. in geology. The unfortunate thing about a B.A. in geology is that it is almost without value unless you go on to earn a Master's Degree. So I enrolled in graduate school. I took the graduate record exams for post graduate studies and scored in the highest percentile in mathematics and in a lower percentile

(89 I think) in geology. All my fellow geology students who were going on for a Master's Degree scored in the high 90's in their tests of geological knowledge. I was somewhat embarrassed by my relative lack of geological prowess.

The first term in graduate school I took a heavy load (had to get those math classes in) and came out with straight As. When the professors found that I had achieved the highest grade in my differential equations class, they thought that I should probably be thinking about going on for a Ph.D. in geology.

Shortly before I had received encouragement to pursue a doctoral program, the Geology Department at the University of Oregon had undergone a significant change-over in personnel. The argument presented to me by the Geology Department was I did not need to attend another school to get a doctorate degree. I could get the benefit of new thinking and new teaching just by remaining at the University of Oregon. Then they threw out the carrot that I could not help but grab. I was told that if I wanted to go on for a Ph.D., I would be given a fellowship that would pay my tuition and books, and a tax-free sum of $250 per month. All I could think of was that this was too good of an opportunity to pass up. My father was making about $355 per month at the time and here they were going to give me $250 tax free. In the vernacular of some of my Central Oregon ranching friends I had to "get me one of them Ph.D.'s."

In 1967, still taking mathematics classes each term (to help me maintain a good grade point average), I happened to glance at the class requirements needed for a degree in mathematics. The more I looked at the details the more certain I became that I was entitled to a B.S. degree. So, one day I walked over to the mathematics department and said I wanted to be put up for a degree during the upcoming graduation period. I remember the departmental secretary looking at me and saying, "Who are you?" My credentials were checked, and I walked through the subsequent graduation ceremony, proud as could be.

Then I took a class in theoretical mathematics. I was in a different world. I remember walking into class listening to a lecture and then thinking, "What the heck is he talking about?" I took the first assignment back to my graduate office and looked at the problems. I did not even understand what was asked of me. How about this problem, the one I chose to work on first since it was the shortest of all the problems we had been assigned: "Prove that a function is one to one if, and only if, it is onto." That course, and I did complete it, ended my career as a mathematician. I could only wonder how I could do so well in applied mathematics and be so inept in theoretical mathematics. I concluded it had to be how one's mind is wired, and I had to have had a few circuits disconnected.

I completed my class work requirements for my doctorate in the academic year 1966-1967, and I had spent the following summer gathering data for a dissertation related to a geologic study of an area located in Curry County, southwestern Oregon. I had previously spent parts of three summers in Curry County mapping and collecting rock samples. During two of those years, I was assisted by my younger brother, Steve, who took to the hiking and climbing like I thought he would. When one goes into rugged terrain and into places where few people have ever gone, it is good to have someone with you in the event you fall and hurt yourself. There are areas of the northern Siskiyou National Forest that were (and may still be) virgin timber lands. There were times when we were in the far reaches of some of the canyons where that I thought we might just be the first Homo sapiens to ever come this way.

I returned home in Prineville after completing my 1967 summer field work in southwestern Oregon. I was sitting on our living room couch and my mother, Mabel, resting in her favorite rocking chair, looked at me and said, "Did you know that Shirley Hill has moved to Eugene?" Then, without even a hesitation, she said, "You ought to look her up." My mind was racing even as she said this. I wondered what had triggered her to move to Eugene. Could it be that she was *available?*

When I returned to the University of Oregon a few days later, I called Shirley to see if she was home. She answered and, after the preliminaries were over, she suggested we might want to get together sometime soon. She said she was excited to see one of her favorite and dearest friends. She had no idea how excited I was. My expectations were rather low, but I was definitely interested.

It had been nearly seven years since Shirley and I had last seen each other and that was when I had left for the University of Oregon. In the meantime, Shirley had obtained her Dental Assistant degree and she had worked for dentists in Prineville and in Portland. I knew she had given up dental work and was most recently an executive secretary in La Grande, Oregon. I could not imagine what had brought her to Eugene.

I went to Shirley's apartment the day after I called her. When I rang the doorbell she came to the door, opened it, and then gave me a big hug. As I was getting this much welcomed hug, I looked past her to a table where a handsome young man was sitting with a cup in front of him. My heart sunk a bit. I realized there was no way Shirley could be anywhere without some debonair young man moving in on her. I would have preferred she was alone. The young man looked at us and he could see we had a lot to catch up on, so he politely dismissed himself and returned to his downstairs apartment. Shirley mentioned that he had come up to borrow a cup of sugar. And she believed it.

Shirley and I chatted as if it had only been yesterday since we had last seen each other. I thought, "She is as beautiful as I remember and even more charming, if that is possible." Although our conversation covered many topics, the one bit of information that caught my attention was that she had moved to Eugene because her latest "love experience" had ended up on the rocks. Hey, maybe the big boy had a chance.

I called Shirley the next day and offered to take her to the Oregon coast during the upcoming weekend. During the previous day's visit she had mentioned to me that she had never been to the coast and was looking forward to making a trip there now that it was only an hour drive away. When I made my offer, she surprised me by saying she would love to go on Saturday.

When I hung up the phone I began to think about Shirley and the possibility of our friendship blossoming into romance. I made two decisions that day. First I would go on a diet and I would lose weight: I was 6' 4" and weighed approximately 300 pounds at the time. Second, I knew that Shirley loved to dance and if I was to ever have a chance with that gorgeous woman, I would have to be able to take her dancing. I called up the Arthur Murray Dance Studio and made arrangements to take private dance lessons. I needed an accelerated course and I needed it now.

Our Saturday trip to the Oregon coast was all I wanted it to be. I took Shirley to the best part of the coast where the scenery is at its spectacular best. We walked along sandy beaches and took long strolls onto several rocky headlands. We stopped to look at numerous tidal pools, many having star fish, flowering anemones, small fish, and hermit crabs. I took mental notes on all she said and the manner in which she took in the beautiful scenery and sea life. I photographed Shirley looking into the various tidal pools, walking along the beaches, and resting on precipices while watching the pounding surf. We had dinner at a small café on the way back to Eugene, and we chatted like two very good friends, friends who had not seen each other in a long time, and who had a lot of time to make up for. I dropped Shirley off late Saturday night and went back to my apartment. I knew what I wanted to do next.

I had the film developed on Sunday. A putative collage of the photos taken during our trip to the coast was placed on a classroom table near my office. When the layout was just right, I put the photos on a large sheet of white cardboard, and underneath each photograph I added quotations from the comments Shirley had made during that part of the trip. I amazed myself. Some of my fellow students in the Geology Department (I wanted them to see that I had a very pretty "girlfriend") had pitched in and offered artistic help in turning out a high-class poster board presentation. I called Shirley Monday morning and asked if I could come by her apartment that evening as I had something I wanted to give her. I said I would only take a minute. She broke out into a great big smile when she opened the door and saw the poster board I lifted up for her perusal. I kissed her on the check and said I would call her later in the week. I left her knowing she had been favorably impressed

Courtship and Marriage

with my efforts, and that her feelings towards me had certainly warmed a bit.

We spent almost every weekend going out over the next couple of months. Trips were made to visit mutual friends in Washington, back to the coast to visit my geologic study area, and to Prineville via a commuter plane since Shirley had never been airborne and she had an intense desire to do so. We went to movies, took long walks through a nearby public rose garden located along the riverbank of the McKenzie River, and danced the polka in vacant parking lots during late evening strolls. All of this was serious courting on my part. Then it came time to ask Shirley out for dinner and dancing. The Platters were playing at a local night club and it seemed that this was the right time to play my dance card. I had lost nearly 40 pounds (you can do that when you keep your calorie count below 1000 per day) and I had progressed my dancing to the point where I could expect to be ok.

On dance night, we had a wonderful dinner. Shirley had mentioned that she really did not drink but when I ordered her a vodka gimlet I lost control. She absolutely loved the drink. Had I not known better, I would have questioned her not being a drinker. After dinner we moved to the lounge area, site of a rather large dance floor. I asked Shirley if she cared to dance. You know the answer. I took her in my arms and took my first steps of the classic ballroom Fox Trot (the music had the slow beat that only the Platters can pull off). I did just fine. When you dance with a lady who is a gifted dancer sometimes it makes even a feeble effort look remarkable. A few swing dances were mixed in but mostly the songs were soft with a slow beat, music for lovers. I was in heaven. Shirley remarked that she was surprised I was such a good dancer. I never let on that she should be thanking Mr. Arthur Murray.

We returned to our table and more vodka gimlets were ordered. I was getting worried since I did not have a credit card and my cash supply was almost depleted. The drinks came and we were sitting there looking at each other over red hued candlelight. I felt a tap on my shoulders and turned to see what that was all about. There, to my chagrin, was my private

Arthur Murray dance instructor. She was attired in a very revealing bright red, short skirted cocktail dress. She was in the lounge working as one of the extra cocktail waitresses brought in to serve the large crowd drawn to the Platters event. Before I could say a word, she looked at Shirley and said, "Bob, it is so good to see you here practicing your dance steps." The jig was up. I had been found out. Rather than be disappointed in me, Shirley seemed to think it was sweet that I had taken the time and spent the money so that I could dance with her. I was on a roll.

When my money ran out, and this was after only one more glass of water for me and another vodka gimlet for Shirley, we left for Shirley's apartment. I had high expectations for what might happen. When we entered the apartment, Shirley turned on the light and said she was going to slip out of the magnificent black and white polka dot dress she was wearing. Now I was really getting excited. When she came out of her bedroom she was dressed only in her black slip. She sat down on the couch beside me and said she hoped I did not mind, but she had just gotten the dress out of the cleaners and she did not want to get it wrinkled. No, I did not mind at all. I took her in my arms and pecked her on the neck. She then got up and offered me a drink. A failed attempt but things still seemed to be looking good. But do you know what? Shirley really was only interested in not messing up her dress. I never got to peg one that evening. It was then that I realized she thought of me as a very, very good friend: more like a brother than a lover. What a crushing defeat. I drove home that night wondering where our relationship would go from that point on.

We drove over the Cascade Mountains so that we could spend the Thanksgiving Holidays with our respective parents. We talked a lot, as do good friends who enjoy being with each other. I missed her while we were at home and when we got back in the car to head back to Eugene I had a real ache in my loins. There was no doubt in my mind that I was in love with this woman. During our drive back to Eugene she was discussing with me how things in her life were not necessarily going the way she wanted them to go. She mentioned she was considering making application for the Peace Corps. I could not control myself. How could such a beautiful, talented lady want to sign up for a cause, perhaps even a noble one, that would take her away from what would surely turn out to be an exciting and wonderful life in a normal world. She was not Peace Corps material. She had more to offer some special man than to direct her talents into a path that would take her far from the beaten path. This just could not happen. Before I knew it we were in Eugene, and it was time for her "big brother" to drop her off at her apartment.

The next day I thought a lot about the conversation Shirley and I had during the drive back to school. Shirley went back to work at the pharmaceutical company where she was employed as an executive secretary. I was back in my graduate offices preparing for the most critical period of my graduate career; written and oral examinations that would determine whether or not I was academically qualified to be a bonafide Ph.D. candidate. In a month I would face three full days of written tests and a grueling day of oral examination conducted by a panel of professors. Shirley had my destiny in her hands. If she and I were not comfortable going forward in a "loving" relationship, then I feared I would be so rattled that I would not be able to study for, let alone pass, my upcoming examinations. I had been quite diligent in my studies and in my preparation for the exams, but I was losing concentration.

I called Shirley at work and asked her if she would care to go for a drive with me during her lunch hour. I picked her up and we drove above Eugene and into a woodland park. We were chatting innocently when we came to a place where the trees form a canopy over the narrow road. I stopped the car, looked at Shirley, and said, "I no longer wish for us to think of ourselves as 'friends'. From now on I think we should be lovers." I leaned over and gave her a very loving kiss. When I backed away, she looked at me and said, simply, "Ok". And so it was from that time on.

I dropped Shirley back off at work and then went back to the library and my studies. I would see Shirley again on the weekend but not before then. I had too much to prepare for.

And There We Were

We went out to dinner the following Saturday, it was now early December, and Shirley looked absolutely stunning. We went to a local steak house, ordered a bottle of cabernet, and had a most pleasant meal. When we returned to her apartment, she opened the door and I gave her a warm kiss, one to which she responded as never before. It was not long before we found ourselves necking on her bed. The defining moment in our relationship was now at hand. I did not know what either of us would think after we made love, but I knew that anything else in my future would pale in comparison to the fact that I was about to make love to the most desirous female I had ever known or would likely ever know.

I wish I could tell you all the details and that the earth moved for both of us, but that is out of school as is, more than likely, this entire narrative. But something moved. In the midst of our amorous adventure, a clock fell onto Shirley's head, a potted plant on the overhead headboard fell and spilled dirt on my back, and then at the most inopportune time, the slats in the bed collapsed and the mattress fell to the floor. I had done all I could. If the two best friends were to become serious lovers, it would be in Shirley's hands. I, for one, was already there.

Shirley wrote in her diary the next day that she knew now that she would marry Bob Lent. When she told me what she had written, I became the happiest man alive. I went back to my studies and it was the most peaceful interlude I have ever had. I knew Shirley was mine and that I did not have to worry about our relationship. I poured my efforts into preparing for the upcoming exams. I often reflect on what I would have done if Shirley had not chosen to be my lover and if my preparation time for the exams had been clouded with the possibility of a failing romance or even one that required intense nurturing. I was so very fortunate. I forever reminded Shirley how incredibly appreciative I was that she was there for, and with, me when I was about to take my qualifying exams. Fifty years later I still had the same love for Shirley as I did then. That feeling is a gift to me from above.

Shirley and I were married on July 6, 1968. I was as proud

a bridegroom as ever lived. I still had to finish writing my dissertation, but our future looked bright. I received my Ph.D. in Geology at the conclusion of the spring term, 1969. We packed our car, drove to Prineville, where we spent a few days with our parents. We said goodbye to Son and Marie Hill, and then to John and Mabel Lent. We headed east on our great adventure, not having a clue as to what that might be. I had a job as a geophysicist with Pan American Petroleum (Amoco) in Denver, Colorado. That was a good starting point.

FIGURE II. BOB AND SHIRLY LENT ON THEIR WEDDING DAY
JULY 6, 1968

And There We Were

Chapter 10

Family and a Career
The Denver Years

Much could be written of the 24 years Shirley and I spent in Denver, but that part of our life is rather like any other couple that buys a home, has children, and then is witness to the growth of a career and children. A brief summary will likely suffice, although the 24 years we spent in Denver are as memorable as was our courtship. Our son, Tobin was born January 27, 1970. We moved into our first home, a modest three-bedroom brick bungalow in 1972. Our second son, Taran, joined us on May 1, 1974. Shirley had early on made the decision she would remain a housewife and a homemaker. Any ambitions she had concerning a professional career were set aside. She would be a team player. I believe that such a sacrifice, by any woman, is most commendable. I certainly believe the sacrifices Shirley made in this regard are as noble as one can make.

There are many wonderful, even poignant stories that could be told about our years in Denver, but I shall not go there. In 1977 we sold our home in Arvada, a western suburb of Denver, and moved to Chicago (our home was in Naperville, Illinois) where I took a temporary assignment with Amoco in the General Headquarters. When we returned to Denver in 1978, Shirley and I chose to live in Englewood, a suburban community located near the southern border of a then rapidly expanding Denver metropolis.

Our boys, with their mother being a steadying and nurturing influence, went on to become quality student-athletes. Both boys attended Cherry Creek High School where the enrollment was typically around 4000 students (in grades 9 through 12). Tobin played on a Colorado State Champion football team as a junior and was named an All-State player during his senior year, a year that ended with Cherry Creek being the State Runner-up. Taran played on two State Champion football teams and was placed on the All-State team after both his junior and senior seasons. Tobin accepted a football scholarship to Stanford, and Taran chose to matriculate at Dartmouth. Both boys graduated in four years from their respective colleges. Tobin gave up football after his second year but Taran went on to start three years at Dartmouth and he was the team Co-Captain his senior year. Taran's high school teammate, Peter Oberle, was the other Dartmouth Co-Captain, the first time two players from the same high school team had ever served as Co-Captains in the same year at Dartmouth.

In 1993, during Taran's freshman year at Dartmouth, we faced an unsettling situation. My career had taken many unusual turns over the previous 24 years, but it now looked like we might be faced with leaving Denver, not on a temporary assignment, but permanently.

Up until that time, my career had been an interesting one. It was unusual in that one can rarely spend 24 years in the oil industry without moving to another city, especially a city such as Houston, viewed by many, as the oil center of the world. At Amoco I was initially employed as a geophysicist, even though I had never had a course in that subject in my entire academic life. With a Ph.D. in Geology and a B.S. in Mathematics it was deemed I would most likely make a good geophysicist. I worked as such for three years and then I made a request to change disciplines, back to the one where I had my greatest degree of expertise. My career took a backward step for awhile. I had to catch up with those geologists that now had three more years of experience on me.

Several years of quality work followed and that work caught the eye of several mentors who took me under their wings. I

Family and Career, The Denver Years

was given more assignments of greater responsibility and then came the opportunity to move to Chicago, where I would be working directly with the senior oil and gas management team running Amoco's worldwide exploration program. The time spent in Chicago was exciting, but it was also very trying. Shirley and I loved the big city, the first real big city we had seen. Denver was a large metropolis, but Chicago was a big city. My door-to-door commute from Naperville to my office in downtown Chicago was a commute of one hour and fifty minutes one way. The children had a fun and safe place to live but I had to pay the price in travel time.

The time spent at the Amoco General Office was one of the most difficult times I have had to endure in my professional career. I was sent to Chicago, as were several others, so that the Company could see if I was senior management material. All went well, except the one person who did not view me in a favorable light was the Company President. Wow! Can you imagine that? I really did not know what was going to happen to me. Heck, for all I knew, I would be let go. Maybe I had gone from the proverbial penthouse to the outhouse.

Under a cloud of presidential disfavor, I was given a temporary assignment to assess the potential of, and to formulate an exploration plan for, an Amoco concession in Tunisia. The task force that was assembled had six months to come up with a recommended plan of exploration. The team did an exceptional job, and when the assignment was completed, I was presented with two opportunities for promotion. One opportunity was to return to the Denver office where I would be Western Division Geologist. The other opportunity required that Shirley and I move to Egypt where I would serve as Exploration Manager, North Africa. Both positions on offer had to have been approved by the President. It must have bothered him a bit, but I was elated. We returned to Denver in 1978.

I left Amoco in 1980. The regional exploration team had been successful at Amoco and the oil industry was booming. Amoco managers were in high demand and it was time to reach out for the brass ring on life's merry-go-round. In May of 1980 I became Vice President of Exploration for Chandler and

Associates, Inc., a small oil and gas firm operating out of Denver. This was a rewarding and exciting time in my career, but this came to an end in 1985 when I moved several buildings down to become an employee of BWAB, Inc. BWAB was owned by four individuals whom I had admired over a long period of time. I also had good friends who worked at the Company. I was employed at BWAB for 8 years and was serving as Vice President of Exploration when I left the Company in 1993. And that brings us to the beginning of events that resulted to the writing of this manuscript.

During the winter of 1993, with Taran at Dartmouth, where he was busy consuming a lot of capital (the Ivy League schools do not give athletic scholarships), I met with one of the owners of BWAB and had a very frank discussion. It had become apparent to me that they were keeping me on as a Vice President mainly because they were fond of me, not because I was needed to run a much-reduced exploratory effort. I felt that I was still young enough and talented enough that I should probably move on. That would allow BWAB to reduce its overhead to a level more in line with their ongoing exploratory efforts and it would allow me to find a new job which would likely be one to carry me through to my retirement. I did not have a job lined up, but I felt it was time to move on to another challenge. We agreed with a date of separation. And then it hit me. I had a son in an expensive Ivy League school. Our savings were not robust. We were financially alright for the time being, but if I was not able to find another job in a reasonable amount of time, we were toast. With those thoughts on my mind, I walked into our Englewood home and gave Shirley the news. I remember she looked at me and said, "You did what?"

To say that women are more emotional about things than men is probably an understatement. Security is fine, but to men integrity and doing the right thing come first. I had done the right thing from a career perspective, but I had probably not done the right thing when it came to homeland security. I was confident I would be able to find work. After our discussion I knew that the book *Women are from Venus, Men are from Mars* was an accurate depiction of the differences of psyche in the sexes. Shirley saw her life coming down around her and she was terrified.

I had been previously contacted by an old friend, Luke Corbett, who was then senior vice president of exploration at Kerr-McGee Corporation. Kerr-McGee had come to me 18 months earlier and had offered me a managerial position with the Company. I eventually turned down the proposal I was offered, and this was not an easy decision. I admired Mr. Corbett, and the fiscal stability of BWAB was something that had concerned me, even then. The reason I turned down the job offer was primarily due to our son Taran being in high school. He was completing his sophomore year at Cherry Creek, and that is a heck of a time to move a child from one high school to another. I had seen the effect this had on kids many times before. I was fairly certain Taran would have been ok with the move, but I was not willing to take a chance, especially when it was not really necessary. In football, Taran was one of the first sophomores to ever start on the varsity at Cherry Creek. He not only started but he had been named second team on the prestigious Centennial League football all-league team.

I thought about it and thought that with the existing press that came from his brother having been a Colorado all-state football player, and his early success on the field, underscored by his all-league selection, Taran had a chance, if we stayed in Denver, to play on a team that would contend for a state championship. Furthermore, he probably had a good chance of becoming an all-state football player. I felt that I just could not make a move and deny him of those possibilities. Certainly, with his talent, he likely would have been a star player in Oklahoma (Oklahoma City is the corporate headquarters of Kerr-McGee). But being a star is a long way from making an all-state team and from playing with a group of kids who have the potential to win a state football championship. This way of thinking may sound a bit muddled, but to me it did not. Even today I continue to think that way. I wish I would have spent more years with Kerr-McGee, but that is the only regret I have.

When I came home from my eventful day at BWAB the first thing I did after telling Shirley about my decision to leave

BWAB, was to call an intermediary, a headhunter, who had worked with Mr. Corbett during their previous courtship of me. I informed him that I was now looking for a job and I would be interested in talking to Kerr-McGee. I had to assume I had not burned any bridges when I previously turned down the Company's offer of employment. I made a few other contacts with companies in the Denver area and a few feelers sent to companies whose employment would have entailed a move to another part of the country.

During the time that I was actively seeking employment I found out something about human nature. Friends and neighbors have an exceedingly difficult time in knowing how to talk to you when you are newly un-employed. Conversations are forced and eye contact is much more difficult. It is almost like someone has died. I remember feeling so good about myself, but when I had contact with friends it was like I was among the living dead. I have since heard others talk about this type of reception when they too, have become unemployed. Hey! I initiated my unemployment. Right or wrong, I had chosen to go down this path. I had nothing to be ashamed of and no reason to be unhappy. I had a touch of angst about finding a job in a timely manner, but I was not in a panic mode. Perhaps I would panic if I was unable to find employment in a month or two, but not in the weeks immediately following my unemployment. Anyway, I certainly felt like I was almost a leper in the neighborhood. How very interesting.

After about a week, while Shirley and I were sitting at the dinner table, the phone range and it was the headhunter getting back to me after having made contact with Kerr-McGee. I was told Luke Corbett would like me to consider taking a position in London that would lead to me becoming Vice President and Managing Director with responsibility for Kerr-McGee's exploration efforts in the North Sea. The assignment would require Shirley and I move to London and that we remain in the United Kingdom for a period of no less than three and no more than five years.

When I heard what was being offered, I pumped my fist and suppressed a great big *Hurrah!* Shirley was looking at me, and she wondered what the heck was happening. When I hung up the phone, I relayed what had been said. "We would live in London for three to five years, and I would head up the exploration efforts in the North Sea." I did not necessarily get the response I had anticipated. It was then that I realized that I was asking Shirley to leave the city where her two sons had been born and reared. We would be moving from the home where the boys had spent most of their childhood. Shirley would be leaving friends and closing friendships that she had cultivated over 24 years. All the friendly store owners and her favorite shops would have to be replaced by new ones. In other words, her whole life was going to be turned upside down. Where I had experienced elation, Shirley was now facing despair. That I would have a job did not make up for the price we would have to pay. She was going to need some time to get herself together so she could be there for me.

This brings me to something I found out about Shirley Lent at this time. It also was underscored several other times in the future, but it was at the time of this move, the one that would take us first to Oklahoma City, and then on to London, that I learned Shirley had a remarkable ability to adapt to change. There is no one I know who abhorred change as much as my Shirley, but there is also no one that I know who embraces change as well as she did. She proved it during our move to England. She proved it again at the time of our move to China. And then she surprised me with how she proved her adaptability when we returned to the United States and to the city of Houston. Because of the climate and the city's reputation, Shirley had once remarked that she would go with me anywhere, but "Please do not take me to Houston." I can tell you now that when Shirley was faced with a relocation to Houston, she adapted. She adapted so well to living in Houston that we chose to spend our retirement years in this fantastic city. Our dream of returning to Oregon in retirement went out the window.

On April 1, 1993 I reported to Kerr-McGee in Oklahoma City. Shirley stayed behind as we prepared to sell our home in Englewood, Colorado. She began the long process of saying goodbye to her many friends. Tobin was living and working in

And There We Were

Minneapolis at the time and Taran was in Hanover, New Hampshire, finishing up his first year at Dartmouth. In June I flew out to Denver and helped supervise the packing as we prepared for our departure.

I was saddened to be leaving our home on Jasmine Court, but the sadness was somewhat tempered by the impending adventure of an overseas assignment. I shed tears and probably for a reason some will not understand. When our oldest son, Tobin headed off for Stanford, Taran somehow talked his mother into acquiring a pet dog. Taran's logic was that a dog could be considered as a replacement for the loss of Tobin. Except for a pet parakeet, Sparkles, we had never had a pet and I had been close to certain we would never have one. But Taran, after making an almost absurd promise to his mother, gained approval for the acquisition of a small pet dog. The promise, by the way, was that Shirley would have the final vote of approval on Taran's selection of a wife. So it came to be that the Lent family acquired a small piece of fluff that we named Tabor. Tabor was a Shih Tzu. This was Taran's dog but everyone in the family became very attached to him. I could not believe that I could feel as I did toward this small mutt.

When I was a young boy, we never had a pet and I was convinced that Bob and Shirley Lent would never have one. Then Tabor came along and he stole my heart. He was my buddy and I learned what dog owners all over the world have learned. These animals offer you unconditional love. They never seem to have a bad day. No one else in the family ever greeted me the way he did when I came home from work. Tabor would head for the door when he knew it was about time for me to come home. He would listen and try to look under the crack. When I pulled into the garage he would begin to bark and jump up and down, "Hey guys, the alpha male is here." Once the door was opened Tabor was all over me. I usually picked him up and held him for a while. Then I placed him back on the floor and he returned to a more normal state. Ok, why do I bring up a pet in this story. I bring it up because as I said, there were tears when I left Denver and they were related to my love of this dog.

One of the sad events related to our pending move to England was the then absurd English law pertaining to the quarantine of pets. A pet coming into the United Kingdom had to be quarantined for 6 months before it could be returned to the owner. This would have meant that it would have cost us about $2700. As a provision of the quarantine, we would only be able to see Tabor once a week. We did not want our mutt to spend six months in a pound without his family. We also struggled with the cost. The decision was made to find Tabor a new home.

A girl friend of Tobin's had a younger sister and this beautiful child had taken a liking to Tabor, even taking him to school one day for Show and Tell. We asked if the family would be interested in adopting our puppy. They were most happy to do so and I must say that by going with this adopting family, the little guy moved up in the social circle and into a much better neighborhood.

On the day we were to leave Denver, I awakened at 2:00 am, dressed, and looked down at Tabor. I said the word "walk", a word association that Tabor understood. Even at this un-Godly hour, the little fellow jumped up and down and was ready to go. I put a long retractable leash on him, and we headed out into a rather large open space near our home. We walked for over an hour along moon lit trails. All I could think was that after today I would probably not see the little guy again, and that he was totally unaware of what was about to transpire. Early in the morning, Taran (he was back from Dartmouth for the summer) and I took Tabor over to his new owners. I began to weep. A 300-pound macho man and a 12-pound Shih Tzu make a very strange couple of bedfellows. What a puss I was. But I loved that dog. Tabor went on to live a good long life and he was in the arms of a loving owner when he had a seizure and passed away.

Shirley's tears were a bit more justified I fear. We loaded up the car and headed east; Shirley took one last look at skyline of Denver, framed in the snow-covered mountains beyond, and then she looked ahead at the road we were about to travel. What a road that turned out to be.

And There We Were

Chapter 11

OKLAHOMA CITY

Kerr-McGee had asked me to spend at least six months working in the general office in Oklahoma City. There was a twofold reason for this deployment, but I was somewhat naïve in thinking there was only one. I was told that Kerr-McGee did not wish for me to fail when I went overseas to run the London office. The company wanted me to know how the company was run and what the corporate policies were. There had been many exploration managers in the London office, but they had either been terminated or had resigned every six to nine months. They suffered from not knowing the *Kerr-McGee* way of doing business. The only successful manager, a vice president, was a long time Kerr-McGee employee who had been sent to London to "straighten" things out. Kenneth Crouch was a successful manager and explorationist, but he was needed back in the States. I was to be his replacement.

I reported to work anxious to learn more about Kerr-McGee. What I learned was that it was very much a command-and-control type of management. One was expected to communicate with senior management when key decisions were made. Command-and- control is not necessarily bad, especially when the stakes are high, but one has to understand the difference between fiscal authority and discretionary actions. I am certain beyond a doubt that I would not have had a successful stay overseas had I not learned *the Kerr-McGee way* of conducting business. My predecessors who had failed were not aware of the corporate culture. The time spent in Oklahoma City, nine months rather than six, was a gift to me from those who ran the company. Had I not spent the time in the General Office I am sure I would have gone down the same precipitous path traveled by those who went before me.

The second reason I was brought to Oklahoma City was for the senior management to evaluate whether or not I had the talent and the social skills to handle the overseas assignment. I should have expected this, but like I mentioned previously, I was a bit naïve. I proved myself to the local management, but I would still have to prove myself to the London employees and to the vice president who was currently in charge.

When I was finally informed that we would be moving to London in December of 1993, it was with the understanding that I would serve as an explorationist and advisor for a period of six to eight months. Not only was I going to have a trial period, it was going to be much longer than I thought it would be. In the meantime, both in Oklahoma City and in London, the staff I worked with were not made aware that I had been hired to run the London office. This bit of deception was part of *the Kerr-McGee way* of doing business. I had reservations about the lack of openness, but if that was how things were, I would be a good soldier. It was then that I realized becoming a vice president at the company required I be subjected to prolonged periods of scrutiny. I do not disagree with that line of thinking, but I had not thought it through until I was an employee of the Company. One has to understand that I had been a vice president in the oil and gas industry for 13 years at the time I was hired by Kerr-McGee. I expected to have to earn my spurs, but I expected that my work experience would have been an indication that I had mettle.

Before Luke Corbett, who later became the Chief Executive Officer of Kerr-McGee, brought me into the Company he asked me to meet with his direct report who was in charge of worldwide exploration. I would need his approval before I was brought on board. It was important to Luke that there be a mutual expectation that we would be able to work together.

When I first met Mike Webb, the manager whose approval I needed, I remember thinking, "This guy might be funny but then, again, maybe not." It turned out Mike and I were able to work very well together. This British born, Canadian raised gentleman went on to become not only a very much respected supervisor, but also a close personal friend. It was only after working with Mike that I learned he is indeed a very funny person. His sense of humor is so dry it takes a certain degree of sophistication to appreciate it.

As Shirley and I drove through eastern Colorado and then Kansas, I knew that the time we would spend in Oklahoma City would be difficult for her. We had sold our comfortable and exquisitely decorated home and our household goods had been portioned into three different categories. We were going to live in an apartment in Oklahoma City until we moved to London, so we needed to furnish it with one shipment. The rest of our household goods went into storage and were partitioned into two compartments. Those household goods not taken overseas would be placed in long term storage. The rest would be kept ready for transport to a home in the United Kingdom, and this home had not even been identified. How do you know what to pack when you have no idea as to what will be needed? Can you imagine how difficult it was for Shirley to have the movers running around our Denver home while she was trying to make sure that this piece of furniture goes overseas, this one goes to Oklahoma City, and this one to long term storage? I think it must have been any housewife's worst nightmare.

We had opted to rent an apartment in Oklahoma City since the short time period made it difficult for us to lease a house. Buying a house made no sense whatsoever. I asked a lot of my elegant lady. I took her from a beautiful home with a lovely yard to an apartment in an enormous complex. It was as if I had taken her back to the days right after we were married when we lived in what could be called, student housing. We were back to living in a building where we heard toilets flush, people yell at each other, and lovers scream in ecstasy. We were impressed by the apparent sexual prowess of our neighbor whose performances were made up close and personal as a result of the sounds coming from adjacent fireplaces that shared the same vertical flue. I knew I owed Shirley a lot. Why would anyone subject his lady to this type of misadventure?

Even though we were only in Oklahoma City for nine months we thoroughly enjoyed our stay. Our apartment was so bad that we never wanted to be "home". That meant we went to every new movie, musical, and comedy show. We visited the zoo, an air show, and all the local Hall of Fame establishments. We not only saw all that was on offer in Oklahoma City we also branched out into nearby communities like Guthrie. On a visit to Tulsa, we visited longtime friends and took in the musical, *Oklahoma*, performed in an outdoor theater called *Discovery Land*. Shirley found that the shopping malls in Oklahoma City were full of wonderful shops and when she left our apartment she was usually out and about shopping. Still, we did live in a pit. Sorry about that Shirley. But both I and Kerr-McGee made it up to her.

After school was out in Hanover Taran had flown home to Denver. He then drove with us to Oklahoma City and spent the summer in our apartment. Taran was seriously into athletic training the entire time. We bought him a membership in a local gym, and he lifted weights and ran nearly every day. His workouts were brutal and that is the way he likes them. One day when he was on the track at a local high school, Putnam City High, he was running alternate sets of dashes, 220 yards followed by 440 yards. It was hot, *very* hot. Taran always excelled at strength and conditioning. He was number one on his high school team and later went on to become a collegiate All-American - Strength and Conditioning. I mention this because on one hot summer day when Taran was blazing around the track, looking "chiseled" from all his weightlifting, the Putnam City football coach walked across the stadium floor and asked Taran if he was a new kid that had transferred into the area. I believe every high school coach has that dream where out of nowhere there comes a kid who works hard and who is loaded with physical ability.

When Taran finally reported to Dartmouth for the start of football daily doubles he was weighed and found to be a lot lighter than expected. He told the head coach, "Don't worry, I have been training in Oklahoma and I will likely gain weight over the next couple of weeks." The coach was incredulous that anyone could gain weight over a period of time when practices were held at least two and sometimes three times a day. But Taran did gain weight, thanks in part to the extreme conditions under which he had trained in Oklahoma City.

When Taran left for Dartmouth at the end of the summer he took our second car, a Jeep Grand Wagoneer, with him. Since Shirley needed a car during the day, I chose to take the local bus to and from work. I had "bussed" many of the years I lived in Denver and it was something that was acceptable to me. What I had never done was to commute through a neighborhood filled with financially challenged minorities and Caucasians. I found that I was usually the only one on board who was wearing a suit. Typically, the same people got on the bus in the morning and, although a different group, the same people rode home together in the evening. Although the etiquette on public transportation is that you do not initiate a conversation, it is inevitable that you do so when you see the same people day in and day out. I would sit down next to one of the passengers and at some point we would say "Hello" or comment on something we saw or heard from the vantage point of our seats. I eventually came to be acquainted with a number of the bus riders. One lady once remarked that I must be someone important since I always wore a suit. I assured her that was not the case. But I did find out where most of my fellow commuters worked, what their family life was like, and what they did with their spare time (e.g., travel, weekend activity, and evening entertainment). I enjoyed learning when one of their children was getting ready to go off on some adventure, be it school, work, or the military.

I knew that the locals liked me, but it came to the fore one evening when two muscular young men of color hopped on the bus. They appeared to be drunk and the first thing they did was to belittle a nun; not an indication of good things to come. They made disparaging remarks about her habit and then walked back towards my seat. When they saw me, a well-dressed white man in a sea of black faces, they reached out and grabbed my shoulders and were about to give me a hard time. My fellow riders, and especially a little old lady, immediately and almost in unison said, "Leave him alone", and they did. I was moved by this and when I left Oklahoma City, I took that poignant moment with me and I put it into my bank of memories.

My evening walk to the bus stop took me through a part of the Oklahoma City that was on the decline. I think one could even say it was decaying. When I passed one vacant building (it had once been the home of a real estate firm), I observed that the building's previous occupant had written the company's name in wrought iron and the script was anchored to the wall with a pair of iron bars. If one looked hard, he or she could see past the script to the bars, but you had to look, not just walk past. I do not know why, but one day I put a dime on the back of the iron name plate. I knew that there were a number of derelicts that would snap up that dime in a minute if they saw it. After that first day, I made sure I always had a dime in my pocket, and each day I placed another dime on the bar, eventually stacking them in piles, 10 coins to a pile. When I finally left for England there was maybe $10-12 in dimes resting on the metal ledge. The dimes were quite visible from the adjacent sidewalk, but not so unless one glanced through the sign. I was visiting our general office approximately one year after we moved to the United Kingdom and I thought of those dimes I had placed on the sign. I was curious so I walked down the street and peeked at the bar. The dimes were still there. I was shocked. The next time I made the walk, and that was after another year, the building had been demolished. I only hope that some poor street person stumbled across the cache before the wreckers moved in.

Chapter 12

Wecome to the United Kingdom
A London Landing

     I reported to work at Kerr-McGee on April 1, 1993 and on May 12 I made my first visit to the London office. I went with Mike Webb on a trip primarily intended to review the prospects the office had generated. I was introduced as a technical advisor and that did not create a stir.

    I still had my childhood dreams of travel and the trip to London was exciting, both for the immediacy and in anticipation of experiences that were likely to be in our future. In 1993 I was 52 years old and I had traveled considerably within the United States and Canada, but I had only made one trip overseas and that was to Paris in early 1978.

    The trip to Paris had been a disaster. I had flown Air France on a big jumbo plane, most likely a Boeing 747. With no expectations, no experience, and no clue, I allowed Amoco reservations to purchase an economy seat in the middle section of the aircraft. I opted to eat and drink everything that was on offer: I did not know that they were going to stuff us throughout the flight. My pants were tight, I felt bloated, and I did not want to bother my neighbors, so I unrealistically curtailed visits to the toilet. A movie was played but one had to purchase a headset. When the movie came on it was in French. I watched the first part (it was quite a bad presentation) and then put down my headset and tried to sleep. I was too full to sleep and the narrow seats and tight seat belts made it difficult to even breathe.

And There We Were

When we landed in Paris, we went directly to the Nikko Hotel, which is part of a Japanese Chain. I was an American staying in a Japanese hotel, in France. Amoco reservations could not have made it any more difficult. To compound the difficulty my traveling companions told me that no matter what I did I should not take a nap. So we hired a tour guide and toured Paris. When we returned to the Nikko in late afternoon, I was a zombie. The rest of the gang went to the hotel bar to have drinks and I said that I was going back to my room to review my presentation even though our business meeting was two days away. I asked them to give me a ring when it was time for us to go to dinner. One gentleman had made reservations at an upscale French restaurant. I went to my room and hopped straight into bed. I was going to take a 30 minute nap and then get dressed for dinner. I went into a deep, deep sleep and when I was awakened by the phone I picked it up and heard, "Bob, we are ready to leave." I was so disoriented that my mind processed the information as the group was ready to go to the Total Oil Company offices for our meeting. I shaved, jumped in the shower, and then just as I was toweling off I realized that all we were doing was going out for dinner. I went down-stairs and apologized for being late.

We took a cab ride, actually the driver took us for a ride, to the restaurant, but not before we traveled throughout the city under the guise that he misunderstood the name of the restaurant we had given him. When we finally arrived at the restaurant, we were seated at the only center table. All the other tables were in booths lining rectangular walls. I noticed that the ladies were dressed in attire like that seen on the fashion walkways and the men all seemed to be wearing pin stripe suits. Furs were hung as the patrons entered.

My fellow workers were indeed the ugly Americans. They had not spent their time at the bar idly. Our group was loud, obnoxious, and obviously very irritating to both the staff and to the other diners. I actually got up at one point just so I could distance myself from my fellow Americans. We made it through the evening but when it came to dessert one wag commented on the small portions we had been receiving. The chef came out and brought a large pan of chocolate mousse. He took a big silver spoon and plopped it onto our dessert dishes. I ate my dish and that was not a good idea. To this day I think the chef coughed, urinated, or did something else quite despicable to the dessert. When we got back to the hotel room, I became very sick, and I did not recover for two days.

I spent most of my time in Paris staring at a bidet, the first one I had ever seen, or sitting through meetings. I was far too sick to tour with the rest of the guys. On the last day prior to our departure, I managed to join the group for a tour of Versailles Palace. That was the high point of the trip. So much for foreign travel, or so I thought at the time. I had found the French to be a bit hostile and not all that helpful in communicating with us. Yes, we did not speak French, but most of the French we encountered could speak English. However, they chose not to do so. I rationalized my not having a speaking knowledge of French (remember I had passed a test of my command of written French as part of my doctorial qualifications) since I was not likely to ever return to France. Little did I know that in the future I would make many trips to various French cities. Indeed, I would come to love Paris and the French citizenry.

The trip to London with Mr. Webb was an introduction to what foreign travel can be. We flew in business class. Our seats were spacious, and the food was of high quality. The movies were in English and the stewardesses were friendly. I was so pumped up that I did not sleep a wink. Once again, when we landed, I heard the axiom: do not sleep or you will never get on the local time schedule. Later in this tale I will give you my ideas about that line of thinking, but for this London trip, my second trip overseas, I listened to the advice of my fellow world traveler. After we checked in at the Britannia Hotel, a magnificent hotel facing picturesque Grosvenor Square, we strolled to the Davies Street office to check in with Kenneth Crouch. Kenneth has a motor that runs a hundred miles an hour so the first thing he did was to take us on a running tour of the London Underground. And by running, I mean just that. We raced down the escalators as fast as we could as if we were in a track meet. When we were on an Underground carriage, we were able to catch our breaths, but only for a few minutes. When the train stopped, we raced to get off the train and then quick stepped our way up two escalators. We popped up at Piccadilly Circus and walked to the Savoy Hotel for a cocktail. Kenneth rarely drinks but he thought we ought to taste the hotel's famous Bloody Mary. After our libation we were off to Leicester Square, and that was followed by a walk back to the office. I think Kenneth was happy that he had given his boss, Mike, and me, the rookie, a look at how one travels while in the City. Mike and I were left on our own, so we stopped for a pint at a local pub, The Barley Mow, followed by a casual dinner. I did not know one could be so tired. I had a lot to learn about international travel.

Upon my return to Oklahoma City, I could barely wait to tell Shirley all about the trip. I knew she would be excited to hear the details. I told her about business travel on American Airlines, and that the seats were spacious. I brought her back menus given us before our in-flight meals. I described the accommodations at the hotel. But mostly I gushed about the beauty of London, the sights and sounds of the city, and the marvelous black cabs that seemed capable of turning around on a dime. Shirley was going to love living in England. We had come a long way from those days when I sat on that Central Oregon rim rock dreaming of a trip to Mexico, and she living a dream by taking a 100 mile commuter flight across the Cascade Range. Like it or not we were going to become world travelers.

In August of 1993 Shirley and I took our first trip to London in search of housing. There was certainly an aura of excitement as we departed from Will Rogers International Airport. Our first stop was at the Dallas-Fort Worth airport where we caught an American Airlines flight to London. Even though Shirley was now an experienced flyer, a trip over the ocean traveling business class was a big, big event. I looked at her and it felt so good to see the sparkle in her eyes and to hear the excitement in her voice. Why is it that the *first time* for many things are so special and memorable, almost heart stopping? Many years later when we finally repatriated to the United States, we were jaded. A flight from Beijing to Houston was just another tiring overseas journey. But that first trip to London was filled with excitement and adventure.

On the short trip from Oklahoma City to Dallas we found that the corporate controller, Deborah Kitchens, was also on the flight and that she would also be on the American flight to London. Deborah, being the veteran traveler took Shirley under her wing. When we landed in Dallas, Deborah rushed us to the American Lounge so Shirley could experience the benefits offered to international travelers traveling business class. Shirley and Deborah ducked into the ladies room, and what a pleasure it was for Shirley to find the facility un-crowded and clean. We had just enough time to have a complimentary cocktail and to test the soft leather sofas. Such pampering Shirley had never seen. Then it was time to board the flight to London.

The business class seating and service was something Shirley took up on immediately. I could see that it would not be long before Shirley would expect to travel this way all the time, even when we traveled on our own dime. The adrenaline flowing through Shirley's veins kept her from any sleep and when the plane began its descent into Gatwick Airport Shirley was at the window looking out at the green and open British countryside. I think Shirley was looking for castles, stone fences, hedge rows, chimney pots, kings, knights, and peasants, everything she had imagined about England. I want you to understand that to this day, I share Shirley's look of expectation and wonder, and I have flown into Gatwick some 60 to 70 times, maybe more.

We arrived in London on August 21 and we were not scheduled to depart until September 6. It was intended that I would report to the office and be available for meetings and technical reviews, but that most of our time would be spent looking for a property where we would reside following our transfer to the United Kingdom.

We said a temporary goodbye to Ms. Kitchens who, wisely, caught the Gatwick Express to downtown London. A town car had previously been arranged for us with our destination being the Britannia Hotel. The wise and learned traveler will of course realize travel into the City by motor car is a very slow and trying experience. It was a weekend and one might think the traffic would not be all that bad, but the day seemed to be one of national celebration and we were detained on our journey by numerous parades and civic fairs. It seemed like it took forever to get to the Britannia.

When we checked into the executive suite at the Britannia Hotel, we found a basket of scented soaps, flowers, and a box of candies along with a card welcoming us to London and wishing us a very enjoyable and productive stay. It was not obvious from the card who had gone to all the effort, and we assumed it was the Hotel management. In retrospect I think the arrangements were most likely made by the local Kerr-McGee staff.

Shirley loved the room and the hotel. Our room looked out onto the gardens in Grosvenor Square. The American Embassy, a towering and majestic eagle above the front foyer, was the singular building framing the western edge of the Square. From our window we could see across the Square to the building where Dwight Eisenhower had directed the allied efforts in World War II. And we were in the heart of one of London's most prestigious and exclusive residential areas, the Mayflower District. Of course, we did not know much about the Mayflower District at the time. We just knew that the Britannia had a certain elegance and atmosphere that we took to be "British". The service was impeccable, and the hotel lobby was quiet and unhurried. We noticed that many of the guests were from the middle east. Indeed, some of the rooms on the lower floors had the names of the guests emblazoned on the door with brass nameplates (for example Mr. Hassan). We later found that these guests were those that came to England for the summer and then returned to their country of origin once the hot weather in their homeland abated.

I recall that the first thing to catch our attention shortly after we checked into the hotel was how expensive everything seemed to be. The room was more expensive than any we had ever stayed in and the meals seemed to cost about twice what they did back home. This was our introduction to the high cost of living that was to be with us during the nearly five years we lived in the United Kingdom.

I stopped by the office and spent a couple of days 'working' although I must admit that the work I did was of questionable quality. The local staff still did not know what I was there for: they only knew I was eventually going to be transferring into the office on a permanent assignment. I remember on that first day, the sky was sunny and clear, and the temperature was just right. I called Shirley from the office on Monday morning and said, "It's a beautiful day in London town isn't it my dear." She responded in the same jubilant manner, "It is a marvelous day in London." We were certainly off to a good start.

On Wednesday of the first week we were met by a management relocation expert, the owner of Tricia Townend Associates, who was going to lead us on a two-day search for housing. The search would start in London and then expand out into the outlying communities. This search proved to be most interesting and incredibly informative. If we thought the hotel room and meals were expensive, we were about to get a taste of what it would cost to live in London or in the outlying villages.

On Wednesday, August 25, we visited 8 properties in London. Most of the properties were in the West End. The rentals ranged from 900 to 1,200 British Pounds Sterling and this was per week, not per month. The exchange rate at the time was one pound for approximately one and one-half dollars making 1,200 pounds equivalent to about $7,200 per month. Despite the high prices for which these units were renting, we did not see anything that really fit our needs. What I took from this first day was fact that I did not want to live in Knightsbridge. One of the flats we visited had a view of Harrods through the front window. The proximity of this elegant and expensive retail establishment so close to 'home' would be frightening. The Company might not be able to pay me enough to weather that storm. I also learned that when an address was in a mews (e.g., Belgrave Mews West) we were looking at apartments that had been converted from the stables where horses were housed in the pre-motor car era. Agreed, the transformation from horse stalls to elegant apartments was done with great care, but to me the apartments in the mews were still horse stalls. I was probably not all that open minded.

My poor attitude with regards to the housing search resulted in my being encouraged to work in the office during the next day of the search. It was argued that I would better be served by having Shirley preview the homes to be visited in St. Georges Hill, Ascot, Virginia Water, and Weybridge – villages/communities located to the west-northwest of London. Shirley returned to the hotel in the evening and was excited about what she had done and seen. I was not prepared to handle such exuberance. I heard about homes with fabulous gardens, spacious kitchens, wooded forests, and fabulous interiors. The typical rental was 4,000 Pounds per month, somewhat cheaper than what we had seen on offer in the City. Of course, I would have to pay for the commute and spend time on the train, but that was not of an immediate concern to my precious Pearl.

Shirley was most impressed with her luncheon stop at the Wentworth Golf Club in Virginia Water. The view from the dining room was onto the golf course and a nearby lake. She had wonderful piece of salmon and a glass of wine served by waiters who were friendly and solicitous, almost overly so.

Shirley had seen one home, in Virginia Water, that was close to what she wanted. It had been recently refurbished and there was an abundance of dark wooden trim. The kitchen was airy and bright. The bedrooms were on an upper level and the back yard (garden) was expansive. It would be available in January, about two months before our household goods would arrive in the United Kingdom. The owners were going to be living abroad and would not likely return for at least three years. With the exception we would possibly be facing an in-country relocation in three years, it seemed like we had found the place we wanted. The property rented for 4,000 Pounds per month. Everything seemed to fit. We would take another look at this place the following Friday, September 3, a few days prior to our departure back to the States. The relocation company would also take that time to show us a few more homes in the Ascot and Sunningdale areas.

On the Friday evening of our first week in London Shirley

Welcome to the United Kingdom

and I purchased tickets for Lloyd Webber's musical, *Phantom of the Opera,* which was playing at Her Majesty's Theater. It was billed as London's most popular show and the evening gave us our first viewing of the London theater. Even though tickets were hard to get on short notice we found that one firm specialized in getting premium tickets for its customers. Lashmars Theater Tickets had access to tickets and, indeed, proved over our years in London to always have premium seats for popular shows. At the time, Lashmars was located on Duke Street, only two blocks from the Kerr-McGee office on Davies Street. I would hope that the company is still in business and is continuing to provide easy access to quality seats for premium shows.

Shirley and I loved the music in the *Phantom of the Opera,* but the show did not move us as it did for so many. We found we enjoyed the experience and the incredible setting in the Her Majesty's Theater. The exterior of the theater, located in the Haymarket District, is ornate and has multiple levels and columns set in a Victorian façade. The foyer is wood-paneled and the black and white checkered floor is under a Tudor ceiling. The velvet walls, red carpets, and white marble staircases add an elegance that remains even after many years of wear. Even though we were not necessarily enamored of the *Phantom,* we were totally captivated with London Theater.

The following morning, Saturday, we had made plans to take an Evan Evans tour to Dover, Canterbury, and Leeds Castle. This was a great way to see the English countryside and to experience a bit of English history. As it turned out the tour was one given in both Italian and in English, and this was a bit of an inconvenience since each time the guide spoke she had to repeat what she said in another language. It was not apparent how many Italians were on our tour bus but one gentleman, a tourist dressed in Bermuda shorts with a mismatched colored shirt, got up and asked if it was possible for the tour talks to only be conducted in "American". I wanted to crawl under the seat. In one quick move he had insulted the Italians and the English driver and the tour guide. I thought, "My God! This is shades of Paris!" The ugly American is everywhere.

Leeds Castle was a wonderful stop. It is one of the more

picturesque castles in England. Located at Maidstone in Kent, this castle, called by some, "The Loveliest Castle in the World", was originally built in the 9th Century although it was probably well into the 13th Century before its final battlements were emplaced. The castle extends partially out into a lake on a seemingly manmade peninsula. The lake and castle are themselves framed by green parklands that take your breath away. Even though we were on a tour, we knew we would be back to this castle many times during our stay in the United Kingdom. The tour stop at Leeds was made memorable by two events. One was a historical anecdote narrated by our tour guide, and the other an act of defiance perpetrated by an angry farmer.

The anecdotal tale relates to an event in that took place in medieval times. The story as told by our tour guide went something like this: One of the kings of ancient England was traveling through the Kent countryside with his entourage when he decided to send one of his attendants ahead to Leeds to let the Lord and Lady of the castle know the king would be spending the night with them. The lady did not favorably respond to this news. She told the attendant that the king and his entourage were not welcome at the castle. When the king heard of this, he declared he would take the place by force and so he did. By the time his lordship, the naughty lady's husband, heard what she had done it was too late. Both the lord and his lady were slain, and the castle became the property of the crown for the next three centuries. I do not know if the tale is true, but it was a good story. There are probably countless times in the history of mankind when one mate or the other has made an egregious error in judgment, whereupon both have suffered from an active and undisciplined tongue.

Leeds is known for love, romance, and happiness. I believe I shall take that thought with me always. It is a beautiful place, and I am sure that more people have left Leeds with warm feelings than those of hostility.

When we were at Leeds, I noticed that there was a terrible smell in the air. I could not see anything that was the obvious cause of the foul odor. I did see a massive stage that had been set up on a grassy slope leading down to the lake. It appeared there was going to be a concert and the crowd would have a view of the stage with Leeds Castle across the lake and in the background. I asked about the smell as we got back on the bus. The answer given was that the famous tenor Pavarotti was giving a concert in the evening and many in the local community were not happy with this event taking place on the Leeds property. One of the farmers had apparently taken it in his hands to spread wet manure all up and down the fence line adjacent to the historic park and gardens. I could imagine this farmer busy with his manure spreader driving up and down his field spreading the vilest stuff he could find. I am sure Pavarotti gave a wonderful performance that evening, and I am equally certain those in attendance suffered immeasurably. I know we suffered, and we were only there to take a quick look at the Castle. Only a change in wind direction could have alleviated the situation. When I looked at the water and the leaves, I could not see any evidence of wind as we drove off the grounds.

Canterbury was a fun stop for Shirley and me. She had not previously seen the beauty and the grandeur that goes along with the massive architecture characteristic of historic European churches. I had visited several massive and ornate churches while in Paris so our stop at Canterbury Cathedral did not have the impact on me that it did on my Shirley. She was awe struck by the size of the rooms, the ornate stained-glass windows, the crypts, the archways, the ornate external carved panels, and the rural setting. Canterbury, like many great churches in Europe was a site of worship extending back to a time that is poorly documented. It is known that in 11th through the 15th centuries there were alternate times of great construction, and also times of conflagration when much was destroyed.

But many great churches like Canterbury also are the sights of events and inspirations that are remembered even as much as is the architecture. When we left Canterbury, I remember being impressed by three pieces of information.

First, Canterbury was where Archbishop Thomas Becket was hacked to death because King Henry II uttered, "Who will rid me of this low-born priest?" Subsequently four of his knights took a December 1170 ride to Canterbury to carry out the King's wishes. Only the king was not serious, he was just speaking rhetorically. I guess when you are king you must be careful what you say, and to whom you say it. The king did not care for Thomas Becket, but he apparently did not mean for him to *really* be slain.

Second, Canterbury is the site of inspiration for Geoffrey Chaucer's *Canterbury Tales*. We studied the *Tales* when I was at university and I must admit I had a hard time with the language, it was written in archaic verbiage with which I struggled. When I had been in England for a few years I found my copy of Chaucer's book and tried to read it once again. Even at this later stage of life, at a time when I was much more patient, I found that it was still a bunch of gibberish. Sorry Geoffrey.

And lastly, Canterbury will remain in my memories because it is the final resting place of the Black Knight. Doesn't that name conjure up great images? You can really let your imagination run rampant. When I saw the sarcophagus of the Black Knight on the south side of Trinity Chapel, I thought that this must be one of those knights that charged across an arena with lance locked, battling for the honor of a maiden, or, if not a good guy, then in combat with the one who was fighting for the maiden's honor. It did not matter to me whether he was good or bad, he was a knight of old. In truth, the Black Knight was Prince Edward, the eldest son of King Edward III. The prince was a military leader who led the English against the French with such bravery and ferocity that he was feared by friend and foe alike. His death was a huge blow to the British in the coeval war(s) with France. The Black Prince died in 1376, about the same time that Chaucer was penning his *Canterbury Tales*.

We left Canterbury when the "Road Warrior" gave her command to load up for departure. Our guide, the small woman that she was, had earned the Road Warrior moniker by deeds and words. Many on the bus found it easy to switch from her given name, only none of us had enough nerve to speak the *Warrior* name in her presence. Whenever we pulled off, she would give us a lecture on the timeliness of departure, and then she would march us off to see the sights and to give us her patented spiel. Heaven help you if you did not pay attention, or if you were a laggard coming back onto the tour bus.

Our next tour stop was Dover Castle, an ancient battlement located above Dover Harbor and the coastal town of Dover. The White Cliffs of Dover were known to Shirley and me through movies, books, and songs. I had also read of the chalk cliffs as part of my geological studies in university. As we drove up the grass covered slope to Dover Castle. I was filled with excitement because we would have the best view we yet had of the English Channel, and we just might get a glimpse of France if the haze was not too bad.

The Road Warrior took us immediately to the great tower, or keep, built by King Henry II sometime in the 1180s. This four-sided tower commands the highest elevation and each of the four battlements atop the tower give panoramic and spectacular views in all directions of the compass. I raced for the southeast battlement which I expected to provide the best view of the English Channel and the Continent. The haze was there but I was able to see France, and maybe the village of Calais. If what I saw was Calais, then Dunkirk had to be off to the left (northeast).

When I had sated my desire to view the ocean and the lands far beyond, I peeked over the tower to look at the buildings within the fortress. The tower is surrounded by a stone blockade, called a curtain by the locals, part of which is stone-fronted residential buildings, and part simply walls and towers. A moat separates this inner defense from an outer wall that encircles all that is Dover Castle. The outer wall has many towers from which archers and later gunneries could bombard aggressors. When one visualizes the open spaces between the encircling walls green with grass (even the moat is grass covered), one begins to get a feeling of how beautiful this setting is.

When we were sated with the views from the tower, we made the short walk, still within the castle complex, to the buildings that are "ancient". Mind you, much of what we had already seen was built in the 11th and 12th Centuries. But in the 1st Century AD the Romans had built a lighthouse, called a

And There We Were

pharos, on a knoll about 200 meters from the keep. Adjacent to this lighthouse is the Church of St. Mary-in-Castro (what a name), built sometime in the 10th Century by the Anglo-Saxons.

The Roman lighthouse held the most interest for me. I marveled that it was still standing, and I was intrigued by the stone construction. Many of the stones in the walls consisted of chert, or flint, if you will. The Dover chalk cliffs have many nodules of chert and these weathered or mined stones seem to have been the preferred construction material in the walls of both the church and the lighthouse. I could not but wonder what the Indians in the American West would have given to have such an abundance of material for use in the making of arrowheads and fire. And the early builders at Dover just mortared these stones right into the walls.

As with any place one visits you take from it certain thoughts and observations. Would you believe that it was one of the sieges of Dover Castle that most impressed me? When I think of sieges, I think of assaults on the battlements by battering rams, ladders, cannons, etc. But at Dover Castle one of the most effective attempts to invade the fortress came in 1216 when the forces of Prince Louis of France tunneled through the soft chalk and caused the North Gate structure to collapse. The English defenders rushed in and blocked the breach with timbers and were able to hold off the French. Thereafter Dover Castle no longer seemed so impregnable. Talk about "thinking out of the box". I think someone in the army of Prince Louis army could teach the class.

Dover Castle was never built to be a residence for royalty. Unlike Windsor Castle, for example, Dover was primarily intended to be a military barracks. Still, that did not keep one King Charles I from making a singular attempt in that regard. In 1625 King Charles I had Dover Castle renovated. He created royal apartments to which he brought his young bride Queen Henrietta Maria. What a big mistake that was. I think King Charles I did not have a clue as to "what a woman wants". Queen Henrietta was most unimpressed, and she left it to her chamberlain to write,

> *"The castle is an ancient building constructed after the manner of olden days, in which the queen was ill lodged in poorly furnished apartments, and her retinue treated with very little magnificence considering the importance of the occasion."*

I have my feelings hurt when Shirley is disappointed with a birthday gift. Can you imagine poor ol' King Charles I?

The last thought I took with me as we pulled out of the Dover Castle complex was the role the place played during World War II. By 1940 many tunnels had been excavated beneath Dover Castle and along the English Channel coastline, and it was in these tunnels that some of the key decisions and plans were made as England prepared to rescue the British Expeditionary and French Forces from the Continent. I do not know how many boats sailed from Dover for Dunkirk, but many had to have left Dover harbor. Many of the rescued soldiers were taken to Dover and then, via train, back into the English heartland. The master planners working in the tunnels beneath Dover Castle and its surrounding chalk hills were responsible, along with their fellow countrymen, for the rescue of 338,682 British soldiers from Dunkirk. In nine days, May 26 to June 4, 1940, British war ships, fishing vessels, and many small boats, rescued the British soldiers and another 139,000 French troops from the burning and bombed French coastline near Dunkirk Harbor.

We looked back over the English Channel and the Cliffs of Dover as tour bus climbed the hill and headed back to London. We could not possibly know it then but two of the ten most exiting experiences we would have over the next five years would take place in this rural area of England.

We were tired when we left the tour in London and returned to the Britannia Hotel. But we both were appreciative that we had had this introductory opportunity to see a bit of England. We decided that next weekend, time permitting, we would sign up for a tour to Bath, Stonehenge, and Salisbury. But before then we still had to find a home in England.

I spent the week at the office and Shirley found her way

around the West End. She made her first visit to Harrods, Selfridges, and Bond Street. In the evenings Shirley and I walked to Piccadilly Circus and Leicester Square. We went to the cinema one evening, but mostly we just walked around the City and ate in small and inexpensive restaurants. We had reserved Friday for a re-visit of the country homes Shirley had found interesting.

The Friday trip to Berkshire and Surrey was my first and I fell in love with the countryside just as Shirley had done on her trip the previous week. We toured 6 residences in Virginia Water, Sunningdale, Ascot, Weybridge, and Walton. Lunch was at a pub, The Thatched Tavern, an establishment famed for fine food and its small, cozy atmosphere. During our luncheon Shirley and I came to the conclusion that the home on offer in Virginia Water, near the Windsor Great Park, was the one place we had visited that met our financial and spatial requirements. It had its flaws, but it would be acceptable. The relocation firm was asked to work with our office in preparing an offer. Because we offered what was asked, we expected to get the rental.

Our plane back to the United States was not going to leave until Sunday so Shirley and I decided to take in one more tour prior to our departure from England. The trip the previous weekend to Leeds and the Kent countryside had been a lot of fun and we had found this type of touring to be a great way to get a taste of the more popular tourist areas. We thumbed through the Evan Evans Tours booklet and chose a one-day trip that would take us further out into the countryside than did our trip the previous weekend. We would be going to Stonehenge, Salisbury, and Bath. We made reservations, paid the fare (62 Pounds each), and walked to the Park International Hotel, one of the designated departure pickup points.

As always, the newness of travel abroad makes for a riveting experience. I recall being excited even as we traveled through the City prior to getting on the motorway that would take us to Salisbury. I viewed the countryside with the same fascination as I had on the tour we had taken through the Kent countryside the previous weekend. The boy from Prineville could not take his eyes off the hedgerows, the cultivated farmlands, the rural housing, and local pubs. Everything was new and exciting. I wanted to take it all in and to never, ever, lose my first impressions of this scenic and ancient country.

Our first stop was Stonehenge located on the Salisbury Plain near Amesbury in Wiltshire (Southern England for those not having access to a map). Most people have either seen pictures of, or read about, the strange megaliths (also known as rocks) that typically stand vertically in pairs with some having flat stone lintels across the pairs. For those familiar with the movie *European Vacation* these are the same rocks of antiquity that were visited by the Griswold family.

When we pulled into the parking lot and disembarked, I noticed a mobile concession stand (eats and trinkets). I thought it odd that we would be visiting a historic monument, and this commercial venture was so close by. But, when I thought back on other historic places around the world and what is going on around them, the concession stand did not seem so out of place. It was just that the grass was so green, and the monuments so isolated that any, and I emphasize *any*, form of modern construction would just seem out of place. That was my first impression of Stonehenge.

Shirley and I walked towards the monument with our tour guide and saw that the ruins themselves were roped off, so we would only be able to view the large monoliths from afar. I can tell you now that the 60 mile drive out to this locality is a little much if you are a tourist and this is the only site you will visit. After about 10 minutes of looking at the stones and reading the informational boards you begin to feel guilty that you are not more reverent. Shirley was ready to head back to the bus. I wanted to hear the tale the tour guide was to give but mostly, being a geologist, I was interested in the composition of the rock. No doubt I would have created quite a stir had I walked over to the stones and taken a chip out of them with a rock hammer. I did not have such a tool, so I had to rely on visual observation from 30 or 40 feet away. It appeared to me that the larger stones, that is, the ones standing tall with flat blocks overlying them, were composed of dense sandstone or even quartzite. The funny bluish grey rocks, the Bluestones, standing by themselves were probably fine-grained igneous rock. Later, after we had returned to the States, I dug out a reference book and read that my guesses were correct, although scientists had given more detailed names to the igneous rocks (for example, dolerites, etc.)

Stonehenge began as a place of worshipping or gathering nearly 5000 years ago. Most of the stones were probably emplaced by the year 3000 B.C. Most of those in the public realm relate Stonehenge with the Druids, a religious sect that first held celebrations during a period extending from the 16th through the 20th Centuries. We probably know more about the source of the stones at Stonehenge than we do about the people who made the structures. The massive pillars (13 feet tall and 6.5 feet by 3 feet at the base) and their lintels (usually 10.5 feet long) likely came from outcrops less than 20 miles distant. But the dense and heavy Bluestones had to have come from a quarry no closer than 240 miles away. I cannot imagine the time and the manpower it must have taken to cut, haul, and emplace these massive stones. It did not take long before I was ready to get in line to get an ice cream cone and then to board the bus.

One last thought about Stonehenge. I apologize if you have not seen the movie *European Vacation* starring Chevy Chase and Beverley DiAngelo but I must harken back to the one scene in the movie in which the Griswolds back their car around as they prepare to leave. The car hits a pillar, and then like dominoes they fall against each other, leaving only a jumbled pile of stones. As odd as this black humor is, something like this did happen in the year 1900 when tourists toppled two of the massive stones. Of the 30 upright stones that originally formed the Sarsen Circle only 17 now remain standing. Without the rope to keep the modern tourist separated from the ruins I fear that the number of standing stones would be much reduced.

It is only 6 or 7 miles from Stonehenge to the city of Salisbury. Although the city is famous for flourishing markets; its colorful old buildings; and its proximal location to many antiquities, it is uniquely recognized as the home of one of the most picturesque cathedrals in all of England. Salisbury Cathedral is a magnificent structure. Continuously constructed over a 46-year period (1220-1266), the Cathedral can be seen from a considerable area of the Wiltshire countryside. The site chosen for the construction was a field called Myrifield. Unlike most other cathedrals that are space constrained by nearby buildings, Salisbury Cathedral was built with an abundance of open ground. The towers have a gothic appearance, and the primary spire rises more than 400 feet above ground level. The rural setting is aptly captured in many paintings, one of which now hangs in our home. In that painting there are several cows pictured grazing on the grounds adjacent to the Cathedral or drinking in a pond along the edge of the grassy fields. The only manmade building is the magnificent Cathedral.

When we pulled out of Salisbury and on our way to Bath, I wondered what I would recall in years to come about the Salisbury visit. I thought, "I will remember the rural Cathedral and that magnificent spire, and I will remember that the builders covered the roof with 400 tons of lead."

It was only a short time before the bus came around a turn, and we began our descent into Bath. There is so much that could be written about this beautiful city that it would be an injustice to try and capture its essence in a paragraph or two. I will, for now, say our first visit to Bath on the tour bus left us wanting more, and more we got, for in the years to come we would return there many times over. The bus took us on a quick ride through the city and up to The Crescent, which in Victorian times was the rural retreat for those in high London Society. We dropped down to the River Avon and parked the bus. It was only a short walk over to the city's namesake, the Roman Baths. As we approached the "baths" I could see "Roman" statues. I later learned that these were statues created in the 18th or 19th Centuries and that the Roman Baths were in the deeper part of the open area that is known as the *Kings Bath*. The Kings Bath is now an abandoned bathing area that was once used extensively by royalty and the aristocracy. Surprisingly, it was not until the mid to late 1800s that the Roman ruins were uncovered and efforts made for both excavation and study.

And There We Were

The tour of the Roman Baths was interesting and captivating. The Romans began construction around the natural hot springs in AD 60, and over the next hundred years after an elaborate plumbing and heating system was engineered, Bath became a sanctuary for both bathing and worshiping. Elaborate pools, their floors lined with sheets of lead, settling ponds, lead conduits, and saunas became a part of the overall architecture. Hypocausts directed hot air to dry rooms. To me these conduits were the most fascinating of all the Roman works. The idea was so simple, and it must have been so welcomed by all of those coming out of the cold air, from cold pools, or even from the hot water pools. Furnaces fueled hot air that moved beneath the floors of rooms built over stacked columns of tile. The air, most likely containing smoke from the furnace fires, then passed up wall flues to the surface. I found the concept to be fascinating.

The elaborate bathing pools were warm and decorative, but the builders did not forget the Gods. The temple to honor the Goddess Sulis Minerva was built along one end of the main bathing pool. On one of the temple walls was an image of a Gorgon's head that was probably a God associated with water.

The interesting bit of information regarding the Roman Ruins at Bath is that they are constantly being excavated. During our stay in England, we went back to Bath many times and each time I was continually surprised by the extent of the new excavations. The Romans must have surely liked their baths. I read somewhere that a Roman was once asked why he bathed once a day, and his answer was that he did not have time to bathe twice a day. In the cold, hostile climate of an English winter I am sure that many Roman Centurions would have preferred to spend the day at the bathing pool rather than out on patrol.

The tour guide said it was time to load up and head back to London. I had enjoyed Bath, and found Salisbury and Stonehenge to be interesting but not exciting places to visit. On the motorway back to the hotel I was in idle thought, and I found myself thinking of construction materials. I could not help but wonder where the lead mine was that sourced the roof at

Salisbury Cathedral and the pool linings at Bath. When you are a geologist you think about such things. As for my Shirley, I noticed that she had nodded off.

We made plans to leave the Britannia Hotel and to catch the plane back to Dallas and then to Oklahoma City. We had had a wonderful introductory trip and we were both thrilled with what life in the United Kingdom might entail Although we were still neophytes when it came to international travel, we were on our way.

Back in Oklahoma City things were going smoothly. Work at the office had taken an interesting turn in that I was given a research project that proved to be both fun and challenging. It gave me a chance to make my first meaningful contribution to the Company. Shirley found a large lake which had an encircling trail that was an ideal place for her to take the walks that she had so loved in Colorado. Even the heat was not all that much of a deterrent. The Company had yet to tell us exactly when we would be leaving for the United Kingdom, but we were led to believe it would be in either December or January. We preferred it be in December as that would give the boys a chance to spend Christmas in London.

And then word was received from the relocation firm that the owners of the home in Virginia Water had signed a rental agreement with another couple. The renters of choice had offered more than the owners originally wanted. It did not matter that we had agreed to the amount that was on offer. When we checked into whether this was possible, we were told that in England that is the way they do business. You can agree to a price but until the papers are signed it is still "open season". What a disappointment this news was.

The Company agreed that we should return to London once again, and this time to only search for housing. I would not be working in the office so the trip would be short and focused. We wanted to make the trip in October, but the relocation company informed us that a number of weeks would be needed to prepare a new list of properties for review. We had looked at many properties and found them to be unsuitable, but Tricia

Townend, the relocation specialist said she knew what we wanted and what our needs were. She was sure she could come up with a great list of properties for our perusal. Tricia made the comment, and I remember it well, "I always get my man." This is, of course a parody, of those in law enforcement but I remember looking at her and thinking, "Maybe not this time."

One might wonder why it was so difficult to find the "right" property? It was not that many of the places would have been workable, it is just that if a company is going to relocate a manager it ought to make sure the housing arrangements are adequate for the furniture to be moved and the setting and layout of the property is acceptable to the wife. We were most fortunate to have a Kerr-McGee executive in London, Kenneth Crouch, who knew how important the match of housing to housewife was. Without his support I wonder just how our stay in London would have turned out. We eventually spent all the time in the United Kingdom that the Company wanted us to spend there. There was no possibility we would leave due to domestic stress. I think all companies should follow Kerr-McGee's model. It is a considerable cost, both financially and politically, to move key personnel around the globe. A failed assignment not related to performance is something to be avoided.

We returned to London on Sunday morning, November 14, 1993. We met representatives from Townend Associates on Monday morning and over the next three days we looked at 20 properties. On Monday we returned to the Sunningdale, Ascot, and Weybridge villages. Our list of sites to visit also included a number of new villages, Englefield Green being one of those. Interestingly, of all the properties on the list, there was one we could not visit because the house, in Ascot, was in a state of refurbishment and the owner was not available. In hindsight this omission proved to be momentous.

As for this first day of the search please let me add a few comments. One of the properties we visited was located along Bishopsgate Road in Englefield Green. Bishopsgate Road continues into Windsor Great Park, but the road is gated and motor access restricted. After we visited the property, and it had been newly constructed, we stopped at a nearby pub, *The Fox and Hounds*, for lunch. This is an outstanding pub and one of the finest dining establishments in the area. But it is a pub, and when we entered there was an old gentleman standing by the bar, pint in hand, with his dog curled up near his feet. Our experience with pubs and pub food had been the *ploughman* sandwiches and other such food served in the London public houses. We had not been impressed. We were greatly surprised when we were escorted into the back dining area of *The Fox*. We were seated at a table covered with red and white checkerboard cloth and presented with a chalkboard with the daily specials. I will not list the hot dishes that were available, but I will tell you that the food was superb. This restaurant eventually became one of Bob and Shirley's favorite dining places; another being its sister pub, *The Thatched Tavern*. I jump ahead a bit, but The Fox and Hounds was one of Nicole Kidman and Tom Cruise's favorite eating places when they were an item. It is also the favorite haunt of many other celebrities. The food and ambience *are* that good.

After we had finished with lunch and before we stepped back in the car, Shirley and I walked to the gated entrance on Bishopsgate Road. It was only 100 meters or so, and there was a guard standing near the gate. We talked a bit with this very prim and proper gentleman. Several questions were asked, and we got good, but very short, answers to most of them. The Bishopsgate Road access is just one of many places where pedestrians can gain access to a myriad of pathways in Windsor Great Park. We asked him if there were guards at all of the entry points into the Park and he answered, "No." We then asked, "We see pathways with signposts telling visitors to go this way or that way to see special attractions within the park, but we also see a paved road without a marker, and it appears to be a continuation of Bishopsgate Road. Where would that take us if we walked down it?" This time we got a two-word answer (he was obviously opening up), "Tower Hill." We did not understand his response since Tower Hill is a famed and historic place for imprisonment and execution. After a pause, the guard looked at us and politely said, "The Queen Mother lives down that road."

After we had been dropped off at the Britannia Hotel, we stopped by the lounge and had a drink. We were disappointed with the properties we had seen. I was sure Shirley wanted to live in the countryside, and I was equally certain I did not want to live any further out than Virginia Water. Each train stop beyond Virginia Water would mean an increase in both time spent on the railroad and an incremental increase in the cost of the commute. I was in no hurry to replicate the 150-minute commute I had while working in Chicago. The next two days of our search would be spent looking closer-in to the City. After the first three days we would pick the top two or three properties for a final re-visit.

On Tuesday we had a later start to our day since all the properties we would visit were nearby. All were in London and in the Kensington, Knightsbridge, Chelsea, Regents Park, and Belgravia neighborhoods. The flats and multilevel homes we visited were nice, but they were much smaller than those we had seen in the country, and also the prices were much higher. The rentals went from so much per month to so much per week. It was scary. I could not imagine the Company willing to pay the asking prices of 1,200 to 1,485 Pounds per week (approximately $7,200 to 8,900 per month). It was really a depressing time in our search.

But there are a couple anecdotes that relate to our search on that Tuesday. The first took place when we visited a multilevel apartment located at Eton Place in Belgravia. Four of us rode the elevator up to the third-floor entrance to the apartment. The elevator opened directly into the living room. The place was obviously not lived in by the owner and the renter, a middle-aged woman, looked a bit uncomfortable having us look around the bedrooms, kitchen, and family room. I notice a stairway leading up from the living room, but I did not ask nor was I interested in where it went. This place was the one that was to let for 1,485 Pounds per week. It was a no go regardless of what Shirley thought of it. Thankfully she felt the same as I, and we agreed that we had seen enough. But as it was when we came up the elevator, we could only go down in two trips. I stayed behind when the other three got in and the door closed. No sooner had the door closed than I heard an upstairs door open and the soft patter of feet. I looked up the steps and coming down were four young ladies (aged 18-20) dressed in see-through lingerie. When they saw me standing by the elevator they turned and raced back up the stairs. The lady in waiting blushed red and by that time the elevator had returned for me. There is no doubt in my mind that this apartment was being used as a brothel and that the owner wanted these tenants out of there. Shirley and I were not the answer to his search for new renters.

The other property of special interest was located along the southern edge of Regents Park. This, too, was a multi-level place and each level (floor) offered wonderful views onto the gardens of Regents Park. We pulled into a circular driveway, and we were met by the realtor who was handling the rental. This property did not have elevators, or if did we were not offered that luxury. As we walked up the stairs, we noticed a number of pictures of a very well dressed and beautiful woman. When we got to the top the realtor said that we must surely have seen the photos of the famous London actress and star of the theater. She gave us the name and it meant nothing to us, and I remember feeling bad that we could not give the realtor the response she wanted. The great lady had recently died, and the heirs were obviously anxious to rent the property. They apparently had not yet come to feel comfortable with the idea of selling the place. The more we looked around the more saddened I became. The lady's creature comforts were still in every room. She must have been quite old, and the place had the look of a home where an elderly person with wonderful memories of "what was" lived. I remember thinking that when Greta Garbo or Kathryn Hepburn die, this is what their apartments are likely to look like. Great was the life experience, but how sad that what follows cannot be appreciated by those who were not a part of it. This home, with all of its wonderful past, was not the place for us.

We had seen little to interest us on this, our second day

of the search. The following morning we left to a look at properties a bit more removed from the City, but still within what is considered to be London. When I glanced at the itinerary for the day it had properties in St. John's Woods, Hampstead, and Kensington Green. The price of rental had dropped a bit (now in the 900 to 1,100 Pounds per week range) but the places were still expensive.

We found the small homes, and many of these were in stand-alone buildings, had attendant gardens. There were grass lawns in what could only be called postage stamp yards. The communities were located near an American school and the properties were and probably still are in high demand for parents with children transferring to the United Kingdom from the United States. We found several of the units to be empty. It is really depressing to visit a property where the rugs have just been shampooed, and there are fans blowing to accelerate the drying out process. We found blowers running on two occasions. We had to take off our shoes and walk through with our footwear. I do not know about Shirley, but my socks were soaked and just about the time they were getting dry it was time to go into another property with wet carpeting.

While we were being dropped off in the courtyard of the Britannia we sat with Tricia Townend and gave her the list of properties we would like to return to for a second look. Two were in the country at Virginia Water and Weybridge, and two were near London City at St. John's Wood and Knightsbridge. If we had time, we would very much like to take a look at the Kier Park, Ascot property that we had not been able to visit on Monday.

On Thursday, the last day of our search, we stepped into the car and I could see that Shirley was distressed. We had seen multiple places that might work but she had not seen anything that was as good as what we had back home. I knew that whatever we ended up with she would make it work, but I had hoped for so much more for her. Especially after the debacle surrounding the Oklahoma City apartment rental.

The second time around in St. John's Wood confirmed our

wish to live in the country. Those two near city homes were deleted from the list. We were left with two homes, one in Virginia Water and the other in Weybridge, and the one long shot located in Ascot. After the second look at the two country homes, we were down to the Virginia Water property. I could see that this presented many problems for Shirley. I began to hear how the colors did not match her furniture, that we would not be able to accommodate all our furniture, and that the kitchen and closets were just too small. And this was the best of the best. I was beginning to think that we might just as well live in a dungy apartment as to spend a lot of money on something she did not like. The Badgers Hill home in Virginia Water, the best place we had come up with, rented for 4,100 Pounds per month. The Company would probably go for this although it was probably on the high end of what they wanted to pay.

We headed for Ascot and all the time I was telling Shirley that whatever this place looked like it would most likely be a stretch. The place was listed at 4,000 Pounds per month but the owner was considering raising the rental since the place had just had its interior completely redone. And I was still adamant that I did not want to extend my commute. I had checked the cost of commuting and the cost, including the Underground trains in London, would be approximately $400 per month.

We entered Kier Park, Ascot late in the afternoon. This residential area is one where large homes have been built in what was, until a decade ago, a large estate. Massive Beechnut trees (over 100 feet in height) covered the high ground that rose 50-60 feet above and behind the houses built along one side of the Park. The narrow road traveling through Kier Park separated homes that occupied opposing sides of the street. Behind one of the homes on the relatively flat side of the parkway we thought we caught a glimpse of a large open pond. There were Beechnut trees behind the lower lying homes too but the trees here were arranged in groves rather than in the seemingly row-like ones that dominated the ridge line. Several of the properties we passed had extensive front yards. One or two of the homes were set back from the road and the driveways into these domiciles curved through large grass yards. We passed a massive tree that was not only tall, but also spacious, and it had great symmetry. What a tree it was. We passed this majestic tree and then came to a fifty-foot-long hedge that was 4 to 5 feet in height. The driver slowed the car until we could read the address displayed on one of the two brick pillars that framed a reddish bricked driveway. The address, a name, was emblazoned on a golden metallic nameplate. Each of the two pillars, including the one with the nameplate, was topped by three-foot-long standing lions. It was not unusual that the address was a name, and not a number, as we had seen many such addresses in other homes we had looked at. The property on offer in Kier Park was *Muirfield*. I remembered, correctly, that *Muirfield* was the name of one of the Scottish golf courses where the British Open was sometimes held. I never really made any connection between the Muirfield we were about to visit and the famous golf course, but as we would find out much later, there was more than a casual tie between the two.

We pulled up into the brick driveway and as we approached the closed iron gate, it began to swing open. It was sensor driven so there was no one there to greet us. We pulled into a spacious brick courtyard and I remember looking up at this exceptionally large and beautiful home. Rose bushes framed the entrance portico that had a semi-circular raised brick, two steps, base. The covered portico was supported and framed by four 10-foot white pillars. A three-car detached garage was accessed at one end of the courtyard, and it looked as if there was a swimming pool and terrace along one side of the house. My first impression was that Muirfield was more than acceptable: I was awestruck. I remember thinking, "This place might be too good", and we had only seen the courtyard and the exterior of the front of the house.

The interior of the house was somewhat of a disappointment, not for what it would be, but rather for what it was. There was no carpeting and no drapes. The walls and the ceilings all appeared to be freshly painted. This property was most definitely being refurbished. When we asked why there was so much work ongoing, the answer surprised us. It seems that this home, built in 1987, was later purchased from the previous owner, but then not occupied. The new, and present, owners left town but chose not to turn the heat on. As fate would have it, there was a cold spell that dropped the temperatures low enough to freeze and break many of the pipes, especially those on the second floor. When the thaw came water poured throughout the house for several weeks. The ceiling eventually collapsed and all of the walls had to be rebuilt. When we showed up the property was at the point where it would be rentable in about a month.

If you think it is hard to get excited about a wet carpet in a potential rental you have to appreciate how we felt looking at this Kier Park property. Not a word was said as Shirley looked around the house and climbed up the winding staircase to look at second floor bedrooms (there were five of them). I peeked out and found that there was indeed a swimming pool, and the surrounding area was all paved in flagstone. A cabana and dressing room offset the pool on the backside. The pool was separated from the backyard by a short white picket fence. Along the side of the pool facing the house were shrubs and a cherry tree. Behind these plants there was an 8-foot-tall hedge row that not only bordered the pool, but also formed a boundary with the adjacent property.

The backyard, the locals call it a garden, was simply stunning. A grass lawn some 35 feet wide extended from the house to a brick wall that separated the lawn from a raised and grassy, but also tree covered, terrace. A brick stairway gave access from the lawn to the terrace. The impressive Beechnut trees we had seen in other parts of Kier Park were in a grove near the back of the terrace. As I walked back amongst these, I saw a 20 to 30-foot-wide expanse of rhododendrons, azaleas, and other assorted evergreens and shrubs. These grounds were certainly not anything like what we had seen in the City or in St. John's Wood. As a matter of fact, we had only seen one other property out in the country that had gardens anywhere near the size of those found at Muirfield.

Shirley had walked through the house and was impressed by the open kitchen area. It looked out onto the backyard and the view was as impressive looking out as it had been for me looking in. She took me upstairs to the master bedroom and I could not believe we were in England. The room was 28' by 18' and there was a built-in recess for a queen-sized bed, with small built-in bedside chest-of-drawers. Floor to ceiling built-in cabinets braced the smaller bedside stands. Along one wall of the room there were floor to ceiling cabinets that served as closets. The adjacent bathroom suite was huge. It covered an area of nearly 160 square feet. How very un-British this was.

The guest bedroom was also very large, and it had its own ensuite bathroom. I was struck by the length of this bedroom. It was nearly 30 feet long. Muirfield had obviously been purpose built by someone who loved American-size bedrooms, bathrooms, and kitchens. Even with no furniture and without carpeting and curtains I knew this home would be something very special. Still, I never heard a word from Shirley.

I went downstairs and visited with Martin, our driver for the day. I looked all around and told him that if this is not something Shirley likes I am in deep trouble.

Shirley loved the place! She said later that when she saw Muirfield she just fell in love with it. And Muirfield did not disappoint us. The property was magical. We would always consider the time we spent there to be a gift from above. We asked Tricia Townend and her relocation company to work with our office to make an offer. We wanted to close this deal and if possible, we would like to meet the owners so that they could see who would be renting the property. This turned out to be a good idea, as the owners befriended us and for the next four years this family did all that they could to keep us on as tenants.

We will leave Muirfield for now, but many of the wonderful experiences we had in the United Kingdom came from our living in this wonderful home. When it comes to the 10 most exciting and interesting places we visited during our stay in the United Kingdom, Muirfield will be at the top of that list and it belongs there for reasons that, hopefully, will become obvious.

On Friday morning, November 19, 1993, Shirley and I left

Gatwick for our return trip to the United States. We were pleased with the home we had found and were now looking forward to our move from Oklahoma City to London. We still had not been given a transfer date, but we assumed that would be forthcoming since we now had a destination in England for our household goods.

When I returned to the office the Monday following our house hunting trip to London, I was met by my secretary who asked when I would be leaving her. Many with whom I worked were now aware that I would be transferred to the London office, but no official announcement had been made. As was my secretary Mary, all were wondering when the move would take place. Some of the staff thought I would never leave. I had after all, been hired in May for the London assignment; few knew that at the time, but it was beginning to become common knowledge. Several employees working on other floors would drop by to see if my name plate had been removed, a definite sign that I had left. But "Bob Lent" remained on the brass holder and we all waited.

After discussions with management, it was decided that the movers would pack up our goods from the Warwick West Apartments and place them alongside our "London" furniture that was in temporary storage. All of the household goods would then be shipped to England once the lease on Muirfield had been negotiated, and my United Kingdom work permit had been granted. The movers came on November 30, 1993. Bob and Shirley left for England on December 4. Little did I know that on the workday following my departure to the United Kingdom, my secretary had a new brass name plate engraved. Bob Lent had been replaced with Bob Went. The Bob Went was still in front of my old office when I returned for a business meeting in late winter, 1994.

Company policy said that we could have an air shipment of goods that we would need prior the arrival of the shipment coming over by boat. We had made plans to stay in a Company leased flat while our shipment was in transit and this flat was fully furnished so we did not see the need to airship a container. But I had certainly underestimated the quantity of personal items my wife would need for the two or three months we would be staying in the London apartment. Unknown to me, she had purchased a steamer trunk that would be one of her two pieces of luggage checked through to London.

The steamer trunk caused us no end of grief both at the airport in Oklahoma City, but also in customs at the Gatwick airport in the United Kingdom. At the Oklahoma City airport the porter placed the luggage on the scales. The clerk looked at the weight and called over her supervisors. First, if this was shipped, we would be facing a significant excess weight charge. But before the airline personnel could even talk about that fee the airline's union would have to agree to handle the excess weight. The issue was: should these goods be shipped via freight or can they be shipped as baggage. Well, shipment by freight would mean that we had to go across the airport to the freight terminal. Such a decision would throw everything out of sync (i.e., our flight, the car waiting for us at Gatwick, etc.). All the while this discussion was going on all I could do is look at Shirley and think, "Does she really need that many clothes?" The union agreed to handle the shipment as luggage, so we paid the fee and boarded the plane.

At Gatwick, we picked up our luggage at the carousel and with two luggage carts stacked high we came to the *Goods to Declare* and *Nothing to Declare* partition. Not knowing what was meant by all of this declaration business, I decided that we should error on the side of being too cautious rather than boldly trying to push a ton of dresses through customs. In all the years we traveled to and from the United Kingdom this is the only time that we ever opted to go through the *Goods to Declare* door. But this time we did. When we rounded the corner we entered a large room with long tables, and sitting on these tables were three attendants who were obviously enjoying the paucity of traffic coming their way. I pushed the trunk laden trolley up to one of the tables, and Shirley nearly running over me pushed the other cart to an adjacent table. I asked, "What do we do now?" I did not have a clue as to what the customs personnel wanted to see or even if we should have come this way. They asked what we were bringing over and I said, "Mostly clothes for my pretty wife." The custom officials looked at Shirley, always the looker, and then at the trunk. "How long are you going to be here in London?", was the first question asked. When we told them that we were immigrating and that our main shipment would be over in several months they began to understand. They asked if we were bringing any gifts over, which of course we were since the Christmas holidays were coming up and our boys were going to join us in London. Shirley took over at this point and in her soft sweet voice said that there were presents for our adult children, but they would be taking these back to the United States when they left in early January. The officials, who did not want to even begin sorting through the steamer trunk, waived us through. And then they went back to chatting amongst themselves.

Customs officials are highly trained, and I am sure that they had the situation summed up correctly. We did not look like smugglers. But custom officials are human, and you never know what they might do. In this case, even thought we were bringing an unbelievable amount of baggage into the United Kingdom, the officials chose to waive us through rather than sort through so much luggage.

In other circumstances, the humanity of custom and immigration officials shows up in all too predictable ways. On one flight several years later I noticed this stunningly beautiful young lady, maybe 23, who was attired in a very short, but fashionable brown leather skirt and matching top, but the top was open enough to show more than a modest bit of cleavage. Shirley had visited with the lady during the flight, and as we were walking out through *Nothing to Declare* I told Shirley that there is no way that this beautiful, and sensual, lady is going to make it through immigration without being checked. Sure enough, it came to pass. All she had with her was a small suitcase and an overnight bag, but she had not taken three steps when a young, slightly overweight, officer stopped her and asked that she open her luggage. The young lady was being harassed, no doubt about it. The young man sorting through her garments only wanted to be able to see her up close and to chat with her. No doubt about that either. It all was just too predictable.

When we cleared customs and walked out through the confining ropes, we saw a well-dressed gentleman with our name on a placard. We had requested that the London office have a van pick us up since we would come with a 'significant' amount of luggage. Even with this forewarning, the driver was still stunned by the number of suitcases, and by the steamer trunk. For a while I thought we were going to have to have him clear loading the baggage through his "union".

On our way into London, the driver, surprisingly engaging for a British citizen, inquired as to the purpose of our visit. When we informed him that we were moving to the United Kingdom, he began a never-ending dialogue meant to enlighten us. First, he wanted us to know that many of the most populous nations in the world drive on the left side of the road. Never mind that many of these populous nations have few cars. Then we got an explanation of why the English chose to travel on the left. The driver said that in medieval times, the knights carried their lances in their right hand so it made more sense to travel on the left side of the country roads, the arenas, or wherever. I took this with a grain of salt, but the driver was on a roll.

Next, he wanted us to know that the best television in the world was British television. I had never heard much about local television, so I inquired what made it so. He responded that firstly, they had Richard Attenborough and his many documentaries on travel and wildlife. The driver's primary argument for British television excellence was the public broadcasting shows relating to science and travel and the network shows with their wonderful comedy. Open minded, I did not argue but I had my doubts, which proved to be well founded. When we checked into our apartment, I turned on the "Telly" and found four channels whose programs were of little interest to me. There are many things British that I learned to love, but I must say, given the same discussion we had on that first day with our driver, I would now argue his point as to the excellence in British TV broadcasting.

Thus was our introduction to England as new, albeit

temporary, immigrants.

The driver pulled us into Three Kings Yard which was the courtyard off of which the Company apartment was located. Our rental address was Flat B, 17 Three Kings Yard. Our neighbor in the courtyard was the Italian Embassy. Across the Davies Street entrance to Three Kings Yard was the five-star hotel, Claridge's. We were certainly in an elitist neighborhood.

Now Flat B is not at street level. All of our luggage would have to be hauled up a narrow stairway to an apartment two levels above the brickyard. Most drivers willingly offer to help with the luggage, but this time I could tell that the driver was not all that sure that he was up to helping me haul all of the suitcases, especially the steamer trunk, up the stairs; too much *Telly*. It was hard work, but the two of us did get all our baggage up the stairs and into the rental property. I paid the fellow for his efforts, but I am sure that he left shaking his head at the travel habits of the Yanks.

After traveling all night and having to worry about our luggage I was very tired and all I could think of was taking a nap. But Shirley thought we should stock our refrigerator with essentials so that we could have coffee and breakfast in the morning. The nearest place to pick up items was two blocks from us, but this was a kiosk selling predominantly non-perishable goods. Four or five blocks distant, on Oxford Street, was the large department store, Selfridges. Selfridges like many of the large department stores in the United Kingdom (e.g., Harrods, Marks and Spencer, etc.) carry an extensive variety of high-quality foodstuffs. I always found it somewhat incongruous that one could be looking at socks and shirts only to look through an open door at a fresh 50-pound tuna nicely displayed on a bed of ice. I played for the team and went with Shirley to Selfridges where we bought five bags of groceries, all that I could carry.

Three Kings Yard would be our home for the next two and one-half months. By the time I had obtained my work permit, and our household goods shipped and delivered, it would be mid-February before we would be able to move into Muirfield, our Ascot home. Furthermore, once the work permit was obtained, we would have to fly back to the United States and then re-enter under the work permit. The permit and re-entry would allow us to live and work in the United Kingdom. Until the work permit was granted, I would officially be considered to be working in the country on a temporary assignment.

One could say, almost predictably, that we began to sample and to live the international life when we took up residence in our Three Kings Yard apartment. I was about to be reminded of a personality trait Shirley had exhibited while we were dating, one that had been somewhat subdued by the demands place on her by twenty-three years of parenting. The pretty and elegant lady had always remained active and outgoing, but she was not compulsively social. Even though she found time to play bridge and shop with the girls, her sense of well-being, self-worth, and contentment was not tied to what she did outside of the home. She loved to have fun, fun that could come from interactions with her children, her husband, or her friends. She had successfully avoided the routine and the drudgery that had seemingly been a part of her mother's housekeeping and child rearing efforts.

Shirley took care of her personal appearance like Aunt Mildred did, but she had not had the opportunity to live the carefree lifestyle she perceived Mildred to have lived. The demands of child rearing left Shirley precious little free time; the desire or the need to be doing something all the time was suppressed. She was a hands-on parent who was much involved in activities related to the curricular and extra-curricular functions at our son's schools. As long as the children were living at home there was no need to be continuously active across a broad social front.

Once freed from the daily chores related to rearing of children Shirley found herself wanting to sample all that life had to offer. Shirley in London was about to realize that she did not want to miss out on anything that might be the least bit exciting and/or interesting. With the yoke of responsibility having been significantly reduced, she was free to pursue anything, anywhere and anytime. The seed planted by Aunt Mildred was to bear fruit. The little girl from Big Summit Prairie was about to find all of the elegance and the excitement that once was a part of her dreams.

I believe Shirley began to want to be "busy" around the time Taran left for college and we moved to Oklahoma City. At the time I thought her restlessness was related to our living in a dumpy apartment, but looking back on it now I believe the pretty lady was just getting ready to spread her wings. She was fledging and I just did not recognize it.

On the first Monday of our first day living in London I took a call from Shirley that indicated she was restless and that she felt all alone in the City. I picked up on the mood and was concerned she might be struggling with our relocation. After the call, I worried about her and was concerned about her ability to cope with our new life. In less than a year I had uprooted her from her comfortable home and her friends in Denver, transplanted her to an apartment in Oklahoma City, and then dropped her into temporary flat in London.

I was busy in the office, and about the time I was to head for home, I noticed there was a red message light flashing on my desk phone. The familiar sweet voice informed me that she would not be home until late in the evening. She had made some friends and they were going to go to a wedding apparel fashion show. Dinner would be served and she would tell me all about it when she got home.

Later in the evening I heard the door open into the stairway leading to our apartment and in came Shirley, dressed to kill and absolutely bubbling over with excitement. It turns out she had gotten up in the morning, had breakfast, administered her make-up, and then picked one of her favorite dresses prior to going to Selfridges on Oxford Street. Once in this large upscale department store, she found herself in the cosmetics department. She wanted to see the variety of the products carried, but especially she wanted to see if they had her favorite lip stick, rouge, eye shadow, etc. While she was moving around the cosmetic area a tall and attractive young lady of color came up to her and asked if she would help her. She had noticed how nice Shirley looked with her makeup and was bold enough to ask for some advice. The young lady was with her mother and they were in London for a week, having come from Nigeria. The girl was to be married in a couple of months and she was in the City shopping for her wedding gown, veil, shoes, and other related goods. She also wanted to try on some make-up that would complement her looks.

 It is not surprising that the young black lady came up to Shirley. Shirley always dressed well and put on her make-up and manicured her nails, even when she was just doing housework. One of Shirley's friends, and a neighbor once remarked that whenever she came over to our house, even in the morning when Shirley was mopping the floor, she found Shirley looking like she was almost ready to go to church. Her hair was made up and her make-up spot on. As a matter of fact, she told Shirley that she even liked calling her since Shirley always had nice mood music playing on the radio. This very close friend said that she was going to turn over a new leaf come the next morning. She would have music playing and she would get up and apply her make-up before starting her housework. Well, the next morning the young lady called Shirley, and sure enough there was soft music playing in the background. But this same girlfriend said that after she had made herself up, she looked in the mirror and had come to the conclusion she looked too fine to do housework. She was going to the mall to shop.

 I make the point only because it was not unusual that the young African woman came up to Shirley to ask her advice. In addition to her make-up Shirley also had an unusual hair style that elicited comments from peoples all around the world. The hairdo was unusual, and I cannot adequately describe it but I will tell you the key to it was her wavy silver bangs and her ability to elegantly put her hair into a compact bun. Even when people did not come up to her and make a comment about the hair, I would frequently see them looking at it. Once, in China, I was several steps behind Shirley and three or four young ladies fell in line behind her just so that they could take a good look at her hair style.

 Shirley worked with the young lady at Selfridges and they spent several hours trying on various products with an assortment of colors. After the betrothed had finally selected the make-up needed for her special day, she asked Shirley if she would join her mother and her at a bridal fashion show that was by invitation only at Debenhams, also on Oxford Street. The lady wanted Shirley's help in selecting a wedding dress and a wedding veil. Dinner would be served and there was no question that the young lady would be able to get Shirley an invite. So it happened. Shirley Lent, on her first full day in London went to a fashion show and had an elegant dinner with a wealthy young African and her mother. On her wedding day this lithe and beautiful young lady wore the make-up and a wedding dress and veil suggested by my Shirley.

The time spent in the City allowed Shirley to explore many fine department stores, restaurants, and hotel lobbies. She visited Harrods, Liberty, and Harvey Nichols department stores for the first time. She found she loved shopping in these stores, and she was taken by the service offered and the special attention that was given to her. Mind you, Shirley and I were not wealthy, but you do not have to be wealthy to look wealthy and that is the way it was with Shirley. When you dress well, carry yourself with good posture, and present your face and hair in an elegant manner you attract attention. When you have the attention and then show that you also have charm, wit, and a captivating smile people simply do not forget you.

To make my point, I will relate an anecdote about an attentive doorman at the Liberty Department store. Shirley liked to shop at Liberty, and there is a doorman there who greets one and all with a big smile. He also helps you out with your bags and will call a taxi if needed. Shirley and he became good friends. Two years after we left England we had an opportunity to return to London on a business trip. Shirley took me down to Liberty and as we walked up to the door, the doorman came up to her and said that he had missed her. He looked at me and remarked that she had never brought me with her before; that it was good to see her husband this time. It was like they were old friends. She had similar experiences at Harrods and Harvey Nichols but that is not for now.

I previously mentioned that our apartment at Three Kings

Yard was directly across the street from the Claridge's Hotel. Claridge's is the epitome of elegance and opulence. It drew Shirley in almost immediately. She found herself walking into the lobby and then into a rather large tearoom that also serves as lounge in the early evening. Live music plays daily, and it can be a violinist, a pianist, or a musical ensemble. Anyone can sit at one of the fashionable tables and order a drink. The only caveat is that you must meet a certain dress standard. When the boys came over to spend the Christmas Holidays, Shirley took the boys and I over to Claridge's to listen to the music, have a drink, and to look at the Christmas decorations. A hotel representative approached us as we walked through the lobby on our way to the lounge. The man was very diplomatic, but he said that coats and ties were required to be seated in the open lounge. The boys and I were offended, but Shirley was not. She said that the dress code made it special and that it was not asking too much to abide by that code.

In case you think the dress code at Claridge's is meant only for "commoners" I would like to pass along a bit of Claridge's folklore as presented in the book *An Affair to Remember*. This book, written by Christopher Andersen, chronicles the love story between Katharine Hepburn and Spencer Tracy. When the couple was in London, Spencer Tracy chose to stay at Claridge's, and Katharine Hepburn down the street at the nearby Connaught Hotel. By staying at separate hotels the couple was able to keep up the façade of being just "friends". However, Katharine would visit Spencer nearly every day. When the hotel management finally approached Spencer Tracy about a delicate matter, it had nothing to do with their trysts. Instead, it had everything to do with Katherine's attire, for she always wore pant suits and not a dress. The matter was finally resolved when it was determined that Katharine could use the freight elevator rather than elevators in the guest lobby. Both loved Claridges and they would have stayed in the hotel together if had it not been for potentially bad publicity. Spencer Tracy is reported to have said that when he died he did not want to go to heaven: he wanted to go to Claridge's.

Claridge's remained a special meeting place for Shirley and

I, even long after we had moved to the country. When Shirley came into London, I could count on her wanting to meet me at Claridge's for a pre-dinner cocktail. We had more cocktail hours at Claridge's than dinners. Most of our dinners we had there were prior to us going to the theater or when we were dining out with business associates.

The Claridge's cloakroom attendant came to know Shirley quite well. The woman was taken by Shirley's charm and though Shirley was not a hotel guest, the attendant would offer to keep Shirley's packages until later in the day when she would be meeting up with me.

I recall that Shirley first uttered her famous line, "I think I would die if I did not have elegance in my life", one evening as we sipped Grand Marnier and listened to classical music in the lounge at Claridge's.

I will relate one final anecdote on Claridge's and about those who stay there. It is said that once you stay at Claridge's they will remember all of your personal tastes and they will do whatever they can to make sure that you are provided with any special need or preference you have made known to them. Something simple, like taking a certain brand of scotch from your ensuite bar is easy. But Michael Crichton in his interesting book, *Travels*, has an anecdote that shows the degree to which Claridge's will go to make their guests happy. I will not go into all of the details as the reader can find them in *Travels*, but Mr. Crichton once had need to use scotch tape in his room and he did not have a dispenser. He taped all of the brass handles on the room's chest and drawers with long strips which he then cut as needed. He came back years later and found, to his surprise, the brass handles on the chest and drawers covered with long strips of scotch tape.

Shirley spent most of her days exploring the city. During the evenings she and I went to plays, stopped at a local pub for a pint, and sought out a variety of dining establishments. We discovered elegant restaurants and a great number of lesser ones where the ambience came from simple decorations and an abundance of caring and friendly service. It is amazing how enjoyable a meal becomes when you are greeted by an owner or waitress/waiter who says simply, "Mr. and Mrs. Lent, it is so good to see you again." They remember your name and make you feel special. And this cordiality was there for all former customers who walked through the door. It is no wonder these rare places became some of our favorite retreats when it came to dining in the City.

We learned much about London during our time spent living in the apartment. We traveled the Underground at will and no place in the City was out of striking distance. We could pop in at the Bond Street Tube Station and climb out at Baker Street where we were only a block from Madame Tussaud's. We could go to Leicester Square or to St. Johns for a movie. We also loved the black cabs. Travel by cab was simply superb for it provided a good sensorial feel of the City. We walked and walked for there is no better way to feel the pulse of London and to experience its quaintness than to walk the narrow streets, nearly all of them packed with people.

Several of the staff at Kerr-McGee suggested we might like to purchase a copy of *Time Out*, a magazine that provides details of everything happening in and around London. *Time Out* proved to be an invaluable resource, especially when it came to choosing entertainment and selecting a place to dine. Information was available across a wide range of activities ranging from exhibits at the museums to cabaret shows. We mostly used the magazine for details pertaining to the time and performances for London Theater and for the cinema.

One of the listings in *Time Out* made us aware of an activity that proved to be fascinating. *Time Out* had, and probably still has, a section showing the times and the topics for a wide variety of London Walks. These Walks may be unique to London. The Walk descriptions go something like this: "Pub Walk Along the Thames", "London – 2000 Years of History", "The Haunts of Jack the Ripper", or "London Dungeons". My recall of the names is likely a bit off, but you get the idea. A gathering place is listed, say at the street level entrance to Monument Tube Station. Those individuals who are interested in taking a tour gather at the appropriate time and are greeted by one or more tour guides. After a modest fee is collected from each person, the group begins the narrated walk. Shirley and I took several of these, but our first Walk was by far the best one. It allowed us to learn much about the city of London.

We chose "London – 2000 Years of History" to be our first "Walk". I was a bit skeptical about how this Walk might go. My gut reaction was that we would emerge from the Tube Station and would not be able to find the tour leaders. London swarms with people. Off to one side I saw a group, maybe 15 or 20 in number, who had money out and were paying a middle-aged man. In answer to my inquiry, I got this response, "Yes, this is the London Walk."

Although the Walk covered only one square kilometer of London, the topics covered by the guide were captivating. We stopped near London Bridge and heard the history of the Bridge, from 40 AD to the present. It was fascinating to learn of the wooden and then stone bridges that had been built, and how these bridges effected commerce and the social flow into and out of the City. The guide took great delight in telling the group that a crazy Yank had purchased the third stone bridge and had taken it, piece by piece, to Lake Havasu, Arizona.

Our next stop was near Pudding Lane, where the Great London Fire of 1666 began. We lingered before the mural showing the progression of the fire and we gazed up at the Monument to the Fire built by Thomas Wren. Our guide gave us details concerning the number of people who died (only 6-8), the drought conditions (14 weeks without rain), and the wind direction (from the east). We learned that the closest and most effective fire fighting equipment was in one of the nearby buildings which was amongst the first to burn. There were many other facts or factoids that related to the fire, and many of these were stories of individuals, both heroes and villains.

We went into the city to visit the business sector of London. We visited Lombard Street and learned of its importance to London business and we visited the Royal Exchange, the first indoor shopping market built in London. The Roman ruins, then being excavated were viewed from platforms. We heard of the great destruction that came from World War II bombing and of the Barbicon Convention Center which was rising over this devastated area. It was a great Walk!

During our time in London we went on other Walks that were similarly interesting, Walks that anyone, tourist or resident, can take. The London Walks are a wonderful and cheap way to get a feel for the highways and byways of London.

Even though we found ourselves dining out quite often we still tried to maintain a well-stocked larder. Grocery shopping proved to be a bit of a problem as it did not make common or economic sense to routinely shop at Selfridges which was more a specialty store than a "grocery" store. The nearby kiosks were great for emergency items, but they had much higher prices and a limited variety of goods. Shopping became much easier when I discovered I could take the Tube to a nearby supermarket, shop, and pack my grocery bags into a cab for the return trip. Even this was not without problems. On one trip back to Three Kings Yard, a quart of milk spilled and, unnoticed, it leaked out onto the waffle-like rubber mat on the back seat floorboard. When I prepared to exit the cab, I glanced down and saw a sea of white milk. I asked the driver if he had a cloth with which I could clean up the mess. His answer, so very British was, "Don't you worry about it. It needed a good scrubbing anyhow." Here was a guy that needed to keep his cab running to earn money and I had just messed things up. I added five Pounds to his tip, but that extra sum was probably not enough to make up for the trouble I caused him.

Speaking of cab rides and Three Kings Road. Do you have any idea how difficult it must be to find such a small courtyard in a city the size of London? I came to appreciate the quality of the service given by London cab drivers during the time spent at our apartment by the Italian embassy. All we ever had to do was step in and say "Three Kings Yard" and off we would go. I once asked a driver how he could possibly know all of the nooks and crannies in the city. He responded that, to get a license, it was necessary to know the location of all streets. Each driver also had to ascertain the shortest distance between pick-up and drop-off. Not in time, but in distance. The gentleman I chatted with said that each driver usually spent months riding a bicycle to out of the way places like Three Kings Yard before taking their practical driving exam. Can you imagine a cab driver in one of our major cities having to undertake this type of training and testing?

Getting the groceries into our apartment was just one of the adjustments we had to make. Another one was becoming accustomed to the appliances that were in the apartment. The front-loading washing machine for clothing was a tiny little thing. It made the loudest noise, and this noise came in periodic pulses (Whrrr, Whrrr, Whrr…. Pause………Whrr, Whrr, Whrr… etc.) We later learned that some washing machines serve dual purposes; they can be used to wash both dishes and clothing, although not at the same time.

One of the most embarrassing experiences I had with appliances occurred on a Sunday morning after Shirley asked if I would cook breakfast. The request was for scrambled eggs and sausage. I decided that to cut down on the smell from frying I would put the sausages in fry pan and place it in the oven. I looked at the settings on the oven knob. The temperatures went up to 500. I did the math on this and determined that the degrees could not be in Centigrade. Even though England used the metric system, the conversion of 500 degrees Centigrade to degrees Fahrenheit was too great a temperature (932 degrees Fahrenheit) to have in a kitchen oven. One should be apprised that lead melts at 621 degrees Fahrenheit.

I took the sausage laden pan by the two black handles and placed it into the oven. I dialed in 400 degrees and left for a few minutes. When I returned, I got a whiff of a very acrid metallic odor, and I ventured a peek into the oven. The sausages were blackened and the handles had melted from the pan. The gauge was indeed metric. I cannot imagine why or what anyone in the United Kingdom would cook at such incredible temperatures. Forging iron I understand, but cooking, I don't know.

The boys showed up for the holiday season and this was really a special occasion for the entire family. Tobin had come in from Minneapolis where he was working for Dain Bosworth (an institutional brokerage firm), and Taran had flown over from Boston after driving down from Hanover and Dartmouth College. We fed off their excitement and took them to many of the tourist haunts and to our newly found "favorite" restaurants. One evening in an attempt to obtain a cheap meal I suggested we go to a pizzeria. The meal still cost more than $100 in U. S. currency.

Christmas in London, 1993, was a wonderful experience. There were few people out and about. Cabs were hard to find and almost all establishments had shut down for the day. I was pleasantly surprised I could not hear the Underground trains running Christmas morning. On all other days I could tell time by the frequency and volume of noise coming up into our apartment from the ground deep beneath us, and we were nearly two blocks from the nearest tube station (Bond Street). It was a treat being able to walk around the City without having the sidewalks jammed with people, and the streets not packed bumper to bumper with buses, cabs, and automobiles.

The relative calm lasted from Christmas to New Year, although the Tube trains did run and the cabs were back at it. We were anxious for the boys to see where we would be living. One day we took the train to Ascot where we hailed a cab that took us to our new home. The boys were impressed, and they could hardly wait for us to move into Muirfield. On their next visit they would be staying in their own bedrooms, and Taran would be once again sleeping in his waterbed, a bed that he had once fought long and hard to get.

After we left Muirfield we turned left and went down Cheapside Road to The Thatched Tavern. Shirley and I had found the food and the ambience of this local favorite to be something quite special. Once in the pub, everyone but Shirley had to duck to avoid hitting the cross beams. The Tavern was built in the 1500s when the average height must have been somewhere around 5'6". There was a fire in the fireplace and an open wooden table in front of it. We seated ourselves and I went to the bar to get four pints, including one for Shirley who had come to enjoy her favorite pint, a Newkie Brown (Newcastle Brown Ale). After the men had several pints we were seated for dinner. The menu, presented on a chalk board, featured salmon, lamb shoulder, sirloin tips, bangers and mash, rosemary chicken, and several other dishes, all of which came with a family style serving of vegetables. The boys were hooked. Tobin much enjoyed the shoulder of lamb, a dish that he thereafter rarely failed to order. When we walked out the door to our waiting cab the boys let us know they envisioned spending many evenings at The Thatched Tavern, sitting in front of the fireplace, listening to the rain fall, and watching the fire burn. And they did. On several occasions, they brought young English lasses with them.

New Year's Eve, 1993, was a strange one in that the boys wanted to see the New Year in at Trafalgar Square; they and a hundred thousand other people. Shirley and I went somewhere special, but I cannot now recall where it was. It had to have been somewhere special because we always went somewhere special on New Year's Eve. We left the boys on their own. Our only advice was that they stay together. It was good advice if I do say so myself.

Shirley and I tuned on the television to see the celebrations taking place throughout London and England. The first scene shown was the almost unruly crowd that had assembled at Trafalgar Square. Later, on New Year's Day 1994, we discovered the boys went to a local pub and met a few girls with whom they had drinks. This was mostly a platonic encounter because the young people were primarily interested in getting out onto Trafalgar Square. As the New Year approached, the Square became lined with Bobbies on their horses. Entrance was being denied. There were too many people in the Square. Taran said he was going gain entrance anyway. Tobin warned him against this brash behavior, but Taran waved and said not to worry. He walked across the street, and when a nearby Bobby was not looking, he dove under the belly of his horse, and into the mass of humanity circling the Square. Where there is a will there is a way.

Tobin saw the New Year in and he waited and waited but saw no sign of Taran. He walked back to our apartment and sat on the sidewalk leading to the stairs. He did not have a key, Taran had that, and Tobin did not want to awaken Shirley and me; we had asked the boys to stay together. About 2:00 in the morning Taran came strolling into Three Kings Yard. He waived at the Italian guards and walked over to Tobin. It is a good thing that our sons have the utmost respect and love for each other as I cannot imagine how that confrontation could have ended. It ended with the boys climbing the stairs and letting us know they were home. They knew we would be awake. Years later we learned what happened in the missing hours. Only Taran's quick thinking got him back to Three Kings Yard without having had his honor impugned. Two girls had talked him into taking a train to their apartment in a village west of London. At one of the stops along the way, Taran got to thinking about what Shirley and I had told him. He stepped off the train and caught one returning to London. Had Taran not come to his senses it is entirely possible that Tobin could have spent the entire night waiting outdoors in cold and foggy London.

New Year's day, 1994, was unusual in that the Lent family walked about eight blocks over to Piccadilly Street to watch what was billed as a parade featuring "1000 American Cheerleaders". It was not until several years later that we realized cheerleaders in England are uncommon, but on this January day we were glad to see some vestige of what we had left behind. There were indeed a great number of young girls marching down Piccadilly Street. They must have been cold on what was a very damp and chilly day. After watching the parade, I was left with the feeling that these young girls must have very loving parents who would pay for a trip to London so that their perky daughters could perform for the Brits. The English department of tourism deserves a lot of credit, for by putting on the parade they not only insured that the girls would come to London but that these girls would bring with them innumerable members of their families. To this day I commend the young girls for their performance. They came down streets lined with very few spectators, and they gave it their all. Their performances were certainly not appreciated like they would have been in the United States. Despite the muted appreciation, I imagine that each of the girls who made the trip will never forget it. Such it is when one travels abroad, and especially when one travels to London.

Before this narrative jumps from London to Ascot, I will mention one more thing about our Three King's Yard flat. We had heard from several people that flat B at 17 King's Yard was one of the places where John Profumo took Christine Keeler during his torrid affair with the promiscuous beauty. The Profumo Scandal that brought down Harold Macmillan's government was a seedy affair that began at Cliveden, the former Astor Estate overlooking the Thames near Maidenhead, but the trysts that followed probably found many lairs. Whether any of these was indeed flat B is problematical, but for Bob and Shirley who lived in the flat, if only for a short time, it was exciting to know that British history might have been made in the same rooms where we slept and ate. An elaboration of the Profumo Scandal will be further discussed when much is written of Cliveden, the magnificent country estate that is high on our list of the most memorable places visited during our stay in the United Kingdom.

We were notified near the middle of January, 1994, that our household goods would arrive in the United Kingdom on approximately February 26. After a few days to clear customs we could expect to move into Muirfield sometime during the first week of March. We were more than ready to be reunited with all our home furnishings. Those minimal pieces of furniture coming from the Oklahoma City apartment were now in the same sea container as our other furnishings. These household items were those that had been placed in temporary storage in Oklahoma City. It is odd how you find yourself wanting your favorite chair or your favorite cup. I was ready to get my Pearl back into a "real" home. It had only been 8 months since we packed and moved from our comfortable home in Englewood, Colorado but it sure seemed much longer than that.

And so it was that we moved to Ascot and into our wonderful home, Muirfield. Shortly after we moved in we learned that the home had originally been built by Nick Faldo, the British golfer who had been ranked number one in the world for several years. Mr. Faldo had built the home shortly after he won the Open at Muirfield in 1987. I guess it is only fitting that he would give the name of a great golf course to his home. Even though neither of us was an avid golfer, it was interesting to know that someone as famous as Nick Faldo had once lived in the house we now called home.

It soon became apparent that everyone we met in the Ascot community wanted to make sure that we knew whose "home" we lived in. Having the mailman, the cabbies, and the various shop keepers tell us about the previous owner of our habitat soon got to be wearing. But I will give Mr. Faldo credit, he built one heck of a home. It has been said that he loved this home but that when he switched out wives his first wanted nothing to do with Muirfield, and the second was on the same wavelength. Fortunate for us, but it was sad for Nick.

So it was that the two kids from Prineville, Oregon became ensconced in a magnificent country home in Ascot, Berkshire, England. This is where our story really begins to unfold, for from the moment we moved into Muirfield until we returned to the United States seven years later Bob and Shirley lived a life unlike anything we would ever have dreamed possible. If we had been sheltered during the 1950s living in a small but vibrant community, we were about to experience life at an entirely new level, where excitement reigns supreme and new adventures are always just around the corner.

Shirley was soon to be in her "element". After all was said and done, I have to believe that if we have former lives Shirley must have been royalty for that is how she lived, both in England and in China. I do not know how else she could have done the things she did and met the people she met.

Our stay in England was magical from day one. That being said, I was sobered by a question asked of me during one of our return trips to Prineville. While seated on a sofa at a friend's house I was asked how life in England was going. I said life was great and that we just absolutely loved living in the United Kingdom. Our friend then looked me in the eye and asked if I could I tell him about our adventures. What was a typical day like in England? The truth of the matter is that I mentioned a few really fun things we had done but I realized that I was not adequately portraying what life in the United Kingdom was like for Bob and Shirley. I had been writing friends letters, and sending back annotated photographs, but I was not systematically keeping track of those day-to-day experiences that make living in London and England so very special.

In an attempt to better document life as we lived it in the United Kingdom, I began to keep a diary. My English diary covered the years 1996 and 1997. I stopped keeping a diary when, in 1998, we were transferred to China. I captured our Asian adventures by once again writing letters to those back home. Much of what you will read in this tale will have been excerpted from episodes recorded in the diary and from the letters I wrote to friends.

I hope I do justice to what became the highlight of both my professional life and Bob and Shirley's social life. Every life should have such a lofty apex of satisfaction and exhilaration. This euphoric ride lasted throughout the time we spent in England and in China, and like many expatriates we experienced a certain period of sadness when we finally re-located back to the United States. It was good to be back, but how were we ever going adjust to life at home after living the life as we had been living it.

FIGURE 12. MUIRFIELD, KEIR PARK, ASCOT
BOB AND SHIRLEY'S FAVORITE PLACE IN ALL OF ENGLAND

FIGURE 13. THE POOL AND CABANA AT MUIRFIELD

Chapter 13

"England, My Beloved England"

Our stay in England was special. No, it was more than special. We were mesmerized, captivated, and thrilled by the myriad of experiences we had during our stay in the United Kingdom. We knew almost from day one that each day we spent in England was like living in a dream; we felt we had been given a gift of unimaginable value. Several years after we had relocated to the United States after having lived abroad, Shirley told me she had never been as utterly and totally happy as she was during the time we spent in England.

Twice during the final hours we spent on English soil Shirley had the occasion to utter the phrase "England, My Beloved England." And even after she returned to the United States there was one last opportunity to pass along her sentiments when she said, on television, her endearment to a former member of the royal family.

With our household items packed Shirley and I found ourselves being driven along the A-30 near Windsor Great Park. We were working our way to Heathrow where we would catch a flight to Beijing, China. With tears in her eyes Shirley looked over at the trails filled with day walkers and whispered, "England, my beloved England."

When we came back to England for an oil field inauguration in the fall of 1998 Shirley had the opportunity to chat with Prince Charles, and she told him that even though she now lived in China, England would always remain, "England, my beloved England."

After we had been repatriated to the United States and to Houston, Shirley found her way onto the Debra Duncan television talk show where Sarah Ferguson, Duchess of York, was a celebrity guest. Selected from the audience, Shirley spoke to the Duchess and concluded her conversation saying that she had left her heart in "England, my beloved England."

I am sure that those who read further will come to understand why my wife had this love affair with the nation, a nation filled with elegance and grandeur, and overprinted with royalty.

My dilemma is choosing a place to begin. I could tell anecdotes and give descriptive narratives of the most impressive places we visited. Maybe it might be best to write about our most memorable experiences. Perhaps I should start with the people we met, for they are many, and they are indeed fascinating subjects.

In English society there does appear to be a social layering, and all are aware of this seemingly endless division of classes, with the apex of society being the royal family. Many in England will no doubt say the old class structure has dissolved, but from what we saw and what we experienced there is no doubt in my mind that, individually, the population has a strong sense of their place in the hierarchy. Given this observation I shall begin with the people we met.

Chapter 14

MEMORABLE PEOPLE ENCOUNTERED IN THE UNITED KINGDOM

*W*hen we first moved to the United Kingdom, we were in our temporary living quarters at 3 King's Yard in London. To escape our rather small apartment, Shirley one day accepted an invitation and joined a new acquaintance who was on her way to play contract bridge at the nearby Piccadilly Hotel. Walk-ins were welcome, although not encouraged. Little did my sweet wife know but playing at this gathering were some of the world's best bridge players. When she was seated, she found that she and her partner were paired against Omar Sharif (actor in *Lawrence of Arabia* and *Dr. Zhivago*) who was in 1994 ranked among the top 50 bridge players in the world. Sharif had already written two books on bridge. Shirley told me she was in way over her head. She never went back to the Piccadilly to play bridge. She said she did ok, but that it was hard not to stare at Dr. Zhivago. She did tell Sharif he had beautiful eyes. His response was a muffled laugh. She also kept the score card from her game with Omar. Every so often she brought it out just to remind me of her encounter with Dr. Zhivago.

I think it would be an understatement to say that many, perhaps even most, English are reserved. They tend not to be officious and many do not particularly appreciate outgoing, gregarious, and loud Americans. The English probably share that level of affection for Americans with the rest of the world.

Yet, nearly every Englishman we met, once engaged, turned out to be most gracious, and genuinely warm and outgoing. It is just that most do not wish to emerge from their cocoon of reserve.

Once, Shirley and I were riding in a first-class cabin on a train traveling to a social event in Kent. The two other passengers in our cabin were mature gentlemen, both dressed in sartorial splendor. The older of the two gentlemen had a pocket watch chain dangling from his pant pocket, and he was wearing a striped shirt with a bow tie. The other gentleman was a bit more conservatively dressed; he was busy reading a newspaper that he conveniently used to shield himself from the other gentlemen and ourselves. Shirley, bubbly as always, asked me a question about a magnificent complex of buildings we were passing near Epsom Downs. I did not know the answer, but I could tell by the older gentleman's body language that he had heard the question and that he probably could give Shirley an informative answer. I merely mentioned, "I would imagine that this gentleman could answer your question." When we both looked at him his face broke into a big smile and he begin to speak. He told us about the grand buildings and about the family that lived in the multi-roomed mansion. He then opened up and began to speak on a great number of things, including national politics. It turned out that he was a former Minority Whip in Parliament and, even though retired, still had some influence in matters: a man in a gray suit as it is said in England.

The gentleman reading the paper abruptly said, "I can see that I am not going to be able to read my newspaper on this trip." I was afraid that we had really offended the guy, but he surprised us by immediately entering the conversation like he had been a part of it for the past 30 miles. He was equally delightful. He turned out to be the United Kingdom Managing Director for a major motion picture studio. I think it was MGM. Anyway, this very proper Englishman, who had been so aloof and maybe even a bit rude, suddenly began speaking as if we were the best of friends. When we finally left the train many miles down the track, I was struck by the thought that the stimulating conversation we had just experienced would not

Memorable People

have occurred if Shirley had not broken train etiquette and kept talking about what we were viewing from our train window. I would not have wanted to miss what had just occurred. These men were incredibly engaging and interesting, and, except for a simple query, we would have remained captives of our own thoughts.

I also met an engaging couple at the Ascot train station. I can say now that they were engaging, but that was not the case when I first saw them. Every morning I would arrive at the station and would wait either inside or outside, depending upon the weather, for the next train going into London. There are many early morning commuters who ride trains, but after a time you begin to recognize faces. I tend to be a bit outgoing, a result no doubt of my being an obtrusive American, and on several occasions I made a remark or two about the weather, a fellow passenger, or even the train service. This couple, both of whom worked in London, were straitlaced and polite but neither was particularly approachable. But after about a month of my banter they begin to open up, and open up they did. I began to look forward to our chats in the morning. I learned much about the English vernacular and what the English worker was like from these two. They could say what they wanted to me about anything. I was not a part of their careers or even of their very private social circle.

One day when I was away from London and missed the train, they asked if I had been "skiving", a term I learned was our equivalent of "playing hooky". I once told them a story and they said they were "gobsmacked" (stunned). My English vocabulary grew by leaps and bounds. I heard words and phrases I had not heard before, words like "cock-up" (a foul-up), "bollocks" (our B.S.), "car boot sale" (flea market), "bonnets and boots" (car hoods and trunks), "wobbly legged" (week in the knees) etc. But mostly I was excited to learn about their experiences at work, their plans for vacation, and any other matter they wished to comment on. They never visited with anyone else at the train station, yet I found these individuals to be open, sincere, and gregarious. I can tell you with absolute certainty that if you were to go to Ascot train station today and encounter Frank and Margaret you would find them to be stereotypical Brits: prim, proper, and reserved. When I left England these two were fast friends, the barrier between us was no longer up. So it would be with you if only you took the time.

One Saturday morning I entered the only supermarket in Ascot. A big "Budgens" sign greets you as you pull into the small parking lot. I had been shopping at Budgens for months and I usually saw the same people (clerks, managers, and shoppers) in the store. Remarkably, no one had ever said a word. I could go through the check-out line, and if I did not make some comment requiring a response, there would be no verbal exchange. However, on this particular Saturday morning, I walked into the store, gathered up my groceries, and proceeded to the check-out stand. In the front of the line was a little old lady. She had a cane and was bent over in the back. She was busy counting out her coins when she suddenly stopped and remarked to the young clerk, "Sonny, I am getting tired of you only having French apples in this store. Why don't you get some proper English apples?" Her comments turned all heads. I was stunned. I had previously learned that you do not mess with little old English ladies carrying canes. They will beat you to death if you jump a queue or if you undertake something that is forbidden.

The lady in line behind the troublemaker suddenly spoke up, "Yes, why must we always have French apples. We are supporting their economy while ours suffers. And besides that, we have been at war with them for centuries." "My God!" I thought. "How long has it been since the French and the Brits fought? Certainly not in this lady's lifetime." Then the third guy in line chimed in, "English apples are small and mushy. If you want good apples you should stock New Zealand apples." The guy was obviously from New Zealand. The humped-over lady who had started this dialogue grabbed her sack of groceries, looked back and said, "I'm sorry I created all of this commotion."

I left Budgens thinking I had just witnessed something quite remarkable. I did not think much about the exchange until the following Saturday when I went back once again to the store. As I walked in the side entrance, there in front of me was a huge pile of sacked English apples. Each bag weighed about 5 pounds. My first thought was that the little old lady who had raised the ruckus would not, and could not, buy a bag of this proportion. She would not eat that many apples in a month. Since I had been witness to the exchange the previous week I knew what the store had done to address the complaint (request) of a customer. So I bought a bag and took the apples home with me. I could hardly wait to try them. I took one out, cored it, and then took a big bite. It was soft and mushy, just like the New Zealander said. The apples were awful.

Each Saturday for the next four weeks I returned to Budgens and to the stack of English apples. The pile was not going down one bit. Each time I shopped I bought a bag and took the apples home, leaving them outside for the critters in our yard. I tried my best to acknowledge the efforts of the store's management, but one guy just cannot solve the marketing problem. In the end the pile disappeared in one fell swoop. I would have liked to believe that they caught on and were sold, but realistically I feared they ended up in the dumpster.

On November 25, 1997 Shirley and I attended a dinner to celebrate the launch of a new book written by The Right Honorable Baroness Thatcher. What a title, but to me she was the former Prime Minister Margaret Thatcher whom I remembered simply as The Iron Lady. There is no doubt that Margaret Thatcher is one tough bird. You have to be tough to survive in British politics: you can get a good idea of her strength of character if you read memoirs written by her peers on the international political stage. One of my favorite anecdotes relates to a meeting she had with German Chancellor Helmut Kohl, who once remarked that Prime Minister Thatcher had engaged him in a very heated debate and just when he was getting ready to lay into her, she said, "Helmut, may I serve you tea?" Chancellor Kohl remarked to the press, "I do not know how to handle this type of diplomacy." The first president George Bush wrote that he was worried on several occasions that a resolution would not meet with her approval and he was concerned about the consequences of this disapproval.

What, you ask, does this have to do with Bob and Shirley

And There We Were

Lent formerly of Prineville, Oregon. Well, 45 minutes prior to Margaret Thatcher giving a speech on *The Collected Speeches of Margaret Thatcher* she mingled with a room full of businessmen and their spouses who represented companies that were members of The British-American Chamber of Commerce. Never mind that nearby there were nearly 500 people filing into Grosvenor House for dinner and the talk, The Baroness was matriculating and was in great form. She was alternately solemn and politely gracious as she worked the receiving room. And then she came to my Shirley, who had politely made her way up to the front of the circle of dignitaries and businessmen waiting to greet the Prime Minister. When Shirley extended her hand, the Pearl said, "Hello, glad to meet you, and, by the way, how are your children, especially your son in Durban, South Africa." The Baroness inquired as to how Shirley knew about her family in Durban. It turns out that one of Shirley's dearest London friends had recently moved to South Africa and had met Margaret's son. The conversation went on for some 5 or 6 minutes and concluded with Margaret asking about our sons, Tobin and Taran. Where did they live, and what were they doing? Then Margaret suddenly remembered where she was and she said, almost apologetically, "I must be moving on". So it came to be that we have a lovely photograph of "The Iron Lady" chatting with Shirley about our boys. As is usually the case, and you will hear this refrain many times over, I was not in the photo. It was just Shirley and The Iron Lady with a few other well-wishers looking on.

When it came time for the speech, the Baroness made reference to the fact that it is not often one gets up to give a speech about the speeches one has given. This elicited a bit of laughter, and it demonstrated a bit of her warmth. After the speech, Margaret took questions from the audience. One wag made the mistake of asking her why England should support the United States on what was a contentious issue of the day. She ripped into the guy and said, "Why wouldn't we support the United States? Friends stand by friends! Surely you would." You could have heard a pin drop. She is a tough lady and I respect her more each time I read about her.

Memorable People

Figure 14. Former Prime Minister Margaret Thatcher and Shirley Lent

In this section on memorable people I have chosen to record an observation, not of an individual but of a mass of people. The event was the Henley Royal Regatta on the Thames River. The Regatta is one of the social events of the British "Season". It is a big-time affair. Shirley and I had wanted to attend the event, but it was a chance meeting at Marlow Weir one day in 1995 that led in the following year to our being invited for lunch at the Leander Club (the Members Reserved Marquee) with reserved seats in the Stewards' Enclosure. Our host was Mr. Dick Dunham, a former member of the United States Olympic Rowing Committee. Mr. Dunham was an avid supporter of Dartmouth Big Green Football and as such was also a fan of our son Taran who was a Co-captain during his senior year. We had met Mr. Dunham, by happenstance, when our paths crossed as we were walking with Taran across the Thames on a bridge at Marlow. Dick had recognized Taran and

And There We Were

he rushed over to chat with us. When Shirley expressed an interest in attending the Regatta Dick said he would make sure that we were invited the following year. And he delivered on that promise.

Dick Dunham was a member of the Leander Club, the world's oldest and most famous rowing club. To be an ordinary member one is usually elected by having shown proficiency at rowing, coaching, and administration, usually at the Olympic level. The club is exclusive: its membership consists of individuals from around the world. Oddly, the logo on the club's coat of arms is a pink hippo. Members are usually attired in blue blazers, often double breasted, with pink ties being a common accoutrement.

I would say that the Leander Club epitomizes the British ability to bring class distinction into focus. Proper attire is mandatory if one is to be admitted to the Club grounds and to the Stewards' Enclosure. I say this without one ounce of criticism or distaste. As we were entering the Steward's Enclosure, there was a lady in a line next to us who was arguing with the Stewards. They told her that the dress she was wearing was too short and that she would not be admitted. I have to tell you that this woman looked like a million dollars and her dress must have cost a fortune. But it was too short! She was arguing that she could pull it down a bit, and, indeed, she bent over and did just that. But the Stewards said simply, "Yes, it is acceptable now, but as soon as you enter and stand, the dress will ride up and it will become unacceptable." They turned her back. She watched the Regatta, but she did not watch it on the grounds within the Stewards' Enclosure.

But I digress. The point I wish to make about The Henley Regatta has to do with class distinction, and this distinction of classes can best be seen by walking the asphalt path that starts in front of the Leander Club and ends at the starting point for the Regatta races some 2112 meters (6930 feet or 1 mile 550 yards) away. The Thames is straight over most of this difference and one gets a good view of the racing from start to finish no matter where you might wish to watch the race. Of course, the view from the Grandstand and the chairs along the

Memorable People

riverbank in the Stewards' Enclosure offer the best views of the finish line. As there are 19 events and/or championships being contested, and there are multiple entries from around the world, ample time is available to stroll on the grounds and to walk the length of course if he or she desires. Shirley and I decided that it would be fun and refreshing to walk down to the starting line and then back to the Leander Club. So we walked.

I remember passing in front of the marquee where we had lunch. The tables were under a covered building and the service was superb. Pimm's was poured for one and all. This welcoming drink was followed by copious quantities of champagne and fine wines. There were well dressed waiters hurrying between the tables and the hidden kitchens. Everyone was dressed in their finest, especially the women who all wore hats. Many of the men also wore hats but they were Panama in style and not the derbies we had seen at other events comprising the social "Season". As we walked we next came to a covered pavilion, I think it was named Fawley Court. Here the people were still dressed in their Sunday best but not quite to the hilt as they were in the Stewards' Enclosure. Waiters served the guests, but they were dressed in more comfortable attire. I noticed that at the next big partition the covered awning was now over a buffet line and individuals were walking through the line and returning to tables on the lawn. Some had on sport coats and others did not. The women looked beautiful and were stunning in their dresses. After another couple of hundred yards, we came to a wide open area where there were large grills kicking out smoke from grilled meats. It appeared as if no special ticket was needed for this area. If you had the price for the meal and for the drink you could order what you wanted and sit as seats became available.

Things began to change rapidly once we left the enclosed and partitioned dining and sitting areas. The big smokers soon were replaced by individual grills that were cooking up bangers and chicken. The wine and champagne that were so predominant up around the Leander Club had now been replaced by beer or malts. Then the barbecue grills were gone and we saw a plethora of picnic cloths and baskets, all with sandwiches and other finger foods. Dress in this area was much more relaxed. The patrons here were attired in slacks and shorts and a few of the women wore tops that were scanty, and at times quite revealing. The people seemed to be having a great time. More children were visible in the crowds.

As we approached Temple Island, a grand place in the middle of the river, we could see more catering across the water but on our side of the river the grass banks were now teeming with young people. Many were reclined and in various modes of clinching; much like a bunch of mating snakes. Six packs of beer were abundant, but blankets seemed to be in short supply.

It struck me that in this short walk I had seen the entire gamut of English Society. Individuals in each segment seemed to be having a great time, but I could not see those at the Leander Club wanting to watch the races from the starting area and I was absolutely certain that those individuals sitting and laying on the grass at the starting area were not welcome in the Stewards' Enclosure, nor were they the least bit interested in being there.

The Henley Royal Regatta has been a significant event in the "Season" for over 150 years, and I will bet that in all that time there has been a similar de facto separation of classes like that we saw as we walked the course on that wonderfully sunny day, July 7, 1996. I personally think it is just great that one could attend the Regatta and drink beer and lay in the grass, or if he or she preferred to dress to the tens and experience the elegance and tradition available to those invited to the Stewards Enclosure. I suspect that the beautiful lady in the expensive and marginally short dress would have been heartily welcomed by the lads and lasses at the starting line. But I doubt it if she was of a mind to go there.

Henley was a memorable experience for us, and Mr. Dunham was a most gracious host. It is a bit remarkable to know that a former United States Olympian gave us one of our greatest insights into the people of the United Kingdom. By the time we left the country, Shirley and I were of the opinion that no one in the world can 'put on the dog' the way the British can. When they want elegance, they demand elegance. But don't try to crash the party.

Before returning to recounting people Shirley and I met, I would recommend that anyone touring the English countryside, especially if they find themselves in Oxfordshire, take the time to visit Henley, even if the Regatta is not being contested. The village has been around for over 2000 years and is truly delightful.

We went back to this market community several times and even found time one Sunday to have brunch at the historic riverside pub, The Angel. The wonderful rowing races make Henley the Mecca for oarsmen but the community is magical in its own way, racing or not. On almost any day but those during the July Regatta it is possible to walk the silent shores of the Regatta course, all the while eating an ice cream cone purchased from a local vendor.

Unlike Americans and perhaps numerous other foreigners, the British do not undertake something if it is not proper. A proper Brit just does not consider improper actions as being in the realm of possibility. When they come across someone whose demeanor appears to be honorable and respectable, they assume that such a person would not make an improper request. I am not saying that Shirley did not make an improper request or two, but her curiosity and her insatiable desire to experience everything created avenues of access to events not normally made available to English citizens, or to foreigners.

Shirley had a penchant for attendance at famous churches. She was moved by the beauty and the historical aura she found in churches throughout the world. Even though she had gone to many of the London churches, including St. Paul's, the big-name house of worship nearest our home in Ascot was St. George's Chapel located on the grounds of Windsor Castle in Windsor. The church is a large one and serves the local citizens of Windsor and other surrounding communities. Shirley had been to St. Georges several times and she always wondered why there was a section of the church where only a few people were seated. The Chapel is shaped like a cross with the main seating area for the parishioners at the bottom of the cross. There are several hundred seats in the rooms that comprise the "arms" of the cross. And at the top of the cross is an ornate enclosure where there is room for a hundred or so worshipers. The pulpit is situated so that worshipers in any of the seating areas have a view of the speakers.

Shirley was attracted to the ornate room at the head of the Chapel and on one Sunday morning she walked over to it and made the comment, "Why is this blue rope here?" The church official who was the closest attendant looked at Shirley, beautiful as she was and elegantly attired, and said, "Sorry Madame", and he lowered the barrier so that Shirley could gain access to the special area. When Shirley had asked her question she had rolled her right hand at the rope and the official had taken her question to be, "**Why** is this blue rope here?" He assumed that anyone asking such a question was expected to be seated in the reserved area. It did not cross his mind that this person was just asking a simple question.

Shirley found herself seated in the Choir of The Chapel. The Chapel consists of beautifully carved wooden stalls above which hang the banners of each Knight of the Garter. Below each banner hang the knight's helmet and his crest. The Choir of the Chapel is the host for an annual service held each June when the Sovereign of the Order of the Garter, that is, the Queen, attends as do each of the Knights and Ladies of the Order. Except for when the Order of the Garter is in attendance anyone can sit in the Choir of the Chapel. It is just that no one in the local community would dare. As a consequence, The Choir is used almost exclusively by members of the Royal Family who are in residence at Windsor Castle on any particular Sunday morning.

When Shirley sat down, she found herself seated next to Princess Margaret. The Queen, when she comes to church, usually sits across from where Shirley was seated. Of course, Shirley was not aware of all of the protocol exceptions that were at play. She looked at the surrounding lamps, wooden enclaves, and the beautiful banners and thought that this was just grand. The church administrators soon realized that Shirley was most likely not royalty, so to avoid embarrassing the church or Princess Margaret, a bishop came and sat next to Shirley to make sure that she knelt when she should and took communion as was appropriate.

The really strange thing is that whenever Shirley went back to St. George's Chapel to worship she would be seated in the Choir. Indeed when her mother, Marie, came to visit the two Prineville girls went to church and were escorted into the Choir. What a treat it was for Marie. Unless the rules have changed anyone can still attend church and sit where Shirley and Marie sat, but the locals would never do such a thing as it would not seem to be proper. If the Queen were in attendance, they would be mortified to even think of such an audacious move.

Shirley Lent fell in love with the Royal Ascot, which is one of the traditional events on the British social calendar, or "The Season" if you will. The Ascot experience will be discussed in another section of this narrative, but Shirley and her friend, Rita Gunter, made history of sorts by gaining entry into the exclusive "Royal Enclosure" without either of them having proper credentials. Kerr-McGee played host to a group of oil industry partners at the June 19, 1997 Royal Ascot. The Kerr-McGee table was located in one of the marquee pavilions but none in our group had credentials that would allow access to the Royal Enclosure, the seating area where the Royal Family, including the Queen, come to watch the races and to place bets. To gain access to the Royal Enclosure one must make a written request to one's country ambassador who then makes a formal request through the staff at St. James' Palace. If the request is honored, tickets and credentials can be picked up at St. James. Many local citizens of the United Kingdom find it impossible to gain entry into the Royal Enclosure. Entry into the Royal Enclosure is elitist to the nth degree.

Following a pre-race card luncheon catered by the best that London catering had to offer, the Kerr-McGee guests were invited to tour the Ascot grounds. We had seats reserved for our guests in the Grandstand Enclosure, although many chose to remain at our lunch table, proximal to the nearby open bar.

And There We Were

The races could be viewed on nearby television monitors. Betting was available in the Marquee so it was not necessary to join the masses crowding to the various on-site bookies or to the betting booths in the Grandstand. Shirley took Rita and a group of other wives on a tour of the Ascot grounds. Shirley had been here many times and was intimately familiar with the layout. After the group had visited the Pre-Parade Ring and the Winners Enclosure, most of the ladies chose to join their husbands in the Grandstand or in the Marquee. Shirley took Rita, who had husband Jim in tow, towards the entrance adjacent to the Winners Enclosure where the horses enter the track. As Shirley began to walk through a gate she realized, belatedly, that there were a host of stewards watching credentials as the patrons walked into the open area leading to the Royal Enclosure. Rita realized that the stewards were turning back everyone who did not have the proper badge on display and she mentioned this to Shirley. Jim Gunter was very high risk as he had neither the coat and tails, nor the derby hat, nor the badge required for entrance. He was dead meat. But Shirley looked over at Rita and whispered, "Walk with purpose." And they did, dressed in their very best, with hats displaying the pinnacle of elegance. Who could possibly question that these brisk-walking ladies were without proper credentials. It never crossed the Stewards' minds that these proper ladies were doing something improper.

Shirley and Rita breezed through but the two stewards converged on husband Jim and said, "Whoa there sir. You are in the wrong area!" Jim turned away and then looked forlornly back towards Rita. When Jim mouthed, "What am I to do", Rita returned his silent query with the mouthed response, "Go Back." Shirley and Rita spent the rest of the race card in the Royal Enclosure. The Queen was about 25 feet to Shirley and Rita's right. Rita could not stop looking at the Queen and noticing what she was doing. There was a glass partition between them but that did not diminish Rita's experience. When the two ladies returned to the Marquee to have a final drink with our guests, they were abuzz with what had happened. Shirley related that she was not trying to be deceitful, but when they found themselves so close to the Royal Enclosure, it just seemed like the right thing to do, so they kept on walking.

The type of rigor mortis that can set in when a commoner meets royalty is interesting to behold. Shirley, as she did almost every day, was walking in Windsor Great Park when she came up behind a middle-aged lady walking her small dog, a Shih Tzu. As both walkers crested a hill they came upon a car with both back doors open. It was parked beside the walkway. Because only park employees and royalty are permitted to use the park road, Shirley was quite sure a member of the royal family must be close by. Sure enough, Shirley saw Princess Margaret with a friend. The Princess was standing on the pathway and pointing to something that had caught her eye. She hardly noticed the walkers coming upon her parked car. But the car did not escape the notice of the free running little dog. He was obviously tired, and when he saw the car with its doors open he must have thought, "Good, its time to go home." He ran to the car and jumped into the back seat where he promptly sat down and looked as content as a puppy can be. The dog's owner was mortified. She looked into the car and froze. She too had recognized Princess Margaret and now her dog was sitting on the Princess' car seat. Princess Margaret looked back and saw the dog and began to laugh, but she did not attempt to remove the happy little fellow. Shirley smiled, walked over to the car, gently lifted the dog, and handed it to his master. Both the Princess and the dog owner thanked Shirley who, hardly breaking stride, continued her walk.

To appreciate how unexpectedly warm and gracious the British citizenry can be, you could reflect on an experience we had on the Thames River near the town of Marlow in Buckinghamshire. Shirley and I had made reservations at the Compleat Angler Restaurant at Marlow weir for ourselves and our two dear friends, Paul and Sharon Hess, who were in the United Kingdom as our houseguests. The Compleat Angler and the town of Marlow will be the subject of their own special section later in this tale, so I will relate here only that the Restaurant has a riverside docking area from which guests can depart for leisure rides up the Thames. All manner of boats are available

And There We Were

for rental if one calls in advance. We had made plans for the four of us to take an hour-long trip up the Thames in a shallow draft and covered boat that had seating available for six. Captain Jack, I am not sure that his name was "Jack" but we referred to him by that name and he responded accordingly and without rancor so "Jack" it is.

Paul loves his beer as much as I do, so we made arrangements to have the boat stocked with iced British brews, champagne, and an assortment of nuts. Paul and Sharon were surprised when we parked our car and walked up to the restaurant only to walk right past it and onto the boat dock. Shortly after we were seated in the craft, we began a slow journey up a very picturesque segment of the Thames. It was quiet except for our chatter, and we passed many ducks, geese, and swans. Walkers along the bank waived to us as we slowly drained our beers and the champagne. The only time demand we faced was the dinner reservation at the Compleat Angler, and we would have plenty of time to meet that demand.

We passed an island with an inlet leading off of it. This inlet appeared to go back into an area where there were some very large and ornate mansions. We asked Captain Jack if he could take the boat back into this stretch of backwater. He said, "No, this is not allowed." We proceeded up the river drinking and chatting and making friends with the Captain. When we arrived at a weir, small dam, Captain Jack announced that this was as far as we were going. He reversed course and headed back down the river. When we came up on the island and the intriguing inlet, we once again asked if we could make a quick side trip to see the impressive homes.

By this time Captain Jack had taken a liking to us and, and against his better judgment, he turned the boat into the inlet. We traversed up to a turning basin and there made a wide sweep as we prepared to return to the main part of the river. As we made the turn the engine and the propeller began to make sounds like the life was being choked out of both. We limped over to the nearest dock, in front of the nicest home we had seen. No sooner had we pulled along shore than a door opened and out came the couple who owned the property. We

Memorable People

whispered to the Captain, "Don't worry, we will tell them we made you do it. We will tell them that we are from America and we just wanted to see how the wealthy British people lived." The Captain looked at us as if we must be daft and then he went back to frantically working on the propeller. He soon found that he had not pulled in a trailing rope and that when we made the turn in the basin the rope had become entwined in the propeller, thus killing the engine and preventing the blades from turning.

When the couple, a doctor and his wife, reached the dock, they wanted to know what we were up to. We gave them our spiel. When they found out that we were from the United States they became very animated and most effusive. They noticed that our champagne bottle was empty so the man returned to his house to bring us down a bottle of their favorite bubbly. As the Captain worked to get the propeller free the six of us sat and sipped champagne. And then when it became apparent that this was going to take a bit of time the lady went back to the house and returned with a large sheet of birthday cake. Trailing along was her daughter who was celebrating her 23rd birthday. The couple thought it would be nice if we would share the cake with them. And there we were, sipping champagne and eating the young lady's birthday cake. But Captain Jack was having a bad run of luck. He informed us that the boat would have to be towed back to the restaurant dock. He suggested we might want to call a cab as it was going to be some time before he could get us back down river.

When the lady of the house learned that we had dinner reservations she immediately insisted on driving us back to Marlow. Whereupon the biggest surprise of our day unfolded before us. She opened her garage, and in it was a vintage automobile, a purple beauty built sometime in the 1920's. It was incredible. She immediately retrieved a can of fuel, maybe it was oil, filled various vents with the fluid. She took a crank from the boot and went to the front of the car where she made a number of turns of the crank. After only a few turns, the engine coughed and then roared to life.

As we started down the road Paul suggested we should keep

our chins low so that our heads would not snap back. That was funny! The car could not do much over 25 miles per hour. What a treat the trip was! When we pulled into the parking lot of the Compleat Angler, many of the arriving diners watched as we poured out of the car. We paused to take many pictures and to thank the lady for her hospitality and kindness. She gave us a big smile and waived as she headed back to her home. We shall never forget her or the good doctor. It was a special treat, indeed, for the four of us crazy Yanks. I wonder if we in America would have been so kind or so accommodating.

We later returned to the Compleat Angler and rented a much bigger boat. The Chief Executive Officer of Kerr-McGee, Mr. Luke Corbett and his wife Becky, were the guests of honor on this trip. Captain Jack was again at the helm and he seemed to have forgotten the trouble we had gotten him into. I was delighted and grateful that Jack never mentioned to Mr. Corbett or the other 10 guests that we had once experienced a difficult time on the river. I can assure you that we did not take the big boat into the inlet.

I would like you to believe we once met Princess Diana as Shirley would have loved to have done. Our paths crossed Diana's many times. Indeed, one time a local newspaper showed her having tea on the patio of the Compleat Angler, at table that was one of our favorites. We were often seated at this riverside table where we served our pre-dinner drinks. But Diana had enough people chasing her. She was probably better off not having to handle another couple of Diana-philes.

Given that we did not meet up with Diana, Princess of Wales, you might wonder why I bring her name up. The truth is that if you were to come into our home you would see a very nice photo of Diana and Shirley. Diana towers over Shirley, with one of the ladies being 5'5' and the other 5'10". Both are dressed in elegant dresses although Diana's is much more formal than is Shirley's. The picture was taken at Madame Tussaud's during a Kerr-McGee's office Christmas Party. The Company had reserved this tourist attraction for one evening and our dinners were served on tables located in the hallways betwixt and between the wax figures of famous and notable

Memorable People

characters. I remember that at our table it appeared as if Mikhail Gorbachev, Francois Mitterrand, and Indira Gandhi were all looking over our shoulders to see what we were eating.

Following dinner, Shirley and I walked amongst the various exhibits. We came to one portraying the Royal Family in a receiving line. A nearby photographer asked if we would like to have a photo with the Royal Family in the background. Shirley said she wanted one of her standing next to Diana. The photographer was aghast. "You cannot cross the rope and go there." But before he could even finish his protest, Shirley had hiked her dress and stepped across the barrier. When she stood next to Diana the picture was taken. Diana looks-life like and the photo might be considered to be genuine except for the fact that Diana is solemn and looking down the receiving line and Shirley is looking at the photographer with a great big smile on her face. So we met Diana that night, only she was not aware of it.

By the way, we also met Nick Faldo, the first homeowner of Muirfield, that same evening. We have a photo of Nick handing Shirley the keys to our house. I am sure that Mr. Faldo would not be amused. But we were and so it goes.

Princess Diana died tragically in a car crash in Paris on August 31, 1997. Shirley and I were in different countries when we learned of the accident. I was stunned by the news when I turned on the television in Muirfield on Sunday morning. Shirley was in Nice, France. In order to capture events around Diana's death I have chosen to insert my diary entries relating to the Diana tragedy:

August 29, 1997

Today Shirley and Tobin left for Nice so that they might attend Aaron Hendleman's wedding to his French bride, Christine. The rehearsal dinner was this evening and the wedding is an all-day affair tomorrow, Sunday. On Tuesday morning Shirley and Tobin will tour the Mediterranean coast as they travel from Nice to Monaco.

August 31, 1997

Today I woke up to the tragic news that Diana, Princess of Wales, had died. My first reaction as I saw the dash between the dates on television was one of utter disbelief. How could she have died? Before it was announced where she had died, I was trying to remember where she was yesterday. She was on a boating holiday on the Mediterranean Sea with her new boyfriend, Dodi Fayed. Was it a boating accident? God, did she commit suicide? All of these questions raced through my mind. Then the word came that she had died in a horrific car accident in Paris, and that Dodi had also been killed. What a sad day it is. I will remember her as a tragic figure in the monarchy, one who was dealt a bad hand but who somehow had come through everything with dignity. She was obviously a good mother and the two boys may turn out to be the best thing that has happened to the royal family in generations. She was loved by many, and that included the two of us. She had a very magnetic personality and her royal manner was splendidly blended with her ability to relate to others no matter what their station in life. A real loss for England.

September 1, 1997

Today I left for the United States. I have not been able to contact Shirley so I do not know how she took the death of Diana or even if she had heard the news. (Of course she had heard the news, even in the Kalahari Desert the nomadic tribesman had heard of the death of Princess Diana). Later after Shirley returned home she told me that she had heard the news from a maid in the hotel where she was staying. The young girl came in and said, "Di dead", and Shirley said, "yes, Diana". But the maid insisted that "Di dead" so they turned on the television and heard the tragic news.

Before I left for the States I purchased all of the British papers I could buy and they were each filled, front to back, with stories of Diana. It soon became apparent that the lady was loved by all. How can that be I thought? I do not even know her and yet I want to cry for the loss. It is really puzzling to me but the more I think about it the more I come to realize that I really did know the young princess. She was in the news every day, she appeared on the front page of almost every fashion and ladies magazine, and she was on television or radio every day. We knew when she exercised, when she saw her kids, when and with whom she flirted, when and where she shopped, and so on. I do know Diana because whether I like it or not she was a very real part of my everyday life here in England.

When I deplaned in Houston there was a television reporter waiting to interview passengers coming off of the flight from London Gatwick. I was stopped by the reporter, but I told the reporter he really should be interviewing the Brits and not an expatriate. He insisted, so I began my interview. He asked how I thought the people in England were taking the news of her death and this was my response to that question. I quote it only with the caveat that it is what I remember saying... it might not be totally accurate, but it is how I remember as I made this entry into the diary. "The people of England are totally devastated. You can see it in their faces and you can tell by the silence that exists on the trains; there is a somber mood in the air as people exit and enter subways. She was a great ambassador for England. She was loved by many and despite her shortcomings, and she had a number of them, she had the ability to make an impact on society, and by that I mean world society. She was a lovely lady, fragile and caring. She will be deeply missed."

SEPTEMBER 2, 1997

Shirley and Tobin return from France and I begin the Exploration and Production Managers meeting in Houston. Having brought a number of newspapers from London the people in the office are very much interested in having a copy or at least being left to read what was written in the local London press.

SEPTEMBER 3, 1997

Shirley makes a trip into London and she takes flowers to the gate in front of Buckingham Palace where she places them beside a cherub pot. Her note is enclosed in plastic and both she and our son, Tobin, are overcome by the emotion shown by the masses. It is truly amazing that so many people care. The queue to sign the book of remembrance at St. James Palace is nearly 10 hours long. Shirley and Tobin go to the chapel at St. James and they walk by without stopping. Diana's coffin is lying in state at the chapel and the number of people milling about is huge. Shirley wants to go to Harrods (Dodi Fayed's father Mohammed Al Fayed owns Harrods) and does so. Tobin is reluctant to go there but once there he finds the pictures, flowers, and the crowds to be very emotional.

SEPTEMBER 5, 1997

Return to London. It is interesting that the plane is filled with common people from the United States who are coming to London to attend the funeral of Princess Diana. As we boarded the plane in Houston, a local television crew had its cameras focused on the departing gate which read, "London Gatwick".

SEPTEMBER 6, 1997

Today is the funeral of Diana. The pomp and ceremony for a non-royal (she had been stripped of her royal title by the divorce decree) is unbelievable. The nation found that its citizens were not as prim and proper as believed. England has never known a period of such un-requiting grief or a period where its populace was so willing to show its grief. I have to believe that if the entire Royal family had died the nation would not have shown as much grief as it did today. A beautiful lady, in the prime of her life, struck down in a tragedy that will be remembered through the ages. Two hundred years from now people will remember Diana, Princess of Wales. She will be the Ann Bolyn of the Twentieth Century. I have great faith that the nation will be well served by her sons. Whatever is said, I believe that Charles and Diana both loved their children, and that they went to exceptional ends to make sure that they were raised as normal children...royal, but normal. Many were more beautiful than Diana, many more intelligent, many more articulate, many more confident, but none were more influential.

Thirty-million Americans got up between 1:00 and 3:00 a.m. to watch the funeral. It is said that in a desert in South Africa nomads placed a picture of Diana by a pile of stones and they had their own ceremony.

The above diary entries covering the dates during which Diana died and was buried may be a bit too detailed for many, but the words were written from the heart. The written words were my attempt to capture the events of the days as viewed by a foreigner living in an adopted homeland.

When we first met Mr. Michael Portillo we were sure that he would one day be Prime Minister of England. The Right Honourable Michael Portillo is a handsome and charismatic leader. He is also a bright individual and is an accomplished conversationalist. Mr. Portillo worked for Kerr-McGee in the early 1980s and did so once again for a time in the late 1990's, but his claim to fame in politics came after he was elected to a seat in Parliament, a seat he held from 1984 until 1997. As a part of the Government, he rose through the ranks to become first Secretary of State for Employment and then Secretary of State for Defence. His surge towards the Prime Minister position was badly derailed when he lost his seat in Parliament in 1997. Even though he was re-elected in 1999, the sweeping defeat of the Conservatives in 2001 set his plans back. When he was not able to gain leadership of the Conservative Party, he opted to leave the House of Commons in 2005. Afterwards, though sidelined for the time being, Mr. Portillo still had many political battles yet to fight.

Because of Mr. Portillo's past associations with Kerr-McGee we had the opportunity to meet with him and his wife, Carolyn, on multiple business/social engagements, most of which were business dinners. One of the first involved a dinner with a delegation that had come from China. I could not have known at the time that I would be working with members of this delegation when I transferred to China in 1998. Dinner was at a restaurant overlooking Chelsea Harbor, and the Chinese leaders were immediately taken by Michael. The Chinese respect power and what could be more demanding of respect than having dinner with the Minister of Defence of one of the world's military powers.

The Chinese had brought their own special liquor, Mao Tai, which is a drink that they revere but which usually stuns foreigners with its taste, its strength, and its ability to induce an offensive body odor that seeps through the pores of the individuals who drink the stuff. One does not want to spill this drink on your clothing or in your travel bag.

Shirley, the Chinese called her Mrs. Robert as our societies can never come to an agreement on which goes first, surname or given name. Anyway, Mrs. Robert was offered Mao Tai and when Shirley sipped it she smiled. The question posed to her through the interpreter was, "Do you like Mao Tai?" Always the diplomat, my Mrs. Robert smiled and said, "Good", although the good may have come out a bit more like "*Gooood.*" Shirley and I had been a bit concerned as to how we would handle dinner etiquette with the Chinese but when the delegation leader, Mr. Zhou Shou Wei, bit into a lobster tail, chewed on it for a while, and then spit out the shell we knew that we need not be concerned whether or not we used the right utensils.

Although there were twelve people at the dinner table that night, the Chinese spent most of their time speaking directly to Mr. Portillo. I was the Vice President and Managing Director of Exploration for Kerr-McGee, but had it not been for my wife I do not think the Chinese would have paid any attention to us. After we had moved to China, Mr. Zhou Sho Wei and his family became friends both with us and with our sons. It remains a friendship I cherish.

Another evening when we dined with Mr. Portillo and Carolyn, I found myself sitting next to Carolyn at the dinner table.

We made small talk and I thought, "now this woman is an interesting lady". And she must surely be one. As masculine as Michael Portillo seems to be, the British tabloids and internet message boards constantly rip him as to his sexuality. Michael has made a few comments about poor discretions in his past and that is good enough for me. If Carolyn is a wife of convenience so be it. There is no doubt in my mind that Mr. and Mrs. Portillo are great friends. Carolyn surprised me when she and I got into a conversation, wherein she offered as how she "would do anything in life once." Boy did that leave the door open for thought.

When we left England, we hoped we would see Mr. Portillo elected Prime Minister. The Liberal Party was in control at the time, but in politics the favor of the populace can turn on a dime. I believe that a man with Mr. Portillo's leadership qualities would have made a great Prime Minister. But now, some 20 years on, Mr. Portillo's time has come and gone, an opportunity missed.

Another character that comes to mind whenever I think of Michael Portillo is Frank Sharratt, who was Kerr-McGee's Director of Government Affairs. Frank was also a close friend of Mr. Portillo. On the organizational charts submitted to the government Mr. Sharratt was listed as Chairman of Kerr-McGee United Kingdom, PLC. As such you would think he would have been my boss, but he was not. I reported initially to Mr. Michael Webb who was Senior Vice President of Exploration. Mr. Sharratt reported directly to our Chief Executive Officer, Luke Corbett.

There is no doubt that a very interesting book could be written about the life of Mr. Sharratt. He was very influential in British politics. He was a man in a gray suit; an inconspicuous person in the background who wields power through influence. Someone once told me that Mr. Sharratt was one of four or five men in the United Kingdom who could possibly bring down the government of John Majors. Frank denied this but I am not so sure that it wasn't true.

Nothing was ever as it seemed with Mr. Sharratt. He hid an

early, and probably failed, marriage that many consider was "beneath the stairs", that is he married below his station in life. Frank's family owns a landed estate in northern England and he had partial ownership in at least one ocean view Castle. He apparently has a son, but he referred to this young man only as his nephew. Mr. Sharratt ran with a number of individuals who appeared to be effeminate, but at the same time he was rumored to be a ladies' man and to have courted a number of young ladies, some less than half his age. He was definitely a moving target.

The influence Mr. Sharratt had with the Royal Family came from his life-long friendship with the late Queen Mother. For many years they played cards together and their friendship was an open book. I did not witness it but one of my associates told me that once the Queen Mother was riding through a crowd in Hyde Park when she spotted Frank. She had her carriage stopped, stepped out, and walked over to have a chat with Frank. I can believe it. When Kerr-McGee wanted a member of the Royal Family to be present for the inauguration of our production vessel which was to "sail away" for the Janice Field oil development, all it took was a request by Frank Sharratt, and the guest speaker was none other than Prince Charles.

We appreciated the influence that Mr. Sharratt had with the Department of Trade and Industry and especially those in charge of licensing. We never got any special treatment, the staff at the DTI are too honorable for that type of collusion, but we did get audiences that permitted us to make our case for the acquisition of licenses or for favorable treatment with respect to some larger oil companies that appeared to be taking advantage of Kerr-McGee.

Mr. Sharratt would most likely disapprove of what I have written, and I do not write to be disrespectful. He was one of the most memorable characters I ever met. When my mother, aged 81 at the time, met him she fell in love with this English gentleman. She referred to him as that delightful old man, even though at the time he was 15 years younger than she. Frank was equally respectful and cordial both to me and to my wife. He was a smooth operator.

Memorable People

World leaders find their way into the United Kingdom for all manner of reasons. Sometimes, if one is in the right spot at the right time, you can have an unexpected encounter with a dignitary whose path you would never have expected to cross. Such it was one Saturday evening in the village of Bracknell. The nearest cinema to our home in Ascot is located in a mini mall in Bracknell, a village only 4 or 5 miles from Ascot. We frequently attended the cinema to take in the latest movies.

On the Saturday night under discussion Shirley and I had read in the local paper that the Whoopi Goldberg film, *The Associate*, was playing in the Bracknell multiplex. Having nothing else planned we decided to take in the movie. The mini mall at Bracknell has several restaurants on a lower level and an escalator brings movie goers up to a second level where the concession stands and the theaters are located. Shirley went to the ladies' room before the movie started. I walked over to the nearest concession stand and bought a large bag of popcorn. I leaned back against the glass counter and waited.

As I was waiting, I glanced over at the rising escalator and noticed that there were a number of men, all in suits, coming off the moving stairs. The suits kept coming, like bread off of a conveyor belt. My first reaction was "Come on guys, give it a break. It is Saturday night at the movies. You ought to lighten up." I could not believe that at the Bracknell cinema there would be men wearing suits.

As I watched I noticed that they were coming right towards me. And in the middle of the suits was this relatively short fellow who was looking around and trying to make eye contact with the locals. As everyone in this segment of the lounge was waiting to enter the various theaters, I was one of the very few who was looking back and into the face of this gentleman. I immediately recognized him. It was His Majesty Hussein, King of Jordan. I could not believe my eyes. As he walked by me, he looked at me and broke into a great big smile. Not a word was said but I was captivated by the obvious contact we had made. I think that ability to make contact must be a trait all great leaders and politicians have.

And There We Were

    After King Hussein had passed, I saw a beautiful tall lady and a 13-or 14-year old boy walking behind him. It was Queen Noor! I found out later the young dark-haired boy was their son. Just as a trailing group of suits passed, I saw Shirley coming out of the ladies' powder room. When she reached me, I told her what had just happened. We walked up to the ticket taker, all the while looking down the hall towards the royal contingent. The young attendant handed back our ticket stubs and said, "Second door on the right." But we were not really paying attention to what he said as we were watching to see which theater King Hussein would enter. When the group turned right into a theater, I could not believe my eyes. They were also going to see *"The Associate"*. My first impulse was to wonder why King Hussein would come to England, and to Bracknell, and spend Saturday night watching a Whoopi Goldberg movie. It just blew me away.

    Shirley and I turned into the same theater where we saw King Hussein make his way and we looked for our seats. In the United Kingdom all seats are reserved and you sit where your ticket says you should sit. I remember looking at the stub and, keeping one eye on the Hussein entourage, found that we were directly behind the King, but about four rows back. It appeared as if no tickets had been sold in a security area around King Hussein and Queen Noor. The lights dimmed and the trailers came on. Just before the movie began, I leaned over to Shirley and remarked, "Can you believe that King Hussein wants to see a Whoopi Goldberg movie." Instantly, to the sound of loud music, a title flashed onto the screen. It was *Conair*. We had entered the wrong theater! We did not leave, remaining seated to watch the Nicholas Cage action movie along with the other patrons. Lucky for us our seats had not been sold to anyone else.

    Later, when I read that King Hussein's 14-year-old son was attending a boarding school in the area I finally got it. The King had probably asked his son what he would like to do on this Saturday night and the boy had said he wanted to go to a movie. And his movie of choice must have been *Conair*.

    We followed the Royal group out of the theater and into the

Memorable People

hallway. The pace was fast, and this time King Hussein was walking directly into the faces turned towards the theaters. Many people recognized the King and there was a steady hum as people pointed and spoke his name. But the suits quickly moved the group through the lounge, down the escalator, and into a line of black limos waiting in front of the mini-mall entrance. Shirley had hoped she might be able to catch up with Queen Noor, but it was not possible. The Queen was shielded and moving much too fast.

I was saddened when, in 1999, I learned that King Hussein of Jordan had died. For a singular moment he and I exchanged smiles. It was a magical moment for me, and probably a most forgettable one for him. But the night at the movies in Bracknell will be remembered always.

Obviously not all the memorable people we met while in England were citizens of the United Kingdom. Another fellow I met was a business associate from Japan. Akio Suzuki was, at the time, Managing Director for Nippon Oil Exploration & Production U.K. LTD. He is a great fellow, and we shared many marvelous times together, some professional and some social. I will not relate the details here, but on one occasion when Kerr-McGee hosted a group of our partners on the Orient Express, a Valentine's Day Luncheon Excursion, Akio and his wife Yoshiko were two of the invited special guests. I am sure that their memories of this excursion, like ours, will not be diminished by the passing years.

One might ask, "Why write of Akio, you met many fantastic businessmen during your stay in the United Kingdom?" That is a legitimate question. But I shall never forget Akio, and my memory of him was cemented one very wet day, June 26, 1997, during and after a round of golf.

Mr. Suzuki had invited me and Michael Webb, my former boss and at the time the Senior Vice President for Strategic Planning, to a round of golf at the London Hatfield Golf Club. Hatfield is an immaculately kept club whose membership is mostly Japanese. Michael became ill and had to cancel his participation at the last minute. Akio found another mutual

And There We Were

industry friend who could join us, but when we arrived at the Club rain was falling in sheets. It was raining as hard as I had ever seen it rain in England.

When we sat for lunch, our place settings were chopsticks only. No pretense as to the wishes of the club patrons. Our lunch was a bit fishy, but quite delicious and the meal was washed down with several bottles of cold Japanese beer.

As we were about to get in our carts the rain began to come down even harder. Massive sheets of water were running down the paths and the paved road. We went back inside and said we would wait five minutes, but after five minutes we had seen no change. For whatever reason, the three of us decided to go ahead anyway. As we were heading out, we encountered a foursome of Japanese ladies walking from their carts towards the club house. They looked like a bunch of muskrats that had just come out from under a waterfall. There was not a single smiling face amongst them.

I had a rain slicker, but it was a joke. By the third hole I was so wet that my watch had water condensed on the crystal and my billfold was wet down to the last little piece of paper. The sand bunkers on the course were filled with water and pools of casual water were randomly distributed on the greens. When we putted, the balls would roll across the greens with rooster tails trailing behind them. When the balls dropped, they disappeared into cups filled to spill. Fun huh! Actually, it was.

As we drove up to a par five hole, I was chuckling at the water pouring off the tops of our electric golf carts. There must have been some sort of funneling action because the water, hose like, only spilled from each of the four corners. I had taken off my golf glove and just as I was about to tee the ball up, Akio handed me his new "Big Bertha" driver and encouraged me to use it since I could probably carry the lake and cut off the dog leg. I did not want to do this, but he insisted so I gripped it and ripped it. When I swung hard with wet hands, the club slipped and started doing loop-to-loops towards the lake. All I could think was "Please! Oh please!! Do not let it go into the lake!" It stuck shank down in the mud about six inches into the water.

As we were nearing the end of the round Akio approached me and said that he had a big surprise for us. We were going to get in a big "bus". I looked at him, and said, "And where are we going?" He looked stunned. "We are going to get warm in a 'bus'. You know b-a-t-h."

Boy was that ever a surprise. He got that one right, a big surprise indeed. When we got back to the clubhouse, I undressed, buck naked, and sauntered into this big room. I sat down on a Tupperware-like bucket where I was expected, proper etiquette required it, to wash myself. The hose was about 18 inches from the floor and the bucket could not possibly have held even a small fraction of my weight. As I squatted I turned my head to see 20 of my newest and best buddies, all Japanese, relaxing in the pool, each with his head out of water much like snakes in a Chinese restaurant aquarium.

Now I do not usually take my body out for a spin in public. It is not really a pretty sight. But the time had come for me to join Akio in the tub. As I rose and began walking towards the steps I must have looked like a sumo wrestler, maybe even Okebono; the only thing missing was me tossing rice flour. I did not know if the 40 eyes were looking at my body, my hernia, or my genitalia. It was quite an experience.

Later I told Akio that I had wanted to get to know him, but that I had not wanted to get to know him that well. Over the course of several years I did get to know him, and I would hope that he still has it in him to call me "friend".

Ainsley Harriot is a black chef who is known for his very humorous and energetic cooking antics. He has had his own television show and has published a number of cookbooks. On October 10, 1997 Shirley and I were invited by Kvaerner, an oil industry construction and management company, to a dinner at the Savoy Hotel in downtown London. The entertainment was to be Ainsley Harriot. The bad news was that October 10 is Shirley's birthday, and I was taking her to an industry function.

Shirley had come into London earlier in the day and had gone to Asprey, an upscale jewelry store on Bond Street. She had hoped that she could get a ring that went with a bracelet I had given her for Christmas the previous year. When they told her the ring was on display in Hong Kong for another couple of weeks she realized that 1) it probably would cost too much for us anyway and 2) she was most likely not going to have any present on this birthday. Sadly, she was right on both counts.

After her Asprey visit Shirley went to a Petroleum Wives Luncheon and then out to lunch with a bunch of the girls. Still raring to go, she took a black cab to Chelsea Harbor where she had a short visit with Minoz, a former neighbor of ours who had recently relocated from Kier Park. At 5:00 p.m. she gave me a ring at the office and asked what I was doing. My response was, "Nothing I cannot get away from, what did you have in mind". The sweet thing then informed me that she had room 302 at the Savoy Hotel reserved for the next 2 hours. Before I could get my hopes up, she quickly informed me not to get any big ideas. The room was let so that she, and maybe myself, could get a short rest before the Kvaerner dinner later in the evening. I told her that I would finish up at the office and that I probably would not be over until 30 minutes before the reception. When I hung up I was left wondering how she knew one could access a room at the Savoy for a few hours.

The evening turned out to be enormously entertaining. Ainsley Harriot is a very funny man. Not only can he speak of humorous things related to cooking (he has a book *Can't Cook, Won't Cook*), he is also bald and has large lips that he can quiver on demand. I swear he can make you laugh just by looking at you.

Somehow Ainsley discovered what October 10 meant in the Lent family. During his opening monologue he pointed to our table and said there was a man in the audience who was at this Kvaerner function with his wife on her birthday. He said, "What kind of man brings his wife to a free dinner on her special day and expects her to share it with 100 total strangers?" He then proceeded to sing happy birthday to her, gave her a signed copy of his latest book, and had a picture taken with her. All things said and done, the Pearl had a blast. I would never have predicted that this evening would go like it did.

Memorable People

Sometimes you ask a question and are "gobsmacked" by the answer. Such was the case one evening when Shirley and I were sitting with two lovely girls who had immigrated to the United Kingdom from Sri Lanka. Shirley had met the girls' mother in Windsor where the lady owned a hair salon. For a year or more Shirley kept saying that the girls ought to meet her boys. The lady was saying the same thing. I guess that is what mothers do. Anyway, our oldest son Tobin was in the United Kingdom, and even though he was about to depart for Vietnam in four days, plans were made for Tanya and Sanya to come to Muirfield and for Tobin to take the girls out for a drink at the nearby Thatched Tavern. When the two girls walked into the house I was stunned by their beauty and by their height. Each stood somewhere close to 5'11". Their dark blouses were partially open. To say the least, they were marvelously endowed. Their make-up was spot on. Their nail polish was just the perfect color and applied as if done by a manicurist. Impressive specimens!

The girls were seated, and we made small talk. I was wondering how Tobin's evening might play out. It was not likely that anything serious would come from this initial "date", if going to a local pub can be called a date. As we sat and chatted, I realized Tanya was the "available" one of the two. She mentioned that she was an airline stewardess. I picked up on that and asked her if she had ever met anyone famous during her travels. She said that on one flight Mikhail Gorbachev was in her first-class cabin. They had chatted and he seemed to be quite a nice fellow.

After what seemed like a few minutes of silence Tanya added, "But in my other job I have met a number of celebrities." Inquiring as to what that job might be she said that she was a masseuse at Pine Wood Studios, the major film maker in the United Kingdom. When we asked who some of her clients were she said that Tom Cruise was one, and that Nicole Kidman was always with him when he had his rub down. Others were Bruce Willis, Pierce Brosnan, Val Kilmer, and a list that just went on and on. Names were dropping like mad and I just sat there with my mind racing.

I glanced at our son sitting next to Tanya I asked the obvious question, "You are a beautiful girl. Have any of these guys tried to date you?" She replied that she tried to keep her Pine Wood business separate from her private life. She did reply that Pierce Brosnan had been to her apartment for a massage but that he was polite and proper and it never went anywhere. She said that Val Kilmer was a bit more persistent. He asked her out and she declined and then one night he called. Sanya had answered the phone and when Val asked for Tanya, Sanya stood close by so that she might listen. When Val asked Tanya out for a date, she replied as before, "I do not wish to complicate my life by dating someone from the Studio." When she looked up at the eyes-dropping Sanya she saw her sister excitedly mouth, "But its Val Kilmer!" Right then and there I realized that even though my son might be good looking and well educated, he was way out of his league. When a girl has turned down Pierce and Val, how is she ever going to be interested in Tobin.

Well, the three kids did have a great time. Tobin said that when they entered the pub it was the only time in his life when he was with someone who made mouths drop and conversation stop. The girls were that stunning. Tanya and Tobin did have two other dates before he left for Vietnam and they seemed to hit it off. After he left she asked for his phone number in Vietnam. She later placed a call to his apartment but the lady who answered, most likely his Vietnamese maid, never left the message for Tobin. Whatever might have been never was.

We had wonderful neighbors around us in Kier Park, Ascot. Sir Guy and Lady Marsha were across the street and the neighbors next door was a couple from Iran, Mohit and Minoz. Mohit left Iran when the Shah was deposed and he, along with a number of his Iranian buddies (all classmates) made fortunes in the United Kingdom by, of all things, exporting sanitary products to the Soviet Union.

While we were living in Muirfield, Minoz gave a birthday party to celebrate Mohit's 50th birthday. It was a birthday bash to end all birthday bashes. A large tent was put up in the gardens and a parquet floor was laid. Ten large tables with linen tops surrounded an open area left for dancing. An ethnic band was hired and, best of all, there were tables full of wonderful middle eastern foods. Minoz had invited all the neighbors since she did not want to offend anyone with the loud music. It was a good idea. When the music reached decibels that hurt the ears, Sir Guy became embarrassed and rushed his elderly wife back home. Shirley and I stayed a while, but soon we thought it best to leave the party to the Iranians. Upon our departure the fun really began. I do not know how the women did it but that shrill sound that came from their mouths built to such a crescendo that I thought there must be a jet landing nearby. It was a one-of-a-kind experience for us, and it must have been an absolute ball for Mohit.

But we had other neighbors. Shirley took a walk nearly every day in Windsor Great Park, but occasionally she just wanted to walk out of the house and through the neighborhood. On the rare times she went for a local spin, she would walk down Cheapside Road and just before she came to Water Splash Lane she would turn left onto a rather quiet street then up into a secluded part of our neighborhood. This north to south street connects Cheapside Road to the B383, and is the main access to Sunninghill Park, home to the Duke and Duchess of York, that is, Prince Andrew and Fergie (Sarah Ferguson). A walker on this the street is quickly met by guards who man small booths. These guards do not want people walking near the York residence, but they are mindful that the locals, especially the nearby neighbors, like their walks.

When Shirley walked up this street the guards rushed out and asked her if she was a neighbor. She would always answer, "Yes, we are neighbors." A bit of a fib, I fear. The guard meant immediate neighbors, not ones 10 minutes removed. But he would dutifully ask for Shirley's name, which she always gave, and she would then continue on for her walk. Many times, she looked back and saw the guard thumbing through a list of neighbors, trying as he could to find "Robert and Shirley Lent". They obviously never found the names, but neither did they ever stop Shirley from taking her walk. No one with Shirley's demeanor would have the audacity to say she was a neighbor if she really wasn't one. This is another iteration of, "Walk with purpose". Shirley never encroached on the Duke and Duchess property so no harm was ever done. All Shirley wanted was to take a stroll in the neighborhood.

Shirley and the Duchess of York both had this thing about Christmas trees. There were only two people in all of Berkshire that wanted the tallest and fullest of trees. One was Sarah, the Duchess and the other was Shirley, the lady from Prineville. The place to buy Christmas trees in Berkshire is Long Acres Nursery. Each December, and early in December at that, Shirley would go to Long Acres and ask the staff to reserve the biggest and best tree for her. And each Christmas Shirley would return to Long Acres to find the two or three best trees tagged for the Duchess. No amount of pleading or whining would change the outcome. The Lents always had a magnificent tree, but it paled in comparison to those standing in the Sunninghill Park home.

After we had returned to the United States from our assignment in China, and a number of years after we had left England, Shirley was in our home in Houston and she read in the newspaper that Sarah Ferguson was going to be a guest the next day on a very popular regional television talk show, The Debra Duncan Show. She laid the paper down and informed me she was going to attend the next day studio telecast of the Duncan show. I snickered and said, "That show is always sold out. What makes you think that you can get in on such short notice?" But Shirley never, ever, thought something was not possible. Life is full of excitement is it not, and one should never take anything for granted.

The next evening when I returned home the phone was ringing off the wall. Many of Shirley's friends were calling to say that they had seen her on the Debra Duncan Show. I could not believe it. Shirley then told me when she got to the studio there were three tickets that had become available. The one she got was in the back row and far to the right. She was in the door. Sarah Ferguson, the Duchess of York, came on stage and gave a nice interview. Just before the break for a commercial Debra asked if there was anyone in the audience who might like to ask the Duchess a question. Of course, everyone, including Shirley raised their hands. Two people out of the audience were asked to come down to be on stage with Debra and the Duchess. You know without being told that Shirley was one of them.

When it came time for Shirley to ask her question, she first asked, "Do you still live in Sunninghill Park with your children and Prince Andrew?" This question not only took the Duchess back, it also caught Debra Duncan by surprise. Very few people in the United States were aware that Fergie was living at Sunninghill Park with her girls. She resided in quarters separated from Andrew, but she still lived in his home. Most people knew that Andrew and Sarah had separated and, for most, that meant living in separate homes.

When the Duchess asked Shirley how she knew about Sunninghill Park and the fact that she was currently living there, Shirley replied, "I was once your neighbor when we lived in Kier Park off of Cheapside Road. And furthermore, you were always the one for whom Long Acres reserved the largest and best Christmas trees. I could never get in the queue ahead of you." Tongue in cheek Shirley continued, "And I have not forgiven you for this."

Debra Duncan wanted to talk about a possible reconciliation that might be in the offering between Sarah and Andrew, but Sarah dismissed that and said that living in Andrew's home was great for the kids and it was a financial necessity for her. There went the big scoop.

Shirley and Fergie continued chatting after the station went to break and Shirley concluded her conversation saying, "You must know that I left my heart in my beloved England". Sarah quickly and wittily responded, "And I shall pick it up for you when I return".

Not all the people we encountered in the United Kingdom were nice. Every society has its odd ducks. I met my first one on a Saturday morning coming home from a short bit of work I had done in our London office. At Waterloo Station I boarded the train bound for points west, including Ascot. Since it was on weekend anyone can sit in the First Class cabins, and I chose to do just that. They are more comfortable and certainly quieter. But after a few stops along the line the cabin door opened and in walked this rather large teenager. I remember thinking, "Why would this guy choose to do this?" There were any number of empty First Class cabins. As I sat there reading my papers, I noticed that the young man had taken off his jacket and placed it on his lap. Although I could not actually see what he was doing I was sure that he was unzipping his trousers. I tried not to watch the guy, but I soon realized, what with the hand action and the moaning, that the kid was masturbating under his jacket cover. My first impulse was to stand up and confront him. But I thought, "That is probably just what he wants. He must be a sick person and I would probably make him happy if I got abusive." I decided I would move to another car and just as I was gathering up my work we pulled into a station. But the boy, obviously done with his deed, got up and walked out the cabin and onto the station platform. I settled back and considered myself lucky. The whole thing could have played out so differently.

What would a fellow Brit have done in this circumstance? It is a good question. The British are very proper, and they obey rules. When there are not specific rules, written or otherwise they tend to be passive and/or nonresponsive. I once read, perhaps in one of Bill Bryson's travel books, a narrative that sums up the reaction a British train passenger might have had to the young masturbator in my First Class Cabin. In that narrative a drunken young man and his buxom girlfriend board a late-night train heading out from London. The couple begins to neck and to fondle each other. One thing leads to another and they are soon fornicating right there on the train. The fellow passengers are aghast but there is no written sign stating "No Fornicating". So all of the passengers keep their heads down and say nothing. As soon as the couple have finished, the man leans back and reaches for a pack of cigarettes. As soon as he has one in his mouth and has put the match to it, the entire group of nearby passengers yells at him, "No Smoking"; there is a sign that says just that. This tale may be a bit over-the-top, but I think it captures the British way of thinking.

Memorable People

Another pervert of sorts was encountered one day when Shirley went walking in Windsor Great Park. She often had a cyclist ride past her and then circle back to look at her. This was odd and a bit discomforting, but nothing ever came of these types of mildly aggressive acts. It is just that in secluded parts of the Park you do wonder how vulnerable you might be.

The perversion Shirley experienced involved a fellow walker. Shirley was only an accessory to the incident. As Shirley was walking, she came to an intersection of paths, and an obviously distressed lady came running up to her. She breathlessly told Shirley that she had just walked by a naked man who was chained to a tree. He was about a quarter of a mile back down the trail. She had gone over to the man who said that he had been abducted and that he needed for her to unchain him. She made a quality decision and said that she would run ahead and come back with help. When Shirley heard what had happened, she said that she knew they could contact a Park Ranger at a building about a half mile from where they were. When they got to the Ranger, they told him about the poor fellow who was chained to the tree. The Ranger laughed and said, "Don't worry, that is a guy who comes here and exposes himself. He just wants women to come look at him. I will go back and run him off, or more likely he has already left the Park." So, if you are a lady walking in the Windsor Great Park and you come upon a naked man chained to a tree, walk on by. It's only Ebert the Pervert.

The next memorable fellow was not quite a pervert, but he did leave a lasting impression on Shirley. One late afternoon, following a morning full of shopping along Oxford Street, Shirley opted to go to one of our favorite Italian cafes, Dino's, for a cup of coffee. The small dining room is bright and has a blue sky with puffy white clouds painted on the ceiling. When Shirley sat down in one of the wrought iron chairs she looked around and noticed a handsome gentleman and his friend sitting at a nearby table. It was before the dinner hour so the café was relatively empty. Tony, the café proprietor, knew Shirley and greeted her effusively as he always did.

When the coffee had been served the handsome gentlemen,

obviously of middle-eastern lineage, leaned over and initiated a conversation. Shirley is friendly, and she is attractive, and it was not too long before the questions became a bit more personal. When Shirley asked where he was from the answer came back, "Would it make any difference?" It was a strange answer. Shirley indicated that it wouldn't, so the man said that he was a pilot from Iraq. This encounter occurred after the first Gulf War so there is no telling what the fellow was doing in the United Kingdom. He did give the impression that he was a military pilot and he was on holiday. When he became bolder with his suggestions, Shirley held out her hand and said, "I am married." To that he said, "But are you happily married?" By this time her coffee cup was nearly empty, and she noticed that not only was the flirtatious gentleman's companion becoming nervous, so too, was Tony, who was more agitated than nervous. Shirley got up to leave but not before the dashing fellow insisted on giving her his telephone number. She took it and walked out of the café and never saw the guy again. When she told me of the encounter later that day, she said, "You know, he *was* a handsome devil."

James Spicer, Minister of Parliament, invited Shirley and I to meet with him on June 17, 1996, so that we might have drinks on the Parliament Terrace adjacent to the River Thames, and to join him at a group luncheon. At the time Mr. Spicer represented the Conservative constituency for Dorset West, located near the English Channel in southern England. The luncheon and drinks on the Terrace were amongst the most memorable events in which we participated, and I could easily have deferred a narrative of this experience until a later section, but James Spicer is a character who deserves to be in this chapter about Memorable People.

Kerr-McGee was about to drill a well located in Lyme Bay off the English Channel. Dorset West includes much of the historic and World Heritage shoreline that rims Lyme Bay. Kerr-McGee spent considerable money conducting base-line environmental studies both off and onshore. We also counted birds for one entire year. We developed a computer model that, with input for tide levels and wind, would show where an oil

Memorable People

spill would make landfall and how it might best be mitigated. We met with 46 special interest groups in Mr. Spicer's district and as such we got to know him well.

Before I move on, please allow me to point out that Kerr-McGee and our partners drilled the well in Lyme Bay. We did not find hydrocarbons. It was a big disappointment for us, but we did leave a significant and useful legacy. As we stressed to the audiences we met with in Dorset, Kerr-McGee would not be the company that would create an oil spill. Our record both in the United States and in the North Sea was impeccable. But the software and research data we left with the coastal agencies charged with oil spill cleanup would give these agencies the tools needed to fight an oil spill that would surely occur in the years to come. Realize that Lyme Bay is the haven where oil tankers come to shelter from storms and to repair power and steerage problems. It is probably only a matter of time before a crippled tanker limps into Lyme Bay and finds itself in a situation where it is unable to keep from breaking up, either offshore or onshore. It is unfortunate, but until the Petroleum Era comes to an end, ships will bring oil to or take oil from countries, and this movement of product carries with it the likelihood of incapacitated and drifting vessels.

James Spicer is a chatty guy who is an exceptionally effective fund raiser for a wide number of charities. At least he was when we knew him. On his 70th birthday, to raise money for a charity, he swam across the Thames river and back. He entered the water where the river flows past the Parliament terrace. I am pleased to say that Shirley and I signed up for a contribution. How could we not? During the time we knew Mr. Spicer, he fought many battles for his constituency and for his causes. Like most British politicians, he was quick with his wit and rapier sharp with his tongue.

The luncheon at Parliament was memorable not so much for the great food that was served, but rather for the opportunity we had to mingle with the power brokers. We were delighted to have at our round table the House of Lords Whip, The Lady Doreen Miller. This Chief Whip for the Government gave us several documents of the day, all with her signature on them.

And There We Were

After the luncheon I had to return to the office, but Shirley remained, and Mr. Spicer took her into the House of Commons where she sat in the gallery and listened to debates between the Tories and Labor. I wonder what the little girl skipping through the grasses beneath the massive pines in Big Summit Prairie would have thought of this experience.

But Mr. Spicer had also done something for us on an earlier date that made our June 17, 1996 day at Parliament even more memorable. Most people are not aware that if you can find a Minister of Parliament who will extend you an invitation it is possible to walk up the 292 steps comprising the stairs of The Great Westminster Clock, known to one and all as "Big Ben". James Spicer gave us that invitation, and late one morning Shirley and I met the guide who escorted us to the top of the tower. When we got to the clock room we walked around the interior of the four faces of the clock, ducking as we passed by the rods that support the 14 feet long minute hands and the 9 feet long hour hands. I remembered as we walked "inside" the clock face that we had looked at this clock hundreds of times and not once had I suspected there was a 30-inch-wide walkway behind the four dials. We peeked at the pendulum, 13 feet long and beating every 2 seconds. The pendulum clock weighs nearly two and a half tons. It is wound by an electronic motor, but the oddest and most remarkable thing of all is that this "largest, most powerful and most accurate Public Clock in the World" is kept in time by a number of two pence and one pence coins that rest on the pendulum and speed up or slow down the swing.

Big Ben is the bell upon which the clock strikes the hours. The amusing aspect of this is that this bell was cast by the same company that made the Liberty Bell in Philadelphia. And would you believe it, Big Ben also has a crack in it. There must have been a design flaw. We were only four feet from Big Ben when it struck noon. Twelve blows to the Bell. I shall never forget it. "What did you say?" has now become a part of my everyday conversations.

When we had finished visiting the Great Westminster Clock, Mr. Spicer took us to a cab pick-up point in front of one of the back buildings of Parliament. This location is far removed from the main gates, and I wondered how we were going to get a cab to come pick us up. But, after only a few minutes a cab arrived. Then I discovered the secret. There is a streetlight standing tall near the west shore of the Thames, where the Westminster Bridge crosses. I had never noticed it before, but when the light comes on it means that someone in Parliament requires a cab. Naturally, the cabbies fall all over themselves racing to get to the stand. Even though Shirley and I were not Members of Parliament, the cab driver who picked us up came out even better than had it been a MP, for Americans are bigger tippers than Members of Parliament.

Most of the people we encountered in England were the everyday workers and homeowners. Some we got to know quite well, and some were just wonderful place holders in a panorama of the social drama in which we lived. But one fellow I encountered, I cannot even say I met him, left an image with me that remains burned into my memories. I shall never, ever, forget him.

On one hot summer day I was traveling on a train headed for Ascot following a day at the office. One of my sons was visiting us, I think it was Taran, and he had joined me for the trip home to Muirfield. When we boarded the train, we found a couple of seats in a closed-in compartment. Each train usually has an open seating area, a First Class section which consists of closed in compartments, and a couple of free seating compartments, much like those in First Class but without the comfortable seats. In the compartment we settled into there were four other gentlemen. Three of us on each side faced the three on the other side. Common train etiquette was at play, and little was said during our trip into the country. When we arrived at the Sunningdale Station, there were only three of us left in the compartment. The gentleman across from Taran and I had been sleeping and when the train began to depart the Sunningdale platform, the movement woke him up.

The startled fellow, who was wearing a suit with narrow pin stripes, jumped up and started to get out. This is no easy task as many English trains have this very odd way of opening the door. One has to push in at the top of the window and then slide the window down. Once this is done one has to reach outside and turn the door handle, which opens the door. The man had done this and was about to depart when he realized that he had forgotten his briefcase, which was resting on a rack above the seats. He reached back in and grabbed the briefcase and then walked to the steps to disembark.

The problem the man faced with his disembarkation was that the train was building speed. By the time the man awoke, opened the window, and retrieved his briefcase the train was nearly to the end of the platform and probably moving at close to 20 miles per hour. I remember thinking, "Surely this guy is not going to step off the train." But he did. The last we saw of him he was sliding on his stomach parallel to the train, holding his briefcase aloft in his right hand, and looking at us wide-eyed with that, "What happened?" look on his face. I am sure the guy had stopped by the pub after work to have a few with the lads and that he was a bit under the influence. But what a sight it was, him sliding down the platform at the same speed as we were moving in the train. The pin stripe suit had to have been ripped to shreds and I am sure that were numerous abrasions that would take weeks to heal. What a sight and what a memory.

I am not sure just how this next encounter with noteworthy personages fits into this segment of the narrative, but the experience is a great example of Shirley's power of observation with respect to recognizing something special, wanting to be a part of it, and then having it somewhat stifled by yours truly. That Shirley loved elegance and being part of anything exciting has now been established. But she was also taken by pomp and ceremony and when she spied it she invariably wanted to slow down and absorb the events as they unfolded.

On a beautiful Saturday morning, October 18, 1997, Shirley and were in the library room at Muirfield having coffees. We were discussing the events that were to take place during the following week. The topic turned to Becky Corbett's (the Kerr-McGee CEO's wife) wish to see Blenheim Palace on the following Friday. It was Shirley's task to organize the trip and to escort Becky to Blenheim and back. The conundrum was an important dinner was scheduled for all of us for that same Friday. Time was going to be of the essence. It is approximately 2 and ½ hours from downtown London by car to the community of Woodside and the nearby Blenheim Palace. The return trip back into London, especially on a Friday afternoon, is more like 3 hours. The more Shirley and I talked the more we realized that a chauffeured car trip was out of the question. We next discussed the possibility of taking a high speed train to Oxfordshire and then a car from the train station at Oxford to the Palace.

Shirley jumped out of her chair, got on the phone and discovered that trains left London Paddington Station bound for Oxford. The departures were also quite frequent. Even better, the ride only took 57 minutes with there being only one stop and that was at Reading which is just up the track from Ascot. The more we thought about it the more excited we became about this possibility

Since there were no clouds in the sky and the temperature was going to be in the low 70's we both synched, "Let's make a dry run to see if this works." We jumped up from our chairs, went to Ascot Station, purchased tickets to Reading and, with a switch in trains, on to Oxford. If everything worked out, we hoped to have Becky Corbett, and Susan Kimes, the wife of our Vice President Production meet Shirley at Reading the following Friday, and they would all travel to Oxford together.

When we got to Reading, we fumbled around a bit but we finally got on the right platform and caught a ride in a First Class carriage compartment to Oxford. When we departed the train, we flagged a cab which took us to Blenheim Palace. Everything was working like clockwork.

Blenheim Palace is where Winston Churchill was born. He is also buried nearby in the small village of Bladen. When Winston's mother, The Lady Randolph Churchill - "Jennie" to many, first saw Blenheim she was awestruck. In the Blenheim Palace glossy tourist publication there is a quote from the writings of Lady Randolph Churchill:

And There We Were

> "As we passed through the entrance archway and the lovely scenery burst upon me Randolph said with pardonable pride, 'This is the finest view in England'. Looking at the lake, the bridge, the miles of magnificent park studded with old oaks... and the huge stately palace, I confess I felt awed. But my American pride forbade the admission."

The grounds and the Palace are spectacular and on a beautiful sun-filled day like we experienced the beauty is taken to another whole level of magnificence. The Palace has several halls where Churchill memorabilia are on display and where the Prime Minister's famous talks can be experienced through audio and video presentations.

The Palace was built for the first Duke of Marlborough who was the architect of the British Victory over the French at Blenheim (in Belgium, I think). Anyway, Queen Anne had the Palace built for him and every succeeding Duke of Marlborough has benefited greatly from this gesture of appreciation.

Shirley and I walked the grounds and then retired into the Palace to have lunch at one of the restaurants made available to the public. Our meal was served in the Indian Room, and following this repast we called an Oxford cab for a pick-up at the Palace and a drop off at the train station.

As we had been walking the grounds and touring the Palace, we noticed that there seemed to be an inordinate number of catering companies scurrying about. Marquees were being emplaced on the grounds. Trucks with refrigeration units were lined up adjacent to the west side of the Palace. We did not think too much of the activity until it came time to go whereupon we found that the eastern entrance to the castle had been blocked off. This entrance is where the cab had originally entered and dropped us off, and this is the entrance where we had told the cab dispatcher to send our cab. We were told by palace staff that our only egress was via a paved single lane road that winds around the Queen's Pool (lake) and through the Triumphant Arch and into the village of Woodside.

After about a 10 minute walk we found ourselves walking

the streets of Woodside. Our trek took us by a very old church (as I have said before, I think all churches in England are very old). It seemed as if the entire population of the village had turned out to watch limos pull up and drop off ladies in fine dresses and men in tuxedos. It surely looked like a wedding was about to take place. We thought that probably explained why there was so much catering activity at the Palace. Blenheim would be an obvious place for a reception.

As Shirley and I fought our way through the crowd, Shirley pleaded for us to stop and stay as long as we could. I was more concerned about finding our cab in the mass of humanity. I looked down the street and saw a cab that was obviously looking for someone. I approached the driver and asked if he was looking for "Lent". He nodded, and I opened the door for Shirley to get in. Shirley looked at me and said forlornly she would have preferred to wait until later in the evening so she might see what was taking place.

As we were riding to the Oxford train station Shirley mused as to who might be getting married. She said maybe we would be able to read about the wedding in the newspaper. I scoffed and said I did not think so, and I further remarked that village weddings don't usually make it into the London dailies and tabloids.

When we arrived at the Oxford station Shirley checked the train schedules and looked at the local yellow pages for chauffeured car rentals. She had all the information she needed to plan a very fast and efficient trip for Mrs. Corbett. We took a fast train back to Ascot. As we got ready for bed, we agreed that for a day in which we had not planned anything, the Blenheim adventure was one of our more memorable ones. We reaffirmed to each other that living in England was wonderful.

On the following morning I went to work and, as is usually the case, I was reading the morning Sun. I turned the front page and there was a large picture of three flower girls who were part of a wedding that took place Saturday in Woodside. I read the long article with amazement. It turns out a Greek merchant banker was marrying one of the current Duke of

Marlborough's close family relatives (I think it was a niece). The last paragraph in the newspaper article was most memorable. The officer in charge of security said, "Security here is very tight. This wedding party includes people who are amongst the richest on the planet." To give you an indication of to whom the officer was making reference, one of the three flower girls, just by herself, was worth approximately $2.7 billion. Her name ... Athina Onassis. Athina Onassis (Roussel) was soon to become the world's richest teenager. She is the granddaughter of Aristotle Onassis, the Greek shipping tycoon. She is also the daughter of Christina, the late and only previous beneficiary of Aristotle's fortune.

Shirley had a nose for things that are special, and it was about the time of the Woodside wedding that I begin to accept that if Shirley wanted to see or do something I probably ought to go along with her. There is no sense in arguing against things that I know nothing about. So if she said, "Let's go to a Venetian orchestra playing in a ballroom in Beijing.", I just hopped to it. Approximately 95 per cent of the time I was going to be in for a treat of a lifetime. Such was life living with my Central Oregon girl who, until the very end, maintained her sense of majesty and her zest for life, and who also was able to retain her infectious wander lust.

One of literature's great fictional characters, Anne Shirley, found her kindred spirit living not far from her Green Gables home on Prince Edward Island. Shirley Lent found a kindred spirit when she attended her first meeting of the American Women of Berkshire and Surrey (AWBS). At the time Shirley did not realize the role that AWBS would play in her English life, nor was she aware of a friendship that was born at that first meeting. At the conclusion of the luncheon and business meeting an attractive and statuesque brunette walked up to Shirley just as she was about to leave the building. The lady said, "Pardon me. My name is Joey Baechle and I want you to know that I think you are a beautiful lady." Joey Freund Baechle and Shirley did not become kindred spirits that day but shortly after that first encounter the two women found themselves on one of the frequent AWBS trips the club makes

Memorable People

to castles and ornate country homes. They were seated next to each other on the coach, and what started out as a polite conversation quickly turned into a friendship that proved stimulating to both ladies.

Joey Baechle is an American artist and she is the daughter of artists. A beautiful lady in her own right she has, as a result of her artistic training and upbringing, an appreciation for beauty and architecture that evades most of us. In her friendship with Joey, Shirley found a person to share her excitement in all things ornate, beautiful, elegant, architectural, historic, and/or royal. Joey, like many artists, carries around a sketch pad and she is always sketching what she sees. Shirley was captivated by this constant capture of colored windows, ornate transepts, vaulted and painted ceilings, buttresses, animalistic rain spouts, or whatever it was that captured Joey's eye. "What do you see that makes you want to sketch it?" was a common question. Shirley loved the answers for it put into words what

FIGURE 15. SHIRLEY LENT WITH HER FRIEND JOEY BAECHLE

she was feeling, and she loved that about Joey. But Joey also found Shirley's infectious enthusiasm and exuberance to be equally refreshing and inspiring. The two women just seemed to feed off each other. Shirley had an incredible appreciation for beauty and Joey had the means and the talent to capture it on paper. The two women were inseparable for more than two years.

There are many interesting anecdotes but one of particular interest relates to a luncheon that Shirley, Joey, and two other ladies had at the Georgian Restaurant at Harrods in Knightsbridge, London. Shirley was a regular patron at the Georgian where the staff would typically seat her at her favorite table and immediately upon being seated, a sparkling water with ice would appear. Shirley had made her preferences known to the Georgian staff, and like many successful restaurants, once a preference has been shown it is honored. I might interject that even after we had moved to China and then had the opportunity to return to London, Shirley was at Harrods and the Georgian Restaurant and, without a word being said, a glass of Perrier water with a twist of lime was served.

But I digress. When the girls, Joey included, showed up at the Georgian one day in 1997, several months removed from the tragic death of Princess Diana and Dodi Fayed, Shirley was informed that her favorite table would not be available that day. The waiter, in hushed tones, said that the owner of Harrods, Mohammed Al Fayed, would be having lunch at "Madame Lent's" table. So it came to be, amidst a flourish of activity and a bustling of chairs and waiters, Mr. Fayed, and his entourage burst into the room and were seated only a few feet from the four ladies.

Joey Baechle immediately began sketching Mr. Fayed and the other guests at the table. The Fayed luncheon table came into focus as did the background in the Georgian room. Shirley was impressed with the speed with which it had come together. All at Shirley's table thought the sketch was something special so they decided to write a note on the bottom of the pad with the intent that it might be passed along to Mr. Fayed who was known to still be grieving the loss of his son, Dodi. The note went something like this, "We want you to know that are hearts go with you and we share your great personal loss." The waiter was asked if he would give the sketch and the note with the four signatures to the Harrods' owner. The waiter said that he could not do that, but he would place it in an envelope on a silver platter, and he would then present the platter to Mr. Fayed. If Mr. Fayed wished to look at it and to respond it would be up to him. When the platter was placed in front of Mohammed Al Fayed he opened the envelope and looked at the sketch and he read the words. He immediately rose from his chair and said, "Where did this come from?" The waiter acknowledged Joey, Shirley, and the other two ladies. Immediately he came over and said that the kind words and the wonderful sketch had touched his heart. He said, "Let me do something for you." With that he snapped his fingers, and four staff members were sent on an errand to bring back something special from the Harrods inventory. It took only a few minutes and back came the staff, with boxes of Harrods' chocolates and Harrods' teddy bears, each paired on silver platters, one per lady. He bid adieu to the ladies and said he would not forget their kindness, and he was gone. It was Joey's sketch and Shirley's relationship with the Georgian staff that made this micro-moment in England a special one for all four ladies.

Joey and Shirley's adventures in England were hampered by an almost year long illness that made Joey a near invalid. Just when she had recovered enough to regain her mobility, she and her husband, Bob, moved to South Africa on a business assignment. It was Joey, by the way, that had befriended the wife of Margaret Thatcher's son, a South African friendship that eventually found its way into the conversation Shirley and Margaret Thatcher had the night of the Thatcher speech at the British-American Chamber of Commerce Dinner. The Harrods encounter with Mohammed Al Fayed came during a return trip to London that Joey Baechle and her husband made on their eventual repatriation from South Africa back to the United States.

Joey Baechle not only reserved a special place in Lent family memories, but she also left the family with a very special painting, one that was completed prior to Christmas, 1995.

And There We Were

One day when Shirley and Joey were having tea at a tea garden on the Thames in Windsor, Shirley mentioned that it was too bad that we had not been able to get a negative or a copy of a photograph that had appeared in the Denver Post. Our younger son, Taran, had made a sack of the quarterback in the final seconds of the 1991 Colorado State class 6A football championship game, and, standing over the quarterback, our son had raised his arms to acknowledge the team's win and the culmination of his high school football experience. The photographer took a series of pictures leading up to the sack, but the one with Taran raising his arms on the snow-covered field was the one that captured the beauty and the essence of victory. Neither a duplicate of the photograph nor the negative was available from either the photographer or the Denver Post. Sadly, what we were left with was a copy of the front page of the Denver Post sports page, dated December 1, 1991. The copy was aging poorly and Shirley wondered if Joey could capture the moment in a painting.

Joey poured her heart into the project and, when we finally saw the finished product we could not believe what we saw. Not only had she replicated the moment in oil, but she had somehow added a special touch. In the crowd of thousands there was a small silver bun atop a lady wearing a long topcoat. The image was so subtle that most people would not even pick up on it, but all in our family knew what Joey had done. She had painted Shirley into the piece. What a special and appreciated touch it was.

The Queen Mother, wife of King George VI and mother of Queen Elizabeth II, was in her 90's during the time we lived in England. Like all the royal family, the Queen Mum was constantly shown on television and was pictured frequently in the full range of English newspapers and tabloids. It would be a terrible omission to exclude this magnificent lady from the list of memorable people we encountered during our stay in the United Kingdom. There is no doubt that this lady, who unfortunately died in 2002 at the wonderful age of 101, was the most beloved of all the royals. Whereas Princess Diana had captured the love and attention of the English, the Queen

Memorable People

Mother was beloved and revered by the masses around the globe. The former Lady Elizabeth Bowes-Lyons earned this love and adulation by being a commoner who was in touch with the ordinary people of the country. Tony Blair, the United Kingdom Prime Minister, said this of the Queen Mother: "During her long and extraordinary life, her grace, her sense of duty and her remarkable zest for life made her loved and admired by people of all ages and backgrounds, revered within our borders and beyond."

My favorite story of the Queen Mother relates to the time during World War II after Buckingham Palace had been bombed. Both King George VI and the Queen Mother had remained in London despite the constant bombing. This decision apparently was meant to inspire popular determination and the belief that life would go on as usual. After a bombing at the Palace, the Queen Mother is reported to have said, "Well, at least now we have an excellent view of the East End," a reference to London's East End which lies beyond James Park, a park that fronts the Palace.

I believe the Queen Mother died in her home in Windsor Park. It will be recalled that this is the home at the end of the paved path that Shirley and I had inquired about during our first visit to the Fox and Hounds Pub and Windsor Great Park. Where will that path take us we asked and of course the answer was "Tower Hill". But it also would have taken us to a lovely lady. The press release said simply that the Queen Mother died in her sleep at the Royal Lodge in Windsor.

Did we talk to the Queen Mother? We did not. But we saw her innumerable times as she rode through Windsor Great Park in a carriage on her way to the Royal Ascot. She always made eye contact and waived. Her great sweet smile seemed to be for you and you alone. Shirley and Joey had also seen her when she was in London riding in a horse drawn carriage carrying Nelson Mandela of South Africa, but the closest we came to chatting with the revered lady was one day in July 1997.

July 26, 1997 was a strange day in Ascot. There was to be a day of racing at the Ascot track. We decided to nip down to the track and take in the festivities. The Royal Ascot races had been the month earlier, but on this day the featured race was the King George VI stakes. After we had showered and dressed for a day at the races, the skies opened up and it poured down rain. Nearly 1 and ½ inches fell in an hour. Fortunately, the skies cleared, and we soon found ourselves on the Ascot grounds right before the featured race, which was named for the Queen Mother's husband, King George VI. We, like many others walked down to the paddock area and to the pre-race parade area. We noticed that there was a roped pathway separating the crowd. We walked over to the barricade and saw that the Queen Mother, who had also visited the paddock area, was slowly making her way back to the grandstand and the Royal Enclosure. When the Queen Mother saw Shirley (I am sure that she never saw me, no one ever sees me), she headed straight for her. Just as the Queen Mum was about to say something, a proud father pushed his infant son in front of the grand lady. The young boy, with a binky in his mouth, caught the Queen Mother's attention and she did what was expected, for she was a royal. And then she was gone. Shirley was disappointed that she did not have a moment to chat with the Queen Mother. At the time, I thought Shirley might have another opportunity on another day, but it just did not happen. Still, we left England believing that we knew the great lady. We certainly shared the Country's adulation for this very special member of the royal family.

I do not know how one captures all of the inter-personal relationships that occur over a five-year period. Our stay in England was filled with encounters of interest across a wide range of characters. Our staff at Kerr-McGee was wonderful and consisted of many very unique personalities. An essay on these characters would easily populate another chapter. The same could be said of the professionals and managers that I met in the oil and gas industry. Shirley's encounters with fellow members of AWBS, shop keepers, and the ordinary people were memorable but not necessarily worthy of inclusion herein.

But before we conclude this section on people met and remembered, and before I write of our encounter with Prince

Memorable People

Charles, it is appropriate that I single out one of the expatriate couples who embodied expatriate social life in Berkshire, and then of an exploration manager who had a bit of the devil in him.

Wayne Milloux was president of Pepsi Cola Europe and Asia during the years we spent in Ascot. Shirley met Wayne's wife, Penny, through AWBS and over the years our friendship matured. Wayne and Penny liked to entertain, and they threw great parties. I think it was, and is, in their soul to entertain. We attended three or four big bashes at the Milloux home. On each occasion we had to park along some isolated neighborhood street because every parking place anywhere close to the Milloux home were already taken, no matter how early we arrived. Virtually everyone else showed up early too, so there it is. The Milloux's had a great garden, the lawns were expansive and spilled down a hill into a forested area. Their patio was a wonderful place to have cocktails, chat, and to generally enjoy the wonderful English evenings (can you believe we were never once rained upon?).

One evening at one of the Milloux parties, I found myself around a table of snacks (hors d' oeuvres) chatting with an interesting gentleman. When I asked him what it was he did he said he was the president of Coca-Cola Europe. I about fell over when I asked him if he knew the host Wayne Milloux who had a similar job for Pepsi, and the response came back, "No." Like most of the men at the party it was not unusual that we did not know each other. The women interacted through AWBS, and we masculine types came to parties mostly on the arms of our social gadflies. When I found the gentleman worked for Coke, I grabbed his arm and said, "You just have to meet Wayne." When I mentioned to Wayne that this guest was the president of Coca-Cola, Wayne, without even moment of hesitation said, "I hope you checked your Cokes at the door!"

I previously mentioned how Akio Suzuki had gotten me into a predicament at a Japanese bathhouse, but Akio's intentions were all honorable. However, a good friend of mine, Mr. Rick Mott, who headed up United Kingdom Exploration for Phillips Petroleum, showed me a side not known during a dinner he hosted at the Institute of Directors on Pall Mall Street. Rick had reserved a small room at The Institute for a dinner where six exploration managers from various United Kingdom-based companies could meet the Phillips Worldwide Exploration Vice-President, Mr. Mike Calley, who was in town on a visit. The meal was served and the food was outstanding as it typically is at this venue. A few talks were given, and then dessert was brought in on a cart. Each small serving plate covered a disgustingly molded grey gelatinous mound. Even from two feet away the smell was repulsive. All attendees had the same reaction, but not wanting to offend our host we picked up spoons and sampled what was on offer. It took only one bite for me to know that this was something I would not be eating, regardless of my friendship with Mr. Mott.

Rick rose from his seat and said that Mr. Calley frequently spoke of the terrible food he had to eat when he traveled to different countries, and into areas having different cultures. It particular it seemed that Mike Calley loved to tell of the hardships he endured eating duck feet and drinking snake blood. Rick Mott decided that he would give Mr. Calley something to talk about concerning the culinary hardships as they existed in London, England. Over the objection of the famous chef, Rick had the kitchen prepare baked cod roe covered with a creamy garlic seasoning. Never has anything so vile passed over my lips! I left the dinner that night wondering if Rick's career path might have taken a turn for the worse.

One of our best encounters involving English Royalty occurred after we had left England and moved to China. Kerr-McGee, and our working interest partners in Janice Field, an offshore discovery of some importance, were celebrating the inauguration of the Field at a ceremony held October 23, 1998 at the Customs House, Mill Dam, South Shields, Tyne and Wear (Newcastle, to those that prefer it simple). Since I had been Vice President of Exploration when much of the early drilling and development occurred in the Janice discovery, the Company was kind enough to invite Shirley and I back to the United Kingdom for the festivities. The invitation was most gracious, and it was deeply appreciated by both Shirley and me.

The return to England was, for Shirley, a welcome respite

from our life in Beijing. Although, as it will become obvious, life in China was exciting in its own way, the lure of London was forever deeply rooted in Shirley's psyche. I sent her on ahead and she spent 10 days visiting old haunts, greeting familiar doormen at Harrods and Liberty, and walking the streets of London. On a Sunday morning she went to church at Westminster Abbey. The archbishop who conducted the service that day was the very same one who presided over Diana's funeral. It may by now not be surprising that the ushers put Shirley in a special pew where each seat had elevated wooden sides. Most of the seats in the Abbey are close to the ground and I think Shirley was given seating in an area where she would have a better view of the church services. I am not sure how all of this came about but it could simply have been because the ushers knew she was an American lady; or perhaps an inquiry was made and a special accommodation ensued. It happened so frequently I was no longer amazed when it did. After the church service Shirley walked across Westminster Bridge and then along the Thames, all the while glancing over her shoulders at Parliament and "Big Ben". She walked, and walked, as one often does in London. Her route took her downstream, and then back across the Thames. She walked through St. James Park, past Buckingham Palace, and then into the various stores along Oxford Street. She loved the City.

But let us return to the Janice celebration. On Thursday, October 22, 1998 Shirley and I flew to Newcastle for the Inauguration Party which was to be held the following day. The embossed invitation said the Inauguration would feature His Royal Highness, The Prince of Wales. Frank Sharratt had arranged for Prince Charles to do the honors. What a special treat this was going to be, not only for Bob and Shirley but also for our Kerr-McGee special guests and staff. In a room adjacent to the hall in which the Prince would unveil a model of the Janice offshore production facility and where he would make a few remarks, there was a receiving area. The reception protocols in this area were strict. The top-ranking dignitaries from Kerr-McGee and the partners would greet Prince Charles as he came up the stairs from a meeting he was having prior

And There We Were

to the formal presentation. Since Shirley and I were now not in that hierarchy (having been transferred to China), we were further down the receiving line, almost as if we were commoners. I had somewhat of a problem. Shirley had disappeared. I assumed that she must have gone to the water closet but I was not sure. I became more nervous when the word came back through the ranks, "The Prince is coming up the stairs." And then, like magic, Shirley was standing by my side. I asked, "Where have you been?"

I learned that when Shirley and her friend, Susan Kimes, were looking for the ladies' room, they chanced upon the room in which the Prince was about to give a short talk to the British workers and the engineers who had been instrumental in the construction of the Janice production facility. When Shirley peeked in, she asked the men guarding the door what was happening. One of them described the proceedings in whispers, and then asked if Shirley and Susan would want to sit down in

FIGURE 16. PRINCE CHARLES AND SHIRLEY LENT
BOB LENT IS SHAKING THE PRINCE'S HAND

Memorable People

the back of the room and listen in on the topics under discussion. The ladies were told they would have to keep very quiet, but that they would be welcome. You know the answer. Thus it came to be that while everyone in the room upstairs was making sure the pecking order was just right, Shirley was sitting 10 feet from the Prince, and occasionally they made eye contact. When the meeting in the small room was about to end, Shirley and Susan moved quietly to the door and took a back way up to the receiving room. When I looked and found her by my side, she had just finished listening to the Prince.

Prince Charles walked out of the small room and, escorted by the Kerr-McGee CEO Luke Corbett and his wife Becky, made his way up the stairs to where all were waiting. The ranking dignitaries in the greeting line shook hands with the Prince as he walked into the room. A few pleasantries were exchanged but it did not seem the Prince was particularly enjoying being 'made over'. He must be accustomed to deferential treatment, but there must be times when he tires of such special treatment.

When he approached Shirley and me, my sweet wife looked at the Prince, smiled, and said, "I am delighted to be back here in my beloved England." I had already reached out to shake the Prince's hand but he was looking at Shirley and listening to her. When the photographers took the photo of the Lents and the Prince, only my hand is in view. The framed picture shows the Prince deeply into a conversation with the Pearl. The Prince and the Pearl, how appropriate is that. Prince Charles responded to Shirley's remark by saying, "Where have you been?" Shirley replied, "We now live in China but I shall never forget our times in Berkshire and our home in Kier Park, Ascot." He responded, "Did you go to Royal Ascot and the Polo matches (Prince Charles rides a lot in the Windsor Park Polo Grounds)?" Shirley told the Prince that she never missed an event (isn't *that* the truth). The Prince looked at her and then started to walk away, but he turned his head and said, "If you loved England so much, why did you move to China?" Shirley turned and pointed to Luke Corbett who was just behind the Prince, "Well, that was Mr. Corbett's decision." Prince Charles turned, placed his right hand on his hip, and remarked, "I shall talk to Mr. Corbett about this." And Luke responded just as quickly, "Lent, that is five more years in China for you."

All of us in the immediate area laughed and the Prince moved on. The Prince had in that instant become a favorite of ours, no matter all the bad press he gets. He exuded considerable wit and charm; attributes which, unfortunately, seem not to be recognized by many of his subjects.

As a side note to the Prince Charles meeting, Susan Kimes later mentioned that wherever Shirley Lent went, she was also going because something very interesting was usually in the offing. Further affirmation of Susan's observation is found in our collection of photos. During the time Shirley was conversing with both Prince Charles and Margaret Thatcher the person standing by her side was Susan Kimes. Susan's husband, David, was also a Vice President of Kerr-McGee, and protocol would have placed her proximal to Shirley anyway, but Susan had learned that when dignitaries meet Shirley there is usually a unique exchange.

Chapter 15

A FEW OF OUR FAVORITE PLACES IN THE UNITED KINGDOM

When you reside as long as we did in the United Kingdom, distinguishing places from experiences is difficult. Consequently, this part of the narrative blends places with the experience of being there. Often this blend is the only effective way to convey how extraordinary a place is. I want to get this part right, for our love of England comes from the special places we encountered and the wonderful adventures we had.

If you would have asked Shirley or me "What was your favorite place in all of England?" we would both have said, "Muirfield", our home in Kier Park, Ascot. That discussion I shall save for later and move on here to those places that I hope one and all will visit and come to enjoy as much as Shirley and I did.

CLIVEDEN

"Cliveden is like no other country house on earth."

So wrote George Bernard Shaw in 1939. In the diary of Lady Frederick Cavendish (1863) it is written of Cliveden,

"When one lives in Paradise, how hard it must be to ascend in the heart and mind to Heaven."

And in the fictional *The Romance of Cliveden*, Andrew Deepgrove offers these descriptive words,

> "It is now thirty-four years since I first trod the greensward of Cliefden (sic)...The first time that ever I looked from yonder Terrace upon the glistening Thames, and marked it course between the lofty Cliff on this side, and the broad Meadows on that, till its silver thread passes from sight eight miles away beneath Maidenhead Bridge, it seemed to me that never could the Eye of Man have rested upon a scene of more exquisite enchantment."

These three quotes are only a sampling of those that are documented in James Crathorne's excellent book, *Cliveden, The Place and the People.*

Innumerable magnificent country houses and castles can be found throughout the United Kingdom so for Cliveden to be considered the "best" in class might be a stretch, and the subject of some debate. I once debated a landed English gentleman concerning the merits of Cliveden. His argument was that England had many such country houses and that many were more magnificent than Cliveden. I pondered his argument for several years before I realized why Cliveden comes to the top of any such list. There may be many estates that have houses as magnificent as Cliveden. Many may approach it in historical significance. Many may have been its equal as a center for political and social gatherings. And many may have geographical settings that can similarly take one's breath away. But no place puts them all together as at Cliveden. Shirley and I found nothing like this stately home during any of our English travels.

From the moment we first drove through the entrance gate and along the narrow road that took us through woodland and meadows, we were mesmerized by the increasing and encroaching beauty. Before gaining a view of the manor itself, we came upon a massive sculpture carved from marble. Beside and astride a giant seashell are three partially clad maidens, each attended by a cherub. The marble carvings are nestled on a darker volcanic base. At the time of our first visit water poured from a flask held aloft by a maiden who stands near the apex of the sculpture. The falling water, once it reached the surface of the massive seashell, moved along the flutes of the shell, and then gathering into rivulets, poured as discrete jet streams into a beautiful reflecting pool. The "Fountain of Love" sculpture is a wonderful way to be greeted upon one's first visit to Cliveden. Although we looked forward to seeing the Fountain on subsequent visits, we never felt the impact of its magnificence as intensely as we did on our first visit.

Leaving the Fountain, we turned left onto the Great Lime Avenue, nearly a third of a mile of straight passage. This pea-graveled lane took us to the eight-columned porte-cochere where the doorman opened the door of our sedan. Upon entering the manor, we found ourselves in the Great Hall, a beautiful open area with wooden ceilings, numerous paintings, a massive fireplace, armored sentinels, luxurious sofas and ancient tapestries. We took a quick tour of the ground floor, a tour that led us into a hall with marble busts of who I supposed were great men. Sadly, I recognized none of them.

After a peek into two dining rooms, the expansive Terrace and more intimate French Dining Room, we were escorted outside onto the south-facing grand terrace. It was from this elevated terrace, rising approximately 30 feet above the gardens, that we had our first clue as to why Cliveden was special. The panorama before us included the ornate Parterre and the Thames River; in the far distance across a gully and high on a hill we could see a statue of the Duke of Sutherland. Off to our right, and near the edge of the chalk cliffs was an octagonal temple. We could not see, nor were we aware of at the time, the multitude of magnificent private gardens hidden in the Cliveden parklands.

Our first visit to Cliveden resulted from an invitation we extended to Tricia Townend and her husband, Bob, to join us for dinner as a way for us to show our appreciation for the work Tricia did in finding us our wonderful home in Kier Park. I mentioned to Tricia that cost was not a concern as we wanted the evening to be memorable. The evening certainly was memorable and our experience that night brought us back to Cliveden time and time again. I could have been more cautious with the "expense is not a concern" statement.

That evening in 1994 we found Cliveden to be awash in a sea of humanity. All restaurants were fully booked, and we were left with a reservation at Waldo's, a cozy retreat on the lower level and near a lively lounge. I took away two memories from the visit to Waldo's. The first came after the waiter informed us the evening's special was "Lamb-Four Ways". As a former meat cutter, I assumed he meant I would get a cutlet, a piece of shoulder, a tad of shank, and slice of leg. When I said I wanted the Lamb Special, he looked at me and offered as how I could have Lamb-One Way if I preferred. Which inspired me to ask, "What is Lamb-Four Ways?" His response was a chilling, "A cutlet, brains, sweetbread, and tongue". I immediately changed my order to Lamb – One Way.

As Shirley was fond of saying, "It is always good to ask."

Memory number two was occasioned by a painting of a beautiful woman that caught my attention as we were being seated. I looked closely and then read the underlying caption, "Christine Keeler, a portrait by Stephen Ward." Wow! I remembered Keeler from my days at university. She was the teenage tart who had, in 1961, brought down the government of Prime Minister Harold Macmillan in the Profumo Scandal. Later I would learn considerably more about the role Cliveden played in that political drama.

After we had coffees in the Great Hall, we took one last stroll on the Terrace and then loaded into our vehicle for our short ride, 30 minutes, back to Kier Park and Muirfield. I had much to learn about Cliveden and I was going to be a willing pupil.

I do not wish this narrative to be a history lesson so I shall recount only what I have found interesting about historical Cliveden. The Duke of Buckingham began construction on the original buildings in 1666. You have got to give the Duke credit; he broke tradition and built his estate high on the chalk cliffs above the Thames. The gentry of the time invariably chose secluded areas near the riverbank. The Duke's choice ensured Cliveden would have an enduring magnificence far beyond that related simply to architecture and opulence.

A Few of Our Favorite Places

The Duke of Buckingham was, however, not all that bright. He had a mistress, Anna Maria, also known as the Countess of Shrewsbury. This married lady had many lovers and an even greater number of charms, or so it has been written. The Duke often took both his wife and his mistress to the theatre (refer back to "not all that bright") and on one occasion one of Anna Maria's former lovers, scuffled with the Duke. Even though Anna Maria's husband was not at the theatre, the events led through a very contorted set of circumstances to a duel between the Duke of Buckingham and the Earl of Shrewsbury, the cuckolded husband. The poor Earl lost his life and the unfortunate event began the demise of the Duke of Buckingham. The date of the duel, 1668, is commemorated with the date and a sword, set in stone on the east lawn at Cliveden. Anna Maria would not be the last Cliveden woman who would be responsible for the ruination of a male consort.

I may be prejudiced by proximity in time, but I cannot imagine that any period in the history of Cliveden matched events that transpired during the 74 years in which the primary residents of Cliveden were members of the Astor Family. William Waldorf Astor came to England in 1891. At the time he was considered to be the richest man in America (in today's dollars he was most likely a billionaire), yet he turned his back on his homeland. In 1893 William Waldorf purchased Cliveden and it remained an Astor residence until 1967. It was the money and the effort that William Waldorf Astor invested in Cliveden that gave the property much of the internal and external definition it exhibits today.

After William Waldorf lost his wife, at age 36, and once his daughter Pauline married in 1903, he lost interest in Cliveden. When his son Waldorf Astor and Nancy Langhorne were married in 1906 William Waldorf gave the couple the Cliveden estate.

During the time Waldorf and Nancy Astor were in residence at Cliveden, it became one of the centers of social and political influence. With the exception of intervals during both world wars, when Cliveden was used as a hospital for Canadian troops, the grand house was the weekend destination for people from all levels of society. The Astor family had the wherewithal and the willingness to entertain almost every weekend. Famous guests included Charlie Chaplin, T.E. Lawrence, Bernard Shaw, Winston Churchill, Charles Lindbergh, and all manner of royalty both from the Continent and from within England. It is said that no one turned down a weekend invitation to Cliveden. It was a luxury hotel long before it became a luxury hotel.

Nancy Astor, an American from Virginia, was elected to the House of Commons in 1919 and she remained a Minister of Parliament until 1945. It was during this period that she and Winston Churchill had some very heated exchanges, prompting Nancy to say the famous words, "Winston, if I was married to you, I'd put poison in your coffee". Which prompted Winston's immediate and equally famous retort, "Nancy, if I was married to you, I'd drink it."

The Cliveden Set, as the press preferred to call the personalities and political machinations that took place at the Astor home, elicited a certain degree of contempt. Though the Astors made the point that their gatherings represented individuals of all political persuasions, the press did not choose to view it that way. The excess of attention given by the media reflects the influence the Astor gatherings had on political thinking in the United Kingdom.

The most infamous event in the recent history of Cliveden found its origin in a wild summer fling that took place in the outdoor swim pool. On Saturday night, July 9, 1961 there were two parties held on the Cliveden Estate. One was in the main house where John Profumo, Secretary of State for War, was in attendance and the other was in the Spring Cottage where Yevgeny Ivanov, a Captain and a spy for the GRU (a precursor to the Soviet KGB) was a guest at a coarser and less refined party. The common thread that led to disaster was nineteen-year-old Christine Keeler. When the Spring Cottage party moved up to the outdoor pool adjacent to the main residence, a certain amount of noise drew the attention of the indoor party. Christine Keeler was in the water and topless when John Profumo and the rest of the party arrived to see what was causing the commotion.

Christine Keeler was by all accounts a sexual dynamo. Within days following the pool incident, she seduced the Russian spy and ensnared Profumo in a three month affair. Captain Ivanov later wrote in his memoirs, "That devil of a girl (Keeler) could seduce anybody."

John Profumo's problem was that word of the twin trysts hit the tabloids. Of course, as Secretary for War, he flatly denied the charges. The nation was concerned about national security; John Profumo was focused more on the security of his neck. He was painfully aware that it did not look good for him to be sleeping with a woman who was also sleeping with a Soviet spy. When the truth came out, not only was Profumo forced to resign his post, the Macmillan Government fell with him.

As the Profumo scandal was being sensationalized in England the boy from Prineville read of these shenanigans in the Oregon press. Being hot blooded and young, the events were followed with great interest. The same age as Christine, I could not help but be impressed that she had seductive and social skills capable of destroying a democratic government. And to think decades later, I would sit in a restaurant in the stately home where it all began, and I would be looking up at a painting of the wanton woman as I ate Lamb-One Way. Who would have imagined it?

The Astors turned Cliveden over to the National Trust near the end of World War II. The Astor family was permitted to remain in residence as long as they chose. The Astor era came to a close in 1967 when the last Astor moved out of the stately home.

Stanford University took a lease at Cliveden and used the property as an overseas campus from 1969-1983. In 1985 Cliveden was turned over to a group that now runs it as a luxury hotel. And a luxury hotel it is. The restaurants are top notch as is the service and the amenities which are on offer. It should be, and probably is, a destination hotel for people from around the world. I imagine that each and every Stanford student who ever spent a year, or a summer, at Cliveden has been back there at least once. The magnetic attraction of Cliveden is that strong. Of course, the current tariff is a bit higher and the rooms are much more opulent than when the grand house was a dorm.

Cliveden is special and there is much in the literature about the politics and the history of the estate. I think one has to visit the property to appreciate the beauty and the grandeur. My hope is that these tales will encourage the reader to do just that.

We loved Cliveden and the Lent family had a multitude of very special moments on the estate. We celebrated many holidays and special events, events like our anniversary, Christmas, and New Year. As special as these days were, we came to truly love Cliveden as a result of the many visits there with dear friends. I do not recall we ever had a close friend or relative visit us who we didn't take to Cliveden. Sometimes we had lunch, sometimes dinner, or more likely than not we simply walked the grounds. There is so much to see at Cliveden and all of it is memorable, especially for easily awed Yanks.

When Kerr-McGee's soon to be Chief Executive Officer, Luke Corbett, came to visit our office in England, I asked this business leader, who was also a close friend, to join me for dinner at Cliveden. After a short tour of the manor, we walked out on the terrace so that Luke could see the Thames River and the surrounding countryside. We were seated for dinner in the Terrace Dining Room where we had cocktails and a wonderful repast. After our coffees, I asked Luke if he would like to walk the grounds. Luke is a good sport and agreed: we began what amounted to a recapitulation of the sum total of Bob and Shirley's previous forays into the Cliveden parklands.

From the terrace we descended stairs, first to a landing area, and then on to ground level. At ground level we were within the main Parterre, an arrangement of bedded plants and flowers planted in intricate geometrical patterns. The ground on which the Parterre is located is relatively flat although there is a slight southward slope towards Spring Creek and the Thames River. The walk along the Parterre becomes mesmerizing when one reaches a point in the gardens where, whilst looking back, the full magnificence of the Cliveden Mansion comes into perspective. I have never looked back without feeling a sense of awe and reverence for the beauty. I am sure that Luke felt the same way.

We walked over to the Octagon Temple which stands at the edge of the chalk cliffs. From a viewing area adjacent to the Temple, one gets a magnificent view of the River Thames and the wild meadows that cover the western lowlands. As beautiful as the view is, it is the quiet that gets one's attention. Peaceful and serene probably best describe the setting. We were not able to enter the Temple, which serves both as a family chapel and as the resting place for the ashes of William Waldorf, Waldorf, and William Astor; the 1st, 2nd, and 3rd Viscounts Astor.

A trail from the Temple leads down to the bank of the Thames and to Spring Cottage. As we approached the Cottage, I gave the spiel on the Profumo affair, which began at the Cottage where Captain Ivanov, Christine Keeler, and others spent the weekend of July 8-9, 1961. All had been guests of Stephen Ward, to whom the Astors had granted residence at Spring Cottage. Poor Yevgeny, or maybe not poor Yevgeny, but in any event, Yevgeny Ivanov should never have offered to take Christine back to London that Sunday evening.

As Luke and I walked along the bank of the River we passed the boat house. Moored there were several vessels that are available for use for guests at Cliveden. Shirley and I had seen these boats; one, the *Liddesdale*, is actually an electric running canoe. The more impressive boat is the *Suzy-Ann* which can be used to take small groups on champagne cruises up and down the Thames in the calm waters beneath the Cliveden cliffs. Neither had we made reservations, nor did we have time to take a boat ride, so Luke and I continued walking down the river until we came to a pathway that leads up the southern side of the Spring Creek notch. Shirley and I had found this trail only by trial and error, but I am sure the Cliveden staff have maps that show how one gains access to the trail. The climb up to Duke's Seat, as this part of the grounds is known, is intense but short in duration. Once on the level landing, the view to the south is dominated by a marble statue of the Duke of Southerland, which can also be seen from the terrace at Cliveden. The more memorable view is to the north, after one has turned to look back at Cliveden. From this vantage point the Parterre and the manor house can be seen in totality. It is quite a view. Luke was impressed. I could tell.

From the Duke's Seat there is a nearly flat pathway that winds through the forest back to the main grounds at Cliveden. This path is used by those wishing to ride horses at Cliveden or by those wishing to take a quiet walk through a sylvan setting. Massive yew trees border most of the pathway. Indeed, the trail is known as the Yew Tree Walk

As Mr. Corbett and I walked slowly along the grass and leaf-covered pathway, the softest of music began to filter through the trees. So soft that at first, I was tempted to think I had imagined it. Then, there again, was the soft music. I could tell that it was classical, maybe even Handel. Luke had heard the music too. As we walked the flat pathway, the music became louder and closer. I told Luke I was going to walk through an opening to investigate. When I emerged from the vegetation surrounding the opening, seated before me in an amphitheater was an entire orchestra. There was no audience. I was aware that the Royal Philharmonic Pops Orchestra sometimes performed at Cliveden, but I had no idea which orchestra this was or why the group was playing such lovely music.

I walked back to Luke and mentioned to him that I had planned a little something special for his first visit to Cliveden. I asked him to follow me. When we got to the seated and performing musicians I just smiled, and he looked at me knowingly. Upon asking what was on offer here, we learned the orchestra was having its last rehearsal for an outdoor performance that would take place the following evening. For a few moments Luke and I had experienced something quite surreal. Even today, many years later, I can see the trees, the sun shining through the upper browse, and the music, almost like it was visible, filtering through the forest.

Luke was impressed. Hey! This might be getting me somewhere. We then came to the Water Garden which is an expanse of isolated ponds surrounded by flowering shrubs and bedded plants. The focal point of the Garden is a Chinese Pagoda whose presence makes one feel he or she is in Asia. The ponds are filled with numerous leviathan carp and Koi, many of which are supposed to be direct descendants of those planted in the late 1670s by the Duke of Buckingham (work he had done when he was not busy with the Shrew). A day at play around the Water Garden is probably worth the trip to Cliveden all by itself. At a minimum time spent at the Garden will provide great opportunities for a photo shoot.

Luke and I finished our stroll around the grounds with tours through The Long Garden, known for its linear hedges, statues, and sculptures carved from growing flora, and the Rose Garden, which needs no explanation. We also paid our respects at the Canadian Cemetery, the resting place for those Canadian Soldiers who died at Cliveden when it served as a hospital.

Had I impressed Mr. Corbett with this visit to Cliveden? Luke answered that question when he remarked, "I do not want you to tell others at Kerr-McGee of this place. When Mr. McPherson retires as CEO of Kerr-McGee, I want to have his retirement party at Cliveden." The McPherson party never happened at Cliveden. It was not because it was not the right place, but because it was so far away from Oklahoma City.

In case you are wondering how my schmoozing attempt turned out. When I took Luke Corbett to Cliveden in 1995, I was a Vice President. When I retired in 2003 I was still a Vice President. He did send Shirley and me to China. Maybe I should have worked on my schmoozing techniques.

All our friends and many of our associates at work knew how much we enjoyed Cliveden. On one occasion, June 12, 1997, Shirley had made plans to throw a surprise going away party for Paulette Guion, wife of our Vice President of Production, Jim Guion. Jim and Paulette were being transferred back to the United States and David and Susan Kimes were coming to London to replace them. The Kerr-McGee expatriate wives who lived in London made arrangements to pick Paulette up and take her to lunch. Paulette was not told where they would be dining. The ladies also informed Paulette that unfortunately, Shirley Lent would not be able to join them.

When the limo headed out into the country Paulette found

herself looking for a landmark she recognized. Recognition came when the car turned and drove through Taplow. Paulette looked at the other ladies and said, "If this luncheon is going to be held at Cliveden, it is really unfortunate that Shirley could not join us." Paulette knew how dear Cliveden was to Shirley.

What Paulette did not know was that Shirley had organized the entire luncheon. Tricia Townend, the relocation expert and a friend of both Paulette and Shirley, was also going to be joining the group for lunch. When the London car arrived, Shirley met the ladies at the front entrance and immediately took them on a tour of the grounds and the mansion. She even walked them up the grand staircase so that they might see the paintings and sculptures in the hallway of the guest bedrooms. This is really a no-no with regards to guests who are not registered, but Shirley showed such familiarity with the manor that the hotel staff never said a word. Shirley gave a running commentary on the history and architecture, tidbits of information that can only come from having read the many books on Cliveden and from having been there many times. The ladies walked out on the terrace and then around the grounds. After they left the Water Gardens, they retired to the library room for refreshments, after which it was time for Paulette's luncheon celebration. The ladies were seated in front of the largest window which offered a view of the Thames some 200 feet below.

After lunch Paulette made note of the boats on the Thames, adding that these must be available for hire. Little did Paulette know, but Shirley had arranged for the group to be picked up at the porte-cochere for transport to the Cliveden Spring Cottage and the Cliveden boat dock. Once at the river bank the ladies were escorted aboard the *Suzy-Ann*, the shallow draft covered boat that is available for quiet and scenic runs along the Thames. The canopy-covered seating area of the boat seats six but there is also room both fore and aft where guests can sit or stand outside for maximum sensory impact. Coffees, truffles, and after lunch drinks were served to the ladies who alternated between standing outside and sitting in the cabin.

Paulette was delighted with the special attention and affection bestowed on her. Even the hard to impress Tricia Townend

A Few of Our Favorite Places

seemed moved. But it was Joan Verm and Jackie Davidson who were "gobsmacked" to use the local terminology. The spouses of Kerr-McGee managers, these ladies could not stop raving about the day. Michael Verm mentioned to me the following day at work that after Joan got home, she did not stop talking about the day, even after they turned off the lights and were in bed.

For Paulette, the day's celebration was capped by the presentation of the book, *Cliveden - The Place and the People* and a Cliveden Halcyon enamel box.

Our sons had a special affection for Cliveden. It became an accepted tradition that when either of the boys would have dinner and drinks on the premises, and his brother was far away in the United States or Asia, the diner would write a note on Cliveden stationary. The details of the lunch or dinner were always embellished with the grandest items shown on the menu. I looked over Tobin's shoulder one day to see that he had written the following note to Taran: "Wish you could have joined us today for fine wine and fillet of Scotch lamb with tian of vegetables, Anna potatoes, and a fricassee of wild mushrooms. We especially missed you when, for desserts, we had the crispy tagliatelle, lightly flavored with cinnamon and a quenelle of bitter chocolate mousse on a bed of poached pears. And of course, a glass of port simply topped off a great experience. Hope that your final in quantum physics went well and that Dartmouth daily doubles are not getting you down."

Cliveden is located near the village of Taplow. From the M4 motorway take exit 7 (Slough West). At the roundabout turn left onto the A4 signposted Maidenhead. At the next roundabout turn right signposted Burnman. Follow this road for 2 ½ miles to a T junction with the B476. The main gates to Cliveden are directly opposite this T. Or you could just ask a local for directions to Feathers Inn, a pub located across the B476 from the Cliveden entrance.

And There We Were

Compleat Angler
Marlow, Buckinghamshire

    It took us a while to find this Hotel and its Riverside Restaurant. Uniquely located on the bank of the River Thames this venue became one of our favorite destinations. The location is blessed by four features that bring exceptional beauty to the restaurant and its associated bar and lounge. The most remarkable feature of the location is its proximity to the Marlow Weir, a L-shaped series of broad cement steps that drop the Thames from an upper to a lower pool. At the weir the north flowing Thames makes a perpendicular turn to the east. The roar of the falls and the abundance of white water offer the onlooker a view that is unsurpassed in the Thames drainage. Guests of the bar and the restaurant are free to walk outdoors onto a wooden terrace that is a fringe separating the Thames and the restaurant/bar. If the day is warm and sunny, guests may have tea or other refreshments served on the terrace. The Riverside Restaurant offers window views of the slow-moving Thames above the weir and of the falls as the water spills over the weir.

    There has been a weir at Marlow since well before 1600. Fishermen have gathered in the pool below the weir for centuries. Even today, diners in the elegant restaurant can look out the windows and see recreational fisherman. The Compleat Angler Hotel takes its name from the book written in 1653 by Isaak Walton. This book, the first ever written on the art of fishing, and especially fly fishing, is: *The Compleat Angler or the Contemplative Man's Recreation. Being a Discourse of RIVERS, FISHPONDS, FISH, and FISHING. Not unworthy the perusal of most Anglers.* Isaak Walton wrote his book from a home not far from the present day Compleat Angler Hotel. Anyone who has visited the Compleat Angler, is apt, upon reading Mr. Walton's book to visualize where he must have fished and how he caught his fish. As an avid fly fisherman, I was taken by one chapter, *Observations of the Nature and breeding of the Trout, and how to Fish for him: and the Milkmaid's Song.*

I remember that back in Prineville we had an Isaak Walton League famous for its fishing and hunting activities. I am certain the League once offered a bounty on magpies and porcupines. Just how these bounties related to hunting and fishing I do not know. Maybe the group just got away from the ideals of its namesake.

The view of the Marlow Weir is reason enough to have a refreshment or dinner at the Riverside Restaurant, but there is more. Across the river from the Compleat Angler is an old church (again a bit redundant in England), the All Saints Parish Church. Originally built in the 11th Century, the church was rebuilt in 1835. The length of the church runs parallel to the river. The entrance is crowned with a gothic spire that dominates the Marlow skyline. Separating the All Saints Church from the Thames is grassland that includes a part of the Church cemetery. Many of the tombstones in this cemetery are so old that it is difficult to distinguish the names and the dates.

The roadway in front of the All Saints Parish Church leads immediately to an ornate Victorian suspension bridge. The roadway across the bridge is narrow but the structure itself is stunning. The suspension cables and struts are painted white and are kept in pristine condition. The white suspension and walkway barriers are almost lace-like in appearance. Massive stone arches anchor the bridge on both banks. If you take the bridge across the river from the All Saints Parish Church, the first left turn off the roadway is the entrance into the Compleat Angler.

The Thames above the Marlow Weir is calm and the river way is straight for nearly a mile. The stretch of the river is famous for being the site of the Marlow Regatta and is a recreational area for sailing, canoeing, rowing, and fishing. The Thames Path, a national river trail, runs along the west side (church side) of the river. This path is favored by walkers going upstream from the bridge since the Thames is on one side of the path and open meadows are on the other.

If you put all of these features together you might imagine why the Compleat Angler is so enchanting; Marlow Weir, All

Saints Parish Church, Marlow Bridge, and the Thames River all part of one visual package. As one would expect, it is difficult to book a wedding on the grounds of the Compleat Angler. On nearly every weekend we partook of the amenities, there was a wedding reception taking place.

Often, especially when the weather was nice, the wedding or the wedding reception was outdoors. There were a number of occasions when Shirley and I sat at one of the white linen-covered lawn tables and had a drink served to us, courtesy of restaurant staff who had not yet gotten around to removing tables used in an earlier ceremony.

The terrace along the restaurant also serves as a boat dock, the very same dock from which Captain Jack took the Lent and Hess families on that storied trip upstream which culminated at the birthday party given by the good doctor and his wife. Shirley and I took a number of other such boat rides with other guests from around the world, but none were as interesting as the one in which the aristocratic lady chauffeur, in her purple roadster, returned us to the Compleat Angler for our dinner appointment. That is not to say that there were not a few other "incidents".

We booked a larger boat one evening when Luke Corbett, now the Kerr-McGee CEO, was in town. We had made the decision to bring Mr. Corbett and his wife Becky to the Riverside Restaurant at the Compleat Angler along with four other Kerr-McGee executives and their wives. Shirley and I thought it would be nice to rent the more accommodating boat so we could have pre-dinner drinks whilst taking a quiet and scenic trip up the Thames. The evening was cool, and soon we were searching the boat for blankets to keep several of the women on board more comfortable. During the search I walked up the steps going from one level of the boat to another and hit my head on a low entryway. I groused about the bump, but took no further notice of it.

After we returned to the boat landing after our short trip, we escorted the ladies into the warm restaurant. When I had sat down, those near me, including my Shirley, were aghast.

When I hit my head on the boat, I must have scraped my bald spot across a nail. My head was covered in blood. I looked like I had been under Custer's command at the Battle of the Little Big Horn. The wound was more superficial than it appeared, but that being said, it was not a great way to start a dinner with the big boss. Fortunately, I did find a way to keep his wife from freezing. It never hurts to give the CEO's wife the best blanket on the boat.

On one other occasion I was in Captain Jack's small boat with another Kerr-McGee traveling dignitary, and we found ourselves slowly moving up the Thames. Before we boarded, I had picked up a handful of breadcrumbs. My intention was to feed the ducks and geese that follow boats on the river. As we progressed up the Thames, I noticed a very attractive lady who was walking beside us on the Thames Path. She was walking about the same speed as our boat, so she seemed to always be just out of reach on the bank. Not only was she attractive, she was also scantily attired. It was difficult to not look at her. After about a mile the lady waved at us, flashed a promiscuous grin, and turned to make her return trip down the river. Only then did I realized I still had the sweaty breadcrumbs in my hand, and that the ducks and geese were nearly exhausted from their failed attempts to get my attention.

On one sunny summer day in May of 1996 Michael Webb, then Senior Vice President of Exploration at Kerr-McGee, and I stopped at Marlow for refreshments on the terrace at the Compleat Angler. A few days after our visit and after Michael had returned to the United States a full-page photo of Princess Diana and a friend appeared in one of the London tabloids, most likely the Sun. Diana is shown seated at the exact same table where Michael and I sat whilst we were enjoying our refreshment on the terrace. If you visit the Compleat Angler today, the photo of Princess Diana is sure to be on the Restaurants "Wall of Fame". I sent Michael a copy of the newspaper article, and I told him that we must have good taste if the table we chose was popular with the Royals.

Rod Stewart, the pop star icon, loves the Compleat Angler too. He did not choose to have a wedding on the grounds, but in April of 1996 he chose to renew his wedding vows at the All Saints Parish Church. Such is the attraction of the Compleat Angler and the Marlow Weir that after the ceremony he was taken by horse and carriage across Marlow Bridge to the Compleat Angler. Unfortunately for Mr. Stewart, the affirmation of vows did not save his marriage. The songster continues his pursuit of matrimonial bliss.

The Riverside Restaurant is exceptional in its own right. The place would probably book up night after night even if it did not have great food, but that it has such food is another reason the Compleat Angler is high on our must visit list. A typical meal for me would have been somewhat like the following: Starter - Sauteed Scallops on Jerusalem artichokes with quail egg ravioli, Main course - Filet of Red Mullet and Lobster with sauteed cos lettuce and blood-orange butter sauce, and Dessert – Dark chocolate mousse with white chocolate and orange ice cream. The menus, both for lunch and for dinner are exhaustive; those with discerning palates will not be left wanting.

As to the village of Marlow, it is quaint but not particularly so. It does, however, have a special place in literary history. It was in Marlow that Mary Shelley wrote her novel, *Frankenstein*. Although the idea for the book was conceived one evening in Lake Geneva, Switzerland, it was in Marlow, Buckinghamshire that the authoress seated herself and wrote the masterpiece.

Marlow is approximately 30 miles west of London and can be reached via either the M4 or M40 roadways, connecting then to the A404 and A4155 feeder roads. Once in Marlow, a drive through the village takes one to the Thames and to the Compleat Angler.

A Few of Our Favorite Places

WINDSOR GREAT PARK, BERKSHIRE

One might question why an outdoor park ranks as one of Bob and Shirley's most favored places in all of England. For someone telling others of this grand place it is not easy to know where to begin. The very end of our stay in England might be a good place to start, with a description of the impact Windsor Great Park had on Shirley as we were being driven from Muirfield to Heathrow to catch a flight for our relocation to Beijing, China.

At our Muirfield home we watched as the movers packed and loaded our household goods. Afterwards, we took one last look around the gardens and the house. Empty though it was, we were haunted by the many memories racing through our minds. I locked the door and helped Shirley into the chauffeured car waiting for us. The electric gate opened, and we drove out onto the Kier Park roadway. She turned for one last look and then, stoically, we drove on down the road. She did not have a tear in her eye. I was sure that she would not be able to say goodbye to Muirfield without emulating Niagara Falls.

The ride out of Kier Park was done in silence. I did not say a word: I just looked at my beautiful wife and imagined the anguish she must be experiencing. We turned onto the A329, and then onto the A30. Both of which take motorists past part of the Windsor Great Park. I turned toward Shirley and took a peek as we passed Virginia Water Lake and then again as we passed the entrance into Savill Gardens. When Shirley glanced over and saw people strolling along the pathways in the forest her eyes began to water.

Shirley fell in love with Windsor Great Park almost immediately. From the beginning of our life together, and wherever we lived, she always found a great place to walk; her goal being to walk an hour or an hour and a half each day. The Windsor Great Park covers more than 5000 acres, and it stretches from Ascot on the south seven and one-half miles to the village of Windsor on the north. The terrain includes meadows, hills, dales, forest, and lakes. There are 7 main entrances to the Park, including one in Windsor at the entrance to the Long

Walk. The changing seasons insure the views within the Park are constantly in flux. Changing weather patterns produce a myriad of overhead compositions that create scenic variations even in a single day. Unlike many parts of the world, weather in the United Kingdom is subject to dynamic change. Offshore winds laden with clouds and moisture tend to move quickly across the land mass. Bright blue skies, skies with white fluffy clouds, skies with dark and fast-moving rain clouds, high overcast clouds that diffuse and dull the vegetative coloring, and low hanging heavy rain clouds might all be seen in a day, in a week, or in a month.

The British are adaptable and tend not to let weather alter their outdoor activities. What difference if you have a picnic in the rain or if your walk is not under sunny skies. All know that if it rains, the sun is not far behind and there will, invariably be a "brightening". A sunny or bright day had better be enjoyed because a bright day means rain is on the ocean wending its way onto the Island.

What makes Windsor Great Park special? First, and perhaps most importantly, the Park has benefited immeasurably from the Royal caretakers. Going back to the rule of Edward the Confessor, 1042-1066, the royal rulers have taken active roles in preserving, protecting, and planting of forests and gardens. The major era of tree planting occurred in the late 1500s. King Charles II planted trees along the Great Walk in the late 1600s and he initiated an active period of landscaping. When the royal appointee, William the Duke of Cumberland, was appointed Ranger of the Park in 1746, he initiated a near continuous 200-year period of park development that resulted in exceptional plant and flower gardens. Construction of the impoundment that became Virginia Water Lake, located in the southern part of the Park, began in the Duke of Cumberland's first year on the job. After a disastrous and destructive flood in 1768 the Lake was rebuilt in the late 1780s. Virginia Water Lake is approximately two miles long with a maximum width of one-third of a mile. The shoreline extends for nearly seven miles.

Although a number of monarchs were responsible for the planting of the many specimens of trees found throughout the

Park, it was the guiding hand of King George VI who encouraged Eric Savill to develop the magnificent plant and flower gardens that are now the Savill and Valley Gardens. During spring when these two gardens are in full bloom there are few gardens in the world that can match either for the variety and intensity of color, or for the breadth and magnificence of plant species. In a two-to-three-month period the landscaping prowess of Mr. Savill is on display for all to see and enjoy. A crescendo of color builds as the flowering daffodils, camellias, rhododendrons, and cherries burst into bloom in March and are followed over the next two months by flowering magnolias, alpines, azaleas, irises, primus hostas, and ferns. Plants and flowering trees cover nearly every slope of the Valley Gardens and most of the areas surrounding Savill Gardens. It is possible to walk trails and at every turn look down on a grass-bottomed valley filled with blooming daffodils, and then to look upward into an interlocking mass of giant azaleas, camellias, and rhododendrons covering the slopes of the dales. It would be foolish to try to describe the coloration. Other than actually visiting the Park, the best way to view what transpires in the spring is to purchase the incredible *The Royal Gardens in Windsor Great Park*, by Charles Lyte. Although Mr. Lyte is a consummate professional, even our own private photo albums are filled with spectacular shots of the plant coloration. In a favorite photo Shirley is standing amongst the flowering branches of a massive rhododendron tree. One has to look hard to see her in the wall of flowers, but she is there, pretty as can be.

It would be unrealistic to think that the Windsor Great Park is as beautiful all year long as it is during the spring, but there is so much variety that a walk in the park is a delight during every month of the year. One of Shirley's favorite moments during her daily walks occurred when she chose to end her journey near the eastern shore of Virginia Water Lake. She had discovered a wooden bench where she could watch the sun set over the full two-mile length of the lake. And then she thought how wonderful it would be to have a pint of Newcastle Brown to sip whilst she watched the sun set. She found a nearby pub, the Wheatsheaf, where the bartender would sell her a pint that she could take to the bench. The walk to the pub and back took about ten minutes. Despite the effort, Shirley was in heaven when she could sit, sip, and watch as the sun set over Virginia Water Lake. Many a fellow walker looked at her and wondered where she found the pint - all shared in her appreciation of the scene and the sunset. It does not matter what the season, one can (weather permitting) blissfully watch the sun set over Virginia Water Lake.

One day Shirley walked out of Kier Park and along the road to the Ascot Gate to the Windsor Great Park. It was her intent to walk the length of the park to Windsor. Her route took her up the west side of the Park with superlative views of Queen Anne's Ride and the Copper Horse. Queen Anne's Ride is a wide expanse of grassland bounded on both sides by a single row of majestic oak trees. Many of these massive trees are so old they are beginning to die. But just as trees replanted in previous centuries, seedlings are currently being planted to replace the withering giants.

The Copper Horse is a monument to King George III. Now I would have thought that the guy who lost the Colonies would not have been so honored, but the truth of the matter is King George III handled the French in a much more efficient manner. Furthermore, his son, King George IV, could erect whatever he wanted to, and he did - a monument to his father. The Copper Horse on the top of Snow Hill looks down the three-mile Long Walk. Windsor Castle is clearly visible at the end of the Long Walk, and looking back from the Castle, the Copper Horse is similarly visible. The Long Walk is an impressive straight-line walk, bordered on each side by double rows of horse chestnut trees. Shirley completed her walk to Windsor Castle and Windsor Village. After she stopped at a local tea house for refreshments, she hailed a cab that took her back to Muirfield.

A walk along Queen Anne's Ride usually offers one the chance to see the rapidly building herd of Red deer that were re-introduced to the Park in 1977. Deer had always been in the Park until World War II when they were removed to facilitate farming in support of the war effort. Since re-introduction, the herd has thrived. A walk in the park, especially along the western edge almost always results in a sighting. Indeed, travelers along the A332 often stop to look at the "Royal Herd". For years, the need to concentrate on the road, and the new way of driving (on the left, or wrong, side of the road) left me no time for side attractions. The only "Royal Herd" I saw was the one comprised of milk cows that are part of the commercial farming conducted for the benefit of the Queen. This farming activity was done in meadows on the side of the road opposite the Park.

The deer in Windsor Great Park do not always stay in the Park. When they do get out interesting situations sometimes arise. We once had a yearling take up residence in our front yard at Muirfield. There was no water for the little fellow, but he seemed to thrive. He spent his time at Muirfield in the same general area where someone had nicked our standing ornamental lions so, he was in a danger zone. One day he vanished and we never saw him again. I hoped that after a week of munching on our cherries and green grass he had had enough, and he decided to return to his mother and the rest of the herd.

Not so lucky was one deer that was hit on the roadway leading to the Ascot train station. My early morning driver pointed out the dead deer and the damaged car. The odd thing about the accident is that after my driver dropped me at the station, he drove back up the hill and saw the other driver loading the dead deer into his trunk. No doubt in my mind that the guy was going to enjoy venison for a while. Red deer are better served when they stay in Windsor Great Park.

Polo matches are held on Smith's Lawn in Windsor Great Park, adjacent to the Polo Club. When Prince Charles asked Shirley at the Janice Inaugural if she had watched the polo matches whilst she lived in Kier Park, he was referring to the matches held on Smith's Lawn, where Prince Charles often competed. The public can drive cars into this area and this knowledge allowed Shirley to do something creative and memorable, just for my father.

John and Mabel Lent came to England to visit us in 1996. During their stay Shirley wanted to show dad one of her favorite places, Windsor Great Park. But dad, age 81, was not all that mobile, and it seemed that there was no way for either he or mom to get a view of all those magnificent things Shirley regularly saw in the Park. Not to be denied, Shirley loaded mom and dad in our Honda Legend and entered the park via Cranbourne Gate, a western entry into the Park that provides access to Smith's Lawn. Shirley drove dad down all of the paths in the park, paved or graveled. They saw the Copper Horse, Virginia Water Lake, the Valley Gardens, the Roman Ruins (Corinthian pillars imported from North Africa), the Totem Pole, and the Cranbourne Tower. The three of them even managed an exceptional viewing of the Royal Herd.

Then dad said to Shirley, "You know this is absolutely wonderful, but it is very odd that we have not seen any other cars." Shirley told him that it was forbidden to traverse the park in a car. Dad was immediately taken back and asked Shirley what would happen if a Ranger stopped them. Shirley responded, "I will tell them that I am a lost American and that I am just trying to get to Smith's Lawn and the Polo Grounds." When Shirley told me what she had done I was happy for my father, but a bit concerned for Shirley. As a result of Shirley's daily walks in the Park she was known by every Ranger. There was no way her flimsy excuse could have ever worked. But it probably would have! My dad and mom did see the great park, and to this day I am glad both had the opportunity to do so before they died. I do not, however, recommend Shirley's tactical approach. The better way to achieve the same end is go to Windsor and engage a horse drawn carriage.

The pathways in Windsor Great Park are not always as clearly marked as one would hope, and it is easy to get disoriented. The frequent walker soon learns all of the famous landmarks, and these serve to get a confused visitor back on track. Some of the more famous landmarks are the Copper Horse, Smith's Lawn, the Totem Pole, the Jubilee Bridge, the Plunket Memorial, the Canadian Avenue, Valley Gardens, and the Cascade at the head of Virginia Water. Just remember, do *not* take the roadway across from Bishop's Gate. That road leads to the Royal Lodge and consequently to Tower Hill. The Royal Lodge, the Windsor home of the Queen Mother, was where she was when she took her last breath. The Queen Mum had returned to the park she loved and was near the beautiful gardens that she helped create.

Fall is a wonderful time in Windsor Great Park. The colors are spectacular but perhaps not more glorious than the colors seen in the northeastern United States where the turning of the colors is magnificent in its own right. When the leaves begin to change and drop, the Park takes on an entirely different look. The evergreen copses and forests stand out in relief, and valleys such as Pinetum are just as pretty in December as Azalea Valley is in May.

Farming still occurs on the lands within and around the Windsor Great Park: I believe the number of acres of agricultural land are included when the total size of the park is calculated. The size of Windsor Great Park has already been alluded to as exceeding 5000 acres. Depending on the reference book in hand, the size of the Park varies over a considerable range. One text has the Park encompassing over 14,000 acres, 8,000 of which is forest.

The Royal Estate owns a number of buildings in the Park that are residences for employees of the Royal Estate. When Shirley and I first drove through the agricultural section of the Park, we were told that every building painted "pink", and there were a lot of them, belonged to the Queen. It may be so, but not all that one is told turns out to be the truth. I personally cannot believe there is much profit in dairy end of the Park management, but maybe the Queen likes fresh milk.

I did not share Shirley's desire to go walking each day in the park, but I was a happy husband knowing that such walks made her, in her own words, "A better woman." The fresh smell of pine, lavender, mint, or whatever, scented the wonderfully fresh air that Shirley walked through. When she came back from walks in the Park she had a zest about her I could not but admire. She was probably never happier during our stay in England than when she was back where she began, walking through forest and meadow. Windsor Great Park is a long way geographically and culturally from Big Summit Prairie and the

Ochoco Mountains, yet the feeling instilled by walks through both locales are very much the same.

Frogmore House Gardens and Mausoleum

The northern boundary of Windsor Great Park is near Snow Hill atop of which is the towering statue of King George III astride a copper horse. The scenic Long Walk, a nearly straight three-mile pathway, begins in the Park at the base of Snow Hill and continues north to the King George IV Gate at Windsor Castle. The Long Walk is part of Windsor Great Park, but this tree-lined pathway is only a narrow easement through the private park of the monarch. The Home Park, which might in a broad sense be considered to be the monarch's Windsor Castle 'yard', includes grasslands and gardens south and east of the outer walls of the Castle. The Home Park also includes property reaching north to the Thames River. A public recreational ground (also called the Home Park Public) is situated near the Thames, and this park, with the Queen's "gracious permission," is host to the annual Royal Windsor Horse Show. The Horse Show is held over a five-day period and features equestrian competition and exhibits. A second Home Park event, admission to Frogmore and the Royal Mausoleum, occurs with the approval and at the discretion of the Queen.

Frogmore House is located within a 300-acre enclave of The Home Park. Frogmore originally became part of the Home Park when Henry VIII purchased the property. Originally, the land was low lying and marshy and was, of course, the habitat for croaking frogs.

The original home at Frogmore was built in 1680, but Frogmore House as it is known today was commissioned by Queen Charlotte, consort of King George III (famous for being astride the Copper Horse and for losing the Colonies). Queen Charlotte loved Frogmore House and she spent most of her mornings there painting, reading, drawing, or "botanizing". Being the lady she was, she returned to Windsor Castle in the evenings to dine and sleep with the King. Queen Victoria took control of the House in 1841 and offered it to her mother, the Duchess of Kent, who lived on the grounds until her death in 1861.

Frogmore House became a favorite retreat of Queen Victoria, and she spent many hours there. In 1867 she wrote:

> *"All is peace and quiet and you only hear the hum of the bees and the singing of the birds and the occasional crowing and cackling from the Poultry Yard! It does my poor excited, worried nerves good!"*

Frogmore House is included in this narrative because the grounds are also the site of a remarkable burial ground. Following the tragic and unexpected death (from dysentery) of Prince Albert, the Queen's Escort, in December of 1861, Queen Victoria commissioned the construction of a mausoleum that would be the burial place of not only the Prince, but also of the Queen herself. She ordered the construction of the tombhouse in a Frogmore private garden.

Many of Queen Victoria's ancestors were buried in churches. Indeed, King George III and his family were all buried beneath St. George's Chapel at Windsor Castle. It was an unusual turn of events for the Queen to order a special built mausoleum.

The Royal Mausoleum is beautiful and a visit there is captivating, because of the beauty and because of the sentimental impact. I will leave the beauty to the eyes of the beholder, but what captivated me was the height, 70 feet from floor to dome, and the obviously ornate Victorian paintings, sculptures, and ornamentation. The floor and walls of the central octagon are inlaid with colored marble. Extending off the central room are four small chapels, each exquisite in its own way. The copper-sheathed roof of the Mausoleum has, over the last 150 years, weathered to a malachite-hued green.

But the striking fixture in the Mausoleum is the reclining effigies of Prince Albert and Queen Victoria. After Prince Albert's death at age 42, Queen Victoria commissioned two effigies to be carved in marble. One was of Albert, the other, a youthful Queen Victoria also aged 42. She did not want to live to be an

And There We Were

old lady only to have an aged effigy placed beside her youthful looking husband. The Queen's effigy remained in storage until after her death more than 40 years later.

The two effigies rest atop a massive granite sarcophagus. The memorials, and the ebony and bronze wreaths placed amidst other memorabilia around the base of the sarcophagus leave an impression the ceremony occurred only yesterday, and these were laid there by dignitaries paying their last respects. It is as if the mourners left their mementos and then quietly backed out of the room. There have been relatively few visitors to the Mausoleum over the years and the sanctity of the funeral site has been well preserved.

After Prince Albert died, there were two deaths that resulted in burials in the Mausoleum chapels. Victoria's oldest child and her grandchild both died before the Queen. These tombs tug at your heart, but no more so than another statue that Queen Victoria commissioned for the Mausoleum. This statue has Prince Albert standing erect with a loving Queen Victoria looking up to him. There is no doubt that the lady loved this man.

If the Royal Mausoleum is such an interesting place to visit, why then have so few people visited the site? The answer is that the Mausoleum is open to the public only two times during the year - on Queen Victoria's birthday, which is May 25, and on the August Bank Holiday (the last weekend in August). As mentioned previously, these visitations are allowed only with the discretionary approval of the Queen.

Had we not lived in Berkshire and read the local papers Shirley and I would not have known that we could visit Frogmore House or the Royal Mausoleum. But we did so on August 24, 1996. The visit added another addition to our collection of wonderful memories of Windsor Great Park and the Home Park.

It is interesting to think that in 1861-62, when Prince Albert's death led to the construction of the Royal Mausoleum, Oregon, our native state, had achieved statehood only two years earlier. Some of our ancestors, at least on my side, were in wagon trains wending their way to the northwest.

A Few of Our Favorite Places

The Ritz Hotel London, Claridge's, and Harrods

Her Windsor Great Park experiences took Shirley back to the free-spirited times she spent exploring the high meadows in Big Summit Prairie. The fresh air, the beautiful plants and trees, the capricious weather, and the solitude she found in the Great Park were exhilarating. But the younger Shirley Lent had another side to her. Her love of life, zest, and enthusiasm for all things elegant fueled her dreams and imagination. The elegant hotels and department stores of London afforded Shirley the venues where she finally found the elegance and style that she wanted in her life. If you are looking for elegance, glamour, and service in London you will soon find yourself sampling what is on offer at Claridge's and The Ritz, both world famous luxury hotels. Harrods is in a class by itself only because it is what it is – arguably the most famous and elitist shopping store in all of England.

When the pre-teen Shirley Lent waited up for her parents to return from Prineville's King's Café in the 1950s, she was beside herself thinking how special it must be to have a meal served to one in a restaurant. Up until then she had not been in a restaurant with either friends or family. The wide-eyed girl could hardly wait to hear what was ordered and how the service went. When her parents returned from the evening meal, she wanted all of the details. That her mother had ordered chicken fried steak was beyond belief. That someone brought it to your table was similarly unbelievable. The young curly and blonde-haired girl's definition of service and style at that time was stunted by family life that limited expectations.

Shirley clung to her dreams as she matured. She found herself wanting more elegance and fashion in her life. Yes, she was a home maker, but she could and did continue to dream the dream. She was a beautiful wife and mother, and she still turned heads, but it took our residency in London for her to find the service, elegance, and ceremony that were a part of her dreams.

And There We Were

As a middle-aged businessman I did not find the bastions of elegance to be a significant part of our stay in London. Indeed, it was only during our final week in the United Kingdom that I took the time to walk through Harrods, and that visit was to pick up a few items for myself (gifts to Chinese dignitaries) and few for Shirley. But for the Pearl, The Ritz, Claridge's, and Harrods always remained at the top of her list of favorite places.

Because our time spent at the Three Kings Yard apartment afforded us ready access to Claridge's, it was in this grand hotel that we first experienced the service and elegance characteristic of London's grand hotels. Earlier in this narrative I made mention of specific remarks attributed to Spencer Tracy and Michael Crichton, but any reader of novels and fiction set in London will find Claridge's mentioned over and over again. I suspect most well-heeled travelers place Claridge's high on their list of preferred places to stay whilst in London. Dwight Eisenhower stayed in the hotel while he was planning the invasion of Europe. His choice is not hard to fathom. There were a number of classy hotels proximal to his headquarters off Grosvenor Square, but none could hold a candle to Claridge's.

Shirley looked forward to the music coming from violins, the string orchestra, and the piano during her trips into London. I knew if she had come to the city, we would meet in the foyer at Claridge's after I finished my time at the office. We would have a leisurely drink before departing for dinner, the theater, or home.

Rarely did Shirley and I dine at the restaurant in Claridge's. We ate there when visiting corporate dignitaries were in town, or when there were industry functions during which corporate introductions of new Presidents, Vice-Presidents, etc. were made. Kerr-McGee introduced one of our Vice Presidents, David Kimes, via a dinner gathering at Claridge's. It was the venue of choice if you wanted to insure the attendance of industry movers and shakers, and if you wanted to impress your own corporate leaders, including a Chief Executive Officer (Kerr-McGee's Frank McPherson or Luke Corbett).

Shirley made Claridge's a must stop during her London activities. She never spent the night at the hotel, but she frequently met ladies there for High Tea, or for dinner prior to a ladies' night out at the Theater. She became so familiar to the staff that the hat clerks, the waiters, and the doorman knew her by name, and they were incredibly solicitous when it came to hailing a cab or storing her shopping packages. Sometimes she would come in from a trip down Bond Street, or an outing at Harrods, loaded down with shopping bags. The hat clerk would offer to hold her bags while Shirley continued on her way, either into the lobby for a libation or out for more shopping. One can be treated the "Claridge's Way" even if one does not stay there, but I doubt most people are aware of the special treatment that can be on offer.

 I find it interesting that many of the United Kingdom's royalty and members of high society choose to stay at Claridge's rather than at The Ritz. The reason sometimes offered is that The Ritz is palatial whilst Claridge's is rather more homey. Both hotels are elegant, but The Ritz is certainly more ornate and luxurious. It has been said that members of British high society reside in palaces and grand manor houses, so palatial is not all that impressive to them. I struggle with that assessment but there is a certain logic to it.

 The Queen Mother was a frequent diner at The Ritz, and she had a special table reserved for her proving that not all royalty preferred Claridge's to The Ritz. Of course, each hotel could no doubt offer up an incredible list of "Who's Who" patrons who have spent nights in their respective establishments. To counter Spencer Tracy's comment on life after death, "I'd rather go to Claridge's", one can get Jacqueline Kennedy Onassis' comment on The Ritz, "It is heaven." My read on the situation is that if one wanted to stay in wondrous hotel where you are pampered and remembered, Claridge's is the place. If you want to have a wonderful meal or high tea with an abundance of elegance, opulence, glamour, and style, you probably want to be at The Ritz.

 I enjoyed meeting Shirley at Claridge's following the completion of my workday. Somedays she would come to the office, and I would escort her to the hotel. As soon as she entered our office on the 2nd floor offices of the West One Shopping Center, high above the Bond Street Tube Station, I would usually hear one or another wag say, "Shirley is in the city, eh?" My colleagues came to recognize the scent of her perfume as it preceded her throughout the office.

On many occasions I simply joined her at Claridge's. When I walked up to her unnoticed, she invariably had a big smile on her face. Often, she was watching the musician, or musicians, or maybe even looking at the ornate decorations. I think it must make any man, and especially an expatriate, pleased to see his spouse so happy and full of life. Shirley's attire was characteristically impeccable – no pant suits or other casual attire like that which got Katherine Hepburn in hot water. Shirley invariably felt right at home at Claridge's, like she belonged there.

The Ritz may, or may not, afford one the rooms and ensuite service offered at Claridge's but it is certainly more special in one regard. The palatial setting and the impeccable service at The Ritz create an atmosphere that allows a commoner to feel like he or she is royalty. When one enters the Palm Court or The Ritz Restaurant (sometimes referred to as the Sanctuary), one immediately draws the attention of staff; each responding so as to make sure you are welcome and that you are aware your presence is of consequence. It does not matter who you are. The heads of staff members are always upturned and there are smiles for everyone.

Cesar Ritz, the namesake for the London Ritz, is responsible for the high level of service afforded at both the London and Paris Ritz Hotels. Cesar Ritz revolutionized dining in London, but this revolution did not start at The Ritz. Rather it began at the Savoy Hotel after Mr. Ritz was named hotel manager in 1889. The owner of the Savoy, built in 1884-89, hired Cesar Ritz following his meteoric rise through restaurant services in several famous European hotels. When Mr. Ritz began his career in restaurant services (1866 in Brieg, Switzerland) the apprentice wine-waiter was told by his supervisor that he did not have the special knack or flair for restaurant management and that he would likely be better served seeking employment in another field. That the Ritz name is now synonymous with elegance, luxury, and service (e.g., *putting on the Ritz, Ritzy,* etc.) tells of how far Cesar Ritz went in overachieving the expectations of his first supervisor.

In 1889 when Cesar Ritz became manager of the Savoy (and you may recall that it was at the Savoy where Shirley negotiated a day room rate prior to the Ainsley Harriott *Can't Cook, Won't Cook* dinner) the owner, D'Oyly Carte, expressed his desire to make the Savoy the "hotel deluxe" of London and of the world. One must realize that at this time in London it was not fashionable to be seen eating at a public restaurant and certainly not with your wife. Cesar Ritz changed all of that with service, elegance, style, and innovation in entertainment. He was known to bring Johann Strauss and his orchestra from Vienna so that his patrons could dine and dance to the Strauss waltzes. Bakers and chefs were brought over from the Continent; only the best of cuisine was on offer. It was not long before the restaurant clientele included not only the socially elite from the United Kingdom but also British and European Royalty.

Seven years after taking over the managerial position at the Savoy, Cesar Ritz's success, his unlimited energy, and his relentless quest for perfection resulted in a financial syndicate funding the first hotel to bear the Ritz name, The Paris Ritz. The Paris Ritz, opened in 1898, was the first "modern" hotel built in the City of Lights and was a huge financial success, so much so that the syndicate ownership wished to then build another hotel, this time in London.

Luxury hotels in London had proven to be a huge success and Cesar Ritz had already played a key role at both Claridge's and The Savoy. Ritz's role in building up cliental and patronage in the Savoy was mentioned previously, but probably less well known is the role Mr. Ritz played at Claridge's. The Hotel, on which construction began in 1894, was subsequently bought by the Savoy Company and Cesar Ritz helped organize the new staff whilst he was also managing the Savoy. Ritz knew who he wanted and what he wanted and that had been conveyed to the operational staff at Claridge's. With the success experienced at both the Savoy, and at Claridge's, the scene was set for a new grand hotel, the London Ritz.

Unfortunately, Cesar Ritz's contribution to the building of the London Ritz was limited to his choice of architect, the same one who had conceived of the elegant rooms and enclaves in the Paris Ritz. Mr. Ritz's health began deteriorating in 1902, and by the time the London Ritz opened in 1906 he was no longer a significant hands-on contributor to the operations, but his decision to employ the architects Charles Mewes and Arthur Davis ensured the elegance and glamour associated with the Ritz name endured.

Although Shirley and I infrequently dined at the Ritz Restaurant, it was the Palm Court that captured Shirley's heart and the bulk of her patronage. It is in this ornate side room where reservations for "Tea" can be made. There are five settings each day, and at 7:30 p.m. the day culminates with an "afternoon" Champagne Tea. The Tea does not come cheaply but the setting and the service make the outlay more than acceptable. To illustrate this claim, I offer a quote from the January 1980 Harpers & Queen written by Evelyn Grubb who describes the Ritz Tea experience far better than I could:

"Under the ornate gilt and glass ceiling in the pale pink and cream lounge, seated on comfortable pink velvet chairs and sofas and with gold cherubs looking on, tea at the Ritz is, thank goodness, still magical. The china is white and pale blue, pretty but surprisingly rather modern. Delicate fingers of white bread and butter are striped appropriately with pale pink ham, pale peach (the tint now given to the glass in the ceiling, incidentally) smoked salmon, cream cheese, pale green cucumber. Cakes are delectable: tiny éclairs, fresh fruit tarts, plain chocolate sauces and a huge central gateau with fresh strawberries, cream and the lightest sponge. The atmosphere is totally relaxed, conversation from the intriguing mixture of guests is quiet but not self-conscious and the service is immaculate."

I would only add that Ms. Grubb was somewhat amiss in not making reference to the two Ionic marble pillars that are the only barriers to the hotel central gallery (or walkway), and

A Few of Our Favorite Places

the "La Source" fountain, an extravagantly sculptured and ornate fountain with figures and ornaments gilded in gold. The cherubs Ms. Grubb alludes to are on the fountain but there is much more to the fountain than golden cherubs.

Shirley took advantage of every opportunity to be a part of the Ritz High Tea experience. If we had guests from the United States, or if there were dignitaries visiting on business, or even if it were just a bunch of the Berkshire-Surrey ladies out on the town, it was time for Tea at the Ritz.

When Shirley took several of her girlfriends from Prineville to dinner at The Ritz, they were impressed with the elegant ceiling featuring a Carolina Blue sky with clouds, the eight magnificent chandeliers, the ornate chairs, and the service. The girls were not impressed with the portions or the cost, one of which was minimal and the other maximal. The service was to the extreme, maybe even a bit over-the-top for the small-town ladies. I was once told by a fellow oil man that it would be impossible to drop a fork and have it hit the floor as there were always three servers/waiters near any table and one of them would surely catch it. Not accurate of course, but it drives home the point of attentiveness.

In the Ritz and at Claridge's Shirley found extraordinary elegance, sophistication, and style unlike anything she had previously experienced. Each time she entered either establishment she found the experience to be magical. It was a time of dreams coming true. Her face lit up when she described her experiences. The energy and passion she drew from such outings never failed to impress me. I could hardly wait to hear what had transpired, and I was never disappointed with the narrative.

Harrods is an interesting establishment to which reference was previously made of events occurring at the time of Princess Diana's death and also to the ladies' (Joey Baechle et.al.) meeting with Mohammed al Fayed in the Georgian Room. Shirley's animated discussions following her shopping forays were equally refreshing though she often never bought a thing. A spot of browsing and a nice luncheon in the Georgian Room were sufficient to fuel her enthusiasm and delight.

When I finally took time to walk through the multiple floors and departments at Harrods, I realized how unique the store was. In its own way opulence is found everywhere in Harrods. One must look beyond the conventional department store visage. I was stunned by the ornate paintings and murals I saw when I walked the stairways.

I dare say that nothing comes particularly cheap at Harrods but almost everything is of exceptional quality. When Shirley brought home a 350-pound picnic basket, and by that I mean a 350 pound sterling (about $530) basket I was beside myself. How could any picnic basket be worth that much money? Although it took nearly 6 years before we had our first picnic using the Harrods basket, the money turned out to be well spent. We once had a lovely Valentine's Day outing in Burroughs Park which is located near our home in The Woodlands, Texas. We drank champagne from crystal glass flutes and ate on fine China with elegant silverware; all on a fine tablecloth. We subsequently went on many picnics with friends and family. I loved to break out the Harrods finery. You just never know do you?

As I mentioned earlier, I probably would not have put The Ritz, Claridge's, and Harrods on my "favorite places" list but on Shirley's list they were all near the top and were most memorable. I think Shirley was meant from day one to skip along on a trail that became a path that took her from the grassy woodlands of Oregon to the most elegant surrounds in London.

THE THAMES

How can the Thames be on a list of favorite places? After all, it flows over 217 miles from its source to its emergence into the North Sea. And if you said it is not 217 miles in length, I would agree with you. Just why I am so malleable with regards to the length of the Thames will become apparent when the saga of our search for the source of the Thames has been told.

The Thames is magical. You cannot live in the London area or in the area between London and the Cotswolds without coming to love the Thames. The river is a shining thread that connects not only modern-day England but also the country's historical past to the present. For the most part, the river flows slowly through meadows, alongside villages and towns, and beneath vegetated bluffs. Because of the presence of numerous weirs (dams) there is little white water anywhere in the entire drainage.

The Thames is one of our favorite places because of the many memorable experiences had either on or adjacent to the river. Viewing the river in the meadows of the Cotswolds is no less impressive than watching it flow past the Oxo Tower in London. The Thames draws one to its banks and the urge to float on it is overwhelming; at least it was overwhelming to Bob and Shirley Lent.

Our introduction to the Thames came soon after our arrival when we were trying to learn more about the City of London. As we branched out from our apartment near the Italian Embassy, Shirley and I were looking for ways to jump-start our historical knowledge of the City. The impromptu City Walks we took were helpful and fun. Then someone suggested a river bus that took walk-up passengers from the dock near Charing Cross Tube Station and the Victorian Embankment downstream to Greenwich. We were told the captains on such vessels typically gave a running narrative of the historical and architectural points of interest along the length of the float, both coming and going.

When Shirley and I stopped by a dockside booth to buy our ticket for our first float we were amazed at the minimal cost, at the time about four and one-half pounds sterling ($6.75) for each round trip. The price of the trip then, and I think still is, one of the best buys for one of the more memorable experiences one can have in London.

We were not exactly sure where the boat would load so we went dockside early and waited in a rather long line. It was January and the temperature was in the low 50's. As we waited, I noticed a number of people ahead of us wearing fur coats. The coats were made of sable or mink, and the women looked simply grand.

After a short period of time the captain spoke through the loudspeaker. I looked at Shirley and asked, "What did he say?" I hadn't a clue. The guy had a cockney accent and the verbiage sounded like gibberish to me. Shirley was of no help, so I gently tapped the mink-draped shoulder of the lady in front of me. "Pardon me, Madame, but did you understand what that man just said?" She looked at me and said, "It's your language. You should understand it better than me. We are Russian." The reply not only explained the furs, it also gave us an idea of how attentive we would have to be when the captain spoke during the tour. We would not be getting any help from the Russians, Glasnost or not.

The ticket for the river bus ride from Charing Cross to Greenwich is good for the day so one can spend as much time as he or she wants in Greenwich or at the Tower of London, the two stops the river bus makes. If one wants to spend a couple of hours touring Greenwich and the Observatory, you are free to do so. Just catch a later boat for the return trip.

Shirley and I were stimulated by what we learned on that first trip down the river. The running narrative was captivating, even if we missed a word or two due to the accent. I cannot and should not detail each part of the narrative, but I will mention a few of the juicy tidbits, ones that I still remember as clearly as if the captain had just spoken. The first anecdote, and perhaps it is a bit frivolous, only means something to you if you have seen the movie *A Fish Named Wanda*. It was pointed out that the building on the right was where the stuttering fellow was held upside down out a window. Now when I see a rerun of *Wanda* I look at the scene and think to myself, "I know where that scene was filmed." Another of the Captain's memorable anecdotes described the construction of the wharves and the subsequent discovery of the mass graves where Londoners who fell ill and died from The Plague were unceremoniously dumped. I do not know if the last of these mass graves extends past Greenwich to the village of Gravesend, but I would not be surprised. The Captain made no mention of this, and it is left to the imagination whether or not the long line of wagons and carriages hauling stacked bodies ever made it as far as Gravesend. Gravesend is famous and historical for another reason. It was the port on the Thames where big ocean-going sailing vessels moored and transferred their cargo to smaller vessels.

When the river bus arrived at Greenwich, the Captain pointed out the Cutty Sark and the Gypsy Moth IV, both moored near the dock and available for viewing. I had always associated the name Cutty Sark with a brand of scotch. I was a bit surprised to learn that the name was originally given to the world's last tea clipper. Some say the ship is the most famous ship in the world. A bit strong and I can think of a few rivals to the claim: The Battleship Arizona, sunk in Pearl Harbor; the Bismarck, resting on the bottom of the Atlantic; and the Titanic, resting 12,000 feet down offshore Nova Scotia. At least the Cutty Sark is safely moored and can be visited for a fee and via a ramp.

I had heard of the Gypsy Moth IV but up close this 54-foot ketch looked fearfully small to have sailed around the world. Sir Francis Chichester did just that in 1966-67, aged sixty-five. The sailing ship can be viewed but one has to stay behind a white wire fence, so it is not possible to get up close and personal like one can with the Cutty Sark.

Before we departed the river bus, the captain suggested we might also want to walk the grounds at Greenwich Park, visit the Royal Observatory (and maybe step over the Prime Meridian, straddling both the eastern and western hemispheres), or tour the National Maritime Museum. Eventually we would visit all these Greenwich tourist sites but on our first trip down the river we limited our investigations to a quick visual examination of the Gypsy Moth IV and the Cutty Sark.

Shirley and I later returned to Greenwich many times, always via the river bus. We visited the Museum where we saw the Titanic Exhibit, and we took great delight in taking a slow tour of the Old Royal Observatory. Keeping with our developing love of quality pub food, we also found time to have Sunday brunch at several of the finer Greenwich public houses.

On the way back upstream we passed The Isle of Dogs, where one or more of the English kings once kept fox hounds.

Passing ships would invariably set the dogs to barking so it was not all that hard for the sailors to know where they were, even when it was dark and foggy. I think the keeper of the hounds must have wanted to send the mutts to obedience school. The incessant barking must have driven him crazy, what with all of the traffic coming up the river.

On the trip up the river the captain pointed out some of the famous riverside pubs such as the Grapes, the Prospect of Whitby, and the Mayflower. The Prospect of Whitby really caught our attention for it was along the stretch of the Thames near the "Prospect" that Captain Kidd had been executed (1701). The pub, originally built in 1520, and known then as The Devil's Tavern, was close to execution dock where a goodly number of pirates were hanged. Sometimes the bodies of these nefarious sailors were left for the incoming tide to wash over them, and sometimes the condemned were just chained alive to the shoreline and the tide was left to do the gruesome task. The anecdotes told by the river boat captain were captivating, even if not entirely true. That is what makes the river bus ride so interesting.

As we passed beneath the bridges, and there are six of them (e.g., Waterloo, London, Blackfriars, etc.), we got a running commentary either on the construction or on events relating to each bridge. We also learned where some of the good doctors in the 17th and 18th Century got fresh corpses, and where some of the ships bound for the Orient acquired their crews (as in Shanghaied). It was all good stuff.

When we passed the stone walkway that climbs from the Thames up to Saint Paul's the captain pointed out the stairway where Prince Charles and Diana made their way to the Cathedral prior to being married. In disgust, the captain remarked, "What a waste of time that was!"

We passed the battleship Belfast, now a museum and permanently moored in the Thames. We got a bit of history concerning the ship. Later during our stay in the United Kingdom, I read that a fox had been observed coming down the onramp and onto the Belfast. The ship's resident cat challenged the fox and chased it off the boat. This story interested me, and not just because of the sighting of a fox in downtown London. I had witnessed a similar encounter between a cat and a fox one night at our Ascot home, Muirfield. I was awakened by the sounds of a horrible fight taking place in our back garden. The encounter was obviously between two animals, and from the sound of it, there was a mortal battle underway. I awoke the following morning and was getting ready to go to work when I looked out the back window and saw a black object in our garden. I opened the library door and walked out on the lawn where I found a vixen (a large female fox with swollen teats) proximal to a cat carcass. I chased the fox away, and then took a closer look at what had been left behind. What I found was the partial remains (the hindquarters were missing) of our neighbor's cat, Fluffy. Clearly, the fox had won the battle. I did not want Shirley to see what had happened, so I tossed the carcass out behind a clump of rhododendrons.

That night the neighbors came over and asked if we had seen their cat who had gone missing. I did not have the heart to tell them of Fluffy's gruesome demise. I know I should have done so, but I just could not bear to have them view the remains of their beloved cat. I knew all the calls of "Here Fluffy, Fluffy" were not going to be of much help. When I read of the Belfast cat and how it had chased off a fox I was impressed - Tough cat!! In my opinion, predicting the winner of a fight between a fox and a cat is a toss-up. I felt bad for Fluffy.

Our first trip up and down the Thames on the river bus had been a hoot. We could not think of a better way to see London and be entertained while doing so. We made many repeat trips, and we were never disappointed with the experience. The trip is cheap, entertaining, and historic (with a bit of embellishment). Each captain has his version of the narration so repeat performances are often quite different. And you know what else? It is always peaceful floating down a river as scenic as The Thames.

Later we found another way to float The Thames in London. On Shirley's fiftieth birthday her mother, Marie, came over from the States to help her celebrate. Shirley's Aunt Mildred came too. You will remember Aunt Mildred as the relative who set in motion Shirley's desire for elegance and adventure. For this October 10th birthday we chose to celebrate with a dinner cruise down The Thames on the luxury restaurant cruiser, *Symphony*. This sleek and low draft vessel has panoramic windows, exterior floodlights, and offers luxurious dining and dancing. The music is live, and the service is impeccable. What I remember most about the evening is the sequence of photographs I saw when I looked at the prints a few days after the event. The first photos, taken shortly after we boarded the *Symphony*, had a relatively sedate and remarkably bright-eyed group of ladies being seated and looking out the windows. The pictures taken at the shank of the evening, after several bottles of wine, and a night of dancing, showed Marie and Aunt Mildred glassy eyed with flushed faces. The ladies had had a grand time. Indeed, after we had returned to Muirfield, Shirley walked into Marie's room and found Mildred and Marie sitting cross-legged on the bed, in their nightgowns, chatting like two schoolgirls. Sitting between them was a half-drained bottle of port that they had appropriated from the wine cellar.

The ladies of the AWBS also brought a group of its members and their spouses to London for an evening of dining on a London riverboat. The vessel was much larger than the *Symphony*, and the evening was made even more fun since the guests had boarded coaches in Surrey, and the partying began the minute we walked past the driver. On the evening of the AWBS event we sailed upstream a goodly number of miles, reversed course to cruise downstream to the Thames Barrier, a moveable flood control barrier designed to prevent flooding in London due to storm surges and exceptionally high tides. When the party ended, we were almost ready to start all over again.

One bright Saturday morning in the spring of 1997 Shirley and I were in the library looking out at the budding plants and the new leaves sprouting on the tall beech trees. It was a marvelous day (sunny skies but a bit chilly) and was want to happen on such days (remember our quixotic journey to Blenheim Palace) we pondered where we might travel to experience the grandeur of the day. I suggested that it might be a great day for us to motor into the Cotswold Hills to see if we could find the source of the Thames. We would not have thought of such a quest, but we had read where there was a point source for the Thames, and that revelation spurred our imagination and our interest. I had expected that the Thames formed like many other streams; a number of springs coming together to form a creek and those coalescing to become a river. But that is not what we learned from reading the literature. There appeared to be a singular place where the Thames gushed to life. The description of the source made it sound as if it were almost like a baby born with a full set of teeth.

    I pulled out a road map and estimated the source of the Thames, which was clearly marked on the map, to be no more than 85 miles from our home in Kier Park. And most of the journey could be taken via the A4, a major motorway. The destination village was Kemble in Gloucestershire. The source looked to be less than a mile north-northeast of Kemble, and not far removed from the A429. So we grabbed a few things, and I backed the Honda Legend out of the brick courtyard at Muirfield and we were on our way.

    We connected to the A4 in Reading and this highway took us through a number of interesting villages (e.g., Newbury, Hungerford, and Marlborough) and through the Hampshire, Marlborough, and Berkshire Downs (in England the Downs are Highlands – I never did figure that one out). At the small village of Calne we were hungry and looked for a pub where we might have a light lunch. We stopped at The Waggon and Horses Pub and popped in to see what was on offer. I am easy to please and when I saw the menu included lasagna, I was ready to plop myself down and, to use a word that my fellow Kerr-Mc-Gee workmates used, "Hoover" a plate of pasta. Shirley, as she always did, looked around and made the assessment that we could do better. No need to settle for something mundane when there was likely a much better pub up the road. I had been there, done that too many times to argue with the Pearl. She was usually right, but I never fail to be miffed. I was ready to eat and ready to eat now.

    At Calne, with the Waggon and Horses fading in the rear-view mirror, we turned onto the A3102 and headed north towards the Cotswold Hills. One small road turned into another and we motored on. We did not see any pub that in any way compared to the Calne pub. Finally, only four or five miles from our destination we drove by the Wild Duck Pub in Ewen. The parking lot was packed; the establishment appeared to be popular with the locals. Shirley had been right. This pub proved to be a much, much better place to eat than the one we had passed up about an hour earlier.

A pretty young lass in a ruffled white dress seated us by a window, but not before we had a peek at what those seated at the other tables were having. Everything on offer looked great. We ended up ordering baked chicken (Shirley) and bacon shank. The vegetables were cooked perfectly. The freshly-out-of-the oven breads placed before us in a woven basket were heavy and had a very pleasant yeast taste. We topped off our meal with a delicious wedge of whiskey-soaked sponge cake. I remember remarking that it was too bad this pub was so far from our home in Ascot. Otherwise, we would have been frequent patrons.

It was now mid-afternoon and before we could even get oriented, we found ourselves in Kemble. We crossed a bridge and observed an ornate sign upon which *Source of The Thames* had been burnt into a brown wooden plaque. A small yellow arrow pointed northwest into a broad meadow, in the midst of which ran the full-to-the-banks Thames River. The sign indicated that it was only 1 mile to the source. The signpost actually read "1 m" which, even in this metric nation, was certainly not one meter, so I took it to be one mile. But as I looked at the volume of flowing water I thought to myself, "No Way! There is just too much water for a river of this size to come from a point source less than one mile from where we were standing."

We crossed a walk-over fence and began our trek to the "source". The meadow we walked through is locally called Trewsbury Mead. As we walked along the path, I kept looking at the river; I am an avid fisherman and the water was so clear that I was sure I would be able to see fish if there were any present. I did not see a single fish, but I noticed something else that was rather unusual. The clear, fast-moving water was

A Few of Our Favorite Places

flowing over grass. How strange that was. Most river bottoms are covered with mud or with stones. The Thames river bottom at this locality was grass covered. We met a couple of ladies walking towards us and asked if the source was really only a half-mile (by then) up the trail. They assured us it was and that we would find it on the other side of a manmade stone embankment not far from where we were standing.

When the path made a slight turn to the right we saw a wooden fenced enclosure behind a stone weir three to four feet high. The weir had five four foot-square openings near its base, and it was through these openings that the river was rushing downstream. The stone weir ended abruptly on both sides of the stream. I could not see the utility of this structure which must have taken a considerable amount of effort and time to build. When we reached the point where our view allowed us to look beyond the weir, we saw a grove of trees and a half moon dirt embankment enclosed by a wooden fence. Above and

FIGURE 17. THE SOURCE OF THE THAMES
NEAR KEMBLE IN GLOUCESTERSHIRE

beyond the embankment there was no flowing water. Behind the weir was a circular pool of water and in its middle, flowing out from what looked like a stone-rimmed dark hole was an artesian spring, the source of the Thames. The volume of water flowing from the dark hole was impressive; it actually rose several inches above the pool before spreading out and reaching equilibrium. The embankment surrounding the upstream part of the pool was lined with numerous holes which I took to be rabbit warrens. I walked over to the warrens and looked downstream. The sun was shining brightly and there was silver sheen reflecting off the water as it began its trip down the 217 mile path that would eventually end in the North Sea. It truly was a wondrous moment for us.

As we walked back to the car, I told Shirley that we just had to return and bring our sons here someday. This place was too special not to share it with them. In August of 1997, we did just that.

Shirley and I were exuberant as we told Tobin and Taran about the source of the Thames. Both of the boys were visiting, and we were eager to show them something new that we had discovered. We were so exuberant that there was no way they could say they were not interested in making the trip. We further sweetened the pot when we offered as how they would have an incredible meal at the Flying Duck Pub, one of England's finest. That sealed the deal.

We drove to Ewen and sure enough, the meal was as promised. The boys had a pint of beer with their meal and they were feeling mighty fine when we climbed in the car for the short ride to The Thames. Everything was as I remembered it: the right turn at Kemble, the bridge, and the meadow. But after we crossed the bridge and parked the car behind some leafy green bushes, in my mind I began replaying what I had just seen. Something was terribly amiss. I blurted out my concern, and the family looked at me like I was a bit Looney Tunes.

I opened the car door and stood up so I could look into the meadow. There was no river, not even a small creek. There was no water what-so-ever! How could this be? And then my geologic training kicked in and I realized that the artesian source of the Thames must have ceased flowing when the water table dropped after a summer of little rain and hot weather.

I apologized to the boys, but since we were there, we were going to walk up the path to the Thames source anyway. When we got to the basin where the water had been flowing from a dark hole, we saw only a circular orifice, framed by a cemented ring of stones. There were several large stones in the well, and a rusting pipe that looked like it might be part of an iron grill. We could not see a drop of water even when we put our hands to the sides of our eyes and peered into the opening.

I took a picture of the boys with their mother, standing on the stone orifice. It remains a fine family memento, but I would still rather have been with the boys when water was flowing so that they could say, with conviction, "I have been to the source of the Thames." All we really have visible evidence of is the two boys and their mother huddled over what looks like an abandoned campfire site: certainly nothing to make future members of the Lent clan ooh and aah.

Subsequent to our walk in the meadow on that late summer day I read where the source of the Thames actually moves 5 or 6 miles, depending upon the level of the ground water. So, if you want to make the journey to the source, I would urge you to go in the spring when the rains have rejuvenated the water table. The Thames starts in the meadow outside of Kemble. If you want to make the full trek along the Thames Path, you probably ought to start at the circular urn, water or not.

When we left the Thames 'not flowing' through Trewsbury Mead we thought it might be fun to take the boys back to Ascot along a different route than the one already traveled. During our stay in England, we found that most villages and small cities usually have something that distinguishes them one from the other. Swindon, a rather large city (approximately 300,000 in the city and the surrounding communities) has several museums and points of interest. It also has a hospital, Princess Margaret Hospital, now demolished (and for good reason) where a patient once waited over 77 hours on a trolley, stuck outside of a toilet and forgotten. But I shall remember Swindon for something else entirely.

We had taken the A419 south from Cirencester and I thought it might give the boys something to break the monotony if I drove through Swindon rather than around it. I worked my way through a couple of broad streets and then I saw an unusual sign. It looked like a series of round-abouts with maybe 27 or so different exits. I thought this sign had to be someone's idea of a big joke. I had seen round-abouts back-to-back (called peanut round-abouts) and even a triple once, but I had never seen a signpost with a circular pattern within which were five other circulars. And then, suddenly, we entered a wide-open parkway which looked like an Italian piazza, with circulars everywhere. There are moguls on Rocky Mountain black ski runs that are less intimidating. My first reaction was that I should follow one of the round-abouts until I could find a way to negotiate my way across the open area. I knew where I wanted to go – straight across the piazza. In a moment of reckless abandon, I made the decision to ignore the roundabouts. The circular hubs were low, and I knew our car would clear them, no potted plants or impassable barriers as seen in most other round-abouts. So I turned and went straight across the open courtyard, straight to my exit, bumping over one round-about mound after another. The family was, of course, yelling that I could not and should not do that. But I saw very few cars, and I dare say the ones I did see were just as disoriented as was I, so I just put the pedal to the metal, and before one could say "Hold on" I had cleared the last of the bumps. Now that is what I will remember about Swindon. Forget the hapless chap on the gurney.

We also passed the village of Hungerford on the way home. I looked around as we drove through the village and I made a mental note that the central market area was quaint and that village might be an interesting place to live and work. But each little village has its dark past. Hungerford has been around for centuries, its place in history, however, was punctuated by a tragedy that occurred on August 19, 1987 when Robert Ryan, aged 27 and unemployed, began a shooting rampage that eventually left sixteen people dead, including his mother and himself. Just for good measure he killed the household pets and set fire to his home. Surrounded and under siege, Robert Ryan is reported to have said, "I wish I had stayed in bed". His use of weaponry, including an AK-47 rifle, led to the British Firearms Act (1988).

Many of our experiences on and around The Thames occurred close to our home in Ascot. It was so very easy to spend a special day or evening at what can only be called an idyllic setting. Mostly we tied a special event to a dining experience, and there are many opulent settings along the Thames. We tended to focus on those places in Windsor or upstream as far as Marlow.

One of the more unusual hotel and dining establishments is Oakley Court, only 3.5 miles up-river from Windsor. The grand mansion was originally built in 1859 by Sir Richard Hall in an effort to make his French bride feel more "at home". It must have been a heck of a home she came from. The mansion is situated on the banks of the River Thames on a stretch known as Water Oakley. The Victorian Gothic Mansion has magnificent gardens and, after a make-over, an opulent interior. It is no wonder that Shirley eventually found this place.

When we first visited the Mansion, we were struck by the number of gargoyles facing out into the courtyard. On close inspection these gargoyles are seemingly harmless bears and dogs. But when the sun goes down and the lighting dims, they become incredibly ominous. It is no wonder that the Oakley Court Mansion has been a favorite location for the filming of many Dracula and Frankenstein films. Scenes from the Rocky Horror Show were also filmed at this location. But for all of that, the place remains a wonderful setting for a special dinner or a Sunday brunch.

We spent two Christmas Eves dining at Oakley Court, each memorable in its own way. The first evening occurred after a day a cold front had passed through this part of England. First it had rained and then it had turned into a freezing rain. When the temperature dropped even further, the dense fog over the river began to freeze onto the limbs of the deciduous trees and frozen moisture covered the needles of the evergreens, almost as if they had been flocculated. When we took a post-dinner walk along the cement walkway that runs parallel to the Mansion's dock, we looked across a fog laden river onto trees with fluffy branches laden with hoarfrost. With illumination coming from artificial lighting it seemed like we were walking in a painting of a winter wonderland. It was a most unusual sight.

On another Christmas Eve we had a fine dinner, listened to carolers, and then walked out the front door where we were taken by horse and carriage to a local church for Christmas Eve Services. It was another cool evening, and we were draped in warm blankets. After the church service we returned to the hotel for a late evening snack. We left for Muirfield with our souls comforted and our tummies full.

Whenever we went to Oakley Court, either for lunch or dinner, we usually were seated at the best table in the main dining room. Similarly, if we chose to eat in the smaller restaurant that caters primarily to the boaters (those travelers who tie up at the dock and eat at the hotel) we would also most likely get the best table by the window. Why, you ask, did we get the "best" table? It was because for weeks before our reservation Shirley would stop by the dining room of choice and talk to the chefs, the servers, and the hotelier. Each would be impressed by Shirley's enthusiasm for the upcoming event and how much effort she was putting forth so that the luncheon or dinner was indeed "something special". Shirley made like efforts frequently, so it was not a ploy she used uniquely on the Oakley Court staff. When we arrived for any reservation, Shirley was recognized by many of the staff members. If I were hotel staff and I had a vivacious, outward going, and friendly lady making so much effort to ensure she might have a "special" evening I, too, would make sure she got what she wanted. Even if it meant bending the rules a bit.

On one bright Sunday day we had lunch at Oakley Court, then walked down to the dock and boarded an excursion boat that took many of the diners and guests down the Thames for a Sunday afternoon cruise. On this sunny day the boat ride was simply a perfect ending to a wonderful dining experience. Oakley Court has so much to offer, a visit to this unique facility is a *must do* for those wanting something out of the ordinary when they are out in the English countryside. But as Shirley did and does, plan your trip and make sure that you are on the grounds when something special is happening.

Monkey Island is less than a mile upstream from Oakley Court. Once in the small community of Bray, motorists can reach it via Old Mill Lane. One has to park and then access the Island and the hotel/restaurant by a walk over a white swinging bridge. There is a gate at both ends of the bridge, presumably there to keep varmints and foxes from having their way with Monkey Island's plethora of peacocks and rabbits that inhabit the beautiful and secluded riverside gardens. Some people access the grounds via a helicopter, but that seems to me to be a bit over-the-top.

Visitors come to Monkey Island to explore any number of different and, perhaps, individual preferences. My attraction to Monkey Island is two-fold. First the big glass windows in the Pavilion Restaurant offer scenic and panoramic views of the Thames as it flows around the upstream tip of the island. The second draw is the sitting room (also known as The Monkey Room) where at first glance, the ceiling has paintings of mundane human activities like fishing, hunting, and boating. When one looks closely, however, the figures are all monkeys, not humans. It keeps with the "Monkey Island" theme and that touch enhances the ambience. This small room with an ornate fireplace is a perfect setting in which to have pre-dinner and after-dinner drinks. Though some may come to the Island just to see the animals and birds, this was not a major plus for me although we did enjoy watching the male peacocks preen. Many of these big birds were seen roosting in the island's big trees.

It should not surprise you that the name of the Island was not always Monkey Island. The name came from an early order of monks who were given the fishing rights along this stretch of the river, including the island. Over time the Monk became Monkey and so it is Monkey Island.

And There We Were

We once took a group of oil industry associates on a dinner outing to Monkey Island Restaurant and, following dinner, we toured the island, watching the strutting, roosting, and omnipresent peacocks. I recall the ladies were all dressed in their finery and the walk was sufficiently interesting that we soon found ourselves treading on a sodden dirt path. The Thames was at its best that day and the scenery was so captivating that no one seemed to care, and we just walked on.

Waterside Inn is probably the most famous of the Bray riverside restaurants. The Waterside was opened in 1972 by Michel and Albert Roux, arguably England's finest chefs. The Waterside Inn located on Ferry Road in Bray, is immediately adjacent to the Thames. Indeed, the ducks, geese, and swans make daily trips up the sloped cement river landing in search of scraps from this Michelin Three Star restaurant.

The Waterside is a small restaurant and is the dining choice of many high spending customers from the Middle East, Europe, and America. But what makes the Restaurant special is that you can be Bob and Shirley Lent and still be not only made to feel welcome, but also given service and food that matches that presented to royalty. Such is the atmosphere and dedication to service for one and all.

One evening Shirley and I were seated at a Waterside river view window, watching the ducks and swans and having our drinks. Amidst a flourish of waiters and managers we noticed an elegantly attired gentleman of obvious Middle Eastern heritage who entered the dining area with a spectacularly beautiful young lady. The gentleman was obviously a high roller. He and his companion were immediately escorted to a small, secluded octagonal building attached to the restaurant and located on a rock sub-structure that extended a short distance into the Thames. Once the couple entered the enclosure, the curtains were drawn and we never saw them the rest of the evening. Their meal had obviously been prepared and served prior to their arrival, and the couple had only the river and each other to look at. The intimacy and the uniqueness were impressive, but, never-the-less, I felt like the prettiest lady in the restaurant that evening was dining with me. That being said, I knew I had witnessed a sterling example of what money can buy.

On April 21, 1996 Shirley and I read in the local newspaper that Queen Elizabeth, in residence at Windsor Castle, was going to celebrate her 70th birthday with a few friends at an "exclusive local restaurant". I remember saying to Shirley after reading the article, "You know, the only local place that would have the intimacy and the quality of food fit for the Queen and a few of her friends would be The Waterside Inn." I was convinced that the Waterside must be the restaurant of choice and looked forward to reading the papers the next morning to see if I was right.

I proved to be an astute visionary as the Waterside Inn was where the Royals had planned to celebrate. Unfortunately for the Queen, word had got out. The Waterside was surrounded by newspaper reporters, paparazzi, and a crowd of local well-wishers. When the Royal Family (sans Princess Diana and Sarah, Duchess of York who had not been invited) approached the Inn they saw the crowd and retreated to Windsor Castle. In the end, the most interesting aspect of the evening was the meal that had been prepared for the Queen was delivered to the Castle by the restaurant staff. In effect, the Queen had "takeaway" on her 70th birthday. On her 60th birthday she had been honored at a dinner with more than 1000 in attendance. Her Majesty may have been showing her age.

If you are ever in the vicinity of Bray, please visit one of the three riverside restaurants/inns that will leave you with a memory not to be forgotten. Oakley Court, Monkey Island, and The Waterside Inn are each worthy of a visit.

I will mention one more river restaurant experience before we conclude this section on the Thames. There are a number of other restaurants that merit attention: each left us with a number of memorable experiences, ranging from romantic to comedic. But Boulters Inn, upriver from Maidenhead and downriver from the cliffs at Cliveden has its own unique place in our memories of England.

By now you know that Shirley rarely goes anywhere without making sure the experience will be memorable. I was almost numbed to this fact and consequently did not pay much attention when, one Sunday morning as I sat in the family room by the fireplace reading the Sunday Times and listening to it rain, Shirley walked in and said, "Don't you think it would be fun to go up to that restaurant on the Thames where you can dine looking down onto an old mill run?" We had talked a bit about Boulters Inn previously and had agreed that we ought to eat there someday. We knew it was a popular place for Sunday mid-day meals (supper to some, luncheon to others) so I just snapped, "We can't get reservations at this late date." I was perfectly happy to have my coffee and read the paper. The thought of dressing and heading out on the English highways was not all that appealing to me. And to think we might be making a trip up to Maidenhead on the off chance that we could get in on a cancellation put a burr under my butt.

I am, however, a princely husband (maybe a bit overstated), so I agreed and headed up the stairs to take a shower and to dress. We got in the car and made good time as we traveled to Maidenhead. When we arrived at the Thames we turned onto a river frontage road that took us north to Boulters Island, and the Boulters Inn. We found a place to park our car in the crowded parking lot and walked into the reception room. When Shirley approached the hostess, the lady asked for her name. I knew then that we were dead-in-the-water. We did not have reservations. Or at least I thought that was the case. The hostess smiled, looked at Shirley, and said, "Oh yes, Mrs. Lent we have your table by the window." I should have known. We had the best table, with an unobstructed view of the mill run. The reservations had been made more than a week previously. Shirley had only waited until Sunday morning to tell me we were dining out.

During our stay in England, we went to many wonderful restaurants and we met a great number of exceptional staff. And Shirley never, ever, failed to make the experience special for me or for her/our friends. At some of our favorite places (e.g., Oakley Court), the staff came to know us, and as soon as we made reservations, we knew that we would have a great seating and we would be greeted like we were people other than who we were. As said previously I believe most individuals in the restaurant industry want to please people and they want to show off their professional skills, be they waiters, water boys, managers, or owners. Once they know you appreciate these skills, they seem to just go overboard making sure your dining experience is something to be remembered. Establishing this depth of rapport with the staff is not always easy, but it is a talent worth developing. Shirley had it pretty much mastered.

One example of Shirley's charm relates to a reservation we had made for us at a local Berkshire restaurant. We were living in China at the time and we had been called back to England for a special event. When a secretary at the Kerr-McGee London office called the restaurant to make reservations, the hostess immediately inquired, "Are these the American Lents?"

In late March of 1997, there was a strong atmospheric "high" located over England. Saturday had been a warm and sunny day, and Sunday promised to be even better. Shirley, ever the adventurer, suggested that we take a run over to Runnymede and have brunch at the Runnymede Hotel on the banks of the Thames. Little did we know that this simple decision would lead to one of our more interesting forays onto the River Thames.

The Runnymede Hotel and Spa is located along the banks of the Thames near the southeastern part of the Runnymede flood plain. The Runnymede meadows are associated with many historical events, the most significant of which was the signing of the Magna Carta on the Runnymede grasslands in 1215. The low-lying marshlands and meadows have been kept from residential development by the frequent inundation of water that comes when the Thames reaches flood stage. There are only a few such places along the Thames reach. They are nature's gift to us and to future generations, for along these infrequent strips of land we get a glimpse of the drainage system as it was prior to the arrival of humankind.

Runnymede is a great locality in which to learn something of English history and in which to take wonderful walks with interesting destinations. Shirley and I visited Runnymede many times, but even before our first visit to Runnymede Park, we had driven by the meadows and grasslands on our way to Heathrow Airport, or on our way to and from Windsor. We knew that history had been made at Runnymede, but we had not yet become familiar with the details. Once we visited this National Trust Park we fell in love with the site, and we subsequently took many of our American visitors for short walks along the numerous trails. On such occasions we would entertain them with historical anecdotes we had picked up during our earlier visits.

When King John signed the Magna Carta in 1215, he initiated the first democratic process for the English people, and especially, for the twenty-five barons who had pretty much backed King John up against the wall. The barons demanded and were granted a number of personal freedoms for the people, and democracy was born. Reading the Magna Carta document, one is struck by the range of rights granted, some quite profound (e.g., protection of personal property and the rule of law as it relates to an individual's rights) and some quite frivolous (e.g., standard measures of ale throughout the kingdom and the right of a widow to forego debts to certain groups of people). All in all, the document was incredibly beneficial to those long oppressed by royalty and aristocracy.

Several monuments on the Runnymede plain commemorate the signing of the Magna Carta, but the exact location where the document was signed is unknown. The location most visitors come to is the memorial to the Magna Carta that was built by the American Bar Association on an acre of land given to the Association by the Egham Urban District Council. This memorial and the surrounding land are located on a gentle slope immediately adjacent to, and west of, the Runnymede flood plain. The center of the small circular monument is comprised of a stone monolith inscribed *To Commemorate Magna Carta Symbol of Freedom Under Law.*

Not far from the Magna Carta Memorial is another memorial, also located on land donated by the English people. This memorial, to John F. Kennedy, on a three-acre plat of land amidst a copse of oaks and pines, was created after assassination of the president in 1963. The walk up the hill, via a number of shallow steps comprised of hand-hewn granite setts, After lunch we walked through the wedding party to the banks of the Thames and seated ourselves on a cement casement of stairs that permitted stadium seating for those wishing to watch boats traverse the Bell Weir Lock. It was warm, and it was most entertaining to see the wide variety of boats working their way up and downstream. Watching the boaters having so much fun made us want to take a float on the Thames. It was that kind of day; warm and balmy, and one of those days that makes you feel good. We thought about where we might catch a river boat and decided that our best bet was a few miles up the Thames at Datchet where a river bus was known take fee passengers on float trips.

When we arrived in Datchet, located a mile downstream from Windsor Castle, we found the float boat had already departed and would not be back until much later in the day. We were disappointed, but then I saw a large *Boat Rentals* sign. After a short discussion, I convinced Shirley that we ought to get a four-hour rental and tour the river on our own. As much as my sweet wife likes adventure, she was concerned that I lacked the ability to navigate a powered craft on a river. Neither of us had ever maneuvered a boat on open water. But, what the heck, it seemed like the thing to do. After all, I am an educated man.

We negotiated a rental for a small cruiser with the controls located in mid-section. This pristine white craft was big enough that we felt safe, but not so big that we could not maneuver it. When we pushed off, after getting instructions how to restart the engine in the event it failed, we began a slow powered downstream drift. We were amazed by the solitude and the presence of so many swans, geese, and ducks. The vegetation appeared to have overgrown onto the river, and on the Windsor side of the drift we did not see a single home. We opted to drift along the vegetated side of the river. I kept commenting that we were certainly lucky that there were so few boats on the river. No need to be concerned that we were breaking boating etiquette or that we were in danger of being rammed by or ramming another boater. Life was good.

And There We Were

Before we rounded a bend in the river, we had made the decision that we probably had sufficient time to float all the way downstream to the Runnymede Hotel and to the Bell Weir lock. We should have known that with there being 45 locks on the river that we would need to traverse at least one lock before making the drift through Runnymede Park.

As we made the turn in the river, we saw a weir and a lock, but there appeared to be very few boats waiting to go through the lock. We felt good about ourselves and our chances of negotiating the lock. But I have to tell you, when we finally arrived at the lock, we found a wide assortment of craft already in the holding waters. There were cruisers, long boats, barges, mini-cruisers etc. It was just awful! I had to make sure that I entered at the right speed as I did not want to ram the big cruiser in front of us. So I throttled forward and back like I knew what I was doing. When we finally reached the side of the lock and had come to a stop, I asked Shirley if she would climb over the front of the boat and get the rope tether and secure us to the bollard, not that I actually knew what a bollard was. I just asked her to secure the rope to the t-shaped iron post. She looked at me like I was crazy, but she climbed over the glass window and onto the bow. When the rope was pulled tight, she threw it around the bollard, and tied the rope in a knot. We were not going anywhere. The sweet thing looked at me and slapped her hands together: job well done. And just about then, the water began to drop.

When we began to tilt to the left there was all kinds of commotion above us. The lock master (lock keeper if you will) and the captain of the cruiser came running over to our bollard and yelling that we had to let the rope slip through the bollard as the water dropped, otherwise we would be left hanging from the rope. We never had a chance to untie the knot; the lock master had it done before we could respond. When he found out that we were Americans and that this was our first time on the river, he became a bit more understanding. After he talked to my pretty wife, he became even more solicitous regarding our trip downstream, and especially our return trip back through the lock. He was going off duty in ten minutes and he told us we would have to operate the lock by ourselves on our return trip.

We motored downstream a few hundred yards below the lock and made the prudent decision to turn around, foregoing a drift through Runnymede. We did not wish to have to man the lock apparatus by ourselves. Old Windsor Lock, the name given this particular lock, is operated by a hydraulic system, and power is made available for public use after the lock master goes home, but one still has to make a few critical decisions, least of which is to make sure that the gate is not closed while there are boats still in the queue waiting to come downstream.

We turned around and went right back up to the lock where the lock master came to our craft and said he thought we had made a good decision. He was concerned that we might be disappointed by our abbreviated day on the river so he gave us a few tips as to how we might get the most out of our trip back upstream. He suggested that when we came to the first island, we would see a big sign that said, *Kept Left - Extreme Danger to the Right*. He told us, "Go Right." That will take you along a quiet arm of the Thames and alongside of the back gardens of Eton College. He also said that from this location one would have an incredible view of Windsor Castle which commands the heights.

When I queried him about the *Extreme Danger* sign he said, "As long as you do not go beyond the large white house on the right, you will not be in danger. Beyond that point you will run aground on a dangerous and shallow rock pile." So, I thought to myself, "Go right, turn around at the white house." I got it!

When we came to the island, I saw the signs and with more than a bit of trepidation, I steered into the waterway on the right. What was interesting was that there is a walkway along this quiet section of the river and there were many individuals out for a walk on this most pleasant of days. Whenever I looked shoreward, I saw people looking at me and giving me that, "Didn't he see the sign?" look.

When we arrived at the shoreline adjacent to Eton College I glanced up and looked across the river to Windsor Castle on the high bluff. The view was simply magnificent. We had previously enjoyed many spectacular vistas of Windsor Castle, often during our many walks through Eton. But the view from our boat at river level, looking across an island covered by trees, made the scene most medieval. Without the presence of buildings, roads, and streetlights we could have been looking at a view seen by peasants and barons some three or four hundred years ago.

The back gardens at Eton were memorable to me but to Shirley they were even more so. Each year on the Fourth of June, Etonians celebrate George III's birthday (you will remember King George as the guy who lost the colonies) with a celebration attended by the Queen and the parents of the Eton College students. It happened that the Fourth of June Celebration in 1996 was held on May 29th so go figure. Shirley called Eton College to inquire as to how one gained admission to the celebration. The lady at the College assumed that Shirley must be a parent of one of their students, so she told Shirley how to negotiate the campus to the riverside gardens.

The Fourth of June Celebration is one of the most colorful and pageantry-filled events that occur on the Thames. The Eton boys, dressed in coattails and colorful hats, float their dragon boats past the Queen and once in front of her, each doffs his hat (filled with rose petals) as his name is called out. On that May day in 1996 Shirley was only a few yards from the Queen and from her perspective she could see each of the boaters and also many of the parents who were in attendance. The most famous of these parents were, of course, Prince Charles and Princess Diana, who were there for their son William.

The front pages of the London newspapers covered the Fourth of June Celebration and the following day they made a big 'to do' about the fact that the estranged couple stood by each other, and that Princess Di gave Charles a kiss on the cheek when she left. It is just as well that a photograph was not taken of that kiss, for in it we would have certainly seen Shirley, the interloper. She was that proximal to the royals.

The Fourth of June Celebration that Shirley attended made history. When the last boat load of boys passed before the

Queen, one of the lads stood as he prepared to doff his hat. When he rose he lost his balance and the dragon boat capsized. It was reported in the paper that in the nearly 300 years of the celebration only one other boat had capsized.

We motored slowly past the Eton gardens, and we saw the great and dreaded white house ahead of us. I turned around and we began our downstream trek to the dock. After the entrance into the bay had been successfully negotiated and the boat had been tied to the dock, we looked back on the Thames and agreed that we had experienced one of our more memorable days in England.

I mentioned previously that the Thames has a reach of 217 miles, plus or minus. The river begins in the Cotswolds highlands and it ends when it flows into the North Sea in the Thames Estuary. There is a pathway along the entire length of the river, and one could, if he or she chooses, walk the entire distance. Some of Shirley's friends in the American Women of Berkshire Surrey (AWBS) set out to do just that. I do not know of any who completed the entire walk, but I am sure that a number of the adventurous American ladies saw the journey to its end. Most try to do it in segments, eight or nine miles at a time.

For those that want to take shorter walks along a segment of the Thames and to follow those walks with a pint of ale and lunch or dinner, there are a number of books to help you find your way. In January of 1996 we purchased a book written by Liz Roberts: *Pub Walks in The Thames Valley*. Robert's book details forty circular walks that can be taken adjacent to the Thames. Each walk, 1 ½ to 7 miles in length, starts and ends at a country pub. Detailed maps accompany the narration of each walk and a detailed history of the pub, the type and quality of the food on offer, and the selection of beers at the tap are also made available to inquiring minds.

Shirley and I took many walks along the river, most of the time we were looking for something unusual. Like the upper limit of tidewater (at Teddington), the oldest bridge over the Thames (near The Swan Hotel in Radcot), and the source of the Thames (Kemble of course) just to name a few.

One day shortly after we had purchased Liz Roberts' book, we decided to have a Sunday brunch in Medmenham at the Dog and Badger Pub and, depending on how we felt after the repast, take one of the Roberts' walks. The food on offer looked interesting and the place was supposedly where the noted (not known to us but never-the-less noted) Satanist, Sir Francis Dashwood came to drink after his Hell-fire club meetings. We found ourselves seated at a table by the window and near us were two Brits who were having a quiet discussion. I noticed that they were looking around like maybe they were not locals. I was more than surprised when the lady reached into her purse and pulled out a copy of *Pub Walks in The Thames Valley*. They were reading Liz Roberts' book! Upon engaging them in a conversation, we found they were checking off the various pubs as they completed each walk. We had come across the ocean to do the pub walk; they had come out from London. It is a small world isn't it?

A visitor to England has to be selective in choosing to visit a famous landmark or to observe a renowned event. Time usually does not allow the casual visitor to sample what an in-residence foreigner has at his or her fingertips. But no matter what the time frame, a visitor to England will be captivated by the Thames. The problem is, of course, what to do first. This brings us back to the Thames River buses. There is always time for a ride down to Greenwich and back to Charing Cross. The buses are the best way to get an incipient feel for what is a most grand and mystical of rivers.

The Tower of London

When friends ask us what one should do when traveling to London for the first time, our first suggestion is always, "take the river bus ride." But the second suggestion we make is, "take the Beefeater's Tour of The Tower of London." The river ride will offer the visitor a sense of history, the spatial setting of the city, and a view of famous London landmarks. The Tower of London tour is a history lesson, with elements of horror sprinkled liberally throughout. In a sense the Tower represents the dark side of London, the one many of us think of when we recall the fog and smog filled scenes from any number of macabre motion pictures or narratives in novels.

Tower Hill and its role in English history are riveting. But if one were to just purchase a ticket and tour the Tower of London grounds, I would think it would be a rather mundane part of one's stay in London. However, when you follow the Beefeater guide on a tour the history lesson becomes spell binding. There may be a Beefeater, they prefer the moniker Yeoman Warder, who does not give a captivating performance, but I doubt it very much. We took the Beefeater tour of the Tower many times, and on each occasion we were spell bound by what was said, even though we had heard it all before.

The first glimpse I had of the royal palace and fortress that comprise the Tower of London was following a business dinner during the first trip I took to London with my then boss Michael Webb. When Kenneth Crouch, the then Managing Director of Kerr-McGee, U.K. hailed a taxi to take us back to the Britannia Hotel, he had a side conversation with the driver. Instead of heading west (upstream along the Thames) the cab turned onto Embankment and went east (downstream). The road changed names several times, most noticeably from Embankment and then to Upper and then Lower Thames Street. As we were driven along the north shore of the river, we had an impressive view of the Thames. We came up on a small rise, and to our right, was an incredible complex of buildings. I had no idea what we were looking at. It was a fortress with massive rock walls forming a perimeter, and within the walls were massive stone buildings; one building seemed to be more than 10 stories in heigh, with four impressive battlements rising above each of the four corners. The wall and buildings were illuminated with flood lights. I had never seen anything so stunning. Not wanting to seem ignorant, I did not ask the question that anyone else equally as uninformed as myself would likely have asked,

"What is this incredible complex?" The view and the structures were so magnificent I felt, at the time, my question would have been comparable to someone in Washington D.C. looking at the White House and asking, "What's that building?" It was only later that I put it all together. The magnificent sight I had seen was the Tower of London.

The Tower of London is located upstream a short distance from Tower Bridge in an area that was originally near the southeastern corner of the walled Roman city that later expanded to become modern London. Constructed over a period from 1066 to 1285 the Tower of London has served as a royal residence (palace), an arsenal, a treasury, and a state prison; not necessarily all at the same time. It also was and is currently the home of the Crown Jewels. Tower Green located within the Tower of London grounds, and the nearby Tower Hill, located outside of the stone perimeter, have served as primary places of execution – executions typically done with an axe at the neck.

When Shirley and I took our first tour of The Tower of London, we entered thinking that this impressive collection of stone buildings and battlements was likely just like many other ancient artifacts of a civilization that flourished during medieval times. Were we ever in for a big surprise!

When the White Tower became a royal residence, beginning in the 10th Century, things were quite benign; the dark side was still to be revealed. William Duke of Normandy gets credit for having the vision to build what became The Tower of London. Approximately 10 years following William's coronation in 1066 the White Tower was ready for habitation as a royal residence. The Tower is 90 feet in height and has a base that is 118 feet by 107 feet. But the most impressive statistic is that the stone walls are 15 feet thick. The Beefeaters are ready, of course, to tell you how the lower rooms that served as a dungeon made use of this extraordinary measure of rock.

During the first five hundred years there were events that made footnotes in history, but it was left up to Henry VIII and his immediate descendants to transform the arsenal, palace, and treasury into something much more sinister. To be sure, there were the occasional executions, even murders, during the first half-millennium. The most chilling murder, maybe it should be an alleged murder, is told in the tale of two princes who disappeared once they entered Tower Hill. The elder of the two princes was Edward, the son of King Edward IV. Obviously, Edward the younger was in line to become King Edward V. Unfortunately, King Edward IV requested his brother keep the two princes in the White Tower for safety following his death. When the king died, the princes could not be found, and the king's brother and the boys' uncle, Richard, became King Richard III. The disappearance of the young princes was certainly one of convenience for Richard. During an excavation in 1674 a trunk with two skeletons of children was found near the White Tower. When Victorian painter John Millais captured the princes on canvas as they apparently awaited their fate, the macabre tale was visually burned into the annals of history.

Henry VIII changed forever the way history would perceive The Tower of London. It was during Henry's reign that the Tower became the official state prison. Henry VIII had need for such a facility. Firstly, he did away with the Catholic Church in England and replaced it with the Church of England with the royal monarch as head of the church. That meant that there were a great number of potential prisoners and a considerable number who would be beheaded. If you wanted to remain a Catholic and to protest the new Church of England, you stood a good chance of losing your head. Among the well-known prisoners who found their way to the Tower gallows were Thomas More and John Fisher, but many other less well-known dissenters found themselves traveling through Traitor's Gate via what the Beefeaters call London's first one-way street.

Henry VIII made the biggest waves when he had two of his wives beheaded at the Tower Green. Anne Boleyn whose courtship and marriage triggered Henry into doing away with the Catholic Church was arguably the most famous of those who lost their heads either at Tower Hill or Tower Green (the place of execution within the walls of the Tower of London). Not only was Anne Boleyn a passive player in the overhaul of the church, she also gave birth to the future Elizabeth I who later became one of the great monarchs in English history. Anne Boleyn's tragic end put a flourishing touch to the drama and horror that would forever be associated with the Tower of London.

Actually, Anne Boleyn is only one of three queens that were beheaded on Tower Green. The other two were Catherine Howard (Henry VIII's fifth wife) and Lady Jane Grey also known as the Nine Days Queen. After Henry's death, Lady Jane was brought to Tower Hill to await her coronation (a tradition for many centuries) but she ended up losing her crown (to her half-sister, Queen Mary I) and her head.

Anne Boleyn's daughter Elizabeth (the future Queen Elizabeth I) spent two months in confinement at The Tower of London as she was being investigated in plots against Queen Mary I, the successor to Henry VIII. Although she was later freed, it must have been a terrifying experience staying in the Queen's House facing Tower Green, the site where her mother met her fate not so long ago, and all the while wondering if that was to be her fate too.

The Beefeaters have it all down pat and just who was killed and when it happened is great stuff for the telling of stories. I will leave the last of the Beefeater anecdotes to those who take the tour, for if you do you will end up in the Chapel of St. Peter and Vincula and the tale told there will send chills running up and down your spine.

There are a few additional comments I would like to make before we abandoned this discourse on London's most famous place of execution. Not all recollections involving The Tower are macabre. Some are tragically funny. Like, for example, the various prisoners who tried to emulate earlier successful escapes, escapes made by tying sheets together and dropping them out of high-rise cells. Needless to say, some people are good at tying knots and some are not. At least one of them fell to his death when his sheets became untied.

And even though The Tower of London is a most formidable structure, many of the defenders who manned the bastions lacked fortitude. Twice during the Tower's history defenders just gave up without a fight. The first time this happened was during the Peasant's Revolt of 1381, and the second time was in 1460 during the War of the Roses when the defending garrison opted to surrender rather than fight for a lost cause. When we lived in China I was awestruck by the Great Wall. Then I learned that this monumental feat of construction was rarely effective when encroaching armies wanted to breach the barrier. The Chinese defenders in selected outposts were invariably seduced with liquor and women, and the gates in the valley bottom were opened from within as the armies advanced. I think barriers to intrusion are only effective if the construction is formidable and the defenders have fortitude. One without the other seems not to have worked if we use history as an indicator.

Ancient combat armor is on display in the Royal Armory. I found it very amusing that the armor made for King Henry III had a metal protector built around the family jewels. The armor built for others appeared to be lacking this additional point of protection. What with all the ladies King Henry served I guess it is only logical that he would want to protect his manhood. No one was going to injure the King with an up-thrust of the attacker's sword.

If, after one has visited the Tower of London and he or she would like a bit more of the horror that was London in the days of yore, drop by the London Dungeons, a tourist locality on the south side of the Thames where all means of torture and execution are on display, along with wax figures that portray the hapless victims.

The English Public Houses

A discussion of our favorite places would not be complete if I did not include a segment on the public houses, or pubs. Life in England in a sense is pub oriented. The culture lends itself to such. Young lads and lassies can drink at 18 and many probably drink in pubs before that age. And why not? Their parents have most likely brought them to a pub for dinner or Sunday brunch since they were wee ones. In most small communities the public houses have a drinking area and a dining area. And on the grounds of the pub there is often an open space for children to play. This arrangement is not always the case, but it is usually so.

A typical British pub, be it in London or in a smaller city or village, does not make our list of favorite places. There are many pubs that serve mediocre food and do not distinguish themselves as being "fun" places to spend time. There are a number of pubs that could make a list of our favorite places but many of them, even though they served great food and were fun places to visit were too far removed from our home base (e.g., The Flying Duck Pub in Ewen) to be on the short list that merit inclusion in our favorite places list. There are four pubs that were amongst our favorite haunts; where we could go for excellent food, a pint of beer or a glass of quality wine, and friendly repartee.

Three of the pubs were owned by two gentlemen, Bobby King and Jon Mee. King and Mee were hands-on owners and they made sure when you walked in the door you felt like one of the "locals" even when everyone knew you were from the "States", or from some other foreign country. The Fox and Hounds on Bishopsgate Road in Englefield Green, The Thatched Tavern on Cheapside Road in Ascot, and The Cottage on Winkfield Street in Maidens Green (Winkfield) are three of the finest pubs in all of England (my opinion). In the United States these would be considered outstanding local restaurants with a bar. Food and drink are great attractions in each, but even more compelling is the ambience that comes with each establishment.

The fourth pub on our list of favorite places is The Winkfield off the A330 in the village of Winkfield. The food in the restaurant at The Winkfield did not measure up to that in the three pubs previously mentioned, but The Winkfield was an exceptionally fun place to eat and to celebrate special occasions. The owner, Mike Hawksworth, had an unusual flair for hosting great semi-private celebrations for his favorite patrons: more about this establishment later.

A Few of Our Favorite Places

Reference to The Thatched Tavern and to the Fox and Hounds was made earlier in the text. As a matter of fact, the first really good pub meal Shirley and I ate whilst in England was at The Thatched Tavern. This was at the time we were exploring the countryside searching for a home. We knew after that first meal, and we ended up living anywhere near this pub, we would be frequent diners at the establishment. The food was outstanding, and the ambience was spot on. We felt the same way when we ate our first meal at the Fox and Hounds.

The Thatched Tavern is housed in a very old building (constructed in the late 1600's if not earlier). When you walk in the door you are taken by how quaint it is. The ceilings are beamed and hang very low. This was great when the populace was mostly 5'6" or so but for the modern populace you best heed the sign *Duck or Grouse*. The bar is on the left as you enter. Wooden bar tables are located to the right in front of a stone fireplace. The modern facilities are in the dining areas where the ceilings are higher and the tables covered with red and white checkered table clothes.

The host, usually it was Bobby, was friendly as was the bartender and the waitresses. Heck, even the cooks were friendly, and you could see them through the opening in the wall that served as the dispensing area. Most of the patrons were equally friendly although there were, on occasion, wealthy (and stuffy) patrons who came only for the food and who were not at all interested in having "loud" Americans seated near them.

Whenever we visited The Thatched Tavern we usually sat by the fireplace, had a pint or two, and then were seated for what was always a great meal. The half shoulder of lamb or a lamb joint was invariably the favorite of our sons (who were then in their mid-twenties). Salmon, beef, chicken, and wild game dishes were tastefully prepared, and the meals came with mixed vegetables (new potatoes, carrots, broccoli, and onions) that were invariably cooked to perfection. No matter who we brought to the Tavern they never left without thinking the food and the experience was something to be remembered.

We had many visitors whilst we lived in Ascot. And whether

these visitors were business associates, family, life-long friends, acquaintances, friends of friends, even sons or daughters of friends, we without exception took these guests for a meal at the Thatched Tavern, The Cottage, or The Fox and Hounds. Guests always raved about their experience. Not once was anyone ever disappointed.

Our elder son, Tobin, who lived with us for a period of 9 months whilst we were in the United Kingdom, had many memorable experiences at the Tavern. Sometimes we were not even aware of how much time he spent at the pub. But when we walked in with one or more of his friends who were visiting from the States, we sometimes were surprised how well Tobin knew the staff. When he introduced Bobby, Jon, or the hostess we only smiled but when he said that he would like the guys to meet Flower (only one of many), the cute bartender, we were sometimes taken aback, as we were not that familiar with the hotties.

On the night when Tobin took Tanya and Sanya (the Sri Lankan beauties) out for the evening he took them to The Thatched Tavern. This was the place, mentioned previously, where he had walked in and subsequently realized that he had never before been in a place where all eyes turned and focused solely on the women he was with.

One cold December Shirley and I made evening reservations at the Tavern. When we arrived, we found 10 to 12 rowdies still drinking after having had a Christmas office party luncheon. Space was limited in the bar area, so the group kindly invited us to sit and join them in celebrating the holiday season. This we did. I think the invite is typical of friendly gestures that can be expected in many country pubs. But it is hard to play catch-up with a group that has been pounding pints since noon. We soon bid them adieu and took our pints to the dining area. The lesson we took from this encounter is: when you are imbibing at a pub it is best you be at the same stupor level as your table mates.

One evening my boss from the United States and several business associates were having dinner with Tobin and me at the Thatched Tavern. Tobin freshly back from an extended stay in Vietnam, looked around at the hostesses and the cute barmaid and said, "It is great to be back in a country where women have breasts." I am glad to say that my boss, Michael Webb, thought the statement was humorous enough that he coughed out his salmon. It could have gone either way.

We found The Cottage when Jon, one of the owners, told us that he and Bobby owned not only the Thatched Tavern but also The Cottage. We had to try it out to see if it was as good as the other two places. It was.

The Cottage is not only a pub and restaurant it is has rooms to let. The grounds are small but well-kept with flowering plants that bloom most of the year. The parking lot, at least whilst we were in England, consisted of pea-size gravel. Parking space is limited. Indeed, one food critic who was having a difficult time finding a place to park was asked by a party just arriving in their car, "How's the food at this place?" The critic responded, "If I can find a place to park, I will let you know!"

Parking spots, by the way, are also limited at the Thatched Tavern where many cars pull in and park one behind the other. When a party wishes to leave, someone must ask the diners and/or drinkers to move their car. We found early on that the best place to park when we went to the Thatched Tavern was on the shoulder of the very narrow Cheapside road. This basically made the road a one lane street: it was necessary to look down the road for oncoming traffic before proceeding through the narrow passage. Fortunately, all the locals knew the situation so there was rarely a problem. First time visitors were often annoyed but they, as we did, soon learned how to play the game.

The Cottage parking was more expansive but finding a place was still a challenging. The parking lot at the Fox and Hounds was also limited, but proximity to a large parking area for visitors to Windsor Great Park, a few tens of yards past the pub, provided a convenient solution.

One of the vagaries of living in England is that adequate parking is not a given, not only for popular pubs but also for grocery stores, high street shops, and village malls. What complicated matters for folks like Shirley and me is that we tended to lease vehicles larger than those driven by the typical

Englishman, so the available parking spaces are not only limited but they also very narrow. Some people were known to step out and fold back their side mirrors just so they could fit into a parking spot. I never saw the logic in that method: even if I found myself in such a narrow spot, I would never be able to work my way out of the car. When we finally returned to the United States, one of my great joys was parking my normal size vehicle (large by British standards) in parking lots with abundant extra-wide spaces. I had plenty of room to exit and enter my vehicle. Boston might be an exception to that rule in the United States, but then most of downtown Boston was built at a time when the Brits controlled the colonies.

Back to the Cottage. One of the things Shirley and I liked about the Cottage was that when you entered the pub (off of which is the restaurant), you were immediately taken by the chatter and relaxed atmosphere. There was usually standing room only in the bar area, but sometimes we could work our way to one of the few bar stools. The British would rather stand than sit at a pub. Although I stood more times than I ever sat, I still liked to sit and observe the patrons whilst sipping my pint.

As a result of always wanting to sit at the bar, we became close friends with the barmaids, especially one tall blonde who was not only attractive but also quite witty. When she saw us come in, especially with either Tobin or Taran in tow, she knew she would be making multiple and time-consuming Bloody Marys. At the Cottage this drink was made from scratch; no pre-mixes here. And they were made one or two at a time. Those wanting a draught had to wait while the Bloody Mary drinks were prepared. And as soon as our order was filled, it seemed we were ready for another. It is entirely possible that the logistic bottleneck has been overcome with the use of mixes, but I hope not.

The menu for the Cottage had entries from many countries but our favorites were always the English entries, especially the lamb and beef dishes. I once passed on the sirloin tips, the shoulder of lamb, boiled gammon with crispy crackling, and the baked plaice so I could sample the steak and kidney pudding. I found the kidney pudding to be about as disappointing as Yorkshire pudding. But I did relish the other fixed dishes, and the many other entries that drifted in and out of the menu. The Cottage served one dessert we always looked for, but it was infrequently on the menu. This dessert was a chocolate tart served with an unbelievably rich and tasty chocolate sauce. In our travels we have only on one or two occasions found a chocolate sauce that is so similarly delicious. Speaking of rarities, one "soup of the day" was a tomato soup served on one Sunday, and one Sunday only, while we were patrons. I reluctantly ordered it, and it turned out to be the best tomato soup I have ever been served in a restaurant. That soup never made it back on the menu and to this day I cannot imagine why. It was so good that maybe there was something illegal in it. Of course, I know that is not true.

One Sunday we were at the Cottage when Bobby told us Tom Cruise and Nicole Kidman had shown up at the Fox and Hounds. Shirley was ready to cancel her salmon order and head for the Bishops Gate establishment, but common sense prevailed. The British patrons at the Fox and Hounds surely accepted the movie stars as just any other guests. Any Americans who were at the Fox and Hounds probably made a mess of the matter.

The rich and famous, and the not so famous (like Bob and Shirley), flock to the Cottage, the Thatched Tavern, and the Fox and Hounds for their famed high-quality food, first class service, relaxed atmosphere, and, especially to foreigners, their unique and wonderful ambience.

After we moved to China, and on to subsequent postings, we always visited one of these fine pubs whenever we returned to England. Indeed, the last time we were in England we visited old friends at two of the pubs. In each case the local management refused to let us purchase a pint of beer. It was nice to be remembered even after years had passed.

The Winkfield, the fourth of our most favorite public houses, is in a class of its own but it is not because of the quality of the food. We found the food to be good, but it sometimes it was hit or miss when it came to variety and to overall quality.

What made The Winkfield so special was the proprietor Mike Hawksworth and his fun approach to pub life. Mike, his wife, and young daughter lived above The Winkfield. When a special evening was planned, it was as if Mike and his wife were hosting a private party in their home.

The first unusually fun evening we had at the Winkfield occurred on New Year's Eve in 1996. We had been frequent patrons at the Winkfield and had become friends with several other couples who were close to Mike. On one Sunday late in November, Shirley and I were having Sunday brunch. Mike asked if we would accept an invitation to celebrate the New Year at the Winkfield. The only caveat was that if we accepted, we should know that it was to be a black-tie affair. Oh boy!

Because the boys would be home for the holidays, we accepted the invitation. We realized that it might be fun, or maybe not, but at least the Winkfield was reasonably close to home and we would not have to hire a driver. If we had any reservations about having fun, we should not have. The entire family had so much fun that we hoped Mike would have a repeat party the following year (which he did).

I found a tuxedo rental in the City (London) and was measured. That was all well and fine, but I found I had two problems come the night of the party. First, I had gained a few pounds and the pants were too snug. Second, the coat given me was the wrong size: I looked and felt like a stuffed sausage. But the tuxedos the boys received were perfect fits, and when we arrived three of the four of us looked dashing and/or beautiful.

The crowd included a considerable number of beautiful young single women, and there were times when I saw one of my sons dancing with two, even three young ladies at one time. These beautiful lasses wore gowns with bare shoulders. Considerable cleavage was in evidence (once again, Tobin was back in the land of women having breasts).

Hors d'oeuvres were placed all around the bar. Tables were set for a grand meal that would be served in time for the tables to be cleared for the dancing and partying that would welcome in the New Year. The cash bar was busy with the revelers purchasing beer, wine, and champagne. The youngsters intermingled and got to know each other. When Taran came back to us after being amongst the lovelies, he offered the opinion that some of the men at this function might be gangster types. He didn't explain why he thought this. I think it was a suggestion from one of the beautiful ladies he had been chatting with. There was never a confirmation of this assessment, but I was on the lookout for the boys to make sure that they did not overtly offend anyone, especially the fathers of the scantily clad ladies.

After dinner we danced and drank and then danced some more. As the midnight hour approached, I saw Taran and one young lady standing close to each other. I could not hear what was being said but there was considerable laughter.

The New Year came in with a cacophony of sound. Around 1:30 a.m. many of the older people headed for the parking lot. Snow was falling and several of the young ladies who had come out to see their parents off to home and to bed were shivering in the cold. The strapless gowns looked awesome but they offered no protection from the cold and the snow.

When the youngsters returned to the pub the party was on. Tobin and Taran were driven home at 4:45 a.m. This was a bit much as Taran had a 10:30 a.m. plane to catch back to the States. Upon his arrival in St. Louis, he had a connecting flight that would take him to Japan where he would play in a football game; Ivy League All-Stars against Japanese All-Stars in the Epsom Bowl.

On the way to the airport, I was chatting with Taran and asking him if he had had a good time. He said he had a wonderful time; that it was fun flirting with all the young ladies even though the flirting never led to anything. I took advantage of the moment and asked him what he had said to the gal he was talking to at midnight that made her laugh so hard. He said she had asked him what his best pickup line was. He responded, "You remind me a lot of my first wife, and I haven't been married yet." The girl smiled but she had heard that line before. She then asked, "What's your next best line?" He said he looked at her and then said, "F--- me if I'm wrong but isn't your name Helga?" She was laughing at that line when the clock struck midnight.

Mike told us that we ought to make dinner reservations for Sunday, November 3. He said that all of those that were at the restaurant would be in for a special treat. He had a "big event" planned for the evening. Shirley and I found two other couples and we reserved a big table near the center of the restaurant. We had our meal, and after a few after dinner drinks I was beginning to doubt there was going to be any 'big event'. And then to considerable fanfare and the blare of music, we found out that "Elvis" was in the house.

Elvis *was* in the house, perhaps with a bit of an English accent but never-the-less it was Elvis. The impersonator put on a great show. His jokes were funny, the music was good, and we danced the evening away. Mike, the proprietor, was proud as punch at the size of the crowd that showed up for an event that he had held close to his vest. He had a sellout, and amongst the crowd were more attractive young ladies than I had seen at any event since we had moved to England, Ladies Day at the Royal Ascot being the sole and obvious exception.

On January 25, a Saturday night, we attended a dinner at the Winkfield to honor the Scottish Poet Robert Burns. "Bobby (Rabbie) Burns" night is celebrated by Scots everywhere, and the celebrations in his honor occur on the anniversary of his birthday (January 25, 1759). The celebration at the Winkfield was done properly with the serving of Haggis and an accompanying performance by a bagpiper. Toasts were made with Scotch whiskey, and the *Ode to a Haggis*, one of Burns' most famous poems was read aloud. At the end of the evening, we were serenaded with that most famous of Burns' songs and poems, *Auld Lang Syne*. Although usually sung during New Year celebrations everywhere in the English-speaking countries, this song is also played ubiquitously on Rabbie Burns night. The Winkfield celebration of Burns birth was as well done and as memorable as any we enjoyed whilst we were in England.

Shirley and I went to other Bobby Burns parties during our stay in England. One such party was hosted by a proud Scot who invited four couples to join his wife and him at their home to celebrate the great man. A typical Scottish meal was served (Haggis and a mash of potatoes, turnips, and carrots) along with Scotch whiskey. What made this celebration so memorable was that the host not only read the poem *Ode to a Haggis* he also explained the words, words that puzzle many English and American citizens.

If I did not include at least the first few lines of the Ode to a Haggis I would do injustice to the impact the poem has on a Bobby Burns celebration. I came to love the poem, even though I still have to rely on the translation my Scottish friend gave me the night of his party.

Ode to a Haggis

Fair fa' your honest, sonsie face,
Great chieftain o' the pudding-race!
Aboon them a' ye tak your place,
Painch, trip, or thairm:
Weel are ye wordy of a grace worthy
As lang's my arm

The groaning trencher there ye fill,
Your hurdies like a distant hill,
Your pin wad help to mend a mill
In time o' need.
While thro' your pores the dews distil
Like amber bead.

We attended another Bobby Burns party in central London hosted by my colleague Jim Guion and his wife Paulette. This party was held in a multi-story, multi-apartment residential complex, with gardens in an open atrium enclosed by apartments. Three things distinguished this fun-filled party.

First, the primary alcohol served was the "classic six" of

Scottish Whiskey. This is all well and fine, but some individuals do not hold their whiskey well and one individual, a fellow Kerr-McGee employee, embarrassed himself by falling down a flight of stairs and implanting himself headfirst into the dry wall at the foot of the stairs. Thankfully, he was not hurt. Only his ego was damaged.

Second, the Guion's had engaged a bagpiper to play Scottish music whilst we partied. The only problem is that a bagpipe in an apartment is bearishly loud. Even when the bagpiper was moved to a landing several floors above the party room the music was too loud to be comfortable. Eventually, the musician was walked out into the cold open area in the yard where he played his instrument while we were inside with the doors closed.

Third, the hosts felt that fireworks would be a great way to end the evening. Large coils of inch long firecrackers were placed on and tied to numerous plants and tree limbs. No one realized how powerful the firecrackers were. When they exploded many of the trees and all the plants lost leaves and limbs. The noise was so loud that I feared the government might think that Whitehall was under an IRA mortar attack. Fortunately for us, there was only one interval of blasting and it was hard for anyone outside of the building to get a fix on where the explosions came from. To deflect the attention away from ourselves we walked out onto Grosvenor Street and looked around like we too were looking for the source of the explosions. Meanwhile, in the interior garden others were busy with rakes and brooms sweeping up the debris. Such is Bobby Burns night in England. I miss the fun.

On a March 18 Mike Hawksworth invited us to celebrate St. Patrick's Day at the Winkfield. This date is the feast day which annually celebrates one of the patron saints of Ireland. At the Winkfield the March celebration was "St. Paddy's Day". When we arrived, a harpist was playing soulful Irish music and singing an assortment of ballads. The guests had several rounds of Irish whiskey and then we returned to the less intoxicating and more delicious pints of Guinness. The dinner on this evening consisted of Irish Stew and our choice of salmon with bacon and cabbage or corned beef and cabbage. A large stuffed pork loin with crackling was an alternative main dish. Predictably, the meal came with both brown bread and soda bread. The dessert menu included spotted dog and barmbruch (Irish fruit cake). Mike sure knows how to throw a party.

But Mike at the Winkfield was still not done. The patrons *of* the pub had so enjoyed the black-tie New Year's party in 1996 that he organized a repeat in 1997. The 1997 party was just as much fun as the original function, but the second time around was not as exciting as the first. And we also attended the celebration realizing we might be about to spend our last New Year in England. I was already aware that we might find the Lent family in China early in 1998.

Another pub, The Wells, was close to our home in Muirfield. It was 742 steps from our doorstep in Kier Park – I counted them several times to make sure the number was correct. We often frequented the pub because it was nearby and because we liked John and Carolyn, the proprietors. The food was not particularly good nor was crowd particularly friendly, but John and Carolyn were amenable to fixing us a hamburger and chips even when they were not on the menu. They were also owners of several slot machines which I believe was the source of John and Carolyn's holiday funds. Although the Lent family played these machines many times, I do not recall any of us walking or driving home with any of the money we put into play. Sometimes we would be ahead, but it was only a matter of time before our "winnings" were gone.

The Wells had an expansive play area for children, making it a favorite haunt for young parents who took their families out for a Sunday meal. Several times John set up an inflatable bouncing playroom. The kids loved it. On one Sunday evening our son Taran, the college football player, had had a pint or two and decided to go into the play area and jump on the inflatable play station. When he walked out, a little boy came running up to him and told him he was too old and too big to be playing in the yellow and red inflatable house. The little lad was absolutely right. The next morning as my driver drove me past The Wells, I saw the inflatable flat to the ground, just like a wilted lettuce leaf. I felt bad about the situation, but by the time I returned home that evening John had found some tape and the bouncing house was once again inflated and awaiting the youngsters – but not those that were 6' 2" and weighed 220 pounds.

During our stay in England, we were in the midst of the "mad cow" scare. I was concerned about eating beef in the pubs until I discovered that only 86 people had died in nearly 20 years, and that the incubation period for the disease was likely beyond my life expectancy. I thereafter ignored the threat and was a beef, lamb, and pork eater for the duration of our stay on the great island.

I understand that Mike recently sold the Winkfield, which is now known as "The Slug and Lettuce". I like Mike's name for the establishment considerably better. After we left England Bobby and Jon sold The Thatched Tavern and The Fox and Hounds, opting to keep and operate only The Cottage. From what I hear the food served at The Thatched Tavern and The Fox and Hounds has remained the same. I would think the booming voices of Bobby and Jon are sorely missed. The Wells has been closed and is no longer an operating pub.

We here take leave of our favorite pubs. They indeed deserved to be amongst our most favorite places.

Ascot and Windsor Villages

Both of these villages were our hometowns whilst we lived in England. And like most hometowns the more one shops, drinks, walks, dines and uses the services the more one comes to appreciate the people and the establishments. Even today, over five decades later, I remember the sounds and smells of our hometown of Prineville, Oregon. For many years I was sure that I knew 80 to 90 percent of all the people in our small Central Oregon community. Some memories begin to fade with the passage of time, however, and given the changing population,

A Few of Our Favorite Places

both Shirley and I had almost become near strangers when we returned for our yearly visits.

It seems like only yesterday that I was walking the streets of Ascot, Berkshire but it has now been over twenty years since I last took a hike down Ascot High Street. My memories of those pleasant times will surely fade but some memories will stay with me forever.

Except on days when there is a race at the Ascot Race Course, Ascot is a small, quiet village, with few people walking along High Street. We eventually learned that the people who man the stores, pubs, and restaurants know who is walking the streets. Once, after we had been living in Kier Park for several years, Shirley stuck her head into a shop she had never been in, and during the course of conversation Shirley mentioned that she was from the States. The clerk then said, "Oh yes, I know who you are. You live in Nick Faldo's home in Kier Park. I see you walking all the time and I wondered when you might come in to visit us." When Shirley told me of this encounter I wondered if other the shop owners kept similar tabs on the locals or was Shirley memorable because she had a striking coiffure and a bearing that matched it.

I got the same treatment one evening when I called Ann Marie's Patisserie to have a pizza delivered to our home, Muirfield. Anne Marie's was a bakery during the daytime. When the bakery (*patisserie*) closed, the ovens became available for pizzas. The first time I called to order a pizza, Anne Marie answered, as she usually did. When I asked for a pizza to be delivered to Muirfield in Kier Park she laughingly responded, "Oh yes, you are the ones who had your lions nicked." She was right! In the middle of one night thieves had pulled up in front of Muirfield and quickly jack-hammered off two beautiful stone lions Nick Faldo had so carefully put up. For all the years Shirley and I lived in Ascot the locals knew we were the ones that had our lions nicked (stolen). The postman and others would often tell us they were sure they had seen our lions at this place or that. We never pursued any of the leads. We were renters, not owners.

And There We Were

Once Anne Marie mentioned she knew where we lived, I always called, ordered our pizza, and asked that the delivery man bring it to the house where the lions had been nicked. Anne Marie would chuckle and send the boy (or man) on his way. Even four years after the lions went missing, I was still able to order our pizza in that manner.

Whenever Shirley chose to shop on Ascot High Street, she would conclude her trip with coffees at Ascots, a trendy little French café, or with a light lunch at Ciao Ninety where Ramon, the maitre d', would always greet her like she was royalty. Ramon treated almost every customer that way, and Ciao Ninety was consequently very popular with the locals.

I was responsible for most of the shopping at Budgens, the High Street grocery store, and for the many visits made to Brooks, the dry cleaners and laundry shop. Shirley's haunts were mostly the clothes stores or the antique shops. There were a number of Ascot High Street pubs where we occasionally made dinner stops, often just for a change in diet. There were five or six such pubs: the ones I best remember are The Stag, Ollies Bar and Diner, and The Dukes Head.

When there are races at the Ascot Race Course, and especially during the week of the Royal Ascot, the town becomes unbelievably crowded. To say that the local population is put under a bit of stress due to the considerable influx of visitors to the Royal Ascot is an understatement. During race days it was almost impossible to move around the village via a private auto or taxi. My normal manner of travel to and from the Ascot train station (for my train ride to and from central London and the Kerr-McGee office) was by a private driver to the station in the morning and by taxi home in the evening. Muirfield is a seven or eight-minute drive, or thirty-minute walk, from the Ascot train station. During the Royal Ascot one can pretty much forget taking a taxi anywhere so I could only make it back to Muirfield on foot.

The first year we lived in Ascot I was stunned by the number of people on the trains coming into Ascot, and by the attire of the racing crowd. Viewing the passengers and those lining the train platforms at Ascot, Sunningdale, Virginia Water, and Staines, I could imagine that this is what it must have been like in Victorian times. Everyone was dressed to the nines: I had never seen so many beautiful ladies wearing such ornate feathered hats.

One evening during the first year we spent in Ascot, I arrived at the Ascot train station following the Gold Cup Day (Ladies' Day) at the Royal Ascot meeting. I was greeted by a large crowd milling about in the drop-off and pick-up area at the station. The party goers had spilled out of a nearby pub. There were hundreds of well-attired patrons drinking pints and glasses of wine in the area where a taxi would normally be waiting.

The pub at the train station, Jazz at The Station, was one of our local favorites and I often stopped by for a pint while I waited for a taxi to become available. Shirley and I had also become friends with John the owner, a very nice middle-aged man who loved jazz and who wanted to make a jazz club out of the pub. He was successful in doing so and today the pub is known as the Jagz Bar. But back in 1994 The Station was just another pub. Owning a pub in Ascot during the Royal Ascot is akin to a python swallowing a calf: 90 percent of the pubs' annual earnings result from patronage during these racing days.

When I realized I was not going to be able to take a taxi home, and it would be impossible to work my way up to the bar at The Station, I began to walk up the hill to Ascot where I would then walk along High Street to Cheapside Road, off of which is the exit into Kier Park. I felt like a real outsider as I walked up the hill on that June afternoon in 1994. It was hot, and I was walking against the flow of the crowd with my briefcase swinging from my arms.

Walking down the hill were the most amazing people. One beautiful lady, quite obviously drunk, was weaving as she walked. Despite wearing a lovely white feathered (with black tips) hat and an obviously expensive white dress, she was a total mess. Someone had spilled a large glass of red wine on her. Had it not been for her inebriated condition, I am sure she would have been devastated. As it was, she walked past me with a glass of wine swinging back and forth as she jawed with a girlfriend.

I thought the lady might be a one off, but I had only walked thirty yards further up the hill when I found four elegantly dressed ladies laying prone on the grass by the sidewalk with their hats pulled over their heads. They were either sound asleep or passed out.

I was in a sea of humanity as I walked down High Street. Whenever I came to a pub the chatter volume went up, and the crowds became more compact. I remember thinking, "How in the world would one get a pint in one of these pubs?"

When I finally made it to The Wells pub, I decided to work my way through the crowd and get a pint for myself. I thought it might be timely to take a break before I made my final push home (only 742 steps left). Even though The Wells was a second-tier pub, it was almost impossible to put in a drink order. The only thing that saved me was that John, the proprietor, saw me and yelled over the crowd for my order. You can see now why I played his slot machines and funded his holiday travel.

In 1995 Taran came to England to visit us during the week of the Royal Ascot. It was then that Shirley took a number of her girlfriends, including Paulette Guion, to the Royal Ascot races. Shirley had not yet discovered how to gain entrance into the Royal Enclosure, and she did not yet know all the ins and outs of grandstand seating or the drinking establishments available to the racing patrons. This lack of knowledge did not keep the girls, and our son, from dressing up and going to the races. Somehow, they were allowed to tailgate in the infield open area within Ascot Heath. Now tailgating at Ascot is a bit of a misnomer as we are talking Dom Perignon Champagne, crystal, linen, and finger cakes. Some "tailgate" parties were served hot meals from the back of Rolls Royce automobiles with the servers being the chefs of the well-to-do owners.

When I arrived home after the day's events, I saw Shirley, Paulette, and our son. They were in great shape, but they appeared to be exhausted. Paulette stayed late waiting for the traffic to thin out before having her contracted driver return her to London and her home. I chuckled the next morning when my friend Jim Guion said Paulette came into the house, hugged everyone, and went upstairs to change into something less formal. The children and Jim waited downstairs for Paulette to return and to tell them all the interesting things she had experienced that day. It soon became apparent that something was wrong. When Jim walked up to their bedroom there was Paulette sound asleep on the bed, still dressed in all of her finery.

Many years later I asked my son Taran what was the most interesting thing he had done during his visits to England. Without even hesitating he said, "Attending the Royal Ascot on Ladies' Day." I was puzzled by this answer, especially coming from a young man in his twenties. He clarified his answer by saying, "The Royal Ascot is the world's largest cocktail party where racing plays second fiddle to elegance and celebration."

Shirley eventually got "Ascot" right. We solicited the United States Ambassador to recommend the Lent family for admittance into the Royal Enclosure during Ladies Day (aka Gold Cup Day) at the Royal Ascot. Our access badges were issued to us at St. James Palace in London. Tobin, Taran, and I dressed in topcoats and Shirley wore a specially purchased dress and hat. Our badges were in order and we had free rein of the Ascot grounds. After we were seated in the Royal Enclosure, one of our sons doffed his hat saying that it was really quite warm. He was sweating profusely. He had no sooner dropped his hat to his lap than an usher tapped him on his shoulder telling him he had to have a hat on to remain in the enclosure. Wow! Not only is it hard to gain entrance to the Royal Enclosure, the rules on decorum are never relaxed.

Mention was made previously of several other times we attended races at Ascot. Altogether, we went to 25 or 30 racing events (only four or five of which were run during the Royal Ascot). Shirley eventually discovered the best restaurants, the best grandstand seats, and the most convenient places to park. We ended up buying all manner of Ascot memorabilia including beautiful Ascot crystal pint glassware that to this day adorn the wet bar in our Texas home.

A day at the races invariably was accompanied by an elegant dinner, either on the racetrack grounds or at Ciao Ninety on Ascot High Street. The key to enjoying any attendance at Ascot is to allocate plenty of time to dine or drink whilst the crowds thin out. Because we lived less than 10 minutes from the racecourse, we were comfortable dining after the races. I always felt sorry for all of those poor souls who had to travel by train, bus, or private car back to London or to some other far destination.

Shirley loved the elegance of the Royal Ascot. I think she reveled in the tradition, the ceremony, and the opulence that was on display. Some days during the Royal Ascot Shirley would walk to an outdoor viewing area where she could see the Queen and her entourage coming by carriage down the path in Windsor Great Park, a path that eventually led to the grasslands and the entrance that were part of Ascot Race Course. When the Queen became visible from the grandstands, the music began, and the people stood at attention. Several times Shirley stood by the entrance to the New Mile and looked on fondly as the Queen waved to those few souls who were far removed from the crowds that would soon greet her and Prince Phillip.

The New Mile racetrack could be seen over the tall fence behind our Muirfield home. I often told Shirley that if she wanted, I could hold her up and she could wave to the Queen as she traveled down the course on her way to the grandstands. I never detected even the slightest interest in this offer. My Shirley would see and receive the Queen on her terms, not mine.

The trips I made to High Street were not always because I had errands to run. There were certainly a great number of trips I made to Budgens, Brooks, and the Patisserie. And I often went to Martins-the-chemist (pharmacy), Oddbins (wine merchants), or the local hardware store. But one fun thing I did was something I chose to do each Sunday morning.

During the time we lived in Ascot there was a significantly large park off of Ascot High Street. This grass covered area served as a parking and marquee area during the Royal Ascot.

A Few of Our Favorite Places

FIGURE 18. BOB AND SHIRLEY'S SONS TARAN (L) AND TOBIN (R)
DRESSED FOR ENTRANCE INTO THE ROYAL ENCLOSURE
AT THE ROYAL ASCOT RACES

At all other times of the year, it was pretty much left ignored. One exception to this rule was that on most Sundays during the year a very, very large car boot sale was held in the park. In the United States we would call this a flea market. I loved getting up early and driving the short distance to Ascot where I would park and walk to the grounds. There would be hundreds of vendors trying to sell articles, most of which I had no interest in. But once every four or five weeks I would find an article that caught my fancy. Sometimes it would be an ornate tin (made of real tin), a painting, old coins, or even a small piece of furniture. I usually bought an item with the intent of giving it to a friend who collected such things back in the States. It is amazing than none of my purchases ever made it to the intended recipient. Invariably Shirley would see what I had purchased and opt to display it in our home. And such it was that these items became a part of our household decorations not only in Muirfield but also in Beijing and in Texas. I apparently had good taste. Another the fun thing: whilst I was walking the aisles at the car boot sale I could munch on all sorts of pastries and breakfast goodies. If the weather turned bad, I just hightailed it home to Muirfield.

One interesting event that did bring the car boot sales to a temporary halt was the arrival one week of a very large group of gypsies who arrived with their caravans (house trailers). There were hundreds of families in the group and they quite simply just moved in and took over the park. These itinerants are not dummies. They got rent-free space for nearly six months which is the amount of time that is needed in England to evict someone who is trespassing on public lands. The gypsies know the legal process and when it is five months and 20 days they just move on. I found the whole thing to be most interesting. I missed the car boot sales, but it was fun watching the locals respond to the angst caused by the unwanted guests. I think in the United States such a gathering of itinerants would be greeted by a group bearing firearms. In Prineville, Oregon the gypsies might be lucky to make it out of town alive.

When it was finally known that we would be leaving Ascot a number of the merchants went out of their way to say their goodbyes and to wish us Godspeed. Shirley received one very nice card from the owner of Ascots. The owner thanked Shirley for her patronage and expressed her sincere wish that Shirley might someday find her way once again back to the lady's coffee shop. Anne Marie cried not so much because I was leaving but more so because her pizza sales were going to take a big hit.

The town of Windsor is only two or three miles from Ascot and it is no wonder that it became as much our home town as did Ascot. Ascot is quaint and when the races are in progress the village is vibrant. But Ascot has only a number of make-do shops. The grocery store is "ok" and the good restaurants are limited (Ciao Ninety and The Thatched Tavern). Windsor on the other hand is vibrant on almost all days. It is a hub of shopping and tourism and there is much on offer for everyone. There is even a downtown shopping mall. As much as Shirley enjoyed walking the streets of Ascot, she really felt that Windsor was her town.

After Shirley and I found that we would be living in Muirfield – Kier Park, Ascot we took a train to Ascot with our sons to show them our new home. After we pulled into the Ascot train station, we were driven through Ascot village on our way to Muirfield. There wasn't much to do at Muirfield as our furniture was still at sea and the house was barren and vacant. We opted to have our driver take us on a quick trip over to Windsor so we could view the castle and to get a feel for the scenery in the countryside around both Ascot and Windsor.

All of us were smitten with the beauty of the English countryside. We could not believe the open area that existed between Ascot and Windsor. Later we would learn that most of this open area was a part of Windsor Great Park. The driver was quick to point out the Queen's properties. He informed us you could identify a royal property by the pink paint that covered the buildings. The driver took us on a quick tour through Windsor, and then he dropped us off at the Thatched Tavern where we had dinner.

My first impression of Windsor was that it was crowded and looked like it might be a difficult place in which to drive an auto. Shirley remembered it quite differently. She saw the beautiful Windsor Castle, St. George's Chapel, the monument to Queen Victoria, and a quaint and tilting(?) tea house. She remembered the bridge over the Thames that separated Eton from Windsor and the quaint restaurants that bordered the Thames. It was only months later that I saw what she had seen that first day.

Even after we moved into Muirfield, and I made my first shopping trips to the grocery store in Windsor, my attention was not drawn to the scenic or historic landmarks. I was focused on how I might negotiate the small streets whilst driving on the wrong side of the road. It had been years since I had had to think about driving. Back home in the States I just got in the car and drove, no thinking required, or at least that is how it seemed.

And There We Were

The second trip Shirley and I made to Windsor occurred just before we were to take delivery of our new Honda Legend. We had been advised that it might be a good idea to get a driving instructor to give us a few pointers before we went out on the English roads. We would be able to use our United States licenses for a while. It would be some time before we would be able to take an English driving test.

The driver who arrived to take us out for our lessons showed up in a very small car with a stick shift. I had not driven a car with a stick shift since I was fifteen and here I was, about to go on the road driving a small car, steering wheel located on the right, and the transmission driven by a stick shift. Shirley was facing the same challenge, but she was not nearly as vocal about the inequities of the situation as was I.

We were told by the instructor that it was not a good idea to have one lesson involving two people, especially when the two were married. We told him we appreciated his concern, but as we were about to take delivery of our new car, we needed to gain at least some familiarity with being on an English highway.

I was first up and soon found that I was very uncomfortable driving on the left side of the road. My first reaction was that I felt I could not safely judge just how far I was from the roadside. A right turn made across on-coming traffic was simply mind boggling. And then there was all that traffic coming towards me on the right. The first round-about totally confused me: I made it through only because I was able to slow down to a crawl thereby allowing the instructor to guide me through the two circulars (it was a double round-about, one the locals call a peanut round-about). Then he took us across the Windsor Great Park and into Windsor during full tourist season when the streets and sidewalks were filled with tourists. From King's Road we entered Windsor High Street and dropped down below Windsor Castle through a series of twists and turns to Barry Avenue, the road that runs along the Thames. After a short drive along the river the driver told me to pull over. Shirley who had been in the back seat laughing at every mistake (and there had been more than a few of them) was next up.

A Few of Our Favorite Places

Still within Windsor Shirley now found she was facing the same problems as I had. Only she was much more vocal than I had been, and when she was confused she just let it all hang out. At the first round-about she let out a loud yell – a mild form of profanity. She asked the instructor how she could be sure to know what the other drivers who were in or about to enter the round-about would do. He said the best thing was just to remember the right-of-way rules and to focus on what she did and not on what others might do. That sounds good but it is not at all comforting. In any event, Shirley did make her way out of Windsor and we soon found ourselves back home at Muirfield. I had laughed all the way back home as I found Shirley's driving escapades to be just as funny as she had found mine.

When we bid goodbye to our instructor, he asked when it was that we would be taking delivery of our car. After we told him, I asked why he wanted to know. He replied, "I just don't want to be on the highway the day you first get out on the road."

We did learn to drive the English roads, and it was not long before Shirley wanted to make a shopping trip to Windsor. We had long ago decided that the best grocery store in our area was the Marks & Spencer store on Peascod Street in central Windsor. Our first shopping trip was tentative at best. Shirley visited a few shops, we had coffees at a tea house and then bought our groceries. All the time we shopped I felt like a fighter pilot who fears his return to, and landing on, an aircraft carrier. I dreaded the moment we had our groceries and would be leaving the multi-story parking garage where I would once again be driving on the busy streets of Windsor.

The truth is that over the years that we lived in England I probably made 50 or more trips to or through Windsor. And I never was comfortable driving those streets. I would have much preferred taking a train to town. That was not an option open to me.

Both Shirley and I did learn to enjoy Windsor. It is a historical and fun town to visit. The town grew up around Windsor Castle, and the Castle draws the tourists. Windsor Castle has been a royal residence for over 900 years. It remains today one of the four main residences of Queen Elizabeth. Like all other tourists, and probably most expatriates, we toured the Windsor Castle and saw the changing of the guards. And, of course, Shirley made St. George's Chapel her church of choice.

I never failed to view the statue of Queen Victoria without being impressed by her monarchy. She was ruler of the British Empire during its golden years. All public visitors who tour the Castle grounds enter via the Castle Hill entrance, where they pass by the towering bronze statue of the monarch, scepter in hand. Even those that walk along Windsor High Street see the Queen looking down on them. Her bronzed effigy remains, even today, one of the great memories I took with me when I left England.

Not far from the marvelous statue of Queen Victoria is a McDonalds hamburger shop. The McDonalds is down the hill and across Thames Street (High Street becomes Thames Street at the point where the road begins its descent towards the River Thames) from Windsor Castle. Now why would I bring forward that bit of trivia? The answer relates to a story told of Princess Diana.

When the newly married Princess was in residence at the Castle, she was often bored and bothered by the stiff protocol required by those running the Castle. These insiders did not like Diana visiting with the staff as she was often want to do, especially late on evenings when she sneaked into the kitchen for a snack. But, as the story is told, Diana often just wanted to be a normal person again, and she reportedly would open a Castle door that led to Thames Street and from here she would walk across the street and get in line to get a bite to eat. I cannot comment on the veracity of this story, but the locals insist that it is true... and they loved her for it. If Diana did do this, she probably was able to do so only early in her marriage to Prince Charles. It was not long before every move she made was documented by the paparazzi. Whenever I walked by the McDonalds, I would get a smile on my face; just thinking of Princess Diana in the queue delighted me. I think she was the kind of person who would do such a thing, and that is probably one of the reasons that the commoners loved her so. I choose to believe that the anecdote is true.

I often went to Windsor with my wife when she had errands to run, and I had nothing else to do around the house. One day, we parked the car and visited a number of the shops. Shirley stopped by her beauty salon to pick up some make-up and then we split up while Shirley visited her favorite shops, and I visited those shops I found of interest. After meeting at the pre-arranged time, we went to the Rendezvous Restaurant for coffees and a snack. This particular dining place has a great name but marginal food. It remains a convenient meeting place for those who shop along Peascod Street and then find themselves on High Street.

After we came out of the restaurant, we walked by the Parish Church on High Street and saw a notice that informed passers-by that a recital would take place at 2:00 p.m. It was nearing that time, and Shirley insisted we enter the church and listen to this recital. Knowing Shirley's ability to find something of interest but never fully believing it will happen, I agreed to join her. As we entered the church I muttered to myself, "I cannot imagine how bad this could be." The recital was by a Tara Noval, a violinist aged 20. The music and the performance were unbelievable. When we left, I told Shirley that we would someday hear more from this lady. Indeed, we later learned that Ms. Noval performed with the Philadelphia Orchestra and had gone on extended tours of the Far East. She now has her own trio and has performed a number of solo concerts. Because of Shirley's intuition we walked into a church in Windsor and heard beautiful music. It sometimes does pay to take a chance.

During our frequent trips to Windsor, we came across any number of surprising events similar to the recital we witnessed in the Parish Church. One day we found ourselves walking Peascod Street in the middle of the Windsor Festival, an event where musicians and other performers fill the street with their acts. I was reminded of the many Shakespearian and Renaissance festivals we have back in the United States. Only here in England we were not very far removed from the locations where such festivals actually took place.

Shirley and I also attended performances at the Windsor Royal Theater where we saw *Aladdin* and the *Music of Vienna*, usually having drinks before and dinner after the shows. We eventually visited most of pubs and eating establishments in Windsor. Some were quite memorable and some certainly less so. Two interesting, if not contrasting restaurants, nearly face each other across the pedestrian bridge over the Thames, a bridge that connects Windsor to Eton.

As one looks from Eton across the Thames to Windsor, the Orangerie Restaurant in Christopher Wren's House Hotel faces the water to the right of the pedestrian bridge. We ate at this restaurant several times, but no visit was more memorable than one on Valentine's Day after I had flown in from Ireland following a business trip. We had made reservations at the Orangerie, which for Valentine's Day had a set menu. Shirley was lovely as ever and our son Tobin was able to join us for this special occasion. The soft music and the fresh flowers on our table created a lovely setting and a nice ambience. Waiters emerged from the kitchen carrying platters which contained our first courses. With the waiters came a most unpleasant odor. When the silver tops had been removed from the serving trays, we found ourselves looking at a serving of squab (pigeon breasts).

As Tobin said afterwards, the taste and smell of the cooked pigeons brought a whole new meaning to the word "gamey". This dinner took place about the time a gentleman was caught trapping pigeons in London's Trafalgar Square. The local press reported that the trapper was selling his catch to local restaurants. Only later did we learn that most of the "local" restaurants were Indian "curry" houses. On that Valentine's Day at the Orangerie I was sure that we were being served squab obtained from downtown London. Whatever the truth, we never ate the fowl, and we never returned to the Orangerie Restaurant. The restaurant offers a great view of the Thames, but what a memory to have of a meal! The previous meals we had had there were good, so perhaps we were not justified in boycotting the establishment following that Valentine's Day fiasco.

On the Eton side of the Thames and located to the right of

the pedestrian footbridge as you look from Windsor to Eton was one of our favorite restaurants in England, The House on the Bridge. The restaurant faces the Thames and looks upwards to Windsor Castle. There are numerous tables on two levels, three levels counting the riverside courtyard, where seating is available at tables looking out onto the river. We often took special guests and family members to this restaurant. The view of Windsor, the Thames, and Windsor Castle is unparalleled, and the quality of the meals matches the view. What a wonderful restaurant it was and is.

We often went to the House on the Bridge for special occasions, such as our anniversary or for one of our birthdays. We took Shirley's mother and my mother and father to dinners there. One of my favorite photos of my father, who passed away in 1999, is of him standing on the pedestrian bridge with Windsor Castle looming high overhead. He has this tremendous smile on his face. The photo was taken moments after we finished our meal at The House on the Bridge.

One of the more humorous events occurring during our stay in England came from a luncheon Shirley and our friends Paul and Sharon Hess had at The House on the Bridge. Paul and Sharon are small town Oregonians who are uncomfortable in a place or at a function where they might be deemed to be inappropriately dressed. Most of us are probably the same way, but Paul and Sharon are especially sensitive to that ethic. When Shirley invited them to lunch at The House, they asked what was suitable to wear. And the truth is, at lunch time during the week, smart casual is just right. Some people always dress business casual, but you should not feel uncomfortable if you dress less so. That is, except for the day Shirley took the Hess' to lunch.

Shirley had made reservations far in advance; this was probably not necessary except that she wanted to make sure Paul and Sharon could have a meal at a window table where the view would be magnificent. When the three of them (I was working in downtown London) arrived for their luncheon reservation the restaurant was packed to its limit – and this was on all three levels. And not only was the place packed but every single person in the restaurant was dressed in robes and gowns with numerous medals and colorful sashes hanging from their shoulders. You cannot imagine anything more formal than the scene Paul and Sharon encountered. Even though they were dressed smart casual, they were totally under dressed when compared to all the diners around them. To this day I still have to calm Paul down when we talk about what he walked into.

One day a year the Queen invests the new Knights of the Order of the Garter. On this particular date the Queen, Sovereign of the Order of the Garter, attends a service in St. George's Chapel for the investiture. Also present are all of the Knights and Ladies of the Order. In other words, Paul and Sharon innocently walked into a luncheon following one of the most formal gatherings in the United Kingdom. It was no wonder that most of the knights and ladies came to the House on the Bridge for lunch. There is no better place in Windsor (the exception being a royal invite to the Queen's private quarters) or Eton in which to eat. I still laugh when I think of my good friends Paul and Sharon hobnobbing with the elite of England. The Hess' must have felt like they were peasants crashing a royal banquet. Shirley of course is comfortable with such surroundings: she loved the elegance, the royalty, and the pageantry that was on display.

Eton should be considered a part of Windsor and we thought of it as such. The locals may argue the point but if they do it is a moot point. Windsor is a small enough town that you can negotiate nearly all of the streets and not be pushed. And if you walk the Windsor streets you will eventually come to the pedestrian bridge and you will take a stroll to Eton and walk Eton High Street. The House on the Bridge is the first building one passes but it is not many steps before you come to other famous establishments such as the Cock Pit restaurant, once the site of cockfighting (17th and 18th centuries). Today the pub and restaurant can be identified by a pair of stocks and a pillar box located near its entrance.

Eton is known worldwide as the home of Eton College, one of the most elite schools in the world. Many of England's greatest and grandest matriculated at Eton. Even today it is a desired academy for scholars worldwide.

Eton College was established in 1440 by King Henry VI. Although originally founded to provide for the education of poor scholars it became a fashionable school for sons of nobility in the 17th century. The young boys, all between the ages of 13 and 18, wear pinstripes, tailcoats, and wing collars. Graduates of Eton include 20 prime ministers and giants in the fields of science, economics, literature, and architecture. Seventy scholarships are made available to all students through competitive exams. Other notables (e.g. Prince William, son of Charles and Diana) are admitted by appointment.

The greatest patron of the school was King George III whose long reign (1760-1820) was mostly accomplished from his residence in Windsor Castle. This proximity to Eton College led to a love affair with the students and faculty. Eton reciprocated with the love and respect by making the king's birthday, the Fourth of June, a holiday. Remember if you will that a Fourth of June celebration was where Shirley once invited herself to the activities, including the Procession of Boats, which she watched while standing near Prince Charles and Diana.

Now you know why there is a Copper Horse commemorating the King George III. The loss of the Colonies was insignificant. What really mattered was the king's long reign, his whipping up on France, and his love affair with his subjects, especially those who attended Eton College. Of course, it helped to have a loving son who could and did erect the Copper Horse in memory of his father.

One of the memorable experiences you may have when you are out and about on the streets of Eton is an encounter with Eton students walking about in their formal attire. To me the experience was like visiting one of the military academies in the United States and watching the very best and brightest of our young men walking about campus.

Yes, Windsor was our town, but it is compact and so interesting that it can be any visitor's town no matter how long the stay in England. Expatriates have the advantage of going back many times, ensuring they get it right, but the reality is one can experience Windsor, Eton, and Windsor Castle in a day or two, especially if you wish to put your feet on the cobblestone streets. It would probably be best to avoid the squab at The Orangerie.

Before leaving Ascot and Windsor, and Bob and Shirley's list of favorite places, it is worthy to note two properties whose one-time Berkshire/Surrey owners and residents left behind legacies that will be part of local lore for years to come. Royal Holloway College and Tittenhurst Park are not located within the Ascot or Windsor communities, but they are close enough that it would inappropriate not to include anecdotes that relate to these facilities. Royal Holloway College is approximately four miles from Ascot; Tittenhurst Park only a mile and a half.

Just across the A329 (aka London Road) from the Royal Berkshire Hotel is a 70 acre property that figures prominently in historical and anecdotal lore. We became familiar with this property when we traveled the A329 on many walking, dining, or shopping trips. It was on our route to the Fox and Hounds and to several entrances into Windsor Great Park. We were always impressed with the massive 10 to 12-foot-high upscale brick wall that extended seemingly forever along one side of the A329 just past the Sunninghill exit. If we slowed down, we could peek through the massive iron gates and view what appeared to be a palatial estate. One of the limo drivers who occasionally took us to Heathrow Airport identified the property as Tittenhurst Park, and he told us it was once been owned by John Lennon who had sold it to his fellow Beatle, Ringo Starr, who in turn sold it to a sheikh from Abu Dhabi. We knew little about the sheikh, but we were impressed that Lennon and Starr had once been owners. But long before all of these Johnny-Come-Latelies there was an owner and financial giant who lived on the property from 1867 until 1883. This man was Thomas Holloway.

Mr. Holloway was a most interesting and incredibly successful businessman. He made a fortune in Victorian times simply by creative packaging and mass marketing of ointments and pills. The products he sold claimed to help in the relief of a number of aches and pains many, if not most, of which would self-cure over time if left untreated. There was no documented medical approval for his products which could be purchased over the counter. Even though the pills and creams were relatively expensive, middle class Victorians aggressively purchased the products for nearly 60 years, minimally from 1840 until 1900.

Thomas Holloway and his wife Jane became very wealthy. Unfortunately, there were no children born to the couple. About the time of Jane's death in 1875, Mr. Holloway remarked that it was seemingly much easier to make money than to spend it.

Thomas Holloway, as philanthropist, chose to spend his money on the building of two magnificent buildings. One was the Holloway Sanatorium that opened in June 1885 and the other was the impressive and ornate Royal Holloway College. It opened in June 1886. Unfortunately, Mr. Holloway had died in December of 1883. His legacy is of two remarkable buildings that are impressive even by today's standards.

Remarkably, the large and ornate college was built to educate and house middle class women. The first students to take up residence numbered only 28. Today the College is known as Royal Holloway, University of London and the student population, both male and female, numbers nearly 7,500. The buildings with their ornate rooflines, towers, and turrets still seem massively large. For those first 28 women the place must have seemed overwhelmingly spacious. Thomas Holloway not only bequeathed the buildings, he also left money to help run it, along with an art collection that today has a value beyond calculation.

Now back to Tittenhurst Park and the rest of the story. Because of Royal Holloway College, which Shirley and I toured several times with friends and family, we became aware of Thomas Holloway's wealth and the philanthropy. Recognition of the connection between the Royal Holloway and the massive, enclosed compound we saw as we drove by on the A329 led us to think more about the ownership chain.

We were impressed that two members of the Beatles had once owned Tittenhurst Park. John Lennon purchased the property in 1969. He paid 145,000 pounds sterling for the

And There We Were

house and the surrounding 70 acres. In 1971 Lennon sold the property to Ringo Starr who lived in the Georgian house until 1988. The price Starr paid Lennon is unknown, but when Starr subsequently sold the house and property to Sheikh Zayed al Nahyan, the sheikh paid nearly 5,000,000 pounds sterling to Starr.

A bit about the sheikh and then the anecdotal suspense will unfold. Sheikh Zayed bin Sultan al Nahyan died in February 2004 aged 85. The sheik was one of the richest men on the planet when he died, with income from massive deposits of oil discovered in Abu Dhabi in 1966. Sheikh Zayed Al Nahyan was ruler of Abu Dhabi and was the founder and president of the United Arab Emirates. In the Middle East only Saudi Arabia and Iran produce more oil than do the Emirates.

Tittenhurst Park underwent a prolonged period of development once the Sheikh began to pour money into the property. It is now estimated that land and the complex of buildings is worth somewhere in excess of 30,000,000 pounds ($55,000,000). When Shirley and I lived in Ascot we were always amazed by the number of trucks coming and going from the Tittenhurst property. The construction just went on and on. We were not surprised one week when we picked up the local newspaper to read that the neighbors near Tittenhurst had protested the endless noise coming from the construction. I thought at the time these homeowners might just have a point. Ten days after the newspaper article appeared I happened to drive along the A329 and could not believe what I saw. There are four, maybe five houses proximal to Tittenhurst. All of the buildings appeared to be deserted with iron gates across their driveways. My only conclusion was that the Sheikh had just made the owners offers they could not refuse. The owners not only sold their homes, but they had moved out in just a matter of days. It was impressive to see what serious money can do. I am near certain some of the homeowners did not wish to move, but they were offered so much money that selling became a no-brainer.

For months afterwards I drove by the abandoned homes and never saw a car parked in the driveways nor any sign of

A Few of Our Favorite Places

life. Pretty impressive if I do say so. I may someday go back to see if the houses remain; if they are now occupied (the construction must be over, and the Sheikh is dead); or if the land is now behind an extended brick wall and an extended part of the original 70-acre landscape. If so, I wager that where the houses once stood there are grasslands and gardens.

Just before we left England we read in the same local paper that Sheikh Zayed bin Sultan Al Nahyan (or more likely his representative) had petitioned the local council for a permit to build a road and tunnel under the A329, creating a private access from Tittenhurst to the neighboring Royal Berkshire Hotel property. It turns out the Sheikh was a true horseman who owned horses that raced in the Royal Ascot. He invited many guests to these races. The problem is that when you fly in plane loads of people even a place a big as Tittenhurst just cannot house all the guests. The Sheikh wanted the tunnel access to the hotel so his guests who lodged at the hotel could safely and quickly drive back and forth from Tittenhurst to the hotel. During the week of the Royal Ascot the A329 is filled with bumper-to-bumper traffic and egress and ingress to the Royal Berkshire property is nearly impossible.

Astonishingly, the council denied the Sheikh's application. I thought that was gutsy, but the councilmen and councilwomen were looking out for the best interests of the populace. Good for them!

Several months later I picked up the paper and saw that the application had been resubmitted and that the permit to build a tunnel had been approved. In the same paper was an announcement that Surrey would now be funding a number of new public works projects, and further, that this work would be done without the use of the taxpayer money. It did not take much imagination to connect the dots. I have not been back along the A329 since we left England, but I am anxious to see if the tunnel has indeed been built: I am sure it has.

I spent a considerable amount of time on the platform at Ascot train station as I waited for a train to take me into London and work. I remember standing on the platform on sunny days, on rainy days, and on cold grey days when massive cloud banks raced over head. But the view one has from a platform is certainly different from the one he has as a train passenger looking out when departing a station. I can tell you to this day what the platforms are like all the way from Ascot into London.

On my train ride in during the morning I typically read a newspaper or two, only occasionally looking out the window when we stopped to pick up passengers. On the way home I read the afternoon newspaper and often power napped for 10 or 15 minutes, a practice that energized my evenings with Shirley.

Having commuted by train for years in England, and in Chicago during my assignment there, I was always on guard against two mishaps: first leaving my monthly ticket on the train and second, nodding off and sleeping through my train stop. In Chicago, nodding off would have meant a 20-mile taxi ride back to my home in Naperville. During my residence in Ascot, I would either have to get off at Martins Heron, the next stop, or I would have to go on to Bracknell or even to Reading.

Thankfully, while in Chicago I never lost my ticket (we had to clip them to the seat in front of us so the conductor could easily validate our travel) and I never missed my train station by nodding off. During my stay at Ascot I never lost my ticket. The obvious omission here leads to my final Ascot anecdote.

Each year The Institute of Petroleum hosted a dinner attended by 1200 or more of the industry movers and shakers in the United Kingdom. During my time spent in the United Kingdom as Kerr-McGee's Vice President and General Manager of Exploration, I attended most of these dinners. The dinners were black-tie affairs and I faithfully paid the 40 pounds sterling rental fee to go attired in Austin Reed finery. Why I never purchased a tuxedo is another matter.

In 1995 I attended as an invited guest of one of our industry partners. Wine and hard drinks were served at a pre-dinner reception in a private room. When we were finally seated for dinners and the presentation, we were in great spirits. Wine flowed freely and by the time dinner was concluded, and we had returned to the reception room for one final night cap, I was feeling no pain. Around 11:00 p.m. we parted company and most of the managers met their carriages (limousines) for transport to their urban or suburban homes. I made the mistake of thinking I did not need to incur all that expense on behalf of the company; I would just get a taxi to Waterloo and take the train out to Ascot where I knew there would be a taxi waiting at the pick-up point. Bad decision!

When I stepped on the train to Ascot, my shiny shoes, coat, tails, vest, and bow tie certainly stood out. I was a dandy, obviously and sorely out of place. I took my usual 10 or 15-minute nod-off, and then watched the platforms as we made one stop after another; Staines was followed by Virginia Water. Next would be Sunningdale and Ascot. The train lurched and I awoke from a nod-off I did not see coming. I looked out the window as the train began to pick-up speed. The platform was totally foreign to me, but just as we left the end of the platform I turned and looked at the signpost on the incoming side. It read "Ascot". I did not recognize my own platform at first because I just never saw it as the train departed outgoing. I was always off the train by that time.

I wracked my brain thinking what was next on the line. Oh yes, it would be Martins Heron. I had no idea what this train station was like, but I knew it was only a few miles down the line from Ascot. Surely there would be taxi waiting for late arriving passengers. I was also aware that I was on the last train of the evening and that there would be no further ingoing or outgoing trains until morning. It was now nearly midnight.

I was the only passenger who got off at Martins Heron. There was not a soul to be seen after I took the crossover to the station and looked around. I then came to the realization that I was in the middle of an industrial complex and all the workers had long ago departed. There was no taxi standing by. I did see a pay phone, but when I worked my way over to it, I learned that in this remote and untended location the only form of payment the pay phone accepted was a BT pay card. It did not accept either coins or other credit cards. Damn!

And There We Were

Out of immediate rescue options, I walked along the road out to the A329 (the London Road and the way back to Ascot) where I remembered there was a service station. The station would surely be closed, but like all service stations, it most likely had a "normal" pay phone from which I could contact the taxi dispatcher. Typical of my evening, the station did not have an outdoor pay phone.

So... there I was, 4 miles or so from Ascot, with nothing left to do but walk towards town. If I was lucky, I would arrive at an inn about 2 miles down the road before they closed at 2:00 a.m. I thanked my lucky stars that it was not raining. I even felt a bit comfortable with the fact that there was no traffic on the road. I could just see some wag driven by and seeing this 6' 4" fellow walking along the highway in a tuxedo. The shoes remained shiny, but the cummerbund was riding low and my pants kept slipping down. I had decided earlier to release my tie and had stuck it in my pocket.

I negotiated the two miles and then, sweating, walked in the door of the inn as they were about to lock the door. When I asked if I could use their phone, they directed me to a pay phone right outside of the front entrance. The desk made change for a five-pound note so I could make a call.

I reached the taxi dispatcher, identified my location, and asked for a ride into Ascot. I made the erroneous assumption the cab would come from Ascot, and I looked that way to see if any lights were coming my way. I decided I did not need to wait at the inn. I could walk along the highway and wave down any oncoming vehicle. After walking about a mile, I realized there would be no cab coming to my rescue. I hitched up my pants and begin the long walk down the road to Ascot. When I got into the village, I went to the pay phone in front of Ascots, the coffee shop, and called Muirfield. It was now nearly 2:30 a.m. When Shirley answered I simply said, "Come get me. I am in front of Ascots." She did not even ask why I was making this call. She knew something was not right.

I was never so glad to see that sweet woman as I was when I saw the car lights and then saw her pull over to pick me up. I told her my tale of woe as she drove me home. I went straight to bed, but it was nearly 3:15 a.m. before I fell asleep. My alarm went off at 4:45 a.m. which was my normal wake-up time. I would be ready when my driver came to pick me up to take me to the train station.

When I recounted my adventure to my boss Mike Webb, he said only that the company was lucky this had happened in the United Kingdom. He said that if I had found myself in similar circumstances on the streets of Houston, Kerr-McGee would almost certainly be searching for a new Vice-President.

I went to a number of Institute dinners in subsequent years, and I always hired a limousine to drive me home, just like all of the other executives did. I had learned my lesson. I can tell you I never fell asleep and missed my stop at Ascot again. And my plan, if it ever happened, was to travel to Bracknell where cabs awaited and the lights were still on.

And There We Were

Chapter 16

Memorable Excursions In the United Kingdom, Ireland and Continental Europe

*T*ourists who visit a country, or a continent, cannot really appreciate the subtleties of culture and location as foreigners who live there do. Often, even the citizens of countries, and I include those living in the United States, do not savor and appreciate the beauty and thrills available in their own country. The local citizenry takes for granted what others see as unique and memorable. If you see something every day, you can come to view landmarks and entertainment opportunities as background noise. There is no urgent need to investigate these, even if they are amazing. Knowing that one will eventually get around to visiting a landmark, because there are years to do so, makes it easy to postpone a visit. He or she can always make the effort when feeling less tired or when other matters are less pressing. For most foreigners living in a country, there is an urgency which compels them to see and do all they can in the time that is available.

When I reflect on the pace of our lives whilst living abroad, I often wonder how we did it. Where did we ever get the energy? Coming home from an event around midnight, and then waking between 4:30 and 5:00 a.m. to catch a 6:00 a.m. train is brutal, especially when it is a repeated experience. When I read my diary of our days spent abroad, I am reminded of how seriously sleep deprived we often were.

One might ask, "How could we have allowed this to happen

repeatedly? Surely we had control of our outings. If it was just up to Bob and Shirley, then that might be true. But there was always more at play than that.

Shirley's calendar was filled with activities selected by the very active ladies who were the American Women of Berkshire-Surry (AWBS). Many of our expatriate friends loved to entertain in their homes. Bob made numerous trips back to the United States each year (an average of 19 roundtrips per year), most of which were business related. Other trips were made to specifically see family members. Our son Taran was playing college football at Dartmouth, and our parents in Oregon were advancing in years.

Left to herself Shirley would have been quite busy just taking country walks, traveling to Europe, playing bridge, and making 2 or 3 weekly trips into London to shop and dine at her favorite haunts. Bob would have been happy just having the occasional dinner at a favorite restaurant along the Thames or popping into one of our favorite pubs. For those who are managers in the English oil and gas industry, however, there is a social calendar that, filled as it is with spectacular events, is often all consuming.

Unlike here in the United States, exploration and production managers in the United Kingdom were expected to be both gracious hosts and gracious guests across a very wide spectrum of dining and entertainment venues. Sometimes, entertainment took the form of dinner in the city, followed by attendance at play or an opera. Dinner in the country was also a possibility, but the vast majority of the entertainment was related to sporting events (rugby, soccer, horse racing, pheasant hunts, and golf to name a few). Most were all day, or several day events.

Kerr-McGee had so many partners in our North Sea exploration licenses that invitations flowed into our office at a weekly or bi-weekly rate. Another very active source of invitations were the vendors who offered us all manner of entertainment to demonstrate how much they appreciated our business. There were also invitations for annual dinners and seminars hosted by the governments of Ireland and England through their respective Institutes of Petroleum.

There were the Licensing Rounds to prepare for followed by presentations to the English Department of Trade and Industry. It was always a dizzying whirl wind of activity and entertainment. But Oh! So much fun!

What follows are some of our most memorable excursions. Although the list may seem long, it does not begin to describe all we did on a day-to-day basis. When our sons came to visit, they noticed the first thing their mother did each morning was pour a cup of coffee, after which she reviewed her calendar to see what was on the day's agenda.

Valentine's Day on the Venice Simplon Orient-Express

Shirley's creative imagination and sense of fun were responsible for Kerr-McGee hosting a remarkably memorable industry function. The company had previously hosted events at the Ascot races and at several rural English golf courses. On this occasion, Shirley suggested we make our industry partners, "Men of Romance". What could possibly please a lady more than to be taken on a Valentine's Day luncheon excursion aboard the Orient Express? Husbands invariably wonder, "What should I do for my Valentine this year?", so I knew each of our managing director partners would be ecstatic knowing they had Valentine's Day covered. The five-hour excursion proved to be even more grand than I thought possible.

The Orient-Express has always been known for glamor and elegance, and this was especially so in the golden age of luxury during the 1920s and 1930s. The original carriages were built in the golden age and the polished wood, grand upholstery, and antique finishings have been meticulously maintained. Over the years, routes have been minimized. Although it is still possible to travel from England to Paris and beyond, travel to Turkey is no longer in the mix. For romantics, a journey on the

FIGURE 19. SHIRLEY LENT ON THE ORIENT EXPRESS, VALENTINE'S DAY, 1995

Orient-Express is a trip back to a time when luxury and service beyond compare were a propriety of all that was grand when it came to "Romance of the Rails."

Kerr-McGee was host to twenty-six guests when we boarded the Phoenix carriage at London's Victoria Rail Station. We had gathered in an Venice Simplon Orient-Express lounge to await departure. When it was time to board, we walked onto the platform and were greeted by stewards wearing white jackets, black bow ties, and white gloves. Once seated at our respective tables, we were offered a glass of Champagne. Everyone was dressed to the nines, especially the women. It appeared that no jewelry had been left at home.

Several of the men and a few of the women were intimidated by the opulence on display. An elderly couple at the table to our right exhibited the behavior one might expect. Although the couple was not part of our group, the lady was beaming, absolutely delighted to be a part of the journey about to begin. Her husband was mortified stiff. This was the last place he wanted to be. His wife kept saying, "Relax, you are going to love this experience."

On our small table was a bouquet of flowers in an ornate golden vase. Menus were off to the side of crystal glasses and table ware. Wine was on its way. The meal was six courses followed by after dinner liquors. Violinists walked the aisles of the carriages playing romantic love songs.

Liquor before, during, and after lunch had relaxed even the most reserved guests. Unexpected good fortune blossomed when one guest (not one of Kerr-McGee's guests) proved to be a musician and singer who wanted to make his lady's day special. After lunch he stood at the end of the carriage and serenaded us all. Soon patrons from other carriages were making their way to our carriage. I had moved to a chair closer to the music, and before I knew it a lady (from New York) walked through our carriage door and plopped down on my lap. I was glad Shirley was nearby, and that she was so forgiving of the behavior of a seriously inebriated woman. What a party! As beautiful as the countryside was the party made the scenic journey almost incidental.

The five hours passed by quickly, and before we were ready, we were back in Victoria Station. Something unusual happened when the train stopped. I had never been on a train that pulled into a train station when travelers did not jump up to leave. No one in our carriage even moved. No one wanted this experience to end. Our day had been that much fun. On our way home to Muirfield, I mused that Kerr-McGee had set a high standard. How could anyone top this for an industry function? As for that elderly gentleman who had been in acute distress after he had been seated, he appeared to have had the best time of his life.

A Weekend in Venice, Italy

It would be hard to top the 1995 romantic excursion we had on the Orient-Express. But romance was, in April 1997, still in the air, for it was then that we flew to Venice for a long three-day weekend. England is a great jumping off spot for trips to the Continent. During our stay in the United Kingdom we made trips to a number of Continental destinations. The trip to Venice was among our more memorable excursions.

Our British Airways flight to Venice took us over parts of France, Germany, and Austria. The weather was clear the day we flew. The snowcapped and rugged Alps were simply beautiful. Shirley was glued to the window, oohing and awing the whole trip. Despite having seen a lot of grand geology from the air, I found this aerial overflight of the Alps particularly captivating. The glacially carved valleys had precipitous walls that rose several thousand feet. There were many isolated villages perched on rugged spurs that descended from the high Alps to the plains of northern Italy. When we began our descent into Marco Polo Airport, I was fascinated by the transition of the landscape to farmland, obviously the breadbasket of northern Italy.

We retrieved our baggage and took a water taxi to the Hotel Gritti, located in San Marco facing the Grand Canal. Our room was spacious and opulent, and it should have been since the room rate was approximately one million Lira (then about $600) per night. We unpacked our luggage and went for a walk through the narrow streets of Venice. We crossed several narrow waterways before coming to the Piazza San Marco, the major plaza in Venice. Although our first impression of the piazza did not compare favorably with impressions of the Grand Place we had seen in Brussels, we found that the more time we spent in and around the piazza, the more beguiled we were by it. Music was coming from multiple locations, most of it played on piano or violin. We continued our walk along the ever-turning streets. We eventually came to the Rialto Bridge, the oldest and most famous bridge in Venice. The Bridge has many shops on the archway, and numerous coffee houses line both sides of the Grand Canal. We could not pass up a gondola ride back to the Hotel Gritti.

We dressed for dinner and ate a gourmet meal at the Hotel's Club del Doge Restaurant which looks out onto the Grand Canal and across the Canal to the Santa Maria Church. After dinner we retreated to the Hotel's piano bar where we listened to some great music, which only got better when the musician realized there were some who were actually listening to him play. When we were not watching the increasingly animated pianist our eyes wandered to the beautiful Venetian glass chandeliers...with orange and green flowers and almost opal like white stems. The color of the glass and room were nearly as intoxicating as our after-dinner liqueurs. Shirley and I were not the only couple holding hands and hugging each other.

On Saturday morning we took a water taxi to Murano and Burano, two of the islands in the Northern Venetian Lagoon. Burano is known for its many multicolored houses, Murano for its glass making. We watched the artisans blowing glass, and we toured several of shops having glassware for sale. The tours through the sales rooms were fascinating. We were amazed at what the Venetians can do with a little silica and pigment. Most of what we saw was beautiful. Bob must be given credit or chastised, however one views the decision, for the purchase of a seven million Lira glass piece that has seven solid glass-colored birds perched upon a green glass blown tree. That piece remains one of the three favorite "treasures" on display in our home in Texas. After making the Murano purchase, I was apprehensive the piece might be damaged during its transport to our home in England. When it finally arrived, all pieces were intact and as beautiful as ever.

We spent Saturday afternoon and Sunday morning visiting sights around the Piazza San Marco. We went atop the Clock Tower, toured the Doge's Palace, and wondered at the architecture of Saint Marks Basilica. Much of what we saw was built at the time Venice was a center of trade between East Asia and Europe. I came to the realization that when wealth is in abundance, beautiful art and architecture flower.

The Piazza floods when the tides are high and the water level rises in the Venetian Lagoon. I do not know how the shops and cafes operate when the water is three or four feet high in the plaza, but they do. I saw pictures of boardwalks crowded with merchants and customers wearing boots. So much beauty, so much worry.

A water taxi delivered us to the airport for our return flight to London. Upon reflection I was certain our Venice trip would be among the top ten experiences of our stay in the United Kingdom. And it was.

The Tall Ship Races

During our stay in the United Kingdom Kerr-McGee drilled an exploratory well in Lyme Bay located off of the English Channel coastline. The award of our exploration license was received with considerable opposition from the local citizens, from environmental groups, and from local governing bodies. Lyme Bay is one of several bays located along an extended stretch of the southern English Channel, designated as a World Heritage Site. The Dorset and East Devon Coast is one of exceptional beauty. Chesil Beach along the east shore of Lyme Bay is one of the most studied beaches in the world. Onshore is the East Devon Area of Outstanding Beauty.

Gaining approval for our exploratory well involved innumerable meetings with local citizen groups and local governing bodies. We also conducted a year-long study of the wildlife in the ocean, on the ocean floor, and in the air to provide a baseline assessment of conditions in the Bay prior to our drilling. If something bad happened, and we had no reason to expect that it would, we wanted to be able to specifically determine whether there was any adverse effect of wildlife caused by our drilling activity. The cost of this baseline assessment was significant.

In July of 1994 the environmental study group Kerr-McGee had commissioned to observe and document all visible birds, cetaceans, fish, and benthonic bottom dwellers on a daily basis, invited Kerr-McGee management and spouses to a special event to commence at Weymouth, a coastal port located along the eastern edge of Lyme Bay. Much attention was given to the vessels competing in the Cutty Sark Tall Ship Races. The ships would set sale that day from the Old Harbor and race one another to the Spanish coastal towns of La Coruna and Oporto before crossing the finish line at St. Malo, France.

The Tall Ships are magnificent and when they set sail it is an unbelievably impressive sight. Over 80 of these ships were anchored in the Old Harbor on the day our group visited Weymouth Port. Limited space in the harbor required the ships to moor side by side and parallel to the shoreline. Both sailors and visitors had to walk from one ship to another to reach the outermost anchored vessel. The world's largest sea going tall ship at the time was the 450 feet long and 190 feet tall (nineteen stories if you will) High Russian Sedov. All ships in the races were manned almost exclusively by young cadets, aged 15 to 25. Setting the sail requires these young sailors crawl out on the cross beams to unfurl the sail sheets. From afar the boys on the cross beams look like pigeons on electrical transmission lines.

We had three memorable experiences during our attendance at the Races. Prior to our arrival at the Old Harbor, we visited nearby Chesil Beach where we toured the Swannery at Abbotsbury, home to two or three hundred swans. These swans and their ancestors have been raised at Abbotsbury from as far back as the 14th Century for food and income. No big deal you say, eh? Not so fast. Most everyone in the England knows that swans are the property of the monarch, today that being Queen Elizabeth. One had better not say he had a fine dinner of roast swan or he/she will end up in Tower Hill. In truth, swans outside of the Swannery are revered and treated like royalty. One day our train into London was delayed for an hour. The reason given us for the delay was that there were swans on the track at Staines. In the United States there would have been feathers everywhere as the train motored on without braking.

We visited the Swannery and chatted with the swan herder

tending the swans and the goslings. He had fascinating tales to tell. The setting for the Swannery is spectacular. It sets amongst the green and grassy shoreline of the Fleet, a narrow finger of water that separates the Swannery from Chesil Beach. A viewing area allows visitors to watch the nesting and feeding swans, while at the same time observing the outstanding beauty of the surrounding shoreline.

After our visit to the Swannery, we returned to the Old Harbor for high tea onboard one of the Tall Ships. Our visit provided a great opportunity to gage the size of the ship, and to visit many of the young cadets. Reaching our host ship required a walk across two other vessels. While Shirley was walking across one of the ships, she encountered two Swedish lads taking a shower, nude as could be. They apologized to my sweet wife, and saying they were sorry, but it was not often they had access to so much fresh water under which they could bathe. She nodded, and simply said, "Well, enjoy!"

Our most memorable moment occurred when the Tall Ships were about to set sail. We were on a yacht offshore and amongst a great many other watercraft gathered to see the ships off on their great race. When the time came our yacht was out front and we were the lead boat heading out into the English Channel. On board for our enjoyment were a lavish seafood buffet, an open bar, and nattily attired attendants. This was indeed a most special adventure.

Several years after the Tall Ships sailed Kerr-McGee drilled the aforementioned dry hole in Lyme Bay. There were no drilling problems, and we did not pollute the waters of Lyme Bay.

Memorable Excursions

The British Open
July 1996

When Shirley and I arrived in the United Kingdom, there was one event I hoped we might eventually attend. I am not into the game of golf, although I do play now and then. I have, however, always been mesmerized by the British Open. Through many hours spent watching the Open on television, I came to appreciate the difficulty of the golf courses and the historic significance of the event. When we moved into Muirfield our connection to the Open became much more tangible knowing we were living in the house built by Nick Faldo, who for several years was the world's top ranked golfer. Faldo won the Open three times, equaling the number of Opens won by the great Jack Nicklaus. I was pleasantly surprised to discover Shirley was also interested in attending the Open Championship. Our dreams came true when we attended the 1996 Championship at Royal Lytham and St. Annes, down the coast a few miles from the city of Blackpool.

Rick Mott, the General Manager of Exploration for Phillips Petroleum, and his wife Leslie invited Shirley and I to be their guests for a day at the Open on Saturday. Friday morning, we were up early and drove 225 miles to Blackpool, located on the eastern shore of the East Irish Sea. The drive from our home in Ascot took us through some beautiful countryside we had not previously visited. After we checked into our hotel, Rick informed me he had made reservations for the two of us to play a round of golf on a sister course to Royal Lytham and St. Annes. It would, he reasoned, be a great way to get a feel for the type of golf we would see during the third round of the Open. I must say the round was an eye-opener. The fairways were hard, the grass short and brown. The bunkers were deep with near vertical banks. It was a hot and clear day. The beer we drank at the end of our round never tasted so good.

Before Rick and I left for our round of golf, I felt bad about leaving Shirley and Leslie to themselves while we were out on the links. When I finally struggled up to our hotel room after

And There We Were

the exhausting round of golf, I was concerned Shirley might have had a boring afternoon - a strange new city and a new acquaintance. I was surprised to walk into an empty hotel room. Moreover, we were scheduled to attend a dinner function in less than an hour, and Shirley needed more than an hour to prepare herself for any industry social event.

As I was about to step into the shower, Shirley came rushing into our hotel room. Despite her late arrival, she was bubbling over with stories of how she and Leslie had spent the afternoon. In a very short period of time they had watched ballroom dancing and had wine at the Blackpool Tower, had ridden a giant Ferris Wheel at the end of the boardwalk, had mounted mules for a ride along the beach, had gone into a loud western bar to listen to *Achy Breaky Heart* and other similar tunes, and had taken a short helicopter ride. They had considered taking a ride on the world's tallest roller coaster, but the 300-foot drop was more than the girls thought they could take. As a result of Shirley's exuberant exploration, I discovered that Blackpool is a vibrant tourist haven. My fun-loving wife and her new friend had made the most of it. I should have known that Shirley would not be moping around the hotel room all afternoon. We made it to the dinner on time, and enjoyed plenty of food, wine, and camaraderie. It was a delightful industry function.

On Saturday we arrived early at Royal Lytham and St. Annes for a day at the Open. We checked into the Phillips' Guest Chalet, where we were given the details for lunch and high tea. Everything was made clear so that we would not get hungry, thirsty, or lost on that hot sunny day. The Lytham course was a typical Open links. We watched a number of great golfers including Jack Nicklaus, Gary Player, Corey Pavin, John Daly, Ian Woosman, and our favorite, Nick Faldo.

The Open was memorable for a number of reasons. On the first hole we watched Ian Woosman plant his tee shot in a steep bunker, the ball up against the vertical edge. I was sure that Mr. Woosman was up against it, with no chance to get up and down for a par. But the short golfer planted one foot against the bank and chipped the ball about 3 feet from the pin. He made his par. Unbelievable.

While we were waiting for the Woosman group to vacate the tee, I heard a very loud CRACK!. I turned and asked a stranger what that noise was. He smiled and said he was sure it was Tiger Woods teeing off on the 2nd hole. And it was. Tiger was 20 years old and playing in his very first Open Championship, and he was not the winner that year. Tom Lehman was the one who hoisted the claret jug.

After lunch, served on linen tablecloths with bountiful amounts of beer, wine, and juice, we were ready for an afternoon full of memorable moments. We were lined up beside the ropes when Jack Nicklaus walked off a green on his way to the next hole. As he walked he looked many spectators in the eye and had a smile for each. One of those spectators was Shirley, who was beside herself knowing it was that Jack Nicklaus had smiled at her.

Later in the afternoon, we watched John Daly prepare to tee off on a very narrow fairway lined on both sides by spectators. I was thinking that had it been me on the tee, all the spectators would have been in mortal danger. Even for John Daly, the safety margin for avoiding a catastrophic or errant tee shot was small. Daly threw down his cigarette, pulled out his driver, and, without pausing, "gripped it and ripped it". The ball faded out of sight around a dogleg. I was dumbfounded. The ball was in the fairway, a long distance from his still smoldering cigarette.

After the round we said our goodbyes to Rick and Leslie and headed for the parking lot. Walking near us was the Shark, Greg Norman. What a way to end our stay.

From Blackpool we headed north into the Lake District. We had reservations at the Lithwaite Hotel on Crooks Road, Windermere. The Lithwaite is located high on a hilltop and overlooks Lake Windermere. The hotel had been voted the best hotel in England, and even though small, the service was excellent. The food and scenic views were unbeatable. Our room had a very large picture window that gave us a view of not only Lake Windermere, but also of the Cumberland Mountains looming high in the west.

After we checked into our room, we took a cab down to Lake Windermere for a peaceful and scenic steamer ride up the lake to the village of Ambleside and back. The excursion put us in the right mood for wine on the veranda and dinner. We reluctantly entered the restaurant as the sun was beginning to sink over the mountains to the west. There was going to be a wonderful red sunset. Halfway through our dinner, the waiter whispered in Shirley's ear that the sunset was at its most beautiful point, whereupon she excused herself and went out on the veranda. Other patrons in the small dining room had overheard Shirley's spoken intentions: it was not long before only the men were left at the tables. When the best part of the sunset had come and gone Shirley rejoined me for dinner - she didn't seem to mind that her meal was on the cold side. After dinner we took our coffees on the veranda. I could not believe it. The red had faded but there was still a purple haze hanging over the distant Cumberland Mountains. What a sight! It was 10:30 p.m. and we were ready to call it a day. What a day it had been.

When we returned to Muirfield on Sunday, Shirley looked at me and said that she was not ready for the weekend adventure to end. It had been a memorable trip in so many ways. The Sawyer's daughter was living the life.

Back at the office on Monday I told members of my staff how beautiful we had found the Lake District. They were in awe. One fellow said he had been to the Lake District four times and had never seen either the sun or the mountains. We had been blessed with clear skies and warm temperatures. Shirley's kind of weather to be sure.

Memorable Excursions

TRAVELS TO IRELAND

The Lent family has had a love affair with Ireland since our sons were toddlers. St. Patrick's Day was a big event in our household. If we were not decked out in green, we heard about it from Shirley. Dinner fare always included Irish soda bread, corned beef, and cabbage. The meal was prepared and eaten accompanied by Irish music. You might think that Bob and Shirley's ancestors came from Ireland. They did not.

During our stay in the United Kingdom we took a number of trips to Ireland. Most of these trips were business related, but I also managed two memorable fishing trips, one with our elder son Tobin. Shirley found Ireland to be magical. If there was a way to make a journey special, we all know by now that Shirley always found a way to make it so.

On the first of our many trips to Dublin, Shirley and I made like tourists. Compared to many other European cities Dublin is small enough that most of the major attractions can be seen by taking short walks from a downtown hotel. Our hotel was the Westbury on Grafton Street. We pub crawled, window shopped, and people watched. We walked the grounds of Trinity College, where I would one day give a talk to the media and faculty on the exploration potential of offshore Ireland, as assessed by Kerr-McGee. Shirley was introduced to Guinness draught beer at the Guinness brewery at St. James Gate. She forever after asked why the Guinness in England and the United States never tasted as good as that which she sampled in Dublin. Many others have asked the same question. We took a short trip south of Dublin to the village of Waterford where the famous crystal is manufactured. We also toured the highlands along the coast overlooking looking the Irish Sea to the east. During our last evening in Dublin, we found ourselves in a pub with 16 drunken English Rugby fans celebrating their team victory over Ireland in a Five Nation match. I doubt that the pub's Irish patrons were impressed with the cacophony, but Shirley and I certainly were.

During one of my last business trips to Dublin I attended

the annual black-tie dinner put on by The Institute of Petroleum - Irish Branch. Kerr-McGee had reserved a table for 10. Our guests included industry representatives from Mobil, Amoco, Marathon, and the Irish Government. The affair was low-lighted by a very boring speech given by the Irish Minister of Petroleum. It was possibly the worst after dinner speech I have heard. The talk was so bad that I did not see one of my compatriots leave the table. I had fallen asleep.

Shirley's most memorable trip to Ireland took place in May of 1997. We, on separate flights, flew to Shannon where I was to attend a meeting of the Irish Offshore Operators Association. The meeting and our rooms were in Dromoland Castle, an impressive five-star hotel located approximately 12 minutes north of the Shannon airport in County Clare. Surrounded by 450 acres of beautifully landscaped grasslands and gardens, Dromoland is magnificent. The Castle's northern baronial facade faces the waters of an "enchanting" lake. The Castle was once home to a line of the Kings of Thomand, whose ancestral lineage goes back to Brian Borug, the last High King of Ireland.

Shirley arrived on a Thursday afternoon so that she might have more time to enjoy the surrounds before I arrived later in the afternoon. Unfortunately, my plane was late and I missed having dinner with Shirley. She had dressed for dinner and presented herself at the formal dining room thinking I would arrive any moment. As she always did, she made friends with many of the waiters and water boys who began to feel sorry for this beautiful woman who was seated at her table alone, a glass of wine in hand. Several of the servers made the inquiry, "Have you heard from Bob?" It eventually became apparent that something had sadly delayed my arrival. Shirley ordered a lobster dinner and followed that up with a glass of port. With the sun still shining, she took a long walk along the manicured green grass bordering Dromoland Lake. She watched the sun set as a mother duck tried to keep her 9 ducklings from wandering too far from the reeds and cattails. I did not arrive until 10:30 p.m., well after dark. I was miserable, Shirley not so much so.

Friday morning I was up early, had breakfast, and attended the Operators meeting. Shirley and several other ladies went on a tour of the nearby Cliffs of Moher. These near vertical cliff faces reach a maximum height of almost 700 feet. The views from the cliff edges are both awe inspiring and terrifying. The roads through the grasslands leading up to the cliff edge offer no indication of the precipitous lip that is only a few feet away. The flat lying strata are composed of alternating layers of sand and shale that form ledges covered with vegetation and birdlife. Only a few of the ladies joined Shirley as she walked over a grassy terrace to the cliff edge.

After visiting the Cliffs, the tour bus stopped at a pub along Galway Bay. It was in one of these Galway Bay pubs that I later, on another trip, had a chat with a charming couple whom I found were tourists from Corvallis, Oregon. At the time there were only four of us in the pub. Time and again it has proved to be a small world.

After Shirley's day out with the ladies and following my day of business meetings, we joined the other couples at Dromoland for an evening of dining and dancing hosted by the Operators Association. It can be quite beneficial matriculating with other exploration executives and their wives, especially when the other executives work for companies active in Irish offshore oil and gas exploration. An Irish violinist and a harpist offered soft background music as we dined.

We were up early Saturday morning for a trip to the incredibly scenic Dingle Peninsula. World class vistas enchanted us as Shirley and I drove the roadway that loops around this most western part of Ireland. Unlike the rock strata observed at the Cliffs of Moher, the Dingle Peninsula strata are steeply dipping, sometimes even standing on end. Numerous narrow bays and inlets are spaced haphazardly between rocky outliers. Before the Peninsula was uplifted to its present elevation, oceanic erosion had carved broad flat terraces that now truncate the tilted rock formations. White sheep graze on these green coastal terraces. Some of the terraces have been tilted by recent (geologically speaking) uplift. On some of the headlands the roadway is carved into the cliffs. When we reached the apex of the roadway loop around the Peninsula, we knew that were we able to continue, we would next set foot on land in Boston.

One of my favorite recollections when I think of the Dingle Peninsula comes from a scene in the movie, *The Spirit of St. Louis*. James Stewart, in the role of Charles Lindbergh, is somewhat lost as he approaches the end of Lindbergh's solo flight across the Atlantic. Looking for a landform he might identify he says, "It is the Dingle Peninsula. I am over southern Ireland."

Two of the trips I made to Ireland were for fun only. They were fishing adventures in Mayo and Galway Counties, western Ireland. Outings like these fishing trips are special since one gets to see scenic areas and to sample life as it is in villages, very much unlike those august locales where business meetings are held. Road trips taken in foreign countries invariably leave me glued to the car window. One gets to witness sights and activities not observable by any other means of cross-country transport. Need I add that the views available on any foreign road trip are vastly different from those along that road to Big Summit Prairie in Central Oregon?

In March of 1996 one of our accountants in London, Kevin Ringrose, invited me to join him on a weekend fishing trip to Ireland. Kevin is a native of Ireland and owns a small cottage in County Mayo near Lough (Irish equivalent of Loch) Corrib, a large freshwater lake (27 miles long, 10 miles wide, 160 feet deep). Ringrose was making a trip to deliver a BMW to his father's home in Corofin. Aware that I was into fly fishing, he thought I might enjoy a chance to do a bit of Irish fishing. I jumped at the opportunity.

We departed downtown London at approximately 1:00 p.m. to drive to Holyhead in Wales for a 6:20 p.m. departure of the ferry that would carry us across the Irish Sea to Dublin. The trip across England took us past High Wycombe, Birmingham, Shrewsbury, Telford, and Oswestry. The beautiful Welsh countryside became more mountainous as we drove westward. The verdant green hillsides were well populated with white lambs, many of which were newborn. The hillside meadows in this part of Wales have an abundance of thyme mixed in with the wild grass, and it is said that the taste of lamb from the area incorporates a hint of thyme. The mountains that lie within the Snowdonia Forest are impressive. Most of the valleys we traversed were carved out by Pleistocene glaciation. We descended to the coastal plain along the Rivers Dee and Alwyn.

About 170 miles from Holyhead we realized that it was going to be tight for us to make our Ferry connection. We increased our speed well above the legal limit, and still arrived at the departure dock at 6:40 p.m., 20 minutes after the scheduled departure time. Some people live right, and the Stena Hovercraft was an hour late in departing. Our good fortune did not keep the lady who took our ticket from chastising us for cutting it so short. We crossed the Irish Sea in 1 hour and 50 minutes, just enough time for several potty breaks, a beer or two, a number of sandwiches, a bit of duty-free shopping (whiskey for Kevin's dad, Jack), and a crack at the slot machines. As mentioned previously, the slots in the United Kingdom are really cash deposit centers: no winners ever.

We arrived in Dublin at 9:30 p.m. and began our drive across a dark Ireland. The trip west was via a major highway which connects Dublin to Galway. At Athlone we probably made a mistake by taking smaller roads (with smaller signposts) cross country. We passed through an interesting mix of small towns with names like Roscommon, Ballymoe, Allyhounis, and Claremorris, before finally arriving in Ballinrobe at 1:30 a.m. We placed coal in the fireplace and retired to our sleeping rooms. An interesting trip - London at noon, County Mayo at bedtime.

On Saturday morning Kevin, Jack, and I loaded our fishing gear and supplies in the BMW and traveled about six miles to Lough Corrib. What a visually interesting place! The lake is dotted with dozens of small islands. They stood out like an invading armada of ships, and they were present along the entire length of the lake. I found the water to be dark in color and highly variable in depth with many large boulders scattered on the bottom.

We fished Lough Corrib for two days. I cast my favorite flies over the open spaces between the submerged boulders. I never got one strike. Kevin, my host, caught a 14-inch German Brown. I would later find (from a ledger kept in a local pub) that the average angler catches one fish in a typical day of fishing.

So, although the fishing was great, the catching not so much so. The rest of the experience on and off the lake was fascinating.

The first day on the lake we took lunch on the lee side of a small island. The grass was green, but the soil was soft and wet giving the ground a spongy rebound as we walked across it. Jack set about making a pre-luncheon tea. He dipped water from the lake with a metal canister known as a "volcano pot". This 'pot' was made by welding an open top and bottom cone inside a metallic cylinder. The interior of the cone is a conduit for the fire, heat, and smoke. The surrounding cylinder is filled with water. A small fire at the base of the cone quite quickly brings the water to a boil. Boiling is good! With all the sheep and cattle doing their thing along the shore line, it was reassuring to have tea made from boiled water.

After our day on the lake, we dropped by the village of Cong for steaks and a few pints of Guinness. Cong is uniquely famous as the site of Ashford Castle, the vacation estate originally built for the Guinness family. Ashford Castle is now a five-star hotel (President Reagan stayed in it when he visited County Mayo).

I found one historical anecdote relating to the Ashford Castle Estate mind boggling. After the Estate was built and the Guinness family was in residence, the property became well known for the enormous population of Woodcocks present in the estate's forest lands. Woodcocks have stocky bodies with long slender bills and a brown or black plumage. Woodcocks are predominantly woodland birds, hence the name. For reasons unknown, the Guinness family took it upon themselves to invite the 10 finest marksmen in Ireland, England, and the Continent on a one-week hunt to prove who was the greatest shot in Europe. The 10 hunters qualified by winning national hunts. The Ashford Hunt, abetted by the use of dogs, continued for a number of years. On the single best day ever recorded, it was reported up to 300 Woodcocks were bagged. Today they stop the presses if anyone so much as hears a Woodcock.

One memorable image I took from my visit to Cong is that of a most beautiful stone house built over the River Robe. The floor of the house is no more than 2 feet above the water level. The living rooms and dining areas would be under water if the level rose 3 feet or more. The house has been there for a very long time so it must not flood. I know one thing, there is no basement.

On Sunday, the second day of our fishing trip we caught no fish, and Jack returned to his home in Corrofin. Kevin and I went to the Red Door Pub in Ballinrobe for dinner and a brew. We walked into a very crowded bar area partitioned in two rooms by an overhanging arch. I bellied (a good term for me) up to the bar and ordered two pints. Having heard how friendly the locals were, I was ready to start a conversation with anyone. You know, say something witty, and apologize for not catching any fish.

Strangely, no one spoke. No one even acknowledged we were there. When we sat down at a table, I noticed all of the patrons in our area had moved through the archway to the other room. When I returned for another pint, I asked the young lady behind the bar if the locals were always so standoffish. She said, "Oh, it's not you." She went on to explain that the people all knew each other and that they were at the pub for a post christening party. Some party! No one laughed or even talked. It had to have been a shotgun marriage.

On our trip down the Irish coast we stopped at Ballyvaughn on the shores of Galway Bay where we had a tasty lunch at the Monk's Pub. As we were seated by the fire eating fish chowder, we struck up a conversation with an engaging couple. They were the couple from Corvallis, Oregon whom I mentioned in the narrative of our trip to Dromoland Castle. When they said they were from Oregon, I was so gobsmacked I expected them to say they were from Prineville.

We traveled by the headlands known as the "Burren". This is a barren landscape, an expanse of dense limestone totally without vegetation. After a visit to the Cliffs of Moher, we dropped off the BMW at Corrofin and were driven to the Shannon airport for our return Aire Lingus flight to London.

My second Irish fishing trip occurred over the 1996 English Bank Holiday weekend (coincides with the American Memorial Day weekend - May 24-26). Our elder son Tobin joined me on this trip as did Kevin Ringrose and Ruth Howe, both Kerr-McGee employees. Kevin was again our host.

Tobin and I flew Ryanair, a very strict no-frills airline, from London's Stansted Airport, located about 70 miles from our home in Ascot. At Connaught International Airport near the town of Knock, we found Kevin and Ms. Howe waiting for us. Kevin drove us to his home in Ballinrobe. We unloaded our luggage and immediately rigged up our fly fishing rods. We walked down a dirt lane that led us to the River Robe, whereupon we walked through green meadows and grasslands to Lough Mask, another large freshwater lake in County Mayo. We roused a number of sheep and deer, and an Irish gentleman who was very polite, but who seemed to have only one oar in the water. His dog was also a bit off-center. We caught no fish, although the water looked good and the scenery was impressive.

After having returned to the house Kevin took us to John O'Conner's pub in Ballinrobe where we had a nice dinner and Tobin discovered the secret of Irish Guinness. After dinner we were entertained by a three-piece group that was seated at the table next to us. They played traditional Irish music. The musical instruments were spoons. Quite a large group gathered around the trio. When we left, we surely were the only ones who were going to go to bed before midnight.

Saturday was a full day, and we covered a lot of ground. After a traditional Irish breakfast, we packed our gear and headed for Newport on the Atlantic Coast. Kevin had reserved a boat to take us deep sea fishing on the outer reaches of Clew Bay. Our Captain was Tom Moran: Tom Jr. was his offshore gillie.

Our boat ride from Newport Harbor into Clew Bay took us through a most scenic area. One author has written that Clew Bay is a "miracle of beauty". He was right! The Bay is bracketed between highlands on both the north and the south and is populated with islands of all sizes. Many of the islands were home to small herds of cattle or flocks of sheep. Because sheep do not need a fresh water source, they are found even on the smallest of islands. Cattle must have access to fresh water, so they only inhabit islands with catchment areas and small ponds. Our trip in the Bay also took us by a number of pens where sea trout were being "farmed". As we approached these fish farms the fish began to jump, apparently confusing us with the boat that brings them feed.

The mountain on the southern horizon of the Bay is Croagh Patrick which is known as the pilgrimage mountain because of the many people who make the trek, some barefoot, to the summit to visit a holy shrine. The mountain trail is visible, even when viewed far from out in the bay. A wall of cumulus clouds formed a backdrop to the mountain, and the pale blue sky on the horizon turned darker shades until it was navy blue directly overhead.

We began fishing with jigs consisting of four to five artificial flies, equally spaced above a heavy piece of lead. The only fish we caught on this apparatus was a five-inch gurnard that Tobin hooked. Tobin did not know it was on the line, so he had taken the small fish on a ten-minute yo-yo ride while he was jigging. No one was more surprised at his catch than Tobin who never knew he had hooked a fish. We eventually switched to bottom fishing with bait and proceeded to land numerous dog fish and bull huss, all of which are members of the shark family. At the end of the day Tobin had hooked not only the smallest fish but also the largest, a ten-pound dog fish.

We sailed back to the harbor dock under bright sunshine. It was a good day to be alive. The grassy green slopes of the islands stair-stepped down to the sea. We rudely disturbed a sea lion on the tip of one of the islands when our boat passed close to shore. The sea gulls stayed with us until we tossed out all of the remaining mackerel bait.

After lunch at a pub in Newport we headed north for an appointment to fish for salmon on the River Moy. Ireland is renowned for its beautiful scenery, more of which we saw on our way to Ballina where we had reservations to fish the Ridge Pool on the Moy. I will not go into all of the details, but fishing for salmon by reservation, in an urban setting, with five other fishermen spaced along a pool is not my idea of fishing. The experience was marred by an old man who insisted on casting directly in front of me and over my line. There is at least one Irishman of whom I will never think highly and there is one American he will not care for.

Jack Ringrose, Kevin's dad joined us for a day of fishing on Lough Mask. Jack is a very good fisherman, maybe even as good as Kevin. He is also a fun fellow to be with. Lough Mask is another of those very large Irish freshwater lakes filled with numerous small islands. The Partry Mountains tower over the western edge of the lake and dense deciduous forests frame the rest of the water. Our day on the Lough was marred only by the mist that gave us what the locals call a "soft" day. Still the islands were bright green and most inviting. We stopped for lunch on one of the islands. An elevated terrace formed an apron around an elongated and mounded hill. Grass was everywhere and there were 7 cows and 14 sheep grazing on the upper slopes of the hill. We had tea, ate our lunch, and fed apples to the cows before catching live May flies for our afternoon of dapping bait. Tobin caught one trout dapping (hopping a live May fly over the top of the water). Jack caught one trout on an artificial fly.

Our trip to western Ireland ended on another sunny day. Kevin prepared us a fine breakfast. We watched a sheep dog herd a flock of lambs and ewes into a meadow across the road from our cottage. The dog then herded the sheep into a pen. It was fun to witness this creature doing a job that brought him great joy.

Kevin and Ruth drove us north to Knock where we caught an early flight back to Stansted. The trip was a lot of fun, especially for Tobin who said Ireland was just as he had imagined it to be.

Rugby, football (soccer), horse races, and outdoor Opera

As mentioned previously, we spent considerable time with our business partners who took us to entertaining venues. Shirley joined me when she thought she might find joy in an event. Otherwise, I was on my own. Attendance at Rugby matches did not include my fun-loving wife.

Although our first encounter with Five Nations Rugby occurred in Ireland, Shirley and I had not attended the match between Ireland and England. We were involved because we had inadvertently chosen to have a pint in a pub where a group of victorious English fans were celebrating their team's victory.

I was an invited guest to three Rugby matches, two of which were Five Nation affairs. England versus Wales was my first exposure to Rugby played at a high level. The match was held at Twickenham with much made of the fact His Royal Highness, Prince Edward was in attendance. The match was a sellout with more than 75,000 in attendance. I found the stadium to be as impressive as any I had seen. It reminded me of Mile High Stadium in Denver. I attended as a guest of Amoco. Another guest was John Brooks who was then head of the DTI Oil and Gas Division. Being the guest of Amoco, I left the schmoozing of Mr. Brooks to Alan May, our host and an Amoco VP. An interesting synchronicity: Alan played on a high school football team (Northglenn) in a 1972 Colorado State Championship football game, a game I attended with my then two-year old son, Tobin. Fifteen years later Tobin played in the same stadium against a Northglenn team. It was a state-semifinal game won by Tobin's team, Cherry Creek High School.

Our group arrived at the stadium at 11:00 a.m. for drinks. Lunch followed at 12:30 p.m. The fare was steak, vegetables, wine, dessert, cheese, and Port. The match went off at 3:00 p.m. Tea followed at 4:30 p.m., with more cheese and Port. A private car met me at 6:00 p.m. for my trip home. England won 25-18 and all was well in England. Nationalism was certainly involved and on display.

It is said that Rugby is a thug's game played by gentlemen in contrast to soccer which is said to be a gentleman's game played by thugs. Go figure. Of all the things one might think most memorable, I found that the half-time break was beyond belief. What with all the drink I had imbibed, I could hardly wait for half-time so I could make use of the facilities. As I was standing in line waiting my turn, I heard a very loud roar. England had scored and I had only left my seat five or ten minutes ago. What I later learned is that half-time is a very short break. The big fellows kneel on the pitch and suck an orange or two and then they are back at it. Even in American youth football the kids get a longer break than the combatants in a Five Nations Rugby match.

In 1997 I attended two other Rugby matches. One was another Five Nation match between England and Scotland. The other was the Pilkington Cup Final that was the 26th final of the Clubs Knockout Competition with Leicester taking on Sale.

Rugby players are physical specimens. One of our neighbors in Kier Park, Ascot had a son who was a junior rugby player. Our sons Tobin and Taran could not believe how spectacularly well-built this young man was. To add to their incredulity, the young man claimed he had never lifted weights. My American football playing sons could hardly believe one could have such a body without having lifted weights.

I attended my first football (soccer) match at Arsenal Stadium in Highbury, England. The Bolton Wanderers team was Arsenal's opponent. Although the stadium was modest, seating about 35,000 fans, the pitch was something else. I had never seen such an immaculate piece of turf. I do not believe a single blade of grass was out of place or cut at a different level.

Our host's suite was stocked with the food and drink one would expect from a corporate entertainer. I do not remember who my host was that day, but it had to be an oil company. While we were in our suite bookmakers kept entering and leaving, taking our bets for all manner of on-field activity. I thought the entire experience was bizarre, especially the zeal of the fans whose in-the-stand abuse was over the top. The soccer on the field was at a high level, as it should have been. It was a Premier League match. Arsenal easily defeated the Bolton Wanderers, and all of the local lads left the stadium in good spirits

I returned for one other match, when Arsenal played Liverpool. Arsenal lost 0-1 with Prince Harry amongst those in the sell-out crowd of 35,000. The stadium, pitch, and our suite were as they were on my first visit to Highbury. What I want to describe here are the sights and smells that surround the Stadium on game day. Upon emerging from the Arsenal Underground Station, one is a met by streets lined with almost continuous stalls, each selling programs, flags, and Arsenal merchandise (mostly clothing). The red and white Arsenal colors give the streets a very festive mix of color. There are Arsenal shirts, shorts, knitted caps, and jackets galore. The colorful flow of fans walking down the streets suggest not only a thriving market in Arsenal merchandize, but it also gives each street the appearance of blood flowing through an artery.

I cannot forget the game day smells. Any space not occupied by a clothing vendor is filled by someone selling and/or cooking sausages, hotdogs, burgers, and/or pita sandwiches. Everything, of course, come with chips (fries) and soda pop. If there were places selling beer, I did not see them. There may be a law prohibiting liquor sales. I can assure you, however, that many English soccer fans show up for a match having had a nip or two.

Following the match and the one-nil defeat I noticed there was a fellow on the street selling some sort of book dealing with humor. He kept yelling, "Don't let the one-nil loss get you down. Step right up and buy this pick-me-upper." Somehow the Arsenal fans were not buying his pitch. I did not see him make a single sale, but I was just strolling down the street. I did not wait to see what happened over a longer period of time.

I walked nearly the entire distance around Arsenal Stadium before reaching the Arsenal Underground Station where I found people backed up from the platform to the entrance to the Underground. I stood in line with the masses and eventually worked my way onto a train going to Waterloo Station. When I finally boarded the train to Ascot, there were six gentlemen seated near me talking about the Arsenal match and how poorly the lads had performed. Such was their passion that this discussion continued for approximately an hour: it would have gone on longer. but they got off as I did at Ascot Station.

Horse Races (other than Ascot)

Although our favorite race venue was and will always be the Ascot races, we attended a number of other interesting and entertaining horse racing events. Two other racing events we attended stand out, not necessarily because they were more fun-filled than the others.

Cheltenham Race Course in Cheltenham, Gloucestershire is host to a number of stunning races. Many of the races are run over long distances - three miles and more. If the distances were not rigorous enough, there were also fences and water hazards the horses had to negotiate. Only older horses have sufficient stamina to compete in these races.

In March of 1995 Shirley and I were at Cheltenham for the running of the Cheltenham Gold Cup a 3 mile, 2-1/2-furlong race for horses five years and older. Pre-race festivities included bands playing at several locations on the track grounds and scattered groups of folk dancers entertaining the strolling patrons. Food and drink were on offer from a number of serving areas. The mood was more than festive, the scenery spectacular.

The long course takes the racers around a track and then high up along the slope of a brilliantly green grassy hill. At times the horses are far from the viewing areas. I remember thinking how difficult it must be for these horses to run so far and to be subject to hurdling so many obstacles. Master Oats won the Gold Cup that day. He was a magnificent looking creature.

Glorious Goodwood! This is the way the locals speak of the

Goodwood Festival and its beautiful surrounds in Chichester, West Sussex. The Festival is a horse racing meet held annually at one of the most unusual and beautiful racecourses in the world. The track is built on the top of a "downs" (as mentioned previously, the English limestone hills are called downs, as in *Water Ship Down*), and the course is not an oval but rather a large sharply bent half oval that skirts a stream-incised valley. Always near the crest of the down, the course swings around the valley and then heads up to the finish line which is far removed from the viewing stands. The grass track is covered with a verdant green grass carpet; looking beyond the track brings the ocean (English Channel) into view.

This affair was hosted by Kerr-McGee for number of oil managers and their wives. Everyone was dressed to the nines and, as always, the drinks, lunch, and tea were catered. The entire outing was quintessentially English. The wives each were given ten British pounds in vouchers and some parlayed this offering into winnings. Unfortunately, my Pearl was not one of them.

Our drive to Goodwood took about 2 hours even though the course is only 45 miles from Muirfield. There is no easy way to get to Goodwood. The roads wind through small villages, each with a high street round-about, and each with a large traffic queue. While we were driving through one village, we noticed a bunch of young men and women getting off their bus and taking to the shrubs to relieve themselves. Several went to a nearby grocery store to purchase beer. We saw these shoppers running hard, cases of beer in hand, to catch up with their departing bus. All this activity seemed odd to us. We attributed our view of the situation to the fact that we must be growing "older". But you get the drift...... traffic was moving slowly.

On the way home from Goodwood we took a different route. The scenery was much nicer, and our route took us through the village of Petworth, renowned for its antique shops. Shirley had been to Petworth with the girls but for me the scenery and the village were a new treat.

Glyndebourne Festival Opera

Why is an outing to an operatic performance included herein? Just as at the horse racing events, rugby, and soccer matches, the Glyndebourne Opera is, if you can believe it, an outdoor affair.

A number of social events comprise "the season" in England, one of which is opera performed at Glyndebourne, East Sussex. This is no ordinary opera as the opera hall is outdoors, and the setting is in the countryside adjacent to the English Channel. As one drives the narrow road leading to the opera grounds, he might reasonably expect to see a village or two, but all of a sudden, the narrow road opens to reveal an old building adjacent to a modern oval structure. The two buildings are the old manor house and opera, and the new opera building. The grass and the wonderful hedges that partition large sections of the lawn are immaculate and well-trimmed.

What made our Glyndebourne experience unique was that the attendees, dressed in tuxes and cocktail dresses, sat on blankets or stood in the gardens drinking Champagne prior to the opera. While sipping Champagne, it was impossible to not appreciate the pastoral setting. Brilliantly green grass hills rose all around the opera house, and on these hills were the whitest ewes and lambs imaginable. One was tempted to take a double look because of the seemingly incongruous mix of farm and fashion.

The opera for our night was *Manon Lescaut*. Like most operas, it featured a sweet (albeit worldly) heroine, a love-stricken suitor, and a tragic ending. The songs and costumes were dazzling.

If the mix of fashion and farm is memorable when one arrives at Glyndebourne, then the way intermission is handled is even more so. After the second Act everyone filed either into the gardens or under a marquis to sit at wooden tables where picnic meals were served. Our hosts, Ray and Linda Charles, had organized a picnic consisting of poached salmon, asparagus, a generous salad, potatoes, and an abundance of wine. Strawberries and clotted cream topped off the repast.

After the opera concluded at 9:50 p.m., and we bid adieu to our hosts and the other couples, who were representatives from Statoil and Enterprise Oil. It was an unusual and memorably enjoyable evening. Our chauffeur returned us to Muirfield around midnight. Such outings were continual reminders of how far we had come from our small town in Oregon.

AWBS Trips to Europe

The American Women of Berkshire-Surrey (AWBS) not only maintained a very full calendar of events on the Big Island, they also organized numerous trips to the Continent. Shirley made two memorable trips to Germany and The Netherlands. One was to Christmas shop and the other to look at blooming flowers. Shirley was able to milk the most out of her trips, sometimes to the amazement and appreciation of her fellow travelers.

In 1996 Shirley and forty fellow members of AWBS took a three-day trip to The Netherlands to view the blooming of the tulips. The ladies flew to Amsterdam on April 29, one day prior to the countrywide celebration of Queen Beatrix's birthday which is a national holiday. The primary destination for the European excursion was the Keukenhof Tulip Gardens in Lisse, The Netherlands.

When the ladies landed in Amsterdam, they checked into the Eden Hotel, a modest hotel overlooking the Amstel River. This north Amsterdam hotel is only 1 kilometer from the famous Red Light District and a little over 2 kilometers from the Anne Frank House Museum. Lisse is about 14 kilometers from the hotel.

On the Queen's birthday, April 30, there were 750,000 to 1,000,000 visitors in Amsterdam, all there to partake in a city-wide celebration for the monarch. A colorful parade of watercraft navigated the main canals of Amsterdam, one of routes being along the canal in front of the Eden Hotel. Unfortunately, the Eden did not have good viewing areas in which to watch the parading watercraft and the waving Queen. Not to be stymied, Shirley found a nearby restaurant with a patio proximal to and overlooking the path of the Queen's parade. Shirley asked the Maitre D' if the ladies could sit at the outdoor tables by the canal for drinks and a mid-day luncheon. The ladies were stunned that Shirley would ask such a question, assuming the tables must already be reserved for the floating extravaganza soon to come down the canal. The Maitre D' was more than happy to accommodate the entire group. The ladies enjoyed a spectacular view of the parade of boats and of Queen Beatrix. If you do not ask, you do not know what you can get. Shirley always, always asked.

I found it interesting that Queen Beatrix celebrated the Queen's Birthday on April 30 even though her actual birthday is January 31. As a way to honor the memory of her mother, the former Queen, Queen Beatrix chose to continue to celebrate the "Queen's Birthday" on April 30, her mother's birthday. Queen Beatrix abdicated the throne on April 30, 2013 making way for her son, William Alexander, to become the next ruling monarch.

While in Amsterdam Shirley talked the touring group into visiting the Red Light District. This is an officially recognized and sanctioned area for prostitution. There are approximately 300 working "windows" behind which beautiful young ladies are on display and ready for customers. Prostitution in the Amsterdam Red Light District is the most visible kind of sex work. It is highly regulated and monitored. Each woman has her own window and a private room. Street prostitution is not allowed.

Shirley saw one attractive young lady sitting in her window display enjoying an ice cream cone in a particularly erotic way and wondered if this was the young lady's method of soliciting customers. Shirley also encountered one very pretty young lady standing in front of her window, taking a break if you will. She asked the girl why she did what she did. The girl's answer surprised Shirley. She said, "I am from a poor family that cannot afford to send me to university. This work allows me to attend school and to make a better life for myself." The AWBS ladies who went on the trip to the District were delighted with the experience. None had even considered visiting the area.

On the way back to the Eden Hotel the touring ladies stopped at a bar for drinks, not realizing the bar was a watering hole for gay men. Shirley found the men to be friendly and wonderful conversationalists. She said one of them came up to her and touched her hair, saying it was the most beautiful hair he had seen on an older woman.

The trip to Lisse and the Keukenhof Tulip Gardens was all that the ladies thought it might be. The Keukenhof botanical gardens, said to be the world's largest, have been called the "Garden of Europe". Over 7 million tulips, daffodils, and hyacinths bloom there annually, with blooming at a peak near the time of the Queen's birthday. The trip to Lisse and back to Amsterdam took the ladies through a rural area where field after field of tulips were in bloom. These spectacular blooms would soon be the source of bulbs sent throughout Europe. Shirley ordered a large box of bulbs from one of the roadside farms, and these must surely continue to bloom in the gardens of our much beloved home in Kier Park, Ascot.

On their last evening in Amsterdam the ladies took an evening tour of the Amsterdam canals. The glass covered boats provided an excellent view of the many scenic and historic areas that make Amsterdam a city to remember. On May 31, the ladies flew back to London's Heathrow airport. For these ladies the outing was just another adventure and another one of the joys of being an expatriate in Berkshire-Surrey. One of my business associates once said to me, "After I die, I want to come back as an American expatriate woman in Berkshire-Surrey."

In late November 1997, Shirley, thirty-eight other women, and one man (?) of the AWBS made a memorable trip to shop in the German Christmas markets at Nuremberg (Nurnberg in German) and Rothenburg, Bavaria. The trip to Germany further underlined the reality that Shirley was continuing to have adventures I never imagined a wife of mine would have. If you think this trip was a tedious shopping trip, you are mistaken - tiring for sure, but certainly not tedious.

Shirley was up at 3:30 a.m. on Friday to make sure she was ready when her driver came for her at 5:20 a.m. The

And There We Were

AWBS group departed London's Heathrow for the short flight to Frankfurt, Germany. A bus then took the soon-to-be shoppers to a Nuremberg hotel, where they spent two nights and three days prior to returning home late Sunday evening.

Nuremberg is located along the Pegnitz River. A central square, the Hauptmarket, is the Christmas Market area. The center piece of the square is the Schoner Brunnen, a multi-tiered array of sculptures that form what the locals call, "the beautiful fountain". The Kaiserberg Castle, the Frauenkirche Church (Church of Our Lady), and a number of red-roofed buildings frame the outside of the square. During Christmas Market the square is filled with shops, stalls, and vendors. The shops have peppermint-colored awnings illuminated with bright lights coming from high up on the surrounding buildings. Choirs sing and music comes from many sources and many instruments. Ginger breads and elaborately decorated Christmas cookies are on sale everywhere.

After two days of shopping in Nuremberg, Shirley had only purchased a beautiful crystal Christmas tree ornament and a silver beer stein. Both of these purchases were hand crafted by a very talented silversmith. Shirley said she would drink beer from the stein, but at a cost of $600 I was inclined to put it into a safety deposit box.

Shirley twice encouraged the group to pass on the pre-paid evening meals available at the Nuremberg Hotel. She wanted her compatriots to take in the fine dining available at nearby elegant restaurants that offered spectacular views of either the river or the central marketplace. After arriving at their first restaurant of choice, Shirley and 11 other companions were seated at a table. A colorful German frau approached their table and began speaking to Shirley. Shirley responded, "I am an American. I am sorry but I only speak English. My German is limited to *'Danke schon'* (thank you), *'Sprechen sie Deutch?'* (do you speak German), and *'Ich liebe dich'* (I love you)." The lady looked at her, somewhat surprised by that alliteration, and then broke out in a great big smile. She reached over and pinched Shirley's cheeks saying, *"Am schonste"* which in German is "most beautiful."

Memorable Excursions

After dinner on the first night in Nuremberg the ladies went bar hopping. They also tried to gain entry to a festive beer hall but were denied entry due to overcrowding. No new customers were being allowed into the hall.

On Saturday the group made a day trip to Rothenburg, a walled city some thirty miles from Nuremberg. A Christmas Market has been held in Rothenburg since the 15th Century. Unlike at Nuremberg, the Christmas shops at Rothenburg are open all year long. The city is enclosed by an exterior stone wall having 42 towers. The streets are made of cobblestones. As in Nuremberg red tiled roofs cover the street side buildings. More color is visible in the hanging and window boxes filled with flowers. The city boasts that it has the "world's most charming Christmas stores". And it does. Shirley bought an elegant and colorful German Santa in Rothenburg. She returned to England with the Santa sitting in the vacant seat next to her on the plane. Today it sits on an ottoman in front of our living room fireplace each and every Christmas.

Rothenburg remains as it has been for nearly seven centuries. Unlike Nuremberg, the city was not bombed during WWII. The ornate medieval architecture has been extremely well preserved. The southern gate to the City is framed by the twin towers of St. James Church. St. James is famously known for the three beautiful interior altars that were carved by a master woodcarver in 1483.

Nuremberg was 90 percent destroyed in 1945 by allied bombing. Although much of the city has been rebuilt, only the Kaiserberg Castle and the medieval walls have been restored to their original state. Nuremberg was the birthplace of the Nazi party and it paid the price for this tie to infamy.

When Shirley returned home Sunday night she was still wired from the frantic pace and the wonderful things she saw, and by the experiences she had, during her her three day stay in Germany. The AWBS did know how to have fun.

And There We Were

THE PAUL SMITH WEDDING

One of the top five memorable events during our time in the United Kingdom was a wedding we attended in 1995. I do not remember the name of the bride: the groom was Paul Smith, a member of our staff in the Kerr-McGee London office. He was a petroleum engineer and a joint venture asset manager. Paul was not one of my direct reports, so the invitation to the wedding came as a surprise to Shirley and me. On the day of the wedding, we took a 40-mile train ride south out of London to the small village of Tunbridge Wells in Kent. We departed London thinking we would enjoy the scenery and a ceremony held in an ancient church.

The church ceremony was not impressive. The vows were exchanged in a stone church, the interior of which was rather non-nondescript. The building was most likely St. James Church, built in 1860, but it could have been St. Lukes Church built in 1895. The point to be made is that the church ceremony did not result in this wedding being ranked so high in our list of memorable events. It was the wedding reception.

After the vows were exchanged, buses delivered us to the Ashdown Park Hotel located approximately 6 miles from the church. After we disembarked from the bus, we were directed to a green lawn behind the hotel and the adjacent Abbey. When we emerged from between the two ancient buildings, one being the original manor house that had been renovated and converted into the Ashdown Hotel, we were greeted with a stunning view. Expansive sloping grasslands left us with an unimpeded view of a distant lake framed by a deciduous forest. One had to look far to the left or far to the right to find a view that was not a hundred percent grasslands. The sun was bright and the colors brilliant. While we were recovering from the shock of the unexpected view, waiters, wearing white gloves and jackets, approached us with glasses of Champagne. There were tables with white linen on which a wide array of hors d'oeuvres were displayed. I recall thinking the view was similar to the view at Cliveden, but of much greater scope. Of course

Cliveden overlooks the Thames while Ashdown overlooks a picturesque lake.

After we milled around for a while, we were called to the Abbey entrance. We were greeted by men dressed in red Beefeater suits who directed us up a stairway to the grand hall. Prior to entering the banquet area, we were stopped by a tall gentleman in another of the remarkable red suits. He held a long ebony rod in his hand. When it was time for us to enter, he pounded the staff on a stone surface and loudly announced our entrance with, "Robert and Shirley Lent." It was like we were courtesans paying homage to a king. The reception dinner was superb, and the wedding toasts and roasts were as poignant and funny as any we ever heard. It was a most enjoyable dining experience.

After the reception dinner, we were invited to a hotel ballroom where we were told the celebration would continue late into the evening. Unfortunately, we were with another companion who did not want to stay for the dancing and revelry. The three of us left Ashdown to catch a train back to London. Shirley was not happy that we were missing what she thought might be a memorable part of the reception. Of course, she was right, but sometimes one does not always get to make the right decision. Our companion was Paul Smith's supervisor and a Vice President at Kerr-McGee. I deferred to this gentleman's wishes out of courtesy, even though I, too, was a Kerr-McGee Vice President.

Paul Smith's wedding occurred early on during our stay in the United Kingdom, and the pageantry accompanying the wedding reception stunned us. We later had other moving experiences, but this was the first one that left us "gobsmacked," as the British would say. It was a year or two before we attended events memorable enough to erode the aura surrounding the Smith wedding.

Pheasant Hunts

I avoided going on an English pheasant hunt the first three years we spent in the United Kingdom. It became apparent, however, that a number of our partners in the North Sea were invited, and had accepted, these hunting invitations. Schlumberger Oilfield Services was always the host. I finally accepted an invitation to a hunt held at Winchbottom Estate on Monkton Farm near the town of Marlow, Buckinghamshire. The site of the hunt was only about 15 miles from Ascot. Ten "hunters" would be a part of the shoot, two of them representatives of our host, Schlumberger.

I had not hunted with a shotgun since I was a young lad. My father and I had often jumped ducks and geese on the Crooked River, and I had hunted on several ranches near Prineville that allowed me to pursue the pheasant and quail populations. When I was young, I was a reasonably good shot, but my stalking techniques needed work. On the English hunts stalking is not a factor. Beaters drive the birds to the hunters. For the first time I would be shooting at birds coming to me, not flying away after they had been startled by my approach.

Once I accepted my first invitation to a hunt, I discovered there was a dress code. It was expected I would arrive dressed in Two by Fours (pants that end at the knees), Wellingtons (rubber boots), a sissy looking flat hat (checkered of course), and a plaid shirt with a tie, a tie preferably with a pheasant on it. Over my clothing I was to have a Barbour raincoat. I ordered the largest Barbour coat available, and the largest Wellingtons on offer. I was surprised that both fit me, but just barely. As for the plaid shirt, well, they just didn't make them with a size 18 1/2-inch neck, at least not without going to the local "High and Mighty Shop" where hunting attire probably wasn't on the list of items for sale. I found one of my Pendleton wool shirts and put a sweater on over it. It would have to do. In full dress I looked large. I also moved with slow and deliberate steps. I was not an athlete in motion.

It was a cool morning when we arrived at Monkton Farm.

Memorable Excursions

The coffees served us were most welcome. I was hopeful the caffeine might help us all be alert to the point that we would not shoot one another. None of us had our own gun so we were given either a 20-gauge or a 16-gauge shotgun and 50 shells. There were to be three drives in the morning and two in the afternoon. We drew for peg assignments, the ten peg locations being spaced out evenly, but not having equal access to the prime areas from whence the birds would come. Each drive consisted of thirty beaters and about twenty yippy little beagles who would be working meadows, grain fields, and woodlands. Each drive offered unique bird overflights. The beaters banged away with wooden sticks to drive the birds (mostly farm raised) to a central area where wire mesh fences required any of the running birds to take flight.

For the first drive I was given peg number 6 which turned out to be the premier peg location for not only this first drive, but for all the other drives conducted during the day. Before I took my location, I was told to make sure that I had plenty of shells. I was certain the fifty shells I had been given would be enough. Well, they were not enough. It had been so long since I had fired at flying birds, I fired and missed at a astonishingly rapid rate. Either I led the birds too far or I shot behind them. When I reached into my pockets for my last two shells the game master was appalled. He gets paid for the number of birds shot. He ran over to me as guns up and down the line were firing away. By the time he got to me most of the birds had passed us by. I had so few birds near me that even the retriever dogs paid me no heed.

After and during the drive, dogs and locals retrieved the downed birds. The birds were paired together in a brace and then hung over rods in a trailer similar in size to a small Hertz rental in the United States. It turns out that at the end of the hunt, guests take whatever birds they want. After the guests have had their pick, buyers for restaurants made their selections. Next up were representatives that sold birds to the local grocery stores. That explains why I once saw pheasants on sale at Budgens (our local grocery store). A note attached to the dressed pheasants warned that the birds might have pellets in them. The remaining birds were divided amongst those who had driven the birds and those who had retrieved them.

After the first drive I asked how many birds might have flown over us. The game master said he thought the number might have been around 800. On this first drive the birds had been driven across a meadow atop flatlands leading to a gully. We, the hunters, were in the bottom of the gully. It really was quite a sight, seeing birds suddenly and unexpectedly fly overhead. There was no warning of their individual arrival. They were just there and then gone.

I got better as the day wore on, but I never again had the prime peg. I think by the end of the day I had bagged just about the average for each of the hunters. But I had surely embarrassed myself on that first drive.

The second drive was in a woodland. The beaters drove the pheasants into the trees where glide patterns took them to the hunters. There was hardly any sound of beating wings. It was eerie. One saw a bird coming and he fired. Unfortunately, not all birds gliding through the forest were pheasants. A few partridges and a woodcock were taken. There may have been other birds who had the misfortune of being in the wrong place at the wrong time. It was pretty much, "If it flies, it dies".

At a mid-morning break, we had soup, Port, and sloe gin. For our lunch break we went to a nearby hunting lodge where we were served cuts from a large leg of pork and an array of vegetables that included swede, potatoes, carrots, and broccoli. Cheese and Port followed. Wine had been served with lunch, which meant the assembled hunters had consumed a fair amount of alcohol prior to going out for our afternoon hunt. I had never been around anyone who had consumed alcohol during a hunt. It was, at least for me, a little scary. During the hunt, mostly to help us keep warm, we were offered sloe gin, cherry, or an occasional nip from a flask. Because I was trying to keep my wits about me, I only sipped the sloe gin during breaks. My lips never touched the flask.

I found it disturbing that we were in the field with 10 guns firing while alcohol was pulsing through the veins. But this is the British way and I never heard of anyone getting shot, at least mortally. On one of the drives where the hunters were shooting overhead, I felt a rain of shot coming down on me. The pellets were light and free falling, almost like a light shower.

After the hunt I selected two pheasants to take home. I would need to dress them if we were to have them for a meal. When I arrived home, I showed Shirley the brace of pheasants. She asked if the male and female were mates. I replied that they probably were (knowing full well that this was most likely a fib). She remarked that perhaps I should have shot the whole family, whereupon she closed the door and left me to find a place in the rain where I could dress the take. It is perhaps not surprising that we never had a pheasant dinner.

To illustrate how packed our calendar was, I had only a few hours after returning from the hunt before I needed to dress for the AWBS Christmas (1996) dinner/dance held at the nearby Wentworth Country Club. I enjoyed the evening, but when I went to bed, around midnight, I was exhausted.

I participated in two more hunts during my time in the United Kingdom. These outings were pretty much the same, although the number of birds taken varied by location. One of the hunts was near West Dean in the hills north of Chichester in West Sussex. I was surprised to learn that the West Dean hunt was located on property only two miles from the Goodwood Race Track. Unfortunately, it was cold on the day of the West Dean hunt; snow was falling throughout the day.

My last hunt was a return trip to the Monkton Farms property. Each hunt was different, different because of the mixture of guests, the weather, and the way the birds were driven to the hunters. I most likely will never hunt again, but I shall remember the British pheasant hunts like they just occurred yesterday.

Across the Sea to Norway

I made three trips to Norway during our stay in the United Kingdom. Shirley accompanied me on the last trip, and as one might expect, that trip was the most memorable of the three.

Kerr-McGee had made the Janice Field discovery in the North Sea, and the results of development drilling had convinced the Company and our partners we had economic reserves justifying construction of an offshore production facility. Kerr-McGee had previously brought an offshore oil field into production by using a Floating Production, Storage, and Offloading facility (FPSO). The FPSO at Gryphon Field was the first purpose-built production facility of its kind. Prior to that all North Sea production had come from production platforms fixed to the sea bottom. The Janice Field partners had agreed to the use of a FPSO facility. Rather than have such a floating vessel built from scratch the decision was made to purchase and then modify an available floating hotel (flotel) that had previously housed workers from drilling rigs and production platforms in the North Sea. This floating facility had to be modified to convert it from a flotel to a production platform. The conversion took place at a mooring in a deep-water fjord in Norway. The lead Kerr-McGee engineer on the project, Paul Doble, invited me to go with him to review the status of the conversion. The Janice discovery had been made during my stay in the United Kingdom. The exploratory test had been approved under the leadership of my predecessor, but the exploratory and development drilling was conducted under my aegis. Mr. Doble's invitation was one of courtesy, if you will, for the work done by my staff bringing Janice to the point where a production facility was needed.

Mr. Doble and I made a day trip to Stavanger, Norway and drove up the coast from Stavanger to the deep-water fjord where the flotel was anchored. We were treated like royalty by those conducting the conversion. I was embarrassed by the welcome because I had no authority over the work being done. Mr. Doble knew what he was doing, but I did not know a thing

Memorable Excursions

about how to make a production facility out of a floating hotel.

I remember walking across the deck looking at what was then mostly a hotel platform. I walked through a large movie theater with 70-80 plush seats, and I was stunned by the size of the stainless-steel freezers and walk-in coolers. I realized that when this flotel had been anchored far out in the North Sea, it would have been a most welcome and convenient habitat for those working 12-hour shifts, knowing they would be spending time between shifts on a flotel rather than flying on a helicopter to and from the mainland. Some offshore production facilities get away from having a flotel by requiring crews to work ten days on and ten days off schedules and housing them on site. For whatever reason, the flotel that would become the Janice production facility had been decommissioned.

I found the scenery in and around the fjord to be incredibly picturesque. The waters were deep blue and the forested mountains brilliantly green. When we departed for our return to Stavanger, I knew I would not likely ever be onboard the completed production platform. That proved to be the case, but I was at Newcastle when the completed facility had its sail away to Janice Field.

On the second trip to Norway, I made a one-day excursion to Oslo so that I might look at a proposal made to Kerr-McGee by a seismic acquisition company who had offered to make all of their seismic data in the North Sea available to us. What they required for this access was a working interest in any exploratory test we drilled using the seismic data given Kerr-McGee. It was a rather startling proposal. Seismic vendors are expected to provide data, but to not be a part of exploration. The reasoning behind that business model is that most seismic acquisition vendors do not want to get into a potential conflict of interest situation affecting the marketability of their data. I looked at the proposal, declined the offer, and made a quick return trip to London. I did not explore any of the tourist attractions that make Oslo so very special. That omission would end when Shirley accompanied me on my next trip to Norway.

In 1997 I made my final trip to Norway. I returned to Oslo

where I was the Kerr-McGee representative at a meeting held by Statoil, one of our North Sea exploration partners. The meeting was cordial and informative and was over in a couple of hours. I brought along two bottles of Scotch whiskey. It is customary to do this type of thing since the tariff on spirits is terribly high on goods coming into Norway. Since I bought the bottles duty-free, the cost to me was minimal. The presentation to my corporate equivalent was well received. Even though I would live in another country, and travel to many other countries around the world, I never again brought spirits to a meeting. Many bottles of spirits were consumed after meetings, but I never again brought bottles as gifts.

Shirley accompanied me on the Statoil Oslo trip. She did not come with me to the Statoil office, but she made sure our two day stay in Norway was memorable. On previous trips to other countries, I had found I did not explore the cultural offerings right at my fingertips. On every occasion when Shirley was with me, I took away memories of experiences that are vivid even to this day. The lady proved time and again she had a way to milk the most out of any situation. Never was this skill more evident than in Oslo, and a number of years later when she joined me on a business trip to Rio De Janeiro, Brazil.

The most memorable outing of our stay in Oslo was a tour of Frogner Park. This 80-acre park contains 212 bronze and granite sculptures created by Gustav Vigeland. All the sculptures are nudes, including one of the most famous ones, The Angry Boy. The parkway of sculptures is nearly 2800 feet long and cuts through grasslands segmented by trees. A pathway bridge populated with sculptures crosses a scenic lake. To tell you the truth, Frogner Park may be the most impressive tourist attraction I have ever visited. Frogner Park, inaccurately called Vigeland Park by some, is Norway's most popular tourist attraction. Up to 2 million people visit the park each year.

The number of sculptures on display at Frogner Park make it the world's largest outdoor exhibit by a single artist. Each of the sculptures is captivating. One can look at a single sculpture for many minutes without feeling the urge to move on. The long park pathway ends on a hilltop above which rises the

Memorable Excursions

most impressive sculpture in the park. The 50-foot-tall monolith, appropriately named "The Monolith", contains 121 human figures entwined in a rising mass that begins with old people at the base and culminates with a baby held atop by outstretched hands.

It took 14 years to carve this masterpiece from a single slab of granite. If I could revisit any piece of art I have ever seen, it would be "The Monolith". Any visitor to Oslo should visit Frogner Park. It is destination not to be missed.

Shirley and I also visited the Holmenkollen Ski Jump Hill where world championships are held in ski jumping. We climbed to the top and looked down on what a jumper would face. Although the view took my breath away, I would not want to be on skis knowing that I would launch on such a terrifying journey. The hill we visited has now been replaced by a new one built in 2008. The view from the top of the new ski jump is no doubt just as intimidating as the one we visited.

We also visited the Viking Museum where three Viking ships are on display. Having observed towering angry waves in the North Sea, I could not imagine setting forth on a journey in one of these ships, destination England, Ireland, Iceland, or North America. We also visited the nearby Kon-Tiki Museum where Thor Heyerdahl's Kon-Tiki and Ra2 boats are exhibited.

On our last day in Oslo the weather was simply stunning. Clear skies and the temperatures in the mid to upper 70s inspired Shirley and I to take a boat excursion through the sparkling waters of Oslo Fjord. As we were boating along, I noticed the rocky shores seemed to be lined with a pink band. I remember telling Shirley that I could not imagine what might be causing the shoreline to be colored pink. A boat filled with locals came sailing by our tourist boat, and we suddenly realized what we were seeing. Onboard the passing boat were young men and women, all topless and basking in the warm sun. That pink band we had seen along the shore....well, it was a goodly number of the more than one million Oslo residents who had doffed their tops to get a little color. We were seeing flesh on display, albeit from quite a distance. Observing the topless youngsters in the sailboat reminded me of the casual young men taking showers in the nude as we walked by during our visit to the Tall Ships. The Scandinavians take advantage of fresh water and bright sunshine no matter what the situation.

THROUGH THE CHANNEL TUNNEL TO BRUSSELS AND PARIS

During 1994, the first full year we spent in the United Kingdom, rail service connecting England to the Continent via the Channel Tunnel was inaugurated when English based Eurostar trains began transporting passengers to Brussels and Paris. Although the 31-mile-long undersea rail line was officially opened in May of 1994, the first passenger train made its debut on November 14, 1994. The Lent family, including our visiting sons Tobin and Taran, took a Eurostar train to Brussels during the 1994 break between Christmas and New Year. Our passports were stamped, coming and going, by a Channel Tunnel immigration officer.

Shirley and I had made several trips to Dover and Folkestone prior to the opening of the Channel Tunnel, but the trip under the sea bottom was especially memorable. As we approached the tunnel entrance, we passed several of the mammoth coring machines that had bored the two 25-foot tunnels beneath the seafloor. Viewing the tunnel entrance while at the same time observing the machines that cut the transportation tunnels was another one of those memorable experiences.

Our trip to Brussels was exciting mostly because we were amongst the first to take the nearly 2 1/2-hour train ride to Belgium. Had we chosen to go to Paris, the travel time would have been about the same - 2 1/2 hours. Following improvements in the tracks, the average speed of the trains increased and the travel times to both Paris and Brussels have since been considerably reduced. The recent record for a train ride to Brussels is one hour and forty-two minutes. The late-in-the-year inauguration of the rail service under the English Channel

Memorable Excursions

limited the number of passengers using the rail service in 1994 to an estimated 100,000. During the first full year of service (1995), nearly 3 million passengers took the Eurostar to either Paris or Brussels. By 2017 the number of passengers using the train service, coming and going through the Channel Tunnel had risen to over 10 million.

At the time of our trip to Brussels, we thought it odd that the train traveled about 80 miles per hour from Waterloo Station to the English coast, then 185 miles per hour from the French coast to either Brussels or Paris. It was like riding in a horse and buggy in England and Porsche in France. With better rails and more efficient trains, the speed of travel in England is now about the same as it is on the Continent.

When one takes what could be construed as a maiden voyage through a 31-mile-long tunnel, on average 165 feet below the ocean bottom, there is room for apprehension. Midway through our trip to the French coastline, the train came to a complete stop. We could not imagine what the problem might be. All I could think of was that over our head was 300 to 400 feet of North Sea water. Fortunately, after about a 15 minute wait the train began to move. No explanation for the delay was given.

Our stay in Brussels came at a time when many of the businesses were closed for the holidays. There were still a number of predominantly American or Japanese tourists out and about. The Grand Place, the main market square surrounded by ornate buildings remains one of the most memorable market squares we have visited. We also took a walk to the Mannekin Pis, the bronze statue of a little boy peeing in a pond. The boy was dressed for the season in a Santa suit, but he was still peeing. The Mannekin Pis is among the world's most unusual water fountains.

We visited several pubs and drank far more Belgian beers than we should have, not knowing the alcohol content of Belgian beer is higher than it is in English or American beers. We learned our lesson, none more so than me. We ate at a fine restaurant, sampled a few Belgian waffles, and had a good night of sleep at our hotel. In the afternoon of the following day, we were ready for our return trip to England.

It was our good fortune that during our stay in England, Waterloo Station served as the departure point for the Eurostar service to the Continent. The rail line that runs from Ascot to London ends at Waterloo. All we had to do was board at Ascot, change trains at Waterloo, and step off in central Brussels (Midi/Juid Train Station) or Paris (Gare du Nord Station). St. Pancras International Station, not Waterloo, is now the departure point for rail trips to Europe.

The convenience of a 2 1/2 hour train ride to Paris enticed Shirley to take numerous trips to the City of Lights, among them an antiquing trip to Paris with the AWBS ladies. She also made several trips with our sons, for no other reason than wanting to spend a weekend in Paris. On one of these trips Shirley and Taran took a number of guided tours. They returned to Ascot amused by the fact the tour guide always said, "very old', when she described a church or building. The guide was probably catering to the Americans in her tour group. After all, we have very few buildings that are even 300 years old - about middle age for a building in Europe.

Shirley and I also took short day trips to Calais and Boulogne via a hovercraft. We found the ancient city of Boulogne interesting. Our visit to Calais was a sentimental journey. The Allied Expeditionary Force had used the port of Calais to facilitate the invasion of Europe after D-Day. Normandy and its once bloody beaches were nearby.

Shirley had an interesting exchange with a candy store merchant in Boulogne. After looking at the candies on display, she had a question or two, which she asked in English. She had looked at the candies in the counter and had a question or two. The French merchant became indignant, obviously miffed that Shirley did not speak French. Shirley's response was, "I am sorry that you feel I should speak French. It was my intent to buy some of your attractive candies, but since we cannot communicate, I will not be able to do so." The merchant then said, in perfect English, "You Americans. You think you can come to our country and expect us to speak your language, and you not ours." Shirley's response was, "I am sorry you are offended, but this may be my only visit to France, and for me to learn French so that I can order candies in Boulogne is not reasonable." The conversation between the two continued cordially, in English. Shirley bought a goodly number of the store's fine chocolates.

Shirley and I later made many trips to France, most of which were after we had returned to the United States and I was then Vice President of International Exploration. The trips we made to Paris were almost always business related, although one trip, following my retirement, was for pleasure only. On that occasion we were in Paris on our way to Burgundy where we would board a luxury barge for a float through Burgundy.

Though Shirley never learned to speak French, she found French attitudes toward non-French speakers changed over the years. The people seemed more friendly and were not openly offended when they found my lady did not speak their language. It is our belief the French are admirable people, not unlike those we encountered in other countries we visited. Of course, the tourist dollar is always welcome.

A Trip to the United States

I realize it may seem odd that a trip back to the mother country makes a list of memorable events formulated during the years we spent in the United Kingdom. More than anything else this event illustrates how Shirley had adapted to living a life of adventure. It showcases her ability to find a way to milk a bit of fun out of a sad situation.

In April 1997, I departed on a business trip back to the Kerr-McGee home office in Houston for three meetings that were spread across six days. When I departed Muirfield for Gatwick Airport, Shirley was in a funk. Tobin had cancelled

And There We Were

his trip home from Vietnam over the Easter break, and I had decided to extend my trip a few days so I might fly to Boston and drive to Hanover, New Hampshire, where I would spend a weekend with our younger son Taran. Shirley had gone too long without being in the company of least one of her sons. She was upset.

After I arrived in Houston and after I had spent time worrying about Shirley, I gave her a ring to see if her mood had changed. She was not noticeably in tears, but she was still down in the dumps. I felt terrible knowing that this lady, probably the happiest person I knew, was sad. There was little I could do for her while I was in the States. I called home again a couple of days later. It was on Friday morning and I would fly to Boston later in the day. Taran was already on his way down to Boston from Hanover. We had decided to spend one night at the Copley Center Marriott in Boston before making the drive to Hanover. Dinner out was a given.

When Shirley answered the phone, her mood had obviously improved. Breathless, she said the first days after I leave on trips were always the worst, but she had a full calendar. She said she really had to run and wished me a great time with Taran.

I caught the plane to Boston and took a taxi to the Marriott. Taran and I planned to have a late dinner and then drive to Hanover on Saturday morning. I checked in and was told Taran had already registered and was in our room. When I got to the room, I slipped my pass card and entered. Taran greeted me with a hug and a very curious look on his face. Shirley chose that moment to jump out from around a corner. That woman never failed to surprise me. She had decided she did not want to be left out of the fun and had booked a flight to Boston. Her driver had been waiting in the courtyard when I made my morning call from Houston. She left me gobsmacked.

It was a great weekend! We ate at exceptional restaurants and toured or hiked in both Vermont and New Hampshire. Taran was the co-founder of a start-up company, Hanover Green Card, and he was proud to show off his new lifestyle and his new offices. Our attempt to go "sugaring" failed when we could not find the man with the maple taps. Taran had helped make syrup previously and thought we might enjoy the experience. During sugaring time, sap flows from the maple trees during the daylight hours, and the cooking occurs at night. At the pace we had been going it was probably good that we did not connect with the owner of the "sugaring" operation.

I left the following Monday morning for a trip to Denver. Shirley stayed another day in New Hampshire to shop and to spend more time with Taran, then caught a plane back to Britain Tuesday morning. I was simply amazed that my sweet wife would take the initiative to make flight reservations on her own. No need to ask about monies. She knew she had that covered. After the Boston trip I knew that there was nothing she could ever do that would surprise me.

Through Sherwood Forest to Nottingham

In 1997 the British Geological Survey invited executives from oil and gas companies active in United Kingdom exploration, both onshore and offshore, to a conference to be held at the BGS office in Nottingham. Called "Petroleum 2000" the gathering was intended to enlighten oil and gas explorers to the work being done by the Survey, and to suggest ways the work might help companies in their exploration efforts.

One Tuesday morning I boarded a high-speed train that took travelers through Sherwood Forest on its way to Nottingham. I was thrilled to have the opportunity to travel through a region made famous by the legendary Robin Hood. I would also spend a night in the hometown of the notorious Sheriff of Nottingham of Robin Hood lore.

"Petroleum 2000" was a bit of a disappointment technically, but it was an excellent opportunity to mingle with many industry leaders, some of whom I knew and others whom I wanted to know. The presentations made by BGS staff were rather boring. Most focused on academic and not practical matters. From a cursory examination of the name badges, I concluded everyone from the Survey was Dr. so and so. The experience reminded me of the scene from the movie *Spies Like Us* where introductions went like, "Glad to meet you Dr., Dr., Dr…" to ad nauseam.

Following the presentation of papers there was a cocktail reception that offered the attendees a chance to mingle and talk business. These discussions were more productive than the conference presentations. Following the reception, a double decker bus took us to Belvoir Castle where we enjoyed a sumptuous feast served in the grand hall of the Duke of Rutland's estate. Belvoir Castle is built on the top of a steep hill overlooking the vale of Belvoir. The word Belvoir is said to have derived from the Old French word meaning *beautiful view*. The castle is well named.

Now we come to the real reason the dinner trip was so extraordinary. Belvoir Castle, at the time of our visit, was the home to the Queen's Royal Lancers Regimental Museum. Sounds rather stuffy, but the truth is of another matter. Belvoir Estate provided the training grounds for the 16th and 17th Lancer Divisions that charged Russians cannons in Crimea, on the shores of the Black Sea. The battle was a rout and is famous for the military incompetence and the imperial bravery that came from a frontal assault on entrenched Russian troops. Most of the 600 who made the charge never returned.

Alfred Lord Tennyson wrote his famous poem, *The Charge of the Light Brigade* to immortalize the bravery of troops sent to their slaughter under withering fire by muskets and cannons, all for a meaningless objective. Tennyson's most famous poetic words from the poem are:

> *"Their's not to make reply*
> *Their's not to reason why.*
> *Their's but to do or die."*

On our way to the great banquet hall, we passed through

passageways lined with over 2000 muskets, bayonets, and swords left without owners when the solders of the Lancer Divisions failed to return. The museum is currently located twelve miles north of Nottingham and is no longer part of Belvoir Castle.

When I boarded the train for the return to London and the connection to Ascot, I was thinking of the contrast between how excited I had been to be in Sherwood Forest and the land of Robin Hood, and my reaction to the sobering exhibits related to the *Charge of the Light Brigade*. Even now I vividly recall walking past the weaponry the departed, never to return, soldiers left behind.

OUT TO SEA, A VISIT TO THE GRYPHON FPSO

Kerr-McGee discovered Gryphon Field in 1987. First production occurred in 1993. During my stay in the United Kingdom the field produced its 50 millionth barrel of oil (As of 2014, total production had surpassed 120 million barrels of oil). A number of the Kerr-McGee staff, myself included, were invited to make an offshore trip to the Gryphon FPSO to celebrate the 50-million-barrel milestone. Having never before been to an offshore production facility, I looked forward to making the trip out to sea. I had visited many production facilities onshore, but never one offshore.

As mentioned previously, the Gryphon Field production vessel was the first purpose built floating production, storage, and offloading vessel ever made operational in the North Sea. A FPSO is designed to receive hydrocarbons produced by itself and from nearby platforms or subsea tiebacks and templates. It processes the production (e.g., removing the associated water coming up with the produced oil) and stores the oil until it can be offloaded onto a tanker. FPSOs are ideal for production in frontier areas and in deep water, where fixed floor platforms are not only difficult to build and maintain, but also very expensive. Based on Gryphon Field's initial 100 million barrel assessment, an FPSO was deemed the most economic method of production.

We flew 175 miles, one way, from Aberdeen to the Gryphon FPSO. Our helicopter ride encountered winds gusting to 70 miles per hour with surface waves near gale force 7. We dressed in wet suits for the flight. I asked why we wore the suits. The answer was that if we crashed without the wet suit, the survival time in the cold waters of the North Sea was 5 to 10 minutes. I asked how long we might survive wearing the wet suits. The answer was, "Maybe 25 to 30 minutes." A sobering thought for sure. I remember thinking it best if we not crash into the sea.

When we reached the Gryphon FPSO, the winds were blowing so hard the helicopter could only touch down briefly before of necessity heading back to Aberdeen. As I stepped out of the helicopter and ducked my head to avoid the rotating blades, a gust of wind caught me and sent me stumbling toward the edge of the landing platform. For a moment or two I (and those watching me) thought I might tumble off the edge. I suspect the captain of the vessel was wondering how he was going to explain the loss of a Vice President to the corporate head office.

Once within the confines of the vessel I was amazed at how calm it felt. A FPSO can be pointed into the wind, which reduces the turbulence that would otherwise result from the ship being at an angle to the cresting waves. When we were in the bridge and looking out under the heliport, I noticed bent tubular supports that were twisted in odd shapes. I asked what had happened up there. The captain said that an eighty-foot wave had caused the damage. Whoa! That damage was well above where I was then standing.

I enjoyed having the opportunity to see how the ship dynamically positioned itself around a central production turret. The vessel could be turned into the wind while the production pipes remained stationary. The turret was kept on location by thrusters working off data incoming from a geo-positioning satellite. I was told that the thruster mechanism was programmed to keep the center of the turret within a 3 foot radius. The ship had ten chains attached to the ocean bottom, but the chains were only safety links to keep the vessel from drifting away in the event of a catastrophic break. Such a break did occur in 2011 and a number of the anchor chains broke. By then operatorship of the Gryphon FPSO had been transferred from Kerr-McGee to Maersk.

While we were on our visit, a tanker arrived for an offload of produced oil. We saw how the transport hoses were attached and how far away a tanker could be and still take on oil. The engineering that made the vessel operational left me speechless. I noticed a small vessel floating near the large FPSO. When I asked about its function, I was told it was a safety ship placed there to rescue the more than 40 crew members in the event of a disaster. Another smaller boat came and left: I discovered it was bringing supplies and mail, both of which were hoisted aboard by cables and winches. I later learned that during a recent mail delivery a crew member had fallen overboard. He quickly climbed up a metal stairway and was treated for hypothermia even though he had only been in the water for a few minutes.

On the flight home from Aberdeen, we were guests on a private jet owned by Rolls Royce Corporation. A Rolls Royce Vice President had accompanied us to the Gryphon FPSO. When the plane took off from Aberdeen the winds were so strong that it seemed for a moment we would be turned upside down. In flight turbulence was so severe that when we made an intermediary stop in Newcastle to drop off the Rolls Royce VP, three members of our staff departed with him, saying they would rather take a train back to London than to fly in such extreme weather. I remained on the plane but remember thinking during the flight to London that it might have been wiser to have taken the train. We landed in London without any problems.

Supper with the King and Queen at Hatfield House

No, we did not have supper with Queen Elizabeth II and her consort husband Phillip. The supper we attended was held in the banquet hall of the Old Palace at Hatfield House where the meal was served in medieval manner on six long tables. As is the custom at Renaissance Festivals in the United States, the king, queen, and their courtiers made a grand entrance into the banquet hall. Mead, red wine, and beer in metal tankards were served to everyone seated at the tables by pretty wenches displaying pushed up and well exposed bosoms. The meal consisted of seven removes (another good British word meaning courses), with each remove brought forth by the pounding of tankards on the wooden tables. It was a truly Elizabethan event.

The meal merits an entry in our list of memorable events not because it was a banquet that can't be replicated anywhere with a number of other different Elizabethan players. The banquet hall where the meal was served is the same hall in which Queen Elizabeth I first held court after learning that she had become Queen following the death of Queen Mary in 1558.

Young Elizabeth spent much of her childhood at Hatfield House, after her father, Henry VIII, had Elizabeth's mother Anne Boleyn beheaded (on trumped up charges and with the help of a fixed jury) so he could marry Jane Seymour, his third wife. When Elizabeth was a young girl she was treated badly, but with time Henry VIII felt more kindly toward her, and he made her living conditions more comfortable. She left Hatfield House in her teens to live with an uncle who physically abused her. Elizabeth returned to Hatfield House where she was in residence from 1553 until 1558. She was effectively under house arrest while her half sister Mary ruled as Queen of England. Elizabeth was seated under an oak tree on the Hatfield Estate when she learned that Mary had died and that she was now Queen of England.

I was so enamored of the life stories of Anne Boleyn and Elizabeth that I left the banquet with the sensation I had actually been there in Elizabethan times as a witness to the drama. Prior to becoming Queen, Elizabeth faced charges of treason and was temporarily placed in a cell overlooking the chopping block and the green on the grounds of The Tower of London. She was 21 years old. I remember thinking how difficult it must have been for Elizabeth knowing she might be about to suffer the same fate as her mother. Ultimately, the charges against Elizabeth were dropped, and she returned to Hatfield House, still under house arrest.

Anne Boleyn's legacy is a poignant one. Her daughter, Elizabeth, was arguably England's greatest monarch. During the Elizabethan Era, English drama flourished with the likes of William Shakespeare; Sir Francis Drake mounted multiple voyages to the south seas; the English enjoyed their greatest-ever military victory when they defeated the mighty Spanish Armada in 1588. Although many have considered and still do consider her reign to be a Golden Age, there were, and are, still detractors. I choose to believe that however history may judge her, Elizabeth's accession to the crown and the cultural, economic, and military accomplishments of her long reign were well-deserved rewards for her incredible mother, Anne Boleyn, who went to her death prematurely and without just cause.

So there you have it. The banquet more than met our expectations and I was thrilled that it was in the Great Hall at Hatfield House where history was once made

Two other incidents at the banquet merit further discourse. Our son Taran and his college roommate Sean Mogan (now a respected eye surgeon) attended the banquet in the Great Hall with us. At one point in the evening's festivities, the Queen announced she wished to know who was the greatest kisser in the land. As her method of discovery, she walked amongst the tables and picked five handsome lads, one of whom was Sean. After kissing all of them, and saying, "Oh my!" when Sean kissed her, she made her decision. Sean Mogan left England knowing that he was the greatest kisser in the land.

A final anecdote: When it came time to pay the bill, I thought it would be appropriate for us to leave a tip for the wonderful service and the friendly banter we had enjoyed with the wenches who served us. I placed a ten-pound sterling note on the table. Immediately a pretty wench said, "Oh no, my lord. You cannot do that." My first reaction was to be mildly irritated, "Why do the British have this aversion to tipping?" We had witnessed this aversion many times, especially in the public houses. On this occasion, however, rather than rebuke me for the gratuity, the wench reached over my shoulder and handed the note back to me, after which she offered up her bound bosoms where I was obviously expected to place folded bill into a deeply accommodating bit of cleavage. It was time to leave. The court jesters took over and coaxed us all into a serpentine dance leading us to the exits.

Thrice to Copenhagen, Denmark

During our stay in the United Kingdom, I made three quick business trips to Copenhagen. Shirley did not accompany me on any of these trips. The first two trips were hum-drum, average in-and-out business trips, but on the third and last trip, I took the time to smell the roses.

The first visit Copenhagen was made to review seismic data available to those interested in filing for an exploration license, offshore Denmark. When I arrived at the office of the seismic vendor, I was asked if I might like a sweet roll to go with my morning coffees. I almost said I would like some Danish before I realized where I was and I revised my response to say simply that such a treat would be most welcome.

After I had spent three hours of pouring over the data, on hand, it was time to head for the airport and the trip back to Heathrow. When the ordered cab arrived, I asked if we might take a short tour of downtown Copenhagen. The driver did not speak English, so my request was mostly done by arm waving and gesturing. We drove by the Central Square, Tivoli Gardens, and Nyhavn Canal. Our final stop was along the shore at Copenhagen Harbor. The driver kept pointing out to the harbor and talking excitedly. He obviously wanted me to see something that was quite special. What I saw were several very large ships being offloaded alongside of a massive dock, and several other ships waiting their turn at the docking facilities. I nodded approval to the driver, but my enthusiasm for the cause of his excitement did not impress him. The cab drove off and we spoke no more until we got to the airport.

It wasn't until my third trip to Copenhagen that I realized the reason for the driver's exuberance. He had taken me to the shore of the harbor so I might view the Little Mermaid, a small bronze statue sitting on a granite boulder at the edge of the bay. The Little Mermaid is the most iconic tourist attraction in all of Copenhagen. I had not seen it when the cab driver took me there because I was looking out into the harbor and not at what was right in front of me. I regretted having disappointed the first driver. He must have thought his American passenger was "thick" in the head.

My second trip to Copenhagen was even of shorter duration than the first one. The purpose of the trip was to sign documents transferring ownership of a North Sea property from Chevron to Kerr-McGee. It was on this property that our Janice Field discovery would be made several years later. Both parties to the signing had flown to Copenhagen to avoid document taxation that would have been incurred by a signing in the United Kingdom. The signing took place prior to formation of the European Union. Simply by flying to Denmark, signing the documents, and having a nice lunch, we saved our companies nearly $100,000. I never understood how the English could have gotten it so wrong,

The third trip to Denmark was an overnighter, the purpose of which was to make the Danish Energy Agency aware of Kerr-McGee's intent to explore all of the North Sea, including the leases that might be available from a Danish licensing round. In effect, we were just introducing the company to the Danish authorities. I was finally going to get to see a bit more of Copenhagen.

And There We Were

The night before our meeting with the DEA we flew to Copenhagen and checked into the Kong Frederick on Vester Voldgade Street. We were near the Tivoli Gardens Amusement Park but it was 10:50 p.m. and restaurants there seemed to be closed. We walked down Vester Voldgade for a few blocks without finding an open restaurant. When we turned around and began our walk back to the hotel, we found an open Burger King. Across the street from this fast-food restaurant was an open Seven-Eleven. I was incredulous! Here we were in downtown Copenhagen faced with eating at the same establishments we might have encountered in LoDo Denver.

Our meeting with the Agency went well and they thanked us for coming to see them. When we invited three of the staff to have lunch with us, they declined saying that governmental policy would not allow us to buy them lunch. Danish standards for ethical behavior are so high that even the appearance of possible bribery or corruption is not tolerated. At the time, I could only wonder how they could interpret our buying them lunch as an attempt to favorably influence a decision to grant us an exploration license.

It turns out Denmark is at the very top of the list of worldwide non-corrupt countries. Kerr-McGee never, ever considered seeking exploration licenses in countries at the bottom of the corruption list. Corruption in countries like Nigeria prohibited us from exploring there even though the country has many oil rich objectives. We sure were not going to have to worry about corruption in Denmark.

My compatriot and I toured Tivoli Gardens and found an upscale restaurant overlooking the park. The dining room was decorated for the Christmas season and a massive buffet table was set for the luncheon customers. We ordered a bottle of Christmas aquavit, a spirit that looks like white lightening but tastes slightly better. After a few pints of lager as a digestive, we visited the buffet table, filling our plates with fish beyond description. I enjoy smoked salmon and herring, so I was in Danish hog heaven. The red and white cabbage dishes and several mystery fish were all delicious.

Memorable Excursions

What I will remember most about this trip to Denmark comes from our luncheon experience. From our seats looking out on Tivoli Park, we marveled at snow so deep it was nearly impossible to see the small children walking down the plowed pathways. I was charmed by the burning piles of coal placed in elevated bowls that resembled barbeque stands spaced regularly along the pathways. The children we saw were dressed in brightly colored and patchwork snow suits, their little cheeks bright red from the cold. As we sat eating the most Danish of lunches, while looking out on a beautiful Danish snow scene, I felt extraordinarily privileged to be immersed in another culture at Christmas time. While I was basking in the warm glow of immersion, Christmas music began to play in the dining hall. The first song, sung in English, was *Rocking Around the Christmas Tree* by Brenda Lee.

And There We Were

Chapter 17

LEAVING THE UNITED KINGDOM

The day we arrived in London we knew we would someday leave. We had been told our assignment would last anywhere from three to five years. From its inception, our life in England was magical. Even after five years, we found the magic had never dissipated. As mentioned in an earlier chapter, there was no other time in Shirley's life when she had felt so utterly happy as during the years we lived in Kier Park, Ascot. Life in England was more magnificent than we could have ever imagined. Twenty years on, Shirley and I both still felt the same way. We had been given a gift, a deeply appreciated gift.

All good things must come to an end. In early January 1998, I was called back to the United States to meet with Kenneth Crouch and Jim Guion, respectively the Executive Vice Presidents of Exploration and Production. I learned the Kerr-McGee London office was being moved to Aberdeen, Scotland. Oil and gas exploration in the United Kingdom would henceforth be directed far from the London exploration hub favored by other major players in the North Sea.

At the meeting in Houston, I was asked to consider a transfer to Beijing, China. The exploration efforts in China were dysfunctional and there was need for a manager with my credentials. If I accepted the assignment, I would become the Vice President Exploration and General Manager of Kerr-McGee China Petroleum, Ltd. with a focus on operations in offshore

China. The writing was on the wall. Shirley and I were either going to be relocated to China or we would be returning to the United States.

Subordinating one's personal preferences to the success of the firm was drummed into me from my earliest years in the oil business. I wholeheartedly believe that a high-level manager should undertake any assignment the company feels is critical to the company's success. If a senior manager indicates he wants to pick and choose what he will do, then he is not playing for the greater need of the team. With respect to the move to China, I replied that I would either undertake the assignment or I would resign. I passed along my reasoning on the matter. Another factor I had to consider was the fact my aging father was in rather bad health. I wanted those in the home office to know my acceptance of the assignment in China would mean I would most likely be burying my father during my time there. That did prove to be what happened.

It was decided that I should take Shirley on an exploratory trip to China to see if this was an assignment we thought we could handle. China is China, and life in this country would expose us to the vagaries of life and culture unlike anything we had ever experienced. There was the possibility that the move, and the potential hardships, might be more than Shirley was willing to face.

In February 1998 we flew to Hong Kong on an exploratory trip that would end in Beijing. The Hong Kong visit was designed to acclimatize us with immersion into a Chinese culture that had a British flavor. Control of Hong Kong had been transferred from the British back to the Chinese only 7 months previously. Life in Hong Kong was going to change, but at the time of our trip the British imprint still prevailed.

We were met in Hong Kong by Bryan Yam, a consultant who gave us a grand tour of Hong Kong and Kowloon, and nearby sites in mainland China the following day.

During our Hong Kong visit we stayed at The Regent Hong Kong, an elegant Four Seasons Hotel located in Kowloon. Kowloon is a municipality within greater Hong Kong, located across

Victoria Harbor from Hong Kong Island. The view from our hotel window was stunning. Our trip occurred during the Chinese New Year (a.k.a. the Spring Festival) celebration. Looking across Victoria Harbor at night, we could see high rise buildings bathed in brightly colored lights, some of which changed coloration after only a moment or two of illumination.

Our tour of Hong Kong took us to Victoria Peak (looking down on Hong Kong), Repulse Bay (an expensive residential area), and the Happy Valley Racecourse (an unbelievable oasis in a sea of humanity). We visited Tian Tan Buddha, also known as the Big Buddha. Another stop was at the Taoist shrine Kwun Yam, where we lit incense candles and watched the faithful release live fish into the ocean off the end of Longevity Pier. We chuckled when we noticed fisherman tossing lines off an adjacent pier, a mere 40 feet from where the fish were being reverently released. Lunch was taken at the Hong Kong Life Saving Society Clubhouse, an exclusive social and athletic club. In the evening we dined at a bayside restaurant where the live fish we selected from nearby pens had been delivered, and then prepared prior to presentation at our table. Shirley had selected a very large live lobster. She was terrified and screamed when a shrimp jumped out of its pen into an adjacent pen of squid, then leaping out of that pen onto her. Shirley's scream left vendors and shoppers alike wondering who was torturing the pretty white woman.

The day following our arrival in Hong Kong we took a ferry to the mainland and visited the cities of Shekou and Shenzhen. Shekou, home to the Kerr-McGee South China Sea exploration office, was the most interesting of the two visits. As was the case throughout our trip, local office personnel were not made aware of our visit, which was made only for orientation.

Late in the afternoon of our second day we flew to Beijing. Shirley and I left Hong Kong with an appreciation of all we had experienced. But mostly we left the city thinking we had experienced an assault on our senses: the sounds, smells, and sights. The mainland visits to Shekou and Shenzhen had given us a glimpse into what to expect when we landed in Beijing. Hong Kong is not the real China, but our stay there did what it was meant to do. We dipped our toes into a "Chinese" culture, but one unlike the one in which we might be living. We flew to Beijing on Dragon Air KA900. We never learned to be comfortable flying China's domestic airlines. But that story is for later.

If Shirley was going to be supportive of me taking an assignment in China, she would have to believe living in Beijing was something she could accept. The first thing I noticed when we emerged from the baggage claim area in Beijing was the sharp smell of sulfur. It had the bite of sulfuric acid. I thought, "Oh no!" I waited for Shirley to make a comment about air quality as we drove into the city. She said not a word. The burning of coal in and around Beijing during the winter creates one of the most polluted pockets of air in the world. It was toxic during our February visit, and equally so during the following winter. We learned to live with it.

We checked into the Kempinski Hotel located a mile or so from the Kerr-McGee Beijing offices. There was nothing we did not like about the hotel. It was the first European luxury hotel built in Beijing. We were impressed with the lively musical entertainment in the lobby, the presence of an excellent German restaurant, and the large comfortable rooms.

During our first full day in Beijing, we drove by the Kerr-McGee office building. We were cautious since we did not want any of the local employees to know we were on a site visit. If I decided to accept the assignment, a big deal would be made of my arrival. On this trip, however, mum was the word.

After the drive-by at the offices we drove out of the city to the Great Wall at Mutianyu. At this location the Great Wall runs along the top of a high ridge. Because it was February and the time of Spring Festival, the cable car to the top of the ridge was not operating. Our host and guide, Bryan Yam suggested a hike up the mountain would be well worth the effort. As we were considering the climb, a group of Chinese villagers approached us with an offer to carry us, for a fee, to the wall on a litter (two long bamboo poles with a chair in the middle). I could not help but laugh. Given my size (300 pounds plus or minus) the little men would have collapsed down the hillside before they could deliver me to the summit. So we climbed. It was a rough trip, but as Bryan had predicted, it was worth the effort.

After descending from the Wall, we returned to Beijing and took a quick stroll through Tiananmen Square. From the Square we walked through the nearby gates into the Forbidden City. Very few people were visible, either in the Square or in the Forbidden City, on what was a bitter cold day. There was not much to see at Tiananmen Square other than the Monument to the People's Heroes and the Mausoleum of Mao Zedong. Along the west side of the Square was The Great Hall of the People. The Square itself was not particularly impressive. What I did find impressive was the incredible number of construction cranes that lined nearby streets and squares. I had never seen so many cranes in such a small area.

As we walked across Tiananmen Square I could not but reflect on the 1989 "massacre" that occurred on this very broad and expansive piece of real estate. I tried to imagine what it must have been like when the young student courageously walked up and faced a moving tank. That image was broadcast around the world and it was deeply imprinted in my mind as I walked away. I later learned that a fellow Kerr-McGee employee, a Chinese national, was in Tiananmen during the protest. His wife said he was lucky to have escaped harm and prison. And he was, lucky that is.

Located near the center of Beijing, The Forbidden City was once a singular walled city surrounded by open space. Today the Forbidden City is an enclosed compound over 3,000 feet long that houses nearly 1,000 buildings. During our trek through the enclave we toured the Hall of Supreme Harmony, the Palace of Heavenly Purity, and the Imperial Garden. When we exited through the north gate, we climbed the hill of the Bell and Drum Tower. By the day's end, Shirley and I had climbed the Great Wall, walked through Tiananmen Square and the Forbidden City, and climbed the Bell and Drum Tower. It was almost too much for one day.

To give us an idea of what our home in China might be like,

we spent part of our second day in Beijing touring villas (compounds) where expatriates lived. Although we did not walk through any homes, we were informed these homes were large and very expensive. We were surprised to learn that the cost of a home rental in Beijing might be twice that for our beautiful home in Ascot.

In the afternoon we toured a number of shopping centers, including one in the Kempinski complex and one in the district known as the Pearl Market (*Hongqiao*). At the conclusion of our day, we dined at the Hard Rock Cafe located only two blocks from the Kempinski Hotel.

We had not seen much of China during our stay in Beijing, but we had seen enough. My sweet wife said she thought she would be fine living in Beijing. She would be experiencing another lifetime event she could not have imagined during her Oregon childhood days. Saying yes to Beijing was saying adieu to Ascot and the United Kingdom. It was time to say our goodbyes and prepare for a big move.

Upon our return to London, I informed the home office in Oklahoma City of our decision to accept the assignment. In early March 1998 the announcement of my assignment was made to Kerr-McGee personnel. Bulletins were sent to the Chinese, and to our industry partners in China.

On March 13th, my last day in the London office, I spoke with each member of my staff and I wished them well. I walked next door at lunchtime and purchased a sandwich, chips, and an apple at one of my favorite sandwich shops, after which I walked back past our Davies Street offices and boarded a red double decker bus on Oxford Street. I bought an all-day pass that allowed me to get off and on at any stop on four different routes without charge. I was about to see London as a sightseeing tourist. When I boarded the bus, I had no idea how sentimental that bus ride would be. The ride through London was an eye opener. In my afternoon of traveling, I passed landmarks that held special memories. I also discovered a number of sites I should have visited but had not. I wished I had taken one of these tours earlier during our stay in the United Kingdom.

At almost every landmark I passed, Shirley and I, together or separately, had an experience that was pause for reflection. Because I do not remember the exact routes the buses took that day as they passed most of the iconic tourist attractions in London, I will describe my impressions of each landmark in no particular order. At Trafalgar Square I thought back to that New Year's celebration when Taran ducked under a policeman's horse and mingled with those in an already overcrowded plaza. Shirley and I had also visited the National Gallery an impressive edifice that looms over the north end of the Square. Passing the Savoy Hotel, I fondly I recalled Shirley's invitation to meet her in a day room she had reserved prior to the wonderful dinner we had one evening with Ainsley Harriott. When we passed Tower Hill, I looked to our left and saw Trinity House, home to the Lighthouse Authority, and the site of an address I made to the European Petroleum Negotiators Group. I remember looking out the Trinity windows onto Tower Hill and the nearby River Thames, with Tower Bridge looming just downstream.

At St. Paul's Cathedral I reflected on Tobin and Taran climbing up to the dome and walking out onto the circular cornice, 100 feet above the floor. St. Paul's cornice is called the Whispering Gallery due to unusual acoustic properties that allow one to whisper on one side of the circular, and hear the sound, as if standing beside the one who is whispering. Shirley also attended several church services at St. Paul's (mostly at Easter). It was on the steps leading up from the Thames that Prince Charles and Lady Diana Spencer walked on the day of their marriage in the Cathedral. I still remember the tour boat captain saying, "What a waste that was."

When we passed by the City of London, I recalled the entertaining guided Walk we had taken shortly after our arrival in the United Kingdom. We had toured Pudding Lane, the site where the Great Fire of 1666 started. Nearby was London Bridge - the new one - the former one now having been dismantled and later rebuilt in Arizona. The original City of London was walled in and rather small, and accessible only by London Bridge which was closed at sunset. We had taken many of our visiting friends and family members to the City of London.

When we passed St. James Palace, I remembered that we had gone there to get our tickets to the Royal Enclosure at the time of the Royal Ascot horse races. It was also at St. James Palace where Shirley and Tobin stood in line to sign the book of remembrances for Princess Diana.

Buckingham Palace was a landmark we passed many times during our stay in the United Kingdom. The route a taxi took from the West End of London always passed by the Palace. My mother and father had toured Buckingham Palace during their visit to London. Tickets for a tour of Buckingham Palace are hard to get, but Shirley had paid a man to stand in line for several hours just so my parents could take the tour. Shirley had also placed a bouquet of flowers at the entrance gate in front of the Palace to honor Princess Diana at the time of her passing.

Passing Westminster Abbey, I reminded of the occasion I was to meet Shirley at the Abbey after she had attended a service. On my way there I stepped into a black cab and told the driver to take me to Westminster Cathedral. When we arrived at the Cathedral, I realized my mistake..... my destination was not adjacent to Parliament like it should have been. Oh well, "Driver can you now take me to the Abbey."

When the bus crossed Westminster Bridge, I looked up at Big Ben and reflected on the climb Shirley and I had made up to the clock tower, and of our walk around the clock, ducking under the clock stems at the center of each face. I also remembered how thrilled we were to have had the luncheon on the Terrace of Parliament, courtesy of in invitation coming from James Spicer, a member of Parliament. I also remembered Shirley had been invited to the House of Commons during one of the sessions of Parliament. Her view of the debates from the viewing gallery was almost as memorable to her as the luncheon she and I had on the Terrace.

We passed by Whitehall and I realized I had missed something special by not having toured Winston Churchill's war rooms. During our time in the United Kingdom, I had learned of the devastating effects the Blitz had had on London. I could only imagine what must have been going on in those war rooms when England was facing its worst hour.

Passing Tate Gallery brought back a memory of a lunch I once had there with an industry colleague. He had invited me to lunch at the Tate for one very specific reason. The Gallery has a massive wine cellar known for its incredible vintage wines. The restaurant in the Gallery, at least during the time Shirley and I were in England, served these high-quality wines at ridiculously modest prices. My colleague wanted me to join him in sampling some of the Gallery's finest vintages, and I did.

I smiled as we drove by Harrods. Shirley had so very many memorable experiences in that store. I also remembered that had we wanted to do so, we could have lived across the street in a flat that was for rent when we first arrived in the United Kingdom. I dodged a bullet there.

We also passed Hyde Park, Notting Hill, Victoria Station, Waterloo Station, Marble Arch, and Madam Tussaud's. At least one memory tied us to each of these localities during our stay in country. Along the way I saw many restaurants that were amongst our favorites.

When the bus tours ended, I felt both sad and glad. I was sad knowing what Shirley and I were leaving behind, but so very happy that what I had just seen would always be with us. These places and this time would never be forgotten.

On March 16, 1998 Shirley and I flew to Beijing to report in for my new assignment. Shirley accompanied me so that she could join me in our search for suitable housing.

And There We Were

Chapter 18

THE SEARCH FOR A HOME, MEETING OUR BUSINESS PARTNERS, AND THE MOVE TO CHINA

O During our search for a home, we found the cost of expatriate housing in the Beijing area to be higher than we would have thought possible. We eventually found the home we liked near the suburban village of Shunyi in a complex of homes called Dragon Villas. Dragon Villas was already home to 10 other oil company families (employees of Phillips, Esso, and Chevron). The Villas complex had many newly constructed homes and a massive central community center that included a grocery store, restaurants, a movie theater, and athletic facilities. The center also provided room rentals for residents who needed additional space when more visitors arrived than could be accommodated in their homes. Our home had neither a name (like "Muirfield" in Ascot), nor a street address like we had in the United States (7294 Jasmine Court). Our address in Dragon Villas was Lot No. 521. The home had 6,600 square feet of living space and the rental was nearly twice what we had paid for our magnificent home in Kier Park, Ascot. Although we were floored by the cost, it was not out of line with what others in our company were already paying.

After we had secured housing Shirley returned to England. She would have nearly two months in England before our household goods would be packed and loaded onto a container ship headed to China, via the Suez Canal and the South China Sea. I knew Shirley would make the most of those two months.

And There We Were

In the meantime, the company made arrangements for me to live in an apartment connected to the Kempinski Hotel, the German based upscale hotel close to the Beijing Kerr-McGee offices. Although I would miss my wife, I was glad to have extra time to focus on all the meetings I knew were coming up with our Chinese partners, and we had a number of them.

Kerr-McGee had exploration licenses in Bohai Bay not far from Beijing, and in the South China Sea not far from Guangzhou (formerly Canton). I met with the senior executives of China National Offshore Oil Corporation (CNOOC) and its affiliate China Offshore Oil Nanhai East Corporation (COONEC). I was also required to meet with the senior management of China National Oil and Gas Development Corporation (CNODC) and its affiliate Jidong Petroleum Exploration & Development Company (JPEDC). Although I met with a number of these company representatives in their Beijing offices, I also traveled to Tangshan, Tanggu, Shekou, Guangzhou, and Tianjin where I was introduced to scientists, engineers, and administrators at technical and joint management meetings.

I was also required to meet our industry partners from other countries, although most of our partner companies were United States based. There were other foreign company representatives active in offshore exploration in China who were also high on the list of people I needed to meet. It seemed as if I was constantly attending technical and management meetings.

I attended one set of joint management and technical meetings held in the city of Guangzhou and on nearby Hainan Island, located southwest of both Hong Kong and Guangzhou. Our operating committee meeting was held in Sanya, a tourist city on the southern tip of Hainan Island, called China's Hawaii because of its warm ocean and beautiful beaches. One of our group's excursions was aboard a submarine and into the South China Sea. The vessel had glass windows that permitted wonderful views of oceanic life forms, including both plants and fish. It was a fascinating outing, and an apt introduction to the many captivating experiences Shirley and I were to have during our stay in China.

The Search for a Home

Before I could get a handle on the ongoing exploration efforts in China, I was called back to the United Kingdom to review a project being considered in the North Sea. During that trip, I enjoyed spending four days at our home in Ascot with Shirley. Prior to returning to China, Shirley and I flew to Oregon so that we could visit our families in the United States, and especially to spend time with my ailing father.

After the Oregon trip I returned to China to continue my whirlwind visits with our Chinese partners. My road trips to cities several hours from Beijing were mind boggling in that I got to view sights beyond imagination. More talk of these observations later, but make no mistake, I never made a trip anywhere in China that did not leave me mesmerized by what I saw.

On May 11, 1998 I flew back to the United Kingdom to be with Shirley as the movers packed our household goods for the move to China. On May 15 we watched the movers load the moving vans that would take our goods to a container ship leaving for China. It would be several months before we would sleep in our beds again. As the movers were leaving, a driver was waiting to take us away from our beautiful home. As mentioned previously, pulling out of our Ascot courtyard for the last time was a very sad occasion. I need not again describe the volumes of tears shed as we drove along the edge of Shirley's beloved Windsor Great Park.

We spent our last night in England at the Runnymede Hotel on the banks of the Thames. By coincidence, my cousin Terry Holden and his wife Cheryl happened to be in England on the day we left Ascot. They altered their plans so they could spend the night with us at the Runnymede. We had a fine dinner together, and their presence helped keep our minds off all we were leaving behind. The following morning Shirley and I departed Heathrow Airport for a flight to Beijing. We were on our way to a new adventure. We hoped our stay in China would be all that it could be. And it was!

On May 16, a Sunday, Shirley and I arrived in Beijing and checked into our Kempinski Hotel apartment. Waiting for me was a message the home office requesting I fly to Houston on

Tuesday for a meeting with senior management. I was not only going to be in Houston for a couple of days, I was also asked to visit the London office on my way back to China. In all I would be gone 5 days on a trip that would take me to Vancouver, Houston, and London, with a subsequent flight back to Beijing. I would be flying around the world.

Shirley did not appreciate the fact that I would be leaving her so soon after our arrival in a foreign land. She said I should have left her in England until such time as I could help her get her feet on the ground in Beijing. I was under a bit of stress myself and responded that I needed for her to be a good mate and for her to handle this inconvenience as best she could. I further suggested she could take lessons and learn a bit of Mandarin. You can imagine how that conversation went over.

I left on Tuesday morning for my trip to the States. Shirley, being the Shirley that we all now know, decided to show me she could do just fine without my help. She found the phone number of the American Women's Club in Beijing in the literature given us by the company. She called and discovered the wife of the Australian Ambassador was to be the guest speaker at a gathering in a nearby hotel. Shirley attended the meeting and struck up a conversation with Janet Smith, the Ambassador's wife. Shirley mentioned how I had dropped her off and then had immediately left for a business meeting in the United States. Janet felt sorry for Shirley and invited her to the Ambassador's residence for high tea.

At the tea, servants wearing long white gloves served not only tea but an assortment of finger foods. During the course of their conversations, the Ambassador's wife said she was planning to go to Tianjin to shop for antiques and wondered if Shirley would like to go along. So, it happened that the following day Janet Smith and her driver picked Shirley up and drove to the coastal city of Tianjin, located approximately 75 miles southeast of Beijing. Tianjin is China's fourth largest city and is known for its beautiful Colonial architecture and for the quality of the antiques found in its numerous antique stores. Shirley did not make a purchase, but she did gather enough information so that she could return at a later date, after we had moved into our Shunyi home.

Shirley was not done having fun. The day after the Tianjin trip she once again contacted the American Women's Club and signed up for a contract bridge tournament to be held that afternoon. She met a number of other expatriate wives. Her social circle was rapidly expanding.

The following day she had a Kerr-McGee driver take her to the five-star China World Hotel and a nearby shopping center, Silk Alley. The China World is a most impressive modern hotel with a beautiful lobby, located in the Beijing's central business district. Shirley had tea in the lobby and listened to music played by musicians seated along an overlooking balustrade above the lobby. Her driver waited patiently for more than two hours in a nearby parking lot, not knowing when she might step out of the hotel entrance. When she finally made her appearance he was there, as if by magic.

Upon my return to our Kempinski apartment, I was greeted by a lady who made sure that I need not worry about her living in a foreign country without me by her side. She, with great exuberance, detailed all the adventures she experienced in my absence. I was relieved, but also a bit worried. What might this lady do in this foreign land?

Our household goods arrived July 10th. Before and after that date we had or would have a multitude of very memorable experiences. Truth be known, we lived abroad for nearly seven years, most of which were spent in the United Kingdom. But if we were to prepare list a top ten list of the most memorable experiences we had living overseas, those in China might be in the majority.

Before I recount those experiences, I will comment on some of the memorable people we encountered during our stay in China. In addition to the individuals mentioned herein, there are thousands of people we encountered, or saw, during the road trips we made in and around Beijing. We had never seen anything like life as we observed it along the highways or in the villages. When we returned to the United States, I missed the roadside activity that so captivated Shirley and me during our time in China. Roadside activity in the United States is dull and boring. Never was it so in China.

Chapter 19

THE PEOPLE OF CHINA

Most of the individuals we met while in China were managers or scientists working for our Chinese business partners. We came to know the Kerr-McGee staff quite well but I shall not write of them, other than to say they were all talented and much fun to be around. I respect them all and it still brings a smile to my face when I think of each, and of the times we shared.

When I reported for duty in China our company was bleeding cash and writing down reserves in the country. Both of these are of high concern for senior management leaders responsible for company growth and economic metrics. As a consequence of the problems faced, the first move I considered was the closing of our office in Shekou. This office had been established to help coordinate our South China Seas exploration efforts with China Offshore Oil Nanhai East Corporation. In my opinion, such coordination did not require that we have an office in both Shekou and in Beijing. The sensitivity of closing the Shekou office meant that I spent considerable time with COONEC executives in Shekou and in Guangzhou.

President Qian Fuhao of COONEC was an interesting man. He was beloved by his staff and must have been a wonderful boss. At one of our dinners, Mr. Qian was described as the "perfect husband". The story told was that he sometimes went home during his lunch hour. If he found that his wife asleep,

And There We Were

he would sit on their doorstep so as not to awaken her. Such a powerful man with such a loving touch moved me. He was always gracious, and at our dinners (banquets as they called them) he made sure that my favorite dishes were ordered, and that a member of his staff was nearby to honor me by placing food on my plate.

It turned out that my best friend in China was the COONEC Joint Management Committee Chairman, Mr. Liu Guang Guo. This senior engineer fought hard to keep the Kerr-McGee office in Shekou. One of his strategies was to make sure we held our Joint Management Meetings (JMC) in exotic locations (e.g., Hainan Island, Shanghai, and Guangzhou). Mr. Liu had a fine sense of humor and it was easy to make him laugh. Although he was disappointed when we closed our Shekou office and laid off the staff there, he made sure to extoll the exploration opportunities that still existed in the South China Sea. Even after we had returned to the United States, I continued to get emails from Mr. Liu. I only wish Kerr-McGee would have given COONEC an offshore discovery.

One of the most embarrassing experiences in my more than 30 years as an executive occurred after COONEC helped lobby CNOOC into awarding us a competitive South China Sea exploration license. After the award was announced, the Kerr-McGee home office executives reversed strategy, and I was told to inform CNOOC we had changed our minds and did not want the block.

Three of the memorable experiences we shared with Mr. Liu were in Shenzhen and Shanghai. One of these, already mentioned, was the trip we took to Hainan Island. In Shenzhen I learned what wealth can do for the Chinese. Shenzhen is in a Special Economic Zone and is a center for exports, mostly to the United States. While we were in the city, we toured a beautiful golf course surrounded by very large homes, mansions if you will. In response to my question about the price of these homes, I was told that most were in the $10 million range. When I asked who owned such homes, I was told that they were Chinese owners. I foolishly asked, "Are these Taiwanese Chinese?" Mr. Liu's answer was, "No, these are Chinese

The People of China

nationals." It wasn't until after we had toured Shenzhen that I got it. Many of the company logos on the high-rise buildings were well known United States companies. Exports to or through these companies, who were partners with Chinese companies, were the source of the wealth we saw around us.

While in Shenzhen we also toured the Window of the World, an incredibly impressive theme park and tourist attraction where Chinese citizens can see many of the famous sites in the world as scaled down models. Amongst these exhibits is a model of the Eiffel Tower. It is 350 feet high, about one-third the height of the Parisian tower. There is a perfect model of the Piazza San Marco in Venice. This model is so large that when we walked through it, I knew where all the paths led. Shirley and I had been to Venice and had seen all the Piazza buildings (like the Doges Palace). The Window of the World has 130 exhibits in total among which are the Taj Mahal, the Sydney Opera House, the Roman Colosseum, Niagara Falls, and the Egyptian Pyramids.

While we were waiting to enter the Window of the World, Mr. Liu talked me into donning an emperor's golden robe so that a photo could be taken by a professional photographer. The funny thing was that after I donned the robe, a circle of amateur photographers gathered around me. I had become the tourist attraction. I am a big man, and I was adorned in a mighty big and manly robe.

Mr. Liu made sure that we held a JMC meeting in Shanghai. What an experience that turned out to be. We stayed in the government Xingguo Hotel and were treated like VIPs. One of the highlights of the trip was an evening spent in the Jazz Bar at the historic Peace Hotel. The Old Jazz Band, a quartet of 80-year-old musicians, was playing the most beautiful music you have ever heard. I was so moved by the quality of the music that I asked Shirley to dance. When we took the dance floor, we were the only ones dancing. Lots of flash bulbs went off, one of which came from the camera of a member of our group. When I see that photo in our photo album, I am reminded of how extraordinary the evening was.

And There We Were

We visited a number of the tourist attractions in Shanghai including the massive 1,350 foot tall Oriental Pearl Tower in the Pudong District. We took an elevator up to the viewing platform, 1,150 feet above ground level. We had a view across the Huangpujiang River onto the Bund, the waterfront area of Shanghai that is home to the Peace Hotel. Shirley and I had photos taken, each seated at a facsimile of President Jiang Zemin's desk. We looked the part of a Chinese leader I am sure.

We crossed the river and spent some time walking the Bund. It reminded us of walking in England, especially when a red double decker bus went by. After our visit to the Bund, we toured You Garden, the "Garden of Happiness". The Inner Garden (there are two gardens) has as its centerpiece an ornate two-story tearoom surrounded by ponds. We took a seat on the second floor and had afternoon teas. It was a beautiful setting. We spent one afternoon touring the Shanghai Museum. There was not enough time to appreciate all of the ceramics, paintings, and Chinese bronze artifacts on display. On our second evening in Shanghai, we attended a special presentation by the Goteborg Symphony Orchestra, the National Orchestra of Sweden. The site of this performance was the Shanghai Grand Theatre. So, there you have it: Shanghai on the run.

Wherever he took us, Mr. Liu always made sure that we were entertained. He and I spent many hours walking the streets of Shekou and Guangzhou. We exchanged gifts when it came time for us to leave China. Mr. Liu also helped me negotiate the purchase of a most beautiful artifact that now stands above our living room fireplace in The Woodlands. Whenever I look at this painting of eight maidens in a garden, framed by a magnificently ornate wooden pagoda-like frame, I think of my good friend Mr. Liu.

China National Offshore Oil Corporation is the parent company of both CNOOEC and China Offshore Oil Bohai Corporation (COOBC). These organizations have been introduced in this narrative previously, but one cannot work only with the personnel of the subsidiary companies. It is critical that any project also involve the executives, geologists, geophysicists, and engineers of the parent company. First, something about

The People of China

the operating practices of CNOOC has to be mentioned. This China national company is as close to a Western oil company as you will find anywhere in the world. CNOOC is well run and collaborates extensively with companies who have been awarded exploration licenses under their aegis. CNOOC is headquartered in Beijing so I had easy access to many of their employees, and none more so than their leader, President Wei Liu Cheng. I had several very rewarding sit-down meetings with Mr. Wei. I believe that as a result of these meetings I was nominated for a very high honor, an honor which I will discuss later. Sometimes a seed for success is created when personal relationships provide the motivation to strive for success. It wasn't until after I had returned to the United States that I was finally able to contribute significantly to oil exploration in China. All that I accomplished was done not only for the benefit of Kerr-McGee, but also for the benefit of CNOOC and COOBC.

Kerr-McGee's exploration efforts in China were focused on an exploration license in Bohai Bay where, at the time of my arrival in Beijing, the company had a marginally commercial discovery on leases covering a very large closed structure. Considerable work needed to be done to develop the indicated reserves, and on exploration that offered the potential for even more significant discoveries.

It is no surprise then that two of the more memorable individuals I met came from our collaboration with CNOOBC. Mr. Zhou Shou Wei was a Vice President and Senior Engineer when I met with him upon my arrival in China. As previously written, we first met Mr. Zhou when he visited England. The occasion, if one remembers, was at the dinner had with Mr. Michael Portillo, Minister of Defense, the primary invitee. Mr. Zhou was rapidly promoted to President and played a key role in directing our exploration efforts in Bohai Bay. I found Mr. Zhou to be a highly intelligent and forceful no nonsense exploration manager who wanted to make sure we knew who made the decisions in the Tanggu office (the company's headquarters). With each technical and management meeting, and there were many, Mr. Zhou and I developed a growing respect for each other. We became such good friends that Shirley and I welcomed in the New

Year on December 31, 1998 at a dinner that included Mr. Zhou, his wife, and his two beautiful daughters.

The New Year dinner was unusual since no representative in the oil industry had ever met Mr. Zhou's wife. We enjoyed a remarkable dinner replete with many toasts and ganbeis (cheers). Mr. Zhou had several of his lieutenants with him and they took it upon themselves to make sure the Lent boys (Tobin and Taran) were well lubricated. It was obviously their intent to drink our sons under the table. When it came time to retire to a nearby dance floor, where there was dancing to live music, the lieutenants were passed out on a nearby leather covered bench. As for the Lent boys......Taran took one of the Zhou daughters by the hand and made a flashy entrance onto the dance floor. He ran, did a cartwheel, and came down in a split on the dance floor. Tobin was accompanied by his newly wedded wife Ha, so he made a more refined entrance. It was a marvelous way to ring in the New Year.

There was one embarrassing moment. Mr. Zhou had presented me with an ornate balsam wood model of a sailing ship. During one of his Ganbeis he slammed his drink down on the ship and broke it into many pieces. I thought, "Oh no!" This is not good. But Mr. Zhou laughed, and all was well.

After I returned to the United States from China, Mr. Zhou was often in Houston on business. He never failed to invite me to dinner, and I was always seated to his right (the place of honor), even in the presence of numerous oil executives from far more powerful oil companies than Kerr-McGee. He invariably had his staff members come up and thank me for my efforts in Bohai Bay. One evening, after a few beers, I looked at my good friend Mr. Zhou and said, "You, on many occasions, had someone watching me, didn't you?" He looked at me and smiled, "No." After a long pause, he added, "I had two watching you". One of the unusual responsibilities Mr. Zhou assumed when he became president of Bohai Oil was also becoming Mayor of Tanggu. Amongst his mayoral responsibilities was birth control. After learning this, I respected him even more. My hands were full directing an exploration effort. I could not have handled being in charge of granting birthing permits.

The People of China

One of Mr. Zhou's deputy director, Mr. Yao Pin Li, was built like a world class wrestler, a truly formidable looking specimen. Prior to Mr. Zhou learning to speak English, Mr. Yao also served as interpreter. Quick to laugh, Yao Pin Li was also quite mischievous. He once dressed up as a policeman, charged into a karaoke room, and told a bevy of foreign oil company workers they were under arrest for lewd behavior. Only after he had scared the daylight out of these men did he break the news that the 'arrest' was just a prank. What a guy!

I mention two other CNOOC employees who were memorable in their own way. Mr. Cao Yunshi was an attorney and the Director of the Legal Department at CNOOC. One day I told my secretary I was going to meet with Mr. Cao. When I pronounced his name, my secretary recoiled in horror. She said, "Mr. Lent you cannot say that. You have just said that he is Mr. (a most crude obscenity)." I never did learn to pronounce his name correctly. To me he was always Mr. F—-.

When I was nominated to receive a high honor and an invitation from the Premier of China, I was told to report to the CNOOC offices to be interviewed by a reporter, Xu Hui Yuan, who said she worked for the China Offshore Oil Press. We met and talked for quite a while. She kept asking me what I thought of Premier Zhu Rongji and his economic policies. After the interview concluded, I realized that it must have been being recorded and that the real story behind the 'interview' was that I was being vetted for the honor I was about to receive. The government wanted to make sure they were not giving this honor to a person who did not respect the Premier. Thankfully, I very much admired, and still do, the efforts Premier Zhu's economic reform efforts.

I met a number of individuals who represented CNPC and their subsidiary China National Oil Development Corporation (CNODC). Most of the meetings we had with both companies were unfortunately adversarial. Kerr-McGee had been awarded near shore licenses in Bohai Bay that required we drill a well by year end 1998. We had not found a prospect worthy of drilling and were working hard either to find a way out of our drilling commitment or be given more time to identify an acceptable prospect. CNPC was reported to have a number of former Red Guards on their executive management team. I remember each individual I worked with in both companies. I found it very difficult to work with the managers and very easy to work with their scientists. When I left China, I thought the onshore potential under CNPC's jurisdiction was incredibly significant, but that this potential might take quite some time to unleash since there were many regulatory barriers that would have to be overcome. I would have liked to have had the time to find a way for Kerr-McGee to explore onshore China. I think the effort might have proven very worthwhile.

Two memorable individuals Shirley and I met during our brief stay in China were our drivers, Mr. Deng Jia Lun and Mr. Zhang Hong Qing. These men were memorable because of the time we spent with them and the insights we gained into their daily lives. For whatever reason, protocol required us refer to them as Lao Zhang and Lao Deng. Lao, meaning senior or elder, is a term signifying respect. We did not understand why the protocol required addressing men in their early 40s as Lao. We spent so many hours with each of these gentlemen that we could fill a book recounting only what we did and observed while they were with us. Included herein are selected anecdotes that stimulate warm and moving recollection of times we spent together.

Lao Zhang was my driver, mostly. He picked me up early in the morning (6:30 a.m.) and drove me to the office. He sometimes brought me home in the evening, or drove me on special outings, but usually he was given the late afternoon and evenings off so that he did not work unrealistically long hours. As with Lao Deng, when you spend a lot of time with each other, day after day, you get insights that are just not possible any other way.

On our drive into the office, I daily observed fascinating sights on and along the road into Beijing. Lao Zhang and I would exchange thoughts when we saw something that was unusual, or sometimes even bizarre (for example, a naked lady walking beside the highway and kicking chickens that were in her way). One day I asked Lao Zhang if he had any children.

He said yes, he did, a boy and a girl. He said the boy was 12 and the girl 9. I thought about this and asked, "Lao Zhang, I thought China had a one child policy." Without smiling he said, "They are twins."

One morning Lao Zhang told me he could not work the following day. The previous day he had received a notice saying his government-owned apartment building was to be demolished. He had been given a choice of two housing locations in different parts of the city. He could pick the area, but not the apartment. His move had to be completed by the end of the week. Shirley and I witnessed two other short notice demolitions done on short notice, both of which involved the widening of a street, and the subsequent destruction of roadside commercial buildings. When the Chinese government makes a decision there is no public hearing to discuss the matter.

I took one afternoon off work and had Lao Zhang drive me into the mountains northeast of Beijing. Shirley and I had been to the area previously, and I had noticed a number of locals fishing for trout in cold, clear water running through cement lined ponds. The locals I had seen fishing were using bamboo poles baited with some sort of meat affixed to hooks tied to the end of a short leader. I saw very few fish caught. When I was told anyone could fish these ponds, I thought it would be fun to return someday and see if a graphite rod and reel, a long leader, and artificial tied flies might induce the trout to be taken more easily and with greater frequency than I had seen when the locals were having at it. If fish were caught, we would have to pay for them, or alternatively, we could have a nearby restaurant grill them and then serve them with vegetables and beer - for a fee of course.

When Lao Zhang and I pulled up I began assembling my gear, all the time thinking what the locals would do or say, if I tossed a line in the water with all that fancy equipment and I did not have any more success than they had had with their bamboo poles. I should not have worried. On my first cast I hooked and landed a 16-inch trout. I had proved my point. I handed the rod to Lao Zhang and asked him to try his luck. As usual, he was attired in a dark brown sport coat over a blue sweater, a dress shirt with a tie, and polished brown leather shoes. Like me, he hooked a fish on his first cast. I have a photo of him with a huge smile on his face. We ate two trout at a nearby restaurant. Before we left, I asked Lao Zhang to catch one more trout to take home to his family.

While we were loading up after our meal, I was waiting near our car when an elderly lady came riding up on her bike. A basket on her handlebars contained firecrackers. I had encountered this lady on a previous excursion Shirley and I had taken up this same canyon. On that occasion, Shirley had gone to a nearby hotel (a small one to be sure) to use the facilities. I did not understand what the lady was saying, but I got the point. She wanted me to buy a few firecrackers. I said no. Looking very disappointed, she rode back up the hill. Later I reconsidered my refusal. Realizing that had I paid her 10 or 20 Yuan (1 or 2 dollars) for a handful of firecrackers; it would probably have made her day. I regretted not making the purchase. When I was in the same place fishing with Lao Zhang, I had a chance to rectify the situation. I gave the lady 20 Yuan. She gave me four firecrackers. The firecrackers were unlike any I had ever seen. They were 3-4 inches long and had the diameter of a United States quarter. They looked like small sticks of dynamite. The lady took my money and peddled off. I looked around, and then carefully hid the firecrackers behind a tree. No way was I going to take that purchase home with me. When we left the fishing ponds, I felt good about myself. We had caught fish and I had made an old lady happier and slightly more prosperous.

When Lao Zhang began driving me to the office, we would connect to the highway coming from the Beijing airport (the old one, a new one was being built). On the highway into town there was a toll station. Lao Zhang would drive up to one of the toll booths, pay the fee, and wait while the person in the booth wrote out a receipt. That process concluded, the gate would open and we were on our way. After several months I noticed that an Easy Pass lane had opened. I had the office apply for a transponder that would allow us to move through a gate without stopping. The first time I talked Lao Zhang into using the lane he drove up very slowly, almost coming to a stop. The red light turned to green and the gate lifted. We drove through. There were policeman watching us and I think that frightened Lao Zhang. Each day I reminded Lao Zhang he could drive much faster, that the gate would always lift, and the red light would turn green. I finally asked one of the office staff to explain to Lao Zhang that he would not be shot if he did not slow down. It took a while, but he finally got it. In my last days at the office, we would sail through the Easy Pass lane without slowing down.

Lao Deng was Shirley's primary driver, and he was at her disposal all day long. She only had to give him a ring and he would pick her up. His command of English was quite good which made giving directions and instructions much easier than if she had been with Lao Zhang. Still, there were occasions when Lao Zhang came to pick the both of us up.

Lao Deng was almost always impeccably dressed. He wore a sport coat or a suit every day. Unless Shirley was in Beijing late in the day, my trip home was with Lao Deng. As with Lao Zhang, there were plenty of times for Lao Deng and I to talk about "life" in the city. Lao Deng, his wife, and a teenage daughter lived in a Hutong where they shared common cold-water showers and toilets with other residents.

Lao Deng's wife was employed, and it took her 40 minutes to ride to work on her bicycle. Lao Deng and his wife were unhappy on those days when she rode to and from work in the rain or snow. Even though he was a driver for Kerr-McGee and had access to an auto, he had to take a cab to our motor pool each morning to get a vehicle. He was not able to help his wife with her difficult trips to work. It was a bone of contention.

One day Lao Deng said to me, "Mr. Lent you are my boss, so I can tell you of a problem I have. My wife and I share a small room with our daughter. It is very difficult for us to have sex with her being so near us." I really did not know how to handle that problem and could not give him any advice, but I was moved by the fact he felt he knew me well enough to voice his angst.

On one occasion Shirley and I were to attend a Thanksgiving

Day dinner party put on by the American Women's Club. Because Lao Deng was driving us, we asked if he would like to be our guest. He stewed about the invitation for several days before he finally told Shirley he was honored to be invited, but he did not know how to use a knife and fork. Shirley gave him a lesson and Lao Deng, proud as a peacock, sat at our table and shared a turkey dinner with us and three other couples.

When we asked Lao Deng to drive us to the Fragrant Hills, he was glad to do so. He was less enthusiastic when we asked him to take one of the two-seated trams up to the top of the mountain. There are actually three separate trams in operation, each one taking visitors further up the mountain. We talked Lao Deng into taking the first segment, but when he reached the transfer platform, he said he was going back down the mountain. We found that people we met in China did not like being alone nor did they like getting out of their comfort zone.

To show our appreciation for the work Lao Deng had done for us, and to give his wife a taste of luxury, Shirley and I invited the Dengs to be our guests for a weekend at the Dragon Villas Clubhouse. We were scheduled to leave China late the following week. We reserved a room on the second floor and encouraged the couple to eat at any of the restaurants, visit the lounge, watch a movie, or whatever. Shirley and I would pick up the tab. I asked that he drive his wife out in the company car and park it in our driveway. We also invited them to walk over and visit us in our home.

We made one trip to the Clubhouse to check on Lao Deng and his Mrs. We found them still in their room. They had taken a number of hot showers and were dressed in the terry cloth robes they had found in the closet. When they finally made it over to our house Mrs. Deng was stunned by the size of our home and by the contents. Mind you, what we had was not particularly impressive had we been living in the United States. But to the Dengs, what we had was unbelievable.

When Lao Deng was ready to depart the Clubhouse, I went with him to check out. The bill came to less than $300. When I saw him in the office the next day, he said to me, "Mr. Lent in my family I am no longer Lao Deng, I am King Deng." I could only smile. There had been no teenage daughter to put a damper on their amorous activity.

Before I left the office, Lao Deng brought me two beautiful vases (about 18 inches in height) that he said were for Mrs. Lent. When I took them home, Shirley told me Lao Deng had been with her when she first saw the vases. She did not purchase them because she thought they were overpriced. Lao Deng had gone back to the shop and had paid the 'Chinese price' for the vases. I am sure they were still expensive, but as we had found during our time in China, all items have two costs: those for foreigners and those for Chinese. There are even two costs for the drilling of an exploratory oil venture, and the variance is considerable. The two vases given us by Lao Deng sit on the top shelf above our family room entertainment center. On nights when I have a fire in the fireplace and sit watching TV, I occasionally look up at the vases and reflect on the thoughtfulness of Lao Deng's gift.

We had an Ayi who came to our house once a week to help keep our house tidy. Unfortunately, neither Shirley nor I could remember her name. Because she spoke almost no English, we had to phone the office and ask one of the office staff to act as interpreter when we wanted to communicate something out of the ordinary. The Ayi had her own small room, with a sink, shower, commode, and a small bed. She never used the bed as far as we could tell, but she always showered. We had given her permission to use our washer and dryer, so she always brought her laundry with her. Even though she was paid very little by western standards, I suspect she would have worked for nothing just so she could take warm showers and use the laundry room. When we transferred back to the United States, we had no use for our refrigerator that used the high voltage outlets we had in both the United Kingdom and China, so we gave the refrigerator to the Ayi. When she and her husband came in a three wheeled vehicle to pick it up you should have heard all the chatter. It does not take much to make some people happy.

Sally Perdue was employed by Kerr-McGee on a contract basis. She was an exceptionally beautiful middle age woman

And There We Were

who helped selected staff members improve their conversational English. Shirley and Sally met one day when Shirley came to visit me in the office and they subsequently became good friends. The two lovely women went on a number of outings together, and Sally even helped Shirley decorate our home for Christmas.

Without divulging the reason, one of our staff members suggested I might Google Sally Perdue and see what came up. I discovered that Sally Perdue was a former Miss Arkansas who had engaged in a four-month affair with then Governor Bill Clinton. Clinton called her "Long Tall Sally", and she was known to sing to him, "*He's just my Bill*". Sally posed for Penthouse (one source said she posed for Playboy) and she later reported that a 'representative' of the Democratic Party threatened her with bodily harm if she did not keep her mouth shut. She received the threat in 1992 as Clinton's campaign for the Presidency came down to the wire. When Shirley talked to Sally, she discovered Sally was in China because of the overt threats to her life. I do not know if Sally remains in China, but I hope enough time has passed since the Clinton Presidency that she has been able to return to the United States and is living a comfortable and happy life.

As mentioned previously at the beginning of this section describing memorable people Shirley and I encountered in China, we observed or were in contact with an incredible number of people who may, or may not, have known how they had captivated us. I hope the following select narratives are of interest to the reader and that they represent a sampling of the humanity of the Chinese people.

Of all the observations I made during our travels on the highways and byways of China, the most poignant came when I saw a very small 4-wheel tractor pulling out of a newly seeded field and onto the roadway. The tractor was pulling a small flatbed trailer that held a hoe, rake, and shovel. Sitting on the bench beside the driver was a small woman who was holding the arm of the man driving the tractor. Her head was against his shoulder. They had obviously just spent the day working their allotted plot of land. Both looked exhausted. As we drove past them, I noticed an apparent deep affection between the two. They most likely did not have much, but what they had was earned by working together.

Several times when we drove through small villages, we passed numerous bicycle riders. On one occasion we passed a well-groomed, well-dressed and very pretty young lady who was wearing a very attractive black and yellow dress. Hanging from her left hand was a dainty yellow purse, much like one Shirley would carry if she went to a cocktail party. Wherever she was going on her bike, the lady was going to make a grand entrance. On another occasion we saw a lady wearing what appeared to be a long silk printed dress. Oblivious to what others might think, she had pulled the dress up above her waist to protect her dress. Her white panties were there for all to see. When she reached her destination, her dress would not be marred by having been caught up in the chain.

Shirley attracted attention. She was beautiful and her hair, in color and style, was captivating. Many times, when we were out and about, on the Great Wall or in one of the cities (e.g., Shenzhen) people, mostly young ladies, would stop Shirley and ask if they could have their picture taken with her. They never asked me such a thing, so I was usually asked to be the photographer. Once, on the way back to our Shunyi home, Shirley saw a vendor selling flowers along the road. She asked our driver to stop so she could look for a bouquet. There was an instantaneous traffic jam on the two-lane highway we were traveling. Drivers of all manner of bikes, tractors, small trucks, and three wheelers stopped to look at the pretty lady buying flowers. Sometimes Shirley was forced to use a public toilet. As she would walk in, women coming out would sometimes turn around and return to the restroom. They wanted to see how this pretty lady squatted over the hole in the floor.

Shirley often visited Silk Alley (also known as Xiushui Market). This market no longer exists (it was demolished and replaced by Silk Street in 2008), but at the time we were in Beijing the narrow alley market was populated with more than 400 stalls. Tens of thousands of people frequented the Alley to shop for items made of silk. Cheap knockoffs of luxury brands were also abundant and available at modest prices. On one occasion Shirley was looking at a blouse that caught her eye. She wanted to try it on, but the seller had no dressing room. Shirley had the vendor hand her the blouse, and she promptly doffed her top and slipped on the blouse. Three women shopping with her tried to shield Shirley from nearby gawking shoppers. Shirley later said it did not matter if people were looking at her, because she would never ever see any of them again. When I got home that evening, Shirley told me of the experience, adding that she had no shame. She bought the blouse.

    Shirley was not the only one who shopped at outdoor markets, street side, or in alleys. I also shopped similar locales. Like Shirley's experience at Silk Alley, I never found a dressing room where I could try on apparel. At an outdoor market near the Holiday Inn Lido, I bought a knock-off Polo shirt for only a few dollars. The shirt' neck size (18 1/2 inch) was right, but when I got home, I discovered that, although there may be Chinese with a similar neck size, there must be none with long arms. The long (?) sleeved shirt was about five inches too short for my arms. I also, at the indoor Hongqiao Market, bought shoes without being able to sit down and try them on. The selected pair of leather shoes was my size 46 (12 in the United States). I hopped around in the walkway until I had one of the shoes on my bigger foot, the right one. My purchase was flawed. It took nearly a month before the shoe broke my foot in.

    Most evenings, when we were not busy elsewhere, Shirley walked out of the Dragon Villas complex for a long walk. Her preferred walk took her by a cluster of small homes built around a common courtyard (a hutong). When Shirley approached the homes one or more mothers frequently opened a door so their children could run out to say "*Nihao*" (hello). During those same evening walks (usually 45 minutes to an hour in duration) Shirley chose a path leading to the Shunyi golf course. She enjoyed walking the fairways late in the day when the golfers were off the course. Men in military uniform standing guard at the point where the path entered the golf course invariably put up theirs hand indicating she should stop. Shirley always smiled and said, "It's ok", and walked on. Not once was she

The People of China

detained. What does one do when a pretty foreigner ignores your warning? A local doing the same thing would likely be hauled away, never to be seen again.

I once went golfing on the Shunyi golf course where Shirley walked in the evenings. Each golfer on the course was assigned two caddies, tiny Mongolian ladies who weighed approximately 90 pounds each. One of these Lilliputians carried my clubs: the other watched where my ball went. They spoke very little English, but I was always given the club they thought I should be hitting. On one hole I was playing to a green on a small island and declined to use the offered club. After striking what I thought was a perfect shot, one of the caddies immediately yelled, "*Shui.*" In the water. "No way", I countered, only to see my shot hit the edge of the wooden rail and fall into the water. At the end of the round the little ladies wanted to know how many of them could fit in my arms. I put four of them together and reached around them, following which I tipped them well.

When I asked why the Japanese foursome who had been playing ahead of us had gone missing mid-round, I was told that a golfer, if so inclined, could take his caddy or caddies into a small cottage located between the 9th and 10th holes. This is where the big tips were earned. My caddies likely received a better tip than the ladies employed by the Japanese, and I am all but certain they were relieved we had not taken a mid-round break.

The Chinese are natural entrepreneurs, but capitalism is still foreign to some at the bottom end of the economic spectrum. They have yet to come to grips with the laws of supply and demand. On one of our trips to the Great Wall we were with Shirley's mother and her husband Claud. I took so many photos that I ran out of film (no digital camera then). I found a man sitting on a blanket selling film. I expected a roll of film purchased on the top of the Great Wall to cost an arm and a leg. I had recently paid 26 Yuan (about $3) for a roll of film in Beijing. The peasant on the mountain top sold me the same roll for 23 Yuan. I would have been happy to have paid three times that much.

The population of China while we were in residence there

was approximately 1.3 billion. There were fewer jobs than there were people to fill them, so manpower was consequently cheap. When we needed work to be done at our home, we were overwhelmed by the number or workers who showed up to beneficially service us. We always had one or two guards standing watch in front of our home in Dragon Villas. There were maybe 20-30 other guards on the streets or in front of other homes. Rotating shifts of these poor souls manned their stations 24 hours per day, 365 days per year. In the winter when the cold winds blew down from Mongolia, they were on duty even when it snowed. Anytime we got up in the middle of the night and turned on a light, we could look outside and see the guard on duty making an entry in a small booklet.

It was always surprising how many workers showed up at our home when we needed work done. When a faucet malfunctioned, four Dragon Villa employees arrived to address the problem. It took 5 to fix a faulty air conditioning unit. When we first tried to use our dishwasher, we found it inoperable. It took 5 workers to pull out the unit, only to find that it had not been plugged into the socket. In the summer 7 lawn care employees would show up to mow, rake, trim, and plant. When a light bulb needed to be replaced, we would find two at the door.

The Dragon Villas management team sent a worker over to help us hang pictures and paintings after our household goods had arrived. We were told the man's fee was 15 Yuan ($1.25) for each piece hung. He surely earned his money that day. The first piece Shirley wanted put up was a large framed mirror with an attached shelf. To make sure the mirror was correctly centered we moved it back and forth until Shirley was happy with the placement. Although the man did not speak English, he understood how we wanted the mirror to hang. He made a few marks on the wall, measuring so that the supports were where they were needed. There was nothing subtle about how he made the holes necessary for the molly bolt anchors to be installed. The man took out a big hammer and a Phillips screwdriver and pounded holes in the drywall. After he had installed the anchors, he hung the mirror and stepped back. Shirley looked and said that the mirror was not centered. How do you tell a guy his work is not acceptable? More holes were pounded in the wall. Before the mirror was finally hung to Shirley's satisfaction, we had to make sure it covered all the errant holes. The rest of the day went more smoothly for the poor fellow. He ended hanging 18 photos and/or frames on our walls. When it came time to pay him for his work, we discovered the man could not multiply numbers. He could add and divide, but not multiply. He was embarrassed that he could not calculate his fee. At his agreed fee of 15 Yuan per picture hung, his take for the day came to 18 X 15 Yuan, or 270 Yuan. This sum was a significant windfall for the picture hanger. The average laborer in China at that time was making about 35-40 Yuan per day.

The employees needed to issue handwritten receipts at the toll booths on the airport highway were amongst many who were required to do unnecessary, at least to me, transactions. I found it interesting that when we bought something in one of the large shopping centers, the salesclerk who waited on us would hand write a purchase order which we would then take to a central cashier station to effect the exchange. With written evidence of payment in hand we could returned to the salesperson and collected our purchase.

After we had moved into our home and the furniture and photos were in place, we put up a bird feeder we had brought from England. It was located in our backyard near a brick wall running along the back of our property. Our yard workers were dumbfounded when they learned we intended to feed songbirds. I quickly learned that in China one does not simply go buy a bag of bird feed in a store. Why would anyone waste money on such a thing? I had Lao Deng take me to a nearby outdoor market where one could buy all manner of meat and grains. After a lengthy search I finally found a merchant selling millet and other coarse grains. When Lao Deng told the fellow I wanted 5 pounds each of three different grains, the vendor asked Mr. Deng to make sure I knew what I had purchased was not suitable for the dinner table. I smiled and took my bags of bird seed home. It took nearly two months before we were able to induce birds to use the feeder. In the first few weeks the feathered ones came and ate only the grain resting on the ground after having fallen out of the feeder. Eventually, though, the birds finally got the hang of it and by the time we left China they were emptying the feeder on a daily basis.

On the day I went to the Shunyi outdoor market to get bird seed, I thought it might also be fun to buy a chicken and a piece of beef. Usually, one bought a live chicken and they dressed it as you watched. For whatever the reason, the vendor I saw selling chicken that day had birds the locals thought of as skillet ready, which meant that even though they were dressed, the birds still had their heads and reptilian-like feet attached. After I had made the purchase, but before I had the lady wrap it up, I asked if she would please remove the head and feet. I thought Shirley might not appreciate having these extra parts laid out on her kitchen table. The lady did as I requested, and then she stunned me. She reached in her pocket and gave me a partial refund. I had not taken all that I had paid for. Wow!

With the chicken already a purchased I stopped by a booth where a man was selling beef. He had a hind quarter of beef hanging from a hook. I made a motion indicating I wanted him to take his knife and cut me a steak. He nodded and went to the hind quarter where he took his knife and removed almost all of the beef round. The hunk of meat he had cut for me weighed over 15 pounds. The cost was minimal but there was no way I had intended make such a large purchase. I took the meat home and, being the trained meat cutter that I am, I sliced off a number of steaks, and I tied up the rest into a nice rolled roast. I never went back to the outdoor market though I occasionally had Lao Deng or Lao Zhang drop by and pick up 20-30 pounds of seed for the bird feeder.

One sight that became a source of amusement for me was the weekly parade of cyclists I saw leaving the Yanjing Brewery on River Road, near the intersection with the road leading to Dragon Villas. Each Friday evening on the way home from work Lao Deng and I passed many cyclists, each one a brewery worker with a case of Yanjing Beer strapped over the rear tire carriage of his or her bicycle. This beer, sometimes referred to as the "Emperor's Beer" is one of the most popular brands of beer in China. I assumed that every worker at the brewery got a beer bonus at the end of each week. Some of the cyclists never made it home with the beer. These cyclists would peddle into the graveled parking in front of a nearby small building that had a television set. They would unload their beer and walk through the door. To this day I can visualize workers drinking beer and watching telecasts that might not have been available in their hutong homes.

Traveling the highways of China always gave us wonderful snippets of the Chinese people as they traveled to destinations unknown and/or marketed their produce and animals. Depending on the season and the region of the country, north and south, Shirley and I would see the most interesting products for sale along the roadways.

When watermelons were in season, we saw pyramids of melons (five by five melons at the base) every quarter to half mile, for miles on end. I rarely saw a melon purchased. There were so many sellers I wondered how anyone could make any money. On the way into work and on the way home I noticed one lady who manned a melon pile with her young daughter at her side. After several weeks I began to feel sorry for the lady. One evening I had the driver stop. I bought 3 melons, one for Shirley and me and one each for our drivers, Lao Zhang and Lao Deng. I felt good about what I had done. Our melon was mushy so most of it went uneaten.

On one of our trips into the mountains we stopped at a junction where many vendors had gathered to sell what they had brought from their nearby farms and villages. We had stopped to use a public toilet and had not intended to make a purchase. A handsome young man dressed in slacks and a sport coat had a gunny sack of chestnuts for sale. He smiled and tried to make a bit of small talk. I took a liking to the fellow because he was the only vendor in the long line of them who showed any interest in marketing his wares. I had our driver, Lao Deng, ask him how much he wanted for his entire sack. The man was dumbfounded. His small hand-held scale could not possibly weigh the big sack. He came up with a price and I paid it. As we were placing the bag in the trunk of the car the man kept repeating "millionaire" over and over again. I took the sack of nuts to the Kerr-McGee office and left them in the coffee room for any employee who might want to take a pound or two of the nuts home with them. At that, it took nearly a month before the nuts were gone.

I mentioned that we stopped at the intersection to use the toilets. As one was about to enter either the respective men or women facility there was a lady standing by the doorway selling small (2X2 inch) squares of tissue paper. Shirley looked at the tiny squares and indicated that she wanted a stack of the tissue three to four inches high (at a cost of much less than fifty cents). The lady would sell Shirley only 5 squares of the tissue. She would have to drip dry.

On one of our trips through the countryside we passed a number of stands selling honey in glass Coke bottles and small jars. Like with the melons, the honey sellers were stationed every few hundred yards, for miles on end. Because I had not seen a flowering plant or tree during our entire journey, I wondered what sourced the honey. Later when I queried one of the Kerr-McGee staff, I was told that we should not buy such honey. It wasn't really honey. Those beekeepers put out sugar water for the bees. What the bees produced from the sugar water was more like a nectar than honey.

When peaches were in season, we saw stand after stand of peach crates tilted so that those traveling the roads could see the beautiful orbs. I noticed some of the vendors spraying their peaches with water. The water made the peaches glisten, but, this being China, I wanted to know from whence came the water.

I previously described coconut vendors I observed while on Hainan Island. The green coconuts sold for 2 Yuan each (about 25 cents) but as with the watermelons, sales seemed to be few and far between. I always wondered what was done with the melons when the vendors went home for the night. Surely, they did not spend the night by the melons or coconuts, and if they were left unattended overnight, they would almost certainly be gone by morning. Maybe I should have waited around after dark to see if someone came by to haul off the melons and coconuts in trucks or other vehicles.

The People of China

When I looked down and across the street from my office window, I could see little stands all in a row, and all offering the same goods, mostly cigarettes and fruit juices. Occasionally there were sweets, like doughnuts on a stick. The same people manned the stands day after day, come rain or shine. During the summer it was extremely hot, and they had no shade. I rarely saw any of them make a sale. I once chuckled to myself, thinking that before I left China I ought to visit one of the stands and make a $300 purchase. A purchase of this magnitude would likely would have cleaned out the vendor and sent him or her into retirement. Of course, I never did this, but I should have.

The reader will recall the elderly lady who sold me firecrackers from her bicycle. She was not the only one we came across selling such explosives. On one promontory near the summit of a mountain, there was a viewing area where locals, almost all of them bicyclists, could purchase firecrackers from a small stand located in a nearby pull off. The viewing area on the point was small, and a rail separated the platform from the edge of a precipitous cliff. Before Shirley and I climbed to the viewing area, I bought three firecrackers, M80 in size. Each firecracker came with a string attached to it. On the other end of the string was a soda pop flip top. We observed others on the platform insert an index finger through the flip top opening and then hurl the firecracker off the cliff and into the void. A delayed fuse detonated the firecracker and the resulting explosion reverberated off the granite and marble walls of the canyon. There were echoes of echoes of echoes. I had made my purchase so that Shirley and I might experience the thrill of our own echo generation. The locals cleared a path for me on the viewing platform. I found I could not insert my finger through the flip top opening. No problem. I pinched the circular opening in the flip top between my thumb and index finger and gave the explosive a big heave. Unfortunately, I could not hold onto the flip top, and the firecracker fell at the feet of the people standing near us. I never saw so many move so fast. Although no one was hurt by my action, I gave the remaining two firecrackers to one of the locals, one with tiny fingers.

The roadways near Beijing, and especially the rural one we took to and from our home in Dragon Villas, were extremely dangerous. I nicknamed our highway the "highway of death". We witnessed several fatal accidents, and the aftermath of others when we passed bodies lying by the roadside. One time our driver had to swerve around a body in the road. Apparently another motorist had hit a cyclist, and the fellow had fallen dead onto the pavement. Because no one had stopped to pull the fellow off the road, trucks and other vehicles continued to drive over him. He was as flat as some of the squirrels we see on the roadways here in Texas.

One of the odd habits of Chinese drivers led to the deaths of two young German men whose parents lived near us in Dragon Villas. For whatever reason, and we heard a number of them, Chinese motorists both in the city and on rural roadways do not turn on their head lights until one hour after dark. Making the practice even more lethal is the fact that many vehicles do not have working taillights. When we passed the accident that involved the German boys, we saw two body bags by the road. Body bags were an indication that foreigners were involved. When a local is killed, he or she is dragged off to the side of the road and left for relatives to pick up. A foreigner is always bagged. It turned out that following a day of drinking, the boys, after dark, were speeding on the highway toward Dragon Villas. When they came up behind a flatbed truck with no taillights, they could not stop in time and drove under the bed of the truck. The German auto caught fire with the boys trapped inside.

Once in the city we saw a cyclist take a head over heels spill when the front wheel of his bike dropped into an open manhole. Whoever was working the manhole had removed the cover and had not put up a warning flag or barrier. It did not appear the cyclist had been killed, but he was unconscious when we drove by him.

One might wonder why people do not stop to offer assistance when there is an accident. We were told that if one does so, he becomes responsible for the care of the injured party. Wow! I do not know if this is actually the case, but it is what we were told.

The People of China

One morning we witnessed a cyclist carrying a styrofoam box containing fish to market. When he was hit at an intersection, 6 large golden carp, each weighing an estimated 5-6 pounds, flew out of the live well onto the street. Fish were flopping everywhere. It was summer and the pavement was hot. I felt really bad for the fellow. Even though he was not injured, the fish would surely die and the market for dead fish, especially golden carp, is nonexistent. Most fish we saw served in restaurants came from in-house aquariums where patrons could see that the fish were fresh.

I was always amazed at how the Chinese squatted along the roadways while waiting for a bus, or because they were idly chatting with others. Most westerners, at least in their home countries, sit on benches or chairs. For the Chinese, squatting was the natural way of taking a load off one's feet. I believe if I were to squat like I saw many Chinese do, I would require surgery for torn ligaments.

Going back to the topic of cheap labor, we saw a number of street sweepers along the rural highways and village streets. They would have long sticks with reeds tied to the end of them. The individuals, mostly women, were seen sweeping the loose gravel off of the roadways. Many times we saw only a cloud of dust ahead, and recognized the street sweepers only as we came upon them.

One of the most unusual sights we came across during our China stay was a mechanical street sweeper. An enterprising man had affixed a drum over a two wheeled axle and designed it such that it rotated when the wheels moved. He had drilled holes into the drum, and into these holes he placed the very same 'brooms' the ladies used to sweep the streets. When we saw the rotating drum moving the reed brooms over the surface of the roadway, we were incredulous. I would have bet good money that in all the world there was only one such apparatus.

I suspect one reason there were so many street (or highway) sweepers is that many of the paved roadways were also used to dry corn or to thresh wheat. On a number of roadways, we saw a traffic lane closed so corn bearing cobs could dry. When the corn was dry enough, shuckers took the kernels off the cobs, and spread the grains out for further drying. After the kernels were sufficiently dry, sweepers gathered the harvest in piles and scooped them into sacks.

On one stretch of road, shocks of wheat were spread out so that the traffic would loosen the wheat from the chaff. I was uncomfortable having our car drive over the wheat, but Lao Zhang assured me it was expected and was actually helpful. Once the grains were separated from the stalks and chaff, the wheat was swept up and bagged. Although the majority of grain Shirley and I saw being harvested was processed in the manner described above, over 85 percent of the grains harvested during our stay in China was reported to have been done with mechanical combines. We did not observe anything approaching that magnitude, but we visited only a very small area of a very expansive country.

An observation that proved to be a source of amusement and interest was the curious rule of the road that allowed unfettered salvage after an accident. During one of our trips to Tangshan, we encountered a procession of cyclists and pedestrians carrying baskets and armloads of cabbages. The procession looked like a line of army ants in the jungle, all emanating from a point source. We finally came upon the point source. It was an overturned truck that had once been filled with cabbages.

Lao Deng and I saw the same type of salvaging when we came upon three wheeled vehicles and small trucks hauling huge rolls of newspaper stock. We even saw a line of people pushing similar rolls down the side of the road. All of the rolls appeared to have burned edges. We eventually came to the site of a collision between a truck carrying the rolls of print paper and a truck carrying drums of a flammable substance. The subsequent fire had burned the outer layers of the paper rolls. I could not, for the life of me, imagine what the peasants were going to do with newsprint paper. It was theirs for the taking and take they did.

Once, on the way up to the Great Wall at Mutianyu Shirley and I found ourselves traveling behind a very bright, and obviously very new, fire truck. Each time the slow moving vehicle passed a cluster of homes the driver blasted his horn, clearly very proud of the vehicle he was driving. I remembered thinking that it was irritating for us to be behind the slow truck, but it was not often that we saw such a flashy vehicle in China. After we walked the Great Wall and had lunch, we drove back down the mountain. At the bottom of a steep hill there was a round-about, and off of the round-about was the fire truck, overturned and on its side. I wondered how much trouble the driver had created for himself. I can only hope he survived the wreck and the punishment that surely followed.

Most of the world knows that China produces some of the finest table tennis players on the planet. What many may not know is that almost all villages, especially in the north of China, have outdoor public pool (or snooker) tables. The tables are under high tarps to protect them from rain or snow. We rarely passed through a village in which a small crowd was not gathered around a table watching a game in progress.

Some of the villages we passed through were tidy, their streets and sideways clear of litter, their crops neatly stored and stacked. Tree branches and broken limbs were stacked neatly beside the houses. These villages contrasted with others where litter and clutter were everywhere. The citizenry seemed not to care how their village looked. I think this contrast in the care of a home or a community must be human nature, and one not peculiar to the Chinese. I remember seeing the same contrast in logging communities Shirley and I passed through when we traveled the roadways in western Washington state. Some villages, towns, have civic pride. Others just don't give a whit.

During our travels we saw many young people enjoying water sports. Some of the swimmers we observed brought forth smiles. Like the young naked nine- and ten-year old boys we saw running and jumping into numerous rural ponds used as fisheries. These youngsters were having the time of their lives. In contrast, we saw a young man swimming in the Liangma River in Beijing. At that time 83 percent of Beijing's sewage was untreated and was discharged into the city's rivers. Severely polluted, the Liangma River was milky gray and stunk to high heaven. The man we saw was swimming near the bridge we took from the Kempinski Hotel to the Hard Rock Cafe on a very hot summer day. Shirley and I were sure that every orifice in the swimmer's body would soon become infected. It was a disgusting sight.

I found it curious, and still do, that huge bodies of water in China, like Miyun Reservoir, have no boats on the surface, no swimmers, and no fisherman on or along the shores. In the United States such pristine waters would be covered with boaters and fishermen. Many small bodies of water did have boats and many fishermen, but the really big bodies of water we saw were void of such activity.

It was not unusual to see fishermen along the shore of the lake, a commercial fishpond, I could see from my Beijing office window. The fishermen were most likely residents coming from a large public housing compound located across the lake from Kerr-McGee's office. Sewage from the apartment complex flowed into two small ponds, separated from the larger lake by a sand and gravel berm. Some fishermen fished off the berm, sewage behind them, a clean lake in front of them. Locals could fish from shore, but when it came time to harvest the fish large nets were worked back and forth across the lake. Truckloads of fish were placed in live wells and taken to market.

One cold winter day, before the fish had been harvested, I saw a number of fishermen out on an obviously thin layer of ice. When curious people approached the holes the fishermen had cut, they were waved off. The ice was too thin to support more than a single person. One day I saw two young boys run out on the ice heading for a wide patch of ice that was dark in color and free of snow. I could imagine them falling through thin ice and dying. I wanted to run out of the office and onto the ice to tell them to return to shore. Had I done so I very likely would have broken through the ice, become stuck in the mud, with ice water over my bald spot. I did not act on my impulses, and I watched the youngsters until they were safely off of the lake. Those small boys were like water bugs scooting across water, only they were scooting across thin ice.

The People of China

We found out quickly that the Chinese people we met, particularly those outside of our circle of business associates, were very outspoken. One day, riding up the elevator in our office building, an obvious foreigner stepped into the carriage. There were a few snickers, and then one lady said to the fellow, "Do you know you have a big nose?" The man did have a big nose, a real Pinocchio if you will. He did not need to have anyone point that out. There wasn't a day in this man's life that he did not look in a mirror and think of his big nose.

When I got in the elevator, I too would hear snickers. One day a young lady said, "*Da Panza.*" Another day I heard "*Pijiu Panza*". More snickers. I finally asked my Chinese staff the meaning of these words. I was told "Big Belly" and "Beer Belly". I thought about it and asked them how one said, "What did you say?" in Chinese. I waited until the next time I heard "*Da Panza*". I turned to the young lady and said, "*Shenme.*" You never saw so many heads turn and look away, much like a dog having just been scolded.

In terms of how Shirley and I were treated personally, we found the Chinese people to be courteous and respectful. Nearly everyone we met was a delight to be around. Some were outgoing, many very shy.

In contrast to how we were treated, I witnessed many altercations that occurred between fellow countrymen. Sometimes these affronts were brutal, other times just rude. We were mildly irritated by the large number of Chinese crowding into long lines ahead of their compatriots. When Shirley and I were in the line we said nothing. After all, when one is in a foreign country, it is not appropriate to behave rudely (and certainly not in a belligerent manner), even when one is in the right. It is another matter when we see a foreigner publicly misbehaving in the United States. Once when we were in Houston, I saw a Chinese fellow jump a long queue at the airport and called him out. I never did that in China.

The physical assaults we witnessed were always disturbing. Shirley and I could not believe what some people did to others. On one occasion, while walking the streets of Shekou, I saw two men jay walking across a very busy street. A taxi driver honked his horn and came to a stop. The two pedestrians opened the taxi door, pulled the driver out, and proceeded to beat the crap out of him. In front of our office in Beijing I saw a confrontation between workers escalate into a brutal fight with the combatants swinging 2 x 4s and metal pipes. It looked like someone was sure to be killed. I learned something watching this fight (from my 11th floor corner office). After about 10-15 minutes everything came to a halt. The police had arrived. The combatants were chatting as if nothing had happened. There were no weapons in hand. I learned from this episode that in China one avoids involving the military or the police. Bad things happen when either gets involved in the matter.

A corollary to this avoidance of police involvement is the behavior that ensues after a car wreck. What happens, at least when the two parties do not engage in a slug fest, is that an agreement is reached wherein money is exchanged to cover damages. The Kerr-McGee drivers carried $10,000 in cash in the trunk of our company car so that any dispute could be reconciled without police interference. Although I witnessed many wrecks, I only saw one where the two drivers went at each other in a fist fight.

Most visitors coming to China soon discover there are many fine restaurants from which to choose. There are also alternate choices if one chooses to eat at fast food restaurants such as McDonald's, TGIF, Arby's, Chili's, or even Schlotzsky's. When we visited small restaurants where the locals ate lunch or dinner, the prices were ridiculously low. In those restaurants the cost of a Coke frequently exceeded the cost of the meal.

A small cafeteria in the basement of Kerr-McGee's office building served a buffet lunch. I decided I would join several of our Chinese workers for lunch there one day. I wanted to see what was served and to have a different luncheon experience from those I usually had. In the cafeteria there was an L-shaped serving table covered with large flat trays containing a wide assortment of vegetables, fish, and rice dishes. Some of the meat on offer looked a bit dicey, but I found the food to be quite delicious. The all you can eat meal cost less than a

The People of China

dollar. The meal was so cheap I did not make a mental note of the exact amount.

On the way down to the basement for the buffet luncheon I learned something very interesting. After I got off the elevator and was walking down the hall towards the cafeteria, I peeked through an open door into a huge room filled with people wearing headsets and phones. I suspected then that every phone call made in our office building was most likely being monitored, if not recorded. When a supervisor saw a large foreigner who had no business being in the basement, looking into the room, he came over and closed the door. From that moment on I conducted my phone calls as if I was also communicating with our Chinese business partners. On one occasion I used this to our advantage. We were in a tense negotiation and the outcome was not going in the direction we wanted. I got on the phone to our home office in Houston and told my boss the Chinese negotiators were being unreasonable, and we really ought to re-think our decision to be operating in China. Later that same afternoon I received a call from the negotiators informing me they could offer us relief on the contentious issue that was on the table. A coincidence? I think not.

The restaurants we sometimes visited, especially in the rural areas, did not have staff who spoke English. Normally our drivers ate with us and would translate our orders into Mandarin. On one occasion, however, on a trip through the countryside, we had our driver drop us off and let him stay with the car. He needed a break since he had driven for several hours and could use a nap. We told him we would have our meal and be out in an hour or two.

When we entered the restaurant the manager, thinking we were with a group of foreigners he was expecting, took us to a private area. The manager quickly realized his mistake and motioned for us to return to the main dining room. No one on the staff spoke English, and we could not read the menu. Several people eating at tables near us thought they could speak English. They tried but it was just not working. I was certain charades would work. We, Shirley's mother Marie and her husband Claud were with us, collectively decided that we would like pork, chicken, rice, broccoli, and soup. I clucked like a chicken and that worked just fine. When I oinked like a pig, we got duck. Rice was easy. I acted like I had a bowl in front of my face and shoveled like crazy. Slurping from a bowl got us the soup. "Broccoli" is hard to convey through pantomime. We were served pea pods. When it was all said and done, we were served a most delicious meal. The soup was so so. It may have been a wash bowl, but we ate it anyway.

Chapter 20

MEMORABLE OBERVATIONS OF ANIMALS, CROPS, TRANSPORT, AND ROADSIDE ACTIVITIES

𝒪 Up until this point there have only been snippets of observations made during our travels within China. The full range of what we observed during our travels is a significant part of our China experience. When we were traveling by car, I often saw things I had never seen before, sometimes in rapid succession - every quarter of mile or so. I was almost always glued to the car window, wondering what would appear next. Shirley was more selective in what she thought interesting but she, too, was stunned by the kaleidoscope of activities and objects that colored our trips, especially the trips we took through rural areas far from Beijing.

The animals Shirley and I observed in transport or in the areas adjacent to the roadways were always a source of interest. In the rural United States, one might pass fenced-in pastures containing horses and cattle, and perhaps a few with goats and sheep. In China we found the roadways frequently filled with animals on their way to market. Animals near the roadways were escorted by a herder or were roaming freely, but some were tied to trees, or tethered to stakes in the ground. I cannot remember seeing a fenced-in pasture containing livestock.

What follows is a recollection of selective observations of livestock that I found to be most interesting, perhaps even unusual:

Pigs

On several business trips to Tangshan (about 4 - 4 1/2 hours from Beijing) we traveled a variety of roadways, some superhighways, others just two-lane paved roads through the countryside and villages. As we approached a cluster of buildings in one small village, we heard a ruckus so loud you could not imagine what was causing it. The squeals were at a high pitch and they were easily audible through our closed car windows. I could not imagine what was causing such a commotion. Out of our car window we saw five 70-80-pound piglets with their hind legs tied together. The entire litter was looped over a hook in an open doorway. There they were, five little piggies hanging upside down trying to turn their heads to see what had been done to their feet. Each was violently kicking (with its front hooves) its brothers and/or sisters. We did not see anyone around, so we did not have a clue why the pigs were where they were. My first guess was that they were hung up like that and they were for sale. The squealing was great advertising. Another possibility was the presence of a nearby pot. That possibility certainly would have explained the pitch of the squealing. Hanging upside down and getting kicked in the midriff is one thing, but going into a pot, well, that takes things to a whole other level. We left the village not knowing the final outcome, but the signs did not bode well for the little pigs.

The roadways leading to Being are filled with trucks hauling animals to market. During one drive into work, we passed a small blue truck (all trucks in China are blue) with sideboards about 24 inches high around the bed of the truck. Five pigs had been loaded onto the truck. There was enough space in the bed that every time the truck stopped or accelerated the pigs all fell down. The hapless creatures were beating themselves to death. A few minutes later we passed another blue truck hauling pigs to market. This time a precaution was made to insure the pigs would not arrive at their final destination with broken limbs. A netting had been placed over the animals. Each time one or more of the pigs tried to get up it looked like they were fighting their way out of panty house. As we drove by, I saw pig faces which reminded me of pictures taken of bank robbers running from a bank with ladies' sheer hosiery over their heads.

On another occasion we came across more pigs in transport. I was appalled at what I saw. Each pig had horrible welts or cuts across its back. It appeared the pigs had been loaded with swords or a whip. Animal rights in China are non-existent, or so it seemed to me. Any protest lodged against the treatment of pigs going to market would be met with total indifference, both by the authorities and by the populace.

One evening on the way home from work I saw a 3-wheel put-put hauling a load of pigs into town. The next morning, I saw a 3-wheel put-put hauling butchered pork quarters and sacks of entrails out of town. A coincidence? I think not.

Geese

On one of our morning drives into the office we passed a man on a bicycle with five white geese tied by their feet to each handlebar. The geese were hanging down with their heads uplifted and turned in the direction the biker was peddling. It was as if they were trying to see where they were headed. I am not sure they really wanted to know that.

During one of our road trips we passed by a junk yard. I looked down a dirt path leading into and through piles of junk where I saw two large geese at a bend in the path, both looking around the corner. Whatever they saw had definitely caught their attention. It could have been a dog, a man, or a cook looking for something to put in his pot. I would have loved to have seen the outcome, whether it was a conflict or just a continuation of their walk. In my mind it was like a painting. To this day I can still see those two geese.

I saw one peasant taking his little flock of geese to market. On the back of his bicycle he had a coarse wire cage (16" by 16" by 30") into which he had crammed eight geese. The geese near the bottom of the cage were being crushed: their long necks were hanging out of the cage and drooping downwards. The peasant had stopped and was examining the miserable creatures. I believe he was going to rotate the ones on the top to the bottom. It is really tough to sell a dead goose.

I saw another peasant hauling his flock to market. He was peddling a tricycle with a flatbed trailing the rider. I estimated the trailer might been able to comfortably hold ten geese, but the farmer had packed twenty of the hapless critters into that limited space. There was no room for any of them to squat and rest. Several heads drooped and were lying across the rail. All I could think was, "Hold on guys! The chop block is only a few miles away."

On one of our drives into the mountains north of Beijing we stopped at a pullout that allowed us to look down on a large river far below. Across the river from us were a number of fields and a cluster of small homes. A very large flock of geese made the river appear white for several hundred feet. We did not see a herder. My best guess was that clipped wings and daily offerings of grain kept the geese close to the village. On a number of other occasions, we got glimpses of geese on a river or pond. If I had been them, I would have made a run for it.

Cows and Cattle

I was always amused, and sometimes mystified, by the way cows were treated. Most of the cows we saw were black and white milk cows, Holsteins if you will. Because many Chinese people are lactose intolerant, it is perhaps no wonder a number of milk cows are misused or abused. We once drove by a milk cow that was pulling a cart filled with potatoes. The cow was one of the sorriest critters I had seen in a long time. Straps from the cart had rubbed sores in the hide, there was dung spread across two-thirds of her haunches, and dried mud covered the front of the body. I would not have wanted to drink milk or eat meat from such an animal. The sight was a total disconnect for me. I could not imagine why the owner would use a milk cow to haul any kind of load. A horse or a donkey would surely have done a better job. But then perhaps he ate the donkey by mistake and kept the cow for his pack animal.

On one of our road trips we passed a milk cow tied to a tree. There was no grass to be seen, only sand and gravel at its feet. The tether was short and attached to a branch near head level. The cow's head was leaning against a fork in a limb: it looked like its eyes were closed. There was no one around. So very strange. One thing about roadside drive-by views is that you see something in a flash and have no idea of what follows. In this case I hoped that the tethered cow was not left un-attended in its awkward predicament for very long.

We came across an untethered and unattended scrawny young black and white Holstein cow munching on scattered watermelon rinds beside the highway. We had previously observed that when the rural Chinese eat melons, they toss the rinds on the ground. There must have recently been a vendor's stall near where the calf was munching as the ground was littered with an abundance of melon rinds.

It was not uncommon to see cows, goats, sheep, and horses that were grazing along the roadsides to take advantage of any grass growing in the bar ditches or under the nearby tree. I once watched as a young calf ran out of a roadside cornfield onto a very busy paved roadway. It stopped midway in the road and began licking rain from its shoulder, oblivious to the traffic swerving around it.

Moving on from the black and white cows, on the way home from work one evening, we came upon a truck taking cattle to market. It was nearly dark and just as we were about to pass the truck, I noticed movement on both sides of the truck. I wondered what the heck was going on. When we pulled alongside the truck, I saw long horned cattle loaded side by side, with one steer facing one side of the truck and an adjacent one facing the opposite side of the truck. Horned heads were protruding from each side and moving back and forth. There was

And There We Were

no room between the cattle. They were so tightly packed there was no way they could not have fallen down. There certainly was no room for any of the cattle to lie down.

Our travels in the south of China took us mostly through densely populated areas. The only visible bovine animals were water buffalo pulling plows in fields being prepared for the planting of rice or vegetables.

Life in southern China is much different than life in the north. Southerners often refer to northern Chinese as "cabbage heads". I believe this moniker comes from the fact that in years past northerners consumed a lot of cabbage (especially in the winter), while those in the south had access to a nearly year-long supply of freshly grown vegetables. Those in the north had to rely on stored produce that was grown during the summer (e.g., cabbage and leeks).

Near the end of our stay in China, during the time I was being honored as a Foreign Expert, the government took Shirley and I on a tour of the Glorious Land and Cattle Company farm. We were given a short presentation on the work the Chinese were doing with artificial insemination. Most of the work, at least with respect to cattle, was centered around the collecting and freezing of semen from a massive and prized 1400-pound bull.

Chickens

Free roaming chickens were ubiquitous throughout the rural areas we visited. We saw chickens along the road, under the canopy of trees, on sidewalks, and in alley ways. They were everywhere. There was no way anyone could say, "That's my chicken." There had to have been some form of ownership that I just did not appreciate.

Once, on our way to Fragrant Mountain, we came upon a truck filled with chickens in cages. Our driver, Lao Deng, became very animated, "Look at all of those black chickens!" I thought the guy must be Looney Tunes. The chickens were as white as white could be. It was not until Lao Deng told us to look at the beaks that we began to appreciate what we were seeing. Black chickens have white feathers, but their beaks, skin, and feet are black. Their meat is all very dark, and apparently very tasty and highly valued.

Several of our Chinese employees told me they had visited a shooting gallery where one could, for a fee, fire AK 47's, throw hand grenades, and shoot anti-aircraft weapons, etc. There was an area set aside for those who wanted to shoot chickens, tethered to a stake, with 22 caliber weapons. The stakes were located at varied distances from the firing areas. Individual chickens had different strategies for avoiding the bullets. Some crouched low when the firing began: others ran around trying to free themselves from the tether. This barbaric practice might have been more palatable if one at least got to keep the chicken he shot. That was not the case. I was incredibly surprised to learn a shooting gallery like this existed in China. Legal ownership of firearms is limited to the police and the military. Enforcement is with an iron fist.

Horses and Donkeys

Horses in China live much, much better lives than donkeys. Ungulates normally spend the majority of their hours grazing or resting. Many of the hapless donkeys we saw were tied to heavily loaded carts on their way into or out of Beijing. They must have been on the road for hours on end. I felt especially sorry for the donkeys pulling huge loads of bricks. The only visible indication of concern for the donkey's welfare were the five or six corn stalks in the back of each cart which provided a measure of nourishment during the day. My observations seemed to confirm the common perception that the owners worked their donkeys literally to death, then replaced them with another one.

And There We Were

The horses we saw were usually in much better condition than the donkeys. Although we rarely saw horses on the busy highways, the ones we did see were usually in pairs and were pulling much lighter loads than the loads pulled by donkeys.

One odd sighting occurred when we came across a man on a bicycle, with four horses trotting in front of him. The horses were tethered to ropes attached to the handlebars of the biker. The sight brought to mind a story I had heard about another bike rider who was leading a Collie on a leash also attached to his handlebars. Something caught the attention of the dog and it bolted at a right angle to the intended path, causing the cyclist to take a monster spill. I chuckled thinking of all the trouble the Chinese cyclist would have been in if his horses bolted. The runaways would not even have known they were dragging the man.

The most memorable encounter we had with horses while living in China occurred at a racetrack less than a mile from our home in Dragon Villas. The racing facility was also used as a site for political gatherings, and on some evenings we could hear men and women addressing the masses over the loud speakers. Amenities at the racetrack were similar to those in England and in the United States. There was parimutuel betting and the enclosed luxury suites were staffed with well-dressed servers who brought bettors all manner of food and drink. But it was not the facility that was so absolutely amazing. It was the fact that all of the betting took place outside of the law. Betting on horse races in China was then, and might still be, against the law.

Because horse racing in China is illegal, the track near Dragon Villas was proclaimed to be a horse intelligence testing facility. Each "race" was a horse intelligence test. I saved several of my betting stubs to prove I was betting on a horse's intelligence, not on his ability to run and win. The irony of the situation is that the horse who wins may be actually saved from going to market. If he or she wants to live another day, it is best that the critter win the race.

The description of the intelligence tests described above

may sound absurd until you understand the process through which the races unfolded. The horses who competed in each race were brought onto the track before the race in long trucks, each containing eight to ten horses. After staggering down the truck ramp on wobbly legs, the horses were quickly saddled and led onto the track by a jockey. Some of the horses were in such poor condition you might think they needed a feed bag. We saw several saddled horses drop their heads to crop the grass growing along the edge of the infield.

Though we obviously could not read the handicapping booklets, it was easy to identify the four or five horses that might be lucky enough to finish a race, or perhaps even win it. We placed our win bets on horses with the best appearance and demeanor. Shirley and I picked six first place winners in nine races. The horses in each race were a motley group of many breeds, some with the square jaws and squatty bodies of Mongolian steeds. Those horses never performed well, and they looked like they should be pulling a cart of leeks or dragon fruit rather than racing.

There was always one sweaty, agitated, difficult to saddle horse in each race. If it also looked like a racehorse, we could count on it winning the race. One horse, No. 4 in the 6th intelligence test (race), was actually led into the starting gate without a jockey. We had bet 300 Yuan on the critter, so we were anxious that a jockey mount him prior to the opening of the starting gate. When the gate flew open, No. 4 had a rider, and the horse won by 20 lengths.

The length of the races at the track near Dragon Villas were only 950 meters in contrast to the longer races we had seen in the United States, and the even longer races we had seen in England. For many of the horses, 950 meters was long enough. Some laggards were running long after the winner crossed the finish line. I suspect these horses may have been running from the butcher after having "failed" their intelligence test.

The only pack horses we saw were during our visit to the Fragrant Hills, also known as Xiang Shan Park. As mentioned earlier, many take cable cars (there are 3 of them) up to the top of the mountain. For those so inclined, there are saddled horses that carry the adventurous ones on a 2-hour ride to a point near the summit of Incense Burner Peak (1830 feet).

Fish

Most of the live fish we saw in China were those swimming in live wells at restaurants. In Hong Kong the live wells were small holding ponds in markets: the fish chosen for dinner were netted and taken to one's chosen restaurant. In Beijing the walls of one very large restaurant were lined with aquariums filled with all manner of fish. When an order was placed, the waiter would tell the cook, who would then come and dip out the chosen fish. One could never say the fish was not fresh. Near the South China Sea, in the cities of Shenzen and Guangzhou, the live fish aquariums were sometimes paired with live snakes. When one walked by one of these covered live wells, the snakes, all with their heads out of the water, would follow you. It was un-nerving. Shirley and I never ordered snake at a restaurant, although we saw a number of others who did. The preparation was not a pretty sight.

We found commercial fishponds wherever we went in northern China. We saw literally thousands of fishponds along the He River during our long drives to Tangshan. Water quality in the ponds was highly variable, and many had reeds and grass growing around the edge of the pond. Some ponds were filled with clear water and some with muddy water, but it was those filled with gray water that gave cause for concern. All the ponds we saw used big electric pumps for aeration, and most had piers from which fish pellets could be disseminated. Youngsters in many of the villages we passed made good use of the ponds and the piers. We saw many naked children swimming and diving in the roadside ponds.

Vertical netting completely crossed some stretches of the He River. These nets were usually green in color and went from the river bottom to a level 3 to 4 feet above the water level. In

Memorable Observations

some stretches of the river, the nets were spaced every third to one-half mile. Barring a hole in the net, nothing migrating upstream was going to pass through these barriers.

We had the opportunity to watch fishermen pole their way downstream on bamboo rafts during a float trip Shirley and I made down the River Li near Guilin. Each fisherman we encountered used cormorants to dive and capture fish. A string was attached to the neck of each cormorant so it could retrieve, but not swallow the fish. Every now and then the man on the raft would untie the string and let the bird swallow its catch. One of my favorite photos from our Guilin adventure shows Shirley fishing with a cormorant tied to a long bamboo pole. She is seen standing on the bamboo raft near a stretch of running water. When the bird flapped its wings Shirley screamed. Such a good memory.

Once when we were in Tanggu on a business trip, we attended what the Chinese call a banquet. It was really a dinner where the staff and executives of our Bohai Bay partners were seated around 4 or 5 Lazy Susan tables. One never knows what is going to be on the menu, so I was totally surprised when the cook brought out a very large fish. It might have been a grouper. I was thrilled. I thought this might be the first time since my arrival in China that I would get a large slice of grilled or steamed fish. Alas! It was not to be. We had four or five fish dishes during the evening, but I never saw a piece of fish bigger than my fingernail. We were served soup, fish flaked vegetables, thinly sliced appetizers, and a potted mix of rice, fish, and vegetables. The cook might just as well have gone to the market and purchased a bunch of minnows.

On the way into work one morning, I saw a man walking down a city street carrying a see-through green bag filled with water. In the bag I could see a live sixteen-inch fish he had either caught at a nearby pond or had purchased at a market. The fish was upright, in a swimming position, and was facing forward. One would likely never see such a sight in the United States. Observations like this made for interesting drives into work.

Ducks

Ducks, like chickens, were ubiquitous. We saw them unattended along small streams, near roadways, and in wooded glens. Sometimes we saw them walking down alley ways in small towns. We rarely saw them in cages on trucks headed to market. I suspect most ducks, like chickens, are harvested on demand by those who think they have ownership.

I observed one roadside vendor who sold pop and cigarettes. Near him were six or seven nice big white ducks. They were resting in the grass near a blanket covered with the marketable items. I initially thought it was delightful the man brought his ducks with him so they could feed on the grass, but after three days of driving past the location I noticed the number of ducks had dwindled to four, and there was a very clear-cut circle where the grass had been nibbled down to the roots. Then came the epiphany. The tethered ducks were destined to be in someone's pot. The remaining ducks probably looked down the road and wished their buddy a nice trip as he headed off to his new home. If only they knew.

Sheep

Shirley and I saw surprisingly few sheep during our travels in China. And I cannot remember having one lamb dish in a restaurant. The sheep (and goats) we saw were mostly in poor condition and were quite dirty. The sheep seen along a roadside were tended to by shepherds.

We observed one flock of sheep, 20 plus or minus, walking under a canopy of trees. They were covered in brown mud from their hooves to their bellies. The grazers all moved with their heads down, their chins nearly touching the ground. They looked like they would benefit from spending more time in grassy fields and not nibbling weeds under trees. They must have spent most of their time in a muddy field or wading in dirty water. I could not imagine eating one of those critters.

We passed a small truck (yes, it was blue) hauling sheep into Beijing. The bed of the truck had sideboards and there were 20 plus sheep on a lower level. Above these sheep, was a fine wire mesh screen onto which another 20 or more sheep had been loaded. The upper level sheep had muddy underbellies and nice white tops. They were riding in style. Meanwhile those in steerage, the space below the screen, were cramped and their wool coats were stained brown and yellow. Had I been one of those sheep under the screen I sure would have hoped that no one was given fluids before the journey started.

Crops and Transport

The practice of using the surfaces of many paved roadways to dry corn and wheat prior to the grains being bagged for sale, storage, or distribution was discussed earlier. Such sights were always captivating, but it was the movement of crops to market or the efforts to sell them roadside that made cross country auto travel so interesting.

Activities in an extensive corn field we could see out our second story bedroom window at Dragon Villas provided insight into how the crops in the north were planted and harvested. The land was rarely left fallow. In the fall, winter wheat was planted, and after it was harvested in late spring, the field was plowed and replanted with corn. In southern China, near the South China Sea, year-round warm weather allowed three plantings of vegetables. Fresh vegetables were constantly being planted, weeded, or harvested when we traveled the roadways in the Guangzhou-Shenzen corridor.

I was intrigued by the methods of corn storage in the areas around Beijing. After the kernel rich cobs were dried, they were stored by stacking them on rooftops, doorway mantles, brick walls, or porches. Some of the racks of corn cobs on rooftops were more than 4 feet high. Corn storage was not confined to the occasional house. It was common to see corn cobs stacked on houses for miles on end. Sometimes there were baskets of corn roadside. Vendors were nearby sitting on stools or squatting on their haunches with baskets of shelled corn beside them. I did not learn how corn was distributed in China. I assumed that under the communist economic system most of the corn was sent to a communal storage area. This may indeed have been the case, as we saw many truckloads of chucked corn in white sacks moving towards villages and into Beijing. My best guess to explain the great stacks of corncobs we saw on the individual rooftops was that farmers were allowed to retain and sell a portion of the corn they raised for the benefit of their local community.

Most of the corn must be used as feed for chickens or pigs. When we were in China, the populace had not yet learned of "sweet" corn. Chinese corn is purely and simply, field corn. I cannot remember ever having been served a dish in a Chinese restaurant that included corn.

Leeks were another crop that caught our attention. These three-foot-long plants were seen loaded on a variety of vehicles with small flatbed trailers on which the green stalks faced outward and the white shanks inward. Most loads were stacked four to five feet high. As with all other seasonal vegetables, leeks were commonly displayed in piles along the paved roadways. Northern Chinese have historically stocked up on non-perishable vegetables (e.g., leeks and cabbages) in the fall, storing large quantities in covered areas outside of their homes. Most of the younger Chinese do not store leeks and cabbages. They know fresh vegetables from the south of China are always available in the north, no matter what the season. People old enough to remember the Mao times still feel the need to lay in a winter supply of greens.

The fall transport of cabbages into Beijing and the suburbs is a sight to behold. Truck after truck (or tractor after tractor or donkey after donkey) bring in tons of cabbage which are marketed street side. The block-long stacks of cabbage are typically three feet high by four feet wide. Shirley always wondered why some vegetables we purchased off the street had such a short shelf life. The answer is that almost all the vegetables were shipped without cold storage. Bananas have the shortest of shelf lives. We never saw a "supermarket" so we, like the rest of the locals, purchased what we wanted roadside vendors or from small open markets.

Very rarely we saw a load of eggplants or potatoes headed to market. Most of what we saw transported on the highways and byways were the same items listed on the Chinese restaurant menus: green vegetables, pork, chicken, duck, and rice. Just for the record, we found that rice is only served near the end of a meal ..... to make sure that everyone is full. The last item served was always watermelon. When watermelon enters the room on a server's tray, one knows the social gathering has been concluded.

And There We Were

Chapter 21

OUR STAY IN CHINA
EVENTS NOT TO BE FORGOTTEN

When one looks back on time spent in any country, be it England or China, there are a few experiences that are more memorable than anything one might have imagined. What follows is an attempt to capture the magnificence of the most memorable events we experienced while we were living in China.

BLACK TIE DINNER AND DANCE ON THE GREAT WALL OF CHINA

We visited the Great Wall many times, almost always escorting family members and guests during their stay with us in Dragon Villas. Shirley and I also made several trips on our own, each of which proved to be an experience unique unto itself. The Great Wall at Mutianyu and at Badaling were close to Beijing and one of these sites was usually where we took visitors. However, the most memorable time Shirley and I spent on the Great Wall was at Jinshanling, an 80 mile 2 1/2-hour bus ride from Beijing.

Shirley was a member of a group of foreign wives, one of whom organized a black-tie dinner and dance held on a Great

Wall watchtower platform located near the bottom of a narrow valley between two steep mountainous ridges. The five-star Palace Hotel hosted and catered the excursion. Drinks were served during the road trip to the Jinshanling Great Wall, and most of us were in high spirits when we departed the bus. Even though we were all dressed to the nines we faced a quarter mile hike up a gravel road to reach the steps that would take us to the parapet where tables were set for dinner. When we arrived on the platform, servers wearing white jackets and white gloves were standing by to take drink orders.

Prior to dinner we were directed to climb the steps to another watch tower where more cocktails and cigars were on offer. The site for the cocktail party was evidently chosen so we could look west to the sun setting over the Great Wall. From our higher vantage point, we also had an unimpeded view of musicians performing on a parapet near the summit of the ridge to the west. The musicians were dressed in Imperial (Ming Dynasty) yellow attire. Their percussion instruments included brass drums, symbols, and bells. The music, dominated by the drums, reverberated up and down the narrow valley. It was an awe-inspiring experience. Some of those at the cocktail party hiked even higher up the wall. One lady called her mother on the phone and said, "I know it is in the middle of the night back home, but I have to tell you what we are doing." I understood her impulse and thought of making my own call home, but I did not think John, Mabel, or Marie would be happy getting such a wake-up call. After sunset, when the music and cocktails were finished, we descended to the valley bottom watchtower where dinner was served on tables illuminated by candlelight.

Our meal was served on tables covered with blue cloth. Tall floral arrangements in the center of each table complemented the blue tablecloths, fine china plates, silver flatware, and the different glasses for red (cabernet sauvignon) and white (chardonnay) wines. Champagne was available for those who preferred it over wine. Shirley and I were impressed by the opulence. The menu included spiced salmon on eggplant tabbouleh, Beijing duck with shiitake mushrooms, endive and romaine lettuce with smoked pancetta and mustard dressing, cilantro- encrusted rib roll with wok fried Asian greens, and a creamy goat's cheese timbale with pear confit. Dessert was a pineapple ginger turnover with lemon myrtle sabayon (custard). More cigars and Armagnac (brandy) were available after dinner. Even the cigar choices were top tier: Don Miguel, Santa Damiana, and Don Diego.

Our dining companions were splendid. I suspect survival in a culture so different from western norms as Chinese culture is requires an uncommonly flexible personality, to the extent that corporations tend to send people who can adapt and have fun in any cultural or business setting. The people seated at our table, and at other nearby tables, were as enjoyable a group as we ever came across during our years of traveling the globe. Stories told by some of the elegantly dressed ladies were ribald in part, and as funny as can politely be told in mixed company.

After the dinner tables had been cleared, a curtain was pulled to reveal a baby grand piano. How that piano was ever hauled to the top of the watch tower remains a mystery to this day. But it was there, and we danced to the music played by the pianist.

The dancing ended at midnight at which time we began our walk back down the mountain to our bus. Once we had boarded the bus a number of local merchants who had been waiting for us all evening entered and walked up and down the aisle trying to persuade someone to make a purchase. I felt badly for them. They had waited a very long time for our party to be over and no one on the bus made a purchase. Perhaps they felt compelled to attempt making sales to the obviously well-heeled foreigners.

We arrived in Beijing around 3:00 a.m. All of us had drivers waiting to take us to our homes. It had been an incredibly memorable evening on a not-to-be-forgotten historic landmark.

And There We Were

RIVER LI AND GUILIN

Shirley and I had a trip to Guilin on our wish list of places to visit in China. The Chinese say that the scenery along the River Li (Li Jiang) downstream from Guilin is more beautiful than any place on the planet. Actually, what the Chinese say is "Guilin's scenery is peerless in the world." Same thing if you will. When we learned we would soon be returning to the United States, we decided to make time for a visit to Guilin. We had a time frame into which to fit a short trip to Guilin. As it happened, we made the trip on what in the United States is Easter weekend. The moving company packers had already spent two days at our Dragon Villas home, and they had several more days of work before our goods could be loaded and on their way through customs, into sea containers, and onto a ship sailing to America.

Nellie Guido, my Mandarin teacher and a most enterprising entrepreneur, put together a guided tour that had us in Guilin for two nights and parts of three days. Guilin is in southern China, about 280 miles northwest of Hong Kong and 1350 miles southwest of Beijing. We made the 3-hour China Southern flight to Guilin on a ticket printed in Chinese except for hand stamped flight and gate numbers. Because the incremental cost was minimal, we flew first class.

After our arrival in Guilin and after checking in to our room at the Sheraton Guilin, our guide took us on a short excursion to Seven Stars Park located east of the River Li in central Guilin. This short excursion gave us the opportunity to stretch our legs and to get a glimpse of the Li prior to our float trip the following day. We crossed ancient Flower Bridge, and then walked through many scenic gardens and past several clear ponds. Seven Stars Park is named for seven peaks, four of which are on one mountain, and three on an adjacent mountain. Camel Hill, another nearby mountain, was the most scenic sight. The outcrop looked like a double-humped camel standing in a grassland with small trees and bushes. We did not see any of the wild monkeys that roam the Park. We also passed on visits to the zoo and the tour of Seven Star Cave.

We were up early Saturday morning for the big event: the river boat float down the Li. The 4 1/2-hour, 35-mile float from Guilin to Yangshuo took us through magnificent scenery, and it offered us the opportunity to observe a wide variety of human activity. As an ardent fisherman, I was stunned with the clarity of the water and the runs that would be available to a fly fisherman. I continually found myself looking at the moving water and playing out in my mind the strategy I would take in fishing these runs.

The scenery along the River Li is dominated by majestic limestone monoliths mostly covered with vegetation. We saw hundreds of peaks (perhaps even a thousand), each peak unique unto itself. Cliff faces on many of the monoliths are stained with naturally occurring manganese dioxide. Some of the staining allows the imagination to run wild. The ancient inhabitants of the region gave many cliff faces on the monoliths unique and imaginative names (e.g., Painted Hill of Nine Horses, Pagoda Hill, Dragon Playing on Water, Chicken Cage Hill, and Yearning for Husband Rock). Many of the majestic peaks were reflected off the smooth surface of clear and still waters. We passed innumerable caves, some small and others quite large. There was no doubt we were traversing a karst topography. Ground and subsurface waters have been molding what was once a most expansive limestone plateau, and this has been occurring for millions of years.

We passed by a number of small villages on our way downstream. We had only a glimpse now and then of buildings as the shorelines, above flood level, were lined with tall and leafy bamboo trees. Once in a while we would see a field or a garden under cultivation. A number of farmers were seen behind water buffalo who were pulling plows. Some women were washing clothes along the riverbank. A most unusual sight was that of individuals who were digging deep round holes in the gravel. They were said to be looking for layers of sand which they could then sell in nearby villages. We saw others working gravel beds, but we could not see what they were after. It might just have been something edible.

There were many boatmen on the river; most of them fisherman on bamboo rafts. On board were the cormorants used to catch fish. Most of the fisherman go out at night and they use large lamps to attract fish which are then easy prey for the cormorants.

We passed many flocks of domestic ducks unattended and swimming close to a nearby village. Sometimes we confused white sea birds with the ducks, but the sea birds flew away at our approach, while the ducks could only stay and await their fates.

I wish we had had a video camera as we came upon a calf buffalo that was walking into the river. He approached a nearby fence protruding into the water. The calf enjoyed his frolic in the water but when he went to return to shore he came ashore on the other side of the fence. A peasant was sitting on the shore where the calf came running. Not only did the calf drench the surprised man, he also caused him to retreat to a nearby tree. I always wondered how the calf got reunited with its mother as she was still on the other side of the fence. But we floated on and I did not see that play out.

Shortly before our float ended, Shirley and I struck up a conversation with one of our fellow tourists who said he was from Norwich, Vermont. We told him our son had attended Dartmouth in Hanover, New Hampshire, just across the Connecticut River from Norwich. The man said he was a medical doctor who had a practice in Hanover. He asked what our son did. We told him that he and a friend were founders of a start-up transaction company called Hanover Green Card. The man startled us by pulling out his Hanover Green Card. He said he used it to get discounts at restaurants and at a local bookstore. We have a photo of the man pretending to pay for a drink on our boat using the Green Card. The female attendant, radiantly dressed in a stylish blue suit, white kerchief, and pill box hat looks absolutely bewildered. It is a small world.

When we arrived in Yangshuo we were informed we had a three hour wait for the car that would take us back to Guilin. Our guide was a bit embarrassed for the delay. We were standing on the dock wondering what to do when two enterprising young ladies asked if we would like to go on a 40-kilometer ride through the nearby countryside. Each woman had a motorcycle with a one-wheeled and canopied carriage attached to its side. I guess you could call it a motor driven tricycle. Two normal sized people could ride in each sidecar. Such began a most unexpected and a most spectacular side trip through the southern China countryside. Shirley and our guide shared one of the sidecars. I rode by myself in the other.

Soon in the rural area outside of Yangshuo, we were immediately traveling past rice patties in flatlands framed by vegetated limestone monoliths in the background. The scenery was simply stunning. We passed innumerable buffalo, some attended and some just grazing by the road. We stopped at a village to visit the maker of bamboo rafts. We bought coins, lanterns, and sugar cane from several of the street vendors. We made everyone a little bit better off. One of my favorite photos from China is of Shirley leaning out of her sidecar with her sugar cane snack in hand.

On the road again, we passed six or seven schoolgirls riding their bicycles. I leaned out my carriage and said, "*Nihao*." The girls looked at me and at Shirley, and then said in unison, "*Hello*." They immediately knew we were Americans, and they were more than willing to let us know they could speak English.

One of the highlights of our tour through the countryside was a stop where we had a view of Moon Hill. Near the summit of this hill is a perfectly round tunnel. When the light is right it gives the appearance of the moon hanging in the sky. Moon Hill is one of the more famous landmarks in the Guilin area, but it can only be seen by taking an excursion like the one we took.

After we returned to Yangshuo, we had time to take tea at a street side cafe with open windows. While we were seated at our table an old lady stuck her head in and gestured that she wanted to sell us something she had in hand. I did not have any Yuan with me so I shook my head indicating she should move on. The lady insisted I look at what she had on offer. It was a small wooden box that opened up to reveal three small Buddhas. The piece looked very old and I was certain this artifact had been dug up from some place illegal (like a grave site). I dug around in my pocket and found a Russian coin I had purchased at the flea market in Ascot, England. I was sure it was worthless, but I showed her the coin anyway. The coin was large, silver colored, and heavy. She handed me the wooden box and took the money. I felt bad knowing she would soon find the coin I had given her was worthless. What I did not know at the time was that the old lady had sold me a priceless antique. After we returned to Dragon Villas and the Antiquities people came to examine what we were packing, the only item they struggled to approve was the box the Yangshuo woman had sold us. In the end they approved the wooden box for shipment out of country. I can only hope that the old lady in Yangshuo got something of value for the coin I gave her.

The morning prior to our departure from Guilin we went for a walk about along the Li. I have pictures of Shirley fishing with a cormorant on a bamboo raft. What a sight! When Shirley had the bird on her bamboo pole, it flapped its wings and made Shirley squeal. One can almost hear the squeal in the photo. We also came across a man with a little monkey. The primate was dressed in a beautiful yellow suit and jacket. He also had on a very small hat. For a price the man would let you have a photo taken with the monkey. I talked Shirley into holding the monkey. While she did this, she also stroked the monkey's small hand. The little guy must have thought Shirley was a loving primate. He began to do what primates sometime do. He jumped onto her shoulders and picked at Shirley's hair, looking for gnats or whatever. Shirley and I both yelled at the same time. Nothing and nobody messes with Shirley's hair. The incident was funny when we recalled it later, but not funny when the silver strands were being pulled out of Shirley's bangs.

During our last walk about, we saw the famous Elephant Trunk Hill, a large limestone rock that looks like an elephant drinking water from the River Li. We also made a tour of Red Flute Cave, a 240-meter-long cave filled with stalactites and stalagmites illuminated by hundreds of artificial lights.

On our flight back to Beijing, Shirley and I agreed that our last travel adventure in China could not have been any better.

The only event left prior to our departure from China was an office party so the staff could say goodbye to us.

TURANDOT

During our stay in China much was made of a historic event that took place in September of 1998. The Ministry of Culture of the People's Republic of China announced that a joint Chinese-Italian presentation of *Turandot*, one of the finest operas ever written, would be performed on location inside the Forbidden City, the site of its inspiration. *Turandot* was the last of the classic operas written and composed by Giacomo Puccini, who finished the work shortly before his death in 1924.

The finest operatic singers from all over Europe were recruited to perform. The Italian Maggio Musicale Fiorentino orchestra was flown in to provide the orchestra and chorus. The conductor and the director of *Turandot* would be Chinese. A Beijing newspaper reported that many famous entertainers from around the world would be present for nine performances. Included on the list of celebrity attendees were Barbra Streisand and Luciano Pavarotti. Even at the astronomical price of $1800 per seat, the demand was equally astronomical. All performances were sold out. *Turandot* was said to be a "must see" event, not only in China, but in artistic circles all over the world. As the reader might expect, Shirley was all over this event. We were going no matter what the cost.

Tickets could only be purchased from a box office that had been opened solely to sell tickets for the *Turandot* production. When Shirley and I sat down to buy the tickets, we gave the lady across the table our credit card. She swiped my credit card and asked me to sign the authorization chit. When I had done this and returned it to her, she looked at my credit card and at the signature. She said the signatures did not match. I knew they did, so I looked at what she was comparing. It turned out she had my card upside down and was comparing

And There We Were

my signature with an upside-down signature on my card. I chuckled, turned the card right-side-up, and made the lady happy. She handed me our tickets. It seemed a silly mistake on the clerk's part, but when I thought about it later, I realized that if the tables had been turned and I had attempted to validate a signature written in Chinese characters, I might have turned the card upside down and made the same mistake.

We had walked through the squares and the halls of the Forbidden City many times, and on each occasion we felt like we were there for the first time. Shirley, with glamorous appearance and an exquisite silver hairdo, was invariably asked to pose by a gathering of Chinese who wanted a picture of her with one of the great halls as a background. Neither of us ever imagined we would be attending an opera performed in the Imperial Ancestral Temple where the Emperors of the Ming and Qing dynasties lived with their attendants and concubines.

We entered the Forbidden City through the Meridian Gate, across the street from Tiananmen Square and diagonal to The Great Hall of the People. Our route took us across one of the five bridges over the Golden Water River to the magnificent square looking directly onto the Hall of Supreme Harmony. The stage for the presentation of Turandot was the upper marble terrace in front of the great Hall. The setting for the performance included several lavish side buildings said to have once been the living quarters for concubines. We had to pinch ourselves to acknowledge we were really in the Forbidden City looking at the pageantry and costumes very similar to those that emperors and their retinues enjoyed over the centuries. The singing and music were sublime, but the stage direction was incredible. Only a Chinese director could have orchestrated the enormous cast of Chinese singers and cast members interspersed with the European operatic performers and the orchestra. I enjoyed the singing, but I liked the Turandot story even better.

The Turandot performance was in three Acts. Between Acts I and II, Shirley purchased a glass of Champagne and stood by a tree in one of the gardens where concubines once lounged. It occurred to me that the concubines must have lounged a lot since there were over a thousand of them. When they sat down for dinner they would look under their plate. If they had an Imperial yellow card under the plate, they knew they were next up for an evening with the Emperor. I suspected that after a couple of years not being chosen, one might look with a little more anxiety. There might have been a fine line between being a concubine and being a nun.

We enjoyed the Turandot performance so much we decided to purchase a number of tickets for members of my staff, these tickets were to a performance held for Chinese only. Ticket prices for this event were much lower, only $300 each, and I bought four of them. The feedback I got from the staff members who attended the "Chinese only" event was that it was a noisy affair with many of the audience dressed in casual clothes. There were no suits and black ties in evidence.

During the performance Shirley and I attended we observed many cameras on beams that moved in, out, and around the stage. The performance was being filmed from many different angles. The film would later air on the Public Broadcasting System's "Great Performances". We viewed the film after we returned to the United States. After the performance we also purchased a beautiful round Turandot clock which adorns a wall on the upper hallway of our Texas home.

Tobin and Ha Lent's Wedding in Hanoi

One of the highlights of our stay in China was occasioned by the marriage of our son Tobin to his Vietnamese sweetheart Ha on December 12, 1998. Even though the Tobin Courtney Lent-Vu Than Ha wedding took place in Hanoi, Vietnam, the memorable experience I will recount involved an unexpected and emotional overnight stay in Nanning, China.

Shirley and I took a Thursday afternoon China Southern flight to Hanoi. Our plan was to meet Tobin for dinner on Thursday evening, and then spend time with he and Ha on Friday. We were fortunate, as there was only one flight per week from Beijing to Hanoi, and our Thursday flight would have us in Hanoi two days before the Saturday wedding. On our way to Hanoi we made a scheduled intermediary stop in Nanning. Following what had been a rough landing, we arrived at our gate where we waited and waited for the exit door to open. There apparently was some mechanical problem with the ramp. After 40 minutes, several passengers (all of them Chinese) began to get loud and restless. The stewards and stewardesses found themselves in hostile situation. One man removed the emergency door near him. That action triggered others to do the same with the remaining emergency doors. Shirley and I had never witnessed such behavior in all our years of flying overseas. Thinking that things might get physical, an Associated Press photographer seated near us unpacked his camera and began filming. Those that opened the emergency doors soon realized that the drop to the tarmac was much further than they had anticipated. The cabin door finally opened, and the passengers began to exit. However, all had to step over, on, or around the emergency doors that were now located on the cabin floor.

Once inside the terminal at Wuxu International Airport, we went through immigration (even though we were emigrates). We were asked to fill out entry cards for Vietnam. I was busy filling out my card when a fellow foreign traveler offered as how I might be wasting my time; the flight to Hanoi had just been cancelled. The Vietnam visas Shirley and I had were for entry by air and were not valid for a water or land entry. In other words, if we wanted to be in Vietnam for Tobin's wedding, we *had* to take the cancelled flight to Hanoi. There was no other option. And the one flight per week from Beijing via Nanning had just been cancelled. Nanning is about 100 miles from the Vietnam border and 150 miles from Hanoi. If we had held visas for a land entry into Vietnam, we could have rented a car, but that was not a viable option.

At the airline help desk, we were told that the flight to Hanoi might still be possible, but the doors had to be checked and re-installed before a decision could be made that would allow the plane to continue on to Hanoi. We were told the decision would come sometime late the following morning. The China

Our Stay in China

Southern staff began to turn off their lights and to vacate the help desk. We inquired about accommodations, and how we might go about getting our luggage off the plane. We got no response, but an airport official told us to exit the terminal and board a bus that was waiting for us. When arrived at the bus, we found our luggage already being loaded into the baggage compartment.

The bus made a stop at the airport guest house dormitory. Shirley, and a number of other foreigners, checked out the rooms and reported back that what was on offer was not acceptable. Shirley said the rooms were at least three times worse than any motel room we had ever stayed in, even worse than one we were once forced to take in Elko, Nevada. That room had leaves on the floor, unwashed sheets, and a broken washroom faucet. Surprisingly, a number of the Chinese travelers accepted the offer to stay at the guest house facilities. The rest of us took the bus into town in search of better accommodations.

We soon learned that Nanning was celebrating 50 years of minority rule, and available rooms in the city were at a premium. Our next stop took us to an accommodation even worse than the one at the airport. Shirley said the sheets were washed once a month and it was near the end of the month. Any room available would be let to three people. To stay there we would require we sleep in filthy bedding in a room with a person we did not know. The cost was $.90 per person, with breakfast included. Back into the bus we went.

We finally found a hotel in the downtown area that was acceptable. When we checked out the room, we found it to look like a hotel room anywhere, except that when we turned on the lights, cockroaches scampered across the bathroom floor and into holes in the bathtub moulding. Shirley said the room would do, but that I would have to plug up the holes in the moulding with toilet tissue, which I did. The room rental was $20. To put that room rate in perspective, twenty years on one can get a room at a 3-star Nanning hotel for $29 per night. A room in a 5-star hotel goes for $59 per night. We were informed that because of the celebration about to take place the following day, we would have to leave for the airport by 6:00 a.m. After that hour all roads into and out of the city would be closed.

We were up bright and early and went downstairs to take advantage of the free breakfast buffet. When the chef learned the hotel had a group of foreigners spending the night at the hotel, he decided to go all out on the buffet. He was beaming with pride as we took our plates. At the head of the buffet table was his dish of honor.... a silver plate filled with spicy par boiled chicken feet. I took two just to make the fellow happy. Shirley politely passed, saying she just wanted fresh fruit. She never even looked at the other hot dishes that were laid out for our dining pleasure.

When we arrived at the Nanning airport, we got the good news. The China Southern flight would depart at 11:00 a.m. We would be in Hanoi in time for Tobin and Ha's wedding. We had not been able to call Tobin to tell him that our flight had been cancelled so we knew he would be worried. He knew the original flight had been cancelled, but he did not know what had happened to us. When we finally made it to Hanoi, Tobin was waiting for us as we exited from immigration.

We checked into the Hanoi Club Hotel on the shore of West Lake in central Hanoi. This hotel was as fine a hotel as one might wish to visit. Ha had obviously gone all out to make her wedding day memorable. She had reserved a room for the wedding reception and dinner, followed by an after-dinner party on the outdoor patio.

We spent most of Friday touring Hanoi. We went to Ho Chi Min's tomb, visited the memorial to the war, and dropped by the Hanoi Hilton where some unfortunate American captives spent miserable years in confinement. At the time of our visit, the U.S. Ambassador to Vietnam was a former pilot who had been shot down and captured when he landed in West Lake. He had spent six years in the Hanoi Hilton. Many leading foreign businessmen in Vietnam were former prisoners of war. I found it interesting that they chose to return to Vietnam.

We found Hanoi to be a beautiful city. We were amazed at the number of motorbikes we saw in the busy streets. We walked along several of the streets looking into shops where vendors manned shops filled with almost anything one might wish to purchase. Many people made comments in Vietnamese as we passed by them. Tobin was fluent in Vietnamese: it was amusing to see the shocked look on the faces when Tobin responded in their native language. It was clearly rare that a tall white foreigner understood the language and responded fluently to what was said.

We had a light afternoon lunch accompanied by three beautiful young ladies playing Vietnamese musical instruments. I did not recognize any of the instruments, although one was stringed, one percussion, and one somewhat similar to a keyboard. In any event, the music was delightful and the dining service first class.

When we returned to the hotel, we sat on the patio and ordered drinks. The sun was setting and the panoramic view was simply spectacular. Nearby fishermen were bobbing for pelagic life forms. Some were fishing from piers near the hotel: others were fishing from small boats powered by foot paddles. Several boat fishermen gave me the impression they were dredging for bottom feeders.

Late Saturday morning we gathered in the lobby. I had never seen so many beautiful young ladies wearing such bright clothing. Even the children were dressed in colorful and elegant skirts and dresses. Shirley was given a beautiful bouquet with colorful ribbons hanging down. After all were assembled, we loaded into cars and vans and traveled by caravan to the home of the bride, Vu Thanh Ha.

When we arrived in the courtyard of the Vu residence we gathered and were led upstairs by a man carrying a ceremonial roast pig decorated with ribbons and flowers. When we entered the apartment, we were greeted by the entire cast of aunts, uncles, nieces, nephews, grandparents, great grandparents and, of course, by Ha's mother Nga.

Ha was in a backroom, but the rest of the family was either seated or standing in the hallways. I felt like I was being sized up by one and all. Some were smiling, some not so much so.

And There We Were

Shirley, as always, looked like a million dollars. I was attired in a pin stripe suit.

After we had been seated Ha entered the room and began pouring tea for those seated at the table of honor. Tobin was also dressed in a pin striped suit. Ha was beautiful in a traditional long red dress imprinted with golden orbs. She wore an elegant hat that matched the color of her dress. Shirley gave her bouquet of flowers to Ha. We presented a traditional basket of gifts, including $1000 in gold to the Vu family. I always say that it cost us a pig and $1000 for Tobin to get a wife.

The ceremony was basically a discussion on and about Ha and Tobin. When all were convinced that Ha would be happy with Tobin, I invited Ha to become a member of the Lent family. At that point, they were married. Legal documents would follow. The blood tests had already been completed. The only reference to the Almighty came when I spilled hot tea on my lap and exclaimed, "God dammit!"

We then traveled by caravan, this time a much larger one, through the busy streets of Hanoi back to the Hanoi Club where there were an additional 150 relatives and friends waiting for the newlyweds. The party was magnificent! Dinners were served not only in the main dining room but also on the adjacent patio under palms and near the waters lapping the shore of West Lake. The main dining room was open to the patio.

Ha arrived wearing a traditional white wedding dress. After many photos were taken, she disappeared, only to reappear wearing a beautiful green dress overprinted with golden flower stems. Her hat, once again, perfectly matched her dress. Everything Ha wore, and the party itself, was first class. Ha paid for it all. She was obviously very well off, much more so than our son. Many of Ha's friends wondered why she would consider marrying a foreigner. With her money and looks she, in their minds, did not have to stoop so low. Although this line of thinking was less than a resounding endorsement of our blond son, Ha was also the lucky one. Tobin was an intelligent and well-educated businessman who would one day provide Ha with two beautiful daughters and a life beyond imagination.

Shirley and I went on Tobin and Ha's honeymoon. At least that is what I tell everyone. Sunday morning, following the wedding, Shirley and I met the two of them in the lobby of the hotel and took a town car on a tour through the city, and then out into the countryside. On our way we passed a number of ornate French Colonial homes and rural cottages. We saw farmers working beautifully manicured croplands and water buffalo plowing wetlands. Like we saw in rural China, chickens were running wild everywhere. I was stunned by how long-legged the chickens were. I had never seen chickens with such long legs. I would certainly not choose to eat one of those skinny drumsticks.

Our travels through the country took us to a boat dock where a speed boat was waiting to take us to Son Tinh Island Golf Club. Located about 20 miles west of Hanoi, this destination resort was the first golf club in Hanoi. Today the resort has been renamed the King's Island Golf Resort. The resort is surrounded by the waters of the Dong Mo reservoir. Nearby Ba Vi Mountain can be seen from the brilliantly green golf fairways. It is a magnificent setting.

We walked several of the fairways before having a light lunch at the clubhouse restaurant. Although we did not play golf that day, we had no trouble imagining the thrill any serious golfer would feel arriving by boat for a few rounds of golf on this spectacular island golf course.

We returned to Beijing on Monday morning. Our trip to Tobin and Ha's Hanoi wedding had proven to be a remarkable adventure. Shortly after take-off from the Hanoi airport, I began thinking about the Vietnamese War. The view I had out the window of our plane was similar to the one American pilots had when they made bombing raids on Hanoi. Ha was a very young child when these raids occurred. Who could ever have thought Shirley and I would someday come to Hanoi to see our elder son married to a Vietnamese girl? Life does take us down strange paths.

Honored in the Great Hall of the People

The most exciting experience we had while living abroad came when the government of China chose to honor me and nine other foreigners for our contributions to the People's Republic. I had begun to hear rumblings in early February 1999 that a nomination for an award might be coming my way. Details were fuzzy, but there were many hints followed by requests for my resume and professional credentials. Then came a note asking for personal details on Shirley and I, information needed for security clearance.

There were 80,000 foreign experts working in China during the year 1998. Ten had been chosen for special recognition. Two of the honorees came from the oil industry, one of whom was my counterpart at Agip, Mr. Franco Rasperambia. Agip, an Italian Corporation, was probably the most economically successful oil company operating in China at the time. One other American was among the honorees. He was the president of General Motors China. I do not remember his name, but he was probably the highest-ranking dignitary in the group.

On February 10, I was called to the Beijing offices of the Chinese National Offshore Oil Company (CNOOC) to meet with their president, Mr. Wei. I was not told why I had been called to Mr. Wei's office, but after meeting with Mr. Wei, I was asked to please stay for an interview with representatives from the company newspaper. I was asked questions like what did I think of CNOOC and what did I think of an opportunity to meet with Premier Zhu. I was also asked what I might like to ask Premier Zhu if I met him. I quickly realized this was not really an interview for a newspaper. It was a way for the Chinese to evaluate whether or not I might embarrass either CNOOC or the political leaders of the country. I doubt that my "interview" ever made it into any company publication.

Following the meeting with President Wei I received a phone call and a written invitation from the State Bureau of Foreign Experts informing us that Shirley and I were to attend a three-day meeting of "Foreign Experts" which would culminate in a reception and banquet to be hosted by Premier Zhu Rongji, the number two man in China and the author and champion of China's economic reform policies. We were instructed to report to the Beijing Friendship Hotel on Thursday, February 11. We were given no agenda for the three days. We were told we would sightsee around Beijing on Friday and that we would attend a State meeting and banquet on Saturday, February 13. We did not know at the time that the banquet on Saturday would be held in the Great Hall of the People.

Despite our repeated requests for more information about the planned activities and the dress codes associated with each activity, the State Administration of Foreign Expert Affairs was reluctant to provide us any details. We learned that when the highest government officials are involved, security considerations come first and one's only option is to go with the flow. We took our cue from the way government leaders dressed on television and surmised that we would mostly be dressed in suits/dresses. Just in case, we also packed more casual wear... sport coats and pant suits.

The Beijing Friendship Hotel is a very ornate and upscale national hotel where foreign dignitaries are housed during official state visits. For security purposes we were only given one phone number that was to be used in case of an emergency. We would be under a blackout for the three days we were guests of the government.

On Thursday we checked into the Friendship Hotel around 5:00 p.m. and were immediately whisked up to our spacious room on the executive floor. Three windows in the room opened to the front of the hotel, and the room was equipped with every imaginable amenity. The bathroom came with both a large round shower and a double bathtub, double sinks, wall-to-wall mirrors, a bicycle exerciser, and a pant and slack pressing device, and, of course, the ubiquitous and cursed weight scale. The heated lid on the toilet seat was a shocking surprise. The bed was appropriately king sized. There was ample room for a variety of comfortable sofas and chairs. The foyer was stocked with liquors, coffee, and fruit platters. In a very large lobby outside our door attendants stood at attention waiting to call us an elevator or to honor any request we might make. Each time we left the room it was serviced. We knew this because the heat on the toilet seat was always switched from off to on during our absence.

There were two dining areas in the hotel, one being a very large open spaced "Chinese restaurant". The "Western restaurant" was a laugher. It was tiny and confined to a small corner of the main dining floor, with very limited menu selections. Room service was available, but we only used it in the morning for fresh coffee, heated milk, and orange juice.

Dinner on Thursday night was one without a host, and it was a typical Chinese banquet with many, many dishes served one after another. There were no surprise servings, and the food was exceptionally good. We dined with several foreigners and Chinese nationals, and we were left to introduce ourselves. The meal was our first attempt to meet and get to know those with whom we would be spending the next two days. A Russian and an Albanian were among those seated at our table, and we found it difficult to communicate with them. Our fluency in Russian was on a par with their fluency in English. It was awkward carrying on conversations with English speakers while looking at the blank faces of the Russian and the Albanian. During the dinner we discovered the foreign experts being honored were from the United States (2), Sweden, Canada, Italy, Germany, Taiwan, and Japan, plus the above two from Russia and Albania.

After dinner we got our first look at the schedule for Friday. The "sightseeing" around Beijing was not at all what we thought it might be. We had assumed we were going to be taken to the normal tourist spots, but this was certainly not the case. We were scheduled to spend the morning touring the Haidian Hi-tech Development Zone, an unknown, at least to us, industrial complex. Lunch was to be served in the Fragrant Hills Hotel, and the afternoon would have us visiting the "Beijing Glorious Land Agricultural Company".

When we returned to our room Thursday evening, we decided to sit in the spacious lobby area and have a glass of wine in front of a large fireplace. The area was just outside of our room and it was filled with large sofas and soft chairs. The attendants were not far away and came to us when we sat down. While we were enjoying our wine, I looked up at the ornate chandelier over our heads. I told Shirley that the chandelier was beautiful, but I was surprised to see two of the lights had burned out. I remarked that in a hotel like the Friendship one would not expect such a lack of upkeep. We retired to our bedroom. Early the next morning I carried my coffee and a newspaper to the same area where we had enjoyed our evening drinks. When I looked up, I saw that the two burned out bulbs had been replaced. I knew then that everything we said was being monitored. I could only imagine what was being observed in our bathroom and bedroom.

After breakfast on Friday morning, we boarded a coach, and with a police escort, began a fast trip through central Beijing. We were surprised by the VIP treatment, as police and the military were stationed at each intersection over a 10-mile stretch. We encountered only "green" traffic lights. All the round-about circulars had access blocked until we went through them. It was amazing just how fast we were able to traverse the ten miles from our hotel to the Haidian Experimental Zone. The license plate on the lead police car, a black Mercedes, indicated that the police in the vehicle were armed with military grade firepower and they were authorized to use it. That was at least one of the reasons the cars parted like the Red Sea for Moses when the flashing lights, the siren, and the car mounted loudspeaker encountered traffic. No one, but no one, failed to respond.

At our first stop in the morning, we were saluted by the guards and met by the Mitsubishi Stone Semiconductor Company's top management and scientists. We listened to a summary of the growth of this private enterprise, and subsequently toured the production facilities. Our next stop was at the "Overseas Student's Pioneer Park" which was described as a "high technology business incubator network"; a part of the "Business launching Service Center of the Haidian Experiment Zone of the New Technology Industries Development and

Experiment Zone of Beijing". For all the fancy words and titles, it appeared this was the Chinese attempt to come up with a way to entice bright young people to create and grow entrepreneurial start-up companies. Some of the companies we saw were focused on high tech urban and residential design, bio-medical manufacturing, and computer language applications. I wondered if somewhere in the group there was another Bill Gates or Steve Jobs.

Lunch at Fragrant Hills was both a welcomed break, and a disappointment. Shirley and I had been to the Fragrant Hills Hotel previously. We were aware of the beautiful setting and of the grand the views from the restaurant windows. Despite the grand setting, we were taken to an interior banquet room with no windows. What a waste it was. After lunch Shirley went for a walk through the Park and she returned just in time to load onto our coach. The day was clear and the temperature brisk, just the way the Pearl liked it. During her walk-about Shirley had come across a wedding procession. The bride to be was being carried on a litter; a beautifully decorated and bright red bridal chair situated between the two carrying poles. Shirley could not see the bride who was hidden behind silk curtains in her carriage. The experience made Shirley's day, and the stop much more memorable for her than it otherwise would have been.

The afternoon trip to the "Beijing Glorious Land Agricultural Company" was certainly the highlight of the day as we toured the hydroponic gardens, reviewed the research being done on both plant and animal gene transfer, and then had a detailed presentation on artificial insemination and embryo marketing. We saw sperm being loaded into glass straws which were then stored in liquid nitrogen tanks. We witnessed the experiments the scientists play with insemination and cell separation. The most entertaining aspect of the entire visit was our stop at the pens of peacocks, sheep, cattle, and the ponds of sturgeon. Shirley was taken by the magnificence of the 1,400-pound brown bull. He was truly a grand creature.

We returned to our waiting coach and began our trip back to the hotel. The return trip took us through a stretch of about 3 miles where outdoor markets selling a wide variety of goods lined the road. People crowded the roadway and they scattered in all directions as our coach and police escort roared through. Not only did they scatter, they also turned and stared, curious to know who or what was responsible for all of the disruption.

The Friday night dinner was a much more formal affair than the one on our first night. Prior to dinner we had begun to learn more about some of our fellow honorees. One gentleman stood out for several noteworthy reasons.

Dr. Peter Wu, a technical manager for Boeing, was probably the most delightful person we met during the three days the 'Foreign Experts' were together. Peter is Chinese but he is Taiwanese Chinese. He is a good looking and articulate fellow who is equally fluent in both Mandarin and English. Born in Taiwan, he came to the United States when he was 21 to pursue a Ph.D. in aeronautics. After receiving his degree, he went to work for Boeing. When we met Peter, he had been in the United States for over 20 years. The remarkable thing about Peter's presence in our group of 'Foreign Experts' is that Peter's father was a general under Chiang Kaishek, and he had remained in the Taiwanese military until he retired. I think it says much about China's Taiwan policy, given that the government honored Peter as a foreign expert despite the fact that his father had fought against the People's army. The Chinese government's stated hardline policy insists that Taiwan be returned to Chinese control, but they, in recent years, had adopted a strategy of conciliatory actions. Honoring Peter Wu was certainly one of those conciliatory actions.

The Mao government was not so kind to the relatives Peter's father left behind when he escaped to Taiwan. Two brothers were subsequently beaten and ostracized. The daughters of the brothers were not allowed to marry. When times changed and the government stance softened, General Wu sent $1000 per month to his surviving brother to make his life easier. This brother showed up at the banquet hall on Saturday night. Although he was not allowed to join us for dinner, he shuffled off to a corner table where he ate, and then waited for Peter to join him for a short visit. Peter told us that in the past his uncle would have been barred from the restaurant. The man was dressed poorly, like one would expect a poor peasant to be dressed.

On Saturday, February 13, the banquets and meetings took on increasing levels of protocol. Over lunch we were briefed on the 1998 economic achievements by Vice Chairman Zheng Silin of the State Economic and Trade Commission of the People's Republic of China. He was a witty and informed speaker. Television cameras covered the event and we later learned that Shirley and I appeared on the local Chinese news broadcast of the event. In all of the meetings we attended I was amazed at how many people took Shirley to be one of the 'foreign experts.' In fact, I suspected several of the dignitaries would have been much happier had I been the spouse and she the honoree. Shirley's habit of asking many questions led the Chinese leaders to think she was an honoree. When one gentleman asked Shirley if she was an expert, she replied that she was not, but that he should remember that behind every 'foreign expert' there was a devoted spouse.

Our lunch on Saturday, served in traditional banquet style, was the best meal we had had so far. In consideration of the foreign tastes of the honorees, the bones had been removed from the chicken and the prawns were peeled and covered in a spicy dough decorated with green pea eyes. Although the food was delicious, we knew we had to back off a bit since there would be a grand meal served later that evening in the Great Hall of the People. Even so, when plate after plate of delicious food is placed before you, it is difficult to forego sampling all that is offered.

After our luncheon I was approached by a reporter from the China International Daily, a local Chinese language tabloid. The reporter was young and I feared what she might write about my observations, not because of what I said, but because of what she might have thought I said. My opinion was that the young lady did not have a clue as to the subject matter she was addressing, but then neither did I.

We returned to the Friendship Hotel approximately three hours before we were to depart for the Great Hall of the People.

Louise Cariedon, the honoree from Canada, who lived near the Hotel took us on a long walk through a number of beautiful gardens woven around several buildings that were part of the Hotel compound. We saw many fountains, some of which flowed down from artificial rock ledges. Ms. Cariedon was a publisher of foreign language books and had been in China for nearly four years. Ms. Cariedon was one of the foreign experts who spoke during the evening ceremonies. Her speech was well delivered and of high quality.

We assembled in front of the Friendship Hotel at approximately 4:00 p.m. and boarded our coach that would take us cross town to Tiananmen Square, the Forbidden City, and the Great Hall of the People. The police escort was as usual, but when we approached the Great Hall it seemed as if the local populace was paying more than their usual attention to our arrival. The locals must see a number of political caravans, many carrying dignitaries far more important than Bob and Shirley.

We exited our coach in front of the Great Hall and climbed the stairs. Television cameras and bright lights lined our walkway. Near our entrance into the main hall were huge red banners that took my breath away. We were escorted to a corner of the Hall where we checked our coats. Each couple and each unaccompanied person had their photos taken. We noticed there were a number of very old people, mostly Japanese and American, who were seated in the same area of the Hall where we were waiting. When we asked about them, our interpreter said that these were elderly 'foreign experts' who had spent 40 or 50 years in China and who now lived in China as pensioners.

At 5:00 p.m. we were escorted into the Great Hall. We found 40 large soft chairs arranged in a square at the center of the East Wing. Behind the large sofas, to the north and to the south, were smaller chairs with tables in front of them. These tables were made of dark wood and were much like coffee tables. Each honoree's name was written on a card placed in front of a chair. The location of one's name and chair was determined by the perceived ranking of the honorees. Shirley and I were in the second row behind the big sofas, on the south end of the seating area. Only a few of the 'experts' were given seats in the soft chairs. On such honoree was Makoto Kobayashi, the President of China Panasonic Industrial Equipment Co. Another was the president of General Motors China. After we were seated the senior foreign experts were brought in and escorted to their seats. The most respected of these senior foreign experts was Mr. Israel Epstein, a Polish Jew who came to China with his father when he was two years old. He had lived in China for more than 80 years and was a member of the standing committee of the Communist Party. I gathered from where he was seated that, other than the Premier, Mr. Epstein, might be the highest-ranking person present at the banquet.

Our entry and seating were recorded by, and shown on, China National Television. We later received a copy of the broadcast tape. It was interesting since it scanned the ten honorees and then zoomed in on Shirley. She always commanded attention, and this was certainly the case when we were being seated. And it would not be the only time during the evening when the cameras made her the focus of attention. After we were seated, we had about 15 minutes before the speeches began to admire the murals, vases, ceiling, chandeliers, and silk brocades on display around the Hall. Three magnificent crystal chandeliers, approximately 12 feet across, hung down 10 feet from the 30-foot-tall ceiling. These were housed in octagonal recesses framed in a brown carved wood brocade that matched the brocade joining the Hall walls to the ceiling. A magnificent mural of the Great Wall covered a width of some 60 feet, and it was a pictorial and panoramic view showing segments of the Great Wall rising out the ocean to the east and then descending to the lowlands with limestone monoliths near Guilin. The north and south walls of the East wing had 10 by 15-foot murals featuring large cranes against a background of colorful foliage. In China cranes are a symbol of good luck so their presence in the Great Hall is no accident as many Joint Venture business contract ceremonies have been signed here. The entrance to the main part of the great Hall was flanked by two ten-foot-tall cinnabar vases, ornately carved. The sumptuous carpets throughout the Hall were thick and the color of dark plums.

Amid a flourish of activity, the politicians entered the Hall and marched to the remaining unoccupied plush seats. As always, the pecking order of the seating told us who was who. It was interesting to hear the introductions and to see the number of Vice Premiers and members of the Politico Bureau. Power is power and it was very much on display. Bob and Shirley were certainly small potatoes in this gathering. Israel Epstein gave a talk which was then followed by one delivered by Panasonics Mr. Kobayashi. Louise Cariedon spoke next, and she was followed by the Russian foreign expert. The Russian had spent most of his career working in China and had just finished supervising the construction of an 800-megawatt power plant. The final speech was given by Vice Premier Li Liang Chen, who then invited all of us to dinner.

We walked across the Great Hall to the West Wing where over 300 people were seated, 10 to a table, for a 35-course dinner. Among the notables at our table was a nine-year-old granddaughter of Vice Premier Li. The food was good, but not exceptional. Silverware was on the table as were chopsticks. The head table was reserved for politicians, the sole exception being the General Motors honoree.

The entertainment was spectacular. Multiple singers, male and female soloists, vocal quartets, and violinists entertained us for over an hour. The highlight of the evening occurred when Vice President Li's granddaughter stepped up to the microphone and sang *"Edlewiess"* from the *Sound of Music*. She sang it in Russian, then in English, and finally in Chinese. She was simply stunning.

At the conclusion of the musical presentations the foreign experts and their spouses were asked to walk through a receiving line of politicians. We were instructed to walk slowly to give the photographer time to take multiple photos. Shirley's walk through the line was so accomplished that by the time she had greeted the Premier and Vice Premier there was precious little film in the camera for photos of me. Digital cameras were not yet in common use. As a consequence, we have many photos of Shirley in the Great Hall and not so many of Bob. But that was usually the case...recall the earlier encounters with Prince Charles and Margaret Thatcher.

And There We Were

We exited the Great Hall bathed in bright lights, thinking we had just had one heck of an experience. Certainly one we would always remember. We had witnessed the trappings of power firsthand. As always, I was very proud of Shirley. She always carried herself majestically in settings dominated by political or business leaders.

FIGURE 20. SHIRLEY LENT MEETING THE LEADERS OF CHINA IN THE GREAT HALL OF THE PEOPLE, BEIJING, CHINA

Figure 21. Bob and Shirley Lent on The Great Wall of China at Mutianyu

Figure 22. The Black Tie Dinner and Dance on the Great Wall at Janshanling

FIGURE 23. SHIRLEY LENT WITH RICE PATTIES AND LIMESTONE MONOLITHS IN THE BACKGROUND, YANGSHUO, CHINA

FIGURE 24. FISHING WITH CORMORANTS ON THE RIVER LI NEAR GUILIN, CHINA

Chapter 22

OTHER MEMORABLE CHINESE EXPERIENCES

The five previously described events were without question our most memorable experiences in China. However, we had many other experiences that deserve to be mentioned. I suspect anyone visiting China would have been thrilled to have participated in any of these less impressive, at least to us, events. Having residence in a country offers the opportunity to experience many profound experiences unavailable to participants in commercial guided tours. What follows are brief descriptions of places and events which, to us, were jaw dropping insights into life in rural and suburban China. We also had the good fortune to attend several dinners at which the entertainment far exceeded our expectations, and Shirley's expectations were always high.

LONGQING GORGE

During our stay in China we took a number of road trips into the Jundu Mountains north of Beijing. We tried to take a different route each time. We avoided the bigger roads, most often taking narrow one lane roads that afforded us more intimate views of smaller villages and a greater variety of scenic and mountainous terrain. One of our trips took us to Longqing

And There We Were

Gorge, 50 miles northwest of Beijing. The Gorge is the site of the annual Beijing Ice and Snow Festival. It would have been quicker to have taken the most direct route to Yanqing, the village nearest the Gorge, but we chose to take a most circuitous route through a number of small villages, along the Liuli, Baihe, and Gucheng Rivers, and over two passes in the Jundu Mountains.

After we arrived in China, we soon discovered road maps were hard to come by, and signposts almost non-existent. We learned from our Chinese friends that road maps are too expensive to make and there are not enough people driving to justify the cost of making them. What we usually brought with us was a sketch map showing the location of villages. It is an understatement to say this was an imperfect system. When, for example, our sketch had us traveling to *Sancha*, we might arrive only to learn that *Sancha* actually means junction, temple, or some other landmark unrecognizable to foreigners like us. Often our travels took us down an unknown road until we arrived at a village that might, or might not, be on the way to our objective. If not, we hightailed it back to the nearest known point and motored on. It would have taken the Oregon Trail Pioneers a hundred years to reach Oregon using our methods.

Our Chinese driver frequently did something we, and by *we* I mean *men*, do not do in the United States. He stopped and asked for directions. Sometimes it took many stops and conversations with a goodly number of individuals before we continued on, or before we took off in a new direction. It was an eye opener.

Northeast of Yangqing village, we took a road up the Gucheng River. When we entered Longqing Gorge we were directed to a large parking area filled with buses and cars. This was the staging area for people attending the Ice Festival. Some, mostly Chinese, walked up the road to the pavilion housing the ice sculptures. Our driver insisted we take a cab that would drop us off at the entrance to the facilities. We paid 40 Yuan each (about $4.80) for admission. Our driver handled the cab fare.

I was stunned when we came to a very tall cement dam

below which was the pavilion housing the ice sculptures. We were in the riverbed, and no water, not a drop, was flowing downstream. Only in China would a dam be allowed to capture all the water, leaving none for the fish, frogs, or other life forms that might inhabit the stream during the summer when water flows to irrigate crops or to provide drinking water for Beijing.

Before we entered the ice show we stopped at a nearby restaurant for a meal of fried rice, chili chicken, cabbage, soup, and *pijiu*. Actually, I had the *pijiu* (beer) with my meal. Shirley and our driver ordered bottled water and tea. The *shaojie* (maiden who served us) brought me a warm beer. I asked her if she would place the beer on the doorstep for 10 minutes. I was sure the cold temperature outside would chill the beer immediately. The young lady could not understand why warm beer was a problem. I subsequently discovered that most young women in China do not drink beer until they are married. It might be difficult to appreciate the difference in the experience of drinking cold versus warm beer, especially if you do not drink beer.

When we stopped for photos in front of the pavilion, we noticed a nearby stairway covered in green and yellow cloth. It was in the shape of a dragon and the enclosed stairway allowed climbers access to the top of the dam. When the climbers arrived at the top, they were disgorged from the dragon's mouth. Those coming down on a return trip had two choices. They could either walk down the steps they had just climbed, or they could take an alpine-like slide to the canyon floor. In either case, those leaving the dragon stairway or the slide emerged from the dragon's tail.

The pavilion housing the ice sculptures was massive. The front wall of the pavilion had two pagoda-like entrance portals cut in a green and gold tapestry. The wall spanned the entire gorge. The walkway along what would normally be the river bottom had been graded and covered with fine gravel. Bordering the two portals were four magnificent colored ice vases that were nine to ten feet in height. Set in the top of each vase were towering bouquets of artificial flowers. A blue and gray canvas covered the entire exhibit area.

The interior of the pavilion occupied several acres of river bottom. Over two hundred temples, buildings, animals, plants, people, and dragons illuminated by bright multi-colored fluorescent lights had been sculpted from massive blocks of ice. Our favorite exhibit was a massive stage upon which was a colorful assemblage of ten beautifully dressed performers: ice ladies in colorful ice sculpted gowns.

Innumerable strings of multicolored small lights, similar to exterior Christmas lights, festooned the interior ceiling. Hanging from some of the walls were ten-to-fifteen-foot strings of light that served as a backdrop for many of the exhibits. After we had finished our tour of the ice sculptures, we exited out a back portal facing the cement wall of the dam. Trees had been cut and tied to the wall. Water sprayed from above had frozen on the tree limbs, giving the appearance of a massive ice fall with adjacent ice flocked trees growing out the cement face of the dam.

I took many photos of Shirley posing in front of the ice sculptures. It would have been impossible not to have noticed that every time I asked Shirley to pose, a crowd of Chinese visitors gathered behind me and also took pictures. I knew they were not solely focusing on the ice sculptures. They wanted to take photos of the pretty Caucasian lady.

As we left the Ice Festival grounds, I looked back and saw a Great Wall of lights that went up a ridge and across a nearby mountain. Installing all those strings of lights had been a monumental effort. Only in China could you get enough cheap labor to string so many lights over such rough terrain.

We returned to our Shunyi home around 9:30 p.m. The next day we were going to Ditan Park where we would mingle with 100,000 people who were there to celebrate the Chinese New Year. The extreme cold we encountered in Longqing Gorge followed us into the city.

Other Memorable Chinese Experiences

Fragrant Hills

During the three days we spent as guests of the Peoples Republic of China we made a stop for lunch at the Fragrant Hills Hotel. The luncheon was between stops on our tour of facilities in and around Beijing. I earlier mentioned that Shirley and I had already spent a day in the Fragrant Hills, and that our stop as part of the government escorted Foreign Experts tour was a disappointment. Our lunch was served in an interior hotel room with no windows, and no time was allotted for those in the group to walk and enjoy the beautiful grounds in Fragrant Hills Park.

Shirley and I had been to Fragrant Hills Park in October of 1998 during the Red Leaf Festival. No matter what the time of year, the Fragrant Hills Park is one of the more popular tourist attractions in the Beijing area. However, during the Red Leaf Festival the Park is overrun with the city dwelling Chinese who come to see the beautiful fall colors. When we visited the Park, we were amazed at the size of the crowds. Not only were the paths near the base of the Western Hills filled with local citizenry, the trails to the top of Xiangshan Peak were also filled with climbers going up and coming down what was a four-hour roundtrip. It took almost the same amount of time for the hikers to come down the mountain as it did for them to climb it. The steep walkways and crowded steps made the going slow no matter which way one walked.

Thankfully for us, there was an alternative way to the top of Incense Burner Peak (Xiangshan Peak). At the base of the 1830-foot mountain is a chairlift facility that gets one to the top of the mountain in approximately 20 minutes. We probably waited in line more than 40 minutes just to get to our lift. There were so many people in line that it serpentined back and forth fifteen times. We passed the same people time and time again. About 20 minutes into the line, an enterprising young man said he could get us up the mountain another way. He said we could go by horseback as there was a trail that came up the backside of the mountain, and the trail end was only several hundred feet below the top of Incense Burner Peak. I looked over at the horses and chuckled. I think any one of the horses would have paid me to carry it to the top of the mountain. I could not see my pretty wife going up on horseback. We stayed in line and took the chairlift.

The trip to the top of the mountain is so far there are two intermediate landings where those traveling by chairlift must switch from one set of cables to another. All chairs on the lifts were two seaters with safety bars in the shape of a T that came down across both passenger's laps. Unfortunately, before I could settle completely into my seat, the safety bar came down and pinned my right leg on Shirley's side of the bar. The only way she could sit was side saddle.

Similar to ski lifts, the chairs moving up the mountain were spaced about 60 feet behind the preceding carriage. Off to the right, and about 10 feet from our cable, was an adjacent cable carrying people down the mountain. Below or off to the side of the chairlifts were paths filled with climbers walking the stairways to the top, or those coming down, after having already been to the top. The crowded walkways had 4 to 5 walkers on each broad step, the entire length of our cable ride.

During our trip to the top, we floated above hillsides covered in pine, red-leafed maple, sycamore, sumac, and persimmon trees. We were also treated to a magnificent view of Beijing from high above the city. The colors were not as impressive as the fall aspen trees in the Rocky Mountains, nor as vibrant as the multicolored trees in the northeastern United States, but the colors were certainly worth the visit.

Our trip to the top not only gave us a great view of Beijing, it also let us view other Park landmarks such as the Fragrant Hills Pagoda located high on a secondary peak, and the Temple of Azure Clouds with its many tiered white spires. As we gained altitude, the Fragrant Hills Hotel shrunk from a massive white complex of buildings to a postage stamp size enclave in a forest of red and green.

At the top of the mountain, we stepped off near Palace Hall. A nearby trail took us to a circular viewing area covered with an ornamental roof supported by red pillars. We had wanted our driver Lao Deng to be with us at the summit, but he had had enough of the high mountain and had gotten off at the first cable car landing. Later would we learn that he had to wait more than an hour to catch a ride down the mountain. During our time at the top we were witness to not only a beautiful view of Beijing but also to views of other interesting areas in the Western Hills.

I chuckled when I looked down the backside of the mountain and saw the landing where the horses had brought the riders. Those dismounting were still left with a long hike to the summit. We were so very glad we had chosen to ride all the way to the top via the chairlift. We were also surprised to see a hidden valley on the backside of the mountain. This valley housed three or four huge coal-fired electrical generating plants. Each of plants was pouring out an abundance of black smoke; all of smokestack emissions hidden from those living in Beijing.

We stayed until the sun began to set. What a glorious sunset it was! No one loved sunsets more than Shirley. One of my favorite photos taken at the summit has Shirley looking peacefully to the west while several Chinese men sitting on the edge of the viewing platform are looking at Shirley, not at the spectacular sunset.

When it was well after dark, we worked our way to the cable car platform where we encountered a crowded platform. We waited 20 minutes in line to get seats on the lift. The trip down the mountain was thrilling for a number of reasons. We saw Beijing all lit up at night and what an enchanting sight it was. I tried to take a photo, but my camera did not capture the subtleties of the scene. As we descended, we heard, but could not see, people stumbling down the trails on foot. We would hear a fall and then, what I surmise, was a string of Chinese epithets. It was funny for us, maybe not so much so for those working their way in the dark. Our two-seater often dropped so low we brushed the tops of trees. Shirley asked why our chair, and apparently our chair only, was making contact with the treetops. I did not have the heart to tell her that our chair was probably carrying two and a half times the weight of the other chairs.

I would be remiss if I did not mention how much we enjoyed strolling through the Fragrant Park grounds near the Hotel. Our walks took us through temples, around lakes, across bridges, and under colorful arches.

Unlike our trip to Longqing Gorge, the travel home took no more than 35 minutes. Because we had remained at the summit of Incense Burner Peak to watch the very last colors of the sunset, we arrived at Dragon Villas much later than we had originally intended. We were amongst tens of thousands of people during our time spent at Fragrant Hills, but we did not see any other Caucasians. We stood out like you cannot believe, and none more so than Shirley.

Ming Tombs, Summer Palace, Temple of Heaven, Drum and Bell Towers, and the Forbidden City (Imperial Palace)

Living in country allowed us to tour many of Beijing's famous tourist attractions in the fall and winter, times when the crowds were almost entirely Chinese. Some of the cultural sites were too large or complex to appreciate in one day, so we often made repeat visits. Each locality we visited left us with unforgettable memories, and we often took out-of-country guests to those places we found to be the most beautiful and the most interesting. We also spent time at many of Beijing's public parks such as Jingshan Hill, Beihai, Zhongshan, Ditian, and Zhonghai Lake. There was not one experience we took for granted. We were living and experiencing a life that we could not have imagined.

July 4th Celebration, Dinner at the United States Ambassador's home, New Year Celebration at the Australian Embassy, St. Patrick's Day Ball, and New York Philharmonic Performance in the Great Hall of the People

Our social calendar was always filled with a never-ending series of events sponsored by foreigners and/or diplomats. Although we did not attend as many functions hosted by our business associates as in the United Kingdom, there were many parties and functions hosted by people and companies representing the national interests of countries around the world. A few of these are described below.

In 1998, the American Club of China, supported by 98 corporate and governmental sponsors, was host to a massive and extravagant July 4th celebration held in the Global Silverhawk Warehouse, not far from the China World Hotel. The seven-hour celebration featured live performances by five American bands and/or singing groups, the most widely known one of which was The Coasters (*Yakety Yak* and *Charlie Brown).* Ambassador James Sasser welcomed the attendees with a message sent from the Embassy. There was a flag raising, singing of the national anthem, and a parade. Scattered around the enclosure were 55 booths available for food, drink, and games. Among those having booths were McDonalds, Coca Cola, Subway, Baskin Robbins, Dunkin' Donuts, and Budweiser, and these were only a few of the many. There were also a number of Chinese companies offering free samples of their products. Most of the Chinese food items were tasty if not interesting. We avoided the wine offered by Dragon Seal Winery. A start-up winery, Dragon Seal wines were made from grape extracts imported from France. The Winery now gets its grapes from in-country and their wine is excellent, but at the time of our stay in China, this was not the case. Expatriates referred to the

Dragon Seal wines as "Dragon Breath".

Shirley and I also attended a cocktail party and dinner at the home of Ambassador Sasser and his wife Mary. I am not sure how we got invited but we certainly found ourselves matriculating with many well dressed and important looking people. I had two very memorable encounters that evening. When Shirley and I were introduced to Ambassador Sasser and his wife, I, trying to make small talk, asked where in the States they were from. When he told me he was from Tennessee, the lights came on, and I remembered that he had been, for many years, the senior senator for Tennessee. I felt like such a dummy. I also remembered a chat I had that evening, over cocktails, with a handsome fellow who inquired about Kerr-McGee's exploration interests in Asia. When I mentioned we had a concession in the Andaman Sea, offshore Thailand, he took a sip of his drink and replied, "I shall never forgive my father for not telling me about Thai women before I married." I remember that exchange like no other I had during our stay in China.

We, along with our sons Tobin and Taran, welcomed in the 1999 New Year at the Australian New Year's Eve Ball hosted by the Australian Embassy. Those Aussies sure knew how to party. This celebration was about as raucous a bash as one could attend. Taran, then a young single businessman living in Hanover, New Hampshire, said he would, at midnight, kiss a girl he had never met before. He furthermore boasted he would kiss her under the bundle of balloons located above the center of the ballroom. Even though young Chinese ladies are reserved when it comes to kissing in public, Taran pulled it off so effectively that the young lady he kissed wanted to show him the after-hours spots in Beijing. We may have saved our young son when we insisted that he come home with us when we left at 2:00 a.m. I can only imagine what an all-nighter in Beijing with a lovely lady might have led to. Among the potential dilemmas, Taran would have had no way home since our driver would have already taken us back to Dragon Villas. Good move by Mom and Dad to be sure.

Sadly, when we returned to our home in Shunyi we learned that my father John had passed away in the Lent family home

Other Memorable Chinese Experiences

in Prineville. We immediately made plans to fly back to Oregon. New Year's Day, each and every year, is now filled with sadness as a result of Dad's passing on that date.

On March 17, 1999 we attended the St. Patrick's Day Ball held at The Great Wall Sheraton Hotel in Beijing. We were guests of The Irish Network China, a voluntary community of Irish people and friends of Ireland residing in the People's Republic of China. Twenty-nine corporate sponsors made sure that there was drink a plenty for those listening to the Irish Bands, "Stockton's Wing" and "Soundpage". The vocals were supported by band members playing drums, guitars, fiddles, and flutes. No one asked for the volume be turned up. I chuckled upon learning that one of the corporate sponsors for the ball was "Durty Nellies", self-proclaiming to be the first Irish Pub in Beijing.

Dinner was impressive. Traditional Irish food was served buffet style and included cold appetizers, soup, a hot buffet, a carving station and a table filled with Irish desserts. The hot buffet included Irish Stew, Shepherd's Pie, Braised Beef in Guinness, Roasted Vegetables, and Boxty Pancakes. The carving stations boasted Limerick Ham and roast leg of lamb. The Irish party hearty but not quite like the Aussies. Still, we had a ball. No pun intended.

In the summer of 1998 Shirley attended a performance by the New York Philharmonic Orchestra. The media was all over the event. The souvenir program prepared for the event was as ornate as any we saw in China. On opposite sides of the opening pages were photos of President Jiang Zemin and President Bill Clinton. Both presidents wrote glowingly of the visit.

Bill Clinton wrote:

> *"I am pleased to extend warm greetings to the people of China on the occasion of the New York Philharmonic's historic visit to Beijing."*

Jiang Zemin wrote:

> *"Music helps people to communicate with each other. I hope the beautiful and inspiring music will usher in the 21st century for the people of China and the United States."*

Of course, both presidents wrote much more but I selected a sampling of my choosing. The performance was held in the Great Hall of the People, where Shirley would return during the celebration honoring the Foreign Experts. I never learned how Shirley managed to get a front row seat, about 30 seats to the left of President Jiang Zemin.

Casablanca Theme Night and a Performance by Rondo' Veneziano

I conclude this recollection of our experiences in China with descriptions of two memorable events we attended only because Shirley insisted we do so. In both cases I was sure we were going to an event I would regret attending. I should have known better. About ninety percent of the time, Shirley was spot on and any performance or experience she dragged me to turned out never to be forgotten. The two events described below far exceeded even Shirley's expectations.

Shirley discovered that on June 28, 1998 there would be a movie - dinner night at the Symphony Restaurant in the Kempinski Hotel. The event had a Casablanca theme and included a set dinner followed by the airing of the 1942 Academy Award winning best picture *Casablanca*. Those with dinner reservations, including yours truly, arrived wearing formal attire. The servers, true to the movie, were dressed in World War II vintage white serving jackets, white shirts with black bow ties, and black slacks. Tables were covered in white linen tablecloths and each had a center piece lamp. The lamps were 20 inches tall and pear shaped, with crystal beads hanging from the base of the shade. A pianist played songs from the movie as we had our cocktails and appetizers. When the song *Knock on Wood* was played we all banged our fists on the tables. And of course, we all were mesmerized by the playing of *As Time Goes By*.

Our meal had Moroccan and Casablanca themes. The *Play*

it Again, Sam, For Old Time's Sake first course was a grilled vegetable couscous salad. The main course, *Here's Looking At You, Kid*, was Moroccan Lemon Spiced Sea Bass. The dessert, *This is the Beginning of A Beautiful Friendship* featured a coconut bread pudding with an orange sauce. The *Rick's Cafe Américain* complimentary dinner beverages were coffee and peppermint tea.

After dinner we were treated to a showing of the original black and white version of Casablanca on a large screen set up in front of the dining area. To stimulate the movie ambiance, cigars were distributed to interested patrons, and those who preferred to smoke cigarettes were encouraged to do so. After dinner drinks were served throughout the viewing. The Symphony Restaurant was as smokey as it was in Rick's Cafe. Rick (Humphrey Bogart) and Ilsa (Ingrid Bergman) were captivating on screen lovers.

The original black and white film was released simultaneously with the Allied invasion of North Africa, when Morocco and France were both occupied by the Germans. Watching the film, I felt as if Shirley and I were back in those times, living as sophisticated refugees in an occupied country. To make the illusion even more compelling, like Rick, I had my own 'Ilsa' by my side. Billed as a "Once in a Lifetime" event, the evening could not have been any more memorable.

When Shirley discovered that the Italian Orchestra "Rondo` Veneziano" would perform in the Jade Ballroom, also in the Kempinski Hotel, on November 29, 1998, I really drug my foot. I had been burned previously by two performances that left me wary of 'symphony tours' (The National Orchestra of Sweden performance in Shanghai) and 'ballet tours' (The Ballet Argentino World Tour in Beijing). Over my objection, Shirley purchased tickets for the Rondo' Veneziano event. I was not prepared for what turned out to be a most memorable event.

Shirley and I arrived at our table in the Jade Ballroom to the sound of canned chamber music from one of the Rondo` Veneziano albums. We were seated at a table with 4 other couples from 4 different countries. The expansive ballroom was filled to capacity. Our menu for dinner featured Italian wines by Rioja and Terrace Rosso. The all Italian four-course dinner began with *Zuppa di Fagioli* (bean soup with penne rigate). *Filet di Manzo al Rosmarino* (beef tenderloin) was the main course.

When the orchestra came on stage we were stunned by the beauty of the highly ornate and extravagant gowns worn by the nine-member all female performers. Each lady was adorned with a silver wig. Most of the musical instruments were string (violin, cello, and viola). One lady stood with an oboe, one with a flute. In the background were musicians seated at a bass guitar and drums.

We soon discovered Rondo` Veneziano plays only happy music. Right from the get-go, the music made one want to tap his or her toe. This mood never let up. One lady in the orchestra took the microphone and told us it was the intent of the performance to let all know life is inherently joyful. The fusion of contemporary and classical instruments, playing the music of some of the world's greatest composers, captivated us. We were told that the musical compositions were ones extremely popular in 17th Century Europe. By the end of the concert, the entire audience was ready to get up and dance. We did not dance, but the lady musicians came down onto the dining area and got those seated to step lively around the ballroom, each group of 40 or 50 people led by a musician. In the end we were led back to our tables and the evening was at an end. Never before had I heard such beautiful music played by such lovely ladies.

When I researched Rondo` Veneziano I found that the group had released more than 70 recordings and had sold over 30 million albums. How could we not have heard of this orchestra? Their music was fantastic. I was stunned that we had never heard of such entertainers. Even after all those years abroad we were still provincial 'Prineville' kids.

Chapter 23

Leaving China

Our stay in China was cut short by a corporate merger. I got a hint of what was coming, but it was not until late October 1998, that a number of newspapers (e.g., New York Times, The Oklahoman, and the Dallas Business Journal) published articles about a proposed merger, which turned out to be a $3.16 billion purchase of Oryx Energy by Kerr-McGee. Shortly after the acquisition was announced, the Kerr-McGee staff was advised to expect staff reductions, especially in management. I was left in limbo, with no indication of what might happen to me. It was possible that I would not have a job.

My father John Lent died January 1, 1999. When Shirley and I flew back to Oregon for his funeral, we decided to spend time in Houston on our way back to China. When we arrived in Houston, we were told that we ought to treat our stay as a house hunting visit. Though we had not been told when we would be leaving China, it became apparent our departure would be sooner rather than later. While we were in Houston, staff cuts were announced: 40 percent of the combined work force in the two companies would be laid off. 525 jobs were being eliminated.

The merger with Oryx was completed on February 27, 1999. By then I knew I was being recalled back to the United States. Although my future position was unknown, I was informed that I would have a position in the after-merger company.

And There We Were

Shirley was in charge of the house hunting efforts. I spent most of my time in the Houston office trying to get a feel for what was coming down the pike. I told Shirley we ought to be looking for a home in the $200,000 - $300,000 range. Shirley's initial search did not allow us in a home that was suitable for our needs. We had been out of country so long that we did not appreciate how inflation had affected the housing market. I didn't know it at the time, but Shirley's search was now focused on homes in the $500,000 - $700,000 range. She had skipped over $400,000 without even mentioning it.

Shirley asked me to accompany her when she went house hunting in The Woodlands. It had become apparent to her that The Woodlands was the community most suited to our needs, and it also had the greatest number of available homes. During our home tour, our realtor showed us a home that, although under contract, seemed to be exactly the home Shirley was looking for. After touring the home, we agreed that it was too bad the new home, in the final stages of being completed, was under contract and was scheduled to close that day.

Then, as we were walking to our car from the realtor's office at the end of the tour, the realtor came running after us. At the contract closing that day, the couple who had put down the earnest money failed to show. The earnest money had been forfeited and the home was back on the market.

On January 23 we agreed to purchase the home at 38 Noble Bend Drive in the Village of Alden Bridge, The Woodlands. I wrote a $16,350 check for an earnest money deposit to secure a contract on the home. Our agreed purchase price was $545,000. The closing would occur after our loan had been approved and after the builder had made all the changes Shirley wanted in paint selection, carpeting, chandeliers, etc. The builder would use the forfeited earnest money on the previous failed contract to cover the cost for these changes.

We had about a week before we were to return to China. During this week, Shirley and I, when she needed my advice, made decisions that would enable the builder to have the home and landscaping completed prior to our return to the United

Leaving China

States. Despite significant time pressure, Shirley made selections that made our home the wonder that it is.

After our January trip to the United States, I learned that the Chinese government was to honor me as a Foreign Expert. I felt badly because I had an exploration plan for China, and it appeared I would not be able to implement that plan. I could only hope in my new position, whatever it turned out to be, I would be able to pursue new ventures in China. I felt strongly in that regard, and in the end, I was able to deliver results beyond my wildest imaginings. More about those results later.

The economic contribution to the Peoples Republic resulting from the exploration plan I was able to effect was incredibly significant. When I look back on it, I suspect the Chinese honored me for what they thought I might yet be able to accomplish when it came to oil and gas exploration in offshore China. My Foreign Expert award was strong evidence our Chinese business partners believed in me.

In February and March 1999, I spent considerable time saying goodbye to business associates, and executives and employees of our Chinese partners. We travelled to Shekou, Shenzhen, Hong Kong, Tangshan, and Tanggu where goodbyes were exchanged, and farewell dinners hosted on our behalf. We returned to the United States the third week in March for the March 17th closing on our Texas home.

After spending a week in Oregon with our parents, we returned to Beijing and prepared for the mover who would arrive to pack and ship our household goods. Before we could pack, representatives from the Chinese Antiquities office inspected all the purchases we had made during our time in China. The initial inspection identified only one item that caused the inspectors to consider confiscation. This was a Ming dynasty vase we had purchased for $1,000. When the inspectors returned after our trip to Guilin, they considered confiscating the small wooden box we had purchased in Yangshou. This was the small box that unfolded to show the three religious looking buddhas (monks?). In the end both the vase and the small wooden box were approved for shipment to the United States.

And There We Were

The packers had arrived on April 1 and packed until we left on Friday, April 3 for our trip to Guilin and the float down the River Li. After we returned to Dragon Villas the following Monday, the packers finished their work. The movers came the following day. We were appalled when we saw the moving truck was an open flat bed. I scanned the skies when our goods left Dragon Villas, covered in a tied down tarp. I could only hope that it would not rain until the truck made it to the shipper's warehouse where the items would be packed into sea containers for the overseas trip to Houston. It did not rain.

We moved into the Kempinski Hotel for three days. The Kerr-McGee office gave us a farewell party. The departure gift they gave us was a 200-pound Buddha head carved in jade. There was no way we could put this on a plane. It eventually arrived in Texas having been shipped in a wooden crate after sailing halfway around the world.

On our last day in Beijing my Chinese language teacher Nellie and her husband dropped by the Kempinski Hotel to see us for one last time. We had lunch together and then went to the elevator where we said our goodbyes. Nellie began crying and gave me a big hug. She said she was going to have a baby and she wanted me to be the first to know. I remember looking over her shoulder at Shirley and at her husband. All I could think was do they think it's mine. Not even a chance. Nellie and I had become good friends and we talked about life more than the Mandarin she was helping me learn to speak. On one of my return business trips to China I stopped by and visited Nellie. She was immensely proud to introduce me to her beautiful little girl.

When we arrived back in the United States on April 12, 1999, I was informed I had been named Vice President of Worldwide New Ventures, and that I would continue be responsible for any further exploration in China. I still had my finger in the pot.

Our household goods would not arrive in Houston until late May. In the interim Shirley and I would be living in a townhouse not far from our new home. It was time to leave the expatriate living style behind and return to life in America. Having been

Leaving China

out of the home office for nearly seven years, I would also have to once again earn my spurs in the Kerr-McGee hierarchy. I was, in a way, the new kid on the block and, as a result of the merger, many of those now in Kerr-McGee senior management positions were former Oryx executives.

Shirley and I had lived a life abroad that was filled with wonderful adventures and experiences we could not have imagined as youngsters living in Prineville. Our world had turned magical, and no one had enjoyed the overseas adventures more than Shirley Lent.

And There We Were

Chapter 24

BECOMING TEXANS

*A*After the merger of Oryx and Kerr-McGee was announced, and before the merger was officially concluded, I knew we would be returning to the United States. When Shirley and I talked about the impending move, she said, "I will go anywhere with you, but please don't take me to Houston." Shirley had lived her life-to-date in localities with temperate climates. She loved to walk, and she hated the heat. Less than two weeks after she and I had this discussion, I got my orders. We were relocating to Houston. I was certain that Shirley, despite her disappointment, would make the most of our new life in Texas, and I was spot on.

Following our April, 1999 arrival in Texas, and during the time we were living in our rented apartment, Shirley began scouting out places where she could go for her daily 60 to 90-minute walks. She soon found Burroughs Park, an expanse of forest, lakes, and grasslands only 15 minutes from what would be our home on Noble Bend Drive, The Woodlands. For over 20 years Shirley walked Burroughs Park almost every day. She made friends with many of her fellow walkers and became the park rangers' favorite visitor. She learned to handle the heat by walking at more comfortable times of day, usually after the high humidity had burned off.

Shirley also jumped in and joined "The Woodlands Newcomers Club", thus paving the way to participation in a wide variety of social groups. She immediately signed up for marathon bridge and the 'Out to Lunch Bunch'. She became involved with politics and was a supporter of a number of successful candidates. We attended fund raisers for senators and congressmen. Shirley was returning to her element. It was not long before she told me how very much she enjoyed living in The Woodlands, Texas. She enjoyed her life in The Woodlands so much that when it came time for us to retire, she chose for us to remain in Texas rather than move to our beloved Oregon.

While Shirley was preparing for our late May move-in, I began work in my new job. I reviewed Kerr-McGee exploration opportunities throughout the world. I even returned to the United Kingdom to review exploration efforts underway in the North Sea. The trip gave me my first look at the newly relocated UK headquarters in Aberdeen, Scotland.

I also took it upon myself to investigate something that had bothered me for the entire time I was country manager in China. Kerr-McGee had two very large concessions (685,000 acres or 1,070 square miles) covering a broad uplifted structure in Bohai Bay. The Chinese had drilled a number of wells on the crest of this structure, the results of which had been condemning. What bothered me was the fact that a number of other geologically similar uplifted highs in Bohai Bay had been drilled, and all had proved oil reserves of 300 million barrels, plus or minus. Kerr-McGee had avoided drilling additional wells near the crest of the structure on which our concessions were located because of the negative test results coming from the wells drilled in the early 1970s by the Chinese. Little did I know at the time, but the work I undertook eventually led to the crowning achievement of my professional career.

Chapter 25

BOHAI BAY BOB'S GIVE-BACK TO CHINA AND KERR MCGEE

I have often reflected on what motivated me to not give up on oil and gas exploration in offshore China. My current thought is that after being honored in the Great Hall of the People, I felt I owed the People's Republic something. If it was the intent of the Chinese government to motivate me to continue exploring in China, I give them credit for what I undertook and for the results that followed.

When I left China and returned to the United States, Kerr-McGee's oil and gas exploration effort in China was hanging by a thread. We had several licenses with drilling obligations, but we were looking for a way out of these obligations. Although the company had made a discovery in Bohai Bay, it was deemed to be uneconomic. We had no plans to further evaluate the two remaining Kerr-McGee concessions in Bohai Bay.

I got to thinking that maybe we should take a more detailed look at the wells drilled by the Chinese on the Haizhong High, an uplifted structure covering more than 250,000 acres extending across our two Bohai Bay concessions. I did not want Kerr-McGee to walk away from 300 million barrels of oil on my watch, but I knew I would have a hard time convincing Kerr-McGee senior management and our industry partners to drill another well on what had thus far proved to be a disappointing pair of concessions.

I asked one of our geologists to get a copy of the drilling and testing reports from HZ-1, the well drilled by the Chinese at the highest structural point on the Haizhong High. I wanted to see the details relating to the drilling and testing, and I wanted to correlate the test results to the suite of electric logs run in the well bore.

The results from HZ-1 were condemning in a number of ways. Only one zone in the well had tested water free oil, and the oil in that zone was of such poor quality as to be economic only if it flowed at a higher rate. All the other zones tested were either water wet or had high water cuts. The viscosity and gravity of oil in many of the shallower zones were of such quality that the possibility of commercial oil production was minimal.

Changling Wu, one of our geologists, sat down with me and we poured over the well data from HZ-1. Mr. Wu translated each entry made by the Chinese. I correlated the testing data with the 1973 vintage log data. We focused on one 'wet' zone that had the same log characteristics as a zone that flowed 302 barrels of oil per day, water free. It did not make any sense that the one zone tested only oil and the other, a much thicker zone, tested water with a minor amount of free oil.

What we found was that the thicker 'pay' zone had not been tested properly. The Chinese had not set an upper packer in the drill stem test. There had been a 3000-foot salt-water cushion putting pressure against the indicated pay zone. I was absolutely convinced that had the zone been tested properly, it would have flowed more than 1,000 barrels of oil per day, water free. A test of that magnitude would have merited commercial development.

With my interpretation of what went wrong in the testing of HZ-1, I began to document the reasons why a well 'twinning' HZ-1 should be drilled. Included in my arguments were the need for modern logs, the information that was needed on the viscosity and oil gravity of the various zones (the deeper zones, even though 'wet', had recovered oil with much more favorable oil properties than the shallower zones), and lastly that there was a thick pay zone that had gone untested and this almost certainly would flow oil at commercial rates.

I presented our findings and my recommendation to my immediate supervisor, the Vice President of Worldwide Oil and Gas Exploration. I got approval on July 20, 1999 to carry my recommendation to the Kerr-McGee senior management team and to the Chief Executive, Mr. Luke Corbett. I was also given approval to present my findings to our co-owners in the Bohai Blocks and to inform them that we might be recommending an exploratory well to twin HZ-1.

One of our partners, with a 41% working interest, opted out of the well and in so doing forfeited their interest in the exploration licenses. This meant that if a well was drilled, Kerr-McGee would be pay over 80% of the cost.

On July 26, 1999 a presentation was made to Mr. Corbett and his management team. The group bought off on my reasons for another well drilled on the Haizhong High. They collectively agreed that Kerr-McGee should not walk away from what might be 300 million barrels of recoverable oil. When I faced a push back on twinning the existing dry hole, HZ-1, I stressed my reasoning. We needed to get all the data possible from the oil bearing zones we already knew were present at the HZ-1 location. We needed this well data more than we needed to prove up a wider area of potential prospectivity. Approval was granted for a test well estimated to cost $2.53 million if it was a dry hole, $4.40 million if it was completed.

In October 1999 the well was drilled. In November the final log calculations were in hand. There was 285 feet of log calculated pay having an average porosity of 32% and and average oil saturation of 70 percent (30% salt-water saturation). All the data were encouraging. It looked like we had a discovery.

On December 21, 1999 a drillstem test of the zone I promised would flow 1,000 barrels of oil per day actually flowed at 1,043 barrels per day. The oil gravity was a very acceptable 18 degrees API. Several other drillstem tests on deeper and shallower zones also flowed oil, most without water.

In January of 2000 Kerr-McGee released a press release announcing the company's exploratory twin to HZ-l was a discovery. The well had been drilled to a total depth of 5052 feet in 80 feet of water. The press release stated, "the first well has successfully confirmed the volumetric potential of this oil accumulation."

In May 2000 a second exploratory well was drilled, a south step out from HZ-1. The big surprise in the step out was the testing of 24 gravity API oil. Not only was there pay in the step out, it was of a much higher quality than that found in the first well.

After recommending the first well, my work was essentially done. I watched over the exploratory and development efforts, but most of the work was being done by the geologists, geophysicists, and engineers in both the United States and China. The discovery and plans for development meant that operations would once again amp up in China. I cannot give enough credit to all of those that carried on the exploitation in the Bohai Bay program. In a sense, most of that staff did the heavy lifting. My work had only been to recommend and get approval for that first well.

On May 14, 2002 Kerr-McGee had a press release stating that the company's board of directors had sanctioned full development of the discoveries in Bohai Bay. The release stated the estimated reserves were 150 million barrels of oil. In August of 2006 Anadarko acquired Kerr-McGee and with it the Bohai Bay assets. In February of 2014, after having already produced 130 million barrels of oil, Brightoil acquired the remaining Anadarko reserves in the Bohai Bay fields for $1.08 billion.

For a number of years after my retirement, Chinese companies invited me to dinner when they had oil and gas management teams in Houston. They always invited other managers who had worked in China, but I was always seated to the right of the primary Chinese delegate. I was honored by this recognition. During the evening and after dinners many of the Chinese visitors would introduce themselves and express their pleasure in making my acquaintance. I finally stopped attending these dinners as I had been so honored and flattered on so many visits that I did not think such recognition could ever be meaningfully increased.

Bohai Bay and Bob's Give-Back

As a result of my being honored in the Great Hall of the People and for my scientific and managerial contributions to the Chinese people, my high school, Crook County High, honored me as one of their Graduates of Distinction. Moved by the honor, I was happy to deliver a talk to the students about the dreams I had and the life I lived. I told them I was proud to be a Class of 1960 graduate from Crook County High School.

And There We Were

Chapter 26

A NEW ASSIGNMENT
A NEW WORLD OF ADVENTURE

I was promoted to Vice President of International Exploration not long after the Bohai Bay results confirmed the presence of commercial hydrocarbons. In my new assignment I was responsible for not only the exploration efforts on existing Kerr-McGee concessions, but also for all exploratory work done in the search for other new venture opportunities. In this new position I reviewed many of the offshore exploratory opportunities around South America, Asia, Africa, and Australia (including New Zealand). My professional travels took me to Algeria, Morocco, Western Sahara, France, The Bahamas, China, Tunisia, and Brazil. Shirley accompanied me on several trips to France and Brazil. Shirley could make any outing an adventure. The trips with her were the most memorable. Trips to Paris and Rio de Janeiro brought out the very best in Shirley, and her best made our trips to these cities unforgettable.

RIO DE JANEIRO, BRAZIL

I made multiple trips to Brazil where Kerr-McGee's had offshore exploratory concessions. I did not take Shirley with me on the first few trips. I focused on work and not the sight-seeing one would normally undertake while in a Rio, an incredibly beautiful and vibrant city. I did not visit the beaches, go to Christ the Redeemer, or take the cable car to the top of Sugarloaf Mountain. My business-related travels took me along the famous beaches (e.g., Copacabana, Ipanema, and Leblon), but I saw them only through a car window as we traveled from one locality to another. When Shirley accompanied me, I was not only a traveling businessman, but a tourist. She made sure I had an equal mix of business and pleasure. As always, she did her part to make her life, and mine, as interesting as it could possibly be.

The first day of the Rio trip Shirley and I took together was, for me, business as usual. I met with the country manager and with the staff responsible for exploration in the oceanic waters offshore Brazil. While I was so engaged, Shirley was provided a driver who also served as a tour guide. She and her handsome (and *yes*, he was) guide visited many of the scenic tourist stops in Rio, but she saved some of the visits to the more iconic Rio landmarks for the day I would be with her. During her day out and about she and her driver had one "Shirley-like" experience that became one of the highlights of Shirley's time in Rio.

Shirley's tour guide thought she might like to visit one of the more beautiful and ornate churches in all of Rio. The guide parked his limo near the front entrance of Sao Francisco da Penitencia Church. When they entered the church, the guide mentioned to Shirley that it was too bad there was no illumination other than the light coming from the decorative stained-glass windows. He said that when services were held and the artificial lights turned on, the gold leafed walls and ceiling were beautiful beyond description.

The guide apologized; she would not be able to see the church in all of its glory. He had just said this, when suddenly, every artificial light in the building came on and people began filing into the church. The driver was nervous and said they should probably leave, because a special service might be about to begin. Shirley, predictably, said they should sit down and see what might be happening. It turned out the unexpected service was a funeral for the 21year old son of one of Rio's most well-known families. The church filled to capacity.

A New Assignment

Shirley later remarked that she was glad she had not asked the guide to sit at the front of the church where the family was eventually seated. During the service she took the time to look at every ornate part of the church while listening to a most unexpected ceremony, conducted in Portuguese, of course. After the service was concluded the family stood outside in a receiving line to thank those who had attended the service. Shirley said there must have been some discussion later on as to the English-speaking lady who had come to the young man's funeral service. As they departed the parking lot, the tour guide said it was good they had decided to stay. There was no way they could have departed earlier since they were boxed in by cars arriving for the funeral.

The following day I took time away from my professional duties and became a tourist. Shirley and I visited many of Rio's finest tourist attractions. Our first stop was at a platform where a cable car took tourists to the top of Sugarloaf Mountain. This famous landmark is nearly 1300 feet high and offers breath taking views of Rio, including its many Atlantic Ocean beaches, Guanabara Bay, the favelas, mountains, and surrounding forests.

The cable car makes an intermediary stop on the top of Urca Mountain a peak about halfway up to the summit of Sugarloaf Mountain. Here we found a number of coffee shops, a restaurant, and a video theater. Most memorable though was the presence of free roaming monkeys. They seemed to be everywhere, but mostly they were in the trees above the landing.

When we finally reached to top of Sugarloaf Mountain we were captivated by the panoramic views. Though there were several fast-food stalls hear the cable car platform, most of the summit area was taken up by fenced-in walkways that led visitors around the summit and along the cliff edges. Many of the spots along the vertical cliffs were covered by low lying bushes. I was sure that one step beyond any of these shrubs would take one on a fall to his/her death. The possibility of such a fall did not keep feral cats from darting in and out of the greenery. Like the monkeys seen on Urca Mountain, we could not imagine how the critters made it to the top of Sugarloaf. I remember thinking that it would be a high-risk endeavor for any cat to jump at birds resting on the bushes.

Our second stop was at the top of Corcovado Mountain (2,300') where the colossal statue of Jesus Christ stands open armed and looking out over the city of Rio de Janeiro. Also called Christ the Redeemer, the statue is 98 feet tall with arms that span 92 feet. There probably is no greater cultural icon in Rio or in Brazil than Christ the Redeemer. I dare say that whenever one sees a photo of Rio it most likely will included both Christ the Redeemer and Sugarloaf Mountain.

We made the trip up Corcovado Mountain via a roadway through the Tijuca Forest National Park. There is a rail line to the summit, but we much enjoyed our ride through the winding road with its verdant cover. At the time we visited Corcovado, our driver was able to drop us off not far from the statue. Today one must take either the railway or a private van to the stairway (or elevator) leading to the platform surrounding the statue.

We were fortunate that during our visit there were only a few visitors on the platform in front of the statue. We had a spectacular view of Rio, and when we turned around, we saw the magnificent Christ the Redeemer looking out over us. It was a memorable and moving experience.

Our driver, tour guide if you will, then drove us 42 miles northeast of Rio to the city of Petropolis, a beautiful city that was once the summer mountain resort for Dom Pedro II, the last ruling monarch of Brazil. Most of the city's beautiful architecture was built in the late 1800s. Dom Pedro II chose to spend the southern hemisphere summers in this part of the Orgaos Mountains which, because of the altitude, offered a cool respite from hot and humid Rio. We did not spend much time in Petropolis, but we did make stops at the Imperial Museum, the Quitandinha Palace, and the Crystal Palace.

The most memorable part of the trip to Petropolis, at least to me, was the drive through the mountains and a luncheon stop we made along the Inhomirm River where we had lunch and beer/wine on an outdoor dining terrace of an upscale restaurant. A stone wall separated our table from the clear and fast flowing river. Since the water level was about halfway up the ten-foot rock wall, I surmised the restaurant, located in a region that receives on average 90 inches of rain per year, had a high risk of flooding. But while we dined, we had the river and a beautiful overhead plant covered trellis to enjoy. I am not sure that we ever dined in a more beautiful outdoor setting.

When we returned to Rio we joined the country manager and his wife for dinner at a famous Rio Churrascaria. We had what Rio residents call "the churrasco experience". Many servers brought us a never-ending variety of meats prepared by cooking over a fire in the "Gaucho" method of roasting. We also visited the restaurant's "Gourmet Market Table." In Texas we would call this a salad bar, but it was a salad bar like no other I had ever seen. Here in Houston we now have a restaurant, 'Fogo de Chao', that comes quite close to offering the same type of meal we enjoyed during our Rio stay. Even the salad bar is world class, as it was in Rio.

On Sunday morning, our last day in Rio, we were taken to an interesting and delicious brunch served in one of Rio's better hotels. The meal consisted of multiple variations of Brazil's national dish, the Feijoada. This dish is a hearty black bean soup/stew made with a variety of slow cooked meats and/or vegetables. There must have been 10-12 big black cast iron kettles, each containing beans with a different meat or vegetable. The meat options were beef, chicken, sausage, ribs, and bacon. The meal came with rice and farofa, a toasted and heavily spiced mixture of cassava, bacon, and plantains. I never imagined that a brunch buffet could be so appetizing yet so singularly composed of bean dishes. Before brunch we had two Caipirinhas, the national drink of Brazil. A Caipirinha is made from cachaca, Brazil's most common distilled alcoholic beverage, crushed lime juice, and sugar. It is a powerful drink, and it is apparently not respectable to consume more than two of these during a meal. We had two and can attest to the powerful impact the drink has on one's cognitive abilities.

We left Brazil for the last time. Although I never found another reason to return on a business trip, Shirley had made sure that neither of us would ever forget our time together in Brazil. To paraphrase Humphrey Bogart in *Casablanca*, we would always have Rio.

Paris, France

I mentioned in an earlier chapter that Shirley and I, together and separately, made numerous trips to Paris. Sometimes Shirley went with her Berkshire girlfriends and sometimes with one or both of our sons. One business trip we took together came after we had repatriated to the United States. I was in Paris to attend an operator committee meeting for a concession Kerr-McGee and our partners had in Gabon. Although our time in Paris was brief, we still found time to visit the Louvre Museum, the Museum d' Orsay, the Arc de Triumph, and the Palace of Versailles. When Shirley was left on her own, she went to the Cathedral of Notre Dame and walked the sidewalks along the Champs Elysees. One of these walks took her to the Four Seasons Hotel George V, just off the Champs Elysees. This hotel is one of the most posh and expensive hotels in the world. In 2000, several publications voted it the best hotel in the world. Shirley walked into the hotel and, in her typical manner, had drinks in the plush Le Bar and a light luncheon at the Le Galerie restaurant. At a later date and on another visit, we returned to this hotel with friends who were with us on a pleasure trip we took on a luxury barge through Burgundy.

The last evening of our stay in Paris we were invited to take a dinner cruise on the Seine River, compliments of Total, the operator of our Gabon concession. I was looking forward to this outing, but Shirley had been cultivating another plan, and when she wanted something, she often got it.

Shirley had a special knack of getting what she wanted, especially when it came to seating at a restaurant or even reservations at a restaurant. She believed that if one was respectful in a request and showed an interest in an employee and his or

A New Assignment

her work, it was easy to make the most out of any situation. Any experience can be made great if one is willing to make a bit more effort or take that extra step.

Shirley asked the concierge at the Marriott Champs Elysees if he could get her dinner reservations at the exclusive Jules Verne Restaurant on the upper level of the Eiffel Tower. The man said, "Oh no Madame, one needs to make reservations there at least six months in advance." Shirley charmed the man, and for the following three days she would drop by his desk and ask if he had made any headway in getting a reservation. "No" was not an adequate answer. She told him that a man of his distinction must surely have the contacts and the clout to get her a reservation. On the fourth day of our stay, the concierge must have used up all of his chits. We had a 7:00 p.m. dinner reservation. We dined gazing out windows high above the City of Lights. I remember looking down on the Seine and thinking we could, and probably should, have been dining at someone's else's expense. No matter what the cost differential, the meal we had at the Jules Verne was one of those lifetime experiences that we talked of always and thereafter.

And There We Were

Chapter 27

RETIREMENT TRAVELS AND ADVENTURES IN THE FIRST YEAR

On December 31, 2003 I retired from Kerr-McGee. Shirley and I then began another era of adventures. I was only 62 but I feared that my medical history and my physical condition might mean my years with Shirley could be limited. I wanted the two of us to have at least ten years of leisure time together. This would surely give us time to experience a life in retirement, and to travel throughout North America. As it turned out, my early retirement was a gift to Shirley and not to me.

Our sons have often told me that their mother and I got an A+ for what we did after I retired. I have to say that I think they are right. We had so very many wonderful experiences. In addition to taking a number of long road trips we also found time for cruise excursions to Alaska and Hawaii. Shirley made a return trip to England when she went with our son Taran to visit the London home of Taran's high school friend Brian Borg and his wife Andrea. During that stay Shirley took Taran and her good friend Joanne Borg, Brian's mother, on an Orient Express trip to Bath. She also visited her old stomping grounds in Windsor and Ascot. She purposely did not drive by Muirfield in Kier Park, Ascot. She said that she wanted to remember Muirfield like it was when we lived there, not as it might be with new residents. She many times said she had never been so utterly happy as she was when we lived in Muirfield as American expatriates in the United Kingdom.

We undertook many North American travels during our time of retirement. Although we had an incredible number of adventures on each trip, it is probably best I conclude this story of "Us" with the narratives that capture what made our travels together so special. More than anything we saw during our travels, it was always the people we met that left us with the most lasting memories. Some people may travel and see the wonders of the world, but if they do not take the time to engage the people with whom they come in contact, they are missing the best of what is on offer. Shirley was a master at engaging others. It did not matter where we were, on a river float or in a remote diner, she charmed people just as she had charmed the celebrities she met whilst we were living abroad.

During my first year in retirement Shirley and I took a number of memorable trips. The narratives from those 2004 journeys may seem excessively detailed, but those trips really defined how the rest of our retirement would play out.

New England and the Maritime Provinces of Canada

Our traveling adventures in North America began with a trip to the Maritime (Atlantic) Provinces of Canada in the Spring of 2004. This adventure actually began in Boston where we went to visit son Taran and his girlfriend Nancy Decker. We rented a car in Boston and drove north through Maine into New Brunswick, Prince Edward Island, and Nova Scotia. Both coming and going we spent several days in Bar Harbor, Maine where we toured Acadia National Park.

I was so excited to get retirement under way that we arrived in the Atlantic Provinces a bit too early. It was late May and snow was still on the ground. Many of the places we targeted for visitation remained closed for the season. We discovered the hospitality and visitor sites are geared up to handle visitors who come to the Provinces in late June or early July. We were so early in the season that we arrived in Canada prior to the opening of the lobster season, which meant menus in New Brunswick and Nova Scotia were filled with fresh fish entries, and not the shellfish for which the region is so famous.

The highlight of our trip came about by accident, and it came after we had driven most of the way through New Brunswick. One of our first stops in the province was at Reversing Falls on the St. John River near St. John, just upriver and inland from the Bay of Fundy. Having studied the effect of the tidal movements in the Bay, I was interested in observing the effects of the tidal surges which are amongst the highest in the world. Our stop in St. John allowed us to observe the flow out of the St. John River during the ebb tide. We took a late lunch at a restaurant on a bluff overlooking the Reversing Falls. There is a natural narrow gap that has been cut through volcanic rock and this constriction causes water to flow in and out of the Bay of Fundy with incredible force. I had never seen a volume of water flowing at such a high rate and with such force. It was a bit frightening just looking down on the whirlpools that were created.

On our way back to Maine we stopped by the same Falls and were stunned. The incoming tide had peaked, and water was about to flow back out into the Bay of Fundy. At this point of equilibrium, the water at Reversing Falls was as calm as one might expect behind a dam. I concluded that if one arrives at Reversing Falls when the tide is either coming in or out the view is stunning. If one is there at the changing of the tide, he/she might wonder what all the fuss is about.

After leaving St. John we spent the night in Moncton. The next morning, we were on the road thinking we were headed east into Nova Scotia. I missed a turn where one major highway merged with another, and we found ourselves heading north towards the Gulf of St. Lawrence. Never one to admit to a major blunder, I told Shirley how lucky we were to be traveling through true Acadia and along the shore of the Northumberland Strait.

And There We Were

Actually, the new route turned out to be terrific. We passed a number of farmlands and coastal villages. We thought we might walk along the beach at Murray Beach State Park, but it was, as were most state parks, "closed for the season". While we were traveling along the shoreline, Shirley spotted a massive bridge on the horizon and asked what it might be and where it went. I quickly looked at a map and found it was the Confederation Bridge, connecting Nova Scotia to Prince Edward Island.

With our original itinerary in shambles, curiosity led us to cross this incredibly impressive bridge just for the experience of doing so. We discovered that it doesn't cost anything to go to Prince Edward Island, but the tag coming back is $28. A gale force wind was blowing across the bridge, and we soon found ourselves tucked in behind a big eighteen-wheeler hauling something sandy. Grit was sandblasting our rental car. I was sure we were going to be liable for a paint job.

Once across the eight-mile-long bridge a sign directed us to a tourist center where we learned we were in the homeland of *Anne of Green Gables*. I believe the tale of Anne Shirley (the Anne in Green Gables) captures the essence of Prince Edward Island. Maud Montgomery, the author that brought Anne to 'life', must certainly have lived a life not unlike that of her most wonderful and fictional character. We bought CD recordings of the musical scores from the *Anne of Green Gables* plays and movies, and we listened to Anne's music continuously for the remainder of our travels in Canada. After we returned home, we bought and watched the Anne movies over and over again. I love that Anne. To me the highlight of our Maritime trip came from our diversion to Prince Edward Island and our introduction to *Anne of Green Gables*.

We bought several other CDs that featured famous local songs of Prince Edward Island (e.g., Bud's Spuds). To me the music of Prince Edward Island sounded remarkably like the music we heard in Ireland and Scotland, but I found that one does not really mention this to the locals as they do not hold much to "off island" influence.

As we were to about to leave Nova Scotia on our trip south,

we saw signs that informed us we were approaching Oxford, the "Blueberry Capital of the World". Wow! This was a must stop! We had no idea blueberries were grown in Nova Scotia. A local museum extolled the town's place in the world order of blueberry and maple syrup production. All of the pipes in a huge processing plant at the edge of the town are painted blue. The air reeks of blueberries. I took a photo of Shirley standing by, of all things, a blueberry totem pole. Our detour into the town of Oxford was a most enjoyable, if unexpected, stop.

Another highlight of our trip along the Atlantic seaboard occurred in Bar Harbor, Maine on our return trip to Boston. After a day of shopping (Shirley) and sight-seeing (Bob and Shirley) we returned to our hotel, the Bar Harbor Inn for dinner. We were seated at what the staff had learned was our favorite window table. We could see and hear the pianist all during dinner. When we were about to leave, Shirley asked the pianist if he would play the theme song from *Dr. Zhivago, Somewhere My Love*. He knew the piece and said he would play it for her, but first he wanted her to tell her of a pretty lady he had seen window shopping on the streets of Bar Harbor that afternoon. He said, "That mysterious and beautiful lady was you", thereby guaranteeing himself a most generous tip.

We returned to Boston and spent time with Taran and Nancy. Taran took all of us out to dinner at the top of the Prudential Tower on Mother's Day. Shirley's gift to Taran was a painting she had purchased while in Bar Harbor. It was of a street in Paris with the Eiffel Tower in the background. Shirley and Taran had gone to Paris on a three-day trip taken via the high-speed Eurostar during the time we resided in Kier Park, Ascot. The oil painting was a great way for Mother and Son to have a tactile memory of their wonderful weekend in France. Trip one in our retirement had now been completed.

And There We Were

Niagara Falls (Canada/New York), Buffalo, and Ithaca, New York

We hardly had time to catch our breath after returning from our trip to the Maritimes before we were off to New York state to attend the wedding of Christian Knecht and Holly Turton in Ithaca on the campus of Cornell University. Christian is the son of our good friends Peter and Renata Knecht who lived near us in The Woodlands.

We flew to Buffalo, New York on an evening flight and crossed into Canada to visit Niagara Falls before continuing on to Ithaca. We had a wonderful room at the Marriott Niagara Falls, Ontario. Our room on the 12th floor overlooked both the Horseshoe (Canada) and American Falls. It was difficult to leave this magnificent view, but we had already made plans for dinner. We had a lovely meal at the Marriott main dining room, and, from our window table, we had a perfect view of the Illumination of the Falls.

The next morning we walked along the shoreline of the Niagara River, both above and below Horseshoe Falls. We also took the elevator to the viewing deck of Skyline Tower, 500 feet above street level. The view was spectacular. On the way down Shirley talked the elevator operator into stopping at the restaurant on the 50th floor. After looking around, she booked a dinner reservation with a window table for the evening following our return from the wedding in Ithaca.

We departed for Ithaca and took our time getting there. We made many stops to photograph the innumerable signs displaying our granddaughter Seneca's name. We took "Seneca" photos of lakes, villages, orchards, a river, streets, etc. Approaching Ithaca, we travelled down the western shore of Lake Cayuga. My graduate advisor, Dr. Baldwin, received his doctorate from Cornell, and in his classes he would sometimes recite poems related to the University and Lake Cayuga. I was looking forward to touring the geology department to see where Dr. Baldwin had matriculated. Arriving in Ithaca, we checked into the Statler Hotel, located on campus a few blocks from the Chapel where the wedding was to be held. The reception following the wedding would be at the Statler.

The day of the wedding Shirley and I went on a walking tour of the campus. We took a trail down to the footbridge that crosses Fall Creek. From the bridge we had a great view of Beebe Lake, an impoundment on Fall Creek. Lake Beebe is a popular tourist attraction, and it is also a locality where young college lovers walk with their sweethearts. It is said that if a couple walks with hands held together the entire length of the pathway around Beebe Lake they will someday wed. I could only wonder how many young coeds had been seduced by this bit of folk lore.

After our trip along Fall Creek, we walked over to Schoellkopf Stadium where Taran had come to play football a number of years ago. I could just visualize him leading the Big Green onto the field as a team captain. Taran also came to this stadium again as a radio color commentator for Dartmouth Football so his presence here covered several years. Interestingly enough, Schoellkopf Field was the only Ivy League stadium we never visited while Taran was a member of the Dartmouth football team. Shirley said walking the field gave her goose bumps, as she could well imagine what the thrill must have been for Taran when he led the team onto the turf in this beautiful stadium.

The Knecht wedding was nice, as weddings usually are, and we had fun at the reception. We danced a little, drank moderately, and slipped off before the rowdies took over. Peter and Renata unexpectedly treated us like celebrities. Their generosity was impressive, given that their participation in the wedding and reception left them precious little free time.

We returned to Niagara Falls, Ontario and checked back into the Marriott, only this time we moved up from the 12th floor to the 15th floor. We had the same spectacular view. Our evening dinner at the Skyline Tower with its rotating restaurant on the 50th floor could not have been any better. From our table we saw a fireworks show at 10:00 p.m. We both believed that the show might have been even better seen from our hotel room.

Peter and Renata took us on a tour of the Niagara area the

following morning. They had both lived in the village of Niagara Falls, and Renata had once been a professional tour guide in the area, so the day spent with the Knechts was quite special. We made a stop at "The Whirlpool", a powerful display of moving water in the Niagara River a few miles below Niagara Falls. Here, the river makes a right angle turn as it flows through a narrow gap. The river is over 130 feet deep. The downstream movement of this enormous volume of water prohibits the swirling water from flowing back across the main current. This creates a volume problem which induces the swirling water to form a vortex that passes beneath the main current on its way downstream. This is one incredible sight. We were told that one goofball tried to swim across The Whirlpool. He went down like a mayfly nymph slurped by a feeding trout. The guy was probably a Darwin award nominee, if not the winner.

After we had spent most of the day with the Knechts, Shirley and I opted to take a ride on the *Maid of the Mist*. This boat takes tourists up the river to the very edge of Niagara Falls. The roar of the water and the encompassing mist at the Falls is simply mind boggling. Shirley and I had donned *Maid* rain slickers. There was considerable squealing and yelling when we reached the Falls. Most of the women were running for cover, not wanting to avoid become wet heads. Shirley was wrapped up tightly and stood at the rail facing the stinging mist. After arriving back at the boat landing, she untied her rain bonnet, shook her head, and walked off looking like she had just come out of the beauty salon. I was highly pleased with this outcome as I would have been in deep trouble had she departed the boat with a wet head.

We never returned to Niagara Falls but we had a remarkably memorable trip. We had visited the Peller Winery and had dinner there while looking down on vineyards. We visited the quaint town of Niagara on the Lake and toured the Queenston Hill Battle Ground (War of 1812). We even found time to lose a few quid at a Canadian casino. It was a grand trip. The time spent around Niagara Falls was the highlight of the entire journey. When we returned to The Woodlands, we had only 10 days to get ready for our next trip. We were perhaps moving too fast, what with one trip in retirement following right on the heels of another.

West Coast Trip
San Jose, California to Vancouver Island, Canada and Back

On June 17, 2004 we flew to San Jose and rented a car for what would be a 31-day, 3,242 mile road trip along the shore of the Pacific Ocean. Our west coast trip began and ended in San Jose where we spent time with our son Tobin and his family. At that time Tobin's family included only his wife Ha and their 3-year-old daughter Seneca. Tobin and Ha treated us like royalty, even giving up their master bedroom for us.

Soon after our arrival in San Jose granddaughter Seneca and her dance troupe gave us a recital that was the highlight of our stay. Infinitely charming in her bright dress and black tap shoes, we were very proud of her when she walked onto the stage and sashayed her dress back and forth like a pro. When she shrugged her shoulders, we wanted to rush on stage and hug her. She was a most talented performer, and her performance was far above the other dancers, many of whom chose to not dance at all. At three years old and in an auditorium full of unknown people, I probably wouldn't have danced either.

We had an enjoyable Father's Day in Los Gatos, a sleepy small town in the foothills of the Santa Cruz Mountains. Considered to be part of Silicon Valley, the number of prosperous residents made it one of the 30 wealthiest cities in the United States. We sat on benches in Vasona Park, located near town center, and watched Senny play with other children. Shirley found time to visit the many shops that help give the village its unique character. Our son Taran called to wish me a happy Father's Day while we were seated at one of the town's upscale restaurants.

During our five day stay in San Jose we spent most of our time sampling the life led by Tobin and his family. We watched Senny swim in a nearby public pool, play in an expansive park across the street from the Lent home on Potrero Drive, attended a birthday party for one of Seneca's young friends, played cards, and ate many of the exceptional meals Ha prepares, no matter what the occasion.

After leaving San Jose, we drove north through San Francisco and across the Golden Gate Bridge. We enjoyed both the oceanic and bay vistas as we drove across the bridge, but we were surprised by the number of tourists walking along the Bridge's pedestrian pathway.

Once across the bridge, rather than continuing north on Highway 1, we took a tortuous secondary road over the mountains to Muir Beach. We had chosen this route so we could visit Muir Woods National Monument. Although the Monument provided our first opportunity to see a grove of majestic redwoods, the monument is small (less than 500 acres) and the magnificence of the trees pales in comparison to the redwood groves we saw further up the coast in the Avenue of the Giants.

When we finally came down from the mountains, we turned north on Highway 1, the coastal highway. As we drove along the coast, we never had a good view of the ocean. Signs identified side roads to state parks and beaches, but there were no ocean views from the main road. We stopped in Point Reyes for lunch and concluded that the village must be a very popular destination for San Francisco yuppies.

By the time we finally arrived at Bodega Bay we were very disappointed, having spent extra hours driving up Highway 1 without seeing anything memorable or scenic. On the return trip down the coast, we would leave Highway one at Bodega Bay and take an alternate route to Highway 101 via the road to Petaluma. This route would save us an hour and a half of travel time and we would not miss anything 'coastal'.

Although Route 1 up the coast to Bodega Bay was a disappointment, the journey on Highway 1 north of Bodega Bay more than made up for this disappointment. Shirley and I had seen world class coastlines around the world (e.g., Ireland, Scotland, Nova Scotia, Oregon, etc.), but nothing compares to that stretch of coast from Bodega Bay to Point Arena. The rocky headlands, sea stacks, isolated beaches, mountain side vistas, and beautiful harbors/coves are something to behold. There are state parks, county parks, and an incredible number of beaches accessible either by driving down a short access road or by parking at a pull-off along the main highway. We observed wonderful shoreline vistas both on our way up the coast and then on our return trip back down it. For over 40 miles we saw so much spectacular scenery we had trouble choosing where to stop next. I actually felt guilty since we drove past a number of fantastic vistas without pulling into a designated pull-out, but we did not have the time to stop every five minutes.

On the stretch of road, about halfway, between Bodega Bay and Point Arena is a resort, *Sea Ranch Lodge*. It is not too far north of the service station/store at Stewarts Point. We glanced at Sea Ranch as we drove north, but we were not looking for a place to stay that early in the day, so we did not stop. Earlier in the day Shirley had seen another inn shortly before we passed Sea Ranch, and she was disappointed that we did not turn into that inn, *Timber Cove Resort*, to take a look. She said we would stop there on the way back down the coast and check it out. We could not have known we would drive miles late at night on our return trip trying to find Timber Cove Resort. I will write further of Sea Ranch and Timber Cove when I describe our return trip to San Jose.

We made it north to Mendocino, California at the end of our first day of travel after leaving Tobin and his family in San Jose. Mendocino is a small coastal village located on a headland surrounded on three sides by the Pacific Ocean. The village has a number of interesting and historic landmarks, several of which we took the time to visit. We were up early in the morning to get an early start on the long trip north to Bandon, Oregon.

Just north of Rockport, California coastal Highway 1 leaves the coast and crosses a mountainous area. The road then terminates at an intersection with Highway 101. The 31-mile stretch of Highway 101 north of the intersection is a world-famous scenic drive through a forest of virgin redwood trees, almost all of which are giants. A segment of the former Highway 101 (now Highway 254) runs parallel to 101 and this stretch of road is called "The Avenue of the Giants". We were awed by the size and number of trees we saw. Humboldt Redwoods State Park offers close up views of giant redwoods not seen anywhere else in the California redwood belt. We made many stops to look at the groves of the super trees, and we took time to walk along several pathways through the fern floored forest.

After leaving the redwoods, we stopped in Eureka, California for lunch at the Woodley Island Marina. Word of the restaurant's reputation for consistently turning out great food reached us through several locals who suggested we take the time to eat there. Shirley ordered a seafood stew (Cioppino) that she said then, and forever after, was the best she had ever eaten. The meal, and Shirley's happiness, made the stop one of the highlights of our trip.

We were not able to observe much of the Pacific Ocean coastline until we reached Brookings, Oregon. From Brookings north to Port Orford we once again were treated to incredible oceanic vistas. The southwestern Oregon coastal views in this stretch are as good as those anywhere.

After we left Port Orford we came to Sixes, a one-store settlement on the Sixes River. While at the University of Oregon I had spent four summers mapping the geology in the Sixes River drainage area in Curry County. This field work was part of the research conducted for my doctoral dissertation. During those summers I made my home in a one room cabin on a terrace above the Sixes River. Shirley and I had spent several weekends in the cabin, including one weekend during our 1968 honeymoon. We drove up the river and hiked down the narrow road (now overgrown and really just a path) to the cabin site. The cabin was gone and there was no evidence that it or the adjacent outhouse had ever been there. I was sentimental about the missing cabin, but I understood why the building had been removed. The owner had had a gold mining claim on the site and shortly before he died, he asked that the claim be forfeited and the cabin torn down. He wanted the site to revert back to the primal condition it had once been. On the hike back up to our car Shirley and I encountered a mother black bear and her cub who ran past our car and up a hill. During my time in the area, I had seen cougars, bears, deer, and many blue grouse, but I had never observed a bear near my cabin. The area had indeed reverted back to that time before human interference.

We left the Sixes area and traveled north to Reedsport where we turned inland and traveled east along the scenic Umpqua River. The river in the canyon is deep, green, and slow moving. The canyon walls are comprised of thick sandstone strata that give the appearance of having been built by a deity, one layer at a time.

We spent the evening in Drain with our long-time good friends, Paul and Sharon Hess. We had a BBQ dinner, a most welcome treat. It was one of the few meals going north that did not include seafood. We had started our trip in San Jose with the intention of eating nothing but seafood until we got to Tofino on the northern tip of Vancouver Island, British Colombia. By the time we made it to Canada and were ready to head back down the coast, we were determined to eat anything but seafood for the remainder of our trip. Too much of a good thing sometimes does not make it a good thing.

Our inland diversion did not end in Drain. After leaving Paul and Sharon, we drove over the Cascade Mountains to our hometown of Prineville where we visited Shirley's mother Marie, my mother Mabel, and my brother Steve and his family. We also enjoyed cookouts with several of our longtime elementary and high school friends. We attended the Crooked River Roundup (June 25-27), a famous (?) rodeo, that featured Shirley's longtime close friends, the Houston girls, as Grand Marshals. Of course, the 'Houston' girls are not now Houston, they have long since been married and are Jean Edwards, Molly Kee, and Carol Dunaway. But to us they still remained and always will be 'the Houston' girls.

We left Prineville early in the morning on July 4th and arrived in Port Angeles, Washington around 6:00 p.m. after, as the Pearl was wont to do, making numerous stops along the way. Not counting stops for potty breaks, our first significant stop was at the Wildwood Recreational Site located along the Salmon River near the village of Welches, Oregon. Wildwood has to be the single best rest/picnic area in the United States. There are many trails, all marked with informative wooden and metal placards. There is a wetlands boardwalk that is accessible by crossing a foot bridge over the Salmon River followed by a short walk through the rainforest. This loop ends back at the Salmon River and the footbridge. There is also a Cascade Streamwatch Interpretive area where children and adults can learn all about salmon migration. An underground bunker with a glass window offers a view of migrating salmon and aquatic life as it is in both the stream and along its bottom. I think it must have taken more than government involvement to make this recreational site the wonderfully informative place it is.

In Portland we stopped at Salty's Restaurant on the south bank of the Colombia River, not far from the Portland Airport. Salty's is a Lent family favorite and it has been so for many years. We were blessed with a bright and sunny day, and our window table allowed us to look down on a variety of sail and sport fishing boats. Midway across the river was Government Island where we saw hundreds of people who had arrived there via motorboats. It appeared most of those on the sandy beach had tossed out big blankets. They also appeared to have doffed their clothes. I saw considerable pink and I could only hope those we saw were decent.

Leaving Oregon, we took Interstate 5 to Olympia and then Highway 101 up the east side of the Olympic Peninsula on our way to Port Angeles. The drive north was uneventful until we entered the Skokomish Indian Reservation where we saw firework stands, all manned by Indians, every half mile and seemingly forever. *Get your low-cost fireworks here. Absolutely the lowest cost. Last chance to buy fireworks.* These were just a few of the signs we saw. Then when we entered the Olympic National Forest, we immediately encountered innumerable signs stating, *Absolutely no fireworks.* I found considerable humor in that whole scenario.

We arrived in Port Angeles early in the evening and checked into our room which looked out on a golf course and Hurricane

Ridge in the Olympic Mountain Range. We asked the young lady at the desk if she could recommend a restaurant where the July 4th fireworks might best be viewed. She said there was a good restaurant at the Port Angeles Marina but that there would be no parking. She suggested we walk to town as that is what she would do if she were us. How far might that be we asked. "A little over two miles" was her retort. Are you kidding me?!*? I was sixty-two years old at the time and was not about to walk two miles there and two miles back just to have dinner and watch a few fireworks.

Shirley, being Shirley, got on the phone to the restaurant and discovered they had an attendant working traffic and that we could park our car at the entrance to the restaurant. And that is what we did. We drove downtown, parked, had a fine meal, and then walked out on the terrace in time to see a 30-minute fireworks show. During our drive back to the motel it occurred to me that the ditz who suggested we walk two miles to town and then two miles back was most likely was near the bottom of her high school class.

It was late in the evening by the time we got back to our room. We had put in the longest day of our west coast journey. I asked the Pearl to get up early the next morning as our ferry, the M.V. Coho, was to leave Port Angeles bound for Victoria on Vancouver Island around 10:30 a.m. The M.V. Coho had the capacity to transport approximately 125 cars and 750 passengers, but it did not accept reservations. Passage was first come first served. We arrived at the dock early enough to be third in line for the mid-morning departure, and Shirley was not happy she had gotten up early just so we could be third in line.

It took about an hour and twenty minutes to cross the Strait of Juan de Fuca on calm sea and under a blue sky. Just the way I like it. As we were approaching Victoria Harbor the captain asked all drivers and their passengers to report to their cars. When I got to the car, a side door on the ferry opened and it was obvious that our car would be one of the first to offload. I had gone straight to our car. Shirley wanted to make one last stop at the water closet. I waited and waited for Shirley. The ferry moved into the dock, the barrier was about to be removed, and the 125 cars and trucks would soon begin offloading. I was beside myself and had come to the conclusion that I would have to offload and then park and search for Shirley before going through immigration and customs. At the last possible second, Shirley opened the door and slid into the car. She had been on deck watching us enter the Inner Harbor. She said the view was fantastic. No wonder men die young and women live into their 90s.

We offloaded and quickly cleared immigration. We drove a short distance, and after making two left turns, and we were at the front entrance to the magnificent Fairmont Empress Hotel, located at the head of the Inner Harbor facing the marina and harbor. There are flowerpots everywhere and the building is large and very ornate (Victorian to be sure). We had made reservations for a deluxe harbor suite on an upper-level floor. When we arrived Shirley asked, and received permission, to see the room we had reserved. The desk clerk also gave the bell boy who escorted Shirley several other keys so she could look at alternate rooms. I remained in our original room, guarding the trolley full of luggage while Shirley and the bell boy made a tour of the rooms on the upper floors. Pretty soon, back came the bell boys saying that the perfect room had been found on a higher floor. The luggage and I moved to another room. I did not let on as how I had used the loo.

Once we checked in and settled in our room, Shirley was anxious go out amongst them. There are shops, restaurants, tea rooms, and things to see everywhere in Victoria. I was looking forward to a short nap and was not at all interested in pounding the cobbled streets. So I took my nap and Shirley went for High Tea at the Empress and followed that up with a shopping trip.

When Shirley returned from her day on the town, she was all bubbly as she usually was. We talked about her day and made plans for dinner. When one is in a new city the choices are almost mind boggling and so it was in Victoria. Our walk around the Inner Harbor to The Blue Crab, a restaurant located along the outer harbor, was just what I needed. The fresh air and spectacular scenery put a bounce in my step. Dinner was great and we reaffirmed our decision to eat mostly seafood as we travelled north along the Pacific Coast.

On the way back to the Empress, Shirley stopped to watch several entertainers perform on the harbor walkway. In England we called these guys 'buskers'. I was uncomfortable in the large crowd, so I opted to walk across the street and to wait for Shirley at the Terrace, the outdoor cocktail lounge on the ground floor of the Empress Hotel. Shirley soon joined me for an after-dinner drink. She chose to have Grand Marnier which turned out to be an absolute set up for the waiter. He immediately launched into his Grand Marnier spiel. He offered Madame a sampling from the Grand Marnier Flight Collection. This collection consisted of three different vintages, the oldest of which was aged 100 years. I checked my billfold. Shirley opted for the sampling and the show began. The orange flavored cognac was poured, swirled, heated, and aerated for nearly an hour. In the end we were given an ornate paper certificate commemorating Shirley's sampling. We had the waiter date and sign the certificate. It is amazing how much can be made of an order for a "Grand Marnier". Because my Scotch and water had been consumed almost at the onset, I had to settle for the show and the beautiful sunset - and of course, a happy wife.

We awoke early on July 6, our anniversary. We had to make it up to the northern tip Vancouver Island and the Wickaninnish Inn near the town of Tofino where we had dinner reservations for 6:00 p.m. One might wonder why we were in such a rush to reach the Wickaninnish Inn on our anniversary. Or for that matter, why we were so Hell bent on going to Vancouver Island. It all started when Shirley read in the Houston Chronicle that Wickaninnish Inn near Tofino was one of the 10 most romantic places in North America and she became enamored with the thought there was no more romantic place than the Inn to celebrate our 36th wedding anniversary.

Once we had checked out and were in the car, I was hot to get to Cobble Hill where our friends Mike and Donna Webb lived. Cobble Hill is about a 45-minute drive north of Vancouver. We planned to have a short visit with the Webbs on the way north, then a more leisurely four day stay with them on our return trip down the Island. I thought it would be nice to at least say hello as we drove by their beautiful hillside home overlooking the Arbudas Ridge Golf Course. My travel plans for the day would allow us to reach the Wickaninnish Inn in time for us to check in and to dress for our anniversary dinner.

My plans for the day collapsed when the sweet voice next to me said, "We just have to tour Craigdarroch Castle." This ornate residence, located on 27 acres just off of Fort Street in Vancouver, was built by a coal baron. Completed in 1889, shortly after the baron's death, the residence was home to Mrs. Robert Dunsmuir, the widow who enjoyed all the fruits of Robert's labors. The Castle is located on a hilltop overlooking Victoria and the rooms have all been restored to the period in which it was completed. There are 39 rooms and 18 fireplaces. Makes one wonder who did not get the heat, eh? Stained glass decorates the windows and the doors. The master stairway is carved from solid oak. We said goodbye to Craigdarroch Castle. Our visit with the Webbs was even shorter than I had planned. After refreshments on their patio, we were off.

Our journey north and west towards Tofino took us through some very scenic terrain. Shortly after we turned west onto Highway 4, we followed a river through an Indian reservation. Numerous roadsides stands had fresh and smoked salmon for sale, and it was easy to see where the vendors got their salmon. The Native Americans had nets across the river every 60-70 yards. Anything moving in the river faced incredible odds against survival. So much for the natives being caretakers of the environment. Oh, and one other thing. The road across the reservation lands was narrow and pock marked. Once off the reservation the road was wide and paved with fresh black top.

Highway 4 takes a traveler through the Sproat Lake Provincial Park, alongside Lake Kennedy, and then through the McKenzie Mountains. The aura of wilderness is everywhere. The only exception is the highway and the cars along it. Beyond the roadway the land belongs to the predators and foragers.

When we finally descended out of the mountains, we got our first view of the Pacific Ocean. After we turned north towards Tofino, we were gobsmacked by the number of young hitchhikers we saw along the road, many of whom were young girls carrying sleeping bags. There were also a number of Indians who first stuck up their thumb, and then a finger as we motored past them. Even older Indians were hitchhiking and some of these appeared to be a husband and his wife (minimally at least a man and a woman). Traffic moved differently as well. We occasionally passed a number of cars weaving back and forth down the road at very low speeds. Almost invariably these drivers were very short. At first, I suspected the local population might include a band of pigmies. The average driver on the road was remarkable as he/she seemed to be traveling right at the speed limit. This was a first for us. We had to be the only Texans on the road.

When we finally arrived at the Wickaninnish Inn, we were greeted by staff who you would have thought we had known us all our lives. "Welcome Mr. and Mrs. Lent, we have been expecting you." And "We are so glad to have you with us Mr. and Mrs. Lent". We checked into our room on the second floor. We were here to celebrate our 36th wedding anniversary, and we were staying in room 36. Our view was through tall fir and spruce trees to Chesterman Beach, a beautiful unspoiled stretch of sand that has a tombolo at one end. I had read of tombolos during my geologic studies but had never seen one. A tombolo is a sand spit that connects a beach to an offshore island.

Room 36 had big glass windows providing expansive views from soft sofas in the bedroom. There was a fireplace and candles in their holders everywhere. The holders were tubes bored into granite cobbles. A rack holding a wide selection of romantic CDs was available to set the mood. Available for bathing were a double soaker bathtub and a very large rock-floored shower. Two heavy duty yellow rain jackets hung in the closet as did two terry cloth robes. Of course, these robes never fit me, but I wore one anyway. A sliding door opened onto a terrace located off to the side of the bedroom suite. Wood paneled walls separated the guest terraces from each other and provided a modicum of privacy. There were two large redwood chairs on the deck. The view was spectacular, and the noise mostly came from the wind blowing through the boughs of the trees, and from the waves pounding the beach and nearby headlands. A pair of binoculars were available for viewing the ocean.

A wide assortment of books describing the fauna and flora of the northwest were on a bookshelf. There was also a diary for those guests who were staying, or had stayed, in room 36. I read many of the diary entries and was moved by what had been written.

We dressed and went to dinner at the Pointe Restaurant which is a circular room looking out onto rocky headlands. Shirley asked for a table that would also give us the best view of the sunset. Shirley never settled for the ordinary.

Dinner was a drawn-out affair. The waiter greeted us with complimentary Champagne. We ordered wine and then scallops and crab cakes for appetizers. Our main dish was the restaurants signature dish, a seafood stew. The stew was presented in a deep clam-shaped bowl and contained generous portions of crab, clams, scallops, and cod. A decorative dessert and coffees finished off the meal.

The Pointe Restaurant was filled with patrons who were celebrating anniversaries, on a honeymoon, or were into a deep relationship. It was easy to pick out the honeymooners and the new lovers. There was a lot of back rubbing, touching, etc. The rest of us affectionately looked at each other and chatted; feeling good about the experience and our lives. I could not imagine anyone coming this far north, spending the kind of money it takes to be here, experiencing the ambience of the restaurant and the scenic setting, then ruining it all by being in a sour mood. I was sure it might occasionally happen, but only to people who had little or no romance in their lives. Shirley and I had a wonderful evening.

On Wednesday morning, July 7th, we drove into Tofino to explore the village and harbor. Tofino is a fishing and tourist village, and it is not that impressive. The population, near 2,000, contains a number of artisans who have chosen this secluded area to live and work. From Tofino one can view wilderness that encroaches upon both the bay and the village. One local legend, Cougar Annie, lived in the nearby wilderness where she killed 18 cougars, and carved out magnificent gardens. When she died, the gardens became a tourist attraction. She must have been one tough old lady.

The concierge at the Inn made reservations for us to go whale watching out of nearby Ucluelet. Our launch time was at 2:30 p.m. After meeting Captain Lance at the dock, we boarded our Aquamarine Adventure Zodiac, the *Sun Dancer*, a high-powered rubber boat with a very strong metallic bottom. There were seats for 12, but our excursion was a small one, only Shirley, me, and three visitors from The Netherlands. Suited up in bright red Mustang floatation suits, the five of us saw 9 different whales, numerous bald eagles, several colonies of sea lions, many seals, and scenery unmatched anywhere. Except for one incident, we had a super outing.

The *Sun Dancer* took us out to the Pacific Rim National Park in Barkley Sound where we spent the afternoon exploring the waters between the Broken Islands, over 100 individual islands, each as scenic as can be. The waves were heavy, and it was a relief anytime we could tuck in behind one of the islands. Many of the islands have populations of black tailed deer that braved the oceanic waters to escape from wolf packs on the mainland. I recognized what must have been the deer dilemma: stay in forest-covered mainland and be predated by wolves, or swim to an island and hope that the Orcas are busy with the seals. Not a nice choice.

During our visit to Tofino the staff at the Indian Gallery, "The House of Himwitsa", mentioned that the Indians who died on the offshore islands were tied to trees so their spirits could more easily ascend to the heavens. When we asked Captain Lance about this practice, he said it was a bunch of malarkey. He had once asked an Indian chief about the validity of the practice, and the chief had said, "There is very little soil on those rocky islands. You would be crazy to try to bury someone there. Better to tie them to a tree."

I took some very good photos, many of Shirley, while we were in the Zodiac. After a marvelous afternoon, we began our trip back to the Ucluelet Harbor.

Now for the incident. The Zodiac was running full throttle when it crested a massive rogue wave and fell into an incredibly deep trough. All of us were thrown about 10 feet into the air. When we landed back on the Zodiac, occupants were scattered everywhere. I found myself draped over the rubber pontoon with my nose six inches from the water. I had momentarily thought I might be going overboard. When I looked back at Shirley, she was just beginning to come back to her senses after having passed out. She was obviously in a lot of pain. I thought she had broken her back or at least some ribs. The captain let the boat drift for about 15-20 minutes while we tried to help Shirley return to breathing normally. We eventually determined she had twisted her back or traumatized her spine. There was no indication of broken bones. The next 20 miles back to the harbor were tough on Shirley. Every bounce on a wave caused her intense pain. The Zodiac had slowed down, but the waves were still very high, especially after we left the lee side of the Broken Islands.

At the conclusion of our 3 1/2-hour trip we docked and got Shirley's out of her survival suite. This was not an easy task. We left Ucluelet Harbor and drove back to Wickaninnish Inn where we had signed up for a clam bake on the beach. Shirley said she wanted to give it a try. We found ourselves a large driftwood log and the staff brought us a wicker basket filled with shucked crab legs and the fixings for our dinner. There were probably 20 other nearby couples who dined on their own log. The experience, as nice as it could have been, was dampened by Shirley's back injury.

The next morning, July 8, Shirley was still in a great deal of pain. For relief, she went to the Inn's Cedar Spa where she was massaged until she was raw. The steam and nimble fingers (male, I might add) helped a lot. I was not too pleased to learn that Shirley had told the male attendant that, "it must be great to make so many women happy." I could only wonder if maybe she had signed up for the full body massage. We had previously scheduled a late morning "bear watch". During low tide, the Zodiac excursions transport guests to remote beaches where the red suited occupants wait for bears to come to the

Retirement Travels and Adventures

FIGURE 25. BOB AND SHIRLEY LENT CELEBRATING THEIR 36TH WEDDING ANNIVERSARY AT THE ROMANTIC WICKANINNISH INN NEAR TOFINO, BRITISH COLUMBIA

FIGURE 26. SHIRLEY LENT WHALE WATCHING IN BARKLEY SOUND NEAR UCLUELET, VANCOUVER ISLAND, CANADA

beaches and turn over boulders and small rocks looking for crab and small clams. I discretely cancelled our reservation. The marriage was perserved.

We checked out of the Wickaninnish Inn and returned to Cobble Hill where the Webbs had planned dinner for us. The return trip to the east coast of Vancouver Island was a repeat of the one coming west except that as we rounded a bend in the highway near Kennedy Lake, a large black bear sauntered out onto the road. He took one look at our car and then shuffled off into the bush. This just underscored my previous comment that civilization ends at the pavement edge.

We arrived at the Webb's lovely home to find several bottles of their home-made wine ready to be consumed while Mike prepared plank baked salmon on the grill. After dinner we sat on the veranda and watched the sun go down and dozens of deer come out. The presence of so many deer led me to think we must be some distance from the nearest Indian reservation.

After a relaxing evening we arose and began a day that was hectic and filled with memorable excursions. We stopped first to tour the magnificent Butchart Gardens north of Victoria. These gardens are incredible and are as beautiful as you will find anywhere. The setting in which the gardens are planted makes the experience even more remarkable. The gardens were created after Robert Butchart made his fortune extracting and processing limestone for his nearby cement plant. When the limestone excavation reached its economic limit, his wife Jennie Butchart stepped in and used Robert's money and personnel from the cement plant to transform the quarry into breathtaking gardens. The deep pits became decorative lakes, the centerpiece of which is the Sunken Garden. A walk through Butchart takes you up and down pathways and through a wide range of plants and gardens. In addition to the Sunken Garden there are Japanese, Italian, and Rose Gardens. A fireworks show ends each day in July and August.

More than a million people per year visit Butchart Gardens. Despite the distracting presence of so many visitors, a visit to the Gardens is still a must for anyone visiting Victoria. The vegetation is so planted as to give a flower show throughout the entire year.

On our return trip back to Cobble Hill, we stopped for a light lunch at the Malahat Mountain Inn. From our table on the patio the view as we looked down on Malahat Bay some 800-1,000 feet below us took our breath away. Across the Bay was a forested and grass covered mountain ridge. We found it hard to break the spell and abandon the incredible scenery.

It was good that we had a very light lunch. Mike and Donna had made dinner reservations for a few hours after we had returned from our trip to the Butchart Gardens.

We took a scenic drive to the Vinoteca Restaurant, a former residence located in the center of a vineyard near the town of Duncan. We celebrated the news that Tobin and Ha were going to make us grandparents for the second time with Champagne. After the Champagne, we sampled the winery's white wine, wine that had come from the grapes on vines visible out the window near our table. Our meal was delicious. Because we were now on our way back down the Pacific Coast, we chose lamb shanks.

We split forces on our last day with the Webbs. The ladies went to Victoria for shopping and traditional English high tea at the Windsor Tea Room. Shirley was in her element. Mike and Bob hit the Arbudas Ridge Golf Course. My game was all over the place, but Mike recorded an 85, one of his best rounds ever.

In the evening, the Webbs drove us across a mountain range to a beautiful harbor on the shore of Genoa Bay. The drive would have been enough by itself, but when we finally came out of the forest we might have been in a postcard. We had dinner at the Cafe Genoa Bay. Our table looked out through an open door onto the marina. The wine and our meals were on a par with the scenery. After dinner we went out on the dock and listened to live entertainment provided by a very good (Shirley's assessment) local band. The audience crowding the docks consisted of locals, diners, and those who were spending the night in their anchored boats. What a memorable evening it was. The experience alone was probably worth the trip to

Vancouver Island.

The next morning, Sunday, the Webbs saw us off after a breakfast of fruit and breads. Each day we were with Mike and Donna we had a good breakfast, always healthy. Donna mentioned she had to have breakfast wherever she went. She then told us of a visit she and Mike had with two of our mutual friends whose only breakfast was coffee. No other food was offered or served. The two couples putzed around the house all morning and then went out to lunch. The host ordered a dozen raw oysters. Donna does not like oysters on the half shell and said she would pass on the appetizer. The host insisted that Donna eat her three very special oysters. Out of courtesy to her host, Donna consumed the oysters, the first nourishment she had that day. Donna now travels with a power bar to provide nourishment in the morning if nothing else is forthcoming.

After exchanging hugs, kisses, and handshakes with the Webbs on Tuesday, we left for Victoria and the dock of the M.V. Coho. If we missed the 2:30 sailing the next one would not be until 7:00 in the evening, and the later departure would make it difficult for us to be in San Jose by Thursday evening. We need not have worried. When we arrived at the dock we were once again the third car in line for boarding. After purchasing our portage ticket, we toured the nearby Pacific Undersea Gardens and the Royal British Colombia Museum. This was the first weekend for the museum's "Eternal Egypt" exhibit and the crowds were massive, even early in the day. After we left the museum, we walked down the street to the Terrace Restaurant at the Grand Pacific Hotel. Our fine lunch was made more memorable by our Chinese waitress. When we spoke a little Chinese, she opened up and did not want to leave our table. Among other things, she told us love had brought her from Hong Kong to Victoria. After a long and drawn-out lunch, we said *zaijian* and walked back to the ferry.

Despite once again being third in line at the loading pen, we were amongst the last cars to board. The first car in line had a dead battery and required a jump start by dock personnel, but we did make it onboard and Shirley was by my side when we drove off the ferry in Port Angeles, Washington. We still had over a thousand miles of adventures and travel ahead of us before we arrived in San Jose at the Tobin Lent household.

When we came off the ferry in Port Angeles, we found ourselves in a long line of cars waiting to clear immigration and customs. I do not know how difficult clearing customs was for other cars, but the official whom we dealt with looked at our passports and then waved us on. I do not think he even considered making a detailed search of our car. We had so many pieces of luggage in the trunk and back seat that he would have been at work way past quitting time.

Leaving Port Angeles, we turned west onto Highway 101. It was our intent to reach Aberdeen, Washington at days end. It never happened. As we traveled west along the northern edge of the Olympic Peninsula, we came across a very large body of fresh water, Lake Crescent. On our roadmap the lake showed up as a bit of blue, but this sucker was 12-15 miles long, maybe longer. The drive was one of the more scenic drives we had during our trip, and we had many such drives.

Near the small town of Sappho two things happened. One, Highway 101 went from and east-west direction to north-south, and two, we left the National Forest. For the next 12 miles the roadside forest had been clear cut with no evidence of any effort or intent at reforestation. We suspected the lands were part of the Makah Indian Reservation. The roadside carnage between Sappho and Forks was in stark contrast to logging practices in Oregon and the rest of Washington where the forest is harvested away from the highways, leaving the roadside scenery looking like it is in its primordial state.

We decided to stop in Forks rather than to motor on to Aberdeen. It was already 6 p.m. and it would have been another three hours to Aberdeen. We checked in to the Olympic Suites Inn located along the banks of the Calawah River. When Shirley opened the window in our room, she scared off a rabbit and a deer that were on the lawn. We had become so accustomed to seeing bald eagles that we hardly took notice of those in the trees outside of our room.

Shirley and I did not remember Forks, Washington for the

wonderful room we had at the Olympic Suites. We remembered it for the meal we had at the Plaza Jalisco restaurant which we chose because we were headed south and were going to eat anything but seafood. So how far from seafood is Mexican cuisine!

The restaurant was packed with tourists and locals.

We were greeted at the door by the Mexican mother, seated at the table by the Mexican father (also the bus boy), and then handed our menus by a rather large raw-boned lady who had lavender comets over her eyebrows, a pierced metal object in her lower chin, and massive tattoos on both arms. She looked like she might be Greek, but my guess was that the Mexican genes got a little mismatched when mom and dad did their deed.

At a booth behind us was an extremely tall fellow, somewhere north of 7 feet, his wife, and their two very tall children. The guy was meek, but he still had enough spunk to tell his wife that they could not afford to dine out like this. Whereupon she immediately showed him who was calling the shots in the family (as if he needed to be reminded of same) by informing him that she could not fix a meal like this for the price the restaurant charged, and besides, there would be leftovers they would be able to take home. I later glanced over the back of our booth, and if there were leftovers, they had to be isolated grains of rice stuck to a spoonful of refried beans. I reached across the table and hugged sweet Shirley. Of course, she winced in pain from back injury and the affectionate embrace was dismissed.

Our meal, cooked by the lavender waitress' boyfriend, was tasty but the spices, well, they snuck up on me. When I rolled over in my sleep, I burped, and a flood of pure undiluted acid flowed up around the epiglottis and onto the tip of my tongue. I wanted to rush out into the courtyard to look for a limestone pebble; or anything carbonic that might dilute the acid in my stomach.

We took a turnoff on our southward journey that took us on a splendid 40-mile loop through the Quinault Rain Forest, along the north and south shores of Lake Quinault, and down a stretch of the Quinault River. What a splendid journey this turned out to be. As we drove east the forest closed in over us and it became quiet and still. When we stopped to take in the scenery, we saw a giant moss-covered tree that dwarfed all others. It stood like a majestic sentinel guarding all entry to the underworld beneath the forested canopy. As we drove on, we found the moss-covered trees and the fern mats on the forest floor to have a most special kind of beauty. Giant ferns came right up to the edge of the road. When we returned to Houston, we discovered the latest issue of the National Geographic Magazine had a spread on the Olympic Rain Forest, but the article and pictorial never really captured the beauty of what we had seen. The rain forest has to be seen to be appreciated. The area gets more than 180 inches of rain per year: it is no wonder that everything is green and covered with two to three feet of moss.

After turning back west on our loop, we traveled along the Quinault River. The amount of gravel we saw along the stream banks and islands gave every indication the Quinault must be a raging torrent when the monsoon rains come. The river looked like it might be an awesome trout stream. No one was fishing, but we later saw several brochures that extolled the trout, salmon, and steelhead fishery in the river.

When we arrived at the southern shore of Lake Quinault, we came upon the impressive Lake Quinault Lodge. We stopped for lunch and for a walk around the gardens and the indoor/outdoor facilities. I thought the Lodge would be a very fun place to vacation.

After we completed our loop through the rain forest, we turned south onto Highway 101. We drove through some towns where civic pride was sadly missing (e.g., Aberdeen) and some towns where civic pride flourished (e.g., South Bend). It is amazing how nice a town can look when the homes are kept up, the streets clear of clutter, and hanging flower plants provide a decorative flair.

By the time we reached Ilwaco Junction we realized that we would be spending the night in either Astoria or Seaside, Oregon. But first we took the road out to Cape Disappointment,

And There We Were

the impressive headland overlooking the mouth of the Columbia River. It was on this bluff that Lewis and Clark completed their epic journey of discovery. When we arrived at the overlook, we saw the mouth of the Columbia River at its very best. The sun was dropping low on the horizon; the sky was Carolina blue. The ocean was calm and there were many flocks of birds flying in a V-formation below our vantage point. We could see the impressive north and south jetties that guard the river's mouth. On the day we were there, it was hard to see why the Columbia River mouth is one of the more dangerous ports of entry along the west coast. The name "Cape Disappointment" is a testament to the many ships (historic and modern) that have foundered trying to cross the bars at the mouth of the Columbia in gale force winds with high water levels.

We spent the night at the Best Western Motel in Astoria. It was the pits, most unusual for a Best Western. There was no nearby restaurant, so we ate an apple and drank a glass of wine and went to bed. I retired expecting the next day to be a great travel day. I thought we might even make it to Crescent City, California. Covering a distance of 325 miles seemed like it would be a piece of cake. It never happened.

Having had essentially nothing to eat the previous evening we left Astoria early in the morning and, via Highway 101, drove 18 miles south down the Oregon coast to Seaside. From my high school days, I remembered Seaside as a dumpy tourist town. Crook County High School played Seaside at home in two basketball games during the 1957 and 1958 seasons. Each time we went there I found the town to be dreary, and 'dreary' was a pretty strong opinion for a kid who rarely got out of Prineville. My perspective on the town was about 45 years out of date.

When we arrived in Seaside, I asked Shirley if she would like to drive through the village. She gave an affirmative nod, and I thought, "Boy, she is not going to like what she sees." We discovered Seaside had re-invented itself about 20 years previously. The beach front hotels were impressive. The central mall was paved with bricks and framed in potted flowering plants. Almost all of the shops were of high quality. There were recreational opportunities everywhere. I didn't say anything, but when Shirley said, "This place is darling," I knew our travel timetable was in trouble. I had to agree, the new Seaside was 'darling'. We parked our car and commenced walking up and down the colorful streets, in and out of various stores, and finally into the Pig 'N' Pancake Restaurant. We had a great brunch.

When we returned to our car, I made a few disparaging remarks about the fact that it was 2:30 p.m. and we had only traveled 18 miles. I would have been better served keeping quiet. We drove on without a word said for the next 30 minutes. As we approached Tillamook, Oregon and the famous Creamery, there was a slight thaw in the air. We both agreed the Creamery would be a great place to tour. I dropped Shirley off at the entrance (her back was still giving her considerable pain) and went looking for a parking space. All the car spaces in the Creamery's large parking lot were taken, so I went to the area designated RV ONLY. It worked for me. I was driving Robert's vehicle (an RV).

Shirley and I enjoyed the tour of the Tillamook Creamery. We observed the entire cheese making process. From our elevated perch we looked down to a room where one young man was looking after 15 huge vats. Mostly he was just watching a number of dials. Looking down onto the workplace opposite of the vat room we saw approximately 100 people cutting, wrapping, and packaging cheese. Conveyor belts kept the people working at a feverish pace. I made a comment about the discrepancy in the workload, but I had to agree with one of our fellow tourists who said the man was likely a scientist and was deserving of the job he had. I thought it was kind of him to defend the geeky, long-haired custodian of the tanks. And after all, who was I to argue against scientists having easy jobs that pay well. We bought three blocks of cheese and some smoked salmon before retrieving my RV and turning back onto Highway 101. We had many miles to travel, or so I thought.

We had been on the road for about 20 miles when Shirley spotted a 'cute' coffee shop located in a small boutique shopping center. The owner was a friendly local gal who said she could not live anywhere else. She told us she and her husband had run the coffee shop for 7 years, and that this, the 7th year, had been the most trying one. We paid for the coffees, left a nice tip, and were back on the road. I hope the proprietors of the coffee shop make it. If not, they will surely have to live somewhere else.

We drove south with short stops at Depoe Bay, Yachats, and Winchester Bay. During our stop at Winchester Bay, we visited a shop where I knew, from previous stops, we could get tasty crab and smoked salmon. This time we found that the few pieces of smoked salmon in the display case were dry and not at all appealing. But next to the salmon, however, were stacks of smoked oysters on a stick. The oysters had been shucked, put on the skewers and smoked in a Texas like BBQ cooker where hickory chips and heat did their magic. We bought six skewers of the oysters and put them in our little traveling cooler. We ate the last of these oysters with Tobin and his family when we visited a beach south of San Francisco. They were delicious to the very last bite.

It was now late in the day and I wanted Shirley to see Shore Acres, Sunset Beach, and Cape Arago. These are State parks along the Oregon coast south of the small village of Charleston. Shirley and I had honeymooned in this area in 1968 so there were sentimental reasons to revisit the parks. We were about 1 and 1/2 hours from sunset. We never made it to Cape Arago, but we did see the beauty of Sunset Beach and Shore Acres. This stretch of the west coast is not the most spectacular, but it is beautiful. Shirley walked through the gardens at Shore Acres and I walked out onto the cliff edge to see the sedimentary strata that were tilted and facing into the oncoming waves. There was a powerful explosion of water when each wave hit the sandstone. The gardens Shirley toured had been magnificently restored by the "Friends of Shore Acres". Well done 'Friends'. The English Captain who, long ago, built Shore Acres for his young English bride would have been most pleased to see that the place still retains the beauty that was his inspiration.

Back on Highway 101 we raced south to Bandon, Oregon and the Sunset Hotel in hope that we might still see the remnants of a magnificent sunset. We were fortunate to be given a ground level room on the sea cliff, and Shirley saw a great end to a beautiful sunset. I hauled luggage back and forth and spent a few moments in between snapping photos of Shirley. Finally, I poured myself a drink and looked out onto the darkness that still carried with it the roar of the incoming oceanic waves.

We were up early in the morning. After traveling many miles less than we had planned the previous day, we had to have a good travel day. And we did! In fact, we drove so long and made so many miles it put us in jeopardy of finding a place to stay late in the evening. More about that later.

We crossed the Sixes River and continued south through the town of Port Orford. As we traveled along the scenic coastline near Humbug Mountain, I mentioned to Shirley that it was good that we were making this trip in good health, that such a trip would lose all of its joy if one of us was terminally ill. I asked Shirley if there was anything she would do differently if she knew she only had a limited time to live. Shirley, thinking for a minute, said she would not change anything. We drove for another 30 minutes and then Shirley said, "I would change one thing if I was terminally ill." I could not imagine what she might do differently. Maybe she would smother me with affection, or visit her children, mother, and grandchildren more often. Those were my guesses. And then she spoke, "I would eat lots of chocolate and I would eat it every day." Shirley's Aunt Mildred was waiting for us in Crescent City, California.

After we crossed the Oregon-California border we were bound for Crescent City where Shirley's Aunt Mildred, Virgil Hill's sister lived. Shirley had called ahead, and Aunt Mildred said we could visit her if we arrived between 12:30 and 2:00 p.m. Aunt Mildred was aged 81, so you would not think her schedule was so tight. Our schedule was also tight, so spending 45 minutes to an hour with Mildred would be just about right. We arrived in Crescent City a few minutes too early, after which we pulled into a Walmart to use their water closet and do a bit of frivolous shopping. I looked at my watch and told Shirley it was time to see Mildred.

And There We Were

When we pulled into Mildred's place, she came out to greet her 'favorite' niece. Mildred had come to England to see us when we were living in Ascot. She came with Marie Hill on the occasion of Shirley's 50th birthday. Mildred was a good British tourist until she discovered that when she exchanged money, like $200, she only got 120 pounds sterling. She insisted this was just not right and after that first exchange, she never had money to spend on anything. It was a good way to avoid paying for meals, etc. but the logic eluded me. Anyway, Mildred could be cantankerous. She could also be a sweetheart. You just never knew which side of the 50% line you were on.

When we sat down at the table to begin our visit you would have thought that a glass of water, a cup of coffee, or maybe a soft drink would have been offered. Nope. We sat at the kitchen table and were immediately into a conversation updating us on the work Mildred was doing with an older (?) patient who was afflicted with Alzheimer's disease. The details were not that interesting, but the clock was running and whatever Mildred wanted to talk about was what we would talk about. After a short while - perhaps she could see the pain on my face - the subject changed to family, and then to our travels.

Some remark triggered a discussion concerning the previous days travel. On Monday we had traveled 18 miles by 2:30 p.m. Now please remember that I too was involved in the decision to spend considerable time in Seaside, Oregon. I went on, with my own sense of humor, talking about the late start, the quick diversion into Seaside, and then stops for cheese and potty breaks. I was having a great time: we were not talking about changing the shorts and the linen for the Alzheimer patient. Only I was a bit out of sync with what Mildred would do with this teasing (done in jest). It seems that Aunt Mildred had a thing about how long it took Marie and Shirley to get ready in the morning. I had just offered up evidence supporting the family wide perception (fueled by Mildred) that the Hill ladies did not go anywhere unless they were clean, manicured, and well coiffured. Hey, I appreciate clean and coiffured. I really like clean.

After an hour on the dot, we bid adieu to Aunt Mildred and again headed south. No sooner than the car door had closed than I heard all about how I had played into Auntie's hand, and about how the rest of the family would soon hear how horrible it was for poor ol' Bob to travel with the Princess. What could I say? Sometimes I am a funny guy, sometimes not so much so. I would have been better served encouraging Mildred to describe the contents of the old man's soiled shorts.

When we were back on the road, Highway 101 south, we planned to reach Fort Bragg or somewhere beyond. After we had passed through the area of the old growth redwood trees, we turned off Highway 101 and onto the coastal Highway 1. Remaining on 101 would have made the return trip to San Jose much faster, but we had been so much in awe of the beautiful stretch of coastline south of Port Arena that we chose to try to make it to at least Fort Bragg.

After turning west onto Highway 1 we came to the place where we had experienced some road work delays on our way north. There was no work taking place now, but we could not help but reflect on an event that occurred when we were caught up in the traffic stoppage three weeks earlier. After some 20 minutes in stalled traffic, without a single car having moved in either direction, a girl (about 16 or 17) in the car ahead of us got out and headed into the deep green foliage along a nearby creek. She moved aside several clusters of stinging nettles and then quickly ran back to her car, wringing her hands. I remarked to Shirley that this girl looked like she really needed to go potty. We said nothing more of it. Then the delay reached 30 minutes and the girl got out of her car and walked around to the right-hand side of the vehicle. She opened the front and back doors before dropping her trousers and squatting. The doors perfectly shielded her from the waist up but her cute little bottom and her activity were perfectly visible out our car window. Shirley did not quite know what to make of this mild display of vulgarity, but my view on the situation was pretty much the same as I imagined the girl's to be. She was never going to see us again and if this was the only way she could relieve herself so be it. After waiting another 10 minutes, I began to think I might be emulating the young girl. But the traffic soon began to move, and we were back to our normal drive and potty routine.

We passed Fort Bragg. Shirley wanted to make it to the Timber Cove Resort she had seen on our trip north. Although we were uncertain how far south of Fort Bragg the resort was, we were sure we could make it there before dark. The sun was beginning to hang low on the horizon. It was 35 miles to Point Arena and another 10 to 15 miles further south to the coastal village of Gualala. It was my recollection that Timber Cove Resort was somewhere south of Gualala. We weren't sure how far south we would make it, but we knew we did not want to drive the beautiful coastline south of Point Arena in darkness.

We were treated to a most colorful sunset as we drove south toward Point Arena. Shirley watched the colorful panorama and describe it to me. On those occasions when the road made a hairpin turn, I got a glimpse of the magnificent view of Shirley had described. It became obvious as we raced on that the sun would set before we could find lodging. On one long straight stretch of the road Shirley said, "There it goes" and we found ourselves driving in dusk, that sometimes beautiful but unpredictable period between twilight and darkness.

We passed Point Arena. After seemingly endless miles we finally came to Gualal. Timber Cove Resort must be only a few miles down the road. At each bend I looked for lights or for a sign to the Resort. After traveling 10 miles I began to worry that we had missed Timber Cove and we might end up traveling all night to San Jose. I saw a light in the distance and thought that this must finally be the place. We slowed down and looked in the direction of the light. We could see it was some sort of inn, but it was too dark to see what it might be like. By then it was 9:30 p.m. Shirley suggested we drive another couple of miles down the road and if we didn't find another place, we could return and stay at the place we had just passed. We drove the two miles, saw nothing and then turned around.

The inn we returned to was The Sea Ranch Lodge. We hoped they had a vacancy. A sign at the registration desk indicated it was closed, but if we wanted to register we should go to the lounge and talk to the bar keeper. Happily, the good news was twofold: a room was available, and the bar was still open. The bad news was that the Lodge was a very expensive place to stay. We took a high-level suite overlooking the ocean and sea cliff - shrouded in darkness at the time of our arrival. I was so happy. We returned to the bar, ordered drinks, rejoicing in the knowledge we would not be traveling all night or stopping at some 'no tell motel'.

When we went out to bring in our luggage, we found a skunk milling around our car. He was a small fellow with a stinker he chose not to use. Because Shirley's back was still causing her considerable pain, I made a several trips to the upper level and room 9. We were anxious for morning to come so we might see the view we had.

When Shirley pulled back the drapes in the morning, we found ourselves looking out on a blue and calm ocean, and at a rugged coastal cliff with many rocky headlands. The flat sea terrace beyond the cliff edge was covered with grass and patches of scrub brush. An old barn, bleached gray by the sun, was near the cliff edge just north of the Lodge.

Sea Ranch Lodge was built on a ranch that began raising cattle in the late 1800s. Included in the 5,200 acres that comprise the present-day resort are some 10 miles of trails along the sea cliffs and several private coves and beaches accessible to guests. A number of the trails penetrate nearby forests. Notable headlands are Buhler's Point and Black Point. The cliffs at Sea Ranch are ideal for watching the annual migrations of gray whales who apparently venture close to the resort on their southern (October) and northern (April) migrations. We loved our stay at Sea Ranch Resort. We agreed to return again someday. On our next visit we would make sure we had sufficient time to watch what would most certainly be a grand sunset.

After checking out we drove south down Highway 1 and in a little over four miles came to the long sought-after Timber Cove Inn. Shirley asked that we stop so that she might check out the rooms on offer. With keys provided by the registration desk, she checked out several ocean view rooms and came back disappointed. The place had not been kept up very well and the rooms were not impressive. We had dodged a bullet when we turned around and went back to stay at Sea Ranch Lodge.

The Wickaninnish Inn was the best lodge we stayed at during our trip. The Sea Ranch Lodge was the next best.

On our return trip down the California coast we left Highway 1 a few miles past Bodega Bay and took the short secondary road over to Highway 101. By taking this route, we saved an hour or two by avoiding a heavily congested stretch of Highway 1 from which there is really no view of the ocean. We pulled into San Jose in the early afternoon. Our journey of 3,442 miles was over.

We spent a few additional days with Tobin, Ha, and granddaughter Seneca before departing for our trip back to Texas. While we were in San Jose the five of us enjoyed a day at the beach. The sand, tidal pools, and fellow sun worshipers combined to make a good day a great day. One of the interesting, but most disappointing, of our coastal adventures occurred when granddaughter Seneca tossed a 'message in a bottle' into the sea from atop a rock wall. The bottle contained a photo of Seneca with a note asking the person who found the bottle to contact Seneca at her San Jose address, or Shirley Lent at our Noble Bend Address. We watched the bottle as it floated in the ocean. The incoming waves brought the bottle back to shore where four excited teenagers fished it out of the surf. When the youngsters discovered that Seneca had thrown the bottle from nearby, they waded out as deep as they could and gave it another toss. I feared it most likely was destined to be washed back onto the same stretch of the beach. We probably would have had better results off had we given the bottle to one of the wind surfers who was paddling so far out to sea that we could hardly see him. A bottle so far out might have benefited from longshore currents and the changing of the tides. Fifteen years later no one has contacted us saying they had found the bottle. It is either still floating out at sea, or it is in some waste disposal dump.

As I close this west coast narration, I must make something very clear. Shirley was a wonderful traveling companion. I kidded her about getting ready to go in the morning but, despite the back pain or whatever, she was always willing to leave whenever I wanted to leave. I just never pushed her. It was comforting for me to realize we could take such a long trip and in the end feel more loving towards each other than we did when we left. Of course, one could challenge this statement by asking, "What shape was your relationship in when you left?"

Northern Nevada and Montana Fishing Trips

After Shirley and I returned from our overseas assignments, I twice yearly went on Spring and Fall fishing trips to the Bighorn River near Ft. Smith, Montana. These memorable outings continued for more than 15 years. My long-time fishing buddy Paul Hess and I were the guests of Jim and Ray Brownlie who had memberships in The Big Horn Club. The Club has a very large log cabin located on the bank of the Bighorn River. The view from the cabin windows is onto one of the premier fishing runs in the river. Paul and I always looked forward to our bi-annual trips as the fishing was great and we fished with four great guys: Jim, Ray, Leonard Baldassari, and Mark Maring. Our evening meals were prepared by the Club caretakers and drinks flowed liberally both on the river and in the lodge. Many were the nights when we sat before logs burning in a mammoth fireplace and talked about fishing and other less worldly endeavors.

In 2004 Paul and I added what would become an annual fishing trip to the Pine Mountains of Northern Nevada. Our first Nevada trip came the month after Bob and Shirley's west coast trip. Paul and his brother Dick had fished in the high mountain lakes of Northern Nevada for a number of years, but after Dick began to opt out of such ventures, Paul invited me to join him on what became our yearly and most anticipated fishing trip. I was always appreciative that Shirley and Paul's wife Sharon allowed us to make these week-long trips each year for a recreational activity that Paul and I enjoyed so much.

And There We Were

In August of 2004 I flew to Eugene, Oregon where Paul picked me up at the airport and took me to the Hess home in Drain. We had a memorable evening that featured steaks on the barbie and card playing in the family room. We awoke early the following morning and spent most of the day traveling to Winnemucca, Nevada where we acquired fishing licenses, drank, gambled, and spent the night. We were most successful with regards to the license procurement and the drinking.

There was no nearby motel or inn where fishermen could stay if they wished to fish the Pine Mountain high lakes. It was much too far to travel back and forth from Winnemucca which was 90 miles from the turnoff to the dirt road that took anglers on a 20-mile journey to the Onion Creek and Knott Creek reservoirs. Paul had discovered a ranch at the base of the Pine Mountain Range where the owners would let rooms and provide meals for those that worked or recreated in Northern Nevada. The rancher's wife, Delia Nuffer, said she would have two rooms for us and would provide a substantial breakfast and dinner each day. Delia told Paul she was a good cook, and Paul passed along to me that she was a gourmet cook. Somehow, 'gourmet cook' and 'working ranch' seemed incongruous to me. It turned out that Delia was a very good cook, but the meals were very much ranch fare (e.g., steaks, potatoes, homemade bread, and salads).

After we had checked in at Rob and Delia's Woodward Ranch, we left and headed north on Highway140 to the exit that would take us into the Pine Forest Mountains and to our primary destination, Onion Creek Reservoir, an impoundment behind Onion Valley Dam. We had not had a drop of brew since we left Winnemucca, but when we turned off the paved road onto the dirt access road, we popped our cooler. Our first pit stop was in a canyon and along a creek bottom filled with numerous shrubs and bushes. We walked over to the steep bank and were preparing for our activity when all of a sudden, the whole creek bottom exploded with chukars. These large gray and black partridges flew in every direction and seemed to rise in waves, one after another. We later learned hunters come from all around the country to hunt chukars in Nevada.

Henceforth we always made sure to make a potty stop in this part of the canyon, just to agitate the birds. It should be noted that it was only going to be a few weeks before humans walking to the edge of the bank would have something more lethal in their hands. Hunting season was about to open.

We arrived at Onion Creek Reservoir a bit after noon and prepared to don our waders. Paul brought out two lawn chairs Sharon recently had re-strung. We would have a place to sit while we slipped into our waders. My lawn chair immediately collapsed into a pile of aluminum and bright strands of woven fiber. I felt bad, but Paul was kind and said the chairs were quite old. Of course, he used his chair for the rest of the trip with no problem. I must have gotten the defective one.

When one fishes a stream or lake for the first time, one has to experiment to find the right fly and to identify the more productive water. Paul had fished Onion Valley Reservoir many times and was convinced the best artificial fly to use was the 'zug' bug. I opted to start fishing with a fly recommended by the fly shop in Winnemucca. After we had fished for several hours, Paul decided to wade ashore and take a nap. We had caught a number of trout (Paul 21, Bob 15) but the action had not been as exciting as I had been led to believe it would be. I walked around the lake to another stretch of water near the road coming down and across the dam. I changed my fly to the zug bug and waded out amongst a bunch of weeds growing from the lake bottom. I made a cast and caught a fish. This happened almost every cast. The fish were fighting hard and doing a lot of jumping. Paul finally raised his head to see what was causing all the commotion. By the time he joined me on the bank I had caught and released 26 trout (as we always did, and I still do). The chair collapser was now in the lead 26-21.

We continued to fish in the same general area and the trout were taking the flies at a rapid rate. We caught fish at our feet, behind us, and several times when we left a fly in the water while we stripped moss from our fly lines. By our 5:00 p.m. quitting time (we had told the Nuffers we would be back for dinner at 7:00 p.m.) we had caught 104 fish between us. We could have caught more but there was no reason to do so; we would be back tomorrow for another go at them. The trout we had caught were mostly rainbows with a few cutthroat and cut-bows. The average length was 10-12 inches with some going up to 14 inches. All the fish were in great shape and took to the air once hooked.

We took off our waders and boots, opened the cooler, and popped a couple of brews. It was time to head back to the ranch house. The trip back to the ranch would take about an hour so we had plenty of time to savor our beers. The routine went something like this - stop and get beer from the cooler, take a leak, and drive on until the beer cans were empty. Repeat. By the time we got back to the ranch house I had a nice buzz on and Paul, well, he was pretty much lit up. Paul is funny and exuberant when he has had a few, and the people at the ranch loved him. For those that think we were drinking and driving in a socially irresponsible manner, allow me to point out that we almost never saw another vehicle on any of the flat dirt roads we traversed. Please know that this is also the part of our country where signposts warn, *Next Services 90 miles*.

At dinner the first evening, Paul and I were joined by two members of a BLM road crew. The beer we drank before dinner (Rob offered cocktails but we declined) was a rather insignificant add-on to our previous happy hour. Our 2-hour dinner consisted of salads, steak, mashed potatoes, squash, rolls, and dessert. We hustled off to bed around 9:00 p.m. and were asleep before 10:00.

Rob was up at 3:00 a.m. to put coffee on and was out feeding the horses by 4:00 a.m. I went down to join Rob and Delia around 4:30 a.m. The BLM road crew showed up at 5:00 and Paul joined us at 5:30. Breakfast was served on demand. The fare was sourdough pancakes, sausage and bacon, and eggs. I felt somewhat bad as my plate was piled higher than Rob's, and he was about to head out for a full day's work. Rob was in the middle of the roundup season for himself and his neighbor. His work for the neighbor was contract work. Rob also broke and shoed horses to bring extra cash. His ranch did not look to be a prosperous one, so the extra cash earned by Rob and by Delia likely made life a bit easier.

Rob and Delia kept a large number of animals around the ranch house. Delia said they had 6 dogs (Paul thought he saw a dozen), five peacocks, 25 ducks, and unknown numbers of cats and chickens. One dog, Booger, a large mutt with a complex heritage, was the alpha dog in the barnyard. Paul was warned about Booger. After a rather traumatic first encounter they became 'friends' of a sort. Booger knew he could blow by Paul and into the house whenever Paul opened the screen door. Once Paul had opened the door just a bit, Booger would press against Paul's legs and use his mass and speed to force the door open for entry into the house. I suspect Delia let Booger in the house every morning, but she acted as if that was not the case. I think she just did not want the dog in the kitchen when all of us were at the table eating a meal.

Booger, by the way, was found by the Nuffers tied to a milepost along a remote stretch of a desert highway. Some evil person had brought the dog into the desert and tied him to a milepost, leaving him with no water or food. The assumption must have been that someone, like the Nuffers, would take pity on the dog and adopt him. It is sad to think what might have happened had Rob and Delia not stopped and taken the dog back to their ranch.

After breakfast we decided to return to Onion Creek. We stopped at the bushes to roust the chukars, but it had rained the previous evening and our water, as compared to that passed by nature, was not enough to roust them out of their habitat. When we arrived at the reservoir it was 38 degrees and raining. There had been two camping groups at the reservoir when we left the previous evening, but by the time we returned the next morning all we could see were muddy tire tracks. The campers had had enough of mountain camping. I thanked Paul profusely for having made the decision to stay at the Woodward Ranch rather than to camp at the lake. We would have had a miserable night and early morning.

We waded into the reservoir and began fishing with our zug bugs. Not only was it cold, but the low hanging clouds and fog made it hard to see across the lake. We caught about 40 trout each in those miserable conditions before we decided to drive across a nearby canyon, Crane Creek Valley, and up and over a mountainous road to Knott Creek Reservoir. The descent into Knott Creek is steep and remarkably rugged. As we began our descent, we passed over a very large outcrop of smooth granite. There appeared to be no way we would ever be able to travel back up the road we were descending. I thought to myself, "Was this excursion worth it?" Well, it was.

When I first got a glimpse of Knott Creek Reservoir I was in awe at the beautiful setting. The backdrop for the lake is a wall of granite that has been unevenly eroded by weathering along massive joints. Outliers stand out like sentinels guarding the valley. Within the lake, a granitic outcrop looks like a medieval fortress. The lake is the moat that surrounds the silent island of solid rock. Encircling the lake, a massive 30-40 feet wide weed bank makes fishing from the bank almost impossible. The only way to really fish the lake is for fishermen to come equipped with float tubes or rubber rafts. There was only one break in the weed bank. Below the cement dam face there was a ledge overlooking water so deep that nothing could grow up from the bottom. Paul told me I would catch very large trout if I could find a way to get a fly to the bottom. I did both. I fished off the bottom caught two trout, both of which were fat and nearly 20 inches in length. After I fished a while longer, we decided to give up fishing for the day. We still had that damn road to negotiate on our drive back out of the canyon.

I should point out that Knott Creek Reservoir has been designated a "Premier and Trophy Trout Fishery". That designation means the waters must be fished with barbless hooks and that only one fish per person is allowed to be taken from the lake. The lake contains many very large trout, to 24 inches, and it is a destination fishery for fly fishermen from around the world. On the day we were in the valley, there were no other fishermen to be seen. My only thought was that if the road into the impoundment deteriorated any further, no one would be able to fish it.

When we came to the stretch of road that had seemed so impassable when we first saw it, Paul shifted our pickup truck into low range four-wheel drive. We crawled up the mountain road and successfully over the smooth granite slab. I was never so happy.

We came across multiple herds of wild burros on our way down the dirt road that would take us to Denio Junction. Feral burros are quite testy and have been known to chase after tourists who stop to take photos. I was driving at this point and when we stopped for beers, I made sure Paul had room to make it to the ice chest and back before a burro could reach him. Sometimes I stopped closer to the herd than usual just to see how fast Paul could pee and retrieve.

Our second evening back at the ranch was pretty much uneventful. We had a massive dinner that ended with our introduction to a dessert known as 'a poor man's pie'. The pie is made with pie crust and a filling consisting of vinegar and sugar. It is topped with meringue. The pie was not very good. Rob and I each had a piece and we never saw the pie again. I suspect Rob told Delia it wasn't at all good.

After a breakfast of bacon, sausage, eggs, and toasted homemade bread served with apricot jam made from apricots harvested from Delia's apricot tree in the orchard, we headed out to fish new waters. Our first stop was at Bilk Creek Reservoir, located in the lowlands about six miles from the ranch. When we got to the reservoir the impounded water looked like it was part of a sewage treatment pond. After a brief conversation, we decided we could find better fishing by driving some 100 miles north into Oregon to fish Mann Lake, known for its population of large cutthroat trout. When we took on gas at Fields, Oregon, 50 miles north of Bilk Creek Reservoir, we read a fishing report on Mann Lake: "Water is low and the fishing for cutthroat trout is slow." What the heck. We headed north and found we were the only fishermen there. Mind you, Mann Lake is one of the great fishing destinations in North America. The highway next to the lake serves a dual purpose, one for cars and two for the aircraft that bring fishermen to the lake. A windsock hangs along the roadside. We donned our waders and worked our way out into the lake. After fishing for 90 minutes without getting a single strike, we decided to leave Mann Lake and head back up into the mountains and Onion Creek

Reservoir for one last shot at those less-than-wily trout. It was just after noon and Onion Creek was some 2 1/2 hours driving time from where we were.

When we turned off the highway and into the canyon that would take us to Onion Creek, we once again stopped to flush out the chukars. We were getting pretty good at this. We reached the reservoir around 3:00 p.m. After we fished for several hours and caught 45 fish between the two of us, we decided we had better head for the ranch as we did not want to be too late for dinner.

After we loaded up our gear and brought out a couple of beers we drove around the lake and over the dam. I was driving when Paul said I should stop and look at the water. The entire reservoir was erupting with feeding fish, some leaping high in the air and some just porpoising near the surface. The more I watched, the more intrigued I became. I finally pulled off to the side of the road and said to Paul, "I am sorry, but we are going to be late for dinner." I pulled out my fly road and walked down to the sandy shoreline near the dam face. Whenever a fish rose to the surface, I would cast my line to the radiating circle and, wham, I had a fish on. I caught nine fish in about a half an hour. I had 5-10 other fish on that got off, and I missed many, many strikes. I was laughing all the time: Paul said he had never seen someone have so much fun fishing. Paul, bundled up in his warm coat and cradling a suds in his hand, was a great cheerleader. I finally broke off on a fish after which we decided it was time to get the heck out of the mountains. We still had time to do our drink, pee, and repeat routine on the way back to the ranch. When we returned to the Woodward Ranch it was almost 9:00 p.m. Rob said that had we not returned by 10:00 p.m. they would have gone out looking for us. Just where they would have gone looking would have been anyone's guess. When we left that morning, we had told them we were going to Bilk Creek and to Mann Lake.

Dinner included massive T-bone steaks, scalloped potatoes, multiple salads, cinnamon rolls, tapioca pudding, and a cake. Delia had cooked two huge pans of scalloped potatoes, enough to feed forty. Late that evening two of the Nuffer nephews showed up. They had come to hunt on the first day of the antelope season.

Paul woke up early on Saturday morning to say goodbye to Rob before he left for work. When Paul got down to the breakfast table at 5:15 a.m. he learned that the Nuffers had had guests who showed up at 4:00am., ate breakfast, and had already left. The two nephews had also left for their hunt. Rob was finished with his breakfast and I had joined him in this repast. When Paul discovered all that had happened before he made his appearance, all he could say was that he felt like a 'bottom feeder' for sleeping in so late despite having been up at 4:30 to take his morning shower. He said he was in deep sleep deprivation.

Our trip back to Drain was uneventful except that Paul directed the trip so that we went through Burns, Oregon and then across the high desert, down the Crooked River Canyon, and into Prineville, Oregon. We spent an enjoyable evening with Mom Lent and left early enough the next day to visit Shirley's mother, Marie, before she went to church. Marie and Paul hit it off famously. Paul sweet talked Marie by telling her that he could now see where Shirley got all of her beauty. Marie, uncharacteristically, said, "We had to dig pretty deep into the beauty gene pool to make that Shirley".

After leaving Marie, Paul and I took a leisurely trip over the Cascade Range. Our chosen route was the spectacular McKenzie Highway which takes one through high mountain lava flows and is proximal to the Three Sisters volcanic peaks. When we arrived back in Drain, Paul and I dropped in on his 90-year-old mother, Irene. I felt honored to finally meet her as I had heard so many stories of her and her efforts to raise her six children, absent a husband. Irene eventually remarried and Paul thought the world of his stepfather, Tony, who had passed away a number of years before.

After Sharon returned from an outing with her sisters to the Oregon coast, the three of us drove down Interstate 5 to the Seven Feathers Casino in Canyonville, Oregon. We lost a modicum of money that was offset by a delicious buffet dinner given to us as a gratuity (I think for Sharon's patronage over the years).

Paul and I returned to the Pine Mountains and the Woodward Ranch for many years. Each trip was a variation of the one described herein. We never went back to Bilk Reservoir, but we did add Catnip Reservoir in the Sheldon National Wildlife Refuge to our list of fishing spots. We were saddened when Paul's health issues, and the Nuffer's sale of the Woodward Ranch, ended our fishing adventures in Nevada. I hope that somehow my sons and their children find a way to spend time in this beautiful part of our country.

Kansas City and Branson, Missouri (September 20-27, 2004)

I had been back in Texas less than a month before Shirley and I flew to Missouri to attend the wedding of Adam Wells and his fiancé Leigh Gregory. Adam and his parents had lived down the street from us when Shirley and I lived in Englewood, Colorado. Taran and Adam were close friends who, with other younger boys, played together in the Jasmine Court and Geddes Circle neighborhood of Homestead.

The Kansas City wedding was to occur on September 25, 2004 at the Second Presbyterian Church. The reception was at the nearby Webster House, a magnificent 19th Century Romanesque-style school.

Prior to the wedding and a gathering of old friends in Kansas City, Shirley and I rented a car and headed south to Branson, Missouri and the hills where Marie Taylor had spent her early school years. We had four days to sample the entertainment in Branson and to tour the Missouri haunts of young Marie.

Our trip to Branson and the Ozark Mountains was one of the few times Shirley exercised her talents in the planning process for one our trips. She played a key role in all we did during the time we were in Kansas City and Branson. She took command because, as she told me, "I do not want to be disappointed." We saw the best shows, stayed at the best places, and ate at the most interesting and exquisite restaurants. We also took a wonderful journey back in time to the Taylor family homestead near Eagle Rock in the Ozark Mountains of Missouri.

Our flight to Kansas City arrived around noon. We checked out a silver Mercury Grand Marquis rental and loaded our considerable luggage into the trunk and headed south towards Springfield and thence on to Branson, a distance of approximately 250 miles. The geography from Kansas City to Springfield is dominated by lakes and low-lying grasslands. South of Springfield on Highway 65 the land gradually becomes hilly and is covered with broadleaf trees. There are a few needled cedars but for the most part white oaks seem to fight for supremacy with sycamore, dogwood, and walnut trees. The geologist in me was intrigued by the road cut excavations between Springfield and Branson. Incised into the hummocky hills, the road cuts exposed thin-bedded limestone layers, stacked one over the other, almost like pancakes on a platter. I had not seen road cuts like these anywhere else in my travels around the United States.

We drove ten miles past Branson and turned into a winding road that took us to the Big Cedar Resort. The road was cobbled, and motorists were forced to ford small streams on their way to the reservation center. Shirley had researched the lodging available in the Branson area and had determined there was no better place to stay than at The Big Cedar Resort. The resort is tucked into the rugged landscape of the Missouri Ozark Mountains, and it overlooks Table Rock Lake, a sprawling clear lake created by the Table Rock Dam on the White River. At the resort we had several lodges and lakeside cottages to choose from and Shirley had chosen the Falls Lodge. One of the newer lodges, Falls Lodge overlooked a cold and clear spring creek that flowed over a series of small waterfalls, and it was only a short walk downhill to the Devil's Pool Restaurant. Near the end our stay at Big Cedar we had a remarkable experience at the Buzzard Bar, located below the Devils' Pool Restaurant, but more about that later.

Our arrival at Big Cedar occurred about an hour before sunset, and Shirley wanted to find a place where we could both dine and watch the sun set as it went down over Table Rock Lake. After we checked in, we hustled up to the nearby Top of the Rock Restaurant, built on what was said to be the highest viewpoint in the Ozark Mountains of Missouri. We had the Lodge call ahead for a reservation, but the restaurant had no table available until 8:00 p.m. The sun would set at approximately 7:15, so we decided to show up early and have a drink on the restaurant's terrace. Once at The Top of the Rock we found there were a number of available dining tables on the terrace, under a beautiful copper and wood canopy. The tables were all arranged around open 4-foot-high circular gas-fired fireplaces where the view of the setting sun was even better than the view indoors. After we were seated and had ordered a glass of wine, Shirley took a walk around the terrace and then along an adjacent golf course. She watched the sun set from a special spot on the mountain, and then she re-joined me for a lovely dinner. Shirley's behavior on that evening was so very typical of her. She always got the best seat, the best view, etc.

After dinner we returned to our room at the Falls Lodge which had a wonderful veranda with several rocking chairs made from the limbs of hickory trees. We soon found that the veranda was also a mosquito feeding station and this complicated matters. After that first evening, we left the veranda to a feral cat at night. In the morning we again became masters of the universe and took advantage of the rocking chairs and the panoramic view.

Our room had two queen beds, a Jacuzzi, a big walk-in shower and a wall decorated with an assortment of stuffed wild animals. Looking down on us were the taxidermist's versions of pheasant, deer, fox, bass, and grouse. The Jacuzzi and the beds were separated from each other by a glass wall with curtains to give the bather a bit of privacy. We were both in our sixties, and it was not really a special treat to see the other stepping into a bath. Newlyweds who stay in the room probably leave a wet path running from the bathing area to the beds. I can assure you that the path in our case was mighty dry. Romance was still in the air, but it was better experienced in the dark.

On Tuesday morning we awoke to a clear sunshiny day. We dressed and hiked down the hill to the Devils Pool Restaurant to take advantage of the breakfast buffet. Sarah from Cheshire, England was cooking the buffet omelets on what was her last day at Big Cedar. She was going to begin the trip back home at the end of her morning shift. It was probably just as well. Sarah was a lovely young lady, but she sure could not make a quality omelet. We ate our breakfast seated outside at a table looking down on Table Rock Lake and a nearby children's fishing pond. The Bent Hook Marina was visible in the background as were the rental cabins in the forest beyond the inlet.

After breakfast we took a short walk, and then made the long, steep climb back up the mountain to our lodge. I was a sweating mess when I arrived, but Shirley took her time and looked like she had only walked across the street. An interesting feature of staying at Big Cedar is that one must walk on trails since a walk along the roadways eventually leads one to a stream crossing where the only way forward is to take off one's shoes and wade.

Then we were off to Branson to catch the Branson Scenic Railway which would take us on a 1 hour and 45 minute ride through the Ozark Mountains and several valleys in Missouri and northern Arkansas. I was not looking forward to the train excursion, but Shirley was really excited about the ride. In the face of her exuberant enthusiasm, I opted to be quiet. Boarding was in the order of ticket purchase. Our numbers were 195 and 196 which made us among the last to board. Shirley, as she would, wanted to be seated in the first club car on the train which had a vista dome and an expansive seating area. I expected that, being among the last to board, we should not even think of going to the front of the train. Surprisingly, we walked the length of the train and ended up with great seats. The train's engineer, 'Bob', took a liking to Shirley and insisted I take a photo with his arm around her. So I did.

To my surprise, the train ride was a lot of fun. The trip

And There We Were

took us south into Arkansas and through some of the great hill country that comprises the Ozark Mountains (hills if you are from anywhere in the western United States). We crossed several high trestles (155 feet and 120 feet respectively) and passed through some very long (3,000 feet plus) tunnels that had been carved out of limestone strata. But what made the trip really special to me was the never-ending view of the forested hills and the stream bottoms. Up close we saw eastern cedar, white oak, sycamore, hickory, ash, pine, walnut, dogwood, and red bud trees. All during our trip there was the most beautiful music coming forth from overhead speakers. The music was soft Cajun, hillbilly, and western played on a variety of instruments (e.g., banjo, violin, harmonic, fiddle, etc.).

As it was always with Shirley, we were the last two people off the train. A conductor followed us through the six rail cars and then insisted that I take a picture of Shirley and him by the big red engine (Number 98). Over the years I had gotten used to people wanting me to take pictures of them with my beautiful and charming wife. After a quick stop at a nearby water closet, we were ready to pound the streets of historic downtown Branson. For a small town that has over 60 theaters, the downtown area of Branson is small, maybe only 4-6 blocks, each block packed with shops and eateries. After visiting most of the shops, we stopped for an ice cream cone. The waffle cone was out of this world, homemade and tasted good enough that I thought I might come back for just the cone itself - but I never did. We walked around the town one more time to make sure we had not missed anything and then stepped into a unique coffee shop where the young owner offered us coffees and a spiel on the proper way to roast coffee beans. After the coffees, we headed back to the train station parking lot. We still had to find the outdoor theater where we had evening tickets for the *Shepherd of the Hills*.

We drove west along the Shepherd of the Hills Parkway until we reached the hilly terrain that comprises the Shepherd of the Hills Outdoor Theater. It was only 4:00 p.m. A small crowd was nearby attending a late afternoon "Sons of the Pioneers" dinner performance. Because we pretty much had the run of the grounds, it was easy for us to pick up our tickets to the 7:00 p.m. Shepherd show. Afterwards we visited a number of the small shops. In one of which we met "Sparklie", who was a real hoot. Sparklie got her moniker from all of the flashing and sparkling souvenirs she sells. We bought two videos and several copies of the *Shepherd of the Hills* novel. When we left Sparklie said she would see us again when we checked in for the evening performance as she usually packed all of her flashing gadgets down to a stall near the main entrance to the theater.

We decided to head back to Big Cedar for a short nap prior to returning to the Outdoor Theater. What a mistake that was. After I drove 35 minutes back to Big Cedar, we had a 30-minute nap, then hopped into the car for the return trip. Shirley had planned on us having dinner prior to the show, but we were so pressed for time the dinner plan went out the window. As a dinner substitute, we purchased large pretzels, dill pickles, an ice-cream bar, and a couple of bottles of water. We were seated in the first row, center, with only a rail separating us from the arena. We placed our "dinner" on the plank running along the rail bar and watched the pre-show. The warm-up performance consisted of a cowboy humorist (?) and a big rawboned cowboy who sat astride a very ominous looking long horn bull. Periodically, the bull rider performed roping tricks and acrobatic hands stands aboard the bull. We were close enough to the action that we could smell the critters (mules, sheep, horses, and other farm animals) brought in for the *Shepherd of the Hills* performance. We were most appreciative when one of the stagehands brought out a shovel and a gunny bag. I glanced at Shirley who was beginning to think that the foul smell was coming from her pretzel or pickle.

Accompanied by the increasing sound of the cicadas, darkness became complete, and the show began. The Shepherd of the Hills performance originates from a book written by Harold Bell Wright in 1910. Mr. Wright was the first American author to realize $1 million in profit from his writings and for three decades he was the most widely read American author. His *Shepherd* story, which takes place in the Ozark Hill country, has all the elements one would want in a drama; love, hate, villains, martyrs, humor, and saints. The story is populated with memorable hill country characters. *Shepard of the Hills* has been made into 4 major motion pictures, the most famous of which was the 1942 release that starred John Wayne in his first film in Technicolor.

We enjoyed the performance and thought the story was interesting, but the quality of the acting and the lack of any music or singing left us feeling we had really not had any 'fun'. Outdoor performances like this one and others (e.g., *Oklahoma* done at Discovery Land outside of Tulsa) are unique. There are not many places where wagons roll into the set and cowboys ride in from the surrounding hills and forest. Where else can one see 50 sheep run through the set as the actors continue on with their dialogue. As interesting as the performance was, we departed looking forward to the shows filled with fiddling, singing, and comedy we would see in the upcoming days.

On our way back to Big Cedar from the *Shepherd of the Hills* performance we stopped at the 5-star Chateau on the Lake Hotel/Resort where we thought we might be able to get a late dinner. It was after 10:00 p.m. and all the dining options were closed so we visited the lounge where we could hear live music. A tall and statuesque blond brought us a large bowl of trail mix and we ordered martinis. Shirley had looked over the bar menu and discovered a chocolate martini on offer. She loved it so much we would return the next night for another one. Our tall blond bartender, aged about 23, looked Swedish, but she told us she was from Poland. I left the lounge thinking that the lady was a lot of woman.

Shirley was not going to go through another night without a quality dinner, so she utilized our time at the Chateau to tour the Chateau Grill with the hotel manager. Although the restaurant was closed for the night, he showed her the best table for viewing the sunset, the expansive (and expensive) menu, and took her reservation for the following evening. There would be no more pickle and pretzel dinners on this trip.

It was late when we returned to our room at the Falls Lodge, and I was bone tired. After only two days in Missouri, I was exhausted. Right after we had jumped into our beds, we heard a lot of thumping going on in the room above us. We could only imagine the noise was either coming from a couple on their honeymoon, or from 5 or 6 young children. Because the thumping and running around continued until 1:00 a.m. and resumed again at 5:30 a.m., we concluded kids were not responsible for all of the action. Our noisy overhead neighbors were with us for all three nights we spent at the Falls Lodge.

Day three in Missouri began with that long trek down to the Devil's Pool Restaurant. The British egg destroyer was gone, but Shirley was convinced she could get a better omelet if the chef in the kitchen did the deed. I asked our waitress if the kitchen personnel would make the omelet or if they would simply have the cook in the buffet line make it. Assured that the kitchen chef was up to the task, Shirley decided to order off the menu rather than go through the buffet line. The ordered omelet came out big and overcooked. I found it interesting that the new cook on the buffet line appeared to be turning out soft and fluffy omelets of high quality. Go figure. This day was our last day having breakfast at the Devil's Pool Restaurant.

After the morning meal we went on another long walk, and then made long ascent up to our lodge. I had learned my lesson: shower after breakfast.

Before we departed in our rented Grand Marquis, we attempted to rescue a small kitten that had cried all night and was still at it in the morning. The hotel staff had been trying to capture and feed the kitten, but it was feral (most likely the offspring of the female cat that slept on our veranda...bad mama) and not easily corralled.

We drove 37 miles through beautiful hill country to Eagle Rock, Missouri. As we approached Eagle Rock, we noticed the hills were becoming less forested. Grassy knolls, many capped by oak or spruce trees, were predominant. The land looked like it would be excellent livestock pasture, and some of the bottom land looked fertile, like it might be good farmland. However, if any of the local inhabitants had engaged in either activity, we saw no evidence that such activity had led to affluence.

Our trip to Eagle Rock had two primary objectives. One, we wanted to visit the cemetery where members of the Taylor family are buried, amongst them Shirley's great grandfather (Marie's grandfather). Two, we wanted to see if we could find the Taylor homestead where Marie had lived as a young girl. We stopped at a local country store, Roy's, to ask if anyone had heard of the Munsey Cemetery. We got an affirmative and instructions on how to get to it. A crusty old fellow said, "Go down the road (Highway 86) until you come to the Baptist Church, turn left into the parking lot, but do not stop, the road continues into the holler. Cross the bridge and go about 2 miles until the road makes a sharp turn to the left. Don't go left. Turn right past the big barn and travel along the fence line. You will find the cemetery on the right." We did eventually find the Munsey Cemetery, but with the directions we had been given, it took several trips up and back before we found the right turn offs.

Despite being in a very rural area the Munsey Cemetery was in remarkably good shape. There had been a recent burial, sadly, a 20-year-old boy whose picture was burned into a granite marker. Shirley and I opened a gate and walked to the highest point in the cemetery. We looked around and were quite sure we could see the remnant foundation that would have been the elementary school Marie had attended. If we were looking at the site of the old school then we were fairly close to the northeast edge of the cemetery, and probably not far from where Shirley's great grandfather Taylor was buried. Shirley took out her cell phone and called Marie. Surprisingly, the call went through and the two chatted for a short while before contact was lost. When we stopped back at the country store and mentioned that Shirley had placed a call to her mother, the old man said that was not possible. He fished in the nearby stream and had never been able to make a phone connection. Shirley replied that an Angel must have intervened so that she could chat, if only for a short time, with her mother.

We discovered the Taylor family grave sites were not marked. When great grandfather Frederick Alonzo Taylor died in 1932, the family (Shirley's grandmother Jennie) sent money back to

Eagle Rock to purchase a headstone. The receiving relative, for whatever reason, decided to put up a wooden cross. The wooden crosses (and there were other Taylor family members buried near great grandfather) have all disintegrated. Apparently, when the decaying wooden crosses were removed for being eye sores, the cemetery caretakers collected large stones from a nearby stream bank and placed them where crosses once were. Marie had mentioned that the Taylor family grave sites were now marked by a trio of large stones. Using Marie's description to guide us, we were almost certain we had found the right burial sites. Shirley was much more emotional than I thought she would be. Being close to where her mother had played and schooled; where her much loved grandmother Jennie had lived; and where many of her ancestors were buried moved her to tears. As we were standing by the grave sites, Shirley said she suddenly had so many questions she wanted to ask her mother and her Uncle Paul.

We did not have enough information to find the old Taylor homestead, but we assumed it was upstream from the cemetery and probably off to the east and over a grassy knoll. We saw a cluster of trees in the distance and thought that might be where the home had been located. No matter what, the land was of such poor quality that it would have been very difficult to carve out a living there. It is no wonder that the Taylor family eventually packed up and moved west.

We returned to Big Cedar Lodge where we had a short nap prior to leaving for the Chateau on the Lake dinner reservations Shirley had made the previous evening. When we arrived at the Chateau Grill, we were seated at the table with the premier views of Table Rock Lake and of the setting sun. Because we were going to the Shoji Tabuchi show that began at 7:30, we knew we would have to leave prior to the actual setting of the sun, but we still tracked the slowly descending ball of fire as it worked its way down the mountain ridges far off to the west. Shirley ordered filet and lobster and I had a stuffed chicken dish. The food was excellent, and the ambience was absolutely perfect. Shirley sipped her Chardonnay and gazed out onto the lake. She told me she would just die if she did not have elegance in her life. Continuing, she said the fine draperies, the lovely carpet, the fine China, the piano music, and the excellent service just made her come alive. The pickle and pretzel dinner of the previous evening was long forgotten. The price of the meal had, however, gone up considerably.

The Shoji Tabuchi Show is held in a privately owned and purposely built Las Vegas style theater that seats approximately 2,000. The show we attended was lively with spectacular video effects. An entertainer, Shoji arrived in the United States in 1967 with $500 in his pocket. He has done very well. Almost all his performances, sometimes two a day, are sold out. The exterior of his theater is awash in shades of purple (Shirley's favorite color), almost to the point of being gaudy. Our visits to the restrooms were worth the price of the admission to the show. The lady's washroom contains seven marble wash bowls perched on serpentine pedestals that face large mirrors with gold plated decorative frames. Fresh lavender, white, and green floral arrangements were (in 2004) woven into the chandelier, over the mirror tops, and into an arrangement centered over an ornate tile floor. Colorful settees offer ladies a chance to sit and take in the incredible view. I thought that one might just forget to go potty. The men's room is also spacious, and it has a side room containing a full pool table and several rows of posh chairs so that the tired male might rest while his significant other is out fighting the masses in the gift shop.

The Shoji Show is dominated by dancing and singing, and Shoji plays all forms of string instruments. He is also a gifted singer. On the evening we were there his talented daughter Christine performed with him. Christine's mother is Caucasian, and the daughter has acquired more of her mother's Caucasian looks than her father's Oriental features. We were disappointed that Christine's mother Dorothy had taken the night off as she was reportedly quite talented in her own right. When I saw Shoji up on the stage, I was moved to recall all the talented musicians we saw performing while we lived in China. I wondered how many "Shojis" there might be in Beijing, Shanghai, or Hong Kong who could come to America and replicate what Shoji had done. The Japanese born Shoji had certainly lived the American dream.

After the show we returned to the Chateau on the Lake and the cocktail lounge where we once again ordered drinks served by the tall Polish blonde. Shirley had her chocolate martini and I, a creme de menthe on the rocks. We sampled the trail mix, but we found it not as tasty as we had the night before (following our pickles and pretzels dinner). We chatted with the cocktail waitress and learned that, although she was homesick, the people in Branson had been most kind to her. She nodded in the affirmative when I asked if she had found the Branson men to be attentive. I could only imagine how attentive they might be.

It was once again after midnight when we returned to the Falls Lodge at Big Cedar and settled into the room we hardly ever saw. The next morning we were going for another long walk on the grounds, and that big hill would still be waiting for me. I went to bed in a sweat just thinking about the long climb back. The overhead neighbors were obviously still finding it difficult to sleep.

We hiked down to the Bent Hook Marina Thursday morning. The skies were cloud free and the sun was burning brightly, as they were for all of stay at Big Cedar. The Marina store has an opening cut in the floor through which the shopper/visitor can look down at giant carp, blue gill, and small bass. I remember thinking that each youngster coming into the store most likely tosses a Ding Dong, Twinkie, or cracker into the opening. The Table Lake fish must cruise around as they patiently wait for their next meal. The carp were huge, maybe up to 10 pounds, and each looked like it could gulp down a Hostess cupcake without any effort.

We stopped at Tom's Smokehouse for breakfast. After we each ordered a breakfast burrito, I added an incremental order for Tom's cinnamon roll which, when delivered, turned out to be the size of a dinner plate and delicious. I could only hope the caloric content was less than 2000.

After breakfast we walked along the lake and saw wild berries, grapes, crab apples, currents, and an incredible number

And There We Were

of fallen acorns. The ground was covered with food for rodents, and the marmots (ground hogs?) we saw were gigantic. It is no wonder the resort gives guests a quick lesson on the poisonous snakes inhabiting the grounds. The forest floors are very likely populated with large and small rodents who are scavenging the bountiful food supply that is there for the taking. Almost as surely, there must be snakes waiting under the leaves for a tasty morsel to run by them. The copperheads we saw in the lodge photos made me want to walk anywhere but near the edge of the trail. Shirley thought I was hogging the trails we walked, but I was just thinking of self-preservation.

Shirley had booked a late afternoon excursion on the Branson Belle, a showboat that plies the water of Table Rock Lake. Dinner reservations, after all this was a dinner showboat, were made at the onboard Paddle Wheel Club. Shirley made sure we had the premier seats on the third deck looking right out between the two giant red paddle wheels. On a vessel that seats 700 there is a select set of tables reserved for 24 people who choose to order off the menu. The cost for a meal in the Paddle Wheel Club (in a secluded and closed off area) is only $15 more than one would pay for seating elsewhere on the paddle boat. For this extra $15 one can get a huge (up to 20 ounces if you wish) rib eye steak, a salmon filet, or a combination of the two. The protein dishes came with delicious side dishes and dinner was topped off with a monster piece of strawberry or chocolate dessert. After dinner we were taken down to a premier viewing area reserved for those who dined at the Paddle Wheel Club. I would think that everyone on the boat would pay the $52 per person cost for such treatment. Anyone unwilling to part with the extra $15 is relegated to paying $37 for their meal and sitting at long tables with the other 674 people onboard.

The after dinner show we experienced on the Branson Belle was the best theatrical presentation we saw during our stay in Branson. The singing and dancing were uplifting, the acrobatics and ballet dancing performed by a Russian couple was spectacular, and the comedy act by a ventriloquist was the performance of the trip. The comedy act featured two dogs, one of which was a bulldog. Both dogs moved their mouths as the ventriloquist poured forth his dialogue. Everyone laughed until their sides hurt. Such smart-assed canines you have never seen.

Once again Shirley was the last one off of the showboat. Just when I thought they were going to close the gang plank, down she came, fresh from a tour of every deck and a visit with every member of the crew: Branson Belle meets the Houston Belle.

Onshore we decided to while away our time browsing through the nearby gift shops, thereby avoiding the large incoming crowd about to board for the late evening showboat excursion. I shopped and bought a few items but, when I tired, I walked over to a rail, leaned against it, and did a bit of people watching. I happened to glance into a nearby and crowded gift shop where I saw Shirley laughing like only she could. She also had the clerks laughing and smiling. Her infectious wit and humor touched everyone. It was no wonder that she went through life bringing so much happiness to herself and to those fortunate to come in contact with her.

After the Branson Belle show we headed back to Big Cedar Lodge. I was thinking, it was only 7:30 p.m. and this looks like it is going to be one of those nights when we might get to bed early. Wrong! Shirley said we really should go to the Buzzard Bar which is located beneath the Devil's Pool Restaurant. I remembered the breakfasts we had at the restaurant and how bad those experiences had been, at least with respect to the quality of the breakfasts. I did not want to go to the Buzzard Bar.

We found a table near the small stage and ordered drinks, Shirley a glass of soda water and her customary Chardonnay and I a pint of beer. We chatted with the bar hostess, no tall blonde foreign lass here, more like short, chunky, and definitely local. She turned out to be a real sweetheart. The more we chatted with her, the more we learned about the handsome cowboy, perched on a nearby stool, who was going to give a performance in an hour. I mentioned to Shirley that an hour was a long time to wait, but the cocktail waitress said it would be worth the wait, and she would even send the singing cowboy over to introduce himself. We ordered another round and then Clay Self, the cowboy, came to our table. He said he was from Grand Junction, Colorado, and that he had quarterbacked Fruita High School to the 1983 state football championship game. The young man was so personable we decided to stay for his show. Clay Self proved to be a very funny fellow and his guitar playing and singing were nothing short of marvelous. He had us and the rest of the packed bar roaring with laughter. Before we knew, it we found ourselves once again going to bed after midnight. Shirley Lent did not believe in nice quiet evenings.

Friday morning was another beautiful day, and it was also time for us to checkout. We loaded up the Grand Marquis and returned to Tom's Smokehouse where I ordered another cinnamon roll and a small order of biscuits and gravy. A boy has to eat you know. Shirley had coffee, a bran muffin, and part of my cinnamon roll. We hit the road and left the Falls Lodge at Big Cedar to our thumping neighbors. Shirley had all the information she needed in the event we ever returned to Big Cedar with Marie and/or our sons and their families. She knew it would be a wonderful place to bring the grandchildren and even knew which cabin by the lake she would reserve. I had seen so very many fun things to do that had I been a young kid I would have thrown a fit if my parents did not bring me to Big Cedar on vacation.

We timed our arrival at the Marriott Country Club Plaza Hotel in Kansas City so that we might meet up with our good friends and former Homestead neighbors, Greg and Sandy Hemming. Waiting for us in our hotel room was a beautiful basket of goodies, compliments of April and her husband Larry Baughman. We also had a note from Sandy Hemming informing us they had made dinner reservations at the Plaza III Steakhouse, about a five-minute walk from our hotel. Shirley decided that after a day of traveling she needed to go for a walk and for a Starbuck's coffee located on the Country Club Plaza. Shirley did not know what she was getting into. A major arts and crafts festival had brought thousands (maybe tens of thousands) crowding into the Plaza and overflowing into the surrounding streets. By the time Shirley returned to our hotel after her 'coffee break' it was time to meet the Hemmings in the lobby.

Being in Kansas City. and at the dinner Plaza III Steakhouse, we each ordered a steak. All our steaks were dry-aged, large, and incredibly tender. Our dinner was grand! We took an after-dinner stroll amongst the masses attending the festival and discovered that one trip around the block was all we needed. We returned to the Marriott and ordered after dinner drinks in the lounge. While we were there I thought, "Hey, this might be an evening when we get to bed at a reasonable hour." Wrong.

No sooner had I completed my thought than Sandy jumped up from her chair and called out to a passing guest. The lady was carrying a basket like the one we had received from April Wells. It was obvious the couple was also in Kansas City for the Wells-Gregory wedding. After introductions, we found that Mike and Carol Daffner were from, of all places, The Woodlands, Texas. They dropped off luggage in their room and returned to the lounge where we ordered another round of drinks. It was still reasonably early in the evening, maybe 9:00. Then we got a call from April and Larry who had just concluded the rehearsal dinner at a restaurant across the street from our hotel. There would soon be six of us. When the Wells arrived, we ordered more drinks and had a great time. Finally, around 11:30 p.m. April and I decided it was time to call it an evening. Hugs and kisses were exchanged, and we stumbled off to our respective rooms. Another midnight had come and gone, and the Lents were still not in bed and asleep. It had been another enjoyable day, even if most of it was spent driving on the highways of Missouri.

The following morning Shirley ordered room service coffees and juice. This turned out to be a big mistake as the coffee tasted like it had been brewed with a couple of dirty copper pennies in the pot. Shirley said she was going to make another trip down to the Plaza for a Starbucks coffee. I decided that a long walk in the nearby park was more to my liking, so I put on my shorts and tennis shoes and took off. I walked a little over two miles (also up and down hills) and returned to the lobby to cool down. As I sat in a large lounge chair sweating like you cannot believe, the Daffners walked by and they hardly recognized me. The bright red face and the film of sweat must have distorted my image. The Daffners were also going for

And There We Were

Starbucks coffees. I told them to say hello to Shirley.

At four o'clock we left for Adam and Kelly's wedding at the Second Presbyterian Church. We arrived early enough for Shirley to get a seat near the aisle and close to the family. Kelly was a beautiful bride, statuesque and well-tanned. We had not seen Adam since he was a teenager, so it was delightful to see both he and his older brother Chris as mature young men. Shirley and I were proud of both: Adam for his choice of bride, and Chris for the loving father and husband that he shown himself to be.

The wedding reception was held in downtown Kansas City at the Webster House, an ornate building, once a school, that had been transformed into a restaurant and an antique gallery. After having drinks on the veranda, we were called into the main building for more drinks, appetizers, and a buffet dinner. The Hemmings, Daffners, and Lents were seated at a table near the colorful bar. The wedding party was disseminated into three different rooms, and this was bothersome to Shirley as she wanted to see all members of the family and to watch them on the dance floor. Because it was a very short trek for a refill, the bar was great for Greg and me....and there were refills, so many that Greg was benched prior to half time. We had a lot of fun that evening, and I was delighted that Adam had found such a beautiful and personable young lady to be his wife.

The following morning, we were up early to attend a 9:30 Sunday morning brunch at the Baughman home. The brunch was just right. We had tasty breakfast goodies eaten outside on the patio overlooking the lawn and gardens Larry had manicured to the Nth degree. The gathering included the bride and groom, relatives, and friends that had travelled from afar.

Following the brunch, Greg and Sandy Hemming left for the airport. Shirley and I returned to the Marriott for a restful afternoon. We joined the Baughmans and the Daffners that evening for dinner at Stroud's, a famous Kansas City landmark located near/under an overpass. Stroud's is a dumpy looking restaurant known primarily for its chicken dinners. When we arrived at 5:30 p.m. there were people waiting in the line to be seated. After a 45-minute wait, we were called into the dining area. Although the chicken is pan fried and greasy, it is also very good and is served with sides of mashed potatoes, house fries, cut fries, beans, and a salad. Dessert was what must be a Missouri favorite, giant and rectangular cinnamon rolls. Even though several in our party split their orders there was still enough left over for take away. I was probably the only one who ate my full order of fried chicken, and I was stuffed when we returned to our hotel room. I was so full that I undressed only when Shirley went to do her toiletries. I was not a pretty sight.

After rising early, we checked out in time to have breakfast at the Cheesecake Factory in the Country Club Plaza where I ate a giant breakfast burrito and Shirley a quesadilla. We left for the airport and caught our Continental Express flight to Houston. Even though we landed at an unscheduled terminal, our limo driver was there to greet us.

The trip was another very enjoyable one and we were extremely happy we had taken the time and spent the money to attend Adam Wells' wedding and to spend precious time with our old friends, Greg and Sandy, and April and Larry. Our side trip to Branson and the Ozark Mountains was memorable.

Our first year in retirement had been a crazy one during which we had travelled like it might be our last year in retirement. Of course, the year was not over, and we had already planned another trip.

San Antonio on the occasion of Shirley's 60th birthday (October 8-11, 2004)

Despite all of the traveling we had done during the year, October 10, 2004, Shirley's 60th birthday, was looming on the horizon. I had felt the pressure to have a celebration commensurate with the event building all year long. Shirley did not like to be disappointed, and she did have great expectations.

And There We Were

Shirley and I were increasingly worn down by our year-long travels and my plans to celebrate Shirley's special day became less ambitious than the celebration I had considered earlier in the year. In the Spring I had entertained the idea of flying the pretty lady to Bora Bora, the tropical South Sea island of paradise. James Michener, the noted novelist and world traveler, considered the lagoon at Bora Bora to be the most beautiful place on the planet. But our major excursions to New England, the Maritime Provinces of Canada, New York, Niagara Falls, the west coast of Oregon, Washington, and Vancouver Island, Denver (twice), Kansas City, and Branson took the starch out of our desire to fly halfway around the planet, no matter how beautiful the place might be.

In late Summer I had considered taking the Pearl to Las Vegas to fulfill her dream of seeing Celine Dione perform at her new purpose-built theater in Ceasar's Palace. It had been my intention to bring two of Shirley's most special people to the glitzy city for her special birthday. These two people were Shirley's longtime friend Carol Dunaway, and her mother, Marie Hill Binam. I looked into the ticket situation and found I could get three tickets, front row center for $400 each. Although that seemed a bit stiff, I considered it a good buy. I would take the ladies to the show and wait for them at the exit. But then I realized I would still need to purchase airplane tickets and hotel rooms for the four of us. I got weak kneed thinking of the total cost for the trip.

Shirley had always wanted to visit San Antonio, so San Antonio it was. Lest one think I am a cheapskate, I should point out that I was already going to fly Marie and my mother Mabel to Houston for Thanksgiving.

What started with dreams of Bora Bora, and then of Celine, ended as a four-day getaway to San Antonio. We awoke early Friday morning and took our time getting ready to leave on the 3 1/2- to 4-hour trip to San Antonio. I anticipated we might arrive sometime around 5:00 p.m. so we left the house around 11:00 a.m. and pulled into the Marriott River Center Hotel early at 3:30 p.m. after making stops in Columbus for coffees and in Seguin for lunch.

Once we checked into our hotel suite overlooking the San Antonio River Walk we walked down to the waterway and boarded one of the scenic tour boats that take tourists along 2 1/2 miles of the famed, "Paseo del Rio". The talking tour boat took us through midtown San Antonio beneath all of the hustle and bustle at street level. It was a great way to get oriented. The meandering waterway is flanked and canopied by beautiful Cyprus trees, palms, and other massive forms of vegetation. There are walkways on both sides of the River Walk and these are themselves flanked with shops, restaurants, and sidewalk cafes, art and gift shops, and trendy hotels. There is color everywhere: bright lights adorn the trees, and the walkway establishments go out of their way to put color in their competing tablecloths and umbrellas. Music plays in many of the alcoves and it is seemingly the intent of each eatery to convince those coming into their restaurant that their patronage is the 'in' thing to do.

After our boat tour we walked to the nearby Rivercenter Mall where, on the steps facing the waterway, we listened to a Mexican musical group perform with an ensemble of reed flutes. We looked around the mall, located the Imax Theater where we would go the next morning to see the special production of "The Alamo". We then decided to take a stroll along the walkway to the Arneson River Theater where a group of Mexican dancers were about to perform dances from the various states of Mexico. The stage at the Arneson is on one side of the waterway, and amphitheater seating is on the other. The seats are grass benches that step down to the water level. Shirley looked at these seats, then looked around and found special adobe enclosed box seats that no one was occupying. She asked an usher if we could sit one of these special boxes, and he said, "Certainly." So there we were, looking down on the dancers and their colorful dresses, all the while sitting in comfortable chairs. Meanwhile, my attention kept wandering to two scantily attired young (18-to 19-year-old) ladies wearing short dresses with nearly see-through soft fabric. They were sitting nearby on the grass benches. I imagined their butts must have itched from exposure to the coarse grass upon which they had positioned themselves.

As the dancers performed on stage there was a never-ending parade of boat tours that came around a sharp turn in the waterway and proceeded to pass right in front of the dancers on stage. The occupants on the boats would cheer, clap, and snap photographs. Each occupant must have wished he or she was in the amphitheater watching the entire performance instead of the fleeting glimpses available from their boat as it floated along the waterway.

One other happening was, to me, especially noteworthy. Occasionally a group of 15-20 mallard ducks would swim around the bend in the waterway. When the birds arrived in front of the stage, they would stop and face the performers, no doubt attracted to the music and the dancing. Some of the ducks, especially the green headed drakes, rose up out of the water and flapped their wings like they, too, were dancing to the music. Several times when a big round of applause erupted from the audience, the ducks would turn and face the crowd. Such showoffs I have never seen. After one group swam, it was only a few minutes until another group of birds came paddling around the bend.

As we walked back along the River Walk both Shirley and I commented on the narrow walkways and on the noticeable lack of barriers to prevent strollers from falling into the water. The guide on the tour boat had mentioned that in the shank of the evening there is a high incidence of tourists finding their way into the waterway. The good news is that the water is only 3 to 4 feet deep but realizing we could be bumped into the waterway was of concern to us. The possibility of out-of-control skateboarders and highly inebriated walkers made it easy to imagine being knocked into the water. Needlessly or not, I was constantly on the alert.

Friday night, on our first day in San Antonio we again went to bed after midnight. It seemed to me that whenever we traveled, we always went to bed after midnight. At home there was only one night owl in the family, and she went to bed long after me.

Saturday morning I was dispatched to get a Starbucks

coffee from a shop in the Rivercenter Mall. As I walked along the River Walk, I came upon a white mongrel bitch that obviously had a litter of pups somewhere. I made the mistake of talking softly to her and saying "Nice doggy." Big mistake! This dog followed me everywhere, even bullying her way into the Mall. I am sure everyone thought the dog was mine. I finally ducked into a restroom and waited. When I came out the dog was gone. Someone else must have said, "Nice doggy."

After our morning coffees we visited the IMAX Theater for a viewing of *The Alamo - The Price of Freedom.* Afterwards, we walked across the street and visited the remnants of the San Antonio de Valero, The Alamo. This site is the most visited tourist destination in Texas, and most of the people who visit it seemed to have been there the day of our visit. We waited in several lines to see exhibits, but mostly we just walked the grounds and commented on who was where during the siege of The Alamo. As resident Texans, we were obligated to make this pilgrimage through hallowed ground.

After visiting The Alamo, I returned to the Marriott and watched the Oklahoma-Texas football game over a lunch of beer and snacks in the hotel's lounge. Shirley went shopping and ate lunch at the Las Canarias restaurant in the Las Mansion del Rio, a luxury hotel located along the River Walk. She made reservations for the Sunday brunch in the main dining area of Las Canarias and asked for the best table in the restaurant. After Shirley explained that Sunday would be her 60th birthday, the French Maitre D' promised her the best of the best.

After lunch, and thinking she might attend services on Sunday, Shirley visited a majestic church located just off the River Walk. Candles were burning and photographers were snapping pictures when she walked into the cavernous structure. There were a number of people in the pews, but the place was not packed. Although she thought the presence of the photographers was unusual, she concluded this place of worship must be one where photographers come to take special photos. After Shirley finished looking over the altar and the front of the church, she turned to leave only to face the music. A bride, wearing a long silk dress with a low-cut back was coming down

And There We Were

the aisle toward her. Shirley found herself a participant in a wedding ceremony without an acceptable way to leave. The bride gave Shirley a smile and many of the guests who had turned to look at the oncoming bride also looked at the pretty and older lady. Each of the onlookers must have thought that Shirley was with the 'other' family.

After the 'wedding' and following the end of the OU- Texas football game, we went back to our suite in the Marriott for a short nap. We were going to have an early dinner at Mi Tierra, a famous Mexican restaurant and bakery in the "Historic Market Square".

We took the trolley car out to Market Square and stepped off, thinking we might do a bit of shopping prior to dining at Mi Tierra. After a walk around the Square, we discovered that all the shops and markets had closed at 6:00 p.m. Although we could have had cocktails at La Margarita, a sister establishment to Mi Tierra, we opted to have a drink in the Mi Tierra bar and to put our name on the waiting list for a table in the restaurant.

Mi Tierra is a very large, extremely well lighted eating establishment whose ceilings are adorned with colorful piñatas and other Mexican decorative items. A wide selection of Mexican pastries is encased along one wall. Mariachi bands stroll through the entire restaurant area. And the place never closes.

We found seats impossible to find in the jam-packed bar. I was searching for a place to sit when I turned and saw Shirley waiving frantically at me. Once again, just by asking Shirley had found a nearly deserted enclave off of the main bar area. The room was furnished with dark ornate tables and large ornamental chairs. On the walls were exquisitely framed Mexican paintings. The area even had its own restrooms, with attendants.

A Mariachi group of 7 well-dressed musicians were tuning their instruments in the back of the room. Besides Shirley and me, there was only one other patron in the room which could easily have seated 70. Those waiting in the larger and crowded bar area obviously did not know that they could seated in this exquisite enclave. All that was needed was an inquiry. For whatever reason, the hostess did not encourage people to come into this beautiful part of the lounge.

We ordered margaritas with tequila shooters on the side. After waiting 30 minutes and enjoying our margaritas, we noticed a group descending down a stairway. They were escorted out to a patio just off of 'our' room. Open windows separated our room from the patio which was also partitioned off from the market square by another wall with open windows. We discovered that the musicians tuning their instruments in our enclave were there to entertain one of the owners of the restaurant. He and his wife were celebrating an anniversary. So, we had wonderful music, an excellent bar hostess, and a marvelous room while we waited for a table in the main dining room. We were almost disappointed when, after an hour, our name was called.

As wonderful as our stay in the lounge had been, we were sadly disappointed in the service and the quality of the food we were served in the restaurant. Mi Tierra has been around for nearly 60 years and it is considered a landmark institution in San Antonio, but we found our food to be bland and poorly presented. Shirley's fajita dish and my lamb were huge disappointments. If we ever returned to San Antonio, we would always go back to the lounge where we waited, but never again eat at the restaurant.

After dinner we hailed a taxi and were driven back to the River Walk. It was a short ride for which we tipped the driver very well. I suspect the driver will forever be looking for another big guy and a pretty lady needing a short ride.

Sunday morning came quickly. When we awoke, Shirley was aged 60. We ordered room service. When our server, Norma, arrived she realized the hotel had left off an orange juice order. We chatted a bit and let on that it was a special day for Shirley. Norma left, and returned with the missing drink and two surprises for us. First, the room service order was 'on the house' and second, a beautiful crystal rose was presented as the hotel's way of saying "Happy Birthday". After we had our coffees. Shirley opened the cards she had received from family and friends.

Shirley dressed for church. I watched the first innings of an Astros-Braves playoff game and then was at the church entrance when Shirley emerged following the service. I was there waiting to escort her to Las Canarias for their famous Sunday brunch.

The staff at Las Mansion greeted Shirley like she was an old friend and longtime patron. The prim and proper Maitre D' even cracked a joke when he remarked that while Shirley was in the powder room I had walked off with a beautiful brunette. As promised, we were seated at the best table in Las Canarias. Champagne was served and we began to pick and choose breakfast items from the expansive buffet. As one often does at a buffet, we ate too much. We paid for our indulgence later when we went for dinner at 'Biga on the Banks', a restaurant included on the short list of the 5 best restaurants in the state of Texas. After brunch all I wanted to do was to find a place to go where I had a chance to digest my meal. My target was our hotel room. Shirley wanted to go shopping again and that was fine with me. Shopping is ok. Buying is a bit more troublesome, but I have learned that many women, like my Shirley, shopped a lot more than they bought.

We dressed for dinner around 6:30 that evening. Because we were still full from the brunch, we chose to walk the mile along the River Walk to the Biga Restaurant. It was a nice walk but even though we had arrived somewhat sweaty (I sweat, Shirley glistens) we still had not worked up an appetite. Subsequent to being seated at a table overlooking the River Walk, indoors for this special occasion, we closed the cloth curtain around us and sipped from a bottle of quality white wine. After Shirley took a call from son Tobin, we ordered dinner. The food was perfectly prepared, brilliantly presented, and delicious. The waiter was disappointed when we did not order any of the restaurant's special appetizers or wonderful salads. We were just too full to eat them. We also passed on dessert and this disappointed the staff as it was going to be complimentary. The staff knew we were at the restaurant to celebrate Shirley's 60th birthday. In the end, they brought out a dish of sorbets

(3) with a burning candle on the dish.

We walked back along the waterway to our hotel on a quiet path along a loop where there are few shops and cafes. We stopped and sat on a bench beneath a tree on "Lover's Island", a famous destination for those who will either marry or who want to remain married. After we arrived back at the hotel, Shirley took or returned calls from family members and friends. I think she had a great day. She usually did.

On Monday morning we checked out of the hotel and returned to Market Square to peruse the shops that had been closed when we went to Mi Tierra Restaurant. We shopped for a couple of hours, bought precious little, and then departed for a tour of the Spanish missions.

There are five famous San Antonio missions, the most famous of which is the one called "The Alamo". All of the missions were built in the early 1700s, and all played a key role in the development of what was then the northern province of Mexico. We spent most of our time touring Mission Concepcion, the best preserved of all the remaining missions. After our tour of the missions, we bid adieu to San Antonio and headed for the Texas Hill Country and the famous tourist destination of New Braunfels.

The Guadalupe River in the New Braunfels area is a wonderful locale for water sports. The river is clear and of sufficient size to accommodate the tens of thousands of river floaters who come down the river on inner tubes, rafts, and even life jackets. The city of New Braunfels has built a number of pools, chutes, and falls that are fun to navigate. Several commercial groups (e.g., Schlitterbaum's and Splash Town) have built very large facilities where those of all ages can go and enjoy water sports. There is a satellite community near New Braunfels that is the 'in' place to eat, shop, drink, and lodge. This village is Gruene (pronounced 'green') and it is fun, fun, fun. The food, service, and ambience during our lunch at the Grist Mill Restaurant, located on a forested bluff overlooking the Guadalupe River, were fantastic. We were reluctant to leave. But we did finally depart, and it was well after dark when we finally pulled into

38 Noble Bend Drive.

The San Antonio trip was the last one we took during the first year of my retirement from the oil and gas industry. Both of our mothers would be with us on Thanksgiving, but we were through traveling in 2004. It was one heck of a year. During the remaining years we had together we took many memorable trips and cruises. What we did in that first year of retirement was a template for the years that followed. I may someday write of further adventures but for now I will conclude this story of 'us' with a trip we did not expect to take.

Chapter 28

AN UNEXPECTED JOURNEY
A Trip to France and a Riverboat Float Through the Wine Region of Burgundy
(July 30 - August 11, 2008)

Shirley and I never expected to travel abroad after we retired. We had lived overseas for seven years and we thought that there was not much to be gained by further travel to Europe, South America, or Asia. We had been there and done that. But we made one deviation from this line of thinking. We were talked into taking an aforementioned trip to France for a float trip through the wine growing region of Burgundy. This trip turned out to be one of the more memorable trips we took during our retirement years.

In January of 2008, Lee Mossel, a longtime friend, former roommate, college classmate, and a fellow oil field compatriot contacted us and said that he and his wife Jan were planning a canal/river float through the Burgundy region of France. He said Shirley and I might or might not be interested in floating through the scenic French countryside whilst being plied with fine wines and gourmet food. The real hook, though, was that those filling the luxury barge would all be longtime friends from our days at the University of Oregon and/or oil field professionals with whom we had worked with in the Denver area. Fundamentally, all the trippers would be oil field 'trash'. Six couples and one recently widowed wife of an oil field associate committed to make the trip. Thirteen familiar souls would be aboard the La Belle Epoque as it made its way through Burgundy via the Yonne River and the Nivernais Canal.

And There We Were

Although the float trip was scheduled for two weeks in early August, most of the group agreed to spend time together in Paris both before and after the Burgundy float. For Bob and Shirley this would be our French swan song. Either together or by ourselves, and with others, we had been to France many times, beginning as far back as 1978. Shirley and I knew Paris like few other tourists. The trip gave us the opportunity to show our friends the best of what we thought Paris had to offer. We might have been presumptuous, but we believed we could make our friends' visit to Paris one to remember. I think we did.

Our trip to Paris began with a direct flight to Paris from Houston's Bush International Airport. Our friends Paul and Sharon Hess connected with us at the Houston airport after a long and arduous trip from Drain, Oregon. Shirley and I used 500,000 of our accumulated frequent flyer miles to fly Business First across the Atlantic. Prior to take off, I photographed Shirley with a glass of Champagne in hand as she perused an all-encompassing and expansive dinner menu. Shirley looked at me and said, "I really love and miss this elegance". When we had lived abroad almost every overseas trip we took was on the company dime and included either First Class or Business First travel.

Our good friends from Drain were in the economy section. Paul said he could almost see the window from his seat in the center section of the airplane. Had it not been for our frequent flyer miles we would have most likely been seated beside them eating coach fare cuisine and purchasing our drinks.

After landing at Charles De Gaulle Airport, we took a previously reserved shuttle into the City and to our hotel, the Ampere, on Villiers Street. Our tour group had assembled by late afternoon, some had arrived earlier and some later than we did. Shirley and I thought the group might enjoy our first night in Paris having drinks at the Panorama Bar on the 33rd floor of the Concorde La Fayette Hotel. We had visited this bar during one of our previous trips and we knew it offered a spectacular viewing of the Eiffel Tower and the nighttime illumination of the City of Lights. The bar is stair-cased so all can sit at tables looking out windows with an unobstructed view. We soon discovered that the Eiffel Tower light show would not begin until 11:00 p.m., and by that time most of us wanted to be back at our hotel preparing for a good night's sleep. Still, for those who had never been to Paris before this was a great way to get a feel for the city. To add a bit of adventure to our trip to the Concorde Hotel excursion, we convinced our fellow travelers to take the underground Metro rail both to and back from the Concorde. It was an experience to be sure.

During our first full day in Paris, Shirley and I visited the Eiffel Tower with Paul and Sharon. The elevator to the upper tier was temporarily closed due to high winds, but Shirley bought tickets for all so that we might be ready if conditions changed. And change they did. Although the ride to the upper tier of the Tower was only open for a short time, we were among the few who were able to ascend the Tower for a spectacular viewing of Paris from a height in excess of 1000 feet. After our trip to the top, we dropped down for lunch at the Altitude 95 restaurant on the first level of the Tower, 95 meters above street level. After lunch at the restaurant, we took the Metro back to our hotel where we took short naps to refresh ourselves for an outing Shirley and I had orchestrated prior to leaving the States. The group was going to attend a Can Can show, and it was to the best of such shows in all of Paris - the Moulin Rouge.

Shirley and I were apprehensive about the evening at the Moulin Rouge. Although we had been to the Moulin Rouge and had enjoyed the show, one never knows how performances that feature bare breasted female dancers will be perceived by a group of women in their late 50s and middle 60s. I was not worried about the men. Pouty, perky breasts do not offend men.

Although I had selected a middle-priced dinner/show package and had asked for the best table, I was worried about the quality of the meal and the location of our table. Because my request had been made to the Moulin Rouge staff via a phone call, I had no assurance as to how we were going to be treated. I need not have worried. Our group of 13 was treated like VIPs. We were allowed to skip the long queue waiting to be seated and were taken immediately to the best table on the ground floor, just a few feet from the stage. Wow! I was as proud as could be: the idea for the outing came from Shirley, and I had organized it.

For the first two hours we were treated to songs sung by female and male vocalists who were accompanied by a small combo. Our meal was sumptuous if a bit "Frenchy". The dinner package included essentially unlimited bottles of wine. We consumed eight in total.

The opening act was quite a spectacle. All of the female performers were on stage, each attired in a massive red feather costume that could be folded up to look like a pair of red lips. About 20 percent of the young ladies were topless. The star of the show was a young man who could sing and dance like no one else. There were also comedians, ventriloquists, and gymnasts. The most memorable act involved a massive aquarium that rose out of the dance floor. Our good friend Sharon Hess who was close enough to the stage to see what was in the tank, started to hyperventilate. We thought she might be having a heart attack. As it turned out, the cage contained three pythons who were soon wrapped around a scantily clad young woman after she had jumped into the aquarium.

We took the underground back to the Ampere and were in bed by midnight. We had a big day ahead of us. The group had the following day set aside for tours of choice in Paris. Shirley and I chose to escort Paul and Sharon to the Palace of Versailles, a 12-mile train ride from the center of Paris. We arrived in Versailles to find a very long line waiting in the rain to purchase tickets for admission into the Palace and access to the Gardens. Shirley and Paul went on a walkabout and Shirley discovered we could take a private tour of the Palace with immediate access - no waiting in the rain. We stepped out of the queue and enjoyed a great tour that for the most part avoided other visitors. It was indeed a "private" tour. On our private tour we visited many unique rooms open only to those taking one of the paid tours. And after all, "It was only money."

The next morning the group gathered in the lobby to wait for the bus which would take us to Clamecy. Shirley wanted to stretch her legs, so she took a short walk around the neighborhood. She passed by Petrus, a very elegant and upscale restaurant. She stuck her head in and asked the Maitre D' if she could have a cup of coffee on the terrace. The man was indignant and said, "Madame this is a very fine restaurant and we do not serve just coffees." Shirley's response was, "There is no one here yet, and I know this is a very fine restaurant. That is why I stopped. Perhaps someday I will come back and have dinner with you." She walked out and had not taken more than 20 steps before the man came running after her. He said, "Please have coffee with us." He did not charge her for the coffee and when she left, he handed her a single rose to take with her when she boarded the bus.

We left Paris on the A6 traveling southeast towards Lyon. The journey out from Paris was interesting because it gave us our first glimpse of rural France. We soon passed through expansive croplands: harvested grain stubble, corn, rapeseed and pastures, but we had not yet seen a single vineyard. This stretch of countryside seemed to be sparsely populated. Most of the farmers evidently lived in nearby villages and not on their farms.

About an hour from Paris, we pulled into a freeway rest area where we could purchase water, chips, sandwiches, or whatever, even gifts if one was so inclined (several of our women were). Then after enough time for our bus driver to have a hot meal, we left for our final push to Clamecy where the La Belle Epoque was tethered.

The further we drove the more hilly the terrain became. Hardwood and conifer trees lined the freeway, some seemingly planted in rows. We saw caution signs with *Watch for Deer* and *Next 7 to 20 kilometers* on them. The setting was not unlike that in some parts of the Willamette Valley.

Upon our arrival in Clamecy we were welcomed onto the La Belle Epoque with a Champagne Reception hosted by Captain James and the staff, all of whom we would soon come to know and appreciate. The staff included Louisa, the Captain's Mate; Marie, the chef; and attendants Lola and Olga. This elaborate welcome was our introduction to ever available intoxicants.

Our first dinner onboard provided us with a first look at the elegant place settings. We were also introduced to the masterful skills of Chef Marie who came out before each dish, be it an appetizer, the main course, or dessert, to describe what she had prepared for us. She seduced us all with her enthusiasm. One could not but love this girl.

We soon learned that if you have wine before dinner on the deck, wine with dinner, and then after dinner wines back out on the deck you need to pace yourself. Some of us paid a high price and learned our lesson. Some paid a high price and never learned a thing.

Monday was our first day on the Canal Nivernais which runs nearly parallel to the Yonne River. Indeed, sometimes the canal and the river are one. Captain James began moving the barge into position around 8:30 a.m. so that he would be in position to be through the nearby lock when it opened at 9:00 a.m. Boaters need to be aware that all locks have specific opening and closing times. The lock masters open the locks at 9:00 a.m. in the morning, close from noon until 1:00 p.m. for lunch, and then shut down in the evening at 7:00 p.m. Our floating schedule was closely coordinated with these opening and closings.

Lola and Olga put out a breakfast buffet around 7:30 a.m. It consisted of rolled slices of ham, thin slices of white cheese, cut and whole fruit, and cereal. Best of all, Captain James went ashore each morning and brought back fresh breads and croissants from one of his favorite local bakeries. Marie always had a selection of jams for us, including her famous homemade fig jam. One could overeat or not, as one saw fit. The rolled ham and cheese was the most popular item, so popular that late risers often found this platter empty by the time they were ready to eat.

On our first morning aboard the La Belle Epoque, the skies were overcast and we floated through occasional rain squalls. When the rain stopped all of us would be on deck, when the rain returned most of us retreated into the main cabin. For some reason, Sharon Hess and Shirley Lent rarely came in out of the rain. Often the only ones outside were Sharon, Shirley, and Captain James, who was fully clad in rain gear.

We passed through a number of locks as we floated down the canal. Sometimes the locks were manned by a lock master who lived in a nearby house. Invariably reflecting the care the resident lock master gave them, some were simple structures with no outside amenities or gardens. Others were well kept and landscaped with flowering plants and bushes. The lock masters themselves also ran a full gamut of characters. On the one hand one might see an attractive young lady turning the wheels. On another, a snaggled-toothed old hag in control of the operation. Young and old men also served as lock masters.

One was never allowed to forget that the lock master is king. He/she controls all transport as it moves up and down the canals. Some can be bribed with a fine bottle of wine (to let you through a few minutes after the gate has been closed), but one had better not count on this sort of favoritism.

As became our daily routine, we would float the canal or river in the morning and in the afternoon, we would visit a historic landmark, a vineyard, or a quaint village. On the first afternoon we went ashore to tour the Chateau of Bazoches-du-Morvan. Built between 1170 and 1190, it became well known when Marshal de Vauban, one of the great men of France, purchased the fortress home in 1675. It has been written that every fortress put under siege by de Vauban fell (49-0) and every fortification built by him never fell (160-0). He was MVP of his league for sure.

On the way back to the La Belle Epoque we traveled along several country roads that cut through a section of the 300 square mile Dark Forest, a French National Forest. Captain James and the rest of us got into an interesting discussion concerning the stacks of wood we saw near the roads. We learned that nearly all of the villagers in the area burn wood for cooking and for heating, and that each village is given an area of the forest where marked trees can be cut (part of a thinning out process). On certain weeks during the year members of the villages meet to cut and stack wood for the following year.

When the next year rolls around, the dry wood is hauled back to the village and divvied up amongst the residents.

When I saw so much wood stacked so close to the road, I asked if anyone from another village ever poached another village's wood. Captain James said that such stealing would just not happen in France because each person in a village knows where his neighbor gets his wood. If someone showed up with wood from a source outside the village, then the entire village would likely inform the authorities of the wood thief. My thought was, "Well in the United States we have horse thieves." I'll wager they have wood thieves in France. I don't care what the French say.

On the afternoon of our second day, we visited the mountain top village of Vezelay. This wonderful village is called the Scorpion on the Mountain because its streets and red roofed houses and shops wind down off the mountaintop and into the valley. Looking from on high, the village resembles the body and tail of a scorpion.

On our way back to the barge we expressed our surprise at the absence of any significant vineyards. We were, after all, floating and traveling through Burgundy. Captain James assured us we would see many vineyards in the coming days.

Wednesday, our third day on the float, turned out to be one of the best days of our trip through Burgundy. The skies were bright blue and the temperature was in the mid 70's. We could not have asked for a more beautiful day. The day was made even more memorable for the excursion we took to Noyers, France, a village included in a list of the most beautiful of all French villages. Noyers did not disappoint!

A medieval village located on a loop of the Sereine River, Noyers was settled at its location because of the natural ramparts the Sereine provided on three sides and a high bluff that rises on the fourth (northeast) side. Nature provided the rudiments for a fortress that required only minor modifications. The village is home to the many farmers who work the surrounding pastoral lands.

The entrance to Noyers is through a stone portal that leads

onto cobbled streets bordered by quaint residential and commercial buildings. One is struck by the ancient buildings and the colorful plants that hang off window openings. Some buildings appear to be leaning into each other, as if they needed each other's support to keep from falling over.

The highlight of our visit to Noyers was a luncheon served in the Restaurant les Millesimes in the Place de l'hotel de Ville. We were the only diners in a small room reserved for our group. An elongated window view table was set with wine glasses, china, fine linen napkins; beautiful fresh flowers served as a centerpiece. The walls were lined with oil paintings. One large painting, framed between two tall flower arrangements, appeared to be a scene along the Sereine River, and it towered above a fireplace mantle. Beneath the painting and resting on the mantle were three pieces of ornamental China. When I first walked into the room, I would not have been surprised if someone had said that the setting was a restoration from the time of King Louis XIV.

As soon as we were seated the staff brought out fresh breads and bottles of red and white wine. The red was opened first and left to breathe, but some of us caused a bit of a stir when we poured and sampled the red. The waiter, friendly but firmly, informed us that the red was to be drunk with the main course. He then poured the white. So there we were, drinking white wine and sampling the fresh breads (no bread plates by the way: in France one places the bread on one's linen).

The main course soon was served on warmed plates placed on gold rimmed ornamental dishes that I thought were the main dining plates (wrong!). The main entry was a piece of braised boneless lamb covered with a mushroom demi-glaze. With the lamb came small portions of carrot, onion, celery, and mushroom. Sprinkled around the edge of the serving plate were fine ground seasonings and stems of rosemary. The presentation could have been a model for a painting class, and the food was delicious. We were advised that we could tuck into the red wine now that the lamb was on the table.

Following the completion of the main course, the staff

brought out an exquisite chocolate soufflé resting on a raspberry sauce. Located along a swirl of pink sauce and chocolate crumbs were strawberries, chocolate sauce, ice cream, and thin strips of white chocolate. The red spiral (it had a peach-colored border) expanded increasingly from the center of the plate to the very outer edge. An astronomer might have said it looked like a dessert replica of a galaxy. This dessert was a masterpiece. We asked the chef to come out so we could let him know how much we appreciated his fine work. When he walked out the kitchen door we broke into applause. Such applause was never more deserving than the one we gave this humble man.

Once back on board La Belle Epoque we began our slow journey down the Nivernais and River Yonne on our way to The Caves de Bailly. The beautiful weather induced some of us to take a bike ride along the waterways. Bob's unfortunate luck was that he chose to ride with Jan Mossel, a world class triathlete. As soon as I set on the bike, the seat collapsed downward and bruised my tush. We stopped to raise the seat, but it just collapsed again. So I ignored it, and swallowed the pain as we peddled on.

Jan and I passed fishermen with long (30 feet) rods that blocked the path and we saw a great number of fish schooling along the banks of the canal. The schools scared easily so we never got to stop and admire them. Three or four miles downstream (maybe more), we came to the village where we were certain we would spend the night. It was such a nice day that Jan and I opted to ride back up the canal to see if we could board the Epoque at one of the locks. We rode for a goodly time, leisurely if you will, until we saw a lock about a mile upstream. It looked like the La Belle Epoque was about to be lowered to the next level. Jan and I took off as fast as we could, peddling like gang busters. When we finally made it to the lock, the boat was so low that the only way we could board was to step onto the roof and bring our bikes along with us. We lowered the bikes to the main deck after the barge was under way. I, quite frankly, was winded. We made it back in time, but the long ride with the sprint at the end had taken its toll.

When I was getting ready for bed in the evening, Shirley

looked at me and asked, "What is that purple coloration on the back of your legs?" I pulled down my shorts and looked in the mirror. I was black and blue from the small of my back all the way down to the base of my buttocks. I blamed the bruise on the collapsing seat but who knows; maybe I just pushed those poor muscles harder than they had been pushed in over 40 years. As for Jan, well she looked as pretty and as spunky as ever.

After lunch on the fourth day, we boarded vans for a trip to the Caves de Bailly. These caves have been excavated in limestone and are now used to store wines and Champagne. Visitors drive into the caves and are directed to parking areas near a retail outlet. The air is quite cool. We exited our vans walked over to a large counter where we sampled the fine Champagne. Along a limestone wall behind the sales counter was a triangular stack of bottles that rose nearly to the ceiling. Several of the ladies bought gifts or other items. Shirley purchased a quaint wooden hand carrier that had room to transport or store three bottles of wine.

Captain James told the group Germans had used these massive caves to assemble and store fighter planes during World War II. Apparently, the Allies knew of the caves but bombing did nothing to damage the integrity of the underground fortress.

We were soon back in the van and off to Chablis, passing through the village of St. Ibis on our way. As we worked our way through the streets of St. Ibis, Captain James pointed out a "naughty car". Naughty cars are as small as a golf cart, and they are driven by those who have lost their driving licenses (usually due to driving under the influence) or by those too young to get a license. Captain James said that it was not unusual to see five or six of these naughty cars outside a local pub shortly after its opening hour.

We took a quick tour of Chablis and visited another Gothic church (seen one church you have....), but this church did have an interesting touch. A number of horseshoes were imbedded in one of the main doors. Leaving a horseshoe on the church door is said to bring one good luck. Local lore had it that Joan of Arc passed this way and placed a horseshoe on this very door. Considering what happened to young Joan at the stake, one has to wonder how much good luck placing a horseshoe on the door actually brings.

The highlight of our stay in Chablis was a visit to the Laroche Winery Boutique where we were given a tour and a tasting of the fine Chablis wines. On the tour took we saw an ancient wooden wine press which was balanced on one end by a massive wooden screw and on the other end by a circular wooden press. When the screw was tightened, the press crushed the grapes with a pressure of over 10,000 pounds. The resulting liquid drained into a collection vat. I think wine crushing is more than a little easier now, but it is interesting to observe the effort the locals put forth to squeeze grapes back in the olden days. It must have taken the whole village to load the grapes, press them, and collect the liquid.

The wine tasting was a big hit. I have never particularly liked Chablis wine (a dry Chardonnay) but the real Chablis Grand Crus we sampled were outstanding.

We passed a number of hillside vineyards on our return trip to the barge and we stopped to take a few pictures and to look at the grapes (still about 30 days from being ready to harvest). We noticed that the soil was very rocky; mostly a bit of clay and a lot of small limestone pebbles. Captain James mentioned that we might have noticed a number of rose bushes at the end of the rows of grapes. He told us the bushes are sensitive to disease and fungal infection and function as indicators of the health of the vines. Blight on the rose bushes informs the vintners that the grapes may be in jeopardy, and a treatment may be required.

We were told that once the grapes are ripe, the vintners do not mind if locals clip 2 or 3 kilograms (4 to 6 pounds) of grapes from the vines for their personal use. I found that interesting. In the United States, one might get shot for taking a single watermelon from a ten-acre patch.

An interesting side note to growing grapes is that the quality of the grapes depends, in part, on the amount of sunshine they get. As a consequence, grapes grown on the east and southeast facing slopes are known to produce the best wines.

Friday morning, our fifth day on the La Belle Epoque, meant that our journey through Burgundy was almost over. The day's float would take us down the Nivernais to Auxerre, the largest of the villages we would encounter. The morning broke with rain, heavy at times. A number of the group went out on the deck in rain gear. The Yonne River flowed parallel to the canal at this location, and the current in the river formed many scenic riffles and rapids. It was not long before the heavy rain drove all but Sharon and Shirley into the main cabin. Later, when the really heavy rain began to fall, only Sharon remained on the deck near the bow of the boat. The rest of us retreated to the cabin and began our assault on the beers and wines that were always available.

We docked at Auxerre around noon. For those inclined to do so there was a church to visit (what can I say), quaint buildings to see, and the siren of shops calling out to those needing a last-minute gift for a sister, brother, mother, or grandchild. I for one stayed back at the barge and rested up for the big evening: Friday was the night of the Captain's dinner. The attendants had forewarned us they would be dressed to the nines and the meal would be something to remember.

When Sharon came back from her tour of Auxerre village, I asked where Shirley was. Sharon said she was shopping and that she had wanted to stop by the church on the way back. But Sharon also added, "She will be sorry because they have closed the church to visitors." I suggested Shirley would probably still get in the church. Sharon said that there was a cantankerous old lady manning the front door and that she was sure Shirley would be denied entrance. My comment was, "Don't bet on it." I had seen Shirley navigate such obstacles before and I was sure she would find a way into the church. And she did! When she found the front door closed, she walked around to a side door where she not only found it open, but also found it manned by a friendly gentleman who was more than willing to let her enter and give her a tour. That is pretty much how Shirley's life went. It was almost magical.

During our last evening on the La Belle Epoque, we began to assemble on the deck for pre-dinner drinks. The rain had stopped and the evening was delightfully cool. Each couple surfaced from their rooms dressed in the best attire we had seen during our entire trip. Dinner was supposed to have been formal dress, but only Captain James appeared in a suit. The rest of us looked spiffy but there were no suits. The ladies (Captain James' and ours) were simply beautiful. The real showstoppers were the attendants and our chef. Olga was dressed in a black and white polka dot gown. Her hair was let down and she had on stunning make-up. We hardly recognized her. Chef Marie wore a low-cut white top over a short black skirt. She too sported make-up and wore pendant earrings that matched her long necklace. Louisa and Lola were both stunning in their black cocktail dresses and each came attired in a necklace culminating in an elegant pendant. The girls' forewarning had not been wrong: you might think we look cute now but wait until you see us the night of the Captain's Dinner. They were spot on.

Our last dinner on the La Belle Epoque again featured lamb, cooked to perfection. Our dessert was another one of those delicious French chocolate confections. After dinner we all retired to the deck for one last evening of visiting and post dinner drinks. The wines were soon replaced by after dinner liqueurs and whiskeys. Paul Hess found a bottle of quality Scotch. He handled it well. Ben Peterson brought out the last of his Cuban cigars and all of the men (I think) lit up. We partied until it was dark, then retired for our last night of sleep on the fabulous La Belle Epoque.

Saturday morning found all of us scurrying about packing our suitcases for the trip back to Paris and saying goodbyes to the staff. Shirley caught Olga and Louisa alone and told them how much fun she had. When she added that she hopped that each of them had a long and wonderful life, they cried. Paul and Sharon had a surprise for Louisa. She had dropped a bracelet into the Nivernais at one of the locks. Paul had learned of this and when he found the bracelet cost 20 euros, he and Sharon decided to give Louisa that amount as a special departing gift. She cried.

An Unexpected Journey

It was time to board the bus and leave for Paris. Shirley and I would never again float a barge through Burgundy, but we never forgot either this float trip or the fine crew that served us.

We returned to the Ampere Hotel where Shirley had the concierge call two taxis, then she went to use the hotel toilet. When she returned to the street, the cabs she had ordered had been commandeered by others in our group. She returned to the concierge and had him order two more cabs. And so, early in the afternoon on a Saturday in August, we pulled into the entrance to the Marriott Paris Champs Elysees.

Our adventures that day were just beginning.

The streets along the Champs Elysees were packed with tourists. Due to construction, the cab we took could get us only about 50 feet from the hotel entrance. Paul and Sharon were waiting for us when we arrived, their luggage already having been loaded on a carrier and taken to the second-floor lobby. A porter managed to get our luggage through the mass of people occupying nearly every square foot of the sidewalk. Shirley and I had never seen so many people on the streets of Paris. But this was August, the month when Europe shuts down and everyone goes on vacation. What better place is there to visit than Paris?

As we were checking in the four of us agreed to reconvene at 4:00 p.m. in the lobby lounge overlooking the Champs Elysees. That rendezvous time would allow us to unpack, take a shower, and catch a few winks before heading out on the town.

As soon as we arrived in our room, Shirley said she was going for a walkabout. I knew exactly where she was going. As mentioned previously, one of her favorite places in all of Paris is the most elegant of all hotels, George V. This five-star beauty is only a short walk from the Marriott. When I came to Paris for the meetings with Kerr-McGee's partners in Africa (our Algerian, Moroccan, and Gabon concessions), we often stayed at the Prince de Galles, next door to George V. The Prince de Galles is elegant and very expensive, but with room rates at least $400 per night lower than those at George V. A partners' dinner one evening at the George V was one of the more expensive business dinners our consortium ever had. But the lobby, the indoor café, and the dining areas are beautiful, both in decoration and in the accompanying flower arrangements. I had taken Shirley for a tour of this hotel during one of her first visits to Paris. She was hooked from that moment onward.

Shirley invariably visited the Le Galerie café in the George V where she ordered what she said was the best onion soup (French onion, of course) she had ever eaten. I had accompanied her on several of these occasions, and I know how deeply she appreciated the elegance of the surroundings and the pampering available to all diners, even those having only soups and wine. Le Galerie looks out onto an interior courtyard filled with plants, flowers, and fountains. Live music, either from a pianist or harpist, is present throughout the day. And the prices at the cafe are in line with what one would expect of a more reasonable Parisian hotel.

When Shirley returned to the Marriott after having been gone for nearly two hours I asked where she had been. Her answer was, to George V and Le Galerie, of course. She had been disappointed that only High Tea was being served. Her craving for onion soup would have to wait until another time. But the waiter brought her a cappuccino and scones. And after only a few minutes the pianist was persuaded to play one of Shirley's favorite songs, *Somewhere My Love* from the movie *Dr. Zhivago*. So there was Shirley, seated for a gathering of well dressed (and well healed) ladies having High Tea in Le Galerie. For Shirley, it did not get much better than that.

Shirley retired to our room to freshen up a bit. When she rejoined Paul, Sharon, and me at the hotel bar, we began making plans for the evening. We decided to first take a short walk along the packed Parisian sidewalks. Tightly grouped amongst others strolling up and down the Champs Elysees, we slowly made our way up the street to the Arch De Triumph. After Sharon took a few photos, we collectively decided that the best vantage point for viewing the Champs Elysees was from the platform on the top of the Arch. We rode an elevator nearly to the top after which we took stairs up to the viewing area. The trip to the top of the Arch De Triumph was the first for each of us. What wonderful views we had.

After spending 30 or 40 minutes walking around the top of the Arch, we returned to street level where we witnessed an in-progress ceremony featuring a very formal presentation of colors by a military contingent. It was pointed out to us that each day the French conduct this ceremony to honor specific individuals who have given their lives in service to their country. It was a most poignant ceremony, and we were delighted to have had the opportunity to be a part of the crowd watching this somber salute.

We walked back down the Champs Elysees. When we looked at the cobblestone street, we could only imagine how difficult it must be for the bike riders who conclude the Tour de France with 7 laps around the length of the Champs Elysees. It must be a jarring ride for these tired riders.

We turned down the Avenue George V and came to the Hotel George V. Shirley wanted Paul and Sharon to see the lobby and the atrium, and if they so wished, to have drinks at Le Bar, known as the *rendezvous incontournable* for both guests and Parisians. The elegance of the George V was intimidating to the other three of us, but Shirley moved comfortably through the elegant surroundings and we soon found ourselves seated at Le Bar. This lounge is beautifully constructed with a liberal use of mahogany and cognac-colored woods. Our table near a window looking out on Avenue George V allowed us a view of the entire room, and also provided us a view into the nearby atrium, visible through the open doors leading into Le Bar. We took about an hour to enjoy our beers, cokes, and wines. We were served nuts and olives by waiters who were always attentive to an empty glass.

On our way out of the hotel we passed through the lobby area where several members of the staff acknowledged Shirley's presence. One even commented that it was good to see her back after having seen her in the afternoon. I think the rest of us, not nearly so comfortable in such a posh setting, were more than glad to be back on the streets.

As we walked down the Avenue George V the girls spotted a

majestic church that they wished to visit. As I have said previously, "After you have seen one church...," so Paul and I worked our way down to the Crazy Horse Cabaret, known as the most erotic cabaret in Paris (the naughty ladies dance dressed only in their high heel shoes). We waited in front of the Cabaret and when the girls showed up, we jokingly said, "We were trying to decide if we should go into the church or into the Crazy Horse." A lady standing near us broke in, "The Crazy Horse is a much better choice." Slender and smoking a cigarette, this lady was dressed in a typically Parisian style – neither flashy nor gaudy. We told her we had already been to a performance at the Moulin Rouge and that we suspected the Crazy Horse show was probably similar. The lady knocked off the ash on her fag and said, "The show at the Crazy Horse is better." We asked how this might be and she responded, "The girls on stage at the Crazy Horse are much more athletic." I thought, "more athletic and more scantily clad to be sure." I asked the friendly lady why she knew so much about the Crazy Horse? Was she possibly a dancer in the show? She replied that she worked at the Crazy Horse but was not nearly talented enough to be on stage.

I had seen a performance at the Crazy Horse when I was in Paris on one of our business meetings a number of years back. The show was entertaining, but I remembered the place being on the sleazy side. I tried to project how the lady we had been chatting with might be employed by the club. All I could conjure up was that since she was on the street while the show was in progress, she was either an accountant type (who worked days only) or she was self-employed.

We proceeded down Avenue George V until we came to the Place de L'Alma, a cross street that runs along the Seine River. We found a nice street corner café, Chez Francis, where tables both inside and outside offered a great view of the Eiffel Tower. Shirley approached the hostess and asked for the best table, one where we could dine and have the clearest view of the Tower. The hostess said if we were willing to wait she would get us the table we sought, then she asked that we seat ourselves off to the side of dining area, a place reserved for patrons who wished to have only beers and wine.

An Unexpected Journey

We seated ourselves and were soon approached by a waiter in a hurry. We told him we needed to look over the menus, and could he give us a few minutes. When he came back, we were still looking, whereupon he asked us to please make up our minds. I ordered the huge stein of beer, Paul a smaller glass of beer. The waiter said I had ordered too much, but I told him I could handle it. Sharon and Shirley ordered a coke and a Perrier, respectively. I finished the beer, if for no other reason than to prove to the waiter that I was up to the task. After about 30 minutes of waiting, we were getting a bit antsy, thinking that maybe the hostess could not deliver on what she promised. No sooner had we began to have doubts than she motioned to us. We did indeed have the best table in the house, outside with an unblocked view straight to the Eiffel Tower.

After dinner and around 11:00 p.m., the blue lights bathing the Eiffel Tower began to sparkle and continued to do so for nearly 10 minutes. Paul was so delighted with our table that he tipped the hostess a goodly sum.

We left the Place de L' Alma at midnight and walked back to the Marriott. In our room we found a note from Jan and Lee Mossel saying they were going to join the four of us for a dinner cruise on the Seine on Sunday night. This was great news as it just seemed appropriate that we spend our last night in Paris with our good friends from Drain, Oregon and Denver, Colorado.

Our last day in France began with the skies a dark gray under a threat of rain. Shirley and I had coffees and took a quick run through the complimentary buffet breakfast. As was usually the case when we went through a buffet line, we filled our plates with too much: omelets, sausage, bacon, fruit, cheeses, potatoes, etc. Still, it was nice that a least a few Caucasians were present to keep the numerous Arab guests company. We had noticed that most of the guests in the Marriott and in the George V were Arabs. Apparently, that is how the petro-dollars were being spent - on a great lifestyle abroad.

After breakfast we dressed for church. Shirley talked me and the Hess' into attending International Mass at Notre Dame.

And There We Were

Our 11:30 mass was expected to be filled to capacity, and it was. We managed to weave our way through the masses exiting the church after the 10:00 a.m. mass, and we found great seats about midway back. Sharon took an aisle seat, and we were next to her.

Notre Dame, extensively damaged by a fire in April, 2019, was not only a beautiful church it was also the most visited tourist spot in all of France. In part, this popularity was due to the magnificence of the building, but the fact that there is no admission fee also contributed to its ranking as France's number one tourist attraction.

We watched the highly ceremonial Catholic services and admired the stained-glass windows and the high Gothic ceilings. Afterwards, I was glad we took the time to attend the services, but I surely did not understand the pomp and ceremony. Even so, watching the priests enter the church flanked by young men swinging smoking spherical incense burners was a sight to behold. If the smoke was intended to keep evil and the devil at bay, I am pretty sure it worked.

Seated in front of us during the service was a very beautiful young girl, aged 4 or 5 years who, though she wore a pink dress and looked like a young princess, was not at all well -mannered. When the congregation stood (there is a lot of standing in a Catholic service) she lay on the bench and writhed around. Paul was kind and occasionally winked at her.

It was not long until I looked toward the aisle and saw this lovely young girl sitting on Sharon's lap. The youngster had adopted Paul and Sharon as grandparents. After church we passed the family and the young girl near the exit area. We spoke with the girl's parents and learned her name was Ruby. After a short conversation, we left to find a place of have lunch. We chose a street side café facing Notre Dame. After we were seated, we turned around, and there was Ruby and her parents seated at the table next to ours. Ruby spent most of her lunch time with us. She ate some of Paul's sandwich and she sat on Sharon's lap. She looked up at Sharon and asked, "Grandma, just how old are you?" And she advised Paul not to talk when he had food in his mouth. I don't think I have ever seen such an immediate transfer of affection. Ruby and the Hess' were made for each other.

All of us took a short nap after lunch. We were prepping to have one last wonderful evening in Paris. At 7:00 p.m. we were to report to a Seine riverside dock where a Bateaux Parisiens dinner cruise ship would take us on a twilight-night trip down the Seine and back again. The trip would begin and end at the base of the Eiffel Tower.

When we departed for our dinner cruise, we flagged a cab outside of the Marriott. We were impressed with the driver. His English was impeccable, and he was very friendly. The gentleman was born in Lebanon and raised in Dallas. We liked the guy so much that we arranged to have him take us to the airport the next morning. Paul and Sharon also asked the driver to take them to their new hotel when he returned from taking the Lents to Charles de Gaulle. When he dropped us at the dock, we paid our tariff and tipped him handsomely, knowing full well that a short distance fare with four passengers was not something he or any other cabby appreciated.

Shirley had requested a front-of-the-boat round table which meant we would have to pay nearly $500 per couple for "Service Premier". We had been led to believe there were two of tables for 12 at the front of the glass enclosed dinner boat. The six of us would have one of those tables and we would be seated next to a table of six from another booking. I was nervous and wanted to make sure not only that we had great views, but that the experience was all Shirley had hoped it might be, and that the outing would be memorable for both the Hess' and Mossels.

Lee and Jan had not yet arrived when it came time to board, so Paul, Sharon, Shirley, and I were escorted to the very bow of the boat where there was a singular table for six. We could not have had a table with any better view or more privacy. I gave a big sigh of relief and was pretty much full of myself.

After Lee and Jan joined us and we shared a bottle or two of Champagne. When we pushed off for our trip down the Seine, we were serenaded by an onboard entertainer. Then we simply quietly passed beneath a never-ending series of Parisian bridges (there are reported to be 37 such bridges, some of which are for pedestrians only). One of the first bridges we passed beneath was Pont Alexandre III, the most sumptuous bridge in all of Paris. The bridge is decorated with lampposts and sculptures of cherubs and nymphs. The pillars on the ends of the bridge are topped with large gilded statues. Anyone who sees this bridge knows it is something special, especially when the midday sun is reflected off the golden pillars. Sharon's first remark when she saw the bridge (from the Eiffel Tower) was, "What is that magnificent structure?"

While we floated/motored downstream it was not yet dark so we did not see the bridges at their best. But that would change the moment we headed back in the direction of the Eiffel Tower.

Our dinner started with shrimp, salmon, or foie gras appetizers. After salads we had a choice of duck, steak, chicken, or sea bass. Delicious desserts were followed with a choice of cordials. The female vocalist entertainer periodically returned to sing French melodies. When one of their favorite songs came across the speakers, Lee and Jan excused themselves and went to a dance on a wooden floor in the middle of the boat

Our trip upstream was increasingly more stunning as the bridges and the city lights began to illuminate. As we approached the Eiffel Tower the blue light illumination on the steel became increasingly more visible. When we passed beneath the Tower, the sparkling lights we had seen the night before at Chez Francis were not yet a part of the Eiffel display, and we were concerned that the sparkling light show might only be a Saturday night presentation.

We proceeded up the Seine to the island where the miniature version of the Statue of Liberty towers above the river. We made a turn at the end of the island and the female vocalist began singing, *New York, New York*. This was a special moment for us.

Just as we pulled back into the dock beneath the Eiffel Tower, the sparkling lights began to illuminate. It was magical. We looked up from the departure ramp to see the Tower ablaze with shimmering intense white and blue lights.

We looked for a cab to take us back to our respective hotels, but there were none. A man approached us and asked if we needed a cab. He was a hustler who operated without a license. We asked what the fare was to the Marriott and he said it would be 40 euros (about $65). We had paid 7 Euros (not counting the hefty tip) to get to the dock so this was truly a usurious fare. Eventually, we found another non-licensed driver who said he would take us to the Marriott for 25 euros. At that hour we were glad to load up and head for the barn. I do not know to this day how Lee and Jan made out.

Shirley and my last thoughts as we prepared for bed was that the dinner cruise was a lovely way to end a truly memorable trip to Paris and Burgundy. When we departed France, Shirley was once again luxuriating in Business First. What fun we had!

One might wonder why so much was said of our trip to Burgundy. Shirley and I had experienced so much in living and traveling abroad, and this was the last overseas trip we took together. To me it seems appropriate that this last trip be documented like no other. We had many, many memorable trips ahead of us as we continued to travel throughout North America, but never again did we go overseas.

And There We Were

Chapter 29

FIFTEEN YEARS OF RETIREMENT AND THE END OF THE STORY

*A*s hectic and as full as year one of our retirement was, we continued to take a number of memorable trips, most of which were long road trips in the continental United States. Sprinkled in with these trips were several cruises, one to Alaska and one to Hawaii, and of course the 2008 trip to France described above. Our road trips, usually covering 2,000 to 3,000 miles and taking 5 to 6 weeks, were unbelievably fun. It was a rare occasion when we were not on speaking terms. We covered most of the United States. Our dreams of traveling continually unfolded until Shirley passed away in February 2019. Her heart just stopped beating. Shirley never lost her lust for life or her love of adventure. She was relentless in her search for excellence, especially when it came to traveling and dining. Shirley was a master at engaging others and seduced them with her charm and sweet voice. She almost always got what she wanted.

I recorded narratives of each adventure we had during our retirement years, but these may only be of interest to our ancestors. I will save such write-ups for another time and another document. I can only say that Shirley Lent was the happiest person I have ever known, and her dreams of an exciting and well lived life came true. I am so very glad that my journey through life was made in the company of such a special lady. I knew Shirley for more than 60 years and we were married for over 50. When we met in my junior year of high school, she was a freshman. It did not matter that we were not high school sweethearts. She was one of my best friends back then, and she was my very best friend at the end. She was loved by all, but by none more so than by me and our sons. When Shirley passed, the Sawyer's daughter had lived a life that she could not have imagined in those early years living in the high prairies of the Ochoco Mountains, Oregon. My dreams did come true. I married the most incredible woman. We had two exceptional sons. I traveled far beyond anyplace I could ever have imagined in my youth. My professional career was successful beyond expectation. My retirement years were filled with loving memories of adventures that Shirley and I shared. No man could ask for more.

Retirement Travels and Adventures

Figure 27. Bob and Shirley having dinner at Lake Creek Lodge, Camp Sherman, Central Oregon

Figure 28. Shirley on a granite outcrop above the Rio Grande River. View is across river into Mexico

Figure 29. Shirley in a float boat on the Big Horn River, Montana. Many a fisherman doffed his hat to the pretty lady.

Figure 30. Lent family celebration of Bob and Shirley's 50th Wedding Anniversary, Black Butte Resort, Central Oregon.

List of Photographs

Figure 1.	Aerial View of Big Summit Prairie, Ochoco Mountains, Central Oregon	10
Figure 2.	Ponderosa pine forest with grass and wildflower undergrowth	10
Figure 3.	The aged one room cabin near the Big Summit Prairie Sawmill	11
Figure 4.	Shirley Hill (aged 4) when the Hill family lived at the sawmill camp	11
Figure 5.	Prineville, Oregon as seen from View Point, circa 1950	27
Figure 6.	Crook County Courthouse, Prineville, Oregon	27
Figure 7.	Yell Queen Shirley Hill at Crook County High School in Prineville, Oregon	47
Figure 8.	Bob Lent Crook County High School basketball photo	47
Figure 9.	Shirley Hill High School Graduation Photo, Class of 1962	48
Figure 10.	Bob Lent High School Graduation Photo, Class of 1960	48
Figure 11.	Bob and Shirley Lent on their Wedding Day, July 6, 1968	77
Figure 12.	Muirfield, Keir Park, Ascot. Bob and Shirley's favorite place in all of England	146
Figure 13.	The pool and the cabana at Muirfield	146
Figure 14.	Former Prime Minister Margaret Thatcher and Shirley Lent	155
Figure 15.	Shirley Lent with her friend Joey Baechle	197
Figure 16.	Prince Charles and Shirley Lent. Bob is shaking the prince's hand	206
Figure 17.	The source of the Thames near Kemble in Gloucestershire	253
Figure 18.	Bob and Shirley's sons Taran (L) and Tobin (R) dressed for entrance into the Royal Enclosure at the Royal Ascot Races	295
Figure 19.	Shirley on the Orient Express, Valentine's Day, 1995	318

Figure 20.	Shirley Lent meeting the leaders of China in The Great Hall of The People, Beijing, China	468
Figure 21.	Bob and Shirley Lent on The Great Wall of China at Mutianyu	469
Figure 22.	The Black Tie Dinner and Dance on The Great Wall at Janshanling	469
Figure 23.	Shirley Lent with rice patties and limestone monoliths in the background, Yangshuo, China	470
Figure 24.	Fishing with cormorants on the river Li near Guilin, China	470
Figure 25.	Bob and Shirley Lent celebrating their 36th Wedding Anniversary at the romantic Wickaninnish Inn near Tofino, British Columbia	529
Figure 26.	Shirley Lent whale watching in Barkley Sound near Ucluelet, Vancouver Island, Canada	529
Figure 27.	Bob and Shirley having dinner at Lake Creek Lodge, Camp Sherman, Central Oregon	607
Figure 28.	Shirley on a granite outcrop above the Rio Grande River. View is across river into Mexico.	607
Figure 29.	Shirley in a float boat on the Big Horn River, Montana. Many a fisherman doffed his hat to the pretty lady.	608
Figure 30.	Lent family celebration of Bob and Shirley's 50th Wedding Anniversary, Black Butte Resort, Central Oregon.	608

www.ingramcontent.com/pod-product-compliance
Lightning Source LLC
Chambersburg PA
CBHW061151170426
43209CB000448/1992/J